The Cambridge History of
Latin American Literature

VOLUME 2

The Cambridge History of Latin American Literature
Edited by
Roberto González Echevarría and Enrique Pupo-Walker

The Cambridge History of Latin American Literature is by far the most comprehensive and authoritative work of its kind ever written. Its three volumes cover the whole sweep of Latin American literature (including Brazilian) from pre-Columbian times to the present, and contain chapters on Latin American writing in the US. Over forty specialists in North America, Latin America, and Britain have contributed to what is not only the most reliable, up-to-date, and convenient reference work on its subject, but also a set of books containing innovative approaches and fresh research that will expand and animate the field for years to come. The *History* is unique in its thorough coverage of previously neglected areas, in its detailed discussion of countless writers in various genres, and in its inclusion of extensive annotated bibliographies.

Volume 1 begins with pre-Columbian traditions and their first contact with European culture, continuing through to the end of the nineteenth century. New World historiography, epic poetry, theatre, the novel, and the essay form are among the areas covered in this comprehensive and authoritative treatment.

Volume 2 provides coverage of all genres from the end of the nineteenth century up to García Márquez's *One Hundred Years of Solitude* and beyond to 1990, thus including discussion of Spanish American literature's best-known works. The novel, poetry, autobiographical narrative, the short story, Afro-Hispanic American literature, theatre, and Chicano literature are among the areas treated in this wide-ranging volume.

Volume 3 is devoted partly to the history of Brazilian literature, from the earliest writing through the colonial period and the Portuguese-language traditions of the nineteenth and twentieth centuries; and partly also to an extensive bibliographical section in which annotated reading lists relating to the chapters in all three volumes of *The Cambridge History of Latin American Literature* are presented. These bibliographies are a unique feature of the *History*, further enhancing its immense value as a reference work.

Contents of the other two volumes

The Cambridge History of Latin American Literature

VOLUME 2:

The Twentieth Century

Edited by

Roberto González Echevarría
Yale University

and

Enrique Pupo-Walker
Vanderbilt University

CAMBRIDGE
UNIVERSITY PRESS

Published by the Press Syndicate of the University of Cambridge
The Pitt Building, Trumpington Street, Cambridge CB2 1RP
40 West 20th Street, New York, NY 10011–4211, USA
10 Stamford Road, Oakleigh, Melbourne 3166, Australia

First published 1996

Printed in Great Britain at the University Press, Cambridge

A catalogue record for this book is available from the British Library

Library of Congress cataloguing in publication data

The Cambridge history of Latin American literature / edited by Roberto
González Echevarría and Enrique Pupo-Walker.
p. cm.
Contents: v. 1. Discovery to Modernism – v. 2. The twentieth
century – v. 3. Brazilian literature; bibliographies.
ISBN 0 521 34069 1 (v. 1). – ISBN 0 521 34070 5 (v. 2). – ISBN
0 521 41035 5 (v. 3)
1. Latin American literature – History and criticism. I. González
Echevarría, Roberto. II. Pupo-Walker, Enrique.
PQ7081.A1C35 1995
860.9′8 – dc20   93-37750 CIP

ISBN 0 521 34070 5 hardback

Contents

LIST OF CONTENTS

Contributors

Carlos J. Alonso, Emory University
Daniel Balderston, Tulane University
Sandra M. Cypess, University of Maryland
Aníbal González, Pennsylvania State University
Cathy L. Jrade, Vanderbilt University
Vera M. Kutzinski, Yale University
Luis Leal, University of California, Santa Barbara
William Luis, Vanderbilt University
Manuel M. Martín-Rodríguez, Yale University
Sylvia Molloy, New York University
José Miguel Oviedo, University of Pennsylvania
Gustavo Pellón, University of Virginia
Randolph D. Pope, Washington University
René Prieto, Southern Methodist University
José Quiroga, The George Washington University
John Rutherford, Queen's College, Oxford University
Hugo J. Verani, University of California, Davis

General preface

In 1893, the renowned Spanish critic and historian Marcelino Menéndez y Pelayo published his vastly influential *Antología de la poesía hispano-americana*; not only the first history of Spanish American poetry, but truly the first history of Spanish American literature. The *Antología* appeared just as *Modernismo*, the first poetic movement developed in Spanish America, was achieving its greatest acclaim throughout the Hispanic world. With *Modernismo* Spanish American literature came of age, while the *Antología*, compiled and prefaced by the most authoritative critic of the language, gave it institutional substance and academic respectability. The present *History* appears in the wake of the most remarkable period of expansion and international recognition ever enjoyed by Latin American literature. The consolidation of Latin American literature as an academic discipline and a recognized category in the world book market was made possible by the achievements of writers as diverse as Jorge Luis Borges, Alejo Carpentier, Julio Cortázar, João Guimaraes Rosa, José Lezama Lima, Gabriel García Márquez, Octavio Paz, Mario Vargas Llosa, and many others. García Márquez and Paz attained the ultimate recognition, the Nobel Prize. Without the distinction and accomplishments of these writers, the public at large, not to mention publishing houses and universities throughout the world, would have continued to treat Latin American literary production as an appendix to Spanish literature, dependent on someone like Menéndez y Pelayo for legitimation. It is to them too that this *History* owes its existence. *Modernismo* gave Latin America a place in the Spanish-language literary world; writers like the ones mentioned above placed it at the center of world literature.

Latin American literature today enjoys a truly international currency. Latin American novelists in particular are read and imitated not only in the West but throughout the world. For instance, Leo Ou-fan-Lee, a professor of Chinese literature at the University of Chicago, has written recently that Latin American writers "now exert a powerful impact on many young Chinese writers". As recently as thirty years ago such a statement would have been unthinkable. Given its universal reach and appeal, it is perhaps appropriate that this *History* should be the effort of a group of scholars working in the United States, England, and continental Europe, as well as in Latin America. Latin American literature is today at the pinnacle of the international literary movements that began with the Avant-Garde in the twenties. Those movements, as well as their aftermath, are cosmopolitan in essence.

The *History* attempts to take full advantage of its collective and international cast, while at the same time aiming to be a coherent statement, conceived within a common set of scholarly guidelines and academic values. As an academic history, ours is concerned with historical fact and accuracy, with sources and influences, and with the relationship of literature to history in general. Our work, in other words, takes full account of the past, not only in the object of our study, but in the previous studies of that object. We build on what has been done before, and if and when we do not, we give our reasons. We aim not just to tell a story, but also to tell how that story has been told before. Aside from those givens, issuing no doubt from large ideological investments, ours is a work that is not dominated by narrow philosophical or methodological constraints. In contrast to most others, the *History* is not limited by the ideological or aesthetic values of a single author. In the invitations to participate in the project, the editors asked each contributor to be innovative in his or her approach to the field. Each was consulted about the limits of his or her area of study and about the very assumptions that make it a coherent subset within Latin American literary history. Everyone was asked, in short, to be self-conscious in his or her choices, not merely to review a field and to furnish an *état présent*. In this sense the *History* is not only a history of Latin American literature, but equally a statement on the current status of Latin American literary historiography. While the latitude given to each contributor has resulted in some unevenness, the editors believe that eclecticism enhances the value of the *History*, both as a reference tool and as an intellectual venture. Some literary works that previously had not been given much attention (in some cases none at all) have been examined by our contributors, thus effectively incorporating them into the canon. For instance, this is the first history of Latin American literature to provide detailed coverage of the colonial period, the works of women writers, and the literature written in Spanish by Chicano and other Hispanic authors in various regions of North America. Similarly, this is the first history of Latin American literature to link meaningfully the works of Afro-Hispanic and Afro-American authors. The *History* also brings together Brazilian and Spanish American literatures, giving the former the full individual attention it naturally deserves, but also underscoring their contiguities, continuities, and discontinuities. In short, the editors feel that our *History* is a reassessment and expansion of the canon of Latin American literature, seen in a broad, New World context.

We are fully aware, of course, that large ideological presuppositions underlie our enterprise. The first concerns the very existence of Latin American literature as such. Since its deliberate creation as a concept and field of endeavor in the 1830s, Latin American literature has debated whether it is a literature at all or in fact a series of national literatures that share a common language. The most prominent writers, from Andrés Bello to Paz, have argued in favor of the existence of a Latin American literature that transcends national boundaries; and if one thinks of tradition as being made up by the major works, as we do here, then one can assume the existence of a Latin American literature. However, not everyone has always been convinced, and we do not question that there are peculiarities that distinguish some national literatures within Latin America. The case of Brazil is a special one, of course: there is no doubt that Brazilian literature is a national literature as original and self-contained as French, Italian, or Spanish literature; its ties to a broader Latin American literature, however, are strong, if fluid and ever-changing over time. But Cuban, Mexican, Argentinian, Chilean, and Colombian literatures are also marked by national characteristics that are undeniable. These national inflections are for the most part thematic. For instance, the lives of Blacks and their African retentions play a very significant role in Caribbean literature, whereas in the Southern Cone it is the *gaucho* and his mores that provide a strong thematic strain. There is, however, a certain homology in the way these figures appear in their respective national or regional literatures, one that extends to how the Indian is portrayed in areas such as Peru and Mexico. National traditions stress the differences and remain local. But the stronger authors and works cross frontiers or dwell in the homology. They constitute a kind of overarching literature to which all aspire. Our assumption here has been that the most significant and influential part of Latin American literature is the one engaged in a transnational intertextual exchange. The recuperation of the colonial period, when Spanish America was one, is part of this struggle to constitute a continental literature with a common origin and discourse. This is one of the strongest forces behind the recent increase in scholarship on the colonial period.

The breadth of this undertaking is particularly evident in the chapters on colonial literature, both Brazilian and Spanish American. Until a few years ago, colonial literature was chiefly the object of antiquarian interest, but in recent years this has changed drastically in fundamental and irreversible ways. The editors and contributors have sought to reflect that change. Before the 1960s, few universities (in Latin America or elsewhere) offered courses on Latin American writers of the colonial period, but now many include in their programs of study Sor Juana Inés de la Cruz, Bernal Díaz del Castillo, Garcilaso de la Vega, el Inca, and many others. At the post-graduate level there are now monographic courses dealing with those figures, as well as with Columbus, Gonzalo Fernández de Oviedo, and many other historians of the discovery and conquest of America. Scholarship on these authors has increased significantly in scope and sophistication. There are now international symposia devoted solely to colonial literature, as well as sessions within established, periodical meetings, such as the yearly conventions of the Modern Languages Association of America.

Appropriately, given the nature of the chronicles, this *History* incorporates scholarly materials and methodological tools that are not common to literary scholarship. The interdisciplinary bent of this part of our venture is enhanced by the contributions of Asunción Lavrin (in Volume 1) and Thomas Skidmore (in Volume 3), well-known historians of Spanish and Portuguese America respectively. This productive linkage of disciplines is the natural byproduct of recent scholarship. In the past two decades, the study of colonial Spanish American literature has been enriched by its broad interdisciplinary scope. The reassessment of early historiography of the Americas combines quite freely the findings of rhetorical analyses, historical scholarship, anthropology and archaeology. This unprecedented and expanding convergence of disciplines has made possible forms of scholarly cooperation that are exceptional in Hispanic studies, and that certainly point to the research agendas of the future.

The incorporation of the colonial period into the study of Latin American literature has improved the overall quality of the criticism devoted to this literature by showing the inadequacy of journalistic approaches that are based exclusively on the most recent literary production. This development is intimately tied to the academic legitimation of Latin American literature as an academic discipline, a fairly recent phenomenon. Curiously, this movement also brings out the strong ties Latin American literature still has with Spanish and Portuguese literature, both in the colonial period and in the present. If the Iberian Middle Ages, Renaissance, and Baroque are such a powerful presence in Latin American literature, then this literature shares a living past with its metropolitan counterparts. From a scholarly perspective what this means is that scholars of colonial literature (and one hopes, also of modern literature) must now have a strong background in medieval, renaissance, and Golden Age literatures. A full sixth of the *History* is devoted to the colonial period, and the chapters devoted to the modern periods reflect the weight of that living past.

One reason for this increase in colonial studies is that modern Latin American authors have discovered in the works of the colonial Baroque, or in the chronicles of the discovery and Conquest, the starting point of the literary tradition to which they belong. Octavio Paz's voluminous study of Sor Juana is but the latest evidence of this phenomenon. Carpentier, García Márquez, Neruda, and many other contemporary writers have either written about colonial figures or declared their debt to them in interviews and other pronouncements. Haroldo de Campos has developed theories of Brazilian literature based on the continued presence of the colonial Baroque, or the self-conscious return to it. Many contemporary works, both in Spanish and Portuguese, include topics, characters, and stories drawn from colonial texts. This return to the colonial past, highlighting its pertinence in the present, rounds out the Latin American literary tradition and endows it for the first time with a density of five centuries. It does not matter that, if examined closely, this is nothing more than an enabling pretext, or a fable about origins. Literature creates its own historical fictions, its own history being one of them. Our *History*, while being as concrete and factual as possible, reflects the fullness and influence of that fiction. In this sense, too, ours is a history of the history of Latin American literature.

The editors feel that the *History* is the first to recognize the richness and diversity of Latin American literature in the nineteenth century (preceding *Modernismo*). This field, which has yet to acquire the institutional recognition accorded to the colonial period, has of late begun to draw attention from scholars as well as writers. The chapters devoted to both Spanish American and Brazilian literature of the nineteenth century are among the most innovative, and constitute the area where the freshest research is offered by our contributors. More than a history bringing to closure the study of this promising field, work on the nineteenth century in the *History* may very well constitute the founding of a new area of specialization.

The richness and depth of Latin American literature in the Colonial period and during the past century is one of the features, perhaps the strongest, that distinguishes it from other literatures of the so-called Third World. In the 1960s, in the wake of the Cuban Revolution and other political movements aimed at breaking the grip of colonialism, many Latin American authors allied themselves with authors whose plight seemed similar to theirs. Regardless of the outcome of those political alliances the fact is that if by Third World one refers to countries that emerged from the debacle of nineteenth-century colonialism, then Latin

America, being the product of a much older and different colonialism, had to have a very different literary tradition. The literatures of the Third World emerged, for the most part, in our own century, whereas those of Latin America reach back really to, at least, the sixteenth. The burden of Latin American culture is a Western culture that extends back to the Middle Ages, when the foundations of the Spanish Empire in the New World were set. Latin American culture, particularly Spanish American, was, from the beginning, one of ostentatious viceregal capitals, surpassing in splendor cities of the Old World, often because they had to compete with magnificent urban centers constructed by the Aztecs, Mayas, or Incas. This urban quality of Latin American culture also obeyed Spanish Neo-Scholasticism, grounded on the Aristotelian notion that civilization was, as the etymology indicates, something proper to cities. Latin American colonial culture, in many ways Medieval, is so distant from that of North America, or countries of the Third World, that gross distortions and misreadings are bound to occur in comparing them. Desire for solidarity with the Third World is a significant element of recent Latin American literature perhaps even as a movement, but it does not make of Latin American literature a Third-World literature. Latin American literature is not a new literature, even if one of its enabling pretexts or founding fables is its newness. Our History, we hope, makes this very clear, with abundant supporting evidence.

The question of the new is so poignant in Latin American literature precisely because it is such an old culture, both back through its European roots, and through those of the native and African cultures. The entire history of Macondo, the fictional town in García Márquez's *One Hundred Years of Solitude* which is a microcosmic representation of Latin America, has been written in advance, in Sanscrit, by a wizard; it is a story that emerges from the very origins of history and writing. In those origins writing precedes history. The literatures of the Third World are recent; some came into being in the twentieth century. Latin American writers find predecessors, within what they consider as their own literature, in the sixteenth and seventeenth centuries. Again, Paz's passionate and polemic literary biography of Sor Juana Inés de la Cruz is a case in point. There were Renaissance-style literary academies in Lima at the turn of the sixteenth to the seventeenth century, and hundreds of Petrarchan poets in seventeenth-century Mexico. If anyone should doubt this he or she ought to read Alicia de Colombí-Monguió's superb *Petrarquismo peruano*, and Irving A. Leonard's classic *Books of the Brave* and *Baroque Times in Old Mexico*.

The editors and contributors have spared no effort in making the *History* a reliable, informative, and useful reference work and research tool. Hence, we have been careful to be thorough in providing dates and bibliographic information in general. In fact, we feel that the selective, annotated bibliographies relating to each chapter (printed in Volume 3) constitute in and of themselves a significant contribution to the field. The general bibliography at the end was compiled by a professional bibliographer. In some instances (Carlos Alonso's comprehensive list of regionalist novels is a good example) the bibliographies are the result of groundbreaking research. All secondary bibliographies are selective and the annotations are meant to guide future scholars to the latest, the newest, and the most promising work. Read in conjunction with their respective chapters, these bibliographies should bring a critic to the point where he or she can begin to make the next original contribution. The editors sincerely hope that this will very often be the case and that the *History* will help to provide an auspicious opening to one hundred years of Latin American literary historiography.

The *Cambridge History of Latin American Literature* draws upon a long tradition of collaborative scholarship that began with the *Cambridge Modern History* (1902–1912) and includes the eight-volume *Cambridge History of Latin America*. In its format, general guidelines and scholarly values, the *Cambridge History of Latin American Literature* aspires to the rigor and accessibility for which these predecessors are known.

RGE and EPW

Acknowledgments

A collaborative work such as this is by its very nature the product of many people, some whose names appear as contributors or editors, and others whose contributions are not so obvious. We would like to thank here as many of those as possible, painfully aware that we are bound to make errors of omission. We apologize for them in advance.

First of all, we must thank those contributors who have also helped us in many ways other than by writing their chapters. First and foremost we thank Professor David Haberly, who was our consultant for the volume on Brazilian literature. Professor Haberly discussed possible contributors with us, read the chapters for volume 3 and offered many valuable suggestions about how to shape the material. He also completed the chapter written by José Guilherme Merquior, whose premature death occurred in February, 1991. In editing that volume, we were also aided by Professor K. David Jackson, whose expertise in all matters Brazilian, and abilities as a translator were both crucial. Other contributors also assisted us in similar ways in editing volumes 1 and 2. Professor Cathy L. Jrade read several manuscripts, offered detailed suggestions about various matters, helped us with the prologues, and participated with the two editors in meetings at which critical decisions were made. We acknowledge our great debt to Professor Jrade, who also served as a sounding board for ideas, several of which she helped sharpen or discard. Professor Sylvia Molloy gave us important advice concerning the selection of contributors, and also on how best to incorporate the work of women writers into the *History*. Professors Aníbal González Pérez, Gustavo Pérez Firmat and Kathleen Ross also aided us with their counsel, friendship, and erudition. We are especially grateful to Andrew Bush and José Quiroga. We asked them for important contributions which they had to write in a very limited period of time.

The library staffs at both Yale and Vanderbilt helped with bibliographical matters, and the staffs at the respective offices of grants and contracts were our link to the foundations that made the *History* possible. We should like to single out here Steven H. Smartt, at Vanderbilt, and Alice Oliver at Yale. We have, of course, an enormous debt of gratitude with the National Endowment for the Humanities, which provided a three-year grant that allowed us to continue work during the summers, and to the Rockefeller Foundation for a grant to round out the sum provided by the Endowment. At the Endowment we were graciously assisted by David Wise, who was always patient with our queries and requests. Completion of a project as complex and time-consuming as this would have been impossible without the financial backing of these institutions, and we wish to make public our heartfelt appreciation.

During the five-year period that we have spent on this project, the office for the *Cambridge History of Latin American Literature* has been the Center for Latin American and Iberian Studies at Vanderbilt. We have profited from all the facilities available at the Center, and want to thank Vanderbilt for its generosity in putting them at our disposal. The most invaluable resource at the Center, and the person to whom we owe the greatest debt of gratitude, is Mrs. Norma Antillón, technical secretary to the Director. Given the demands of our many other academic responsibilities, which often took us far from the *History*, Mrs. Antillón was the only continued presence; at times she seemed to *be* the *History*, as the many contributors who dealt with her in our absence know well. It would be impossible even to attempt to enumerate her many contributions, and we would rather simply express to her our profound gratitude for her loyalty, devotion, attentiveness, and unswerving commitment to the successful completion of this work. We also wish to convey our appreciation to Mrs. Sandra Guardo, secretary to the Department of Spanish and Portuguese at Yale University. She was a valuable resource on many occasions. In addition, Mrs. Suzan McIntire, secretary to the Center for International Programs at Vanderbilt, was helpful to us in administrative aspects of this project.

We would also like to recognize Mr. Kevin Taylor at Cambridge University Press (England) for his exemplary attention to all matters pertaining to this *History*. We are also grateful to Mrs. Jay Williams, who provided valuable advice about contractual matters and helped improve the style of several chapters. We also wish to thank the translators, who labored hard to transform Spanish and Portuguese prose into academic English. These are Susan Griswold, Georgina Dopico Black, David Jackson, and Cindy Najmulski.

Finally, we gratefully thank our wives Betty and Isabel for their patience and encouragement, and for making our meetings not only possible, but enjoyable.

ROBERTO GONZÁLEZ ECHEVARRÍA
ENRIQUE PUPO-WALKER

Introduction to Volume 2
Roberto González Echevarría

Spanish American literature's best-known works have appeared in the modern period; that is, from the late 1800s to the present. This volume of *The Cambridge History of Latin American Literature*, therefore, covers the best-known and most studied genres, authors, and works, from Rubén Darío's *Azul* (1888), to Gabriel García Márquez's *Cien años de soledad* (1967) [*One Hundred Years of Solitude*] including the likes of Mariano Azuela's *Los de abajo* (1915) [*The Underdogs*], Rómulo Gallegos's *Doña Bárbara* (1929) [*Doña Barbara*], Jorge Luis Borges's *Ficciones*, Alejo Carpentier's *El reino de este mundo* (1949) [*The Kingdom of this World*], César Vallejo's *Trilce* (1922), Pablo Neruda's *Canto general* (1950), and Octavio Paz's *Piedra de sol* (1957) [*Sunstone*], to name only a few of the high peaks. As considerable attention has already been given to these works, the scholar will find in these chapters of the *History* the most extensive revisionism. At the same time, the general reader will find an introduction to the most dynamic and current areas of Latin American literature.

Whereas in the coverage of earlier periods mostly fresh research into the primary works was adduced, here the study of each work, author or period is accompanied by the consideration of a substantial body of criticism, not to mention an already established historical scheme. It is also in this volume that we reach that most elusive, yet most influential of periods: the present one, which is also, of course, our own. (Elusive because it is impossible to delimit it, influential because it is the moment from which we write.) Coverage of the most recent literature leaves the realm of history to enter that of journalism, which is where our own present-determined biases most readily show. Those making a contribution regarding current trends are clearly taking the greatest risks: what they add to the history of Latin American literature may or may not remain a part of it.

While Spanish American literature has generally followed the historical patterns of modern Western literature in this century, it is characterized by

I

significant and recurrent formal and thematic differences. If seen against an idealized scheme of Western literary development, Spanish American literary movements may at times seem anachronistic (the regionalist novel is one instance), or just late. This, however, would be a misperception caused by a faulty presupposition: the assumption that a given pace of historical development could and should be attained everywhere. In fact, Spanish America's social and political upheavals, its geographic position, and more importantly its position in the world market, give its artistic movements a rhythm of their own, even if within the larger, symphonic score of Western literature. Momentous events like the Mexican and Cuban Revolutions have dramatically brought to the fore some of the peculiarities of Spanish America: in the case of Mexico, the presence of large masses of Indians not assimilated into the economic and political mainstream of society; in that of Cuba the clash between powerful, modern, industrialized North America, and the rest of the Americas. The first of these issues harks back to the Conquest, whose lingering impact is still felt in many regions; the second reflects a more recent if no less pressing dilemma. As one surveys current events in Latin America, especially in Peru and Mexico, the persistence of these socio- and geo-political problems is evident. In literature, no matter how many different guises it takes, the issue always appears as the question of modernity.

Modernity emerges as a self-conscious topic with the appropriately named *Modernistas* [Modernists], reaching its crescendo during the Avant-Garde. How could Spanish America, as Professors Aníbal González and Cathy L. Jrade inquire here in their respective chapters on *Modernismo* [Modernism], burdened with such an onerous and living past, be modern? Yet again, how could it not be, if it is part of the world economy of goods, values, and ideas? On the political side this dilemma has often led to deep socio-political upheavals, and generated figures that contain in uneasy coexistence, the modern and the premodern; for example, *caudillos* of various ilks, from Manuel Estrada Cabrera to Fidel Castro, touting modern ideologies such as bourgeois liberalism or Marxism, but in fact, deeply rooted in Medieval Hispanic patriarchalism. Geographically the conflict has often manifested itself as a clash between the European-oriented cities, mostly coastal, and the "backward" provinces, found in the interior. The former stay anxiously up-to-date with the latest European artistic movements and feel that they are a part of them, as is made evident in Professor Hugo Verani's chapter on the *Vanguardia* [Vanguard]. The latter cling to colonial ways, in which old Spanish or creole values prevail. One could perhaps say that in the broadest possible terms, modern Latin American literature exhibits the same restless coexistence of the very modern with the somewhat archaic and anachronistic. The most egregious example is García Márquez's novel, *Cien años de soledad*, clearly modern in style, yet curiously old-fashioned in theme and strong narrative structure.

In the early modern period the most enduring creations were poetic (Darío, Vallejo), both during the *modernista* period and the Avant-Garde, though a modern novelistic tradition arose early in the century, during the Mexican Revolution, studied here by Professor John Rutherford. The regionalist novel (Güiraldes, Rivera, Gallegos) displays most visibly the dialectics between the old and the new, and between the rural and the urban at the core of Latin American culture in general. Professor Carlos Alonso's chapter on the regionalist novel shows this, and details the continent-wide appeal of this kind of novel. By mid-century, in spite of the presence of major poets like Paz and Neruda, prose-fiction led the way, with the emergence of figures such as Jorge Luis Borges, Miguel Angel Asturias, and Alejo Carpentier, as studied by Professor Randolph D. Pope. The mid to late 1960s saw the efflorescence of the novel known as the *Boom* of the Latin American Novel, which boasted highly experimental works by Julio Cortázar, Carlos Fuentes, Mario Vargas Llosa, and García Márquez. In a way, this "new novel" was really a late blooming of the avant-garde novel, cross-bred with the Latin American regionalist tradition. That is to say, Cortázar, Fuentes, Vargas Llosa, and García Márquez are belated heirs of Proust, Joyce, Kafka, and Faulkner.

One of the more striking trends in modern Spanish American literature is a dual urge to break with Europe and to adopt the ways of the non-European peoples in the New World, specifically Indians and Africans. While it is true that in the broadest sense the artistic movements generated by this desire to deny the West are very much a part of a trend peculiar to the West itself, the fact is that in Latin America, because of the presence of radically different cultures that are nominally a part of the national cultures and polities, they are endowed with a peculiar authenticity and have enjoyed a longer life than elsewhere. *Indigenismo* [Indigenism] and Afro-Antilleanism, analyzed in detail here by Professors René Prieto and Vera M. Kutzinski respectively, are among the most important artistic movements in modern Spanish America. The latter was the context in which various major poets, like the Cuban Nicolás Guillén and the Puerto Rican Luis Pales Matos, began their work. Both movements, particularly *Indigenismo*, had a powerful connection to politics. They have left a legacy in Spanish America that still survives, chiefly in the novel (Carpentier's *Concierto barroco* [1974], and Vargas Llosa's *El hablador* [1988] *[The Storyteller]*, are good examples).

A corollary of this rejection of European civilization, but again issuing from it, is the persistent theme of revolution present in modern Spanish American literature. This topic harks back to the theme of utopia, prevalent since the colonial period, but gathers momentum and artistic expression during the Mexican Revolution, when it gives rise to the subgenre of the Novel of the Mexican Revolution (related to a powerful pictorial flourishing in the work of the Muralists). In the poetic sphere revolution takes on a more cosmic air in works by major poets such as Neruda and Paz. Here, sometimes taking advantage of indigenous cosmologies, revolution is seen as not merely social or political, but as part of a grander design. *Canto general* and *Piedra de sol* are the high peaks of this tendency, which has attained lesser, though considerable, heights in poets such as Ernesto Cardenal. Professor José Quiroga provides a careful study of these poets, as well as of their poetic and historical context.

The clash between the modern European legacy and the backward but persistent Spanish American past has been the spark for a vigorous and sustained essayistic tradition concerned with finding the true identity of Spanish America, as well as that which distinguishes Spanish American culture, including literature. The tradition opens with José Enrique Rodó's influential *Ariel* (1900), and continues in the work of the Peruvian José Carlos Mariátegui, the Dominican Pedro Henríquez Ureña, the Mexicans Alfonso Reyes, José de Vasconcelos, and Samuel Ramos, as well as in the Argentinian Eduardo Mallea, and the Cuban Fernando Ortiz. A neat loop is closed with Roberto Fernández Retamar's *Calibán* (1967), which attempts to revise these interpretative efforts from the perspective of the Cuban Revolution. Poets like Paz, in his *El laberinto de la soledad* (1950) *[The Labyrinth of Solitude]* and José Lezama Lima in his *La expresión americana* (1958) have made decisive contributions to this essayistic tradition, as have novelists like Alejo Carpentier with his *Tientos y diferencias* (1962). The tradition is one of the most characteristic and significant features of modern Spanish American literature, and it is the point at which it links with what could be called Spanish American thought or philosophy. Here, the work of such figures as Leopoldo Zea plays a mediating role of considerable importance. Professor José Miguel Oviedo provides ample coverage of this essayistic tradition in one of the most extensive chapters in this *History*.

The work of women writers has been a focus of attention in the past few years. Earlier writers like Teresa de la Parra and Rosario Castellanos have been the object of numerous studies, and current ones like Elena Poniatowska, Luisa Valenzuela, and Isabel Allende have received considerable critical acclaim. An effort to rewrite the history of Latin American literature to include women writers unjustly neglected previously has met with some success. This *History* has made a deliberate effort in that direction.

Another current trend has been the incorporation of popular culture, perhaps more accurately the culture of the mass-media, into literature both as theme and as a form. This trend, most apparent in the most recent fiction studied by Professor Gustavo Pellón, has a troubling political dimension because much of the popular culture prevalent in Latin America is imported from abroad, mostly from the United States. However, the local *radio novelas*, and more recently the *telenovelas*, have begun to play an important role in more "serious" literature, particularly in Mario Vargas Llosa's novel *La tía Julia y el escribidor* [*Aunt Julia and the Scriptwriter*]. In the Caribbean, Afro-Cuban popular music is absorbed into the works of writers like Severo Sarduy (*De donde son los cantantes* [*From Cuba with a Song*]) and Luis Rafael Sánchez (*La guaracha del Macho Camacho* [*Macho Camacho's Beat*]). The most significant aspect of this trend is that popular culture is not presented in a condescending manner, but seen as an alternative to conventional literary tradition.

As the *History* goes to press García Márquez, Donoso, Fuentes, and Vargas Llosa continue to produce excellent works, some better than those that brought them fame during the *Boom*. Among the poets, Paz towers over the entire continent, north and south, as the premier poet of the moment. The deaths of Borges, Lezama Lima, Carpentier, and Cortázar perhaps marked the beginning of the end of what may very well have been a golden age of Latin American literature. Among the newer writers, Severo Sarduy, Guillermo Cabrera Infante, Luis Rafael Sánchez, Gustavo Sáenz, and a few others, have produced works of considerable value and should be now reaching their best years. However, Latin America lost three of its most original young writers with the untimely deaths of Manuel Puig, Severo Sarduy, and Reinaldo Arenas.

It seems that the major change in recent Spanish American literature is the gradual abandonment of the theme of cultural identity, which was connected to a conception of literature that placed within language the deepest enigmas and potentially the most profound insights into that question. It is difficult to fathom what may be replacing, if indeed anything is, this powerful thematic, whose origins are in Romanticism, within whose central ideas the very notion of Spanish American literature was conceived. Some see in the latest trends an alignment with Postmodernism, an as of today still inchoate movement whose main tenet seems to be a rejection of what have been called "masternarratives," by which is meant the central ideological underpinnings of Western thought and practice. These are to be replaced by local narratives, which, rather than language, are seen as the units of the various existing discourses. Is this the reappearance of a form of primitivistic, utopian thought? Or is it really the result of the emergence of a global culture dominated by the media and communication systems that may replace literature as we know it? Or, again, is it the recurrence of that desire to abolish literature that has often been the motivation of modern literature since its inception?

Another issue that clearly troubles current Spanish American literature is the collapse of Marxism throughout the world, a development that has pulled out the rug from under much politically committed writing in all genres. Though no Marxist-inspired literature of any consequence really emerged in modern Spanish America, with the exception of Mariátegui, Marxism provided a sort of ideological umbrella for much politically oriented writing, particularly in the essay and literary criticism. The sudden breakdown of eastern Europe and the Soviet Union, and the disintegration of communist Cuba has left many writers (numerous but on the whole quite minor) without an ideological underpinning. As of this writing it is difficult to figure out if a new political doctrine will occupy the place Marxism once held, or if Marxist-oriented writers will cling to the old formulas in spite of the pressures of a changing reality and ideological climate.

The contributors to this volume face all of these issues, and at the same time, in their very work, exemplify the current status of criticism on them, as well as the major trends in Latin American criticism.

1

Modernist poetry
Cathy L. Jrade

Attempts to analyze *Modernismo* [Modernism] have now entered their second century. Virtually from its inception, literary observers and critics have struggled to pinpoint its distinctive nature and to detail its primary characteristics. While innumerable studies have contributed to our understanding of the movement, its image is increasingly refined by recent examinations of the profoundly philosophic and political nature of *modernista* [Modernist] texts, their relationship with other literatures and modes of discourse, and the way they reflect personal responses to the general trends of modern life. Though Rubén Darío (1867–1916, born Félix Rubén García Sarmiento) defined his – and, therefore, modernist – aesthetics as "acrática," that is, opposed to all authority ("Palabras liminares," *Prosas profanas y otros poemas*), and even though this feature continues to appear on the lists of fundamental characteristics of modernist verse – (often labeled "voluntad de estilo" or "striving for an individual style" [see Davison, *The Concept of Modernism in Hispanic Criticism*]), Modernism manifests an essential unity which stems from its origin in a shared literary, philosophic, and social context. In the broadest of terms, Modernism is the linguistically rich and formally innovative literary movement that began in Spanish America in the late 1870s and that lasted into the second decade of the twentieth century. Its recourse to European artistic visions and poetic models – primarily French Parnassian and symbolist verse – reflected a dissatisfaction with the restrictive Spanish poetics of the day, a longing for cultural autonomy, and a desire to achieve a sense of equality with the great cultures of Western Europe. With its faith in the poet and poetry, it also proposed a profound response to the crisis of beliefs that surfaced among the philosophers and artists of Spanish America toward the end of the nineteenth century, a crisis similar to the one that had dominated intellectual circles throughout the West since Romanticism.

It was the impact of literary sources, especially the strong influence of

French poetry, that first attracted attention. In his famous letter to Rubén Darío dated October 22, 1888, and written in response to receiving a personally dedicated copy of *Azul*. . . the Spanish critic and novelist Juan Valera (1824–1905) defined Darío's originality and technical perfection in terms of his "galicismo mental" ["mental Gallicism"]. Though Valera's judgments are colored by nationalistic pride and ideological conservatism, one can find in his letter to Darío those salient features of the movement that have repeatedly received detailed critical attention during the one hundred years since it was written. From the outset, major studies sought to pinpoint French models for modernist works, with the earliest criticism focusing primarily on the formal aspects of this influence. Scholars emphasized changes in meter and verse form, the introduction of new rhythm and rhyme schemes, and symbolic and thematic similarities with earlier French texts. Others chose to distinguish between the perfection of form and devotion to beauty attributed to the influence of Parnassian verse and the musical evocation and dream-like suggestion encouraged by symbolist poetry.

This line of inquiry found support in the positions taken by Pedro Salinas ("El problema del modernismo en España, o un conflicto entre dos espíritus") and Guillermo Díaz-Plaja (*Modernismo frente a noventa y ocho*), both of whom continued to characterize Modernism as limited in scope, that is, primarily concerned with aestheticism, the search for beauty, and the renovation of poetic form. Even Max Henríquez Ureña's comprehensive, insightful, and influential *Breve historia del modernismo* reflects this general orientation. In it he holds that the central concern of modernist authors was to break with "the excesses of Romanticism" and "the narrow criterion of pseudoclassical rhetoric." Accordingly, they opted to transpose French innovations into a Spanish key. Repeated and detailed references to Leconte de Lisle, José María de Heredia, Alfred de Musset, Victor Hugo, Paul Verlaine, Catulle Mendès, Stéphane Mallarmé, Maurice de Guérin, Théophile Gautier, Pierre Loti, among many others, reaffirm this focus.

The search for "sources" and influences was not, however, limited to France. As Valera noted with regard to *Azul*. . ., there is a strong and wide-ranging cosmopolitan spirit that runs through modernist verse. All of European and even Middle-Eastern and Oriental art and culture captured the poetic imagination of modernist poets from time to time. Occasionally the influence was direct, more often it came by way of Paris, filtered through Parisian imaginations and interpretations. Sensitive to this cultural cross-pollination, Darío wrote:

> Amo más que la Grecia de los griegos
> la Grecia de la Francia

[I love more than the Greece of the Greeks
the Greece of France]

in "Divagación" (*Prosas profanas*). This cosmopolitanism was originally identified with escapism, a rejection of the stifling restrictions of Spanish poetics and culture, and flight from the immediate Spanish American reality. Later, it was seen as a declaration of cultural independence or as an unbridled pursuit of beauty in any shape or form. It is actually a manifestation of a complex and profound search, a search that led modernist writers to embrace diverse aspects of high culture from all corners of the globe with a dizzying enthusiasm in the expectation of achieving – in apparent contradiction – a sense of identity that is clearly Spanish American.

Aware of their extraordinary place in Spanish American history, modernist poets broke with Spanish models which they understood to be both grandiose and inflexible. They turned their eyes instead toward Europe to find the present and, through the present, the future. This attitude is evident in Darío's selection in 1888 of the term "Modernism" to designate the tendencies of Spanish American poets (see Henríquez Ureña's "Historia de un nombre" in *Breve historia del modernismo*). This choice underscores the Modernists' will to be modern, that is, to become contemporaneous with all of Europe but most especially with Paris. The poets sought to leave behind – either through their travels or their imagination – an anachronistic, local reality in order to establish for themselves a modern mode of discourse in which they could speak for the first time with their own voice and with a clear, critical vision of Spanish America.

As a result, "escapist literature" almost immediately became, as noted by Octavio Paz in "Literatura de fundación" (*Puertas al campo*), a literature of exploration and return. Modernist writers turned their attention from the most up-to-date European trends toward home and resurrected, through flights of fancy as much as through historical fact, a Spanish American past that included ancient civilizations, indigenous peoples, and a Spanish American consciousness. This consciousness is clear in the modernist attitude toward language and poetry. From the beginning, their concern for formal perfection reflected, along with Parnassian influences, a desire to formalize and to found a modern Spanish American discourse. Their pursuit of beauty throughout the centuries and across all borders was a manifestation of their desire to choose freely the elements of their ideal language. At the same time, modernist authors struggled with the dominant poetic and prosaic modes of discourse in their attempt to find their own voice. This founding effort was simultaneously aesthetic and political, with the political becoming more pronounced when the socio-economic pressures that gave rise to Modernism exploded in crisis in 1898 with the Spanish American War and later in 1903 with the creation of the state of Panama as a result of United States intervention.

The change from apparently apolitical poetry, as in the case of Manuel Gutiérrez Nájera (1859–1895) and Darío's early works, to a more assertively Spanish American perspective, as with key poems in Rubén Darío's *Cantos de vida y esperanza* and *Alma América: poemas indoespañoles* by José Santos Chocano (1875–1934), gave rise to the division of Modernism – by critics – into two stages. The "second generation" of Modernists was considered more concerned with achieving an artistic expression that would be genuinely American. In reality, both "generations" dealt with the issues of Spanish America's place in the modern world and the creation of a language and vision appropriate to that place. The recognition of the centrality of these issues to the entire movement not only reaffirms Modernism's essential unity but also clarifies the key role played by the politically committed Cuban patriot José Martí (1853–1895) in the formation of Modernism.

The socio-economic conditions that most directly affected the development of Modernism of course vary from country to country. There were, however, certain key factors that consistently came into play. For the most part, the last decades of the nineteenth century saw a consolidation of power which brought about a new degree of political stability – despite the periodic resurgence of "caudillismo" and anarchistic tendencies. At the same time, economic reorganization and growth brought prosperity and affluence to the upper classes. In urban centers, wealth and international trade encouraged a perceptible Europeanization of life. As Roberto González Echevarría has expressed it (in "Modernidad, modernismo y nueva narrativa"), in exchange for its raw materials, Spanish America received culture, primarily in the form of manufactured products. The turn-of-the-century flood of luxury items filled the homes of the old landed aristocracy, the *nouveaux riches*, and the aspiring bourgeoisie. It also created an image of life that left a lasting impression upon the poetic imagination of the writers of the time, an image that evoked the sense of well-being, ease, and fashionable excess characteristic of the Parisian *Belle Epoque* – that is, of the three decades beginning with the 1880s.

Members of the ruling class allied themselves with foreign financiers and investors, and their primary ambition became the accumulation of capital at the expense of more traditional goals. The political philosophy of the day was the Positivism of Comte and later that of Spencer, both of which became linked with a type of social Darwinism. Auguste Comte (1798–1857) had developed a philosophical system that rejected metaphysics and relied exclusively on the positive sciences. His final aim was to reform society so that all men could live in harmony and comfort. During the peace that followed the political consolidation of the 1860s, Positivism became the philosophy of order, promoting progress, science, and the miracles of free enterprise. Society in Spanish America was to be organized upon a more rational basis than ever before, and humanity was to find itself living in a world without problems. Scientists were believed to be the bearers of a demonstrable truth and trustees of the future. The evils of "modern life" and industrialization were accepted as necessary for national development. In reality, however, Positivism provided the ruling classes with a new vocabulary to legitimate injustice as liberal ideology was replaced by the struggle for existence and the survival of the fittest. Inequalities were now explained, not by race or inheritance or religion, but by science. The Mexican Porfirio Díaz and his "científicos" ["scientific ones"], the oligarchy of the Argentinian landowners, and the Chilean nitrate barons best represented the political scene during this era.

Positivism generated in most Modernists a strongly ambivalent attitude. They maintained a respect for science, its breakthroughs, and its contributions to progress; they rejected it, however, as the ultimate measure of all things. Despite the promises made, it became clear that, far from becoming more understandable, life appeared more enigmatic, and the great inventions and discoveries had not provided answers to the fundamental questions of existence. If anything, Spanish America's growing prosperity and its increasing involvement with the industrial capitals of the world brought about social dislocations that heightened the sense of crisis among its writers. Two essential elements in the social context of modernist art were the disappearance of the old aristocracy along with its patronage of poetic production and the transformation of all products of human enterprise – including art – into merchandise (see Pérus, *Literatura y sociedad en América Latina*). In this situation, poets had to earn their living producing a marketable commodity. Many supported themselves as journalists at the same time that they sought, through their well-crafted poetry, to assert themselves in a world where the items of highest esteem were luxurious, opulent, and usually imported (see Jitrik, *Las contradicciones del modernismo*). Some like Julián del Casal (1863–1893) became marginalized, creating a bohemian response to the vulgarity and utilitarianism of bourgeois society. Others, like Darío in his famous "El rey burgués," scorned the materialism, mediocre conformity, and aesthetic insensitivity of the growing bourgeoisie. Still others, like Martí, put their faith in the superior individual, "el hombre magno" ["the great man"], who could see beyond the pressures of rapid urbanization and commercialization.

With these conditions, modernity, as it is understood in Western culture, arrived in Spanish America – or, at the very least, to its great, cosmopolitan urban centers. Recent studies have emphasized that modernity, as a stage in the history of Western civilization, began as early as the second half of the eighteenth century. Its essential characteristics are linked to scientific and technological progress, the industrial revolution, and the sweeping economic and social changes brought about by Capitalism (see Roggiano, "Modernismo: origen de la palabra y evolución de un concepto"). The ideological adjustments necessitated by these far-reaching alterations in the fabric of life have consistently generated a literary response or, as Octavio Paz notes in *Los hijos del limo* [*Children of the Mire*], modern poetry has always represented a reaction against the modern era and its various manifestations, whether they be the Enlightenment, critical reason, Liberalism, Positivism, or Marxism. Modernism is the literary response to Spanish America's entrance into modernity. It is a response to the spiritual and aesthetic vacuum created by the positivist critique of religion and metaphysics in favor of science as well as by the positivist support of materialistic, bourgeois values.

As the Modernists formulated their reaction to modernity and sought to deal with their feelings of alienation and anguish, they discovered appealing paradigms in the European literature that they had rushed to read in their attempt to create a modern poetic language consonant with the modern times. They found appropriate models in English and German Romanticism, French Parnassianism and Symbolism, for these literary movements too had been reactions to the spiritual upheavals generated by modern life. As a result, the Modernists found their concerns and their poetry to fall within the mainstream of European literary currents. Broadly stated, Modernism is linked to European romantic and post-romantic literary production in the way that they came to formulate the general crisis of beliefs that has dominated Western culture since the Enlightenment and, perhaps more importantly, in the poetic solutions that they opted to follow. Like the English and German Romantics and the French Symbolists, the Spanish American Modernists perceived the anxiety of their age as generated by fragmentation: individuals were out of touch with themselves, with their companions, and with Nature. They longed for a sense of wholeness, for innocence, for the paradise from which they had been exiled by the positivist and bourgeois emphasis on utility, materialism, and progress (see Abrams, *Natural Supernaturalism*). Neither traditional religious beliefs, vitiated by liberal thought, nor the dry intellectualization of Positivism provided satisfactory answers. The hope for amelioration resided in integration and the reconciliation of conflict. The design that the Romantics elaborated for possible recovery and that was later adapted by the Symbolists and the Modernists centers on analogy, that vision of the universe as system of correspondences in which language is the universe's double.

By making analogy the basis of their poetics, these authors – from the early Romantics through the Modernists – made the poet a seer who is in touch with the essence of existence. They also turned poetry into a means of discovery, a way of seeing the supernatural. Poetry became a type of modern religion, replacing traditional religious beliefs which were in crisis. For the English Romantics such as William Wordsworth (1770–1850), Samuel Taylor Coleridge (1772–1834), and Thomas Carlyle (1795–1881), poets were the individuals whose vocation was to liberate the vision of readers from the bondage of habitual categories and social customs – generated in their materialistic environment – so that they could see the new, harmonious world that the poets had come to see. For Charles Baudelaire (1821–1867) and Arthur Rimbaud (1854–1891) and other French Symbolists, poets were the ones who could perceive the harmonious order of the universe behind the chaotic appearance of everyday reality (see Raymond, *From Baudelaire to Surrealism*). In their poetry, as in Baudelaire's influential sonnet "Correspondances," the disordered material of the mundane world is rearranged into an artistic creation that reflects the "dark and profound unity," that is, the orderly soul of both the visionary and the cosmos.

The special language through which the macrocosm and microcosm reveal themselves to each other is the language of symbols, metaphors, and analogies. The mission of poetry is to rediscover this means of communication and to achieve a renewed unity of spirit. To this end, Baudelaire encouraged the free use of words and images, which are to be employed not according to their logical usage but rather in accord with universal analogy, that is, emphasizing the "correspondences" between the material world and spiritual realities as well as among the different human senses. This interrelationship among the senses, which occurs because of affective resonances that cannot be accounted for by logic, provides the conceptual framework for synaesthesia, the term that is applied in literature to the description of one kind of sensation in terms of another. Synaesthesia, which is often identified as one of the most distinctive characteristics of both symbolist and modernist verse, also encourages interplay among the graphic, verbal, and auditory arts, and the appearance of poetic structures based on music or painting. All these features taken together worked to convert the poet's art into an evocative magic.

Stéphane Mallarmé (1842–1898), in turn, sought to increase the magical powers of poetry by separating the crude and immediate from the "essential" condition of words. The "essential" word does not function as an intermediary between two minds, but as an instrument of power capable of awakening the soul to its original innocence. When restored to its full efficacy, language, like music, evokes a pure, untarnished view of the universe. Music, because it is indefinite and innocent of reference to the external world, became the ideal of poetic creation. Paul Verlaine (1844–1896) had written, in his widely influential "Art poétique," "De la musique avant toute chose" ["music before everything"], advocating a poetry of subtlety and nuance that is as elusive and intangible as the scent of mint and thyme on the morning wind. Similarly, Darío in "Dilucidaciones," his introduction to *El canto errante*, addressed the issue of poetry and music and the need for a constantly revitalized and perfectly adaptable poetic form. He wrote: "I do not like either new or old *molds*... My poetry has always been born with its body and its soul, and I have not applied any type of orthopedics to it. I have indeed sung old airs; and I have always wanted to go toward the future under the divine command of music – music of ideas, music of the word."

By viewing Modernism as a movement that sought to confront and respond to conditions and concerns similar to those that appeared in Europe following the end of the Enlightenment, it becomes clear that modernist cosmopolitanism and, more specifically, the stylistic changes and experimentation associated with the modernist adaptation of French models are part of a profound philosophic search in which the sound and substance of poetry are key elements. The purposeful use of the musical resources of poetic language, the internal adjustment of ideas, words, and sounds to the impressions that evoke them, and a return to the ancient Hispanic tradition of rhythmic versification became a way of seeing beyond and even transcending the imperfect here and now. The fossilized language of Spanish poetics was rejected as incapable of attaining the vision that would respond to the collapse of the belief systems dominant at the end of the nineteenth century. While Spanish American poets had read the Spanish Romantics, they failed to find in them convincing models because the spiritual and social dislocations that occurred in Spanish America and that paralleled European experiences had not affected Spain, which remained, for the most part, philosophically and economically isolated. The major exception is Gustavo Adolfo Bécquer (1836–1870), whose emphasis on the sincere expression of profoundly intimate emotions and on the musicality of lyric verse had a strong impact on the Modernists.

In short, the modernist recourse to analogy sheds light on its cosmopolitanism, its obsession with verbal elegance and musicality, and its insistence on artistic freedom, formal experimentation, and heightened individuality. Many of these features, as well as others, were further fostered by the artist's rejection of the commodification, commercialization, and superficiality of "bourgeois modernity," that is, the tradition of modern values which encouraged faith in progress, pragmatism, and the beneficial effects of science and technology (see Calinescu, *Five Faces of Modernity: Modernism, Avant-Garde, Decadence, Kitsch, Postmodernism*). Moreover, the marketplace affected all aspects of life including art and time, and success was judged by the accumulation of wealth. Modernist authors responded to the resulting vacuity of everyday existence with what had become another tradition, namely, the expression of defiantly hostile antibourgeois attitudes. This expression took many forms including "art for art's sake," eccentricity, dandyism, and Decadentism.

The idea of "l'art pour l'art" as conceived by the Parnassian Théophile Gautier (1811–1872) appealed to the poetic imaginations of the early Modernists. With this rallying call they summarized the artist's renunciation of vulgar utilitarianism. Utility was associated with ugliness. Similarly, for some, like the English Pre-Raphaelites, their disgust with contemporary changes in the landscape was such that they came to believe that beauty existed only in pre-industrial settings. The Pre-Raphaelite recourse to allegory and medievalism was another rejection of middle-class values that modernist poets considered and that coincided with the general goal of *épater le bourgeois*. A more radical variation was developed by the Decadents as represented by Joris Karl Huysmans (1848–1907), whose *A rebours* had a tremendous impact on a number of Modernists, most notably José Asunción Silva (1865–1896), del Casal, who corresponded with Huysmans in French, and Darío, who signed his "Mensajes de la tarde" with the name of the novel's protagonist, Des Esseintes.

Nevertheless, neither Gautier nor the Modernists were blind to the benefits of modern inventions. They quickly modified their stand with regard to elements of modern industrial life: they could be transformed through art into a modern kind of beauty. Though, perhaps with the exception of Salvador Díaz Mirón (1853–1928), seldom as adventuresome as Baudelaire, who sought to extract gold from mud or to find flowers in the forbidden realm of evil, the Modernists did come to incorporate aspects of urban modernity in their poetry. This new form of beauty was obviously different from that of classical antiquity. To comprehend the differences as well as the similarities, the Modernists extended their examination of beauty to include all the ages. The resulting syncretism, the extension of cosmopolitanism back in time as well as across borders, is another key feature of modernist verse.

In their unrelenting search for the ideal poetic language, one with which they could address their concerns regarding the life and future of their countries, modernist poets embraced and reconciled varying styles, images, religious beliefs, philosophic perspectives, and modes of discourse. Their ability and desire to incorporate a bewildering diversity of images and ideas is linked, in part, to the economic imperialism of the end of the nineteenth century. Surrounded by an overwhelming proliferation of imported manufactured items, the Modernists created a parallel poetic environment in which things proliferate not in a referential but in an artificial system (see González Echevarría, "Modernidad"). Nature is filtered through any number of aesthetic landscapes from any number of cultures, periods, or artistic media. Modernist art is filled with Versailles-que palaces, oriental gardens and interiors, gods and nymphs, gold and pearls, folding screens (*biombos*), divans, lacquered pieces, urns, and tapestries (see Pacheco, *Antología del modernismo*). These places and things are described, especially in early modernist verse, with sophisticated vocabulary and numerous adjectives that both reinforce a sense of wealth and accumulation and, more importantly, reflect the relationship that modernist poets had with the materialism of bourgeois society. This relationship was strongly ambivalent. On the one hand, the values of the dominant classes are exalted in Modernism's rich language. On the other, however, the emphasis on wealth is criticized as superficial when seen as an end in itself and not recognized as subservient to the poets' profound search for transcendental beauty and universal harmony.

This faith in achieving a harmonious vision of the universe through poetic language distinguishes Modernism from later movements which built upon modernist innovations but which lost its confidence in poetry as a means of attaining a vision of universal accord. The insistent optimism of Modernism as well as its pronounced artificiality, ornamentation, and syncretism have tended to date the movement even though these latter elements reappear – in altered forms, of course, – in the linguistic excesses of the *Vanguardia* [Avant-Garde] and in the neo-baroque stylings of writers like Carpentier and Lezama Lima. The movement's essential modernity is evident, nevertheless, in both its rejection of an obsessive concern for referentiality and its creative reaction to the acute sense of anxiety and alienation characteristic of modern times.

In their syncretic adaptability the Modernists took artistic models that were both traditional and untraditional. They found inspiration in earlier Spanish masters including Berceo, Cervantes, Lope de Vega, Garcilaso, Gracián, Santa Teresa, Góngora, and Quevedo, and they resurrected the irregular versification of old Spanish poetry. More striking, however, is their repeated recourse to Greek mythology and poetics, especially as interpreted by André Marie de Chénier, Maurice Guérin, Charles Marie René Leconte de Lisle, or Louis Ménard. Similarly, the powerful presence of the pre-revolutionary France of the eighteenth century came by way of

Verlaine's *Fêtes galantes*, the writings of the Goncourt brothers (Edmond de [1822–1896] and Jules de [1830–1870]) and the renewal of interest in the paintings of Antoine Watteau (1684–1721). The Nordic mythology that appears in the poetry of Ricardo Jaimes Freyre (1863–1933), Darío, and others invokes the even more exotic and unconventional realities of dark, cold, and distant lands as well as the aesthetic theories of Richard Wagner (1813–1883), which complemented many aspects of the symbolist poetics already discussed. The German composer stressed the interplay of text and music and sought, with his reformulation of Germanic legend, to revitalize Nordic culture which he, like the Modernists with regard to the situation in Spanish America, found to be undermined by crass commercialization. For both Wagner and the Modernists, their artistic formulations were intimately related to the issues of national identity and the formation of national states (see Erika Lorenz, *Ruben Darío "Bajo el divino imperio de la música"*).

For others like Julián del Casal, the Orient held the greatest fascination. Interest in China and Japan can be traced all the way back to the eighteenth century and the construction in the Palacio Real of Madrid of the Salon Gasparini (1764) or in the Palacio de Aranjuez of the Sala China (1784). More immediate, however, was the impact upon turn-of-the-century sensibilities of imported engravings and *objets d'art*, in particular, their transformation of Nature into stylized lines and colors. The literary equivalents, for Spanish America, of these items imported from the Orient once again came by way of France in the poetry of Catulle Mendès, Pierre Loti, and Stéphane Mallarmé, as well as in the French translations of classic Chinese poets in *Le livre de jade* (1867) by Judith Gautier, daughter of Théophile Gautier. The aesthetic innovations introduced as a result of the Modernists' enthusiasm for Oriental art and culture were, as was the case with their other poetic innovations, intimately tied to their search for a deeper comprehension of reality, one which eventually led several poets, most notably Amado Nervo (1870–1919), to explore Buddhism, Taoism, and Zen.

The artistic explorations of syncretism and exoticism were, during the second half of the nineteenth century, further encouraged by the increasingly significant and pervasive scientific explorations of archaeology and philology. They all uncovered unconventional views of beauty and morality, views that offered images of times or philosophies in which spiritual peace, order, beauty, and pleasure appeared attainable. These views increased in importance as the solace offered by orthodox religious beliefs decreased, that is, as the "death of God" was experienced on a personal level. "Science" led the Modernists and their contemporaries further and further away from traditional beliefs (primarily through the positivistic critique of religion) and toward heterodox beliefs (through the archaeological and philological search for origins). These heterodox beliefs generally entered literary circles mediated by a less rigid, more aesthetically pleasing, humanistic – even religious – approach: that of the occult sciences.

The occult sciences offered one great advantage. They explored those "occult" mysteries of life ignored by science with the language of science, giving a certain legitimacy to the spiritual quests of the non-scientist. Darío understood the importance of this phenomenon well. When in 1895 he wrote for *La Nación* about the revival of occultist creeds in Europe at the time, he described the overall goal in the following manner:

> The science of the occult, which before belonged to the initiated, to the experts, is being reborn today with new investigations by wise individuals and by special societies. The official science of the Western World has still not been able to accept certain extraordinary – but still within the realm of the natural in its broadest sense – manifestations like those demonstrated by Crookes and Madame Blavatsky. But fervent followers hope that, as Humanity moves gradually closer to Perfection, a time will come when the ancient *Scientia occulta*, *Scientia occultati*, *Scientia occultans*, will no longer be arcane. The day will come when Science and Religion, as one, will lead man to knowledge of the Science of Life.

This passage underscores certain key elements of turn-of-the-century society. The general malaise of the period – both in Europe and in Spanish America – was identified with a loss, most often that of a paradise from which modern man has been exiled. The ancient way of knowing was considered superior to the modern way, which had opted to consider only physical realities and which tended to disregard the ultimate questions of existence. Despite their limitations, science and technology remained central to the dominant value system, one in which poets had to function. This awareness, as well as the ambivalence that it bred, infiltrates modernist writings. Most Modernists recognized the value and power of science but also felt that they offered in their poetry an alternative vision that was genuinely superior even if it was ignored or misunderstood by the vast majority. The resulting dual perspective becomes evident when one compares modernist prose and poetry. At first the differences appear related to the question of audience and the authors' concessions, in the more widely read prose, to prevalent attitudes. While the public addressed no doubt played a part, a more significant factor is that of modes of discourse. As Aníbal González has shown, (in *La crónica modernista hispanoamericana*) when the Modernists set out to write prose their model was primarily the scientific discourse of philology with second place given to the more commercial mode of journalism. The primary discursive model for modernist poetry was religion with a progressively greater incorporation of the analogical vision proposed by occultism (see Jrade, *Rubén Darío and the Romantic Search for Unity*).

The origin of the distinctive modes of discourse linked to prose and poetry is a romantic tradition that began with Wordsworth. Wordsworth held that the most characteristic subject matter of poetry consists of things modified by passions and the imagination of the perceiver. Wordsworth therefore replaced the contradistinction of poetry and prose with the more philosophical one of poetry and science. Similarly, Coleridge insisted that the essence of poetry, that is, the union of passion, thought, and pleasure, existed in opposition to science and civil and natural history. By the early Victorian period all discourse was explicitly or tacitly thrown into the two exhaustive modes. Religion fell together with poetry in opposition to science and, as a consequence, religion was converted into poetry and poetry into a kind of religion.

When poetry stepped in to fill the void left by the collapse of orthodox belief systems, it found its models in the ancient esoteric tradition that had survived throughout the centuries in hermetic and occultist sects. This tradition is based on analogy and the belief that the universe is alive, harmonious, and responsive. Equally important for the Spanish American poets at the time was the esoteric premise that the ancient wisdom of the sages did not disappear when Christianity became the world's most powerful religion but rather simply assumed the symbolism of the new faith, perpetuating through its emblems and allegories the same truths that have been the property of the wise since the beginning of time. This faith in the fundamental unity of all religions provided those poets who hesitated to abandon their childhood beliefs with a framework in which they would reconcile Catholic dogma with the appealing alternative belief systems. Also, as noted by Darío in the article for *La Nación*, cited above, the syncretic perspective of the occult sciences went so far as to include science and scientific research as well as a wide-reaching eclecticism.

The occultist sects that enjoyed an active revival in Europe during the second half of the nineteenth century were numerous. They included the Theosophical Society founded by Madame Blavatsky and Colonel Olcott, the Rosicrucians headed by Sâr Péladan, and the Independent Group of Esoteric Studies directed by Gérard Encausse, "Papus." They embraced a wide range of systems not always in perfect ideological harmony. There were references to Cabalism, astrology, magnetism, hypnotism, Gnosticism, freemasonry, alchemy, and several oriental religions. The literary circles of Europe were saturated with believers and proselytizers. Recent studies have demonstrated the degree to which romantic and symbolist writings were permeated with cabalistic, hermetic, theosophical, and

Eastern thought. As a result, when tracing occultist influences on modernist verse in most cases it is impossible to determine those that were direct and those that came through contemporary European poetry.

Aspects of these influences have routinely been identified as Pythagorean. It is best, however, to remember that the Pythagoreanism that had an impact upon Modernism was generally reinterpreted through esoteric doctrine and freely combined elements not only from historical Pythagoreanism but also from Neo-Pythagoreanism, Platonism, and Neoplatonism. Perhaps it was the emphasis of esoteric Pythagoreanism on order, harmony, and music that most immediately captured the poetic imagination of this generation of writers and led to the incorporation of a number of unorthodox tenets into what can be called the modernist world view.

As was the case with the Romantics and the Symbolists, harmony as a philosophical ideal associated with divine perfection forms the basis of the modernist cosmology. The entire universe is one harmonious and orderly extension of God, whose soul permeates all and is identical with the great soul of the world. Universal harmony is demonstrated both in the beauty of music and the regularity of the heavenly bodies. The image of celestial music results from the fusion of these two points and distills the modernist view that the universe is a living, rhythmically pulsating extension of God in which all elements are signs that indicate its essential unity.

Since both the individual and the universe are made in the image of God, each being is a microcosm that should strive to implant in his or her soul the harmony seen in the macrocosm. It is recognized, however, that there are certain superior individuals who are more conscious than others of the divine element within them and, consequently, more able to recognize the transcendent order of the world around them. Romantic and symbolist literary theory encouraged the identification of these special individuals with poets. Esoteric beliefs linked this superior status to a highly evolved soul, one that had become perfected through numerous incarnations. While not every Modernist held fast to the idea of transmigration of souls, it is a concept that appears throughout modernist verse either playfully as a dimension of modernist syncretism or seriously as an alternative to Christian salvation.

Another alternative to the strongly restrictive views of Christianity that was supplied by occultism deals with an aspect of modernist art that highlighted its departure from earlier movements. This feature is the modernist elevation of sexuality. Whether sexuality became important as a personal and immediate response to the emptiness of life or as a defiant challenge to the conservatism of middle-class morality (a defiance similar to dandyism in other aspects of life), esoteric tradition supplied a way of looking at sexuality that made it possible for erotic longings to be incorporated in, and to become an essential element of, the modernist cosmology, an element that reinforced and reaffirmed many others already discussed in detail.

As Paz recognized with regard to the Romantics, the exaltation of the natural order of things, especially sexuality, is simultaneously a moral and political critique of civilization and an affirmation of a time before history (*Los hijos del limo*). Erotic passion is a part of nature that has been inhibited and/or destroyed by the social order. Reclaiming its importance becomes linked with intuiting a primordial, more perfect world. For European poets of the second half of the nineteenth century and for the Modernists, the occult sciences provided the framework for this stance. By affirming the sexual nature of the godhead and by appropriating the esoteric myth of primordial man as a cosmic androgyne, sexual love became a means of approximating the androgynous state of the primal man, and, since his fall into evil is identified with his entrance into the world of materiality and two sexes, a return to the union of male and female became a means of perceiving the prelapsarian bliss of unity as well as of intuiting the divine state. The ideal female with whom the poet must join to attain the much pursued perfect vision is often linked with poetic language and the product of their union described in sensuous and seductive terms. Creation, whether poetic, personal, or cosmic, is conceived as sexual. As a result, eroticism and religion are brought together in what is a radically new way for Hispanic poetry.

The experimentation with rhythm and rhyme schemes, verse forms, styles, images, myths, religions, and philosophies that underpins the richness of modernist art began as a search that inevitably turns back upon itself, that is, it is linked to the question of Spanish American modernity and, in broader terms, Spanish American identity. As the modernist poets reflected upon the formation of nation states and the integration of Spanish America into the world economy, they confronted the issue of Spanish American literature. Martí's case is perhaps the most extreme; he aspired to create a new nation as well as a new literature. From this perspective, the political impetus of modernist literature becomes evident – even in the early modernist verse that had been defined by Modernism's first commentators as escapist and superficial. Throughout the development of Modernism, European literature offered models and guidance. The answers that the Modernists formulated were not blind imitations but creative adaptations to their own circumstances and original responses to their unique set of aspirations, tensions, and linguistic possibilities. These answers eventually opened the way for the Avant-Garde.

The modernist movement began in several parts of the continent during the last quarter of the nineteenth century as a development of Romanticism, which had already started to create an original literature for the new, independent countries of Spanish America. It was sustained by the urban affluence and cosmopolitanism of such centers as Mexico City, Havana, and Bogotá in the north and Santiago de Chile, Buenos Aires, and Montevideo in the south. These cities supported the most important literary magazines of the Spanish-speaking world, magazines that were crucial in the diffusion of concepts, trends, and translations and in the formation of a continent-wide movement. They included *Revista Azul*, *Revista Moderna*, *El Cojo Ilustrado*, *El Mercurio de América*, and *Vida Moderna*.

By the 1880s the first Modernists had produced a notable transformation in Spanish literature. The major writers at the time were Manuel González Prada (Peru, 1848–1918), Salvador Díaz Mirón (Mexico, 1853–1928), José Martí (Cuba, 1853–1895), José Asunción Silva (Colombia, 1865–1896), Manuel Gutiérrez Nájera (Mexico, 1859–1895), Julián del Casal (Cuba, 1863–1893), Justo Sierra (Mexico, 1848–1912), and Francisco Gavidia (El Salvador, 1863–1955). It was Darío, however, who became the intellectual center of gravity of the movement, gave it its name, and propelled it forward with driving energy and genius. By the end of the year in which he published the first edition of *Prosas profanas* (1896), a work of revolutionary vision and artistry, he was the undisputed head of and spokesman for Modernism. By the end of 1896 Casal, Martí, Gutiérrez Nájera, and Asunción Silva were dead and the other early Modernists had all written their best poetry. Darío led the younger Modernists in a continued reassessment of poetic language and its relationship to the changing Spanish American scene. The following poets are those who are generally considered the most important younger Modernists (arranged by birthdate): Manuel José Othón (Mexico, 1858–1906), Francisco A. de Icaza (Mexico, 1863–1925), Luis G. Urbina (Mexico, 1868–1934), Ricardo Jaimes Freyre (Bolivia, 1868–1933), Amado Nervo (Mexico, 1870–1919), Guillermo Valencia (Colombia, 1873–1943), José María Eguren (Peru, 1874–1942), Leopoldo Lugones (Argentina, 1874–1938), Julio Herrera y Reissig (Uruguay, 1875–1910), José Santos Chocano (Peru, 1875–1934), Juan Ramón Molina (Honduras, 1875–1908), Franz Tamayo (Bolivia, 1879–1959), Gregorio Reynolds (Bolivia, 1882–1948), Ricardo Miró (Panama, 1883–1940), and Delmira Agustini (Uruguay, 1886–1914).

The early Modernists

While, more than with any other modernist poet, Darío's life and works reflect the major trends and tendencies of the entire modernist movement, the characteristics of his early art had already begun to appear in various places in Spanish America by the time he published his first major volume of work. The features that characterize what would come to be known as modernist poetry included dissatisfaction and disillusionment with the values of the ruling class, anxiety and a sense of crisis with regard to traditional religious beliefs, and an eagerness to establish a new, uniquely Spanish American perspective. The first Modernists aspired to produce a poetry that rivaled the esteemed art and imported items that were entering the great cosmopolitan centers of Spanish America from all corners of the world but most especially from Europe and Europe's cultural capital, Paris. This poetry sought to liberate verse form from the inflexibility of classical norms and to achieve a powerful vision based on an innovative conception of language, one in which musicality was thought capable of evoking profound realities. These founding trends underpin the works of the most accomplished poets of the period. Manuel Gutiérrez Nájera, Julián del Casal, José Martí, and José Asunción Silva are generally considered, along with Darío, the best early Modernists. Even before them, however, others had contributed to the early development of the movement.

Though Manuel González Prada is generally known more for his prose than for his poetry, he published nine important volumes that set Spanish American verse on the road toward Modernism. Part of his poetry was intellectual and didactic, part amorous and sentimental, but above all else it was innovative. After reading Parnassians and Symbolists, he wrote imitations, adaptations, and translation; he experimented with their views of language and their formal changes; he adapted, to Spanish, verse forms from French, English, and Italian; and he incorporated synaesthesia into his work. Justo Sierra also is known less for his poetry than for his work as a historian, educator, orator, and politician, yet in his verse there are clear pre-modernist or early modernist elements. His poetry is graceful, fresh, elegant, and responsive to the new tendencies that came from abroad, from the Parnassians, Bécquer, D'Annunzio, and Nietzsche, to name just a few.

Salvador Díaz Mirón, on the other hand, stands out for his poetic production. Since 1886 when he published his early verse, his presence was felt among modernist writers such as Darío, who praised his dynamic, freedom-loving poetry in one of the "Medallones" of the 1890 edition of *Azul*... While Díaz Mirón's tone was revolutionary and his focus was on the human struggle within the urban, industrialized centers of Spanish America, he wrote with a grace, learning, and attention to style that appealed even to those concerned primarily with the aesthetics of modernist innovations. During his second period, which begins with *Lascas*, his revolutionary concerns were directed toward the formal aspects of his poetry. He experimented with musical effects, with accentual and rhythmic changes, and sought, at the expense of the energy singled out by Darío, a delicate, formal perfection. Another reformer was Francisco Gavidia, who is perhaps best remembered today as one of Darío's teachers. He introduced into Modernism the new rhythms of the French Alexandrine and the Greek hexameter.

Manuel Gutiérrez Nájera

Gutiérrez Nájera was one of the first Modernists to recognize that the stultification of Spanish verse stemmed not from inherent linguistic limitations but rather from a resistance to change fostered by Spain's cultural isolationism. He advocated greater artistic freedom parallel to the cultural openness evident in his beloved Mexico City and in his famous poem "La Duquesa Job." As in this revealing piece, the imported models of elegance and grace by which Mexican society was beginning to judge itself were never proposed as substitutes for uniquely Spanish American attributes. His enthusiasm for European literature, for beauty, musicality, and art for art's sake – without specific pragmatic goals – reflected his faith that art could reveal profound realities, realities he hoped would fill the spiritual void left by traditional religion and by the ideology of the "modern" businessman and scientist. As he repeatedly made clear in his extensive critical writings, he believed that the intuited and evocative wisdom of art would serve the public good as well as national and nationalistic ends. Like the Darío of "Era un aire suave," the Gutiérrez Nájera that has been identified as "Frenchified" cannot be judged superficially. His playful cosmopolitan spirit, his poetic experimentation, as in the Parnassian "De blanco," and his search for the perfect adaptation of image and language, of color and tone are all products of serious reflection upon both the promises and failings of the expanding cultural and commercial environment of the time.

Gutiérrez Nájera knew the changing Mexican scene well. As a professional journalist he kept his readers, many of them women, informed of the events, trends, and fashions of the day. Under various pseudonyms – including his most famous, "El Duque Job" – he wrote reviews, commentary, chronicles, as well as short stories. He actually produced much more prose than poetry, which was collected only posthumously by Justo Sierra in 1896 in a volume entitled *Poesías*. Nevertheless, his poetry was well known and quite influential during his lifetime. It was admired for the vitality and elegance it brought to Spanish verse, even though his innovations were limited to the introduction of new accentual patterns within traditional metrical forms, especially the octosyllable and the hendecasyllable. While Gutiérrez Nájera's confrontation with the spiritual abyss left by the materialistic and positivistic perspectives dominant at the time lends a melancholy and tortured air to much of his poetry, it is its lilting musicality and delicate imagery that leave the greatest impact. His confrontations with the destructive passage of time, the overwhelming presence of death, and the confining limits of human experience are converted into masterpieces that underscore not only the redemptive power of art, as in "Non omnis moriar," but also his unending search for beauty, beauty that could permeate human actions and influence moral behavior. This desire – rooted in Hegelian philosophy and German romantic idealism – to influence, through his art, the course of his nation's history highlights once again the breadth and seriousness of the modernist quest. It also emphasizes the spiritual unity of the movement, for it is perhaps the key element in the works of José Martí, often considered the most imposing figure of the period.

José Martí

It has been virtually impossible to speak of José Martí without alluding to his dedication to the cause of Cuban independence which formed the intellectual backdrop to his political, moral, and philosophic writings and which ultimately led to his death on the battlefield of Dos Ríos. His prose pieces (particularly his speeches), their powerful and innovative use of the Spanish language, and their insightful reflections upon the developments at the turn of the century have tended to receive more attention than his three volumes of verse. His poetry, as he himself confesses, served as a break from his primary tasks of journalism and politics. Nevertheless, those features that have been singled out for praise in his prose are also essential to his poetry and make it fundamental to the formation of the modernist movement. Most important are his sense of moral imperatives and his insistence that language conform to the lyrical impulses that drive it – even at the risk of being shocking or brutally sincere. As Cintio Vitier has pointed out in his "En la mina martiana," Martí not only sought to make a revolution through his words but he also hoped to revolutionize language itself, making it more American and receptive to modern times and, perhaps more importantly, to the future. His famous phrase "La expresión es hembra del acto" underscores the bond between word and deed, suggesting, like the female metaphors that run throughout Darío's work, that language, upon being fertilized, should give birth to verbal children, who, in Martí's case, are the moral equivalent to the acts of just men.

It was possibly this ethical orientation combined with Martí's lasting respect for traditional Spanish verse forms – despite his enthusiasm for the French and North American literature of the day, most notably the visionary figure of Hugo, the sonorous cadences of Whitman, and the oneiric fantasies of Poe – that made early critics slight his contributions to modernist verse. This chronology has now been rectified, thanks in great part to Manuel Pedro González and Iván A. Schulman, who led efforts to have Martí credited with initiating many of the key characteristics of the movement. As a result, the beginning of the movement is now often dated by the publication of *Ismaelillo*, Martí's first collection, in 1882.

In reality, Martí's innovations go to the essence of modern Spanish America, thereby anticipating not only modernist struggles with language but also those of the Avant-Garde. As Martí's own analysis of his poetry in the prose introduction to his *Versos libres* (completed in 1882 and published posthumously in 1913) would indicate, his refusal to temper his structures or images at the expense of his visions, his metaphoric brilliance and novelty, and his acceptance of the difficulty of his verse along with its pure, often brutal, sincerity are characteristics that point to hidden links between Modernism and the Avant-Garde. While a number of studies have examined similarities in the works of Vallejo and Martí, until recently this aspect of modernist poetry has received relatively little attention. Yet it is this willingness – perhaps eagerness – to tap the power of dreamed, unfettered, even illogical visions and verbal structures that is picked up later by Julio Herrera y Reissig and Leopoldo Lugones and that underpins what Yurkievich has called the "causal connection between Modernism and the first *Vanguardia*."

While *Versos libres* was completed during the same year as *Ismaelillo* and contains poems from as early as 1878, *Ismaelillo* is Martí's first published book of verse. It consists of fifteen poems dedicated to his absent son, José Francisco (Pepito), who had been born in 1878. The personal events surrounding their separation and the creation of these poems are of interest in that they emphasize how thoroughly Martí's commitment to the cause of Cuban independence permeated his life and work. While he was living in New York with his wife, Carmen Zayas Bazán, she often accused him of caring more for Cuba than for his family. One day, without notice, she left for Cuba with their son, whom Martí would never see again. Out of the pain of this loss grew *Ismaelillo*, which, in contrast with the texts of the short-lived journal *La Edad de Oro* (1889), is a book not for children but rather about one child. It captures the pure, spontaneous joys of parenthood as well as Martí's hopes for his son and for the future, which come together in the sense of mission and purpose that he aspires to pass on. It is this tension between the lyrical innocence of the child and the moral world of the father that structures the work and also makes it appear so fresh, dynamic, and modern. The son becomes a knight, a shield, a refuge for the father. The work fuses in this way imaginary elements with moral and spiritual comfort and purposeful action. In this regard, Santí ("*Ismaelillo*, Martí y el modernismo") suggests that the title of the collection alludes to the etymology that Martí attributed to Ishmael namely, "Ser fuerte contra el destino" [" to be strong against the challenges of fate"], for the child is heroic despite his not having had to suffer the trials of exile like his true father or his fictional namesake who, along with his mother, was cast out by Sarah, Abraham's legitimate wife.

Despite the fact that *Ismaelillo* was too little read during its time to have been influential, its style represents the best of early Modernism. It makes maximum use of the traditional *seguidilla*, giving it a light and energetic air. Verbs are chosen for their sense of movement, nouns for their metaphoric power, and adjectives for their pictorial qualities. The overall impression is one of activity that borders on chaos, a chaos that reinforces the urgency of the emotions that well up uncontrollably within the loving father.

This sense of urgency also dominates the contemporaneous *Versos libres* and the poems of Martí's next collection, *Flores del destierro* (written between 1882 and 1891 but published posthumously in 1933). There is a verbal abundance, a volcanic flow of emotions and images that suggest the directness and spontaneity of drafts rather than the studied revisions of polished pieces. The adjectives are strong and often surprising and the verbs usually appear in the present, the infinitive, or the imperative, communicating action and activity. Though these works address the same anguish and struggles as *Ismaelillo*, their focus is more universal and the perspective more existential, once again projecting a kinship with poetry of the twentieth century and asserting an unexpected modernity.

All the tensions and pressures that he felt as a committed, conscientious individual are verbalized in what he called the "rough, hairy hendecasyllables" of these poems. With a clearly stated faith in the harmonious order of nature, they explore exile, love, loss, justice, responsibility, and poetry. Anticipating images similar to those of Darío's "Era un aire suave" and "Yo soy aquel que ayer no más decía," Martí in "Poética" describes his verse as capable of going to the salons of the rich and royal, capable of courting ladies and princesses. Yet it prefers the silence of true love and the dense growth of the jungle. There, and not in the urban centers of imported and superficial values, the poet can read the secrets of the universe that he must convey to his readers. His rejection of the city is complete. It represents hypocrisy, fakery, and the masses of poor and suffering. In contrast, the countryside represents purity, sincerity, and contact with the universal forces that give meaning to all the mysteries of life – including love and death. Yet Martí knows, as he makes clear in "Amor de ciudad grande," that the present and future belong to the city, to the world contaminated by time and sin. His poetic response underscores the dilemma of the modern poet – one that haunted Neruda and

Vallejo as well – as he sees himself torn between social action and artistic involvement. Martí finds a compromise that recalls his roots in Romanticism, namely, faith in a sincerity and a purity of purpose that reflects the orderly perfection of nature. All these elements come together later in Poem 17 of *Versos sencillos*, as he envisions his poetry as the musical expression of the loving, knowing rhythm of the cosmos that passes through his soul.

It is in this last collection – with his recourse to the most common of verse forms in the Hispanic tradition, octosyllables, *redondillas*, and quatrains – that his aspiration toward clarity, simplicity, and harmony is most evident. The work's popular tone and its Pythagorean vision of harmony offer a pristine image of Spanish America and of a direct, natural, intuitive wisdom that is easily contrasted with the artifice of Europe and North America. The fusion of art and politics, biography, philosophy, and passion give these simple lyrics a profound and universal transcendence.

Julián del Casal

It is revealing – about the modernist movement and the men in question – that Julián del Casal should in many ways appear to be, as noted by Cintio Vitier (*Lo cubano en la poesía*), the antithesis of his compatriot and contemporary José Martí. These differences stem from different world views, life expectations, and temperaments. Martí's faith in man to act morally and to recreate in his life and art the harmonious order of the universe permeated all that he did and wrote. For Casal life was a constant disappointment, flawed by personal indignities, human failings, and cosmic injustices. He resented having to work as a journalist and lost his job repeatedly, but he had few options and was forced to return to writing for newspapers about the social, literary, and theatrical scene in order to earn a living. Throughout his career, he offended many as he struggled against what he considered crass materialism, ignorance, and bad taste. For the greater part of his life he suffered physical pain and, toward the end, he knew that he would die young.

As a result of all these as well as other philosophic and artistic factors, Casal saw art not as the product of natural forces, as it was for Martí, but rather as something different from and superior to nature. Art was the result of human endeavors; its goal was the creation of an artificial beauty that more often than not elaborated upon other esteemed human creations. As was the case with his best Parnassian sonnets, those of "Mi museo ideal" of *Nieve*, which were based on the paintings of Gustave Moreau, his poems draw upon painting, poetry, and crafted materials of all sorts; they evoke exotic and imaginary settings and affirm the man-made environment of the city and its luxurious urban interiors. Casal makes little effort to hide the influence of his predecessors. The anguished sentimentality of the Romantics (Zorrilla, Bécquer, Heine, Leopardi), the acute and demanding aestheticism of the Parnassians (Gautier, Heredia, Coppée), the subdued attraction to occult realities of the Symbolists (Baudelaire, Verlaine), and the naughty self-indulgence of the Decadents (Baudelaire, Huysmans) are openly present throughout his work, in his first two books of verse, *Hojas al viento*, *Nieve*, and in his third, *Bustos y rimas*, which was prepared during his life but published shortly after his death and which contains both prose and poetry.

This exaltation of artificiality is not the only feature that distinguishes Casal's poetry from Martí's. Casal's dissatisfaction with the *status quo* does not generate, as in Martí, an optimistic, energetic, outward thrust, a push toward change. Quite the contrary, his poetry is marked by an inward turn, the exploration of subtle psychic states, and the presence of suffering, death, boredom, bitterness, inadaptability, impotence, and an inexhaustible longing for escape. As the titles of his first two collections highlight, Casal sought deliverance from the indifferent world that surrounded him in the strange, the foreign (European and Oriental), the sick, the dying, and even the unpleasant.

As different as Martí's and Casal's responses are, it is this rejection of their immediate circumstances that ties them together and makes them both Modernists. Each in his own way struggles to come to terms with the changing Spanish American scene and each finds in poetry – creative, free, responsive poetry – a consolation of sorts. Martí's poetry is more spontaneous, Casal's more studied and refined with a strong emphasis upon pictorial splendor, verbal elegance, and formal innovation – greater accentual flexibility in hendecasyllables, imaginative recourse to nine- and ten-syllable lines, mastery of the monorhyme tercet. Nevertheless the efforts of both poets reflect conscientious attempts to find a language with which to reply to the Spanish America that was taking shape at the time.

José Asunción Silva

Like Casal's, José Asunción Silva's life was colored by an attraction to elegance and indulgence and by a series of tragic events which ultimately culminated with his suicide in 1896. Silva grew up in a Bogotá dominated by a conservative and provincial outlook. His family, in contrast, was known for its interest in and support of the arts as well as its enthusiasm for imported styles, luxury items, and cosmopolitan trends. Silva's father wrote *artículos de costumbres* and the family store was recognized as a center of literary activity. The same store, which carried the latest European fashions that tended to be of little demand in Bogotá, was the source of tremendous financial turmoil and eventually led the family to bankruptcy. Silva's despondency over these economic woes, which forced him out of school and into the workplace, was compounded by personal losses. His grandfather was killed in a violent attack on the family ranch the year before he was born. His great uncle, who had moved to Paris after the attack, died shortly before Silva arrived in Europe. Even greater strains were produced by the death of his father in 1887 and, in 1891, the death of his beloved sister Elvira, to whom his famous "Nocturno" is dedicated.

After resolving the bankruptcy of the family business, Silva sought a diplomatic post as Secretary of the Colombia Legation in Caracas. Though his literary efforts there were received with acclaim, he met political difficulties and returned home a few months later. The ship on which he sailed was damaged on reaching the shores of Colombia and began to sink. Though he survived, he lost the bulk of his unpublished manuscripts from earlier in his life and those that he had written during his stay in Venezuela. This misfortune provided one more devastating blow to the poet, who already felt that life was filled with disappointments and defeats.

Silva had occasionally recited his poems in public and had published a few, but on the whole his work was not well known in Colombia during his lifetime. Twelve years after his death, a few of his published pieces and some fifty other poems were gathered together in a volume entitled *Poesías*, to which Miguel de Unamuno wrote an enthusiastic prologue. Since then at least fifty-three additional poems have been found to belong to the Silva *opus*, which has been divided into three groupings: *El libro de versos*, containing poems from 1891 to 1896 and organized by Silva himself, *Gotas amargas*, and *Versos varios*.

In addition to his poetry, Silva wrote "artistic transpositions," in which he aspired to capture the subtleties of color and shading, and his famous novel *De sobremesa*, which was written in the form of a diary and which evokes the longings, tensions, ambiguities, and anguish of a sensitive and involved intellectual responding to the developing crises in Spanish America at the turn of the century. Like the Silva of "Al pie de la estatua" (written during his last year of life about the disillusionments of the great Bolívar), José Fernández, the novel's protagonist, reflects not only upon artistic, moral, and religious concerns but also upon the changing political situation. Yet it is the obsessive, morose, unstable Fernández and his statements about poetry that reveal the most about Silva's poetic production.

When Silva has Fernández declare that he did not want his poetry to state but rather to suggest, he was speaking for himself. More than any other poet of his generation, Silva wrote under the influence of symbolist poetics with its goal of transforming the music of nature in an evocative language that captures the eternal and profound realities that lie hidden behind the surface of existence. In "Al pie de la estatua" Silva expresses the concepts that Darío, in the same year, placed at the center of his "Coloquio de los centauros" and that Baudelaire had outlined in his famous "Correspondances":

> Fija
> En ella sus miradas el poeta,
> Con quien conversa el alma de las cosas,
> En son que lo fascina,
> Para quien tienen una voz secreta
> Las leves lamas grises y verdosas
> Que al brotar en la estatua alabastrina
> Del beso de los siglos son señales
> Y a quien narran leyendas misteriosas
> Las sombras de las viejas catedrales.

[It [the statue] is the focus of the poet, with whom the soul of all things converses, in a way that fascinates him, for whom the light greenish and gray patina has a secret voice and, upon issuing from the alabaster statue, is a sign of the kiss of centuries, and for whom the shadows of the old cathedrals narrate mysterious legends.]

For Silva nature is eternal, divine, and harmonious; it speaks to the poet whose task is to translate into poetry its cosmic signs and symbols and its hidden and vital forces. Silva's great talent, which is epitomized in his most acclaimed poem, "Nocturno," was the creative use of the rhythmic resonances of the Spanish language – enhanced by a free use of repetition – together with the symbolic evocation of subtle psychological and spiritual states that respect the limits of cognitive comprehension and the impermeability of certain mysteries. In "Nocturno" the interplay of light and shadow, intertwined in the central and structuring metaphor of "la sombra nupcial," suggests a reality that evades precise definition.

In poems such as "Vejeces" or "La voz de las cosas" the longevity of the spirit is contrasted with the fugacity of individual existence. Despite the solace thus evoked there remains in many poems a sense of suffering and loss reflective of Silva's tendency to indulge in a mournful and morose investigation of unhappiness. In some poems from *Gotas amargas*, a collection that Silva seems to have planned to leave unpublished, suffering results from the incomprehension of the scientific community, which is mocked in acerbic and sarcastic tones. The resulting satire highlights the pain, anguish, and anger of the modernist struggle with "bourgeois modernity" and with the dominant positivistic values of the day. With his sights set on the exploration of the mysteries that elude modern science,

Silva had patience neither for Parnassian aesthetic play nor for popular but superficial imitations of Darío's work, a point well made in his satiric "Sinfonía color de fresa con leche."

Rubén Darío

On January 18, 1867, Félix Rubén García Sarmiento was born in a small town known today as Ciudad Darío. The Darío by which he was known all his life was not so much a pseudonym as a patronymic, the last name used by his father as well as his grandfather. Shortly after his birth his parents separated and he was taken to live with his great aunt and her husband in León. Thus began his peripatetic life which took him to all corners of the Hispanic world driven, for the most part, by economic necessity.

By the age of twelve he had already published his first poems. During these early years there were frequent trips between the cities of Managua, Granada, and León with, in 1882, a year's stay in El Salvador. There the poet Francisco Gavidia introduced Darío to French literature – to the formal beauty of Parnassian verse, to the gnostic and pantheistic writings of Victor Hugo, and to the Alexandrine and hexameter. By 1886 when he left Central America for Chile, Darío had read widely among the Spanish classics as well as selected Greek poetry in translation and contemporary French verse published in the *Revue des Deux Mondes*.

His three years in Chile, from 1886 to 1889, offered the young Darío an opportunity to expand the arena of his cultural explorations. They provided a cosmopolitan setting, friendship with many writers and intellectuals, and contact with a society that, because of its growing prosperity, enjoyed sophisticated manners of behavior, dress, and patronage. During this time, Darío wrote for important newspapers like Santiago's *La Época*, developed an elegant and effective prose style, and published his first books of poetry *Abrojos* and *Rimas*. He also wrote the novel *Emelina* (with Eduardo Poirier) and the award-winning *Canto épico a las glorias de Chile*. Even in his earliest poetry there are hints of the metrical experimentation, the emotional depth, and the metaphorical brilliance that would characterize his mature production; still stronger at this point was the influence of his immediate predecessors, most notably Bécquer and Campoamor.

Azul. . . was the work that made Darío famous and by which critics used to date the beginning of Modernism. The already-cited letter by Juan Valera turned Darío into the focus of attention for those interested in the revolutionary but still unnamed literary movement that was taking shape in Spanish America. It is now widely agreed that the greatest innovation appears in the collection's short stories and vignettes, written under the influence of Mendès, Flaubert, Hugo, and Zola. They show Darío's eagerness to experiment with many styles and modes of discourse, his enthusiasm for the various arts, and his desire to break, as the Romantics had done, the restrictive confines of established genres. Most important, however, was the underlying disillusionment – which he shared with many other Spanish Americans writing at the time – with the mundane and pedestrian, especially when they imply a withering of aesthetic and spiritual powers. "El rubí," "El sátiro sordo," "El palacio del sol," "El rey burgués," and, perhaps most directly, the introductory section of "En Chile" all criticize the limited and limiting vision of bourgeois materialism, science, and technology. "En Chile" begins with a paragraph-long sentence that suggests the fundamental focus of Darío's writings at this point.

> Without brushes, without palette, without paper, without pencil, fleeing the excitement and confusion, the machines and bundles, the monotonous noise of the trolleys and the jostling of horses with their ringing of hooves on the stones, the throng of merchants, the shouts of vendors, the incessant bustle and unending fervor of this port in search of impressions and scenes, Ricardo, an incorrigible lyric poet, climbed up to Happy Hill, which, elegant like a great flowering rock, displays its green sides, its mound crowned by smiling houses terraced at the summit, homes surrounded by gardens, with waving curtains of vines, cages of birds, vases of flowers, attractive railings, and blond children with angelic faces.

The world of the modern, industrial city with its traffic, noise, and newspapers (the commercial side of writing) is left behind in search of "impressions and scenes," that is, in search of a nature filtered through, captured in (like the caged birds and cut flowers), and idealized by art (blond children with angelic faces). He leaves the Valparaiso "that performs transactions and that walks like a gust, that peoples the stores and invades the banks" in hopes of finding "el inmenso espacio azul" ["the immense blue space"] – not only the free, clear sky of beauty and tranquility but also the source of artistic vision, which converts the author into a seer capable of recording the profound realities of existence, an existence that is in essence beauty and harmony and not the crass commercialization of the urban setting. This is the point Darío alluded to in his title. *Azul. . .* recalls Hugo's *L'art, c'est l'azur* and therefore evokes the ideal, the infinite, and the eternal – all perceived through and recreated in art.

The poems of the first edition of *Azul. . .* reflect the same tensions and longings mixed with the added element of erotic passion. "El año lírico," which begins the poetic selection, is an escape from the prosaic similar to that found in "En Chile" except the exotic, fanciful, and exquisite settings underscore a fundamental aspiration toward a harmony that is intimately linked to the fulfillment of sexual desire. Woman, more than the poet's Muse, is the other who complements and completes and with whom the poet attains a vision of beauty, harmony, and artistic perfection that is simultaneously in tune with and supported by nature. The distance between this dreamed perfection and contemporary, "civilized" existence is presented in "Estival," where the flow of sexual energy, which is portrayed as the animating force in nature and the inexorable bond between male and female, is disrupted by a cruel and senseless act on the part of the Prince of Wales. Power and modern technology burst upon a scene of lush sensuality and animalistic eroticism interrupting the natural order of things. "Estival" thus emphasizes how uninformed human intervention destabilizes the balance of creation unlocking violence, pain, and discord.

For the 1890 edition of *Azul. . .* Darío added a number of poems that highlight his rapid maturation as a poet. "Venus" continues the themes of the earlier edition while it reasserts – with its unusual seventeen-syllable lines – efforts to expand the poetic potential of Spanish. The idealization of love seen before is maximized as the unnamed object of desire fuses with the star/goddess Venus. Here, however, the unreflective hope for ecstasy of the earlier poems is placed in doubt. The expectation of a perfect union in which personal and artistic goals are achieved is dashed as the heaven from which Venus looks down upon the poet is turned into an abyss of unfulfilled and possibly unfulfillable longings.

The other additional sonnets included in the 1890 edition deal with Caupolicán, Leconte de Lisle, Catulle Mendès, Walt Whitman, J. J. Palma, Salvador Díaz Mirón, and Alessandro Parodi and point to Darío's preoccupation with poetic discourse. Here Darío praises those features consonant with his goals for modernist verse: a soul that is in touch with the world and capable of prophetic powers ("Walt Whitman"), a song that echoes the rhythmic pulsation of the ocean and that contains the mysteries of the Orient ("Leconte de Lisle"), classic grace and intimate knowledge ("Catulle Mendès"), and powerful poetry that proclaims the freedom of the new nations of the New World ("Salvador Díaz Mirón").

Between the first and second editions of *Azul. . .* Darío was confronted by serious financial difficulties that forced his return to Nicaragua in February of 1889. After a few months in Nicaragua he left for El Salvador to manage *La Unión.* There he fell in love with Rafaela Contreras and married her on June 26, 1890. Just then a military coup overthrew his protector, President Francisco Menéndez, and Darío was compelled to leave for Guatemala. In Guatemala he became friends with Jorge Castro, who introduced him to theosophy and other occult beliefs that rounded out the readings that he had begun earlier with Gavidia. While in

Guatemala he also published the augmented version of *Azul.* . . Yet, because of the demise of the newspaper that he was directing, Rafaela and he were once again obliged to move on, this time to Costa Rica, where his son Rubén Darío Contreras was born on November 12, 1891. By May of 1892 further financial problems caused Darío to leave his wife and son as he returned to Guatemala alone. There he was named Secretary to the Nicaraguan delegation to the Fourth Centenary of the Discovery of America to be celebrated in Madrid on October 12, 1892.

In Madrid he met the old guard of Spanish letters including Zorrilla, Valera, Castelar, Núñez de Arce, Pardo Bazán, and Campoamor as well as the Spanish Modernists headed by Salvador Rueda, for whose *En tropel* he wrote a verse prologue. While in Spain Darío extended his fame and consolidated his stature as leader of the modernist movement. After a few months he returned to Nicaragua with a stopover first in Havana so that he could meet Julián del Casal whose *Hojas al viento* and *Nieve* had explored issues similar to those that Darío was confronting in his own work. Upon his return to his homeland he learned of his wife's death in El Salvador. Though he always remembered Rafaela as the ideal bride, he was quickly remarried – perhaps with no choice in the matter – to Rosario Emelina Murillo. In April of 1893 he was named Consul-general of Colombia in Buenos Aires. Darío left Rosario in Panama and headed for Buenos Aires by way of New York and Paris. In New York he met Martí, whose work – especially the prose – Darío had long admired. In Paris, Darío witnessed the heyday of Symbolism and met with Enrique Gómez Carrillo, Alejandro Sawa, Paul Verlaine, and Jean Moréas.

Darío arrived in Buenos Aires in August of 1893. Though the position as Consul-general did not last long, he was not totally without support; he had already been invited to work for the best newspapers in Argentina. During his five years in Buenos Aires, from 1893 to 1898, Darío continued to write both prose and poetry. He founded the *Revista de América* with Jaimes Freyre and published, in 1896, an important and revealing series of articles on modern European and American authors entitled *Los raros*. About the same time he began a novel called *El hombre de oro*.

It was, nevertheless, the publication of *Prosas profanas* in 1896 that marked a watershed in the modernist movement. Darío saw himself at the head of the dominant Hispanic literary movement of the day, in full control of his talents, and in a position to challenge – with his inventive title, his poetic innovations, and the overt sexuality of most of the poems – conservative critics, unsympathetic members of society, and less creative rivals. He was able to assume the responsibilities left to him by the death of so many of the other early Modernists because of his encyclopedic grasp of culture, his syncretic imagination, and his keen sense of direction and purpose. His views stated in the non-manifesto manifesto at the beginning of *Prosas profanas*, "Palabras liminares," and in its three masterly introductory poems constitute a careful, comprehensive, and insightful commentary on Modernism, one reflective of the essential elements that shaped the movement since its inception, one that demands detailed attention.

Prosas profanas is often described as a youthful, exuberant work full of exotic frivolity, playful imagination, and pleasure. When Darío himself refers to the content of the collection and its title he directs attention toward sexual passion – a sexual passion that is inextricably linked to art, poetic creation, music, and religion. He wrote: "I have said, in the pink Mass of my youth, my antiphons, my sequences, and my profane proses . . . Ring, bells of gold, bells of silver; ring every day, calling me to the party where eyes of fire shine, and the roses of mouths bleed unique delights." The proses, like the antiphons and sequences, are verses or hymns said or sung during the Mass. Darío plays with these medieval allusions, breaks expectations regarding the genre in question, and equates divine love and religious devotion with sexual exploits.

While pleasure is certainly at issue, so is "proper behavior" and decorum. However much the young Darío was preoccupied with sexuality, he was also fascinated – not unlike the Romantics and Symbolists before him – by the limits, restrictions, and constraints imposed on behavior, language, and vision by society, perhaps the same limits that tortured Casal and haunted Silva. As a result, the sociocultural context of Modernism is never far from his mind. He begins "Palabras liminares" with regret over the lack of understanding common to the general public and to professionals. It is art that sets him – and the others that he would rally to his cause – apart. Yet art is not imitation; it is the transgressing of limits, it is the reinterpretation and revitalization of habit and custom by each artist.

The interplay between poetry and society reappears as the aristocratic and exotic elements of art are offered in response to and escape from the materialism that flourished at the expense of aesthetic and spiritual concerns. It is this conflict of values that forms the background to Darío's declaration that "I detest the life and times to which I was born." This statement is not, however, a rejection of Spanish America. Quite the contrary, Darío finds poetry in "our America," as he did in *Azul . . .*, in "the old things," in Palenke and Utatlán, in the sensual and refined Inca, and in the great Montezuma. As is clear from his own remarks, the thrust is toward the cosmopolis and the future in both of which the Spanish, Spanish American, and European (Parisian) would find a balance. This future milieu would facilitate the creation of a modern mode of discourse, that is, a poetry that responds to the constraints of modern life by rediscovering the soul of language and its musical nature ("Since each word has a soul, there is in each verse, in addition to verbal harmony, an ideal melody. Frequently, the music comes exclusively from the idea.").

The reference to the soul of language implies a body which, in Darío's poetry, is clearly female. For language to become poetry it must be inseminated with ideas that are in essence "an ideal melody." This image of poetic creation adds a revealing dimension to the role of woman and to the overall sexuality of *Prosas profanas*. For example, with regard to influences, he declares "my wife is from my homeland; my lover, from Paris." Similarly, he concludes "Palabras liminares" with the mandate: "And the first law, creator: create. Let the eunuch snort. When a Muse gives you a child, let the other eight be left pregnant." Despite the jocular tone of this command, Darío is never blind to the possibility that he may not find the female other that he seeks. This concern continues into the first three poems of *Prosas profanas*.

Darío begins with Eulalia of "Era un aire suave. . ." By characterizing her – or, actually, her golden laughter – as cruel, Darío softens the bold and ambitious declaration of artistic goals of the prose preface. He acknowledges the possible recalcitrance on the part of poetic language to be molded to the form he envisions. By calling her eternal, he affirms his aspiration – and that of the other Modernists – to take Spanish American discourse out of its limited and anachronistic present and to have it become "modern" through a syncretic exaltation of the beauty and art of all ages, primarily as they come to him filtered through contemporary French sensibilities. For this reason, the second part of "Era un aire suave. . ." is a series of questions regarding the setting of the first part. The repeated proposing of alternative periods to which the scene described could belong suggests the degree to which Darío aspires to transcend temporal and spatial limitations and to achieve universality. The human, particularistic elements are clearly subsumed to the creation of atmosphere and tone; passion becomes role-playing; eroticism becomes art.

At the perfect point in the timeless evening of the poem (in the last three stanzas of the first section), surrounded by auspicious and evocative music and an ivory-white swan of formal beauty and fluid grace, the poet will join with Eulalia, vanquishing his rivals, the "vizconde rubio" ["the blond viscount"] and the "abate joven" ["the young abbot"]. This reference to the defeat of his social and literary competitors offers some solace, but the poet's happiness is mitigated by the fact that there is no lasting amorous conquest. On the contrary, he remains her page, her servant. Both sections of "Era un aire suave. . ." end with references to Eulalia's mocking laughter.

With this emphasis on Eulalia's aloof nature and the possible intractability of poetic language, "Era un aire suave. . ." anticipates the lament as well as the images of "Yo persigo una forma. . .," which was added as the last poem to the 1901 edition of *Prosas profanas*. Yet whereas "Yo persigo una forma..." pretends to decry the poet's limitations ("Yo persigo una forma que no encuentra mi estilo, / ... / Y no hallo sino la palabra que huya, / la iniciación melódica que de la flauta fluye..." ["I pursue a form that my style does not find, / ... / and I find only the word that flees, / the melodic introduction that flows from the flute..."]), "Era un aire suave..." suggests cautious optimism as Darío enters the *fêtes galantes* and competes with Verlaine and his other (imported) role models and rivals.

This sense of response to the proliferation of cultural elements that dominated European and Spanish American values at the end of the nineteenth century is central as well to "Divagación," the second poem in *Prosas profanas.* "Divagación" is filled with cosmopolitan references, exquisite vocabulary, and esoteric proper names. Moreover, like "Era un aire suave ...," it deals with a beloved that is much more than a possible love interest. Yet, throughout his poetic journey across the globe, he finds that no one woman can satisfy; no one style can fulfill his longing for an original mode of discourse. The poet's aspiration to a comprehensive grasp of reality takes him through a literary "museum," which he ultimately leaves behind. He affirms instead the power of poetry, through which he claims divine knowledge and authority. He makes this claim in the final three stanzas of the poem in which he leads the reader off the map into the world of the transcendental, thereby emphasizing the divine mission that he strives to achieve, a mission he shared with the less self-assured Silva. The savior of poetry appears – as he does in "Sonatina," the next poem of the collection – highlighting Darío's fundamental concern with his own success in choosing the proper vessel to receive his poetic energy, the proper language to inseminate with ideal music.

At the end of "Sonatina" the sad princess is given hope for happiness, love, life, and salvation in the form of

> el feliz caballero que te adora sin verte,
> y que llega de lejos, vencedor de la Muerte,
> a encenderte los labios con su beso de amor!

> the happy knight that adores you without seeing you
> and that arrives from far away, conqueror of Death,
> to enflame your lips with his kiss of love!

No matter how frivolous "Sonatina" appears at first with its nursery-rhyme rhythm and its fanciful gardens and palace, by the final stanza the profound nature of the fairy-tale couple becomes evident. The knight who arrives mounted on his winged steed, victor of Death, is more than the proverbial "Prince Charming" who appears in time to revive the lovesick princess. The linking of the hero/savior with Pegasus, the horse of the Muses, identifies the hero as an artist. His ability to lead his love – and his readers – out of the imperfect present into a paradisiacal future recalls the

Christ-like attributes that become a recurrent feature of Darío's later poetry about poetic responsibility. If the knight who arrives at the end of "Sonatina" most closely corresponds to the poet/hero/savior, the princess who awaits him is the female consort of the male creator. It is here that the central image and the title of the poem show their fundamental union, one that is etymological. The rich, elaborately housed princess serves as a female other, a type of *Muse*, who makes possible the creative articulateness of the male voice. She allows him to fulfill his role as savior by turning language into *music*. This goal is further emphasized by the rhythmic virtuosity of the poem, which is written in superb dactylic Alexandrines. The interplay among language, music, and poet thus delineated in "Sonatina" is a continuation of Darío's attempts to clarify his artistic aims which he had begun in "Palabras liminares," "Era un aire suave . . .," and "Divagación."

Darío holds that poetic language has lost its vitality and color; it is imprisoned in a golden vessel. The *music* that should be heard is silent; the atmosphere is stifling, unimaginative, and uninspired. The objects that have come to be associated with the princess's imprisonment as well as with her physical and spiritual decline are boldy denounced. Yet Darío's detailed rejection is just the opposite of what it claims to be. It becomes a way of possessing, internalizing, and incorporating into his art those aspects that he pretends to disown. He disdains the palace and its wealth as incapable of providing spiritual gratification. In fact they appear as obstacles to knowledge and distractions that prevent the enlightened from seeing beyond the superficial trappings of life (as in "El rey burgués" of *Azul. . .* and in "Poética" by Martí). At the same time, however, he takes possession of the opulence through description.

This ambivalent position with regard to the riches of the palace reflects an even greater struggle – one common among modernist authors. The poet challenges the superficial materialism of the bourgeois society in which he lives. He strives to assert the worth of his creation in an environment that tends to ignore the value of his art, knowledge, and spiritual insight. The poet fights for the respect and esteem that he feels he deserves by taking up the weapons of the enemy – wealth and opulence – and by poetically rendering them impotent. As the princess's wealth is made subservient to the spiritual wealth offered by the poet, the value of poetic vision and artistic achievement is doubly raised above everyday reality ("the life and times to which [he] was born"): as clear a response to the established order of life as Martís, Casal's, or Silva's. Only after the princess (poetic language) recognizes the appropriate (inferior) position of material wealth can the poet fulfill his superior destiny. In short, the poetic goals outlined in "Sonatina" and the other pieces examined point to a political and philosophic awareness behind the frivolity, musicality, and aesthetic play with which *Prosas profanas* has generally been characterized.

Assessments of the collection have tended to be shaped by the overwhelming impact of its formal artistry and conceptual innovation by which Darío continued the discovery or recovery of a large variety of verse forms begun by earlier Modernists. In addition to the dactylic Alexandrine of "Sonatina," Darío resuscitated verses of twelve syllables in "Elogio de la seguidilla" and the poetry of the *cancioneros* of the fifteenth century in "Dezires, layes y canciones." Through caesuras placed at different points and the use of enjambement, he further expanded the musical effect of traditional forms. The great flexibility of poetic prose appears in "El país del sol," and the synaesthetic mixing of music and color is evident in "Sinfonía en gris mayor," a poem inspired by the Parnassian art of Gautier. Yet in all these works the passing pleasure of artistic experimentation and/or of the sexual *pas de deux* is an aspect of profound, enduring, social, and even religious concerns.

The resolution of these and other apparent contradictions is proposed in Darío's masterpiece of this period, "Coloquio de los centauros." On the magical "Golden Island" the centaurs strive for a reconciliation of the tensions within their composite nature and a reintegration into the harmonious and well-working universe. As Quirón helps them perceive what is evident to the poet/seer, namely, that the language of nature reveals the hidden order of the cosmos, they come to understand that the acceptance of the fundamental accord of all existence – the essential unity of the bestial and the divine, good and evil, male and female, life and death – is the key to the paradisiacal vision that they pursue.

The neoplatonic and pantheistic premises of the esoteric Pythagoreanism that underpins the world view of "Coloquio" are further developed in "Las ánforas de Epicuro," a series of poems that was added along with "Cosas del Cid" and "Dezires, layes y canciones" to the 1901 edition of *Prosas profanas*. These delicate and thoughtful poems elaborate, with a new-found grace and transcendent quality, previously expressed themes: the enduring presence of God throughout creation, the harmonious nature of the cosmos, the reconciliation of opposites, love, poetry, and poetic responsibility. By 1901 Darío's perspective, while still influenced by classical and European styles, tends to the universal and timeless. This trajectory would reach its zenith in *Cantos de vida y esperanza. Los cisnes y otros poemas*, in which Darío will reveal himself to be a poet who is more sure of himself and more willing to express his sense of difference – his sense of being Spanish American. The imported models that dominated his poetic imagination in *Prosas profanas* will have receded. His concerns will reflect his sad awareness of the passage of time and of the youthful squandering of energies. They will also address directly the sociopolitical context only alluded to previously.

After living in Buenos Aires for five years, Darío returned to Spain in 1898 as correspondent for *La Nación*. He was to remain in Europe for several years, residing in Barcelona, Madrid, and Paris. He also traveled in Italy and southern Spain, finding much to admire throughout his journeys. Between 1902 and 1905 he wrote a number of articles which he later published as *Opiniones*. In 1906, after a trip to Brazil, he was named Nicaraguan Consul in Paris and then, in 1907, Nicaraguan Ambassador to Spain. Though during these years he was at the height of his career and fame, he never fully resolved the financial and personal problems that plagued him from the beginning. He did, however, find a supportive and caring female companion, Francisca Sánchez, who, in 1900, bore him a daughter and, in 1903, a son, whom he nicknamed Phocás and referred to in a poem published in his next major work, *Cantos de vida y esperanza*. Tragically Phocás lived just a short time. A second son, also called Rubén Darío Sánchez was born in 1907.

Like *Prosas profanas*, *Cantos de vida y esperanza* begins with an important prose introduction that responds to the critics of the day and that clarifies a number of points already discussed. Darío defends his poetry by emphasizing its grounding in the "aristocracy of thought" and the "nobility of art" which, in turn, continue to be offered as antidotes to the mediocrity, intellectual stultification, and aesthetic superficiality that he sees in contemporary society. With pride he recognizes that Modernism, unlike previous literary movements, originated in Spanish America and later spread to Spain, although he slants the historical picture somewhat by proclaiming himself the founder of the movement. Though not the first Modernist, he certainly gave to Modernism a breadth of vision, a philosophy of language, and an intellectual depth that unified disparate elements from diverse countries and allowed him to be considered its head. He also increased, as he notes, against entrenched resistance, the flexibility of Spanish poetic expression, maintaining as his goal a pure and direct reflection of his view of beauty. With this apparently simple statement, Darío reaffirms his links to romantic literary theory and its emphasis on art as the evocation of the profound realities of existence as they are perceived by and filtered through the unencumbered and undistorted soul of the poet. He repeats this position in the first poem of the collection, "Yo soy aquel que ayer no más decía," when he asserts the importance of sincerity and the dangers of artifice. As Darío had made clear in "La fuente" from "Las ánforas de Epicuro," modernist art demands that poets be true to themselves and to the music that they find in themselves. Darío concludes the "Prefacio" by pointing out that this truth includes open and direct discussion of the social and political concerns made more pressing than ever before by the Spanish American War of 1898 and US intervention in the creation of Panama in 1903. In *Cantos de vida y esperanza* there is, in turn, a greater enthusiasm for his Spanish and Spanish American heritage – an enthusiasm that carries over into his next collection, *El canto errante*.

"Yo soy aquel que ayer no más decía" can be read as a poetic complement and continuation of the introduction, a brilliant reappraisal of his literary career and his personal life as well as an insightful declaration of his new orientation. With opening echoes of Hugo's "Celui qui . . .," references to his cosmopolitan embrace of art, and refutations of having achieved formal perfection at the expense of emotional depth and honesty, Darío reviews his early endeavors. It becomes clear, however, that he has now entered a new phase, one in which the primary importance of art is its redemptive power which makes it possible for the poet and reader to become one with the harmony of the universe within the "sagrada selva" ["sacred forest"] of controlled passions and resolved tensions. Darío calmly admits that the promise of salvation is not absolute:

> la adusta perfección jamás se entrega,
> y el secreto ideal duerme en la sombra

> [austere perfection never gives itself up,
> and the ideal secret sleeps in the shadow]

Yet he consoles himself in the last stanza by affirming that the journey toward death goes by way of Bethlehem when virtue and discipline determine the course.

Throughout *Cantos de vida y esperanza* Darío develops the issues presented in these two introductory pieces. He confronts the passage of time and the inevitability of death ("Canción de otoño en primavera," "A Phocás el campesino"); he struggles with his religious doubts and despair; and he affirms the divinity of his poetic mission ("Pegaso," "¡Torres de Dios! ¡Poetas!"). When traditional beliefs fail him, faith in art, in the harmony of the universe, and in the perfectibility of man as revealed by art become the basis for hope ("Mientras tenéis, oh negros corazones," "Helios," "Filosofía," "Ay, triste del que un día. . .," "Caracol"). Even love becomes an aspect of his search for transcendence. Influenced by esoteric thought, Darío's erotic poetry is no longer as playful, light-hearted, or defiantly rebellious as it had been throughout most of *Prosas profanas*; it now evokes the eternal order and perfection of creation ("Por un momento, oh Cisne, juntaré mis anhelos," "¡Antes de todo, gloria a ti, Leda!" "¡Carne, celeste carne de la mujer! Arcilla," "En el país de las Alegorías," "Amo, amas," "Programa matinal"). Yet modern life repeatedly cuts him off from this sense of well-being and belonging, leaving him either to recall the religious answers of his youth ("Canto de esperanza," "Spes," "¿Qué signo haces, oh Cisne, con tu encorvado cuello," "¡Oh, terremoto mental!" "El verso sutil que pasa o se posa") or to suffer the anguish of total despair, a despair which is often exacerbated by an overwhelming sense of guilt ("La dulzura del ángelus," "Nocturno I," "Melancolía," "Nocturno II," "Lo fatal"). Unable to see beyond the chaos and disorder around him, he accuses himself of failing to fulfill the divine destiny he claimed for himself as poet/seer in "Alma mía" of "Las ánforas de Epicuro." While Darío's political poetry – even those poems such as "Salutación del optimista" or "A Roosevelt" that express concern regarding the strength of the United States – often strikes today's reader as naive and outdated, his poems of desperation retain the power of their modernity and the intensity of their suffering. "Lo fatal," the two "Nocturnos" from *Cantos de vida y esperanza*, and a third from *El canto errante* stand out for their emotional energy and for their poetic artistry.

The three "Nocturnos" share a single poetic climate and are united by a serious, almost tragic tone of self-examination. In the first Darío announces their central theme: the dual horror of consciousness and conscience. He confronts the fleeting nature of existence, the halting but inexorable march toward "the unavoidable unknown," and the disjuncture between the artistic and personal goals he has set for himself and what he has actually achieved. The distant clavichord never yielded its sublime sonata to the poet's imagination, and he now fears that he must pay the cost of his search for beauty and pleasure. His only consolation is the belief that life is merely a nightmarish, fitful sleep from which he will be awakened to see a truer reality. This image is taken up in the second "Nocturno."

If life is a fitful sleep, the nights of insomnia become the moments of vision. It is during the dark, sleepless hours that Darío sees with greatest clarity both the illusion of life and the omnipresence of death. He joins in union with all who, in their sleepless self-reflection, have developed an acute sensitivity to the world that surrounds them. They are the ones who, in the mysterious silence of the night, when the past escapes from the prison of oblivion and resurfaces as the voice of conscience, understand the full significance of his verse. By the fourth and penultimate quatrain, it becomes clear that Darío's greatest concern is that he may have failed to be what he should have been and he has lost the kingdom that should have been his. While the poet's unanimity with the beat of universal life suggests the promise of salvation through the assimilation of the divine order, it also reminds the poet of the responsibilities of his vocation and, as is even more evident in "Lo fatal," reinforces the imperatives of the doctrine of transmigration of souls. The resulting anguish is most intensely expressed in the fourth stanza. The alliteration of the *p*'s emphasizes the echo of "pesar" ["sorrow" or "regreat" but also the verb "to weigh," "to be weighty"] in "pensar" ["to think"] and evokes the overwhelming impact of the poet's loss ("pérdida"), while the masculine rhyme of the second and fourth lines intensifies the poet's cry of remorse for his mistakes. With its deliberately ambiguous ending, "Nocturno II" captures Darío's see-sawing emotions, his sense of inadequacy and despondency as well as his hopes and pride.

In "Lo fatal," the last poem of *Cantos de vida y esperanza*, Darío juxtaposes the sense of failure to meet his spiritual responsibilities with the apparent ignorance or insensitivity of the creatures on the lower levels of existence. While he envies their immunity from the pangs of conscience, Darío dreads the thought that his soul may descend from the human to the animal in retribution for having sullied his elevated status with "the flesh that tempts." This allusion to the great chain of being serves as an underlying metaphor which enhances the poem's evocation of downward spiraling despair. By the end there is a total breakdown of grammatical and stropic structures. The poet conveys the stranglehold of fear with sentences and stanzas that remain unfinished, with the purposeful elimination of the last line of what would have been a sonnet.

Like the reference to the "kingdom that should have been his" of "Nocturno II," the line "y el temor de haber sido y un futuro terror" ["and the fear of having been and a future terror"] reflects Darío's obsession with the past and the future, especially with the life that will be his after death. The horror of the future stems from the dual burden of consciousness ("la vida consciente" ["conscious life"]) and conscience ("sufrir por la vida y por la sombra" ["to suffer for life and for the shadows"]). Unlike the tree and rock with which the poem begins, the human is fully aware of his responsibilities and how well he has met them. For the modernist poet who holds that his obligations include fulfilling the visionary destiny of an advanced being, the burden is even greater. In Darío's case, he often alludes to this situation, describing himself as being pulled between the animal and the divine, as being one way but wishing to be another. This tension is central to Darío's entire poetic production and is represented – as in the graphic art of the turn of the century – with extraordinary concision in the many composite creatures that populate his poetry.

Darío's next book of verse, *El canto errante*, incorporates poems from throughout his career, some from as far back as 1885 and 1886. Like the previous two collections, it begins with an important prose introduction, "Dilucidaciones," which reiterates the fundamental tenets of modernist art as Darío conceived them and points to perhaps the work's most salient feature, namely, its diversity of themes, styles, and verse forms. Darío states: "The true artist understands all modes and manners and finds

beauty in all forms. All glory and all eternity are in our conscious grasp."
In *El canto errante* there is a brilliantly executed *eco* ("Eco y yo"), an
extensive and revealing *epístola* ("Epístola," which is dedicated to
Leopoldo Lugones's wife), and a ten-part ode written in memory of
Bartolomé Mitre ("Oda"). There are poems about America ("A Colón,"
"Momotombo," "Desde la Pampa," "Tutecotzimí") including one in
praise of the United States ("Salutación al águila"), poems that evoke the
ancient Mediterranean ("Revelación," "Hondas," "Eheu!" "La canción
de los pinos"), and others that portray the magical worlds of art, fantasy,
and self-indulgence ("A Francia," "Visión," "La hembra del pavo real,"
"Danza elefantina," "La bailarina de los pies desnudos," "Dream,"
"Balda en honor de las musas de carne y hueso," "Flirt"). There are
poems about poets and poetry ("Antonio Machado," "Preludio," "Campoamor," "Soneto") and poems that offer reincarnation as an alternative
to the orthodox view of human destiny ("Eheu!" "Hondas," "Metempsí-
cosis"). As in the first and title poem of the collection, the images come
from all corners of the globe, Greek and Roman mythology, the Bible,
world literature, and modern life. Despite this syncretic vision and the
many bases for consolation and optimism that it offers, Darío is unable to
conquer completely the profound anguish and despair that became
particularly acute with the passage of time and the approach of death
("Sum," "Eheu!" "Nocturno," "Epístola").

In 1907 Darío went home to Nicaragua, where he was accorded all the
honors of a national hero and named Nicaraguan Ambassador to Spain,
thereby achieving a steady if modest income. Upon his return to Madrid,
he was received again with adulation and honors. From then until 1914
Darío spent most of his time in Spain and France, though he did take trips
to Mexico, Brazil, Uruguay, and Argentina. In 1910 he was asked to write
a poem commemorating the hundredth anniversary of Argentina's independence. The resulting "Canto a la Argentina" was published in *La
Nación* on May 25 and later became the centerpiece of *Canto a la
Argentina y otros poemas*. The commissioned work turned out to be
Darío's longest single poem, a masterpiece of civic poetry that reveals
hidden links to other Spanish American literature. Its vision is wide-
reaching and all-inclusive, moving freely from scenes from Greek mythology to the wheatfield of the Pampas to the latest immigrants seeking
solace and sustenance in their new homeland. While some sections are
patriotic and grandiloquent, others are intimate and lyrical. Its overall
exuberance, however, is conveyed by an abundance of images and
detailed, elaborate description. All these elements, the tone, the images,
and, to a certain extent, the themes recall Oviedo's *Historia general y
natural de las Indias*, Zequeira y Arango's "A la piña," Bello's "La
agricultura de la zona tórrida," Lugones's *Odas seculares*, as well as

sections of Neruda's *Canto general* with its drive to rewrite history, to include the common man, and to assert a new, Spanish American outlook. This outlook, while rooted in the past, takes shape and gains strength within the modernist movement.

In 1910 Darío also published *Poema del otoño y otros poemas*. This short collection begins with "Poema del otoño," which continues the philosophic and reflective tone begun with *Cantos de vida y esperanza*. Once again the rapid passage of time, the loss of youth, and the proximity of death overwhelm Darío's viewpoint and encourage modern variations on the ancient theme of *carpe diem*, a theme repeated in the more light-hearted, closing poem, "El clavicordio de la abuela." This perspective is modified, however, by the consolation the poet finds in the harmony, beauty, and living unity of the cosmos. The beating heart of the universe, which appears intermittently throughout Darío's poetic production – most often in the rhythmic echo of the ocean – becomes the central image of the poem's concluding six stanzas. It pumps the vital life fluid throughout all the creatures on the great chain of being, underscoring the erotic power at the core of universal harmony. This fundamental oneness of life is extended to poetry and art in "Vesperal," where crabs leave illegible writings on the shore, and to women, who in "Canción" become works of art of the sacred universal artist. Other poems collected at this time were "Retorno," Darío's masterly reflections on his visit to Nicaragua, in which his homeland is perceived through a veil of art and philosophy, and less serious pieces such as "A Margarita Debayle" and "En casa del Doctor Luis H. Debayle. Toast."

The last collection Darío published, *Canto a la Argentina y otros poemas*, brought together "Canto a la Argentina" and eleven other poems, most of which were written between 1911 and 1914. In "La cartuja" Darío continues to hope for spiritual peace despite the unresolved conflicts within his being. All the visions of order and wisdom remain alien to him as he continues to feel himself pulled toward the bestial while aspiring toward the angelic. As is clear from "La cartuja," till the end of his life, Darío oscillated between the cognitively and artistically satisfying philosophies based on harmony, perfection, and analogy and those simple and direct beliefs about sin, guilt, and damnation that he learned in his youth. This struggle appears in two excellent, uncollected poems written during the last months of his life, "Pasa y olvida" and "Divagaciones." There are nearly fifty uncollected poems that are now regularly published as part of his complete poetic production. Many are equal in quality and interest to those that Darío collected for publication.

During these last years of his life, Darío continued to produce prose works as well. *Letras*, published in 1911, and *Todo al vuelo*, published in 1912, bring together articles written from 1906 to 1909. Darío also wrote two revealing autobiographical works: *La vida de Rubén Darío escrita por él mismo* (1912) and *Historia de mis libros* (1913). In 1914, the First World War broke out and Darío had to leave Paris. Ailing and without means, he found shelter in Guatemala thanks to the hospitality of that country's dictator, Manuel Estrada Cabrera. In 1915 Rosario, his legal wife, came for him and took him back to Nicaragua, where, in 1916, after two operations, he succumbed to years of self-inflicted abuse.

The late Modernists

It is impossible to determine a specific moment at which Modernism reached its plenitude. Generally the "second stage" of the movement has encompassed the heterogeneous group of modernist poets who survived beyond 1896. Somewhere between that date and 1905 – during the period in which Darío moved from Buenos Aires to Madrid – Modernism developed a strong sense of itself and reached its widest diffusion. A number of talented poets continued, to a greater or lesser degree, the predominant modernist tendencies (Enrique González Martínez [Mexico, 1871–1952], Amado Nervo [Mexico, 1870–1919], Ricardo Jaimes Freyre [Bolivia, 1868–1933], Guillermo Valencia [Colombia, 1873–1943], José María Eguren [Peru, 1874–1942], José Santos Chocano [Peru, 1875–1934], and Delmira Agustini [Uruguay, 1886–1914]). Still others drew upon the modernist impetus toward change and pushed further the expansion of the poetic repertoire in Spanish thereby, somewhat paradoxically, beginning the movement's unraveling as it began to anticipate the innovations of the Hispanic Avant-Garde. This tendency is best observed in the works of Leopoldo Lugones (Argentina, 1874–1938) and Julio Herrera y Reissig (Uruguay, 1875–1910).

Enrique González Martínez

If Herrera and Lugones are now recognized as poets who contained within themselves the seeds that gave fruit during the creative explosion of *la Vanguardia* [the Avant-Garde], González Martínez has long been linked with the poetic changes identified with Postmodernism. Yet the work of no other poet shows better that Postmodernism is not an independent movement but rather a continuation and natural development of Modernism, for González Martínez became, despite his longevity and nineteen collections of verse over a forty-nine year period, a poet with one essential concern and one insistent style. In poem after poem González Martínez explores the fundamental *modernist* desire to reveal the hidden order of the universe through the grace, beauty, and harmony of poetry.

Early critics who saw in his work a departure from Modernism tended to view modernist verse as superficial, decorative, concerned only with the formal enhancement of Spanish poetry. Many were unaware (1) that Modernism's recourse to swans, gardens, princesses, palaces, and European cultural models of all sorts reflected profound concerns regarding language, reality, and Spanish America's place in the modern world; (2) that considerably before 1911, as early as the publication of "Las ánforas de Epicuro" in the 1901 edition of *Prosas profanas*, Modernism had already evolved toward a simpler, more introspective, and self-assured style, and (3) that the "swans of deceitful plumage" that he criticizes did not belong to modernist poets but rather, as González Martínez himself would make clear, to the myriad, now long-forgotten hack imitators who echoed the language of Modernism, its opulence, elegance, and ornamentation, without comprehending the underlying issues that defined modernist poetics. He preferred the simpler and unadorned language reflective of his profound and unswerving faith in the power of poetry to establish an unimpeded link between the soul of the poet and the soul of the world, a faith grounded in the pantheism, occultism, and aesthetics of the symbolist poets that he knew well. (He had successfully translated into Spanish Baudelaire, Heredia, Verlaine, Maeterlinck, Jammes, and Rodenbach.)

What González Martínez's poetry does, in short, is underscore the modernist foundation in analogy as well as its ideological distance from the irony, skepticism, and doubt of avant-garde poets. Or, as Octavio Paz would state it, "he offers [Modernism] an awareness of itself and its hidden meaning" (cited in J. O. Jiménez, *Antología crítica de la poesía modernista hispanoamericana*, 280). This meaning was doubly hidden, for Modernism's profound significance was hidden from early readers who failed to realize that it sought to penetrate – through the musicality and evocative power of its verse – the eternal and harmonious order of existence that is hidden by the chaos of every-day reality. This concern provides the background to his most famous postmodernist poem, "Tuércele el cuello al cisne. . ." (from *Los senderos ocultos*), in which the "postmodernist" owl replaces the "modernist" swan. Whereas the swan's natural grace embodied for Darío and other Modernists the rhythm of the universe and the perfection of form, it came to be identified with hollow echoes of modernist poetics and, therefore, with obstacles encumbering the vision of harmony, with deceit, obfuscation, and the inability to "hear the soul of things and the voice of the landscape." While the owl does not have the swan's beauty, it does have the ability to see into the dark and to interpret what others cannot detect. Attention to formal beauty is thus replaced by an emphasis on clarity of perception and an intuitive understanding of the order of the cosmos. For González Martínez, it is this combined ability to perceive and understand that structures his poetry. He seeks a profound beauty that exists in accord with nature – not a showy, superficial distraction.

Like the Darío of "Las ánforas de Epicuro" and *Cantos de vida y esperanza*, he hopes that his poetry will reflect the rhythms of existence, the art of nature, and the harmonious soul of the universe. Yet while Darío's poetry is energized by a tortured uncertainty, González Martínez's is characterized by a relentless optimism and a supreme confidence in the order of things. Darío confronts the gulf that exists between what is desired and what is real; he struggles to replace doubt and anguish with faith and solace; he suffers with the fear that he is not up to the challenge of his mission as poet. These tensions are almost completely absent from González Martínez's work and so the individual poems become variations on a theme, masterful reworkings of one fundamental premise:

> Y que llegues, por fin, a la escondida
> playa con tu minúsculo universo,
> y que logres oír tu propio verso
> en que palpita el alma de la vida.

> [And may you arrive, at last, at the hidden
> beach with your minute universe,
> and may you succeed in hearing your own verse
> in which beats the soul of life.]
>
> ("Irás sobre la vida de las cosas. . ." from *Silenter*)

> Busca en todas las cosas el oculto sentido;
> lo hallarás cuando logres comprender su lenguaje;
> cuando sientas el alma colosal del paisaje
> y los ayes lanzados por el árbol herido. . .

> [Look for the hidden meaning in all things;
> you will find it when you succeed in understanding its language;
> when you sense the colossal soul of the countryside
> and the sighs hurled by the wounded tree. . .]
>
> ("Busca en todas las cosas" from *Los senderos ocultos*)

> Hará que los humanos
> en solemne perdón, unan las manos
> y el hermano conozca a sus hermanos;

> no cejará en su vuelo
> hasta lograr unir, en un consuelo
> inefable, la tierra con el cielo;

> hasta que el hombre, en celestial arrobo,
> hable a las aves y convenza al lobo. . .

[It [the sacred wind] will make humans, in solemn forgiveness, unite their hands and brother recognize his brothers; it will not restrain its flight until it succeeds in uniting, in ineffable consolation, heaven and earth; until man, in celestial rapture, speaks to the birds and convinces the wolf. . .]

("Viento sagrado" from *El libro de la fuerza, de la bondad y del ensueño*)

The exceptions to this replay of themes and symbols (the night, the lake, the wind, the hidden fountain, etc.) are his final works, *El diluvio de fuego* and *Babel*, which have poems that deal with the death of his wife and son, the poet Enrique González Rojo, as well as with gripping historical events. Yet even in these later poems that deal with personal loss and the horrors of Nazi Germany, González Martínez often counters despair with trust and faith.

Amado Nervo

More like Darío and more in keeping with modern sensibilities which are often defined by their uneasy – even unhappy – relationship with dominant beliefs and values, Amado Nervo has been characterized as a poet pulled between opposite poles, between a desire for material pleasures and an aspiration toward spiritual goals, between sensuality and religiosity, and between faith and doubt. His overwhelming longing to see transcendence in what appears limited and mutable, to reach beyond the immediate and the tangible, and to find a philosophic framework that would approve and endorse his erotic nature led him, like Darío and the French Symbolists before him, to explore a wide variety of unorthodox belief systems including pantheism, mysticism, theosophy, spiritualism, Bergsonian Vitalism, Buddhism, and Hinduism. Nervo found, in all these, effective responses to the dry intellectualization of Latin American Positivism in which value derived exclusively from material things and industry was endowed with glories and virtues. He came to see the failure of positivistic thought in its inability to grasp the nature of anything other than the purely mechanical and static. Consequently, he sought to immerse himself in the flow of existence and achieve a knowledge of reality more profound than the fragmented and incomplete visions afforded by modern science and commerce. His *La hermana agua* (1901?) can be read as a statement on the primacy of "fluidity" in this alternate way of viewing the world as well as in modernist poetics in general, which held that to dictate form would be to inhibit what the poet most hopes to achieve, namely, direct contact and accord between language and the universe.

At the same time that Nervo explored untraditional worldviews, he remained tied to his early religious training; his short-lived studies for the priesthood combined with his philosophic curiosity to reinforce the syncretic tendencies prevalent among modernist writers. He easily equates Christ with other divinities – Jove, Allah, Brahma, Adonai – and aspires to a loss of self, of self-importance, and of desire that is reminiscent of both Christian asceticism and Buddhist spiritualism.

It is the recognition of these fundamental tensions of Nervo's work that has generated renewed interest in, and a recent reassessment of, his work. For a period of some forty years following his death, Nervo's reputation declined and critics questioned the value of his poetic production, faulting his writing for its supposed vulgarity, superficiality, and lack of originality. While it may be true that in some of his later collections his poetry suffers from a facile application of various philosophic perspectives or from an artificial cultivation of a sense of intimacy, it is also true that Nervo moved from a mastery of modernist aesthetics, with its aspiration to grace, elegance, and richness of texture, to a controlled, personal, and intimate poetry that anticipated and reinforced "postmodernist" developments. He achieved these changes while addressing diverse issues of fundamental concern – from the political and social to the personal and philosophic – returning repeatedly to the themes of time, change, loss, love, and desire. All these come together in his much quoted "Vieja llave" (*En voz baja*), a sensitive examination of the illusion of immutability and the power of evocation (poetic discourse) in a world of flux and impermanence.

Moreover, with poems like "La raza muerta," "La raza de bronce," "Canto a Morelos," "Los niños mártires," and "Guadalupe la Chinaca" (from *Lira heroica*), Nervo, as José Emilio Pacheco has noted (in his *Antología del modernismo*), anticipates the Chocano of *Alma América*, the Darío of *Canto a la Argentina*, and the Lugones of *Odas seculares*, in attempting to strike a balance between cosmopolitanism and patriotic concerns, a balance that reflects a profound awareness of the movement's extraordinary place in Spanish American history. This awareness is evident as well throughout his extensive prose writings, in which he constantly refers to literary enterprises as a possible antidote to the prevalent stultification of the young and their unbridled regard for money. He also defends modernist innovations in poetic form and language as a deliberate and enlightened response to the movement's immediate context. In this attention to national issues, in his nostalgic vision of provincial life, and in his eroticism tinged with guilt, Nervo lays the groundwork for later poets, most notably Ramón López Velarde.

Nervo's work divides into three periods. The first includes *Místicas*, *Perlas negras*, *Poemas*, *La hermana agua*, *El éxodo y las flores del camino*, and ends with the political *Lira heroica*. In these collections Nervo confesses his personal obsession with erotic passion and religious doubt. Stimulatingly unorthodox ideas offered by esoteric thought appear in the consoling pantheism and universal accord of *La Hermana agua* and in the powerful occultist figure of the cosmic androgyne in "Andrógino" (*Poemas*).

Los jardines interiores and *En voz baja* make up the second stage in which, as Merlin Forster notes in *Historia de la poesía hispanoamericana*, Nervo's poetry becomes more serene as he seeks a place for himself in the material – and materialistic – world in which he lives. In "Mi verso," the second poem from *Los jardines interiores* and a poetic statement of Nervo's artistic goals, he wrote:

> Querría que mi verso, de guijarro,
> en gema se trocase y en joyero;
> que fuera entre mis manos como el barro
> en la mano genial del alfarero.

> [I would wish that my poetry, made of stone,
> be changed to gem and jewel,
> that it would be in my hands like the clay
> in the ingenious hand of the potter.]

The goal is to create objects of transcendent beauty and worth from the mundane and prosaic, objects that, as he suggests in the second stanza, would enhance individual lives as well as have spiritual significance. Yet if Nervo wants to "mint" stanzas and turn verses into gold, it is also in order to be able to move from what he called the "aristocracia en harapos" ["aristocracy in rags"] to the aristocracy of money and power from which he felt excluded but to which he felt – by privilege of merit – he belonged. The poet's aspirations to wealth – even if only verbal – is exemplary of his conflictive attitudes toward the dominant values of the day and the materialistic society that fostered them.

The third period was colored by the death of his beloved wife, Ana Cecelia Luisa Daillez, in 1912, and by a search for consolation that never fully relieved his unremitting grief. The most tortured poems appear in *La amada inmóvil: versos a una muerta*, most of which were written in the very year of her death but which were not published until 1920. The later collections, *Serenidad*, *Elevación*, *Plenitud*, *El estanque de los lotos*, and *El arquero divino*, explore the possibilities for solace and transcendence offered by both Christian and oriental philosophies.

Ricardo Jaimes Freyre

Despite his very limited poetic production Jaimes Freyre continues to be read and remembered today for three important reasons: (1) his active collaboration in Buenos Aires with Darío, with whom he founded in 1894 the short-lived but influential *Revista de América*, (2) his innovative adaptation and enthusiastic defense of free verse, and (3) his syncretic recourse to medieval and Nordic myths and legends to express concerns regarding the general artistic and sociopolitical context in which he wrote.

Jaimes Freyre's practice of free verse developed within the literary circle headed by Darío and Lugones between 1893 and 1898, working, as he stated, a little by intuition and a little under the influence of French, Italian, and Portuguese writers. His first collection of poems, *Castalia bárbara*, was published in Buenos Aires in 1899 and contains six of the earliest examples of free verse in Spanish poetry. They divide into two types, one based on the silva and the other on prosodic groupings. His second and only other collection of poetry, *Los sueños son vida*, also contains three poems of these two types along with "Alma helénica," a complex, polymetric poem. Between the publication of these two books, he published *Leyes de versificación castellana* in 1912, in which he spelled out his basic assumptions and beliefs.

He held that only accent has the ability to generate rhythm and that Spanish verse forms are created by combining "períodos prosódicos" ["prosodic groupings"]. This concept allows him to distinguish between prose and poetry since the latter is characterized by a combination of equal or analogous groupings. His emphasis upon accentual rhythm instead of upon the mechanical counting of syllables provided theoretical support for the type of free verse that he had already begun to write and resuscitates, as noted by Henríquez Ureña (*Breve historia del modernismo*), the irregular versification of old Spanish verse. At the same time, however, this view of poetry considerably restricted the definition of free verse itself, limiting it, within Jaimes Freyre's scheme, to an arbitrary mixture of different prosodic groupings or a combination of phrases without any rhythm at all. Nevertheless he claims for himself the honor of having been the first to introduce free verse in Spanish. He gives 1894 as the date of one of his early pieces, thereby making it contemporaneous with Silva's "Nocturno," which in 1894 expanded Spanish metrics through the free accumulation of clauses.

Related to Jaimes Freyre's attention to the possibilities of versification and the innovation of poetic form is his recourse to medieval and Nordic myths and legends. Through both, he struggles to achieve a poetic vision that is in touch with the primordial rhythms of existence and the visions of a simpler time and place. Like Wagner, whose incursions into his pre-Christian Walhalla reflected changing political concerns and a search for redemption from the crass and sterile realities of nineteenth-century Germany, Jaimes Freyre, with his Germanic gods, heroes, and genies, attempted to respond to his immediate milieu by capturing a world alive with spirits, vibrant with song, and saturated with the lifeblood of existence. While the title of his first collection recalls Leconte de Lisle's *Poèmes barbares* (1854) and underscores a source of inspiration other than the *castalia clásica* of traditional Spanish poetry, the freedom of the verse and the energy of the subject suggest a desire to tap a primitive – not Parnassian – power and a desire to evoke with symbolist magic and musicality an uncorrupted energy that underlies all life and action. Also like Wagner, who achieved a sense of salvation only with the writing of *Parsifal* and a return to Christian themes and imagery, Jaimes Freyre relies on a syncretic blending of pagan and Christian symbols and motifs throughout his poetry. Perhaps the best-known example is "Aeternum vale," in which the end of one world-order, that envisioned in Germanic mythology, ushers in another based on "el Dios silencioso que tiene los brazos abiertos" ["the silent God whose arms are open"] in a redemptive embrace.

His second collection of poetry published eighteen years after the first is less Germanic and more universal, developing both the philosophical and political aspects implicit in many of the poems of the earlier collection. "Rusia," written in 1906, demonstrates a keen political awareness and a profound sympathy for the masses. Politics, however, was not an occasional intellectual exercise for Jaimes Freyre. Once back in Bolivia, after having taught for many years in Tucumán, Argentina, he assumed several high administrative posts and even considered running for office.

Guillermo Valencia

Even more than for Jaimes Freyre, politics was a central activity in the life of Guillermo Valencia. He served in the Colombian Congress, in high administrative positions, and in the diplomatic corps. He was also twice named the Conservative Party candidate for president – though he was never elected. Despite his public service, he maintained an active literary career, a large part of which revolved around translation. His sense of good taste, his solid humanist education, and his knowledge of several classic and modern languages are evident throughout his sensitive and skilled translations, the earliest of which were of his European contemporaries and immediate predecessors – Keats, Hugo, Flaubert, Heine, Baudelaire, Gautier, Leconte de Lisle, Verlaine, D'Annnunzio, Stefan George, Hugo van Hofmannstal, and Oscar Wilde – as well as of the Indian writer and philosopher Sir Rabindranath Tagore. Later, in his *Catay*, he presented idiosyncratic versions of works by Chinese poets such as Li-Tai-Po, Tu-Fu, and Wang Hei based on the French prose translations by Franz Toussaint. The minimalist nature of these oriental pieces reinforced the poetic trends developing throughout Spanish America at the time. During the same period, José Juan Tablada (Mexico, 1871–1945), who is generally classified as a postmodernist poet, was introducing the elegant simplicity of the Japanese *hai-ku* to Spanish.

Valencia's own poetry consists of one book of verse, *Ritos*, which was originally published in 1899 and which reappeared in an expanded version in 1914. His work is dominated by a seriousness and a symbolic density, by a linguistic sophistication, terseness, and polish that have been characterized both as classical and as Parnassian. However, his work defies easy classification, demonstrating in addition a sensual and symbolist attention to the tone and texture of verse. Robert J. Glickman emphasizes Valencia's desire to celebrate "literary rites" that set out to counter the negative forces that impede the spiritual elevation of the individual and society. This effort – encased within a poetry of verbal splendour, encyclopedic breadth, and punctilious precision – links Valencia with other Modernists.

José María Eguren

Equally difficult to classify is the work of José María Eguren. He published his first poems in the magazines of Lima around 1899 and his first book, *Simbólicas*, in 1911; with it he began a poetic career that was generally misunderstood and much maligned. His work contradicted the emphatic and declamatory poetry popular at the time, a poetry epitomized by the work of Peru's soon-to-be poet laureate José Santos Chocano. He remained throughout his career, with the later publication of *La canción de las figuras* and *Poesías: Simbólicas, La canción de las figuras, Sombra, Rodinelas*, a little-known, marginal poet whose supporters – such illustrious Peruvians as Abraham Valdelomar, Manuel González Prada, José Carlos Mariátegui, and César Vallejo – praised his radical independence, his originality, and his unique and solitary nature despite widespread public and critical antipathy and misapprehension.

If Eguren was criticized during his life-time for being difficult, obscure, and "hermetic," he is now esteemed as the supreme representative of Symbolism in Peru and even as a forerunner of the Avant-Garde. His work – with its references to the night, to the tenuous and frightening realm of childhood memories, and to the world of nature turned unreal – reveals the poet's sense of mystery and awe regarding the order of things. From his first texts on, Eguren's poetic imagination provides a type of spiritual idealism offered as an alternative to personal tragedies and social ills. Nature is often viewed with a wonderment that borders on the religious, and this vision is generally presented with the language of the fantastic and a musicality derivative of modernist innovations but more personal and idiosyncratic.

Though Eguren's work was deemed marginal to Modernism because of its symbolist tendencies, its lack of epic breadth and tropical lushness, and the absence of Versaillesque gardens and swans, it manifests key features that reaffirm its placement among that of other modernist writers. As Rodríguez-Peralta has noted (in "The Modernism of José María Eguren"), his poetry is filled with exoticism, oriental fantasies, and references to both classical and Nordic mythologies; his vocabulary includes neologisms, French, and Italianate forms; and there are examples of the frivolous, elegant, and aristocratic details that for many defined much of early Modernism. Yet these standard elements did not obscure his creativity which shocked and alienated his early readers. Today his neologisms and his scenes of childhood innocence turned menacing do not only recall the fanciful inventions of Modernism and its search for the paradise lost to modern man but also the fearful visions of the Avant-Garde, most notably the poetry of his fellow Peruvian César Vallejo. Thus Eguren's work can now be understood to contain a creative mix of elements from Modernism, Postmodernism, and the early Avant-Garde, a mix that underscores the interdependence among, rather than the ruptures between, these movements.

Leopoldo Lugones

An even more extreme and varied mix is central to the poetry of Leopoldo Lugones; for this reason it has virtually become a truism of modernist criticism to say that his work is the product of many Lugoneses. Though the diverse nature of Lugones's poetic production has long been recognized, only recently – with studies such as those by Saúl Yurkievich (*Celebración*) and Gwen Kirkpatrick (*The Dissonant Legacy*) – has the significance of this shifting pattern of imitation and innovation begun to be appreciated. The contradictions and asymmetries within Lugones's poetry are indications of fissures within modernist poetics that result from an evolving artistic and socio-political context and eventually lead to a distancing from and even a disenchantment with literary models – a disenchantment that anticipates the poetic transformations of the Avant-Garde. In other words, the philosophic, emotional, and hierarchical dislocations produced by the continuing changes within the ideological and social structures of modern Argentina provide the backdrop to Lugones's many poetic and political voices.

This feature of Lugones's work, which on occasion has been read as a type of superficiality or artistic fickleness, hides a profound, almost tragic, realization that coincides with what Paz in *Los hijos del limo* specifies as a characteristic central to the transition from Modernism to the Avant-Garde, a characteristic that occurs at that moment when the correspondence of analogy is broken and dissonance takes over. Paz identifies this dissonance with irony in poetry and with mortality in life. Borges, in his famous study, *Leopoldo Lugones*, emphasizes this moment when he describes the poet as a man who:

> controlled his passions and industriously built tall and illustrious verbal edifices until the cold and the loneliness got to him. Then, that man, master of all the words and all the splendor of the word, felt within his being that reality is not verbal and may be incommunicable and terrible, and went, silently and alone, to look, in the twilight of an island, for death.

Borges refers here both to the poet's suicide and to the loss of faith in the decipherability of the universe, a loss that defines an essential change in modernist poetry.

Even though Modernists had rejected a rigid sense of referentiality and had turned away from "realism," for the most part, they continued to idealize poetry as a striving toward beauty and transcendence. The cult of the exotic, the emphasis on sonority, the enrichment of poetic form, and the delight in verbal play remained tied to a romantic faith in the poet's ability to intuite the profound and transcendent. Yet the natural development of modernist tendencies led to a linguistic crowding, an overloading of sensory devices, and a certain formal – and even conceptual – instability that gave way to new poetic possibilities. In this regard the innovations introduced by Lugones and Herrera y Reissig, namely, the breaks in syntax, the eruption of the unintelligible, the irony and self-parody, prefigure the works of later, avant-garde poets and their progressive disenchantment with the power of poetry to fill the spiritual void of modern society.

Almost paradoxically, in spite or because of these fundamental shifts and the cataclysmic dislocations they generate, Lugones rather quickly came to turn his back on innovation and the unknown and chose to affirm the great traditions of rhyme and patriotism. Starting as early as 1910 with *Odas seculares* Lugones's experimentation recedes and conservative values and visions come to the fore. Until then, in his first three collections, *Las montañas del oro*, *Los crepúsculos del jardín*, and *Lunario sentimental*, the impetus is toward the deliberately new.

The modernist delight in presenting the unexpected and unorthodox, the iconoclastic playfulness evident, for example, in the title and poems of Darío's *Prosas profanas*, appear throughout *Las montañas del oro*. Next to prose pieces there are poems in which the verses run on separated only by hyphens, and Lugones purposely replaced the y with i, an orthographic change that later editions do not always respect. More importantly, however, he successfully incorporated into this work the prophetic splendor of Hugo, the resonant serenity of Whitman, the visionary intensity of Dante, and the fundamental power of Homer, swelling the dimensions and enriching the tonalities of the poems. It is with these poets that he aligns himself in the first poem of the collection, which is simply called "Introducción." In it Lugones presents his poetic program, which for the most part coincides with the premises of the modernist verse being written at the time. Most significant are those that underscore the special relationship between the poet and God. The poet hears the voice of God in nature and creates a spiritual force in his verse that moves the earth and lights the darkness of despair and ignorance.

The revitalizing force presented encompasses – by the final pieces of the third cycle – a dizzying array of scientists, theosophists, philosophers, economists, and artists. This syncretic blending of the ancient occult and modern physical sciences together with the arts and philosophy is offered in a frenzied embrace of progress similar to the Futurism proposed by Marinetti twelve years later, but humanized and spiritualized by a faith in a divine and harmonious order. The overall impression, however, remains consonant with Darío's early assessment of Lugones's poetic assimilation as "a rapid collision of glances." The sense of excessive accumulation, artificial overloading, purposeful distortion of forms, and, occasionally, transgressive defiance will continue in different guises and to different degrees in the next two collections.

The publication of Los crepúsculos del jardín in 1905 builds upon Modernism's foundations in Symbolism and the latter's emphasis upon correspondences between the visible and transcendent realms of existence. The visual is the strongest element in this collection in which the presentation of garden scenes, the patterns of fading light, and erotic encounters evoke other dimensions of reality – many of which are menacing and disquieting. It is this feature which links Lugones with Albert Samain (1858–1900), whose Au Jardin de l'infante (1893) is considered to have been a direct influence on both Los crepúsculos del jardín and on Herrera y Reissig's Los éxtasis de la montaña (1904), a confluence of inspiration which led to an unfounded accusation of plagiarism against Lugones in 1912. Along with Samain, the influence of Verlaine and Darío is evident, but most striking is Lugones's reluctance to maintain the sense of mystery and musicality that defines the symbolist substructure of his work. He often interrupts the mood created with an unexpected term, incongruous image, or transgressive allusion. The effect can be parodic, comic, decadent, or – as in "El solterón" and "Emoción aldeana" – a strange cross between irony, nostalgia, and restraint. This last tendency reappears in the pastoral works of Herrera y Reissig and Ramón López Velarde. The most disturbingly moving poems are the twelve sonnets that make up "Los doce gozos." The repeated references to God, violence, parts of the body, and death suggest a mysterious, almost demonic rite that simultaneously plays with the possibility of, and deflects attention from, transcendent significance. In either case, the untamed passions are a haunting commentary on, or critique of, the stable, traditional, and unquestioning nature of bourgeois society, an intriguing and unnerving mix of revolution and revelation characteristic of modern poetry.

It is the revolutionary aspect of his verse that comes to the fore in his next collection, *Lunario sentimental*, written under the influence of Jules Laforgue (1860–1887), his *L'Imitation de Notre Dame la Lune*, and his acerbic mockery of archetypal patterns. In this work Lugones combines prose and poetry, breaks with the affectations of poetic language, introduces colloquial discourse, builds daring metaphors, incorporates unusual adjectivization, dissolves organizing frameworks, and relies upon rhetorical games that underscore his attack upon traditional views of poetic beauty. He supports in his "Prólogo" the freedom provided by free verse at the same time that he insists upon rhyme as the "essential element of modern verse." However, the rhymes that appear are often disturbingly unexpected, as are the images. While the volume is unified by the theme of the moon, this sacred cow of poetic discourse, along with others, is trivialized, caricaturized, and parodied to the point that, as Borges pointed out, the verbal structure becomes the focus of attention much more than the scene or emotions described.

These formal changes and, most especially, the freeing of poetic signs from previous constraints, reflect Lugones's changing attitude toward the role of the poet, one that in its own way pushes Modernism further toward the Avant-Garde. As Kirkpatrick has noted, in *Las montañas del oro* the figure of the poet, either as prophetic leader of humanity or as a satanic visionary, was an interpreter of universal meaning. In *Los crepúsculos del jardín* he became an organizing voice rearranging the chaotic welter of elements of the perceptible realm of existence. In *Lunario sentimental* he turns these roles on their head and underscores his awareness of the inherent falseness of all things. This emotional and conceptual distance from traditional objects of esteem encourages artifice, caricature, comedy, and a disconcerting mix of perspective, tone, and language all of which is offered as a defiant response to a world of appearances.

In what appears as a balancing or stabilizing alternative to the potentially destructive consequences of these insights and innovations, Lugones in his "Prólogo" to *Lunario sentimental* offers a practical and patriotic defense of poetry. He proposes to demonstrate "the utility of poetry in the enhancement of languages." One of its great advantages is its concision: "Being concise and clear, it tends to be definite, adding to the language a new proverbial expression or set phrase that saves time and effort." Lugones sees this power of poetic language as a national asset, one that must be cultivated and cared for. "Language is a social resource, perhaps the most consistent element of national manners and customs." Though for the reader it is easy to lose sight of this fundamental link between the formation of nation states and the creation of a modern mode of discourse appropriate to them – especially in the verbal artifice and fireworks of collections like *Las montañas del oro*, *Los crepúsculos del jardín*, and *Lunario sentimental* – Lugones never does. In reality, it is present throughout his poetry, in the insertion of shockingly prosaic vocabulary such as "cold cream," "alkaline," "hydraulic," and "sportswoman," and in cacophonous rhymes such as "flacucha/trucha," "dieciocho/bizcocho," "botella/doncella," "fotográfico/seráfico." These elements embody the struggle for a language of national identity, one that asserts individuality in the face of traditionalism as well as international trends and pressures.

It is this search for a language of national identity that becomes the focus of Lugones's next major work, *Odas seculares*, published in 1910 as part of the centennial celebration of Argentina's independence. The collection is divided into four parts: the first consists of a single poem "A la Patria," the second is entitled "Las cosas útiles y magníficas," the third focuses on "Las ciudades," and the fourth deals with "Los hombres," including the most typical of all Argentinians, the gaucho. With these poems Lugones confronts history, geography, and national spirit. With them he begins his journey to a simpler, more direct style, one in which his concerns, desires, and reflections achieve a clarity and sincerity that had previously been lost behind embellishment, artifice, and linguistic splendor, a style that reflects another general trend not to the Avant-Garde but to postmodernist poetry. While his next three volumes of verse, *El libro fiel*, *El libro de los paisajes*, and *Las horas doradas*, seem to respond to the same impetus toward traditional poetic form, intimacy, and simplicity, the first is the most strongly confessional, embracing at the same time the delights and despairs of passionate love. The second and third focus more on the exterior world, both landscapes and miniatures. Though less dramatic and certainly less studied than his earlier, more flamboyant, inventive, "modernist" collections, these contain some strikingly beautiful poems that demonstrate Lugones's poetic versatility and skill. He changes key but continues to dazzle in a new, more intimate way.

His final three collections, *Romancero*, *Poemas solariegos*, and *Romances del Río Seco* published posthumously in 1938, continue the dual trajectory toward intimacy and national identity. *Romancero* bears the influence of Heine in its title, its thirteen *lieder*, its opening poem, "Gaya ciencia," and in its overall quietly intense tone. *Poemas solariegos* and *Romances del Río Seco* find the essence of Argentina in the simple elements of life which are captured either in rich, detailed description or minimalist minipoems. These works are a step back from the verbal fireworks of the first three collections, which contain techniques and perspectives that break ground for the poets of the Avant-Garde. The verse that filled the last twenty-eight years of his life offers a reassertion of the fundamental faith in poetry to evoke significant realities, the defining characteristic that makes postmodernist poetry a continuation of Modernism.

Julio Herrera y Reissig

If what defines the link between Modernism and Postmodernism is their shared poetic vision based on universal analogy, a metaphoric system in which the sensorial reveals the spiritual, the early works by Lugones and much of Herrera's poetic production can be seen as an alternate development of modernist tendencies, one that serves as a short-cut to the avant-garde experimentation with poetry as a verbal construct – one tragically or ironically locked within its own structures no longer directed toward a transcendent vision or tied to the imitation of literary models or nature. The early modernist desire to create a poetry based on "the poetic" finds a fertile development in the verbal options opened by these two authors, who build upon what the earlier poets had made possible in Spanish – recourse to verbal correspondences and synesthesia fundamental to the Symbolists, the incorporation of vocabulary and images from high culture and exotic landscapes. Yet they push these elements out of proportion. What comes to predominate is parody, tension, and rupture, a sense of being off balance that is identified with avant-garde poetics.

While Darío struggles – through analogy – to reveal the divine intelligence that imbues the universe with order, Herrera expands the verbal possibilities so that the metaphoric connection between things is less direct and more elusive, more surprising, arbitrary, imaginary, ironic, and critical. His most innovative metaphors are not based on external connections but appear as projections of his own – not always stable – psychic state (hence the repeated allusions to *esplín, jaquecas, neurosis, neurastenias,* and *lo espectral*). The result is violent, shocking, and often deliberately unaesthetic. Whether this poetic vision stems from a tragic awareness, starting at age five, of a congenital heart lesion that would doom him to a short life, or from a rebellious, anarchistic, anti-bourgeois dandyism that would keep him on the margins of society (looking out at the world from within his *Cenáculo* [guest chamber], later called the *Torre de los Panoramas*), or from an eclectic and critical nature that wished to push Montevideo beyond its provincial and unimaginative conservatism, Herrera puts modernist tendencies under a magnifying glass, perfecting, exaggerating, and distorting what he passionately embraced.

It is difficult to trace a clear chronological trajectory of Herrera's poetic development because of the way he chose to publish his work. He organized only one collection of poems, *Los peregrinos de piedra*, which appeared posthumously in the year of his death. It is an anthological compilation of his entire *opus*. From it he excluded pieces that are as important and well executed as those he included. For example, he left out a third of the poems from *Los éxtasis de la montaña* and more than half of those from *Los parques abandonados*. As much as possible, scholars have attempted to date individual poems and group them within their original collections, but the dating is often imprecise because Herrera is said to have worked on a number of collections at the same time and to have revised them over time. What can be safely stated, however, is that most of his poetry belongs to the ten-year period between 1900 and 1910. His early poems belong to the first third of this decade, and those written before 1900 are generally considered his weaker, less original pieces.

As might be expected, the poems from 1900, especially those from *Las pascuas del tiempo*, most strongly reflect the influence of other modernist poets, particularly that of Darío, Lugones, and Casal, whose decadent dandyism finds parallels in Herrera's life-long attraction to images of disease and psychoses. These poems reveal the same preoccupation with elegance, opulence, and European culture that molded much of early Modernism. The famous "Fiesta popular de ultratumba" recalls *Prosas profanas*, especially its first three poems with their wide-ranging exploration of styles and modes of discourse. Though many of Herrera's pieces present a cultural *smorgasbord* similar to Darío's "Divagación," the Uruguayan's unique perspective is already present in the more than occasional ironic remarks that underscore his critical distance from the generally solemn deference given to imported high culture.

The next major collection, *Los parques abandonados*, consists of poems written between 1900 and 1908. Twenty-two were published in *Los peregrinos de piedra* as *eufocordias*; fifty-seven were left out. As Allen Phillips has noted ("Cuatro poetas hispanoamericanos"), Herrera shows a cosmic complicity in these gentle and touching love sonnets. In "La sombra dolorosa," for example, nature shares with the poet the pain of separation, affirming a transcendental unity interrupted by a loss that is linked, by the blaring train, to modern life and unresponsive technology. In "El abrazo pitagórico," the universal and eternal harmony alluded to in the title is found in the unity of the two lovers, their love, their song, and their pleasure – not without, however, the characteristic Herrerian touches of absurdity in the form of intrusive scientific terms and colloquial phrases.

The poems of *Los éxtasis de la montaña*, called *eglogánimas* in *Los peregrinos de piedra*, date from 1904 to 1910. These alexandrine sonnets are pastoral in nature, eclogues full of peace and tranquility. They are, at the same time, among his most original works, containing "pre-creacionista" images and metaphors. The poems reveal a joy in the innocent and ingenuous nature of rural life and an intense pantheism in which the cosmic order is repeated in the apparently insignificant details of everyday existence. The landscape, however, takes on an unreal quality, transmuted into verbal constructs through deliberately archaic references and a baroque sensibility (the influence of Góngora) that helped prepare the transition from Modernism to the Avant-Garde. The fantasy atmosphere is often interrupted by the absurdity of life or by a shocking image, both of which draw attention to and, as a result, mock the poem's literary pretenses. "La iglesia" ends with a flood of chickens, "El cura" concludes with the priest's piety described as licking like a cow, and "Dominus vobiscum" breaks the timelessness of the countryside with the appearance of a "zootécnico," a professor of worms. Within this same pastoral tendency fall "Ciles alucinada" (1902) and "La muerte del pastor" (1907), two narrative poems of great beauty.

Often contrasted with these poems of rural life is another poetic trend that emerges during Herrera's ten years of creativity, one that is more specifically metaphysical in orientation. Yet both tendencies reflect in varying degrees and with varying intensity the same concern with the fragility of life and the absurdity of existence, from which one can only be partially sheltered by community, tradition, or literary imagination. This recognition seems to form the backdrop to Herrera's remarkably "modern" poetry, works that, in their surrender to the dark and troubling aspects of reality, break logical connections and become deliberately difficult, obtuse, and chaotic. The type of angst that appears in Darío's three "Nocturnos," for example, is even more disorienting and potentially destructive in Herrera's "Desolación absurda," written in 1903. Life is defined by death, which tears the soul of the poet apart ("amo y soy un moribundo / tengo el alma hecha pedazos" ["I love and I am a dying man / my soul is torn to pieces"]); unity and salvation become impossible; the best that love can offer is a "parenthesis"; and nature only *pretends* to be a reflection of God. *La torre de las esfinges*, written in 1909 and accurately if self-mockingly subtitled "psicologación morbo-panteísta," is itself a bridge from the playfully optimistic, esoteric syncreticism of Modernism to the morbid, nightmarish visions of the Avant-Garde. In a different way the same is true of another group of poems from 1909, *Las clepsidras*, which are more than "cromos exóticos" ["exotic color prints"], as Herrera calls them. The formal perfection of these sonnets, their rich descriptive quality, and their archaeological fascination with the unusual and unorthodox reveal their grounding in the traditions of Modernism. At the same time, however, they contain elements that will later define the works of the Avant-Garde: shockingly erotic references, illogical and disturbingly evocative images, and language that is disconcertingly innovative. Though Herrera y Reissig remained a Modernist, in love with demanding poetic structures (the sonnet and the *décima*), fond of rich and exotic landscapes and tonalities, and a disciple of the symbolist faith in evocation and suggestion, there can be little wonder that he has been recognized by many modern writers – César Vallejo, Vicente Huidobro, Pablo Neruda, Federico García Lorca, and Vicente Aleixandre, to mention only the most prominent – as a kindred spirit and teacher.

José Santos Chocano

Though José Santos Chocano was one of the youngest Modernists, his poetry did not anticipate the future but rather looked back toward the past. It appeared on the scene as an exuberant affirmation of the painterly, elaborate, image-laden Modernism that had for the most part begun to recede in favor of a more introverted and intimate style. Perhaps because of this very fact – together with his enthusiastic pro-American *Mundonovismo* – his poetry pleased a wide audience accustomed to modernist fare, and he became one of the most popular poets of the time.

It is impossible to determine the factor that had the greatest impact upon his work. He was driven by the idea of becoming "the poet of America" and unselfconsciously called up real and imagined images of South America in order to achieve this title – one that had been foreclosed to Darío by José Enrique Rodó's early assessment of his work. South American geography, history, legend, landscapes, peoples, flowers, and animals are painted in broad and vibrant brushstrokes, for his natural inclination toward grandiloquence, linguistic inflation, and rhetorical expansiveness found a perfect outlet in his purposeful exaltation of American enterprises and wonders. Chocano would recite – with great personal and economic success – these activities and marvels to audiences in Madrid, the Caribbean, Central and South America, and the oratorical nature of these recitals further encouraged his established stylistic tendencies. Thanks to his fame, popularity, and the pose he assumed as he executed his poetic goals, he was crowned national poet of Peru in 1922, though he hardly ever lived there.

Since the end of Modernism, the bombast, hyperbole, excess, and lack of nuance of his work have tended to receive as much commentary as his accomplishments. His reputation as a poet was further diminished by his soldier of fortune life-style. Not only did he spend a year in jail for having killed a young man in 1925, but he himself was killed by a Chilean worker who believed that he had been bilked out of money in one of Chocano's many get-rich-quick schemes. Nevertheless, it is easy to recognize why his verse was received with such enthusiasm during the thirty-nine years between the publication of his first collection, *En la aldea*, and that of his ninth, *Primacías de oro de Indias*, with an especially triumphant reception being given to his principal work, *Alma América: poemas indoespañoles*. His vision was Hispanic rather than European; he even criticized Darío for his recourse to French models and chided other Latin Americans for their fascination with Europe. His pride in America and his hopes for its future – evident, in part, in his vociferous support of the Mexican Revolution – are expressed in a language that is stirringly dramatic, strong, and assertive. The power of his poetry relies upon a keen sense of rhythm and an unflinching sense of purpose. His tone is overwhelmingly optimistic, confident, and direct; philosophic anguish and doubt, as well as poetic suggestion and subtlety, were left to others. "Blasón" from *Alma América*, reveals both his artistic strengths and the egomaniacal nearsightedness that has made him unpalatable to some modern readers.

> Soy el cantor de América autóctono y salvaje;
> mi lira tiene un alma, mi canto un ideal.
> Mi verso no se mece colgado de un ramaje
> con un vaivén pausado de hamaca tropical. . .
>
> Cuando me siento Inca, le rindo vasallaje
> al Sol, que me da el cetro de su poder real;
> cuando me siento hispano y evoco el Coloniaje
> parecen mis estrofas trompetas de cristal . . .
>
> Mi fantasía viene de un abolengo moro:
> los Andes son de plata, pero el León de oro:
> y las dos astas fundo con épico fragor.
>
> La sangre es española e incaico es el latido;
> ¡y de no ser poeta, quizás yo hubiese sido
> un blanco aventurero o un indio emperador!
>
> [I am the singer of native and wild America;
> my lyre has a soul, my song an ideal.
> My poetry does not rock from branches
> with a measured sway of a tropical hammock. . .

When I feel Incan, I render obedience
to the Sun, which gives me the sceptre of its royal power;
when I feel Hispanic and I evoke Colonial rule,
my stanzas seem crystal trumpets. . .
My imagination comes from a Moorish ancestry:
the Andes are of silver, but the Lion is of gold:
and I forge the two lances with epic noise.
The blood is Spanish and Incan is the beat;
and if I were not a poet, perhaps I would have been
a white adventurer or an Indian emperor!]

Delmira Agustini

Delmira Agustini's life and career can be summarized with a few short sentences that belie the power and complexity of their legacy. She began to publish poetry in small journals at the age of sixteen. By 1907 she had published her first volume of verse, *El libro blanco*. In 1910 her second collection of poetry, *Cantos de la mañana*, appeared, and in 1913 she published *Los cálices vacíos* with an opening poem by Rubén Darío. In it she announced her next book, *Los astros del abismo*, which would appear posthumously in 1924 with the title *El rosario de Eros*. Agustini was killed in 1914 by her ex-husband, whom she had taken as a lover.

Because she is so much younger than the other modernist poets, she is often classified – along with Alfonsina Storni (Argentina, 1892–1938), Juana de Ibarbourou (Uruguay, 1895–1979), and Gabriela Mistral (Chile, 1889–1957) – as a Postmodernist. She shared with these later female poets (and with her compatriot and contemporary María Eugenia Vaz Ferreira [1880–1925]) innovative perspectives on art, love, feminine sexuality, and the role of women, that affected her imagery and tone and that distanced her from the earlier male Modernists, yet she maintained during her short and turbulent life a strong affinity for the principal elements of modernist verse. Her vocabulary is at different moments sensuous, ornate, evocative, and exotic. Her descriptions are textured by subtly nuanced adjectives and by references to precious stones, flowers, animals, and opulent objects. Her images affirm their modernist roots in their detail, power, and sensuality but reject established patterns of (male) perception; they are innovative and dramatic, based on shocking connections that assert the individual and idiosyncratic nature of her experience. Her struggle against imposing, inflexible, and unforgiving structures – social and poetic – appears most often and most explicitly in her pieces on love and art and in her repeated allusions to sadness, suffering, and death.

It has been said that love was Agustini's great theme, yet it is not an easy or idealized love that she portrays, for it embraces both pain and pleasure, surrender and rejection, power and impotence. Whether this dark and tortured vision is grounded in decadent art, sado-masochistic tendencies, or in the belief in the voluptuousness of death (as suggested by Doris T. Stephens), suffering and destruction, in an uncannily prophetic manner, are linked to love and love is linked, in turn, to a breaking out and away. What is broken are norms, expectations, traditional male (and modernist) perspectives on sexuality, authority, and transcendence. These very issues forged her views on art as well.

While Agustini shares the modernist aspiration to an art that makes sense of the universe and that is redemptive, she affirms the suffering and despair that constitute the nature of the artistic process as the poet confronts time-honored models, seeks to express the ineffable, and aspires to exceed human, poetic, and stereotypical limitations. As Silvia Molloy has shown ("Dos lecturas del cisne: Rubén Darío y Delmira Agustini"), in "Nocturno," modernist art, its vocabulary, setting, and tone are ritualized only to be exploded in its surprising, touching, and frightful inversion of the image of the swan. Agustini identifies herself as the swan that stains the lake with its blood as it tries to take flight. In this poem as in many others she shouts the danger of reaching beyond. Longing and desire tear at the idealized realms of art and love, turning the passionate poet into what she envisions in other poems as a wild beast, a vampire, or an angel who has lost her wings.

Agustini wrote within the modernist framework at the same time that she struggled against it. Her work is a response, at times violent and iconoclastic, to Modernism, to the poetry of Rubén Darío, and to traditional society. It is this antagonistic relationship to Modernism that has linked her to Postmodernism. Yet her poetry – as well as that of González Martínez, Eguren, Lugones, Herrera y Reissig, and that of Darío himself – under-scores that the demarcation between Modernism and Postmodernism is imprecise. With Darío's turn toward a simpler, more introspective, less decorative style as early as 1901, with the radical innovations by poets like Lugones and Herrera y Reissig as early as 1905, the changes that at one time were identified with Postmodernism can now be seen as adjustments within the modernist movement itself. The true rupture comes with the Avant-Garde and its fundamental loss of faith in the modernist world view, in analogy, and in the power of the word to reveal an eternal order and beauty that is hidden by the chaos of everyday existence.

By 1922, with the publication of *Trilce* by Vallejo, the *Vanguardia* was clearly established. There were, nevertheless, poets still writing in a style derivative of Modernism. This chronologically untidy group continued to alter the face of Modernism but not its fundamental *Weltanschauung*. In addition to the female poets already mentioned, the following are generally considered to be the most important of these writers: José Juan

Tablada (Mexico, 1871–1945), Regino E. Boti (Cuba, 1878–1958), Carlos Pezoa Véliz (Chile, 1879–1908), Enrique Banchs (Argentina, 1888–1968), Luis Carlos López (Colombia, 1883–1950), Porfirio Barba Jacob (Colombia, 1883–1942), Ramón López Velarde (Mexico, 1888–1921), Baldomero Fernández Moreno (Argentina, 1886–1950), Macedonio Fernández (Argentina, 1874–1952), Luis Llorens Torres (Puerto Rico, 1878–1944), Rafael Arévalo Martínez (Guatemala, 1884–1975), Carlos Sabat Ercasty (Uruguay, 1887–1982), José Eustasio Rivera (Colombia, 1888–1928), Alfonso Reyes (Mexico, 1889–1959), Andrés Eloy Blanco (Venezuela, 1897–1955), Dulce María Loynaz (Cuba, 1903–).

2

Modernist prose

Aníbal González

The most cursory glance at the collected works of the major Spanish American *Modernistas* [Modernists] shows that the majority of these writings were prose. An unprejudiced reading of that prose soon reveals that most of it is of a quality equal to the Modernists' best verse works, or to the prose works being written in Europe and the United States at about the same time.

Shortly after the Modernist movement waned in the late 1920s, critics, influenced on the one hand by the prestige of the telluric narratives, such as *La vorágine* (1923) [*The Vortex*] and *Doña Bárbara* (1929) [*Doña Bárbara*], and on the other by the splendor of modernist poetry and that of its successors, such as Gabriela Mistral (1889–1957), Pablo Neruda (1904–1973), César Vallejo (1892–1938), and the Generation of 1927 in Spain, began to value *Modernismo* [Modernism] primarily as a poetic movement and to ignore or reject the achievements of modernist prose. When the Modernists' prose was studied at all, it was usually in a fragmentary manner and subordinated to poetry. Thus, for example, fragments of essays and chronicles by José Martí (1853–1895), Manuel Gutiérrez Nájera (1859–1895), and José Enrique Rodó (1871–1917) were studied for their value as "poetic prose." Scant attention was paid to works in their entirety and to the ideas about art, literature, and society expressed in them, not only because some of these ideas had become unfashionable, but also because many had in fact become deeply ingrained in the fabric of Spanish American writing and were accepted without question.

In the case of some writers, such as José Martí, whose work is mostly in prose, and whose prose is as idiosyncratic in its stylistic and ideological content as his poetry (if not more so), eminent critics such as Juan Marinello (1898–1977) went so far as to exclude him from the modernist movement altogether, letting their preconceived notions about the nature of Modernism obscure the facts of literary history. Indeed, modernist prose as a whole was suppressed or ignored by critics in order to preserve the notion – fomented by *Vanguardistas* [Avant-Gardists] and "Telluric" writers alike – of Modernism as a mostly frivolous and formalistic poetic movement, a sort of "last fling" of the Spanish American *belle époque* before the political and social issues of twentieth-century Spanish American history swept it into oblivion.

In recent years a thorough reevaluation of Modernism has been taking place, spearheaded by the comments of poet–critics like Octavio Paz (b. 1914); particularly in his book *Los hijos del limo* (1974) [*Children of the Mire*] and the explicit evocations of Modernism found in works by writers of the Spanish American narrative "Boom," from *El recurso del método* (1974) [*Reasons of State*] by Alejo Carpentier (1904–1980), to *El amor en los tiempos del cólera* (1985) [*Love in the Times of Cholera*] by Gabriel García Márquez (b. 1928). The attention paid to Modernism by contemporary Spanish American narrators strongly suggests that its legacy is by no means limited to poetry, and that Modernism was, to borrow a phrase from Paz, "a literature of foundation." Indeed, the study of modernist prose on its own terms, as well as in its relationship with modernist poetry, shows Modernism to have been a profound revolution in Spanish American literature.

Although they did not write manifestoes – as the later *Vanguardia* [Avant-Garde] movements did – the Modernists followed a coherent set of ideas about literature that amounted to a virtual program for the establishment of an authentically Spanish American form of writing. As always, Martí was the precursor in this respect; suffice it to recall his notes on how to establish "Literature" (with a capital *L*) in America: "Because we have displays and birth-cries of our own Literature, and raw materials for it, and loose, vibrant, and very powerful notes – but we do not have our own Literature. There is no writing, which is expression, until there is an essence to be expressed by it. Nor will there be Spanish American literature until there is – Spanish America." Despite the frivolous image they assiduously cultivated, the Modernists' prose shows their deep preoccupation with broad cultural and social issues, and particularly with the relation between literature, culture, and society.

It should be noted that the early Modernists (such as Martí, Gutiérrez Nájera, and the young Rubén Darío [1867–1916]) were less interested in achieving autonomy for Spanish American literature than in raising its level of competence. Consonant with the idea of "progress" then prevalent, they wanted to create a literature that could be judged by the same high standards applied to that of Europe; a literature stylistically and ideologically "up-to-date." Despite their later (and essentially political) "Americanism," the Modernists were not cultural nationalists in today's sense of the term. At the cultural level, their nationalism was not so much based on difference as on creative assimilation. Like other Spanish American writers before and after them, the Modernists suffered little if any "anxiety of influence" with regard to their European models.

Modernists prose allows us a backstage glimpse, so to speak, of how the Modernists proceeded to become "modern." An important element in this process was the Modernists' recourse to philology. As the French thinker Michel Foucault has pointed out in *The Order of Things*, "Literature is the refutation of philology (which is, nevertheless, its twin): it submits the language of grammar to the raw power of speech and thus discovers the savage and imperious nature of words." Few Modernists would have disagreed with this observation, nor with Ernest Renan's assertion in *L'Avenir de la science* (1890) that "the modern spirit, that is to say, rationalism, criticism, liberalism, was founded on the same day as philology. *The founders of the modern spirit are the philologists*" (Renan's emphasis). The major Modernists read with passionate interest the works of French philologists such as Renan and Hippolyte Taine as well as those of Spanish and Spanish American philologists and literary historians such as Miguel Antonio Caro (1843–1909), Rufino José Cuervo (1844–1911), and Marcelino Menéndez y Pelayo. Philology, with its encyclopedic cosmopolitanism, its vision of cultural renewal, its interest in religion, and above all its notion of language as an object, as a thing endowed with a concreteness and history of its own, was one of the Modernists' chief models for their literary endeavor.

Another important cultural institution from which the Modernists learned a great deal was journalism. Virtually all Modernists worked as journalists at some point in their careers. The lack of publishing houses in late nineteenth-century Spanish America made journalism the only regular outlet for literary production. Moreover, their work as journalists, which allowed them to make a living from writing, satisfied the Modernists' desire to become professional writers. Journalism, however, probably taught the Modernists far more than they would have wanted to know about writing. Like philology, journalism makes use of texts in its daily activity, and it also aspires to an empirical understanding of the world. Nevertheless, while philology regards texts as objects of knowledge, journalism considers them merchandise; while philology seeks to produce, from textual analysis, a totalizing synthesis, journalism only seeks to capture the instant, the fleeting moment, in all its empirical detail, without attempting a synthesis. In addition, journalism undermines the idea of the "author" – so vital to nineteenth-century literature and philology – because what matters most in journalism is information itself and not the individual who transmits it. In the end, journalism led the Modernists to realize that – philological dogma notwithstanding –

writing is not a transcendental activity, and that literature, like the other arts, has no "essence," that it is, in the Kantian phrase, "purposiveness without purpose" (*Critique of Judgment*, 1790).

The Modernists' acquaintance with philology and journalism, along with the general trend toward institutionalization in nineteenth-century society, led them to also view literature as an institution, with its own coherent rules, standards of quality, and general code of behavior of its members. Their main model for literature as an institution came from French literature, traditionally one of the most institutionalized in Europe, with its schools, cenacles, and academies. As their prose reveals, however, the Modernists were far from being mere imitators of their French models. (In any case, it is questionable whether one can speak of *imitation* from one language to another, and the Modernists were certainly more than just translators.) Their relationship vis-à-vis French literature and culture was analogous to that of Garcilaso, Boscán, and Herrera with Italian literature during the sixteenth century; they studied, analyzed, and critically assimilated certain elements of foreign literatures as a means of renewing their own. From the literature of their European counterparts, the Modernists learned, above all, to subvert philology by using words not only with an awareness of their etymology but also of their musicality. Words were thus turned from historically determined objects of knowledge into objects of pleasure which could be collected and combined anachronistically, in a "very ancient and very modern" way (to borrow Darío's phrase from *Cantos de vida y esperanza* [1905]), like pieces of bric-à-brac upon a shelf.

It is also important to stress that modernist writing presupposes that there is a profound unity and harmony to the cosmos, and that most, if not all, of human knowledge has already been codified and collected in a single place: in other words, modernist writing presupposes the existence of a Library. The metaphor of the Library is shared by both literature and philology. It stands for an ideal plane, a kind of intertextual no-man's-land, where philological and literary texts jostle each other and where their placement within an arbitrary scheme (in alphabetical order, for instance) neutralizes their delicate interplay of similarities and differences. Modernism was, to a large extent, the appropriation and partial reorganization of the Library of European culture by Spanish America. When they entered the Library, the Modernists saw that philology stood, in Renan's terms, for "the modern spirit, that is to say, rationalism, criticism, liberalism," while literature (through a perverse use of philological methodology) had become ever more concerned with an archaeological research of its own nature and origins. However, the Modernists also understood that philology and literature were not merely institutions (with canonical texts, administrators, and locales: the Collège de France or the poetic cenacles), but also discourses, ways of organizing knowledge, and that as such they could be taken up at certain moments and for certain purposes and then abandoned. The Modernists did not choose between the extremes of Renan (in philology) and Mallarmé (in literature in its purest expression): they took from both what they considered useful. Not, it must be pointed out, from mere eclecticism, but because they perceived that both discourses arose from the same problematic of linguistic representation, and that the terms of one could be easily translated into the other as long as philology's claims of truth and authority were placed in suspension.

We have seen briefly how the study of modernist prose can help us to understand better the nature of Spanish American Modernism. Let us now examine more specifically the various modernist prose genres: the chronicle, the short story, the essay, and the novel.

The chronicle was the first prose genre favored by the Modernists and in it, as Ivan A. Schulman has observed ("Reflexiones en torno a la definición del modernismo"), the Modernists' aesthetic first took shape. In many instances, chronicles account for more than two-thirds of the Modernists' published writings, as can be seen in the *obras completas* of such major Modernists as Martí, Gutiérrez Nájera, Darío, Amado Nervo (1870–1919), and Enrique Gómez Carrillo (1873–1927). This genre consisted of brief newspaper articles on virtually any subject, written in a self-consciously literary style. These articles were meant to be entertaining as well as informative. In fact, however, the Modernists made of them much more than they were supposed to be in terms of their content. The chronicles became literary laboratories where the Modernists tried out new styles and ideas and made these known to other writers.

From their beginnings in French journalism of the nineteenth century, the chronicles were at the intersection of three textual institutions: philology, literature, and journalism. As a journalistic genre, the chronicle had to convey news of current events and be subject to the laws of supply and demand, since from a purely journalistic standpoint the chronicle was simply merchandise; as a literary genre, the chronicle had to be entertaining and creative while also possessing the solid, well-crafted nature of a work written with the philological awareness of the historicity of language. Modernist chroniclers also often used the genre to reflect essayistically on the nature of time and history and on the question of modernity.

The Mexican Manuel Gutiérrez Nájera is generally credited with introducing the genre of the chronicle into Spanish American journalism. Taking as his model the frivolous and gossipy *chroniques* published by French dailies such as *Le Figaro* and *La Chronique Parisienne*, Gutiérrez

Nájera made of the *crónica* a versatile vehicle for the Modernists' literary expressions. During his twenty years in journalism (from 1875 until his sudden death in 1895), Gutiérrez Nájera wrote countless chronicles for Mexican newspapers such as *El Federalista*, *El Partido Liberal*, *La Libertad*, *El Cronista Mexicano*, and *El Universal*, among many others. None of Gutiérrez Nájera's chronicles were collected during his lifetime, unless one counts the short stories published in his *Cuentos frágiles*. All of those stories had first appeared as chronicles or as parts of chronicles, and they attest to the purposeful blurring of the distinctions between journalism and fiction that is the hallmark of Gutiérrez Nájera's work in prose.

Among Gutiérrez Nájera's many chronicles, "Crónica color de bitter" (1882) is a good example of how he approached this genre. The subject of the chronicle is a description of an earthquake that rocked Mexico City in June, 1882. This would be hard to guess by judging from the chronicle's first lines, however. The text is in second person, and in it the narrator addresses a young lady, his beloved, with whom he was having dinner at the time of the 'quake, and who has fainted from fright: "Don't tremble any more; rest here, on my breast, while I bring the cup to your pale lips, as if I were giving a sick child his medicine. Would you like me to put a few drops of *cognac* in your tea? There's nothing to be afraid of anymore: laugh, smile. The wineglasses no longer dance upon the table, and the servants'-bell cord no longer strikes the walls. The earthquake is over, and matter, eternally enslaved, has ceased its sudden rebellion: only your heart beats violently against mine." In this chronicle, as in so many others, Gutiérrez Nájera subjectivizes objective phenomena (such as the earthquake) by viewing them from the perspective of the turn-of-the-century bourgeois interior, which, as Walter Benjamin, in his well-known essay, "Paris, capital of the 19th century," reminds us, could be either an office, a bedroom, a library, or a museum.

Gutiérrez Nájera's interior is, like Benjamin's, a place where the self takes refuge from temporality and history. The temporality of the interior is arbitrary and capricious, subject to the whims of the self; Nájera indicates this in his text when he describes how the 'quake stopped all the clocks in the city, but then adds (with an allusion to the myth of the Wandering Jew), "my hand will move the pendulum once again, and time will march on like that unhappy Hebrew who did not give Christ water to drink." The interior is also a refuge for love, for eroticism; the woman's fainting spell during the 'quake is described in terms sufficiently ambiguous to suggest a moment of erotic passion. Lastly, the many descriptions of the effects of the earthquake on the city's public monuments are playful and humorous: this is another trait of the interior, where according to Benjamin, play is substituted for productive work.

The text of this chronicle as a whole is structured as an opposition between the interior (with its arbitrary temporality, its hallucinations, games, and erotic pleasures) and the exterior (with its linear temporality, its monotonous and orderly routine). This opposition may be seen in turn as a metaphor of the tension between literature and journalism present in Gutiérrez Nájera's chronicles. The earthquake appears in Gutiérrez Nájera's text as a gratuitous, almost playful phenomenon, and its causes are described using a fairy-tale terminology: dwarfs and giants caused the earthquake, Gutiérrez Nájera's narrator tells his beloved, because they wanted to scare the lovers. Yet what is more interesting, the earthquake inverts the usual relationship between exterior and interior by collapsing the facades of houses, letting us see what the inhabitants were doing, and turning for a few hours the interior into the exterior. Suddenly, as the interior invades the outside world, imagination and passion run rampant; men, women, and children scream in fright, running out into the streets half-dressed or with whatever clothes they could grab, as if it were Carnival. Indeed, the text suggests a correspondence between the earth-quake and transgression of the conventional, public limits of erotic conduct. The 'quake would thus be the exterior equivalent of the sudden inner movements of passion (whether caused by love or by fear), as well as an emblem of the deep unity between nature and the self from which (in the Modernists' post-romantic view) literature arises. However, this correspondence between interior and exterior, between nature and the self, lasts only brief instants, and the ambiguous moment of literary and erotic plenitude gives way to linear temporality and a feeling of emptiness and death. As Gutiérrez Nájera, with his typical melancholy, reflects at the end of this chronicle: "Fountains dry up, carnations wither, and love dies out."

As a consequence of Gutiérrez Nájera's deep subjectivism, in his chronicles real-world events and objects are seen as if on a stage, and rather than providing knowledge, they provide amusement. They are also miniaturized and, in the end, fictionalized. In spite of their journalistic nature, Gutiérrez Nájera was able to fictionalize his chronicles mainly because they were conceived as forms of entertainment directed towards a predominantly female readership. Yet Gutiérrez Nájera still made use of fiction even when writing on allegedly "masculine" subjects such as politics, as can be seen in his series of chronicles entitled collectively *Plato del día*. In these, he used fictional techniques in order to avoid the censorship prevalent in the press of Porfirian Mexico. Gutiérrez Nájera also made copious use of pseudonyms (his best-known is "El Duque Job," but he used more than twenty others), which again gave him relative freedom both from censorship and from journalistic restraints when writing his chronicles.

For Gutiérrez Nájera, the chronicler's craft was symbolized in the mythical figure of Proteus. This Greco-Roman sea deity was famous for his metamorphosis but also, following a renaissance tradition of which Gutiérrez Nájera was surely aware, he was considered ambiguously both as a founder of cities and giver of laws and as a perverse magician, a creator of disorder and discord. In a similar fashion, the chronicler had to be simultaneously a teacher and a clown, a hard-nosed reporter and a visionary dreamer; in the end, the chronicler had to be all things to all people, even at the risk of abandoning a stable and original literary *persona*.

If Gutiérrez Nájera introduced the chronicle into Spanish American literature, it was the Cuban José Martí who gave it a wider diffusion and greater intellectual depth. Martí's chronicles can be divided into three types: the artistic and literary, the reportorial, and the "domestic." This latter type encompasses the texts Martí wrote during the 1890s for the section of his newspaper, *Patria*, entitled "En Casa." In these he described, in the same lyrical yet familiar style one also finds in his letters, the modest social and political activities of the Cuban emigré community in New York, Tampa, and Key West. The artistic and literary chronicles, on the other hand, were published during the 1880s in such diverse journals and dailies as *La Nación*, *El Partido Liberal* (Mexico), and the *Revista Venezolana*. These consisted of reviews of art exhibits and books, written in the lush descriptive style characteristic of the "artistic prose" of the Modernists (of which more will be said later).

However, it is in the reportorial chronicles that Martí uses the fullest range of stylistic and rhetorical devices. Published during the 1880s and 1890s, and collected in Martí's *Obras completas* under the headings "Escenas norteamericanas" and "Escenas europeas," these chronicles are "reportorial" because they deal with the sort of events usually covered by reporters: political controversies, economic news, crime stories, disasters, etc. However, as is usually the case with Martí, there is far more in these texts than meets the eye. It has frequently been remarked that Martí's "Escenas norteamericanas" have an epic scope, richness of descriptive detail, and vividness of characterization and description that gives them an almost novelistic character in the mold of the vast nineteenth-century *romans fleuve* like those of Balzac, Galdós, or Zola.

Martí's method in writing these chronicles was quasi-philological. Although he lived in New York at the time, he was always short of money and could not personally witness many of the events he described (such as the trial and execution of four anarchists in Chicago, in November, 1887, or the establishment of a frontier town in Oklahoma in April, 1889). Instead, taking advantage of New York's burgeoning press, he bought four or five copies of the major dailies and systematically compared their coverage of the same event, preparing a composite narrative in a style so lively and descriptive that it seemed a firsthand account.

It is difficult to single out from such a prodigiously large and varied body of narrative a specific reportorial chronicle as more typical of Martí's writing than others. An often-quoted and often-reprinted one is "El terremoto de Charleston." Contrast between this text and Gutiérrez Nájera's depiction of the Mexican earthquake is enlightening; while Gutiérrez Nájera subjectivizes the event, scaling it down to the level of a drawing-room drama, Martí's chronicle attempts to describe the admittedly far more devastating Charleston earthquake of 1886, and its aftermath, in all their terrible grandeur. Martí's style in this chronicle is thus highly oratorical and sententious, skilfully blending description with analysis while seeking to create the impression of immediacy through the evocation of the spoken word – "To say it is to see it", in Martí's own phrase – and in his use of the historical present tense. Ever the political leader (which Gutiérrez Nájera was not), Martí also uses the circumstance of the earthquake as a pretext to reflect on the nature of time and history and to present his own ideas about the nature of human "progress."

One interesting aspect about "El terremoto de Charleston" is the considerable attention Martí pays to the role of Blacks in the rescue and reconstruction efforts in Charleston immediately after the earthquake. The natural catastrophe appears at first to have broken not only the buildings but also the spirit of the once proud and beautiful city; but spirits soon revive, and it is the Blacks of Charleston who are the first to rally spontaneously to the task of rebuilding. Martí sees the Blacks as a people endowed with a superlative spiritual strength and resilience that slavery itself could not destroy. In a moving passage of the chronicle, Martí relates how spontaneous "revival meetings" broke out in the streets of Charleston where Blacks and Whites together sang "spirituals" and prayed. He describes with admiration the "sacred elders," the elderly black men and women who emerged from the disaster imbued with "such sacramental power that the whites, the cultivated whites themselves, full of veneration, joined the music of their troubled souls to that tender and ridiculous dialect."

Martí's interest in the role of the Blacks during the Charleston earthquake arises from the need to find in his discourse an element that would explain the renewed impetus with which the people of Charleston begin to rebuild after the 'quake: what is it that stops the people of Charleston, after the 'quake, from becoming disheartened and moving away? From where comes the energy that bridges the gap in the history of the city opened by the 'quake, and assures the continuity of human progress? The Blacks in Martí's text function as mediators between the cataclysmic forces of nature and the power of human creativity. Martí, whose vision of society was influenced by thermodynamics, saw society as a great steam engine which ultimately derived its force from the vitality of the working classes and marginal social groups. In "El terremoto de Charleston," it is the Blacks' inner strength, expressed through the hypnotic rhythm of their "spirituals," that serves to heal the wounds inflicted on Charleston and to bring back the normal rhythms of temporality and history.

Further reflections on "progress" and its effects on literature are to be found in the chronicles of Rubén Darío. After the deaths of Gutiérrez Nájera and Martí, Darío, who was in many ways their literary heir, became the undisputed leader of Modernism. Nowhere is his debt to those earlier writers more evident than in his chronicles. Published and reprinted in Spanish and Spanish American journals and dailies, they were collected in books such as *Los raros*, *España contemporánea*, *Peregrinaciones* (1901), *La caravana pasa* (1903), *Tierras solares*, and *El viaje a Nicaragua*. Darío's chronicles, like Martí's, form a vast body of writings which can be divided into three basic types: the artistic and literary, reportorial, and travel chronicles. Unlike the chronicles of Martí and Gutiérrez Nájera, however, the quality of Darío's is very uneven; far too many (especially the reportorial chronicles) were hastily written occasional pieces. The books mentioned above, however, contain some of Darío's best prose.

Los raros collects the most outstanding examples of Darío's artistic and literary chronicles; these consisted of impressionistic profiles of past and present authors from Europe and Spanish America, selected because of their marginality to their respective traditions. The majority of the authors Darío chose to highlight in these chronicles were French; most were (and still remain) secondary figures, such as Jean Richepin, Rachilde, or Laurent Tailhade, but others, like Lautréamont, were later to be revered by the Avant-Garde. Among the non-French authors, Darío includes only two Spanish Americans, both Cubans: Augusto de Armas (1869–1893) and José Martí. De Armas wrote in French and is a decidedly minor figure; Darío's chronicle on Martí, however, is important because it was one of the first literary evaluations written after Martí's death, and it served to call attention to Martí's stature as a founding figure of Modernism.

Darío's travel chronicles also contain fine prose, and are still worth reading, particularly for what they reveal about his inner life. In them, Darío consistently presents himself as a "pilgrim" (although his final destination is unclear), as a pathetic wanderer – sometimes an exile, sometimes an expatriate – who is also a prisoner of his own celebrity.

Indeed, the major difference between his predecessors' chronicles and Darío's is the latter's frequently autobiographical, confessional tone.

Conversion and its usual aftermath, confession, are topics of turn-of-the-century writing in Europe and Spanish America that are particularly visible in Darío's mature poetry of *Cantos de vida y esperanza* and after, as well as in his prose. Darío's confessionalism arises not only from his increasing celebrity during the 1890s, but also from literary-historical and personal motivations. Darío, unlike Martí, had become fascinated with the works of the French decadents of the end of the century, such as Joris Karl Huysman's novel *À rebours* (1883). Darío's "decadent" phase is visible in the poetry of his *Prosas profanas* (1896) and in the prose of *Los raros*. However, Darío was profoundly affected (like other Modernists) by the Spanish American War of 1898, and the deaths of the earlier Modernists (Julián del Casal [1863–1893], Gutiérrez Nájera and Martí, in 1895, and José Asunción Silva [1865–1896]). Also, already aware of his personal problems with alcoholism, Darío grew disgusted with "Decadentism" and felt the need to change his attitude and give his writings greater social relevance. This impulse is clearly visible in his travel chronicles, especially in *El viaje a Nicaragua*, where Darío tries to come to grips with his troubled personality and his celebrity (and the increased social responsibilities that came with it) while giving an account of his triumphant return to his native country in 1907.

Like every modernist chronicle, *El viaje a Nicaragua* has several levels of interpretation: on the surface, it is simply a travel narrative; on a deeper level, it is the story of a conversion; and on yet another level, it is a meditation on the meaning of history in the context of the issues concerned with the return. As a travel narrative, Darío's text describes in part the poet's itinerary from his departure from Le Havre until his arrival at the port of Corinto, in Nicaragua, after a brief stop in New York (Chapter 1), and Darío's visit to the Nicaraguan cities of Masaya (Chapter 9) and León (Chapter 10). Darío also devotes a chapter to describing his visit to a coffee plantation (Chapter 2). The remaining seven chapters in the book constitute a sort of brief cultural history of Nicaragua, covering aspects as varied as the ethnic background of the Nicaraguan people (Chapter 3), the origins and development of Nicaraguan literature (Chapter 4), and the character traits of Nicaraguan women (Chapter 7).

What brings stylistic unity to all these sections is Darío's "I" which travels through the text, coordinating, explaining, quoting sources as diverse as the colonial chronicler Francisco López de Gómara (1510–1572) and the Nicaraguan historian José Dolores Gámez (1851–?). This is not, however, the overbearing "I" of the philologist or critic; Darío's is much more humble and weak; it is an "I" in search of peace and happiness.

Referring to the coffee plantations, Darío states: "More than once I have thought that happiness may indeed dwell in one of those delightful paradises, and that a certain restless and passionate pilgrim could have taken refuge in those unknown realms instead of crisscrossing the vast earth in search of unattainable ideals and a nonexistent peace." *El viaje a Nicaragua* is structured around an autobiographic "I" that casts the tale of its search for peace as a pilgrimage, a return to the Origin, and a search for renewal. It is not surprising in this context that Darío "Orientalizes" Nicaragua in his descriptions, since the Orient symbolized, in the romantic philology that Darío and the Modernists inherited, the origin of human civilization and a source of spiritual and cultural renewal. In an Orientalist frenzy, Darío compares Nicaraguan soldiers to those of the Mikado, and the city of Masaya to Baghdad. Nicaragua's prime export crop, coffee, grown amid volcanic mountains, symbolizes for Darío the capacity of Nicaraguan nature to reinvigorate his debilitated poetic powers: "One good cup of that black drink, well prepared, contains as many problems and poems as a bottle of ink."

Another interesting aspect of *El viaje a Nicaragua* is Darío's explicit contrast of his country with the United States, specifically with New York, which he had visited on his way home. The contrast is stated, significantly, in terms of temporality and history. Nicaragua, being closer to the Origin, is also a place of "frozen time" (in Darío's words), where time has stood still at the moment of Genesis, and nature reigns in numinous silence and harmony. In New York, on the other hand, where "progress" reigns, everything is in movement; throngs hustle through vast avenues on incomprehensible errands; express elevators hurtle to the tops of huge buildings; time appears fragmented and fleeting, and disharmony and decay are the norm. Nicaragua is a land of poets and poetry; New York is "the vast capital of the bank check." Nevertheless, Darío's attitude toward economic and industrial "progress" (as represented by his comments on New York) is ambiguous; elsewhere, he praises Nicaraguan President José Santos Zelaya for increasing commerce and industry in his country, and – somewhat surprisingly in an author who in *Azul*. . . spoke disparagingly of "el rey burgués" – speaks approvingly of the power of money: "Today, as always, money makes poetry, fills our existence with beauty, brings culture and progress, beautifies our cities, and brings relative happiness to workers."

Among the many other modernist chroniclers, special mention must be made of the Guatemalan-born Enrique Gómez Carrillo, although he is all but forgotten today, because he was in his time ranked among the major Modernists solely by virtue of his abundant chronicles. Gómez Carrillo's chronicles were written at a later stage in the history of Spanish American Modernism, when the movement had achieved a truly international status. As with Darío, numerous Modernists, because of their new-found literary success, traveled abroad during the early 1900s either on speaking engagements, as diplomats, or simply as tourists. Their travels took them to other Spanish American countries, to Europe, the Middle East, and even as far as Japan. Gómez Carrillo, who resided for most of his adult life in France, was above all a writer of travel chronicles. His descriptions of life in Paris, as well as of his travels to Greece, Egypt, and Japan, appeared in newspapers such as *La Nación* and *La Razón*, in Buenos Aires, and *El Liberal*, in Madrid, and were collected in books with titles such as: *De Marsella a Tokío*, *La Grecia eterna*, and *Sensaciones de Egipto* (1918). These texts, written in a deceptively light and elegant style, contributed much to the knowledge many of the less-traveled Modernists had of the world, and, since Gómez Carrillo included in them generally favorable comments on the work of his modernist colleagues, they also served as propaganda for the modernist movement in general.

As Max Henríquez Ureña (1885–1968) observed (*Breve historia del modernismo*), many of Gómez Carrillo's superficially frivolous chronicles are in fact essays rich with information and ideas, which required a long and patient process of composition. Typical of these multi-layered texts is "La psicología del viaje" (1919), a chronicle in which Gómez Carrillo critically analyzes the three interlinked topics of conversion, confession, and pilgrimage that recur in modernist writing after the turn of the century. Gómez Carrillo begins his text with the surprising prediction – particularly in view of his fame as a "travel writer" – that traveling will soon be "bankrupt" as a form of "intellectual penetration and study" (in his words). Paraphrasing the French psychologist Paul Bourget, he asks: "Why travel. . . since we will never be able to know the souls of the people of other countries? Why go to far-off places in search of human documents, when we are not even capable of deciphering the documents of our own homeland, our own family, our very being. . .? The Greeks' *know thyself* is but a deceitful fantasy. We will never know ourselves, just as we will never know our fellow beings."

Gómez Carrillo's reflections on travel and travel writing spring from a deep skepticism toward the strategies of self-analysis and self-renewal of early twentieth-century writers. Not only is the old romantic tradition of the "sentimental journey," of travel as a means of acquiring self-knowledge, useless, Gómez Carrillo points out, but travel itself has become unnecessary as a form of historical and philological inquiry, since there are already innumerable texts through which the researcher can more easily understand the *Volksgeist* of foreign countries. In view of these ideas, what is the function of the travel writer? Gómez Carrillo's reply is that the modern travel writer should simply aspire to transcribe the sights, smells, sounds, and experiences of the foreign lands he visits as they impact on his consciousness. This he must do without attempting to give them a transcendental or psychologistic interpretation, or abandoning the harmonious and artistic style of modernist prose. The modernist travel writer, says Gómez Carrillo, should be a kind of *voyageur/voyeur*, or, better yet, a sort of *medium* who receives and transmits the experience of travel for the benefit of his or her readers, who may never be able to travel themselves, or if they do, will probably fall prey to the banal itineraries of the Baedeker or the *Guide Bleu*. For Gómez Carrillo, the modernist travel writer is the purveyor of a luxury product: a refined artistic reconstruction of unusual scenes and sensations. Indeed, sensationalism, occasionally verging on pornography, is a common trait of many of Gómez Carrillo's travel chronicles.

"La psicología del viaje" is valuable also because it shows the Guatemalan chronicler's awareness of the corrosive effect of the new techniques of representation, such as photography and the cinema, on the nineteenth-century notions of literature and art. Movies and photographs not only make travel for the sake of knowledge and personal improvement superfluous for the ordinary individual, but they also fulfill the desire for empirical accuracy that underlies much of nineteenth-century art and writing, thus posing a challenge for the modernist writer, who must satisfy the public's incessant craving for new sensations. While Gómez Carrillo was not himself an Avant-Gardist (he abhorred Cubism, for instance, as his chronicle "El cubismo" [1914] shows), he was clearly aware of the new forces that were rapidly undermining the foundations of art and life during the waning years of *la belle époque*, and that were opening new possibilities for artistic and literary creation.

The genre of the modernist short story is closely associated with the modernist chronicles. Indeed, Manuel Gutiérrez Nájera, one of the founders of the modernist chronicles, is also considered a precursor of the modernist short story. Many of the stories in *Cuentos frágiles*, the only book of stories collected by Gutiérrez Nájera himself (others, such as *Cuentos color de humo*, were collected after his death), are, in fact, chronicles, or parts of chronicles. As may be seen in E. K. Mapes's edition of his *Cuentos completos y otras narraciones*, Gutiérrez Nájera often imbedded his fictions superficially in a journalistic context, from which they could later be easily detached and collected as short stories; this is the case with tales such as "La novela del tranvía," "La venganza de Mylord," and "La hija del aire." Sometimes, however, the immediately referential, journalistic element is inseparable from the fictional narrative, as in "Los amores del cometa," Gutiérrez Nájera's description of the Great September Comet of 1882, or "La odisea de Madame Théo," whose protagonist is the real-life French singer Louise Théo. Gutiérrez Nájera's stories, like his chronicles, are permeated by a profound subjectivism, and they prefigure the psychological issues that will recur in the works of virtually all subsequent modernist short-story writers, from Rubén Darío to Leopoldo Lugones (1874–1938).

An excessive sense of decorum and concern with poetic form precluded many Modernists from performing in their verse the deep personal introspection that the changing concept of literature at the turn of the century demanded. Instead, the short story, a relatively "new" genre (after its virtual reinvention by Edgar Allan Poe, who also brought to the genre an emphasis on morbid psychology and bizarre occurrences), offered them this possibility. Even Darío, whose poems "Cantos de vida y esperanza" and "Lo fatal" offer some of the most anguished and devastating self-appraisals in modernist poetry, gravitated toward the short story as a means of self-analysis. Although the stories of Gutiérrez Nájera, Darío, Nervo, Manuel Díaz Rodríguez (1871–1927), and Lugones – to mention the major practitioners of the genre – were sometimes little more than embellished chronicles or, at most, allegories of aesthetic theories (such as Darío's "El pájaro azul" and "El rey burgués"), one finds in many of them a recurrent preoccupation with subjectivity, with the psyche. During the same period that Freud was laying down the foundations of psychoanalysis with his studies of dreams, neuroses, and instincts, the Spanish American Modernists were writing stories that focused insistently on dreams, fantasies, and aberrant behavior. Excellent examples of this may be seen in stories such as Gutiérrez Nájera's "El sueño de Magda" (1883) and "Rip-Rip el aparecido" (1890), Darío's numerous and scattered fantastic tales, such as "Thanathopia" (1893), "La pesadilla de Honorio" (1894), "La larva" (1910), and "Huitzilopoxtli (Leyenda mexicana)" (1915), Lugones's *Las fuerzas extrañas*, Amado Nervo's *Cuentos misteriosos*, and Díaz Rodríguez's *Confidencias de Psiquis* (1897), "Las ovejas y las rosas del padre Serafín," "Música bárbara," and "Egloga de verano" (all from 1922).

In "El sueño de Magda" (this title was given by the critic E. K. Mapes, since it is one of those "imbedded stories" found in Gutiérrez Nájera's series of chronicles entitled *La vida en México*), Gutiérrez Nájera evokes the world of dreams in a way that almost prefigures Surrealism. Magda is a woman watching from the balcony of her house as the rain falls in Mexico City; as she watches the rain, the third-person narrator relates how this evokes in Magda the fearful memories of a nightmare she had the previous night. The nightmare, which consists of a vision of universal deluge, ends with Magda falling from the top of a stone cross onto a granite obelisk after having her eyes pierced by the beaks of owls. Gutiérrez Nájera simply relates this dream, leaving possible interpretations to be developed by the reader.

The story "Rip-Rip el aparecido," is also narrated as a dream, although it begins in a more conventionally literary way as a gloss of Washington Irving's "Rip van Winkle" (which Gutiérrez Nájera claims not to have read). Gutiérrez Nájera's version, like Irving's legend, is the nightmarish tale of a man who gets drunk and falls asleep inside a cave, where he sleeps for many years. When he finally awakens, he is already old and is not recognized by his wife nor by his closest friends. In the end, Rip-Rip runs away from the town, and only when he sees his reflection in a stream does he realize the cause of his predicament. Rip-Rip then commits suicide by drowning himself in the stream. This tale may be interpreted as an allegory of personal identity, since the narrator tells us (in a passage that suspiciously resembles a fable's "moral") that Rip-Rip "was not one man, he was many men . . . perhaps all men."

Darío's "Thanathopia" is ostensibly a horror story about a British doctor and hypnotist who is married to a female vampire, but the story's first-person, confessional tone (it is narrated by the doctor's son) allows it to become, ambiguously, a fable about father–son relationships. The protagonist and narrator, James Leen, is an eccentric English professor and expatriate living in Buenos Aires who tells his story to a group of friends in a beer hall. Leen tells how, after his mother's death, his father, who never showed him affection, sent him off to study at a boarding school. The story's surprising ending is prefigured by certain enigmatic phrases spoken by the narrator, which Darío underlines, such as: "Physically, I was the veritable image of my mother (or so I have been told) *and I suppose that is why the doctor looked at me as little as possible.*" The explanation of this and other phrases is seen at the end, when the narrator is taken by his father to meet his stepmother, who turns out to be the corpse of his mother, kept in an "undead" state by the father's hypnotic arts.

"La pesadilla de Honorio," as its title indicates, is the description of a nightmare. Enrique Anderson Imbert has pointed out (in *La originalidad de Rubén Darío*) the story's sources in Thomas De Quincey's *Confessions of an English Opium Eater* (1821), and the narrator himself quotes in translation a fragment from De Quincey's book: "How and when did the following phrase by a dreamer appear in Honorio's memory: *the tyranny of the human face?*" (The original phrase from De Quincey reads: "That affection which I have called the tyranny of the human face.") The nightmare in fact consists of an overwhelming vision of a multiplicity of human faces, which gradually turn into a series of masks that signify the seven deadly sins. In the final sentence, the narrator suggests that Honorio's hallucination or dream might have been simply the product of his drunken revelry at Carnival.

Alcohol and drugs figure more visibly in "Huitzilopoxtli (Leyenda mexicana)." This late story (it was published in 1915, the year before

Darío's death) is interesting mostly as Darío's rather unsuccessful attempt to make sense out of an event – the Mexican Revolution – which contributed to the demise of the modernist ideology and aesthetic. Darío views the Revolution as an act of mass immolation in the style of the Aztec sacrifices. The story's only satisfying aspect, however, is its evocation of an atmosphere of mystery, fanaticism, and menace.

The first-person narrator, a journalist sent to cover the events of the Mexican Revolution, teams up with an American journalist with the amusing name of John Perhaps, and a bizarre Basque renegade priest turned colonel in the revolutionary army, named Reguera. On their way to one of Pancho Villa's encampments, the ex-priest insistently talks about how "the destiny of the Mexican nation is still in the hands of the primitive aboriginal deities." The narrator–protagonist is intrigued, and asks Reguera to elaborate. Reguera argues that Madero's triumph was due to his belief in spirits and specifically to his "contacts" with the ancient Aztec gods. While the narrator and Reguera talk and drink *comiteco*, the American journalist is lost from sight along the winding mountain road. Later, they come upon a group of insurgents but are not allowed to proceed, and must spend the night beneath some trees. Before going to sleep, the narrator and Reguera share some marihuana-laced cigarettes. A dreamlike scene then ensues in which the narrator, unable to sleep and hearing the howling of coyotes nearby, moves into the bush to investigate with gun at ready. After a while, he comes upon a grotesque scene: beneath an enormous Aztec stone idol which the narrator recognizes as belonging to the goddess of death, a sacrifice is taking place. The victim is the American journalist, "Míster" Perhaps. It is never made clear whether this scene is real or only a drug-induced vision; its theme of human sacrifice clearly prefigures the story's ending, however. The next day, after arriving at the insurgents' camp, the narrator has to be treated by a physician. He asks for Colonel Reguera, and is calmly told that the Colonel "is busy right now. He still has three more to shoot."

However, it is in "La larva" where Darío unveils some of his deepest fears. The narration unfolds in a spare, direct style, as a reminiscence of Darío's youth in Nicaragua; the narrator and protagonist, named Isaac Codomano (who is clearly Darío himself), tells of the ghost stories and superstitions he heard as a child in his native land, and of his own encounter with an apparition. In the darkened streets of his hometown, the fifteen-year-old protagonist, coming home from a serenade in a mood for amorous escapades, sees the figure of a woman wrapped in a shawl. He approaches and propositions her. To his horror, the woman shows herself to be a horrible "larva" – a ghost – with the face of a rotting corpse. Although this tale could easily derive from Darío's readings of baroque Spanish theatre (such as Pedro Calderón de la Barca's *El mágico prodigioso* [1637]), the detailed evocation of time and place gives it a powerful confessional resonance that may point to Darío's well-known alcoholic deliriums as well as to psychosexual problems.

Nervo's approach to the psychological issues in his *Cuentos misteriosos* is more light-hearted, and frequently verges on satire, as in "Don Diego de noche," the story of a man who, like Gabrielle D'Annunzio (to whom Nervo alludes in the story), was afraid of decrepitude, and decided never to age beyond his thirty-three years; he finally dies of old age, but his "official" age on his tombstone is still thirty-three. On the other hand, many of the best-known tales from Lugones's *Las fuerzas extrañas* have an underlying satirical thrust reminiscent of Jonathan Swift. Like the eighteenth-century Irish satirist, Lugones shows in these stories a grim and mordant vision of humanity. Lugones's satire is particularly directed toward Positivism and its belief in humanity's inherent superiority over nature. The two most frequently reprinted stories of the twelve collected in *Las fuerzas extrañas*, "Los caballos de Abdera" and "Yzur," are good examples of Lugones's Swiftian temper. The former, despite its mythical Greco-Roman setting, is evocative of the Houyhnhnms episode in *Gulliver's Travels* (1726); the horses of the Thracian city of Abdera are pampered and educated by their owners to such a degree that they become intelligent and ultimately rebel against their masters. Lugones spoils the tale somewhat at the end by the *deus ex machina* introduction of Hercules, who arrives to save the city from the beasts. In "Yzur," however, there is no attempt at a "happy ending"; it is the grim tale of a chimpanzee bought by a linguist whose enthusiasm for language instruction is reminiscent of George Bernard Shaw's character of Henry Higgins in *Pygmalion*. In this case, however, the scientist's obsession with making Yzur speak human words leads to the ape's becoming, in the narrator's words, "sick with intelligence and pain." Yzur's pathetic first words are also his last, as he begs his master for a drink of water.

The title of Manuel Díaz Rodríguez's first book of short stories, *Confidencias de Psiquis*, is highly suggestive in terms of the modernist tendency toward a psychological theme, and indeed, most of the stories in the volume have to do with mental aberrations of various sorts, as some of the titles clearly indicate: "Celos," "Fetiquismo," "Tic," etc. The stories in his second book, *Cuentos de color* were less psychological and more allegorical and "artistic," in the style of Darío's *Azul* . . . In his later narratives, however, Díaz Rodríguez frequently inserted violent and grotesque scenes which break the superficial harmony of his prose. "Egloga de verano," for example, a story set in a creole ambience, tells the tale of Guacharaco, a small-town sheriff who obstinately courts Justa, the virtuous wife of the peasant Sandalio. One night, as he violently tries to break into Sandalio's house in order to rape Justa, who is alone,

Guacharaco is beheaded by Justa. Díaz Rodríguez's description of this act is sensationalistic in the extreme, but despite its gruesome character the whole scene has an artificial, contrived atmosphere that is still a modernist trait: "Guacharaco's head, stretched out in the effort to break in when it was chopped off, jumped, and perhaps in a last convulsion held on with its teeth to the cot's sheet. It was found thus, hanging from the sheet, which undoubtedly did not slip to the ground from the strange weight of the head because it was held tightly on the other side between the cot and the supporting beam of the hut."

Lugones's stories in *Las fuerzas extrañas* and Díaz Rodríguez's later tales, such as "Egloga de verano" and "Música bárbara" point toward the transition between the modernist short story and the more contemporary forms of the genre found in the works of Horacio Quiroga (1878–1937). Quiroga, who began his career as a Modernist, is to the genre of the modernist short story what Julio Herrera y Reissig (1875–1910) is to modernist verse: a writer who innovates by collecting and intensifying materials and techniques introduced by previous writers. In Quiroga's *Cuentos de amor, de locura y de muerte* we find the modernist preoccupation with the psyche and personal identity combined with a more "realist" narrative approach and with the rural or wilderness setting preferred by the later telluric narrative of José Eustacio Rivera (1888–1928) and Rómulo Gallegos (1884–1969).

In terms of their themes and allusions, the modernist short stories also reflect their authors' insistent bookishness: numerous modernist short stories take other literary works as their point of departure – witness Darío's "La larva," which begins with an evocation of Benvenuto Cellini's *Vita* (1562) or Lugones's "La lluvia de fuego" (1906), which is a gloss of the biblical tale of Sodom and Gomorrah. In these and other modernist short stories, the setting is frequently an artificial (specifically, philological) recreation of environments previously encoded in literature – such as the Arcadia of Greek and Roman pastoral poetry, the bohemian world of students and artists of French Romanticism – or of the Orient. Darío's well-known "naturalist" short story, "El fardo," in *Azul. . .* is the exception that proves the rule, since, in the context of the book as a whole it stands out as an essentially literary experiment in the naturalist style, and is as bookish in its own way as "El velo de la Reina Mab."

Partly because of their extreme subjectivism and concern with subjectivity, the modernist short-story writers tended to avoid the realist aesthetic in favor of broad stylistic experimentation and a lyrical tone. Unlike their approach to poetry, however, the Modernists did not attempt to formulate a poetics of the short story; nevertheless, their stories clearly show the coherent and beneficial impact modernist writing had on the Hispanic short-story tradition. Due to the Modernists, the language of the Hispanic short story became more polished, precise, and nuanced, its subjects became more varied, and narrative intensity was emphasized. A greater degree of creative self-consciousness also began to emerge. Indeed, the modernist experiments in narrative point of view, tone, and use of symbolic elements in the development of the plot, were contributions adopted even by later Spanish American narrators who wrote in the realist vein. Furthermore, echoes of the Modernists' interest in "the fantastic" and in bookish and erudite themes for their short stories may be discerned in the narrative of later Spanish American writers like Jorge Luis Borges (1899–1986), Carpentier, Carlos Fuentes (b. 1928), and Julio Cortázar (1916–1964).

The modernist essay, like the short story, is also intimately connected to the chronicle. Many so-called chronicles of Martí, Gutiérrez Nájera, and Gómez Carrillo, can in fact be considered essays. Indeed, if the boundary between the modernist chronicle and the short story often appears blurred, this is even more evident in the essay. Like the chronicle, the essay is an expository prose text that makes occasional use of narration and frequently utilizes poetic and rhetorical devices to present its message. Often the essay, like the chronicle, takes current events as its point of departure. Length is not an important distinguishing factor between both genres, since it could be argued that book-length essays such as Rodó's *Ariel* (of which more will be said shortly) are actually collections of shorter texts united by a common thread of argument, and there are also book-length chronicles: Darío's *El viaje a Nicaragua* immediately springs to mind, along with many of Gómez Carrillo's travel chronicles.

One important distinction between the two genres lies in their *tone*. Generally, the tone of the chronicle is frivolous, superficial, or sensationalistic; description prevails over analysis, and ideas are subordinated to events and things. Martí's work, which could be cited as an exception, actually proves the rule, since what stands out in most of the Cuban patriot's chronicles is his constant struggle to undermine the superficiality and sensationalism demanded of him as a chronicler by his editors (as may be seen in his correspondence with Bartolomé Mitre y Vedia, editor of the Buenos Aires newspaper *La Nación*).

This conflict is particularly evident in Martí's artistic and literary chronicles (as defined by the typology proposed above). In these, he had both to entertain and to enlighten his readers, and the subject matter – new or unknown authors and artists, art exhibits, book reviews – naturally led him toward the essay form. While their introductory nature gives them the status of "news," what makes these texts essayistic is not only their literary or cultural subject matter but also the meditative tone in which they are cast and their abundant digressions, in which Martí reflects on more general social, cultural, or even philosophical questions. Among these chronicles are various highly influential texts Martí wrote to introduce and comment to his Spanish American readers the works of English-speaking authors such as Walt Whitman, Ralph Waldo Emerson, Oscar Wilde, Charles Darwin, and others.

Much of what was stated about the style of Martí's reportorial chronicles can also be said of his essays. The main qualities of Martí's oratory – sententiousness and use of vivid images – predominate in them, sometimes threatening to overshadow his ideas. Nevertheless, these texts convey an impression of intellectual depth combined with a highly effective, if somewhat baroque, use of language. Conversely, if his essays are oratorical, many of Martí's numerous speeches can also be classified as essayistic, despite their abundant rhetorical flourishes. This is the case with his Steck Hall speech of 1880, and his speeches on José María de Heredia (1803–1839) in 1889 and on Simón Bolívar (1783–1830) in 1893, as well as with his very famous and highly oratorical text (which was never delivered as a speech), "Nuestra América" (1891) ["Our America."]. Another important oratorical–essayistic text by Martí, among many that could be cited, is his 1882 prologue to *Poema del Niágara* (1880) by Juan Antonio Pérez Bonalde (1846–1892).

On this prologue Martí, always the perfectionist, later commented with regret that it was like "new wine," too rich with ideas that had not fully matured. Nevertheless, this is clearly one of the most remarkable of the many extraordinary essays Martí wrote. "El *Poema del Niágara*" is outstanding because in it Martí offers a vivid (if rather rhapsodic) synthesis of the changes wrought in Spanish American literature and culture by the arrival of modernity. What first strikes the reader of this essay, however, is its tone, akin to that of a manifesto; "El *Poema del Niágara*" is one of Martí's most sustained attempts at outlining a poetics for Modernism. It is not a poetics concerned with technicalities of verse and form, however, but with the philosophical basis for a new literature.

In his comments on Pérez Bonalde's poem (which is not a particularly memorable or modernist work itself), Martí seeks to come to terms with his romantic background and with the ideas of turn-of-the-century Decadentism. Martí's Romanticism is by no means a residue of the early and rather weak Hispanic Romanticism of Heredia, Gustavo Adolfo Bécquer, or José Zorrilla (although Martí knew and admired some of their works), but rather the product of his belated and marginal confrontation with the more powerful Anglo-Germanic Romanticism of William Wordsworth, Johann Wolfgang von Goethe, and Samuel Taylor Coleridge. Martí, as a Cuban writer from the latter half of the nineteenth century, deliberately studied the earlier Anglo-Germanic Romanticism because he knew that its ideas had only reached America through their dilute French and Spanish adaptations. Martí's interest in Romanticism does not spring from the nostalgia of a latecomer, however, but from his eclectic search for elements with which to lay the foundations of a solid Spanish American literature.

Another reason for Martí's sympathetic appreciation of Romanticism is his own political agenda: Cuba's independence was to be the culmination of Spanish America's Wars of Independence earlier in the century, which had been highly romantic enterprises themselves at both the practical and ideological levels. On the other hand, Martí wished to maintain a critical distance, both for political and literary reasons, from French Decadentism, which was the literary modality then in vogue: as a political leader, he could hardly believe in "decadence" while preparing a revolution, and as a writer, Martí (like Nietzsche, whose works he probably did not read) viewed decadentism as excessively "effeminate" (he referred to the "decadent" writers as "hembras débiles") and life-denying, and considered it unsuitable to form the basis for the new American literature he wanted to create.

"El Poema del Niágara" appears, therefore, as a rather bizarre mixture of romantic topics and diatribes against Decadentism, written in Martí's highly oratorical and image-laden style (which did not escape contamination from Decadentism), leavened with Martí's own perceptive observations (gleaned from his experience of life in New York) about modernity's impact on the life of the mind. Martí's emphasis is on speed, change and uncertainty: "No one can today be certain of his faith," he states, "We wake up with one problem and go to bed with another. Images devour each other in our minds. There is no time to give shape to our thoughts." In a visionary passage that Cintio Vitier (b. 1921), in "Martí futuro," has compared with texts by the Peruvian poet César Vallejo, Martí declares of the new poets: "They have all been kissed by the same sorceress. In all of them boils the new blood. Though they may tear their entrails to pieces, in a quiet corner there still lurk, angry and hungry, Unrest, Uncertainty, a Vague Hope, and a Secret Vision. An immense pale man of haggard countenance, tearful eyes, and dry mouth, dressed in black, walks with grave steps, without rest or sleep, over the whole earth, and has sat in front of all the fireplaces, and placed his trembling hand at the head of every table!"

Martí sees the birth of the new writers and intellectuals as an agonistic process; writers must discard old habits (such as, for instance, the slow, methodic accumulation of knowledge in an atmosphere of peaceful meditation) and must become accustomed instead to working in a more mundane ambience, suffering the continuous and often rending friction of everyday life, and facing an ever-increasing mass of unrefined information. "El Poema del Niágara," is above all a diagnosis of the crisis of the turn-of-the-century writers in Europe as well as Spanish America. Despite its manifesto-like style, it makes few concrete proposals about how the future Spanish American literature should be, save that it should not fall into the trap of Decadentism and should not abandon the metaphysical, transcendentalist search for unity and harmony in the cosmos that was, in Martí's view, the Romantics' greatest legacy.

Needless to say, although many chronicles by Martí, Gutiérrez Nájera, Darío, and Gómez Carrillo, among others, can be considered essays, other modernist prose writers and poets also wrote essays *tout court*, although they are less remembered for this: such is the case of the Uruguayan novelist Carlos Reyles (1868–1938) with his Nietzschean essays in *La muerte del cisne*, or of Lugones's explorations of Argentinian history in *La guerra gaucha*. Nevertheless modernism also produced several writers devoted almost exclusively to the essay as a genre who attempted to distinguish their essays clearly from the ubiquitous chronicles. Foremost among these is the Uruguayan José Enrique Rodó, followed by other less-remembered authors, such as the Peruvian Manuel González Prada (1848–1918), and the Colombians Carlos Arturo Torres (1867–1911) and Baldomero Sanín Cano (1861–1957).

Though it is true that all the major Modernists were acquainted to a greater or lesser degree with philology as a discipline, either in the form of literary criticism or of grammatical and lexicographical studies, the only major Modernist who can be considered a professional philologist is Rodó. Despite his many incursions into Uruguayan politics, Rodó's most constant occupation was what today would be termed "cultural criticism" (criticism of values and ideologies), and literary criticism. Rodó's allegiance to philology as a discipline, combined with his political and moral preoccupations, led him to prefer the essay over narrative fiction or journalism. Although he did write some chronicles (collected posthumously in *El camino de Paros*), a large portion of his work consists of critical essays written in a solemn style and measured tone meant to highlight the profundity of his ideas. His two most outstanding books of essays are *Motivos de Proteo* – which synthesizes Rodó's "ethics of becoming," according to Pedro Henríquez Ureña (1884–1946) – and the well-known and highly influential *Ariel*.

Like Martí's essays, *Ariel* owes much of its rhetoric and structure to the oratorical tradition. The book is in fact presented, in the framing tale that serves as prologue and epilogue, as a long valedictory speech given by an "old and revered teacher," nicknamed "Próspero" by his students because he habitually gave his lectures sitting next to a statue of the character Ariel from Shakespeare's *The Tempest* (1611). Originally published as an integral work, *Ariel* may be divided into six sections, besides the prologue and the epilogue. These divisions were suggested by

Rodó himself after the publication of *Ariel*, when he wrote a summary of the book's content at the request of a friend. Sections 1 to 4 deal with such classic turn-of-the-century topics as the cult of youth, or the appeal to youth as a force for cultural and social innovation; the need for an organic cultural development; the conflict between the self and the outside world; the concept of Beauty in culture; the relationship between beauty and morality; the rise of utilitarianism; the relationship between utilitarianism and democracy, and the need for a redefinition of democracy that will avoid confusion with "the rule of mediocrity" (to use Rodó's phrase). As an illustration of this issue of utilitarianism and democracy, sections 5 and 6 offer a detailed – if, on occasion, factually inaccurate – critique of the civilization of the United States. The crisis of 1898 brought about by the Spanish American War made these comments on the United States particularly opportune, and they are partially responsible for the book's popularity as well as for the controversial reputation it has retained to this day.

In *Ariel*, Rodó tried to outline a program of action for the Spanish American intellectuals of his generation. *Ariel*'s enormous impact on its Spanish American readership was due not only to the ideas it expressed, but also to its programmatic, manifesto-like quality, and to its oratorical rhetoric. There are various styles of oratory, as is well known, and that of Próspero in *Ariel* is one of measured and rational exhortation, unlike Martí's more fiery and poetic style. So balanced and polished is Rodó's style in *Ariel*, that it is easy to forget that its author was only twenty-nine years old when the book was published. Donning the mask of Próspero, Rodó manages to sound like a wise old sage communicating an ancient and unquestionable wisdom.

It should also be noted that Rodó made certain that his work was read and commented by nearly all the major Hispanic intellectuals of his day, from Juan Valera and Miguel de Unamuno in Spain, to the young Pedro Henríquez Ureña and Alfonso Reyes (1889–1959) in Mexico. Rodó sent copies of his book to all of them and wrote asking for their opinion of his work. Through the years, *Ariel* has inspired a long lineage of essays that echo its arguments or reply to them, from *La creación de un continente* (1912) by Francisco García Calderón (1880–1953), through Alfonso Reyes's *Ultima Tule* (1941) to *Calibán. Apuntes sobre la cultura en nuestra América* (1972) by Roberto Fernández Retamar (b. 1930).

If Ariel in Rodó's text is a figure of the purity and perfection to which the modernist artists and intellectuals aspired, in his second major work, *Motivos de Proteo*, Rodó's tutelary deity is very different and in some ways more problematic. Proteus, the variously shaped keeper of Neptune's flocks in Greco-Roman myth, as already mentioned with regard to Gutiérrez Nájera, was an ambiguous symbol of magic and power but also of instability and change. Rodó's Proteus is, to a large extent, the "civic Proteus" of the Renaissance, as seen in the works of Pico della Mirandola and Juan Luis Vives: a figure for the harmonious resolution of multiplicity into unity, as well as a symbol of the multifarious nature of humanistic inquiry. In this sense, Proteus symbolizes for Rodó philology itself, because of philology's wondrous capacity to imitate its object of inquiry and resurrect bygone eras.

It should also be remembered that Ariel, in Rodó's text, appears not as Shakespeare's "airy spirite," but as the statue which adorns Próspero's study; by adopting Proteus as a symbol, Rodó is clearly seeking a less stiff and one-dimensional emblem for his "ethics of becoming." However, the "numen del mar" (as Rodó calls him) is also a sign that stands for the instability and mutability of human nature through time. This deep sense of time's flow is one of the most striking differences between *Motivos de Proteo* and Rodó's earlier essays, which tended toward an ontology based on stony permanence. "Time is the supreme innovator," Rodó declares, and later he states: "We persist only in the continuity of our modifications; in the more or less regular order that controls them; in the force that thrusts us forward towards the most mysterious and transcendent transformation of all. . . We are the ship's wake, whose material essence does not remain the same for two successive instants because it dies and is reborn unceasingly from the waves; the wake that is not a persistent reality but a moving shape, a sequence of rythmic impulses that act upon a constantly renewed object." The problem with which Rodó grapples in *Motivos de Proteo* is how the self can survive in a changing world, in the midst of circumstances which constantly threaten its integrity. If change is inevitable, and "conversion" is the "normal" state of human existence, how can the self control change, and control itself? From a more literary standpoint, how can a writing based on the primacy of the self survive in an age of constant flux and transition? It is the recognition of this dilemma (not the solutions he offers, however) that make Rodó a truly modern writer.

A Peruvian precursor of Modernism, Manuel González Prada enunciated in 1886, fourteen years before Rodó's appeal to youth in *Ariel*, a similar creed which he summed up in the slogan: "Los viejos a la tumba; los jóvenes a la obra" ["The old ones to the grave; the young ones to their work"]. González Prada was, however, a very different sort of essayist to Rodó. A caustic freethinker with anarchistic leanings, González Prada was a polemicist who collected many of his intensely critical essays and (inevitably) speeches in books with such characteristic titles as *Páginas libres*, *Horas de lucha*, and the posthumous *El tonel de Diógenes* (1945). González Prada is also remembered as one of the first Peruvian intellectuals to call attention to the plight of the Indians. However, one of his most interesting essays from a literary-historical perspective is "Junto a Renan" (1894), in which González Prada narrates his personal acquaintance with the French philologist (he attended Renan's courses in Oriental Philology at the Collège de France) and attests to the strong influence of philology on modernist writing.

Closer to Rodó in age and inclinations was the Colombian Carlos Arturo Torres, whose book *Idola fori. Ensayo sobre las supersticiones políticas* appeared with a laudatory prologue from Rodó himself. Torres was an anglophile who had earlier published a series of essays on English literature entitled *Estudios ingleses* (1907). Following Sir Francis Bacon's incipient theory of ideologies in his *Novum Organum* (1620), Torres wrote what is essentially the first serious study of the role of ideology in Spanish American culture and politics. Curiously, for a critic of ideology Torres was rather dogmatic himself, and this is reflected in the highly assertive but colorless style of his book.

Another Colombian essayist, Baldomero Sanín Cano, though ten years his senior, was a kindred spirit to Rodó. Like the Uruguayan, Sanín Cano was primarily a literary and cultural critic. He had read more widely than Rodó himself, and possessed broad knowledge of German and Italian literature. His acquaintance with English literature was particularly intimate, since, like Andrés Bello (1781–1865), he lived for many years in England. Sanín Cano's work, however, never coalesced into a single memorable book, and remained disseminated in journals and newspapers until the mid-1920s, when his concise and elegantly written essays began to be collected in books such as *La civilización manual y otros ensayos* and *Indagaciones e imágenes*.

As we have seen, the Modernists used their chronicles as a sort of "literary scrapbook" or workshop and as a means of informing each other about the latest literary fashions. Their short stories were vehicles for exploring narrative style and the role of subjectivity in fiction writing, while their essays served to reflect on politics, literature, and culture, and to inspire their readers to political commitment in the face of events such as the Spanish American War of 1898 and the taking of the Isthmus of Panama by the United States in 1903. Similarly, the genre of the modernist novel also had its particular *raison d'être*, above and beyond the Modernists' desire to experiment and innovate in all the literary genres.

Like the other modernist prose genres, the modernist novel has suffered from a lack of serious critical scrutiny. To a specialist this statement might seem unlikely, since in fact some modernist novels have inspired important works of literary criticism in Spanish, such as Amado Alonso's *Ensayo sobre la novela histórica. El modernismo en "La gloria de don Ramiro."* Other notable critics and literary historians, such as Enrique Anderson

Imbert (b. 1910) and Fernando Alegría (b. 1918), have devoted essays to specific modernist novels (Martí's *Lucía Jerez* [*Amistad funesta*] for example) and have included modernist novels in their histories of Spanish American literature and of the novel in Spanish America. Yet, on the whole, critical studies that take these texts seriously *as novels* have been lacking. It is typical of most of the early criticism on the modernist novel to view these works as frivolous and unsubstantial, and to consider them chiefly as examples of the Modernists' supposedly excessive concern with style. Scant attention has been paid to the overall formal achievements of the modernist novel as well as to its ideological content.

This relative disdain of the modernist novel has been due in part, first, to the absence of a critically sophisticated and broadly accepted theory of modernist writing, and second, to the ideological prejudices of post-modernist critics, whose concept of the novel was biased in favor of the neorealistic telluric narratives (such as Rómulo Gallegos's *Doña Bárbara*) which arose after the decline of the modernist novels and greatly surpassed them in popularity. In recent years, however, the renewed interest in the study of modernist prose as a whole has given new impetus to the study of the modernist novel.

What at first strikes the student of the modernist novel is the abundance of works included by literary historians and critics in its canon. A cursory survey of the literary histories of Alegría, Anderson Imbert, Arturo Uslar Pietri (b. 1906), Luis Alberto Sánchez (b. 1900), and Max Henríquez Ureña, produces a list of some forty modernist novels, from Martí's pathbreaking *Lucía Jerez* to Carlos Reyles's *El embrujo de Sevilla* [*Castanets*]. Among those that have received serious critical attention over the years are the previously mentioned novels by Martí and Reyles, José Asunción Silva's *De sobremesa* (1896), Amado Nervo's *El bachiller*, Rubén Darío's unfinished *El hombre de oro* (1897), Manuel Díaz Rodríguez's *Idolos rotos* and *Sangre patricia*, *El triunfo del ideal* (1901) and *Dyonisios* (1904) by Pedro César Domínici (1872–1954), *La gloria de don Ramiro* [*The Glory of Don Ramiro*] by Enrique Larreta (1873–1961), and *Alsino* by Pedro Prado (1886–1951).

This plethora of works in the canon is surprising in the light of the critics' general disdain for them, but not in terms of the literary history of the period in Spanish America, since, as Max Henríquez Ureña reminds us, "after the 1880s, novelistic production increases in quantity and importance." The modernist novels were, quite simply, important components of a broad novelistic "boom" that occurred in Spanish America around the turn of the century, in which numerous novels in other modalities, such as *Criollismo* [Creolism] and *Naturalismo* [Naturalism], were also written and published.

The rise, development, and decline of the Spanish American modernist novel takes place within a period of approximately forty years, between the last two decades of the nineteenth century and the first two of the twentieth. Nevertheless, the temporal distribution of works during this period is not uniform: during the first fourteen years of the genre, from 1885 to 1899, only eight important modernist novels were published, while in the following fifteen years, from 1900 to 1915, there were twenty. (The geographic distribution of these works is more uniform – at least in terms of their authors' country of origin: they were produced in the Southern Cone as well as in the Antilles, Mexico, and Central America.) The increase in the production of modernist novels around the turn of the century probably occurred because Modernism was then at the apogee of its diffusion, but also because of extraliterary events such as the Spanish American War of 1898, which, as we shall see, also had an impact on the modernist novelists.

What are the distinguishing characteristics of the modernist novel compared, for example, to the *naturalista* [naturalist], *criollista* [creole] or decadent novels of the same period? At the level of their writing, of course, the modernist novels all share a series of traits that are typically modernist: firstly, the use of the so-called "artistic prose" of the Modernists. Despite variations in style, all modernist novels were written following the principles of "artistic prose" as exemplified in the chronicles and essays of the major Modernists, or as later codified by Enrique Gómez Carrillo in his 1919 essay. "El arte de trabajar la prosa" (*El primer libro de las crónicas*). The notion of "artistic prose" is essentially an outgrowth of the philological idea that language is an object, with a history and a concreteness of its own, and that individual words can be manipulated as "collectables," purely for their aesthetic value, without being totally subordinated to their signifying function. "Artistic prose" was always harmonious, sensuous, meticulously descriptive, full of eye-catching phrases, and was supposed to possess perennial value. The Modernists frequently used terms such as "solid," "polished," "pure," and "marble-like" ("marmóreo") to refer to this form of writing, which, though brilliant at its best, could often become exceedingly hieratic and lifeless. It should be remembered, however, that this writing was considered highly experimental at the time, and that the later avant-garde writing, with its "greguerías" and "jitanjáforas" ["nonsense rhymes"] was mostly an intensification of "artistic prose" principles.

Also important to modernist writing were a series of recurrent topics common to all Modernists: the interior, the museum, the library, the *femme fatale*, the dandy, and the sense of *spleen*, among others. However, at a more ideological level, there are other traits which help to distinguish the modernist novel from the naturalist or creolist works (more will be said about Decadentism shortly). The first, and most general, is the modernist novel's profoundly antipositivistic, critical stance. As mentioned earlier, modernist writing arises from a critical, philological awareness of language's artificiality; the modernist novel extends that critical approach to the ideological framework that sustains both the naturalist and creole novels. Even as they incorporate characters, themes, and topics derived from Naturalism, the modernist novels question Naturalism's attempt to explain, by means of scientific models, a reality that seems to be ever more changeable and chaotic. This is not to suggest that the modernist novelists rejected outright the sociopolitical thrust of naturalist fiction; indeed, that was an aspect of Naturalism in which the Modernists were deeply interested. However, the Modernists clearly approached the whole question of the relation between their literary work and its social context with cautious skepticism. The cosmopolitan and urban thematic of most modernist novels is also in part an outgrowth of this skeptical attitude, which led them to distrust the facile idealization of the countryside typical of most creolist fiction.

It may be thought that the modernist novels are essentially a Spanish American variant of the European "decadent" novels in the mold of J. K. Huysmans's *À rebours*. In fact, although "decadence" – sociopolitical, cultural, or moral – and "art for art's sake" were recurrent topics in the modernist novels, the Modernists' Decadentism was always highly ironic and self-conscious. We must recall that Decadentism was in a large part stimulated by nineteenth-century physics' idea of entropy and its extension to history and society as a sort of "social thermodynamics": it was believed that just as all systems tend to move in the direction of increasing disorder, each society's "progress" must reach a peak and give way to an inevitable decline. However, even the most thoroughgoing Decadentists among the Spanish American Modernists, such as José Asunción Silva and Julián del Casal, realized that their attitude had little correspondence with their Spanish American sociohistorical milieu. They were well aware that from a European point of view, America – both North and South – was still the paradigm of a raw new society full of untapped energy. This awareness is reflected in the Modernists' novels, and thus makes their "Decadentism" rather suspect. For example, José Fernández, the protagonist of Silva's *De sobremesa*, although fascinated by the turn-of-the-century decadent art and lifestyle, nevertheless possessed, we are told, "an athlete's physique," unlike his model, the weakling Des Esseintes from *À rebours*. Fernández was in fact a hyperactive *rastaquouère*, one of those wealthy South Americans who tried to buy their way into the higher levels of turn-of-the-century French society.

A consideration of the protagonist in the modernist novel leads us to another important characteristic which helps to define the genre: in nearly all modernist novels we find the figure of the artist–hero (poet, painter, musician, or sculptor) who tries desperately to define his position and his role within the new Spanish American society of the late nineteenth and early twentieth centuries. The Modernists clearly were not trying simply to imitate decadentist fiction, but were also attempting to go beyond the naturalist and decadentist approach to society and history. They sought a "third way," so to speak, which would help them avoid the hypercritical, ivory-tower attitude of the Decadentists as well as the naturalists' narrow dogmatism that subordinated literature to scientific models and ideological considerations. Indeed, once the modernist novels are subjected to an unprejudiced reading, it becomes evident that far from being frivolous, superficial, or escapist, they were in fact writings in which the Modernists "worked-through" (to borrow a Freudian term) not only their personal problems and aesthetic theories but some of the most urgent issues of their day. If the modernist novel as a genre seems vague and ill-defined, it is simply because it is the record of a profound and sustained search for self-definition by the Modernists, not only on an aesthetic or cultural level, but also on a political plane.

Conversion, as said before, is one of the major topics of late Modernism, and the modernist novels concern themselves with how the sociopolitical and cultural changes in turn-of-the-century Spanish America forced writers to change from being pure practitioners of their art into *intellectuals* in the full modern sense of the term, that is to say: artists, scholars, or scientists who strategically and publicly address issues of political and social import beyond the narrow confines of their disciplines. Most of the major modernist novels may be read as allegories about the conversion of Spanish American writers into intellectuals. In fact, the word "intellectual," which in the romance languages was first used as a noun during the notorious Dreyfus affair of the 1890s in France, first appeared in Spanish in 1901 in the modernist novel *Idolos rotos* by Manuel Díaz Rodríguez. A few years later, the Uruguayan thinker Carlos Vaz Ferreira (1873–1958) would write a book entitled *Moral para intelectuales* (1909). But already in 1900 Rodó had begun to analyze, and indeed to urge, the Spanish American writers' conversion into intellectuals in his essay *Ariel*, though without using the term "intellectual." An often explicit dialogue with Rodó can be observed in many of the major modernist novels of the 1900s, although the issue of the writers' conversion into intellectuals was already being addressed in the very earliest modernist novels, such as José Martí's *Lucia Jerez* and José Asunción Silva's *De sobremesa*.

In *Lucía Jerez*, Martí describes the male protagonist, the lawyer Juan Jerez, in terms reminiscent of the French writer Julien Benda's description of the *clerc* in his well-known essay about French intellectuals, *La trahison des clercs* (1927). According to Martí, Juan Jerez "belonged to that select breed of men that does not work for success but against it. Never. . . did

Juan compromise one bit in that which he considered sacred in itself, which was his manly judgement and his duty not to use it lightly or in the service of unjust persons or ideas. Rather, Juan saw his intelligence like a priestly investiture, which must be kept in such a way that the believers will not see in it the least stain; and Juan felt... like a priest to all men, to which one by one he had to perpetually give account, as if they were his masters, of the good use of his investiture." The nascent Spanish American intellectuals, as represented by Juan Jerez, appear in *Lucía Jerez* infused with "the nostalgia of action" (in Martí's perceptive phrase), anxious to participate effectively in the social and political life of their country, yet unable to do so because of their immaturity and inexperience in the strategies of power and writing that all intellectuals must know.

Furthermore, in his novel Martí portrays the Spanish American intellectuals as individuals stifled by violent sentimental and political passions that do not allow them to become conscious of their destiny. The novel's plot centers around the relationship between Juan Jerez, his fiancée (who is also his cousin) Lucía Jerez, and their friend Sol del Valle. Lucía is engaged to be married to Juan, but their relationship is clouded from the beginning by Lucía's intense and unmotivated jealousy, which leads her to reproach Juan for his slightest delay and his lack of attention (real or perceived) toward her. Lucía professes for Juan an aggressive adoration that borders on insanity; for his part, Juan is more passive, and his love for Lucía frequently takes second place to the ethical and political duties that he, as a lawyer devoted to helping the poor, has imposed on himself.

The course of this already tense relationship is interrupted – at least as far as Lucía is concerned – by the arrival of the beautiful and innocent Sol del Valle (to whom Martí refers in the first chapter as "Leonor del Valle"; as will be seen later, this onomastic ambiguity is significant). Leonor/Sol was one of the five daughters of the Spaniard Don Manuel del Valle. By the time the action in the novel takes place, Sol's father had already died; her extraordinary beauty had allowed her to enter the young ladies school of the city, and had allowed her access to the city's upper class, to which Lucía and Juan belong. Juan knew Sol from the days when he bought a drawing by Goya that was part of her patrimony as a way to help her mother, Doña Andrea, solve the crisis in which Don Manuel's death had left the family finances. Although it is clear in the text that Juan, like everyone else in the city, admires the beauty of Sol del Valle, he never shows romantic interest in her. Nevertheless, when Lucía learns that Juan is helping Sol's mother in some legal matters, and seeing Sol's graduation from the school and her successful entry into the city's social life, she begins to fear that Juan might fall in love with Sol, and begins to feel an ill-concealed hatred toward Sol.

Lucía's jealousy becomes more intense during the concert given by the pianist Keleffy, when the director of the young ladies' school introduced Sol to Lucía so that Lucía will become her friend and counselor. Tortured and delighted at the same time by Sol's nearness and by the confidence she shows in her, Lucía engages in feverish efforts to ensure that Sol does not become interested in Juan Jerez. At the same time the angelically innocent Sol, without realizing Lucía's thoughts, resists Lucía's attempts to manipulate her. The crisis is reached when Sol and Lucía, along with her two sisters and the foppish Pedro Real, travel to a house in the country where Juan will join them later to be with their friend, the painter Ana, whom the doctor has sent there to alleviate her tuberculosis. In the isolated and restricted environment of the country house Lucía's jealousy finally bursts into the open, despite the mediating efforts of the sickly Ana. In the midst of a party to cheer up Ana, Lucía grabs one of the revolvers brought by the male guests and, to the astonishment of Juan Jerez and the other witnesses, murders Sol by shooting her through the chest.

As is well known, Martí wrote this novel as a favor to his friend Adelaida Baralt, who had been asked to write a serialized romance novel for the New York journal *El Latino-Americano*. It was published with the appropriately journalistic title *Amistad funesta* under the pseudonym "Adelaida Ral," and Martí and Mrs. Baralt split the royalties. Although Martí undertook this task mainly for chivalrous as well as financial reasons (he needed money for the cause of Cuban independence), he was as always incapable of producing mere hack work, and his novel is richly endowed with layers of symbolism and interpretation. *Lucía Jerez* contains a critical subtext which encodes a complex allegorical meditation about the role of metaphor in modernist writing.

Following a male-oriented tradition visible in such diverse nineteenth-century works as Huysmans's *À rebours*, Bram Stoker's *Dracula* (1897), and Sigmund Freud's *Studies on Hysteria* (1893–1895), Martí uses female characters as emblems linked to writing and representation. In *Lucía Jerez*, the characters of Lucía and Sol are allegories of two divergent notions of metaphor: Sol/Leonor embodies the traditional concept of metaphor as a spontaneous emanation of Nature, as a transparency that does not displace Nature but rather clarifies it and allows meaning to illuminate the mind. Lucía (whose very name evokes the imperfect tense of the verb "lucir" ["to appear"]) represents the opposing view of metaphor as a play of appearances and as an artificial construct, an "improper" or forced conjugation of very different terms that obstruct meaning by calling attention to themselves rather than to the object to which they refer.

The ambiguity of Sol/Leonor's name is significant in this context because it indicates Martí's doubts about whether there could in fact be a "natural" metaphor; the name Sol is clearly associated with the "natural" view of metaphor, but Leonor, the name Martí uses for this character in the first chapter of the novel (which he never had an opportunity to revise), points, like "Lucía," to the artificiality of metaphor: "Leonor" is a Spanish version (through the Provençal derivation "Élinor") of the Greek name "Helen," which means "torch." A torch is clearly an artificial substitute for the natural light of the sun; by using the name "Leonor," Martí indicates that there is a basic identity between both women and between both notions of metaphor. The "propriety" or appropriateness of metaphors cannot be determined by *a priori* rules, Martí suggests, but rather must be judged by the taste and conventions of a given historical period. Questions of value and judgment are at stake here, and in this context Juan Jerez's role becomes clear; as the emblem of justice in the novel, Juan is called upon to decide which form of metaphor is more "appropriate." The fact that circumstances have reached a point of crisis – symbolized in Lucía's murder of Sol, in the "victory" of artifice over nature – only underscores the urgency of a judgment which Juan is unable to render at the novel's end.

This sophisticated theoretical discussion about metaphor is linked to the dilemma of the intellectual in two ways. First, it is clearly important for an intellectual to explore the rhetorical and stylistic techniques with which to represent his ideas. Second, Juan Jerez's dilemma may be seen as a *lesson* (in every sense of the term) for the nascent intellectual in Spanish America; it is a lesson in hermeneutics, in interpretation. Specifically, it is an anti-symbolist lesson: Quixotically, Juan insists on seeing Lucía as "a symbol of ideal beauty" (as the text says), and he does not perceive her as a *sign*, with all the instability and ambiguity that this entails. A lawyer, an interpreter of laws, and of the words in which the laws are written, Juan must still learn to doubt, to distrust words. This suspicion, this deeply ironic mistrust of everything that seems simple and easy to interpret, is one of the intellectual's most characteristic traits. As Martí says in one of his maxims: "One must trust the best and distrust the worst in people." The "moral" of this "fable" by Martí may be that the intellectuals who do not temper with a profoundly critical spirit their naturally bookish tendency toward idealizations and formulas, will become, like Don Quijote or Emma Bovary, victims of their own fictions.

A similar portrait of the Spanish American intellectual is found in Silva's only novel, *De sobremesa*. More sympathetic to Decadentism than Martí, Silva was profoundly skeptical about the intellectuals' capacity to affect society through their work. His novel's protagonist, José Fernández, a wealthy and energetic social climber as well as an aesthete, is unable to organize his intense perceptions of the world into a coherent system that will allow him to take action. Surrounded by artworks and obsessed by the memory of Helena, a woman he loved platonically, Fernández takes refuge from the chaotic reality of the outside world in a series of fantasies or dreams of order and power.

The problem faced by Silva in his novel is how to defeat "decadence," how to go beyond passive contemplation into action. Silva's protagonist, Fernández, is immersed in a radically aestheticized world in which he not only surrounds himself with beautiful objects but also tries to judge everything (concepts, experiences, and objects) from a primarily aesthetic standpoint. He furthermore tries to steer clear of bourgeois values and customs such as marriage and the family, and when he submits to them (as when he devotes himself to his "business interests" in London, for example), it is always with irony and as a kind of sport.

There are evident affinities between Fernández's lifestyle and the popular notion of Friedrich Nietzsche's philosophy, which is echoed in the text of De sobremesa itself (at one point one of Fernández's mistresses, a German, pays him the supreme compliment by saying: "You are the Overman, the Übermensch of which I dreamed"). A series of "Nietzschean" elements can be pointed out in the ideological content of Silva's novel as well as in its form: ideologically, the tendency to judge everything from an aesthetic rather than a moral or political perspective is reminiscent of Nietzsche's "transvaluation" (Silva uses this term and alludes directly to Also sprach Zarathustra). In its formal aspects, De sobremesa's imitation of the personal diary or journal form produces a tendency toward fragmentation similar to that found in Nietzsche's writings. Nevertheless, it should be pointed out that many apparently "Nietzschean" ideas in Silva's text (the "aesthetization" of politics, the cult of energy, amorality, etc.) were shared by a wide variety of late nineteenth-century writers and thinkers whom Silva surely had read in more detail, such as Ernest Renan, Maurice Barrès, and Gabrielle D'Annunzio.

The image of the Spanish American man of letters that appears in Silva's novel is, as was said before, similar to that in Lucía Jerez (although Silva did not know Martí's work). Like Juan Jerez, José Fernández's ambitions are frustrated by an environment whose complexity and diversity are oppressive. In both texts the role of women is similar: women hold the key to enigmas and to signs; they symbolize the realm of representation, whose control always escapes the men who try to possess it. De sobremesa abounds with femmes fatales, frequently more perverse and dangerous than Martí's Lucía: there are the numerous demi-mondaines that Fernández takes as mistresses – among them the sexually ambiguous Lelia Orloff – as well as the wealthy American Nelly; Olga, the German baroness and reader of Nietzsche; Musellaro, the Italian reader of D'Annunzio, and the Colombian Consuelo, who does not read, and who most resembles Lucía Jerez.

Unlike Juan Jerez, however, Fernández fancies himself a Don Juan, although he also claims to have been emotionally victimized by women. However, there are other, more profound differences between both characters: not only does Juan – as Martí's literary *alter ego* – possess social and moral beliefs diametrically opposed to those of José Fernández, but also Juan and Fernández differ radically in their attitudes toward ideas and language. If Juan Jerez's "tragic flaw" was his incapacity to criticize himself, his surroundings, and language itself, Fernández goes to the opposite extreme by being extremely critical and distrustful of everything and everyone. This hypercriticism of *De sobremesa*'s protagonist is linked with his decidedly sensualist attitude: unable to organize his existence around any transcendental truth or belief, Fernández resorts to the senses (sight, smell, sound, touch, and taste) as the basis for all certainty, only to find that he is flooded with a vertiginous and incoherent flow of sensations and impressions.

In *De sobremesa*, Silva explores in greater detail than Martí the role of the self in literary and artistic production. Throughout the novel, Fernández seeks a transcendental principle with which to "frame" his existence (it is no coincidence that paintings are prominent in this text). He seeks to strengthen his self – which has been weakened by the multiplicity of sense impressions that overwhelm him – and thus become a true "author," a figure of authority in every sense. Like other "Decadentists," Silva believed that entropy was eroding history and society; "progress" was an illusion, world history appeared to be returning to its chaotic origins, and it was difficult to see the direction society would take in the future. The search for order and meaning in history leads Silva's protagonist to take refuge in the turn-of-the-century bourgeois interior. In his mansion, surrounded by the works of art he has collected, "far from the madding crowd," he can carefully filter and arrange the sense impressions that reach him from the outside world, and converse with a few well-chosen friends such as those with whom he has dinner at the beginning of the novel.

De sobremesa means "after-dinner talk," and this is precisely what the novel presents: a select group of upper-crust Colombian men talking after their dinner at Fernández's house. The topic of satiety, of repletion (of food as well as of the senses in general), runs throughout the text and further illuminates the meaning of the novel's title. An after-dinner talk is not merely a trivial conversation but also an interval of digestion when the body begins to assimilate what it has consumed. It can also be a moment of reflection and dialogue, of rumination. Undoubtedly, Silva's novel evokes as part of its background the tradition of the philosophical banquet that springs from Plato's *Symposium*, a work which, like Silva's, deals with the relation between eroticism, love, and knowledge. The basic problem of decadentist art and literature was its contradictory desire to innovate without breaking with tradition; to this end, decadentist writers tried to survey and accumulate the totality of humanity's art and culture (that is why most decadentist heroes live in houses that resemble museums and/or libraries), but this was only a preliminary step in a slow process of selection, of "digestion," of the very best that humanity had produced. From this process of selection and synthesis, decadentist writers believed, a new art would arise.

A similar ambiguity is evident in the Decadentists' relation with politics. Although Decadentism proposed a "strategic retreat" of literature away from mundane topics and toward introspection and self-analysis, Decadentists did not therefore cease to hold and express political and social opinions in their works. Silva did not dabble much in politics, but other important Modernists frequented dictators at both extremes of the political spectrum; good examples are Rubén Darío and his relation with the Liberal General Zelaya, in 1907, and José Santos Chocano (1875–1934) and his long association with the sinister Guatemalan dictator, Manuel Estrada Cabrera. In Silva's novel, his protagonist expounds extremely conservative, even reactionary, views about politics and society. At one point, in a passage that prefigures novels such as García Márquez's *El otoño del patriarca* (1975) [*The Autumn of the Patriarch*], Fernández deliriously outlines a highly detailed "plan" which would allow him to become the dictator, the "enlightened despot," of Colombia.

However, Fernández's extreme and frequently incoherent views should not be confused with those of Silva himself. In *De sobremesa* Silva gave novelistic voice to the existential, political, and literary uncertainties of the writers of his age. It would be risky, however, to extrapolate (as some have done) the opinions expressed by José Fernández into the ideas of his author, José Asunción Silva. This would be like believing Cervantes shared Don Quijote's insanity. *De sobremesa* is a profoundly ironic, critical text that functions partly as an archive of Silva's multiple readings and preoccupations; it would be mistaken to deem it an autobiographical novel or to say that Silva intended to paint his self-portrait in the character of José Fernández. Silva's self-criticism was so intense that he ended up by taking his life: he committed suicide shortly after finishing his novel. If Silva intended a self-portrait in José Fernández, his portrayal is a self-caricature, an anti-narcissistic gesture consistent with *De sobremesa*'s resemblance to an anti-novel. Unlike his character, Silva could not resign himself to living in a world of fictions; even Art could not save him.

Soon after the publication of Rodó's *Ariel* in 1900, the Venezuelan Manuel Díaz Rodríguez published his novel *Idolos rotos*, in which a critique of Rodó's call to action to the Spanish American intellectuals may be discerned. Alberto Soria, the protagonist of Díaz Rodríguez's novel, is a young sculptor who has found in Paris the prestige and recognition he did not receive in his homeland. He is nevertheless obliged to return to Venezuela because of his father's illness. Once there, he enters into conflict with the prejudice and provincialism of his compatriots. He renews his relationship with his childhood sweetheart, María Almeida, and searches for artistic and political projects in which he can become involved. Eventually, Alberto sets up his sculptor's studio on the outskirts of Caracas, where he begins work on a statue of a "Creole Venus." In the political sphere, he participates in the activities of the so-called "ghetto of intellectuals," led by the physician Emazábel, who is trying to reform his country's chaotic and corrupt sociopolitical system.

The narrative contains numerous passages in which the provincial customs and the deplorable moral and intellectual situation of the country are described: Díaz Rodríguez depicts the gossipy social gatherings of the women, the pretentious society balls, and the political cliques that meet to plot and court favors in the plaza of Caracas. One by one, Alberto Soria's projects are destroyed by the narrow-mindedness of his fellow citizens. After the death of his father, Alberto, feeling somehow liberated, distances himself from María Almeida (without breaking off their relationship altogether) and begins an affair with the novel's *femme fatale*, Teresa Farías, a married woman of complex and truculent personality who combines religious fanaticism with adultery. On the pretext of making an allegorical statue of Voluptuousness, Teresa and Alberto meet secretly in his workshop.

Parallel to this plot, a series of political events occur which eventually contribute to the novel's denouement: one of the many scheming military officers unleashes a "revolution" which Alberto's younger brother Pedro joins, and his troops unseat the previous strongman. The new regime, received with naive joy by the populace and with skepticism by Soria, houses its troops temporarily in the School of Fine Arts. Worried about the fate of his statues of the Faun, the Nymph, and the Creole Venus which he had donated to the School, Alberto hurries to rescue them. Meanwhile, María Almeida, notified by anonymous letters that Alberto is deceiving her, breaks into Alberto's workshop, where she finds evidence of his betrayal and in a fit of anger destroys the paintings and works of art with which Alberto decorated the bedroom where he slept with Teresa Farías. For his part, Alberto discovers with horror, upon entering the School of Fine Arts, that his statues of the Nymph and the Creole Venus have been mutilated and sexually assaulted by the soldiers (the statue of the Faun, because of its demonic appearance, has been respected). Beside himself, Alberto Soria then bitterly renounces his fatherland and decides to abandon it forever, in a scene the author describes thus: "Before the iron boots of the new conquerors, the barbarians of today (who also come from the North), write it in a barbarous tongue for the blind, deaf, and infamous crowd to read, the slandered, offended, humiliated artist wrote with the blood of his wounded ideals, in his own heart, over the ruins of his home and the graves of his dead loves, one irrevocable and fateful phrase: FINIS PATRIAE."

The "broken idols" of the novel's title are literally Soria's statues, which, as we have said, are vandalized at the novel's end by the revolutionary peasant army that invades Caracas. Yet the statues are also emblems of the rigid aestheticist and elitist ideology held by Soria and his companions in the "ghetto of intellectuals;" an ideology, according to Díaz Rodríguez, that is bound to be destroyed by the harsh realities of early twentieth-century Spanish America.

The ideology of Soria and Emazábel is to a great extent a caricature of Rodó's. It is an elitist vision which seeks to stir the artists and intellectuals into political action. The "salvation of the fatherland," as Emazábel explains in one of the meetings, will be the result of a "moral regeneration" directed by the intellectuals, who will serve as mediators between the upper and lower classes. Eventually, of course, the intellectuals will rule because of their superior wisdom and merit. However, the only concrete action to which Emazábel's vision leads is a rather pathetic plan to influence national politics by means of public lectures and art exhibitions.

In *Idolos rotos* Díaz Rodríguez suggests that Rodó's "arielist" vision of the intellectual is totally impractical in a society divided by such violent political and class struggles as Spanish America. Díaz Rodríguez's novel is also an exploration of the role of ideology in Spanish American society that reaches back to Sir Francis Bacon's theory of *idola* in his *Novum Organum*. Bacon distinguished four types of "false notions" or "idols": first are the "idols of the tribe," those "deformations" of thought due to the inherent imperfection of the senses and the human mind; second are the "idols of the den," the superstitions and personal prejudices of each individual; third are the "idols of the market," or "false notions" produced by the abuse of language in everyday communication (particularly in politics) and by the inherent ambiguity of language itself; fourth are the "idols of the theatre," those philosophical systems and ideas that because of tradition, credulity, or negligence, are not questioned and continue to exert influence on human thought. This last type of "idol" is the one most similar to our current concept of "ideology": a body of unquestioned political or philosophical ideas which gives cohesion to certain groups in society and guides their actions. Díaz Rodríguez finds examples of some of these "idols" in turn-of-the-century Venezuelan society; thus, the "idols of the den" are represented by the conversation about superstitions in chapter 5, Part 1, which takes place in the living room of Alberto's house. The "idols of the market," or *idola fori* are represented in the novel by the scenes of political gossip and intrigue in the plaza of Caracas. The "idols of the theatre" are the main focus of Díaz Rodríguez's novel, and their most striking manifestation in the text occurs in the description of the meeting of the intellectuals in Alberto Soria's workshop.

This passage is of central importance in the novel, and resembles a *tableau* in its theatricality and immobility: in the meeting, Emazábel is the leader, and he is placed symbolically alongside a lighted lamp (whose light, however, is "weak and faded," according to the narrator); Soria and the others distribute themselves among the statues, "some seated on the *chaise-longue*, others in wicker chairs, others on half-polished pieces of marble and in wooden benches. Beyond the narrow circle of light, in the half-light that bathed the walls, two bas-reliefs showed gigantic mythical battles, and the nymph-raping Faun smiled in its plaster copy." Emazábel is temporarily the master of the *camera obscura* (another venerable metaphor for ideology that Díaz Rodríguez uses), and as he speaks he unconsciously moves the lamp back and forth, casting upon the wall the shadow of the Faun. The Faun is a complex allegorical figure that recurs in this text; in part, it symbolizes the Hellenistic element of Soria's ideology, but it later acquires a broader ironic and demonic aspect that connects it with the figure of the author who, like a mocking demon or demiurge, secretly pulls the strings of the plot in the *camera obscura* that is the novel.

Although like the other Modernists Díaz Rodríguez was obsessed (sometimes to the point of paralysis) with order, harmony, and coherence, his style and the social preoccupations evident in his text already prefigure those of Rómulo Gallegos's telluric novels. As Gallegos would do more successfully later, Díaz Rodríguez sought to transcend the topics of modernist writing to come face to face with the multiple and complex reality of Venezuela; unfortunately, his project did not go past the critical stage: Díaz Rodríguez wished to break the "idols" that symbolized the ideology behind modernist writing, but he could not replace them with a new literary ideology. Nevertheless, not a few aspects of the "novelas de la tierra" are prefigured in *Idolos rotos*: isn't Gallegos's character of Doña Bárbara a rural version of the urban *femmes fatales* like Teresa Farías? It would not be difficult to imagine a "telluric" rewriting of this novel in which the narrative focus would fall on Pedro, Alberto's brother, who runs off to "La Quinta" – the Sorias' rural estate – and joins with his peons in General Rosado's uprising. To write this, however, Díaz Rodríguez would need to have been "possessed" by a different demon: not the Greco-

Roman Faun, but a more Americanized and primitive one like the "jungle spirit" that takes hold of Marcos Vargas in Rómulo Gallegos's *Canaima* (1935).

Another key work in the tradition of the modernist novel is Enrique Larreta's *La gloria de don Ramiro*. As the novel's subtitle, *Una vida en tiempos de Felipe Segundo* [*A Life in the Times of Philip II*] suggests, *La gloria de don Ramiro* is an attempt at an archaeological recreation of sixteenth-century Spain in the style of Gustave Flaubert's *Salammbô*. Nevertheless, despite the subtitle, the life and personality of the protagonist, Don Ramiro, as Juan Carlos Ghiano (b. 1920) has observed in *Análisis de "La gloria de don Ramiro,"* are closer to those of "Decadent" heroes in the mold of Des Esseintes, Juan Jerez, or José Fernández, than to the Spanish hidalgos. Indeed, the character of Ramiro can be interpreted not only as a composite metaphorical portrait of the nascent Spanish American intellectuals, but also of real-life modernist writers, including Rubén Darío. Ramiro's life can be summed up in verses from Darío's "Lo fatal," as a constant vacillation between "la carne que tienta con sus frescos racimos, / y la tumba que aguarda con sus fúnebres ramos," as a desperate tug-of-war between action and contemplation, the senses and intellect, skepticism and dogma. His mixed origins (he is half-moorish) and his constant visions of social, artistic, religious, or martial glory, can be seen as a gloss of Darío's well-known "Palabras liminares" to *Prosas profanas* (1896), where he asks rhetorically: "Are there in my veins drops of African, or of chorotega or nagrandano Indian blood? It could well be, although my hands are those of a marquis."

Larreta clearly proposes a parallelism between the Spanish baroque topic of "desengaño" ("disillusionment") and that of nineteenth-century "decadence": in fact, Don Ramiro's life encompasses the last decades of the sixteenth century and the first five years of the seventeenth. Ramiro lives in a *fin de siécle*, and he witnesses the beginnings of the long Spanish imperial decline that will reach its nadir in 1898.

After leading an egotistic, criminal existence in which he tries to obliterate his racially mixed origins, Ramiro ends his days in America where, after encountering Saint Rosa of Lima, he devotes his energies to works of charity, and becomes known as "El Caballero Trágico" ["The Tragic Knight"]. Ramiro's spiritual errancy and final conversion are comparable to those of many Modernists at the turn of the century, from Darío and Rodó to Santos Chocano and Nervo: after the self-centered but guilt-ridden literary experiments of Modernism's "decadent" phase, the Modernists, spurred by the crisis of 1898, decide to abandon their obsessive *culte du moi* and seek to associate themselves, as "intellectuals," with the great social and political movements of their time. As Rubén

Darío declared in his "Prefacio" to *Cantos de vida y esperanza*: "I am not a poet for the masses, but I know that I must inevitably go towards them."

The parallelism of the novel's dates with those of Larreta's time is deliberately significant: Ramiro dies in 1605, the year the first part of Cervantes's *Don Quixote* (the "Knight of the Mournful Countenance") is published, but also a parallel date to 1905, when Darío publishes *Cantos de vida y esperanza* (which contains, among other things, his "Letanía a Nuestro Señor don Quijote") and Unamuno publishes *Vida de don Quijote y Sancho*. The evocation of Cervantes's protagonist also brings to mind the ideology of "arielism," since Don Quijote and Ariel were symbolic figures that were used interchangeably in modernist discourse about the role of the writer in society. In his novel, Larreta describes the process through which Ramiro divests himself of (in Rodó's words) "the tenacious vestiges of Caliban, symbol of sensuality and clumsiness," and moves closer to the state symbolized by Ariel, "the empire of reason and feeling over the base impulses of irrationality; . . . a generous enthusiasm, a high and disinterested purpose that guides all actions, the spirituality of culture."

Díaz Rodríguez's *Idolos rotos* was an attempt to break with the ideology of Modernism; *La gloria de don Ramiro* aspires to construct a new ideology to replace it. Like many decadentist and post-decadentist works, Larreta's novel is an expression of "the longing to believe, which is already almost a belief" (to use Rodó's expressions in his 1897 essay, "El que vendrá"). In dealing with such a deeply significant subject as the origins of modern Spanish American culture, Larreta tends to sacralize, to fetishize the history and culture of Spain, seeking to lay the foundations of a pan-Hispanic "national theology." It should be recalled that Larreta's original project had been to write "a book about the great masters of Spanish painting; but in such a way that, after analyzing each painter's technique, I could slide off into the study of a different sector of the life of Spain under the House of Austria . . . It was . . . an imposing project. A cathedral. I had not yet laid the first stone and I was already feeling the vertigo of the scaffolding." A good deal of the success of *La gloria de don Ramiro* in its day was due to its "alternance of archaism and modernity" (as Amado Alonso noted), an alternance that resulted from the novel's attempt to fuse an aesthetic, ironic view of religion with a transcendentalist and vitalist faith whose object was culture itself.

Larreta's complex and many-layered text is one of the very few modernist novels to hold a secure place in the current canon of Spanish American literature, a canon that reflects the preferences and prejudices of critics imbued with the realist aesthetic and social orientation of the 1930s' "novelas de la tierra." In many ways, *La gloria de don Ramiro* contributed to the forging of that critical ideology. Although it is not a telluric novel, Larreta's work is nonetheless very much concerned with the sociohistoric origins of Spanish America, and in its re-search of Hispanic roots it returns to the origins of modern realist narrative, to the *Quijote* and the picaresque.

Perhaps the modernist novel that best summarizes the dilemma of the Modernists' attempt to link their work visibly to their society and its problems is Pedro Prado's *Alsino*; in many ways, it can be considered the last great modernist novel. In his novel, Prado explores the tension between the desire for "realism" (in narrative as well as politics) inherent in the Modernists' newfound "Americanism" and the elitist concept of the intellectual found in Rodó's *Ariel*. If other modernist novels can be considered as more or less disguised allegories of this issue, *Alsino* is an overt, extensive, and complex allegory about the destiny of the Spanish American intellectuals.

The symbolic figure that presides over this novel – as in Larreta's – is evidently Rodó's Ariel. Alsino literally "converts," changes his shape from that of a boy to a winged being who in the midst of his conflicts with the surrounding reality, gradually grows ever more spiritual. Undoubtedly, there are also allusions in *Alsino* to the Greek myths of Icarus and Phaëton, but the links with Shakespeare's Ariel, as interpreted by Rodó, are more immediate. As in Shakespeare's character, Alsino's parentage is of no consequence; he has been brought up by his grandmother, an old herbalist whom the people of the area refer to as an "old witch," and who may be seen as a parody (in a positive vein) of Sycorax, the witch whom Ariel served before the arrival of Próspero on the island in *The Tempest*. Shortly after being made hunchbacked in the accident that in the end gives him wings, Alsino (still deformed and Caliban-like) serves Ño Nazario, a parody of Próspero (without Miranda), who does sleight-of-hand tricks with birds and animals. Nevertheless, these are just prolegomena to the main plot, and as soon as Alsino sprouts wings, the narrative moves away from the Shakespeare/Rodó context to become the account of a haphazard, picaresque pilgrimage in which Alsino acquires greater self-knowledge and wisdom.

Toward the end, Alsino is blinded (by means of a love-potion) and his introspection and penchant for prophecy are intensified. This is when Alsino finally begins to talk and act like an intellectual. In chapter 37, Alsino prophesies before a group of sick pilgrims: "Yes, war is upon us, and for many the long sleep. How can we avoid it? It will be fatal to all who participate in it. The winners, like the losers, will be dominated by far-away nations, and only useless blood and ruins will be left everywhere." It is less important to ask to which war Alsino may be referring than to note the fact that he has condescended to make a political pronouncement. Normally, the character of Alsino speaks in a high-sounding poetic prose with little relevance to mundane realities. Nevertheless, by the novel's end Alsino, like the character of Ramiro in Larreta's novel, has decided to move closer to the world of ordinary people. Communion with others and with everyday reality is shown to be the source of true wisdom. However, Alsino has great difficulty in reaching this goal, because although – like a secular Saint Francis of Assisi – he enjoys near-perfect communion with nature, his wings and his blindness make it difficult for him to participate in human society.

Prado summarizes in this section of the novel the insoluble dilemma of the "arielist" intellectuals, whose desire to be closer to the people and to become socially useful, is thwarted by their fundamentally aristocratic notion of intellectual work. This notion posits from the start an unbridgeable gap between the intellectual and "the masses." The "arielist" intellectual (like Rodó himself), although active in politics, lived in perpetual distress due to his continuous confrontation with the harsh realities of government and politics: his participation in the latter was usually limited to the traditional political parties (conservative and liberal) of the Spanish American elites, and in them he usually preferred the role of advisor, of prophet or seer, away from the lobbying and deal-making that typify political life. In such an environment, the intellectual was still regarded at the turn of the century as a kind of freak, an anomaly.

Nowhere else in Spanish America was this situation more clearly evidenced, during the years Prado wrote *Alsino*, than Mexico during the Revolution. This historical upheaval, that erased forever the elitist and positivistic *belle époque* style of politics, was deeply rooted in the peasantry although its ideological orientation came largely from an urban middle class. Mexican intellectuals, many of whom were refined Humanists, were reduced to mere secretaries or advisors to frequently unlettered chieftains of popular origin, like Emiliano Zapata and Pancho Villa. The Novel of the Mexican Revolution, from *Los de abajo* (1915) [*The Underdogs*] by Mariano Azuela (1873–1952) to *El águila y la serpiente* (1928) by Martín Luis Guzmán (1887–1976), is both a pathetic testimonial to, and a corrosive critique of, the Mexican intellectuals' inefficacy within the Revolution. *Alsino* makes a similar point on a more general level and in less precise historical and geographic circumstances.

Clearly, there was no other way out of Alsino's dilemma than a new transformation, a new mutation of the intellectual. In his novel, Prado represents this metamorphosis as a suicide similar to the death of Icarus, after which Alsino's ashes remain suspended in the air and are scattered by the wind (chapter 41). For Prado, as for Rodó, the solution to the "arielist" intellectual's impasse of whether or not to join with the masses remains the dissemination of the intellectual's knowledge through education. The intellectual remains a teacher, an advisor, and – metaphorically – a "sower" of ideas; Alsino's scattered ashes are reminiscent of the last lines of Rodó's *Ariel*: "As the crowd passes, I observe that, although they do not watch the sky, the sky watches them. Over that dark and indifferent mass like furrowed earth, something descends from on high. The twinkling of the stars resembles the movement of a sower's hands."

As may be seen from this brief survey, the refined critical study of modernist prose is still beginning, and there is much work to be done. Aside from some recent and unpublished dissertations, a comprehensive book-length study of the modernist short story is still lacking. Studies of the textual interrelations between the various modernist genres, both in poetry and prose, are also needed: from the intersection of poetry and prose in the prose poem, to the relation between the chronicle, the short story, and the novel. Sophisticated analyses of numerous individual modernist novels are still to be made. Several of these novels deserve to be republished, preferably in critical editions, and brought into the canon.

The study of modernist prose in all its rich variety serves to reinforce the view of Modernism as a founding moment of twentieth-century Hispanic literature. Far from being a frivolous interlude, Modernism was the Spanish Americans' attempt to creatively assimilate the highly refined notions of language and literature produced by Industrial-Age Europe, and thus bring Spanish American writing into the ranks of the West's great literatures. The ample measure of their success is evident today, and that is why many of the major contemporary Spanish American writers have chosen to evoke Modernism and the *belle époque* in their recent works, as seen in Carpentier's *El recurso del método*, García Márquez's *El otoño del patriarca* and *El amor en los tiempos del cólera*, *Canción de Rachel* (1969) by Miguel Barnet (b. 1940), *The Buenos Aires Affair* (1973) by Manuel Puig (b. 1939), and *Colibrí* (1985) by Severo Sarduy (1937– 1993), among others.

It is now clear that without Modernism's contribution to prose, today's Spanish American literature, with all its vitality and richness, is inconceivable. Like their modernist predecessors, today's Spanish American writers, from García Márquez to Guillermo Cabrera Infante (b. 1929), from Mario Vargas Llosa (b. 1936) to Isabel Allende (b. 1942), continue to practice journalism assiduously in texts that are still called *crónicas*, although they differ considerably in style from those of the Modernists. The debt of the contemporary masters of the short story in Spanish America to the Modernists' short story experiments, particularly in their use of erudition, psychology, and the supernatural, is enormous, from Borges, Cortázar, Miguel Angel Asturias (1899–1974), and Juan Rulfo (1918–1986) to García Márquez, José Donoso (b. 1925), and Julio Ramón

Ribeyro (b. 1929). There is also a strong and clear sense of continuity in the development of the Spanish American essay since Modernism, not in terms of style but of ideas: responses to *Ariel* continue to be produced today, as Fernández Retamar's polemic *Calibán* attests. Furthermore, the modernist essayists were the first Spanish American writers to consciously and deliberately address the issue of Spanish America's cultural identity, and were thus the immediate models for the essays of historico-cultural investigation of the 1930s and 1940s by writers such as Pedro Henríquez Ureña, Alfonso Reyes, Ezequiel Martínez Estrada (1895–1964), and Mariano Picón Salas (1901–1965). In the area of the novel, a certain thematic and stylistic continuity can be discerned between the modernist novel and the "telluric novels" of the 1920s and 1930s (as seen in *Idolos rotos* and *La gloria de don Ramiro*); but there are also pre-vanguardist traits in some of these texts (such as *Lucía Jerez* and *De sobremesa*): tendencies toward artificiality, fragmentation, irrationalism, caricature, and linguistic experimentation, that are barely held in check by the old-fashioned modernist desire for formal harmony and coherence.

There seems to be a more than passing resemblance between today's critical concept of postmodernity and the *fin-de-siècle* Decadentism to which many Modernists either responded or owed allegiance. Both postmodernity and Decadentism are ill-defined critical concepts, but beyond that gross similarity there are other more specific resemblances: in both cases there is an aesthetic impulse that rejects absolute novelty and posits instead that all art is but a recombination of previous elements. Both forms of art are therefore compendious: collecting, cataloguing and selecting previous moments of art history. In both there is a feeling of exhaustion, a feeling that art and history can go no further, that masks a hidden millenarism. In both, finally, there is a return to form, though not as an *a priori* category but as a challenge to creativity. It is therefore not surprising to find that many of today's most experimental, "postmodern" Spanish American narrators, such as Miguel Barnet, Elena Poniatowska (b. 1933), Luis Rafael Sánchez (b. 1936), and Severo Sarduy, show an affinity to Decadentism and evoke in their work, as parody and homage, many of the traits of modernist writing.

[3]

The *Vanguardia* and its implications

Hugo J. Verani

The term *Vanguardia* [Avant-Garde] is collectively applied to a diverse range of literary movements – such as *Creacionismo, Ultraísmo* [Ultraism], *Estridentismo*, and numerous other *-ismos* – which appeared in Latin America between approximately 1916 and 1935. Any attempt to establish a chronology of a literary phenomenon is problematic and debatable. While in European literature it is more or less agreed that the manifesto of Futurism in 1909 and the second surrealist manifesto in 1930 can be considered the beginning and ending documents of the Avant-Garde, in Latin America there is no similar consensus. I suggest, however, that we can discern a turning point, a change of direction around the dates I have proposed. Prior to the publication of Vicente Huidobro's *El espejo de agua* (1916), there were only influential precursors and isolated anticipations within the dying rumbles of *Modernismo*; and by the time Pablo Neruda published his second *Residencia en la tierra* (1935), [*Residence on Earth*], the Avant-Garde had fulfilled its historic purpose. Afterwards, there was a displacement of sensibility, a notable decrease in the experimental mood and a sharp increase in the social role of the author; particularly, there was a consolidation of the literary achievements of the period. In other words, around 1935 the Avant-Garde became the dominant mode and Latin American literature moved into different aesthetic and historical concerns, in rhythm with the rapidly changing world.

Distinctly European in origin, the different movements of the Avant-Garde stimulated frenzied cultural activity in Latin America, and evolved from a belligerent and derivative first phase into a wide variety of manifestations, conditioned by the traditions of the societies in which they appeared and central to the development of Latin American letters. The predominant signs of the succession of short-lived tendencies, trends, and movements are the experimental, innovative character of the poetry and fiction, and the conscious opposition to the outmoded literary codes of the preceding time (*Modernismo* in poetry and *Regionalismo* [Regionalism] in narrative). As Peter Bürger observed in the *Theory of the Avant-Garde*, "it is no longer the harmony of the individual parts that constitutes the whole; it is the contradictory relationships of heterogeneous elements." Indeed, the distinguishing features of the Avant-Garde dispute the traditional functions of literature: the Vanguardist discards not only the harmony of the individual parts, the organic and stylistic unity, but all views of literature as description, mimesis, or expression of feelings, in favor of an absolute freedom of invention, which led to broadening of the thematic material and the development of startling innovations in language and structure. Literature was conceived as a construction of the mind, an act of creation free from the controls imposed by traditional forms and external reality.

A reflexive awareness distinguishes the Avant-Garde, that is, the conviction that an effort to radically change literature in modern culture demands an activist role, especially the adoption of an explicitly critical stand toward the dominant values of the times. The Vanguardists were not involved in any kind of systematic theoretical thinking, but, rather, felt the urgent need to formulate combative, irreverent, and iconoclastic documents to develop new means of harnessing the attention of the public. Since Futurism, most movements of the first two decades of our century shared, despite their diversity and contradictory premises, a common bond: a radical rejection of the literature of the past and a commitment to disrupt the continuity of traditional values and ideas. In this respect, critics tend to agree in defining the Avant-Garde in paradoxical terms, as a manifestation of an "aesthetics of opposition" (Yuri Lotman), of "opposition and rupture" (Eugene Ionesco), a "tradition of rupture" (Octavio Paz), or a "tradition of the new" (Harold Rosemberg), implying a new departure and a complete break from aesthetic conventions.

This cult of the new ("Make it new!" was Ezra Pound's challenge) echoed in young artists everywhere, spreading and fragmenting into numerous trans-national movements, under different labels. In the 1920s, in particular, Latin American intellectuals were actively transgressing the literary canon, and the manifesto became a fitting emblem of their activity, a way of self-affirmation and deliberate subversion of conventional writing and bourgeois respectability. Manifestos, proclamations, public performances, open letters, polemics, and the little magazine became a trademark of the period, often more interesting than the literary works produced, as maintained by Guillermo de Torre, one of the participants in Spanish Ultraism and first historian of the international Avant-Garde. To write about literature became the equivalent to making it, and many scholars (Adrian Marino, Bürger, Marjorie Perloff) agree that the manifestos were the movements' distinctive and preferred means of expression. To remain on a conceptual level as a deliberate performative stance was such a widespread practice, that Johan Huizinga contemptuously remarked, in *In the Shadow of Tomorrow*: "It is a pre-eminently modern phenomenon that art begins with proclaiming a movement which it christens with an -ism, and only then attempts to make the corresponding work of art" (p. 182). In rapid succession, groups committed to experimental literature appeared almost simultaneously throughout the continent, as a result of a revolt of youth against the art of the dominant culture and of the inadequacies of the established literary idiom to convey a dramatically changed social and cultural situation. A new historical context – the technological urban society – brought a sense of urgency and a need to invent innovative forms to correspond to the new experiences of a transformed world – in short, a radical change in artistic expression. By 1916, the year Rubén Darío died, *Modernismo* had settled comfortably into aestheticism and had exhausted its inventive spirit.

Historically, the emergence around 1916 of a new sensibility unchained the imagination and opened the way to new explorations of the limits of the writer's creative latitude. The manifesto was the primary project of the new movements; it epitomized a spirit of unrestricted freedom and an erosion of generic distinctions. Its aggressive, polemical, and iconoclastic style was a strategy to provoke a predictable scandal and shock the reader's complacency, while demanding the devotions of a cult. The typographical presentation and a format drawn from advertising posters was an effective practice to arrest the attention of the public. Consider the format of "Actual No 1, " the first manifesto of the Mexican *Estridentistas*. It combines vertical printing, different typefaces, headings, numbered lists, blank spaces, illustrations, capital letters, idiosyncratic spellings, neologisms, and advertising slogans. It disrupts readerly expectations in a way reminiscent of the futurist manifestos. In fact, provocation of the audience by comically absurd mockery of the cultural myths of society is rooted in the futurist movement, founded by F. T. Marinetti in 1909. His flair for highlighting his ideas humorously and aggressively is taken up by Manuel Maples Arce and the *Estridentistas*. Marinetti's amusing plays on words, such as "Giogonda acqua purgativa italiana" ["Gioconda Italian purgative water"] turn up in Maples Arce as "¡Chopin a la silla eléctrica!" ["Chopin to the electric chair!"]. Furthermore, both movements, *Estridentismo* and Futurism, provoke the bourgeois establishment by ridiculing age-old beliefs and the official order with great crudity and in scatological terms. The popularity of these publications rested almost exclusively on scandal, buffoonery, dissidence, and jocular and attention-grabbing dictums. The Futurist's contempt for what was considered worthy (museums, libraries, classical art) was taken up by other movements in Latin America as well. For instance, Marinetti's much quoted battlecry "a roaring motorcar . . . is more beautiful than the Victory of Samothrace," becomes, in the manifesto of *Martín Fierro* in Argentina, "a good Hispano-Suiza [automobile] is a WORK OF ART much more perfect than a Louis XV sedan chair"; and so on. They were strident blasts designed to ridicule worn-out notions and affront respectable public opinion and good taste.

Manifestos and proclamations became an art form in themselves, a model for polemical provocation and tendentious writing, whose major strategy was a radical disruption of the prevailing notions of literature. Behind the various labels there was a unifying experience, namely, self-promotion in an unmistakable language (belligerent, dissident, and dogmatic), predisposed to hyperbole and categorical defiance, aimed at persuading the reader to join the movement. The manifestos varied greatly in type, but most used a journalistic layout and publicity slogans to demythify prestigious literary idioms with mischievously irreverent wit. One of the manifestos of the *Estridentistas* cried out, for instance: "Viva el mole de guajolote" ["Long live the spicy turkey stew"], set off from the text. Furthermore, the manifestos dismantled established notions of literature with expressive typography, syntactical indeterminacy, neologisms, colloquialisms, incoherence, and collages of incompatible thoughts in unexpected contexts.

The Avant-Garde was a group manifestation, but paradoxically their proclamations, written in the first person plural, exalted individualism and the uniqueness of the writers' doctrines and craft. They were collaborative ventures (with the exception of Huidobro's crusades), in which the author diluted his individuality in a collective identity and, at the same time, presented himself as a prophetic visionary and as the leader of a group with wide-ranging programs and international connections. The Avant-Gardists shared a common objective: to turn the text into a public event as a way to establish a space for critical debate to challenge the dominant sensibility and to emphasize their privileged activity.

Virtually all of the movements were promoted by periodicals, often ephemeral, but always a barometer of novelties and aesthetic activity. They functioned as organs for a specific literary current, whose primary purpose was to publish the proclamations announcing the foundation of a new movement and examples of its work, usually poetry. Such periodicals were particularly celebrated for creating an environment conducive to experimental writing and for enabling local writers to read contemporary foreign literature and become acquainted with the leading painters of the times. However, many of the most respected reviews were not attached to any particular tendency. In fact, the four most influential ones cultivated an uninterrupted flow of communication with the newest developments in contemporary artistic trends. Two were primarily literary forums: *Martín Fierro* in Buenos Aires and *Contemporáneos* in Mexico; two others were pluralistic journals, largely literary, which responded to the social concerns of the 1920s: *Amauta*, in Lima, reflected the sensibility and Socialist agenda of its director, José Carlos Mariátegui, and *Revista de Avance*, in Havana, sponsored by a brilliant group of intellectuals – foremost among them, Alejo Carpentier – flourished in a state of cultural eclecticism.

In Latin America, the *Vanguardia* included a remarkable constellation of poets who moved beyond established conventions toward radical linguistic and formal experimentation, aware of the inadequacy of traditional artistic means of communication to reflect the complex, disjointed, and changeable world of the twentieth century. The emergence of Vanguardism is closely linked to the whimsical Huidobro, the consummate tactician of avant-garde attitudes. No poet of his generation wrote more extensively on the process of poetic creation and Oliverio Girondo was the only other writer to prolong an avant-garde stance as a deeply rooted artistic commitment well into the 1930s and beyond. Huidobro's movement, *Creacionismo*, was not only the first but also the most carefully elaborated avant-garde tendency in Latin America. In *"Non serviam"* (1914), Huidobro's earliest manifesto, he outlines his poetic credo, the need to invent new worlds, independent from that of Nature. Art must cease imitating the demands of the external world: *"Non serviam.* I will not be your slave, Mother Nature. I will be your Master." In 1916, Huidobro traveled to Europe and became a participant in the cubist movement, co-founding with Pierre Reverdy the journal *Nord–Sud*, (Paris, 1917), publishing several books of poetry in French, and strengthening his passion for polemics, sustained to the very end of his life. Huidobro's constant theorizing culminates with *Manifestes*, a reformulation of the principles of Cubism, which by then had run its course. Written in French and marked by aggressive defensiveness, it was an answer to André Breton's *Manifestes du surrealisme* (1924). One of the texts, "Creacionismo," contains his main aesthetic tenets: humanize objects and make them intimate by disregarding the conventional idea of space; make the vague become precise, the abstract concrete and the concrete abstract; change the accepted value of the customary associations of elements.

Along with many other Avant-Gardists, Huidobro emphasized the juxtaposition of disparate realities, and the incessant shifting of unrelated images to create an effect of multiplicity and simultaneity. He banned descriptiveness, ornamental and superfluous adjectives, disregarded the conventions of rationality, syntax, and structural coherence, building up a mental construct without any attempt to portray anything external to the literary texture. For Huidobro a "created" poem was "a poem in which each constituent part, and the complete whole, shows something new, independent from the external world, detached from any other reality except its own" ("El creacionismo," in Verani, *Las vanguardias literarias en Hispanoamérica*, 228). The unmistakable identity of his poetry comes from the distinct fusion of apparently unrelated materials and his ability to discover the hidden relations among discordant ideas, the hidden thread which unites the separate realities, and, consequently, his power to stimulate the inner workings of the mind.

Huidobro began experimenting with the visual representation of poetry as early as 1913. His development of the calligram, the graphic arrangement of words to evoke the image described, such as in "La capilla aldeana," from *Canciones en la noche* (1913), printed so that the outline delineates a chapel, is parallel to Guillaume Apollinaire's famous models. However, his first notable example of *Creacionismo* is his manifesto in verse form, "Arte poética," which is included in *El espejo de agua*. In this poem, Huidobro proclaims his faith in the self-sufficiency of art and begins his search for a new poetic expression. Nature is granted new meanings, as highlighted by two famous lines:

> Por qué cantáis la rosa, ¡oh Poetas!
> Hacedla florecer en el poema

> [Why do you sing the rose, oh Poets!
> Make it blossom in the poem]

In the early stages of the movement, Huidobro shifted toward a poetry cut off from common experience. He attempted to replace the depiction of a coherent and definable portrayal of reality and the exploration of a subjective process with the invention of an autonomous entity, with a minimum of correspondences to the external world. He depended heavily on the free play of the imagination, on a fragmented and discontinuous form, and on the use of space to forge an effect of simultaneity.

In 1918 Huidobro published two books crucially important to the development of vanguard poetry in the Hispanic world. The radically revolutionary poems of *Ecuatorial* and especially of *Poemas árticos* [*Arctic Poems*] gave birth to the literary Avant-Garde in Latin America and, at the same time, played a major role in the creation of Spanish *Ultraísmo*, transplanted to Buenos Aires by Jorge Luis Borges upon his return to Argentina in 1921. These books display the innovative formal aspects of his work, which recur with increasing dexterity throughout his poetry, culminating in *Altazor*, his masterpiece. The juxtaposition of unrelated items destroys the associative power of the language and reveals a new kind of poetic expression, stripped of all its customary associations. "Sombra" [Shadow], from *Poemas árticos*, is a characteristic example:

La sombra es un pedazo que se aleja
Camino de otras playas

En mi memoria un ruiseñor se queja

    Ruiseñor de las batallas
    Que canta sobre las balas

  HASTA CUANDO SANGRARAN LA VIDA

La misma luna herida
No tiene sino un ala

      El corazón hizo su nido
      En medio del vacío

Sin embargo
    Al borde del mundo florecen las encinas

Y LA PRIMAVERA VIENE SOBRE LAS GOLONDRINAS

[The shadow is a fragment that departs
En route to other shores

In my memory a nightingale complains

    Nightingale of battles
    That sings above all the bullets

  HOW LONG WILL THEY BLEED LIFE

The moon itself is wounded
It has only one wing

      The heart built its nest
      In the middle of the void

Nonetheless
    At the edge of the world the oaks bloom

  AND SPRING COMES ABOVE THE SWALLOWS]

Poetry becomes visual: typography replaces syntax as a way of establishing relationships between words. Capital letters, absence of punctuation, displaced margins, multiple patterns on the page, and blank spaces are used to achieve a visual effect. Like the Cubists, Huidobro exploits the collage, the juxtaposition of disparate elements freed from accepted logic to create a truly new aesthetic experience. His conscious effort to develop multiple metaphors to bring together opposite or unrelated ideas, without explaining their connection, takes on the character of a deliberately fabricated object, forcing the reader to seek aesthetic pleasure in the discovery of unexpected correlations amidst the seemingly chaotic combinations of words.

Huidobro placed great emphasis on cerebral craftmanship. His most important book, *Altazor*, is a complex but profoundly unified spiritual adventure into oblivion, a remarkable summation of his achievement as a poet. It represents a synthesis of *creacionista* aesthetics and metaphysical concerns, a powerful meditation on the relativity of human values, conveying an anguished sense of non-being, infused with an apocalyptic tone. In *Altazor*, Huidobro pushed to the limit the need to revitalize language, to experiment beyond common verbal and logical connections, transcending the limits of poetic discourse. Written in seven cantos, discontinuous as is modern life, it interweaves a great variety of style, tone, themes, and unrelated stimuli. It combines lyric poetry and narrative stream of consciousness, sprinkled with passages of playful humor and anguished desolation. The speaker portrays himself as an "anti-poet," plunging through space toward Earth in a parachute on a journey which is perceived as a fall into the abyss of existence. Modern society is seen as disintegrating into fragments, reduced to ruins by a crisis of values and by the First World War (the poem was in progress as early as 1919). In the final canto, the efficacy of poetry itself is questioned: Huidobro deliberately interrupts the process of denotation reducing poetry to a combination of sounds generating their own significations. The progressive disintegration of conventional language parallels the shipwreck of humanity, lucidly reflecting the decay of human consciousness in a hostile and ominous world.

Ultraísmo and *Estridentismo* emerged almost simultaneously as self-conscious and combative groups, bent on launching playful attacks upon the bourgeois establishment. *Ultraísmo* began in Buenos Aires in December of 1921 with the distribution of *Prisma*, a leaflet written by Borges and his literary friends, heralding their aims and introducing their poetry. In a similar vein, and in the same month, the *Estridentistas* papered the walls of buildings in Mexico City with their poster, "Actual," signed by Maples Arce and endorsed by a "Directorio de Vanguardia," with 200 signatures. *Prisma* and "Actual" became the opening salvos of rebellious young writers devoted to a radical break with existing norms, drawing attention to their attempts to erode provincialism and introduce new literary forms in the two largest Spanish American cities. In spite of the claims of originality of the main writers of these movements, there is little doubt that their activities were firmly rooted in the European avant-garde tendencies of the previous decades, eclectically borrowing from diverse -*isms* (Futurism, Cubism, Dadaism, Expressionism). The exaltation of metaphor to fuse different areas of experience in order to achieve an elusive and hermetic expression, challenging the reader's imagination, was one of the basic premises of the Avant-Garde. Huidobro's belief that the image is the clasp that unites disparate realities, whose power resides in the effect of revelation, is reiterated and complemented by Borges and Maples Arce. Borges states that the metaphor excited the *Ultraístas* "because of its algebraic way of bringing distances together," while Maples Arce remarked that the *Estridentistas* attempted to "relate or merge disparate terms so that they produced surprise or expectation" (Quiroz in *Siempre!*, May 12, 1971).

In his manifesto, "Ultraísmo," of 1921, Borges provided the definitive ultraist program. Four points sum up the fundamental precepts of the movement: (1) reduction of poetry to its primordial element: the metaphor; (2) elimination of connectives and superfluous adjectives; (3) abolition of ornaments, confessions, circumstantial detail, preaching, and affected vagueness; (4) synthesis of two or more images into one to broaden the power of suggestion of language. These precepts illustrate very well that the ultraist poem should contain a series of unconnected metaphors abruptly juxtaposed, without apparent discernible connection, to expand the expressiveness of language, thus leaving more latitude for the reader's imagination.

In Buenos Aires, the short-lived *Prisma* – published for only two issues – was replaced by two other journals as the forums through which the new sensibility flowed: *Proa* and, particularly, the widely read *Martín Fierro*, the most humorous and satirical avant-garde review. The latter's famous manifesto expressed clearly the strategy and implications of the Argentinian Avant-Garde: irreverence, aggressiveness, playfulness, and caustic irony, as an attack upon the old conventions and a way to ferment activity and to prompt a shift in sensibility. *Martín Fierro* became the center of aesthetic debate in Argentina, indispensable for the development of the environment that modern literature required and for the stimulation of experimental writers. A prime example of avant-garde writing is *Veinte poemas para ser leídos en el tranvía*, by Girondo, one of the editors of the journal and the author of its unsigned manifesto; it excels in its emphasis on visual images arranged in a cubist tableau to bring together conflicting moods, causing an incongruous and humorous effect. Girondo also initiates an anti-literary stance, as he himself stated in an open letter to an association of sectarian comrades: "One finds rhythms descending a staircase, poems thrown in the middle of the street, poems collected as one gathers cigarette butts on the sidewalk." Later books, *Calcomanías* and *Espantapájaros* (*Al alcance de todos*), demonstrate that the avant-garde spirit was not a transitional development, but an intrinsic component of his poetics. The exploration of the dissonance of language reaches its most startling dimension in *En la masmédula*, a very late book.

Undeniably, Borges is the creative genius among the promoters of *Ultraísmo*, but in the 1920s he shared the spotlight with a generation increasingly sensitive to the possibilities of breaking with tradition. The works of Girondo, of course, and of Ricardo Molinari, Leopoldo Marechal, Norah Lange, Eduardo González Lanuza (author of *Prismas*, a book called by Borges "exemplary of *Ultraísmo*, archetypical of a generation"), remain noteworthy standards of avant-garde poetry, as is the narrative of Macedonio Fernández and Roberto Arlt, to be discussed later. Borges defined and exalted *Ultraísmo*, but his contribution to the movement is primarily limited to the use of startling images in his early poetry, published in Spanish periodicals and largely uncollected by him. In contrast to his theoretical writings, his own poetic practice is not prompted by exterior stimuli, but, rather, by an "essential reality," as he called his motivation for writing. In *Fervor de Buenos Aires*, his first book, and in *Luna de enfrente*, his cult of the metaphor is instrumental in transmuting the objective reality of the city into an emotionally charged inner situation, into suggestive recollections of personal feelings, thus diluting and in fact undermining ultraist rules. Borges quickly moves away from Ultraism's aesthetic restrictions – the craving for novelty and metaphorical discovery – into self-reflexive, ironic and metaphysical projections, into imaginative dimensions of time, a practice progressively dominant in his writing.

When Mexico began to emerge from the cultural sterility brought on by the Revolution, José Juan Tablada emerged as a transitional vanguard figure. In *Un día. . .*, he introduced the Japanese *haiku* – a brief poem, usually three verses long, portraying the fusion of conflicting forces into a unique image, whose underlying unity is often difficult to perceive. A classic example

> Trozos de barro
> por la senda en penumbra
> saltan los sapos

> [Chunks of mud
> along the twilight path
> toads hop]

In *Li-Po y otros poemas*, he envisioned quite different artistic possibilities. He introduced space as an expressive factor of poems and created lyrical ideograms, similar in essence and form to Huidobro's calligrams. However, Tablada, who spent thirty years in exile, in relative obscurity, primarily in New York City, exerted little impact upon his contemporaries in Mexico.

With the *Estridentistas*, however, cultural life in Mexico underwent a radical upheaval. As the name suggests, the movement intended to provoke and it stridently extended buffoonery and hysterics to their limits, attaining its initial impetus in a vehement repudiation of prevailing values, norms, and principles: historical tradition and national heroes, reactionary ideologies, religion, morals, and – naturally – the literature of the past. The movement's principal adherents – the poet Maples Arce, the chronicler Germán List Arzubide, the novelist Arqueles Vela and the painter Ramón Alva de la Canal – celebrate the great inventions of modern life, emanating from the dynamics of technological industries (aeroplanes, the cinema, the phonograph, automobiles, etc.), bringing to their work the dynamism of the industrialized world and modern mass culture. The kind of cosmopolitan poetry preferred by Maples Arce, in *Andamios interiores* and *Poemas interdictos*, represents a variation of the radical explorations of the *Creacionistas* and *Ultraístas*. Fragmentation, displacement, simultaneity, and juxtaposition of uncommon images, without transitions and disregarding the conventions of logic and syntax, were dominant once again. Every avant-garde artist claims originality above all, but there is no doubt that *Estridentismo* was an eclectic movement intertwined with similar Latin American tendencies of the period, without significantly different contributions.

The defining feature of the *Estridentistas* was, not surprisingly in post-revolutionary Mexico, a desire to achieve for literature a sense of solidarity with the underprivileged masses, a political activism unlike any other in the early 1920s. Alongside the muralist painters (José Clemente Orozco, Diego Rivera, and David Alfaro Siqueiros), they bear witness to the intense social consciousness of the age. Literature and painting became weapons at the service of social, political, and ideological causes, acquiring in Mexico a distinctive period quality. *Urbe* (1924), by Maples Arce, translated into English by John Dos Passos as *Metropolis* (1929), is a tribute to the workers in a mechanized and alienating city, a glorification of the masses and of socialist revolution.

Like most avant-garde movements, *Estridentismo* was short-lived. However, it radically altered aesthetic traditions and its rebellion left a ferment later to be exploited by more gifted writers. Almost simultaneously with the break-up of *Estridentismo* in 1927, we witness in Mexico a great upsurge of intellectual activity. The works of a new group of writers, centered around a series of journals, primarily *Ulises* and *Contemporáneos*, gradually developed into the country's high point in modern poetry. Its members included the most active young writers of the moment: Xavier Villaurrutia, Carlos Pellicer, José Gorostiza, Jaime Torres Bodet, Salvador Novo, Gilberto Owen, Jorge Cuesta, and Bernardo Ortiz de Montellano. The primary goal of these *Contemporáneos* was to link up Mexican letters with the main currents of contemporary European and American art and literature. On the one hand, they moved away from nationalism and social commitment toward universalism and aestheticism; on the other, they abandoned the unlimited freedom to experiment of the *Estridentistas*, replacing it with an introspective approach to literature, with a convergence of spontaneity and controlled lucidity, effectively taking advantage of the gains of the Avant-Garde. *Nocturnos* and *Nostalgia de la muerte*, by Villaurrutia, reveal an exploration of the dark world of the subconscious, a passionate pursuit of a Surreal nature, unmatched in Mexico in his time; and *Muerte sin fin* [*Death Without End*] by Gorostiza, written at the end of the period, in 1939, represents the culmination of a poetic generation. It is a book-length poem about the discovery of consciousness and its fall into oblivion, and the paradoxical, endless cycle of living and dying. *Muerte sin fin* reflects Gorostiza's idea of poetry which is stated in the prologue to *Poesía*. There he proposes poetry to be an investigation of fundamentals – love, life, death, and God – which is also meant to undermine language, making it more transparent. Such intense reflexion is far removed from the spirit of the Avant-Garde, but the poem "would not have been written," as José Emilio Pacheco has said, "had it not been for the radical experiences of the 1920s" ("Nota sobre la otra vanguardia").

From 1921 onwards, most other countries, in addition to Mexico, had some influential individual or group programmatically calling for an abrupt break with tradition, founding movements, issuing manifestos, publishing journals, polemicizing, etc. Naturally, different cultural, social, political, and historical situations determined an uneven development of the Avant-Garde throughout the continent. While the earliest and most sophisticated manifestations flourished in the main centers of urban culture (Buenos Aires, Lima, Santiago, Mexico City), groups in other countries played an important role in the development of the national literatures and they deserve a brief account in the present context. For instance, a steady stream of *-isms* enlivened the cultural life of Puerto Rico: *Diepalismo* (1921; so labeled for the initial letters of the names of the founders, José I. de *Diego* Padró and Luis *Palés* Matos), *Euforismo* (1929), *Noísmo* (1925), *Atalayismo* (1929). A lasting ingredient of this activity is the discovery of the ethnic roots of the Caribbean and popular rhythms, which please the senses, mainly through the *negrista* [Afro-Antillean] poetry of Palés Matos, the first noteworthy poet to popularize the genre. In Uruguay, a fertile symbiosis of Nativism and Ultraism became the dominant aesthetic trend in the early 1920s, producing a moderate avant-garde tendency. *Agua del tiempo*, by Fernán Silva Valdés, enjoyed sudden, but fleeting fame. *Ultraísmo* was less widespread than in Argentina, but, unexpectedly, a late flowering left at least one book worthy of notice: *El* *hombre que se comió un autobús*, by Alfredo Mario Ferreiro, the co-editor of *Cartel*, the most distinctive avant-garde magazine in the country. Other trends, such as *Postumismo* (1921; in the Dominican Republic, promoted by Domingo Moreno Jiménez), an Ecuadorian variant of Dadaism (led by Hugo Mayo, also in 1921), and the coteries publicized by the reviews *Flechas* in Peru, and *Los Nuevos* in Colombia, among other peripheral manifestations, were all symptomatic of activist attitudes prevailing at the times. They had similar aspirations and provided a stimulating climate for the evolution of poetry in their countries, but suffered from inevitable ephemerality and faded away. *Suenan timbres* by Luis Vidales is perhaps the first consciously avant-garde book in Colombia.

The Peruvian Alberto Hidalgo, an early follower of Futurism, promoted *Simplismo*, a tributary tendency based on ultraist precepts, while living in Buenos Aires in 1922. He also experimented with typography, particularly the use of blank space, and attempted to reduce poetry to a string of metaphors, a characteristic shared by practically all the early Vanguardists. He reiterated that "joining together the greatest number of metaphors in the least possible number of words, should be the aspiration of every poet". Although Hidalgo enjoyed wide recognition, in the end his lasting achievement may well be the fervor of his public activities and avant-garde way of life, a display that still draws much interest today.

At the center of any account of Latin American poetry is César Vallejo, who wrote the finest example of the early Avant-Garde, while transcending the limitations of the movement. *Trilce* is a major literary achievement, a hermetic and baffling book – like the title itself – that makes challenging demands on the reader. It was a book bound to have a profound impact on Latin American literary production; it appeared, coincidentally, in the same year as *Ulysses* and *The Waste Land*, whose effect on their respective cultures is comparable. Vallejo's vision stands poles apart from the perspective of the cosmopolitan Huidobro – while Huidobro writes poetry as an intellectual game, a calculated, elitist and playful end-product, Vallejo, on the other hand, considers poetry as a process of self-discovery, entailing the acceptance of suffering and grief, and as a tool to reach out toward human solidarity. Vallejo lived tormented by the arbitrary cruelty of the world, profoundly anguished by social injustices and a metaphysical agony. Starkly direct verses from an early poem, "Espergesia" ["Explanation"], from *Los heraldos negros*, sum up the sense of helplessness and fatality, the agonizing dimension of his poetry:

> Yo nací un día
> que Dios estuvo enfermo,
> grave.

[I was born on a day
when God was sick,
critically.]

Spiritual desolation looms over the path of Vallejo's poetry: the death of his mother, the break-up of his home and family circle, lost love, misery, and unjust imprisonment were early ordeals that confirmed in him the futility of life. In 1923, the year after publishing *Trilce*, he left Peru, never to return, and lived equally precarious years of deprivation and illness in Paris, until his death in 1938, as if besieged by a tragic destiny. A line from a posthumous poem, "Identidad y altura," collected in *Poemas humanos* [*Human Poems*], captures succinctly the rage which permeates his writing: "Quiero escribir, pero me sale espuma" ["I want to write, but what comes out is foam"]. Haunting, disturbing images acquire a dramatic intensity and an authenticity seldom attained in literature. All avant-garde writers rise to the challenge to innovate, but while other poets were satisfied by merely rejecting traditional poetic idiom (verse lines, rhyme, strophe, conventional syntax, referential language, logical thought), and by finding a special language to heighten their modernity, Vallejo challenged the validity of high culture with a frontal attack on all forms of elitism. His essential achievement as a poet resides in the creation of a personal language, aimed at undermining the limitations of modes of communication, to reveal the deepest emotions of primary existence. This is a crucial difference: Vallejo is not simply an experimenter with imagery or form, who searches for superficially impressive pyrotechnical effects, but rather a poet who seeks to revivify language in order to open unexplored states of consciousness. The obscurity which is characteristic of his poetry is the result of his pursuit of an inner vision, which does not conform to the usual organization of experience. Consequently, to break down conventionalized responses, he ventured into irrationality, incoherence, and incongruity, which render his work arbitrary and incomprehensible for the common reader. He epitomizes the type of writer Irving Howe had in mind when he stated, in *Literary Modernism*, that "the avant-garde abandons the useful fiction of the 'common reader,' it demands instead the devotions of a cult."

Vallejo's Vanguardism is still the subject of disagreement between scholars who cannot concur on the nature of his contribution, if any, to the advent of the movement. The fact that he disassociated himself from all the tendencies, appears to give some validity to the claims of those who negate his place in the *Vanguardia*. Furthermore, he never followed the precepts of any movement, rejecting them all. Nonetheless, he certainly wrote radically new and enduring avant-garde poems. *Trilce* shows that the literary procedures associated with the Vanguard became an essential factor of his poetry: he adapted the expressive possibilities of typography and graphic design (phrases written vertically or in reverse, blank space, capitals), he distorted language by creating neologisms, he used colloquialisms, archaisms and violently incongruous images, he used disjointed syntax by changing the grammatical function of words (made verbs from nouns and adverbs, nouns from prepositions and adverbs, etc.), and he developed a highly elliptic style by suppressing connectives, with no concern for coherent representation. Vallejo's disconcerting break with linguistic and syntactic norms represents an attempt to destroy hierarchies and to develop a poetic language capable of expressing his inner vision, forcing the reader to find unity in the intense underlying emotion. Although his poetry differs greatly from the frivolous and playful image of the Avant-Garde, Vallejo emerged as an unprecedented innovator who carried the tendencies of the new sensibility (ruptures of continuity, dissonance, and incongruity) to their utmost limits.

Vallejo was a puzzling and remarkably contradictory man: he denounced – but did not renounce – poetic experimentation and invention. The posture he adopted in journalistic pieces – for instance, in "Poesía nueva" (1926) and "Contra el secreto profesional" (1927) – reveals both his resistance to innovation and his hostility toward his own generation. He had nothing but contempt for his contemporaries, whom he accused of being incapable of writing poetry concerned with "genuine human inspiration." He seemed distressed by the apparently imitative impulse of Latin American poets, finding that they resembled a "simian nightmare," and going as far as to belittle Borges, Neruda, and Maples Arce and to accuse them of plagiarizing the techniques of European writers. Vallejo was concerned with cultural authenticity and it is clear that he despised the Euro-centered cosmopolitanism of the Latin American *Vanguardia* for its failure to develop a mode of expression indigenous to the continent. He further emphasized his antagonism to all innovative coteries, without exception, in his disdainful articles on Surrealism (especially in "Autopsia del Surrealismo" ["Autopsy of Surrealism"]), a movement that, he felt, did not make a single constructive contribution. Although he repudiated Surrealism as a doctrine, his affinity with the Surrealists' quest for the lost dimension of language, by breaking down rational barriers and disrupting consciousness, is clearly perceivable in his poetry.

Of great significance was the appearance of a remarkable anthology of the new poetry, *Indice de la nueva poesía americana*, edited by three of the most prominent names of the era: Hidalgo, Huidobro, and Borges. They clamored for the formation of "a new sensibility" and each provided a prologue–manifesto promoting his own ideas for poetic reformation. The anthology underlines the continental nature of the avant-garde process and the compilers' awareness of the emerging poetry throughout Latin

America. As might be expected, the poetry of the editors' countries was over-represented (sixteen poets each for Argentina and Chile, and fourteen for Peru, as compared to six for Mexico, out of a total of sixty-two poets included), but there is little doubt that the book is a watershed which stands as a testimony to young writers enthusiastically pursuing poetic innovation. It enables the reader to assess the mutual influences among the various movements and trends, often bitter rivals in their artistic goals, but undeniably similar in their actual results. Although a sharp line of demarcation between the first and second stages of the *Vanguardia* is not to be found, this anthology signaled a turning point.

The first phase of the Latin American Avant-Garde was practically over by 1927. The virulence and scandalous behavior of the pioneering-*isms* was progressively being replaced by eclectic movements and influential journals, which contributed greatly toward generating an intense cultural awakening in the continent. *Amauta* in Peru, *Revista de Avance* in Cuba, and *Contemporáneos* in Mexico appeared at exactly the right moment, when art as shock value and as incendiary outburst had completed its cycle and the consolidation of the Avant-Garde was beginning to take on the attributes of an institutional alternative. These journals welcomed diverse tendencies in art and literature instead of being forums for the promotion of their own programs.

Mariátegui was an advocate of ideologically committed art and of furthering the sociopolitical role of literature, thus renewing the connections between politics and literary–artistic movements established by the European precedents, from Futurism to Surrealism. His political convictions – he was a professed Marxist – made *Amauta* one of the few magazines anchored to a firm ideological base. He intended to name it "Vanguardia," but opted to incorporate the indigenous allusion in its title (the name means "wiseman" or "court counselor" in Quechua), so that it could become a voice for the revindication of the autochthonous cultures. Mariátegui's essays on literature stressed the question of the subordination of art to the social revolution and denounced the dissolution of bourgeois culture. The art of the *Vanguardia*, he suggested, was a symptom of the crisis of a civilization, the "end of an epoch," as he often stated. His main goal was to show literature and politics to be dialectically connected, to associate all domains of cultural and civil life. In "Arte, revolución, decadencia," (1926), he sums up his idea that art is not a diversion or an intellectual game, independent from society: "No aesthetics can reduce artistic creation to a question of technique. New techniques must correspond to a new spirit. If not, the only thing that changes is the ornamental cover, the decoration. And formal conquests are not enough to satisfy an artistic revolution."

Amauta maintained strong ties with *Indigenismo* and the literature of social protest, but it was also a forum for the various experimental Avant-Gardists of the late 1920s in Peru. The magazine promoted, for instance, the work of Carlos Oquendo de Amat, author of a dadaist book, *Cinco metros de poemas*, printed on a page, as a folded-up poster, exactly five meters long, as promised in the title, and of Martín Adán, who wrote "antisonetos," and above all the novel *La casa de cartón*; it also particularly welcomed the French surrealist movement and its early Peruvian followers, such as Emilio Adolfo Westphalen and César Moro, who wrote most of his poetry in French, while living in Paris from 1925 to 1933, where he was the only Latin American writer to participate in the surrealist movement. Contrary to Vallejo's sweeping rejection of Surrealism as a mere "recipe to write poems," Mariátegui considered the movement, in "El grupo suprarrealista" ["The Surrealist Group"] (1926), "not a simple literary phenomenon, but a complex spiritual phenomenon. Not an artistic fashion, but a protest of the spirit," and he clearly deduced its historical relevance to contemporary literature and art.

Revista de Avance was an equally significant focus of aesthetic debate, closely linked to the historical development of Cuba, but open to a cross-fertilization of ideas, with no partisan attachment to a specific creative current. Like *Amauta*, it combined cosmopolitanism and nationalism, without being at the vanguard of social change. In Latin America, only *Contemporáneos* was comparably alert to the new artistic manifestations, which were studied within its covers with perspicacity by Jorge Mañach, Martí Casanovas, Juan Marinello, Félix Lizaso, and others; in addition, European authors and artists were regularly featured and the Latin American experimental writers of those years were customarily reviewed. Its eclecticism was typical of the evolving sense and function of the Avant-Garde in the late 1920s, of the prevailing tendency of movements to be less theoretical, self-conscious, and radical, and to be primarily interested in developing a national cultural identity.

Insurgent movements appeared late in Cuba and experimental activity lacked the aggressiveness of the early 1920s. Nevertheless, one of the most extreme trends in "pure" vanguard poetry, the celebrated *jitanjáfora*, was formulated by Mariano Brull in *Poemas en menguante*. It is an example of delightful virtuosity: sweeping aside all semantic barriers, he produced a type of verse with a pleasing and rhythmic musical effect, attained by alliteration, onomatopeia, and repetition. New words were invented based purely on sound, devoid of any meaningful context. It was a display of consummate artistry, playful and gratuitous, appealing "to the senses and to fantasy," as Alfonso Reyes remarked in his definitive study on the *jitanjáfora*.

The mixed cultural heritage of the Caribbean became a fertile field for literary experimentation. Afro-Antillean poetry, initiated in Puerto Rico, as I have noted, went on to achieve greater prominence in Cuba, particularly with Nicolás Guillén, who transformed a superficial genre into a literary achievement and an affirmation of the cultural ancestry of black Caribbeans. From his earliest books, *Motivos de son* and *Sóngoro Cosongo*, written in the Spanish of black Cubans, he undermined classic notions of poetry with an unexpected artistic turn. In a bold move, he presented collective themes in a popular musical beat, the *son*, an onomatopoeic, alliterative, and incantatory ritual chant. The adaptation of the sensual and percussive rhythms of the *son* as a means of poetic expression became his trademark. With the next book, *West Indies Ltd.*, his poetry grew more overtly political and the seductive harmony of his verse gave way to an increasing concern with racial prejudice and economic injustice. It is important to remember that popular and referential art was irreconcilable with the premises of the Avant-Garde, which rejected any concrete historial dimension. Guillén, writing near the end of the movement, departs from mainstream Latin American Vanguardism and initiates a displacement toward literature as social protest, as an expression of the ideals of a radicalism implicit in the term Avant-Garde (originally a military metaphor, "advance-guard") and explicit in many European movements which combined aesthetic innovation with social radicalism (notably Futurism, Dadaism, Surrealism, Expressionism, etc.). The question of the relationship of revolutionary art to social revolution is crucial when reading Guillén. Clearly, his poetry belongs to the sociopolitical Avant-Garde, of a type which "stresses not only the idea of the interdependency of art and society, but also the doctrine of art as an instrument of social action and reform," as observed by Renato Poggioli in *The Theory of the Avant-Garde*.

Around 1928, new coteries of writers were also appearing in other countries, particularly in Venezuela and Nicaragua. Centered around two journals, *Elite* (1925–1932) and *Válvula* (1928), aesthetic debate proliferated in Venezuela and subjected its literature to radical revision. In this respect, the pioneer efforts of Arturo Uslar Pietri and Julio Garmendia, in narrative, and José Antonio Ramos Sucre, in poetry, display an unmistakable commitment to revitalizing literature. In *La torre de timón* (1925) Ramos Sucre's prose poems still remain close to Symbolism, but the conversational syntax, oneiric and irrational images approach surrealist practices.

In Nicaragua, we find the only deliberate programmatic grouping in Central America, re-enacting iconoclastic patterns reminiscent of the movements of the early 1920s. José Coronel Urtecho prepared the way with the publication in 1927 of "Oda a Rubén Darío," the earliest example of the ongoing effort to break with inherited traditions, a rejection of the greatest heritage in Latin American poetry, that of Darío.

As a consequence, other young writers, especially Joaquín Pasos and Pablo Antonio Cuadra joined him in deliberately unsettling the familiar literary categories. They resurrected the distinctive features of the early Avant-Garde: they founded a group in 1931, under the title *Vanguardia*, and even an "Anti-Academia Nicaragüense" to rally followers, launch manifestos, display outrage in public, etc., until it ran its course in 1933. This ferment of activity led to the development of a cultural renovation of prime importance, profoundly rooted in the vernacular dimensions of the country, while assimilating the distinctive character of the times. *Poemas nicaragüenses* by Cuadra remains a first-rate example of literary skill.

When studying the *Vanguardia*, it is common practice to reduce prose fiction to marginal footnotes in the history of Latin American letters. From our present literary vantage point, the coming of age around 1926–1928 of an avant-garde narrative merits consideration in the larger context of twentieth-century literature. While the poets enjoyed widespread recognition and even acclaim, the prose writers were (and are) neglected and little-read. They were not involved – as were the poets – in self-promotional tactics to convert the reading public, nor were they active participants in the various literary movements. Often they were dismissed as whimsical and self-indulgent writers, working in the rarefied air of lyrical and self-reflexive exercises in technique.

Yet, there were genuine literary innovators in the 1920s, whose influence on contemporary narrative remains largely ignored. Foremost among them are Felisberto Hernández (Uruguay), Macedonio Fernández (Argentina), Roberto Arlt (Argentina), Martín Adán (Peru), and Pablo Palacio (Ecuador), all of whom have recently received enthusiastic critical support. They share with other significant writers, namely Julio Garmendia (Venezuela), Arqueles Vela (Guatemala–Mexico), José Félix Fuenmayor (Colombia), and the Chilean and Mexican poets turned novelists (Huidobro, Neruda, and the *Contemporáneos*), a mode of writing characterized by indeterminacy and the dissolution of the traditional narrative categories. They detached themselves from the *regionalista* tradition, the mimetic and realistic representation of rural life then prevailing in the continent, abandoning the rendering of a coherent and definable experience. Rather, they emphasized introspection, reverie, discontinuity, a free-flowing inventive process, conversational syntax, and fragmentary and unstructured ordering of literary events.

In the 1920s, we witness the growth of fictional strategies that have shaped twentieth-century narrative practices: self-reflexive texts, metafiction, lyrical novels, parodic narrative, the non-fiction novel, the open-ended and unfinished work, all radical challenges to the reader's logical habits of mind and briefly noted here.

Hernández and Fernández – or rather, Felisberto and Macedonio as they are customarily called – are exemplary paradigms of the *Vanguardia*. Both write unclassifiable works and display a compulsion toward self-reflexiveness and experimentation with the powers of imagination. Macedonio is the foremost practitioner of the text about nothing in particular. In *Papeles de recienvenido* he cannot tell a story without digressions, self-questionings, and capricious juxtapositions of chapters, leaving the text in a visibly incoherent and inconclusive form. The book is a heterogeneous miscellany of unconnected fragments, loosely tied together by the misadventures of a *recienvenido* [newcomer] to the literary world. Macedonio encourages active participation on the part of readers, constantly drawing upon their inventive capacity and shaking them out of their passive reading habits.

Likewise, Felisberto's fragmentary stories deviate from the conventions of the well-elaborated and structured artistic whole, developing a truly original modality of writing, prompting Italo Calvino to claim that Felisberto "does not resemble anyone. None of the Europeans and none of the Latin Americans." He manipulates the reflexive dimension of vanguard fiction and deliberately flaunts the mechanisms of textual production. Even in his formative years – *Fulano de tal*, *Libro sin tapas*, *La cara de Ana*, etc. – a narrator aware of the hypothetical nature of his point of view captures the incoherence of mental experiences, the unusual and disturbing relationships between characters and objects. He effaces the limits between determinate and indeterminate elements and juxtaposes the attributes of the abstract and the concrete, of matter and spirit, lifting situations from their habitual function to create enigmatic and irreducible correspondences. Felisberto builds his stories exploiting to the utmost an animistic mode of perception, a procedure peculiar to the Avant-Garde, and a process of defamiliarization characteristic of the uncanny or neo-fantastic.

In a similar way, the principles of dissociation, discontinuity, and disjunction are distinguishing features of the narrative of writers such as Adán, Palacio, and Garmendia. *La casa de cartón* by Adán, perhaps the best novel of the period, *Un hombre muerto a puntapiés* and *Débora*, by Palacio, the latter being the first Latin American metafiction, and Garmendia's imaginative short stories, collected in *La tienda de muñecos*, exemplify the displacement of storytelling by self-reflexive disruptions of narrative structure and by a discontinuous, fragmented, and contextually dissonant fictional discourse.

In the 1920s, it was fashionable for poets to attempt to write fictional texts. *El habitante y su esperanza*, by Neruda, introduces new patterns of perception and expression perfected in his poetry, as we shall see later; Huidobro's narrative – *Mío Cid Campeador*, *Cagliostro*, etc. – negates by means of parody the textual strategies of the realistic novel. Meanwhile in

Mexico, *El café de nadie*, by the *Estridentista* Vela, shares a mood of introspection and subjectivity with a long series of novels written by the *Contemporáneos* – most notably, Torres Bodet's *Margarita de niebla*, Owen's *Novela como nube*, Novo's *El joven* (1928), and Villaurrutia's *Dama de corazones* (1928). In lyrical fiction, the evanescence of experience is evoked through images and figures, and action is substituted by the modulations of memory and by a flowing series of sensory perceptions. *Return Ticket* by Novo merits special mention; written as a travel diary, it is a superb example of a non-fiction novel in Latin America.

At first glance, to include Arlt as an avant-garde writer may be considered an aberration. In *El juguete rabioso* and *Los siete locos* [*The Seven Madmen*], he documents social injustices, class hostilities, deviant behavior, and the conflicts of marginality in the mean city streets. His portrayals of the lower middle class appear to cling to standard norms of storytelling. Yet, his rejection of elitism, gentility, and all forms of "literary" effects is a revisionary impulse. Arlt disconcerts the reader with expressionistic distortions of reality, and, above all, with the blunt authenticity of his colloquial and harsh language, repudiating any norm that stifles the direct rendering of urban life.

The great creative period of the Avant-Garde comes to an end in 1935, with Neruda's publication of his second *Residencia en la tierra*. Like Vallejo, Neruda never was associated with any of the movements that sprang up all over the continent, nor did he make any strident proclamation of modernity; both poets spurned the frivolous traits of the *-isms*, but internalized the innovative techniques inherent to the various movements. With the printing – at age twenty – of his second and most popular book, *Veinte poemas de amor y una canción desesperada* [*Twenty Love Poems and a Song of Despair*], a melancholic farewell to lost love, it was clear that a major poetic voice had emerged. Immediately, however, he radically severed his dependency on traditional poetics and Neo-Romanticism and sought new ways of relating experiences and perceptions. Responding to new stimuli for change was Neruda's fundamental creative propensity; he could be intensely intimate or militantly political; he was able to express the simplicity of elemental things or the complexity of metaphysical despair, to be a chronicler of history, an epic voice of the New World or a conversational anti-poet – in short, to be always in the vanguard of innovation.

Tentativa del hombre infinito, a nocturnal flight into the subconscious and the oneiric in search of "superior man," paralleling André Breton's belief that a "superior reality" can be achieved through the free use of verbal associations, as well as the poems that Neruda began printing in journals on July of 1925 ("Galope muerto" is apparently the first) and later collected in *Residencia en la tierra*, mark a turn toward a surrealist mode. Surrealism was then becoming increasingly dominant and "powerfully contributed to shape the sensibility of our age," as Octavio Paz remarked in 1954. Neruda shatters the usual manner of portraying reality by transforming external correspondences and personal experiences into a dreamlike poetic construction. The art of Neruda lies in blending disjointed, illogical, and discontinuous images of a disintegrating world into a new whole, apparently chaotic, but responding to a deep unity of vision and imagination. The surrealist manner of free association of images, plunging into the subconscious and the oneiric, free from the controls of reason, becomes a familiar trait of his poetry. Neruda's extreme introspection and anguished desolation find an appropriate expression in a modality that allows him to liberate the mind from objective representation and rhetorical confinements.

In *Residencia en la tierra*, the incessant disintegration of the universe, sensorially experienced, asserts the omnipresence of the eroding effect of time. "Estoy solo entre materias desvencijadas" ["I am alone among broken-down substances"] we read in "Débil del alba," ["Weak from Dawn"] and the irrepressible decay of things wearing away and turning to dust becomes an obsessive trait. As a result, his poems overflow with the corroded, the disjointed, the fragmented, the putrid, the wasted, reflecting dusty dreams, withered incentives, and the debasement of humanity in a bleak and crumbling world. The most striking feature of this bewildering mixture of heterogeneous elements is the breakdown of traditional poetic "good taste" and a de-hierarchization of literature. Neruda clarifies the underlying premise in his manifesto "Sobre una poesía sin pureza" ["On an Impure Poetry"], published in 1935 in *Caballo verde para la poesía*, the journal that he brought out in Madrid. A key paragraph reads: "A poetry as impure as a suit of clothes, as a body, with food stains and shameful attitudes, with wrinkles, observations, dreams, vigils, prophecies, declarations of love and hate, beasts, jolts, idylls, political beliefs, denials, doubts, affirmations, and taxes." Without deliberately excluding anything to broaden to an extreme the domain of his poetry, he wilfully gives a literary place to the ordinary, endorsing as a poetic the demythologizing of the aesthetic function of the work of art.

Central to avant-garde writing is the dissolution of traditional form, the exploration of its limits and possibilities. Consider "Galope muerto," the opening poem of *Residencia en la tierra*, which illustrates Neruda's poetic process and sets the tone of the entire book. The first stanza reads:

> Como cenizas, como mares poblándose,
> en la sumergida lentitud, en lo informe,
> o como se oyen desde el alto de los caminos
> cruzar las campanadas en cruz,

teniendo ese sonido ya aparte del metal,
confuso, pesando, haciéndose polvo
en el mismo molino de las formas demasiado lejos,
o recordadas o no vistas,
y el perfume de las ciruelas que rodando a tierra
se pudren en el tiempo, infinitamente verdes.

[Like ashes, like seas being populated,
in the submerged slowness, in their formlessness,
or as they are heard from the height of the roads
the tolling bells crossing,
having that sound already separated from the metal,
confused, weighty, turning into dust
in the same mill of forms to far away,
or remembered or not seen,
and the perfume of plums that, rolling to the ground,
rot in time, infinitely green.]

The poem begins with a simile without a referent, followed by an uninterrupted flow of incongruous and enigmatic images, around an undetermined subject, chaotically evoking the unfolding of an unformed and hermetic experience. The poem is an arresting example of Neruda's paradoxical fusion of disparate elements brought into disquieting new relationships. He passionately recalls the dynamic and opposite tension in the endless process of renewal and attempts a synthesis through paradox, accumulating indiscriminate combinations of images drawn from natural forces, such as the fire and water (ashes and seas) of the first line and the plums rotting on the ground, yet infinitely green, of the last one. The poem does not develop syntactically toward a close, but juxtaposes incomplete and a-syntactical sentences (the stanza is a single open-ended phrase), a form-free flux of sensory impressions that liberates the imagination and disturbs the reader's expectations. This flood of associations and ideas is predominant in the entire poem. *Residencia en la tierra* represents a significant breakdown of established poetic structures: it features a radically different poetic modality, a disjointed, dissonant, and prosaic verse, flowing inward, self-reflexively, thus instituting a new diction in Latin American poetry.

Residencia en la tierra is Neruda's finest contribution to the literature of the Avant-Garde; but a year after he published the second volume in 1935, while living in Madrid as a Consul, there was a drastic change in history, and, as a result, in his social consciousness. In 1936, Fascism was taking over Europe and the outbreak of the Spanish Civil War deeply affected him, and equally outraged Vallejo in Paris. Filled with moral indignation, both embraced a popular cause for social justice. Prime examples are, of course, Neruda's *España en el corazón* (1937) and Vallejo's posthumous

España, aparta de mí este cáliz (1939), which stand at the crossroads of historical periods. Significantly, in a little-read article, "Apuntes para un estudio," Vallejo invented a new *-ism* to apply to Neruda and himself: *Verdadismo*, making an appeal for recognition of the need for human values, along the lines emphasized in the name, "truthism," and opposed to poetry as an intellectual exercise. By then, in the New World, Guillén had written *España: poema en cuatro angustias y una esperanza* (1937) and had evolved toward poetry as social commitment, Huidobro was practically silent, Borges was already writing ludic self-reflexive artifices and the militant groups had disbanded; in short, the historical Avant-Garde was explicitly displaced by a period of consolidation and new departures. Nevertheless, their legacy of radical experimentation fore-shadows later developments in Latin American literature, and each successive generation found in their work an artistic paradigm and a challenge to their own creative ventures.

The Avant-Garde has long been integrated into the mainstream of contemporary literature. In effect, a characteristic strategy associated with the Vanguardists, their self-conscious explorations of the nature, function, possibilities, and limits of the creative act, provides a dominant focus for the aesthetic sensibilities of the postmodern age. If one considers that truly great writers such as Borges, Neruda, Vallejo, Huidobro, Guillén, and Felisberto Hernández, to name but a few, are directly connected with the premises of the Avant-Garde, the movement assumes far-reaching implications. As a consequence, it seems justified to claim that the *Vanguardia* represents a turning point in Latin American poetry and – arguably – narrative of the twentieth century. By creating new modes of expression and insisting on iconoclastic innovation, the Vanguardists altered the practice of writing and rendered possible the creative and critical receptivity to self-reflexive experimentalism that still reverberates in the diverse neo-avant-garde movements of our time. In retrospect, without the aesthetic activism of the Vanguardists in the 1920s there would be no modern literature in Latin America.

[4]

The literature of *Indigenismo*
René Prieto

The history of colonial and republican America is also – in its margins, footnotes, and backpages – the history of the Indian. Not of the Indian as he is but as white and *mestizo* writers from Alonso de Ercilla (1533–1594) to Ventura García Calderón (1886–1959) and José María Arguedas (1911–1969) have chosen to typecast, vilify or idealize him.

The inexorable modification of the first Americans begins with the Arcadian portrayal of Fray Bartolomé de las Casas (1474–1566), a fanciful notion that provides the germ for Rousseau's noble savage two centuries later. This process of transfiguration is not the only feature that harnesses together the colonial perception with that of our contemporaries, however. Curious as it may seem, almost all of the elements that were to typify the literature of *Indigenismo* [Indigenism] in the 1840s are already in evidence in the chronicles of the Conquest and the literature of the early colonial period.

The blend of romantic idealization and social indictment favoured by Las Casas and El Inca Garcilaso (1539–1616), Alonso de Ercilla's vision of warring braves and passionate heroines, the picturesque traditions and unprecedented myths portrayed in the work of Bernal Díaz del Castillo (1496?–1584?) and Bernardo de Balbuena (1568–1627) enter as one unit into the fiction of authors who, since Independence, had been avidly searching for colorful imagery to portray what they saw as the originality of America. And, since independence from Spain came at a time when the romantic movement held sway, a good many of the Indian protagonists during the first three quarters of the nineteenth century developed as exotic objects, faithful reflections of Chateaubriand's and Walter Scott's literary conceits.

At the same time that this chimerical current was bringing to life picture-postcard views of the American continent, a handful of authors was making resolute attempts to vindicate its native inhabitants. It is this focus on social injustice, this determination to champion the cause of a disfranchised race, that distinguishes the literature of *Indigenismo* from the work of *indianista* [Indianist] authors writing in the middle decades of the nineteenth century. Writers of both tendencies share a compassion for the conquered cultures of America but while the *Indianistas* couple a purely sentimental interest with an attachment to the traditions of the past, the *Indigenistas* dwell on social protest and direct their attention to the contemporary rural Indian whom they view from the urban perspective characteristic of the bourgeois novel.

Although agreement prevails regarding the focus and sphere of action of *Indianismo* [Indianism] and *Indigenismo*, opinions differ as to the lineage and idiosyncrasies of both movements. For instance, until very recently, critics hailed the prototypal *Aves sin nido [Birds Without a nest. A Story of Indian Life and Priestly Oppression in Peru]* by Clorinda Matto de Turner (1852–1909) as the first *indigenista* novel. However, in a groundbreaking study entitled *The Andes Viewed from the City: Literary and Political Discourse on the Indian in Peru (1848–1930)*, Efraín Kristal demonstrates that Narciso Aréstegui's 1848 saga of lust and murder, *El Padre Horán*, outstrips Matto de Turner's classic by over forty years.

Questions also arise concerning generic boundaries. Is *Aves sin nido* the crowning example of *Indianismo*, as Concha Meléndez suggests in her foundational *La novela Indianista en Hispanoamérica (1832–1889)*, or, is it, as Julio Rodríguez-Luis (in *Hermenéutica y praxis del Indigenismo: La novela Indigenista de Clorinda Matto a José María Arguedas*) and Seymour Menton (in "La novela del indio y las corrientes literarias") respectively maintain, the first documented work of the *Indigenismo*? What do we make of more recent works such as the controversial *Hombres de maíz [Men of Maize]* by Miguel Angel Asturias (1899–1974), or the five-volume saga, "La Guerra Silenciosa" (1977–1979) by Manuel Scorza (1928–1983), works which, stylistically speaking, are radically different from the canonic examples of the movement although no less bent upon advocating Indian rights than the staunchest of their predecessors?

The differences and similarities, range and scope of these literary tendencies come sharply into focus when we marshal the movements portraying the Indian into three phases – *Indianismo*, orthodox *Indigenismo*, and *Neoindigenismo* – in keeping with Tomás G. Escajadillo's prescription (1971). Drawn to the picturesque and spectacular aspects of the American continent and its autochthonous inhabitants, authors from the first group prefer to set their fiction in the past, at a time before Indian civilizations had been tainted by European culture. The two classic examples of this tendency are *Cumandá: o un drama entre salvajes* by Juan León Mera (1832–1894), a tale of star-crossed lovers who turn out to be estranged siblings, and the loosely historical *Iracema lenda do Ceará*

[*Iracema, the Honey Lips*], another romance of impossible love written by Brazilian José de Alencar (1829–1877) and set in the lush Río Grande del Norte region of Brazil. The child issuing from the interracial union in *Iracema*, a prelusive *mestizo* in the romantic literature of the New World, emblematizes in every way the uncertain destiny of the countless men and women who are alienated in the country of their birth. In fact, it is this paradox of the stranger in a land made strange that constitutes the essence of all New World literature dealing with the Indian and that best describes their social condition.

These social conditions are not portrayed as a problem in literature until well into the nineteenth century. Instead, as Concha Meléndez points out, the subjects that most concern Central and South American authors during the Revolutionary period are: anti-Hispanic feelings, an exultant sense of optimism about the future of America, and an attachment to indigenous traditions, especially those of the Inca.

With one exception, the twenty-four novels studied by Meléndez are most definitely *not* works of social protest, even when they ·share a compassion for the conquered Indian and a sentimental interest in the folkloric aspects of his culture. Such interest is a logical offshoot of independence. Having made a historical break from Hispanic rule, authors begin to consider the mother cultures of America as an attractive lineage for the identity of the budding republics. It is to these cultures that writers of the post-revolutionary period turn with an almost child-like enthusiasm. Unfamiliar as they are with the actual realities of Indian civilization – American ethnology and anthropology are then in their infancy – they idealize the aboriginal inhabitants. Since such idealization is in marked contrast with the deplorable living conditions of the contemporary inhabitants of the New World, they exalt the values of the ancient indigenous cultures and decry the unmaking of their contemporaries, an attitude which translates as an insensitivity to the present in their works of literature. The indigenous past that the *Indianista* authors invent is glorious while the present is simply dismissed from their schemes. This attitude underlies the conception of two novels whose plots are set in pre-Cortesian times: J. R. Hernández's *Azcaxochitl o la flecha de oro* and the Yucatec Eulogia Palma y Palma's *La Hija de Tutl-Xiu* (1884).

In these works as well as in the deservedly famous *Enriquillo* (first published in a complete edition in 1882) by Manuel de Jesús Galván of Santo Domingo, the authors infuse their characters with a typically romantic love of liberty and, in the case of the latter work, go as far as casting the hero as a patriotic symbol. The eponymous Enriquillo, victorious *cacique* who launches a courageous revolt in order to free his people from a humiliating vassalage is a case in point of the process of idealization typical of *Indianista* literature.

As the romantic school recast the long-standing tradition of compassion for the conquered Indian, the developing naturalist tendency fueled by the impact of positivist theories sets off a countercurrent to compassion during the last sixty years of the nineteenth century. As French influence penetrates and permeates the rapidly developing capitals of Chile, Argentina, and Uruguay, the romantic portrait of the Indian becomes substituted by a growing sense that this disfranchised, sapped, and senile race is an obstacle to national progress. It is this vision of a degenerate and vicious breed that authors such as Esteban Echeverría (1805–1851) and Domingo Faustino Sarmiento (1811–1888) respectively translate in "La cautiva" (in *Rimas*) and in *Civilización i barbarie: vida de Juan Facundo Quiroga, aspecto físico, costumbres i ábitos de la República Argentina*, works which postulate the racial and cultural superiority of Europe and storm against "native savagery."

Then, in 1848, alongside the conflicting tendencies to idealize the Indian on the one hand and downgrade him on the other, a novel written by a Peruvian educator turned military hero introduces a whole new perspective and changes forever the course of fiction portraying native Americans. In *El Padre Horán*, Narciso Aréstegui portrays the Indian as a social dilemma for the first time since El Inca Garcilaso's vindication of his race. The novel's action is based on an incident that occurred in Peru in 1836. A respected priest, Father Orós, murdered the daughter of a well-to-do Cuzco family and was brought to trial. Building on the gruesome details, Aréstegui paints the portrait of a greedy and lecherous man of the cloth who benefits from free Indian labor and caps a life of excess and abuse by raping and killing an innocent girl.

As it turns out, the stuff of melodrama is but a stalking horse upon which impassioned political discourse fares forth. As Efraín Kristal indicates in *The Andes Viewed from the City*, the Indian is played as "a rhetorical pawn" in the debate between the landed oligarchy and sectors of the political and cultural intelligentsia in all five countries where *Indigenismo* proliferates: Peru, Bolivia, Ecuador, Mexico, and Guatemala.[1] In the case of Aréstegui's novel, the excesses of Father Horán illustrate how the incubi of commerce (and, by extension, of national development) are individuals who abuse the feudal system. The Peruvian author strongly advocates a protected labor force and hopes for a fully employed society that is justly remunerated for its efforts and will, in turn, participate in the cycle of production and consumption which bolsters agriculture, commerce, and national progress. Kristal goes on to demon-

[1] Needless to say, novels in defense of the Indian have been written in other Latin American countries. A case in point is *Donde haya Dios* (1955) by Argentinian author Alberto Rodríguez. It is in the five countries mentioned above, however, that the literature featuring native Americans has proliferated sufficiently to warrant speaking in terms of a literary tendency.

strate how Aréstegui's views on his country's native inhabitants are really a reflection of certain political stances taken by Peruvian liberals who vindicated the Indian by working to curb the abuses of a feudal order.

The same liberal decrees calling for the exoneration of the Indian labor force enacted by Ramón Castilla (President of Peru in 1845–1851 and, again, between 1855 and 1864) inform the little-known *Sé bueno y serás feliz* by Ladislao Graña (1817–1862), a novel first published in installments in the influential *La Revista de Lima* in 1860. Besides being profoundly didactic, Graña's novel is originally conceived as a story within a story in which frequent incursions into the past alternate with observations about contemporary Peruvian history and politics. It reports the woeful tale of José Huamán, a kind, hard-working Indian whose life is practically destroyed by a greedy governor who earns his wealth through murder, exploitation, and deceit. In the end, following one of the narrator's sallies against those who abuse native Americans, José's virtue is at long last rewarded; in the last published installment of *Sé bueno y serás feliz*, the Indian hero becomes a small property owner while the callous governor who wastes illegally made wealth dies alone, leaving his concubine and child destitute.

In advocating the emancipation of native Americans from forced labor and certain kinds of tribute, Aréstegui and Graña were no doubt mirroring the economic concerns of contemporary landowners who supported these reforms, as Kristal suggests, because "they needed to obtain a labor force in order to increase commerce" (p. 30). In the long run, however, economic motives turn out to be the springboard for a new kind of social engineering. Hand in hand with the need to free a labor force for commerce comes a more altruistic concern with civic ideals, a sort of Benthamism that is no less devoted to the commonweal for being utilitarian. These civic ideals are upheld by a brave new breed of enlightened individuals driven by an apparently incorrupt zeal for improvement.

This type of crusader in favor of Indian rights surfaces as a narrator as early as *El Padre Horán* but does not come into its own as a character until Clorinda Matto de Turner's classic trilogy: *Aves sin nido*, *Indole*, and *Herencia*. In spite of its romantic trappings and tendency to idealize indigenous inhabitants, the first of these – an injunction against the oppression of the "trinity" made up of Priest, Judge, and Governor – is a vehement barrage against the forces that exploit native Americans.

Profoundly influenced by the writings of her fellow countryman, Manuel González Prada (1848–1918), Matto de Turner translates her mentor's social preoccupations into fiction and produces a commanding indictment. The "trinity" she describes had been damned with mordant irony in a novel published four years earlier: José Torres y Lara's (whose pen name was Itolararres) *La Trinidad del Indio o Costumbres del Interior*. This work should be included among the early examples of *indigenista* literature even though it focuses on the abuse and backwardness of the "trinity" in a typical Andean town rather than on the Indian and his pitiful situation. It is a curious mixture in which elements from Menippean satire and Aesop's *Fables* are brought together in order to mock the grossly exaggerated foibles of the corrupt oligarchy ruling over town and country. More curious, even, than the novel itself is that such an iconoclastic tirade could have seen the light, a fact that can only be explained as an extraordinary legacy of the War of the Pacific (1879–1883) waged between Chile and Peru.

Not the most immediately obvious outcome of this debacle was the appalling state of backwardness that shackled the north Andean republic. Underdevelopment was blamed on Peru's precarious social structure, namely that the largely Indian population was excluded from the mainstream of national life – a life controlled by a tight-fisted oligarchy. This belief and the need to recast such an obsolete and ineffectual distribution of power impelled the most revolutionary author of the period, Manuel González Prada, to take a stand against what he labelled the "pus" infecting Peruvian society.

Although an heir to one of Peru's patrician families, González Prada was soon spearheading a group of idealists and intellectuals who wished to take a more active part in political life. Their immediate goal? To redress the social imbalance that hampered national development. The aristocrat turned Socialist took to the podium as well as to the pen, published compelling propaganda in favor of progress and Indian rights and actually campaigned in the newly formed party, *La Unión Nacional*. Never one to sit still or limit his sphere of action, Peru's new-fledged militant poet founded the Círculo Literario in Lima in 1886 with the aim of producing a committed and future-minded literature that would raise national consciousness. It was through this Círculo that he met a young widow freshly arrived from Cuzco, Clorinda Matto de Turner.

At the time, Matto had already published a collection of *Tradiciones cuzqueñas* (1884–1886) aimed at capturing – like the *Tradiciones peruanas* (1872–1883) of Ricardo Palma (1833–1919) – the essence of the past, a fact which demonstrates her ongoing interest in all matters regarding Peru. However, after meeting González Prada and joining the *Círculo Literario*, this interest became focused on the need to rehabilitate the Indian and incorporate him into the mainstream of national life, objectives that this typical representative of the emerging industrial elite was able to voice as editor of the influential *El Perú Ilustrado* and through the no less influential *Aves sin nido*.

No one denies Clorinda Matto de Turner's pride of place, even if her seminal trilogy has been showered with more praise for what was long thought to be its pioneering position as the first work of *Indigenismo* than for any intrinsic merit it may have. Yet the fact that a novel like *Aves sin nido* is romantic and quaint (it includes cooking recipes and household hints) should not detract from its originality. Its author not only outlines the social dilemma of the Indian in contemporary Peruvian society, she also – and this is a crucial step in the development of the *indigenista* novel – portrays her Indian characters as individuals.

Matto de Turner was not a pioneer, however; she acts as a watershed channeling theoretical concerns and topical situations set forth in other mediums and formats. Not only the role played by Indians but, actually, the entire blueprint for *Aves sin nido* can be traced to a remarkable work, "Si haces mal no esperes bien," written by an Argentinian woman: Juana Manuela Gorriti (1819–1892). In their respective works of fiction, both Matto de Turner and Gorriti denounce the oppression of native Americans by an abusive feudal order and dramatize the fatal attraction between members of different races who turn out to be half-siblings. In *Aves sin nido*, as in "Si haces mal no esperes bien," the contemporary Indian – neither Inca prince nor Aztec warrior–has a face and a name. "One-upping" the work of her predecessor, however, Matto de Turner introduces – in the strong-minded Marín couple and their unshrinking friend Manuel – a new type of *criollo* hero, one who neither perceives nor treats the Indian as a picturesque (and therefore alien) phenomenon but, rather, as a human being with very real problems. Solutions to these problems can be found, moreover, provided just men and women are willing to fight in favor of the underdog and, as do the Maríns, to introduce Indians to a culture they had been excluded from up to that point.

In matters of character development and distribution of roles Matto de Turner once again turns to other sources. In this respect, she complies with the three types of Peruvian citizens that her mentor González Prada had inventorized: the enlightened and free individuals (such as the Marín couple), the city folk who waste wealth and the rural oligarchy who amass profits at the expense of Indians (Pascual the priest and Don Sebastián the governor), and, finally, the uneducated Indian masses.

Inasmuch as her pedagogical zeal is concerned, Matto de Turner's trilogy can again be said to hark back to an earlier model; in this case, Graña's *Sé bueno y serás feliz*. As her predecessor had done, Matto de Turner had the aim of enlightening readers as to the hardships of the unjustifiably tormented. To this effect, *Aves sin nido* provides a behavioral guide that illustrates ways and means to redress social injustice. One of the most interesting and certainly one of the most original features of Matto de Turner's plot is the accommodation and recognition of the kind of racial integration she advocated, for instance, in an editorial addressed to President Andrés Avelino Cáceres in *El Perú Ilustrado*: "We call for foreign immigration that can mend our country through the mixture of blood," she declared with a vehemence that would cost her dearly under the next administration and finish by forcing her into exile. But long before that time, she translated into fiction her progressive beliefs by having the white, bourgeois, and enlightened Fernando Marín and his wife Lucía adopt the orphan daughters of the Indians Juan and Marcela Yupanqui while their friend Manuel, stepson of the governor, falls in love with the eldest of the girls. Even though their marriage is impossible (they turn out to be siblings), isn't Matto de Turner's didactic trilogy opening the door to cultural and racial *mestizaje* as a viable solution for Peru's problems? The contrast with Sarmiento's much more successful racist campaign, published scarcely forty years earlier, amply demonstrates how extraordinarily future-minded Clorinda Matto de Turner really was.

Aves sin nido is more than a transitional work, much more than a bridge between *Indianismo* and *Indigenismo*. It is among the forerunners of a militant breed of social protest whose message and method hark back to the indignant accusations of Las Casas and El Inca Garcilaso. Yet even Matto de Turner was not always unprejudiced. Her trilogy suffers from three preconceptions that Antonio Cornejo Polar outlines in his insightful *Literatura y sociedad en el Perú: La novela indigenista*.

First and foremost, the solutions she finds to the Indians' dilemma are not collective; in her novels only a handful of Indians manage to escape a miserable destiny. Second, her perspective is entirely moral; the Indians' suffering is a result of the first families' unworthiness and certainly not connected to the very real problem of land ownership. Third, Matto de Turner's solution to the Indian's quandary is, quite simply, to stop being an Indian and become assimilated into Western civilization through a process of education that will eventually strip the Indian race of its own culture. However, the fact that she was not wholly unprejudiced does not mean that she was not progressive. Matto de Turner's attitude and approach were so ahead of their time, in fact, that they were not taken up again in fiction until well after the Mexican Revolution of 1910 when Latin American authors, saturated with the aestheticizing tendency of *Modernismo* [Modernism], turned once again toward the always elusive question of identity.

Starting around 1919, with the publication of *Raza de bronce* by the Bolivian historian and sociologist Alcides Arguedas (1879–1946), the Indian comes into vogue in literature for the first time since its romantic revival almost a century earlier. By that time, the influential writings of González Prada and his most faithful ally, Hildebrando Castro Pozo (1890–1945) had influenced an entire generation of intellectuals.

Born like González Prada into a family of wealthy land owners, Castro Pozo was soon appalled by the economic situation which shackled the Indian population of his native Peru. In 1916, he published an important collection of short stories, *Celajes de Sierra*, where he exposed what he had experienced during years of contact with the Indian communities. To this experience he brought to bear the stock of information acquired as Chief of Indian Affairs of the Ministry of Development and published a crucial study entitled *Nuestra Comunidad Indígena* (1918).

At this time, Peru entered an era of social and political turmoil; the theoretical concerns of Marx, Lenin, and Engels knew wide appeal among intellectuals after the resounding triumph of the Russian Revolution. Socialism became particularly seductive to countries that had a ready-made apparatus of social protest and a burning cause to defend. The struggle for Indian rights in the five Central and South American republics that had the largest indigenous populations was translated into a literature of social protest geared to redressing the predicaments of native Americans.

Alcides Arguedas had begun his stirring call to arms as early as 1904 under the tentative title *Wata-Wara* (the name of the novel's heroine and victim), but revised and published it fifteen years later, giving it the title we know today. *Raza de bronce* is the second rung – following the phase that concludes with *Aves sin nido* – in the ladder of *Indigenismo*; it connects Matto de Turner's conjunctive work to the second *indigenista* generation composed of Enrique López Albújar (1852–1966), Jorge Icaza (1906–1978), Jesús Lara (1898–1980), and Ventura García Calderón. What its author adds to Matto de Turner's conception is a more profound knowledge of Indian customs and a comprehensive focus on their lives. On the other hand, Arguedas streamlined and oversimplified Matto de Turner's distribution of roles. If, in her *indigenista* novel, there are good Whites, bad Whites, and Indians, in *Raza de bronce* character portrayal (as was to become the case with most works of the period) is narrowly and unrealistically binary, divided between good and evil corresponding, generally speaking, to Indians and non-Indians. The one apparent exception to this rule of two in *Raza de bronce* is a character named Suárez – a flagrant parody of the modernist poet – who turns out to be effete and ineffectual when it comes to actually defending the Indians instead of idealizing them in capricious portraits.

Readers of the novel cannot help wondering if Arguedas's own characterization is not, in fact, as stylized and unrealistic as Suárez's. Certainly the Indians' analysis of the power structure and their doubts concerning the potential hazards of the white man's education are blatant transpositions of the author's own thoughts and perspective. But some measure of stylization should not detract from Arguedas's very real success in enlisting the reader's sympathy in favor of native Americans. His Andean saga – the tale of a young Indian woman who is raped and accidentally killed by the landowner's son and a handful of his friends – is profoundly disturbing. When, at the novel's end, the Indians revolt and burn the landowner's house, it is impossible not to condone their actions. In fact, *Raza de bronce* might well be considered the first South American novel that actively politicizes the reader by suggesting that the answer to the dilemma of the Indian race – depicted as a community and not as isolated individuals – may be no other than violent action.

Unlike Alcides Arguedas, a handful of writers from this second generation of *Indigenistas* were loath to champion social unrest. In his *Cuentos andinos* and *Nuevos cuentos andinos*, the versatile Peruvian judge and author, Enrique López Albújar, focused on the psychology and behavior of the Indian and not on the likelihood of an imminent social rebellion. Despite his lack of revolutionary zeal, López Albújar was, in the words of Ciro Alegría, the first to create flesh and blood Indian characters in the literature of *Indigenismo*. His experience as judge in the hill town of Huanuco distinctly informed his narrative outlook, which is to say that many of the Indian characters in the *Cuentos andinos* were directly or indirectly involved in criminal situations. Given this narrative penchant, the emphasis was on individual cases, on anecdotes that revealed Indian character rather than on social systems. López Albújar's Indian protagonists tend to be violent and, for better or for worse, they are always capable of action. This attitude was in sharp contrast with the passive protagonists of Matto de Turner or of Ventura García Calderón, viewed, these latter, from a downright racist perspective.

From the beginning, Ventura and his brother Francisco made no bones about their prejudice. Ventura saw no way for the Indian to participate in politics and wondered how one could "build a bridge between two races without connections?" (Ortega, *Ventura García Calderón*, 128). He wrote one novel and over two score of short stories that were overwhelmingly well received (he and his brother were even nominated for a joint Nobel Prize by a group of eminent sociologists that included Lucien Lévy-Bruhl). His short stories set in Peru were largely inspired by his own experience as a frustrated prospector roaming across the Andes; they portray a variety of social types and vividly describe a quasi-feudal code of behavior in which honor and a sense of duty play a major part. Among those included in *La venganza del cóndor*, the narrator often transcribed songs in Quechua and showed himself to be drawn to the natives' idiosyncrasies, although merely as a cool and distant observer since he found this race cruel, stubborn, and impossible to understand. Indians were totally alien to him and, as such, ungraspable. Furthermore, given their innate and profound savagery (Ventura's brother, Francisco, warns about the cannibalistic practices that endure among some groups of Indians in his famous sociological study published in French, *Le Pérou contemporain*), the white man must make use of violence in an attempt to – if not civilize – at least control the people that he referred to as belonging to a "vanquished" and "resigned" race.

With the publication of Jorge Icaza's *Huasipungo* and, most particularly, of the unsettling *El mundo es ancho y ajeno* [*Broad and Alien is the World*] by Ciro Alegría (1909–1967), the tradition of rousing political portraits inaugurated by Narciso Aréstegui and continued in the twentienth century by Alcides Arguedas took a further step. The plot of Icaza's novel is very similar to Ciro Alegría's: in both instances Indians are forcefully driven out of traditionally communal lands. However Alegría, who had spent his childhood on his grandfather's country estate, gave a more accurate view of Indian life than his colleague from Ecuador.

El mundo es ancho y ajeno is divided into two parts, the first of which can be categorized as a cycle of defeat (under Rosendo Maqui, emblem of Indian tradition, communal values, and the past); and the second, as a cycle of hope (under Benito Castro who brings to the ancestral communal values the advantages of progress learned in the white man's world). In both novels – Icaza's and Alegría's – the Indian is demonstrably ineffectual when it comes to battling in a society ruled by a white establishment. Yet while the former's characters just run themselves into the ground, the latter's are shown the path to salvation. This path is simply a dramatization of the political program hailed by the left-wing *APRA* party – *Alianza Popular Revolucionaria Americana* – whose leader, Victor Raúl Haya de la Torre (1895–1979), advocated an alliance between workers and intellectuals.

The *apristas* saw in the communal structure basic to the Incario a predisposition or, more exactly, a fertile ground for Socialism. However, in order to bring traditional communities into the present, the Indian had to be taught the culture which governed his country. This is exactly what the character of Benito Castro was charged with in *El mundo es ancho y ajeno*. Because Benito had been forced to leave the community and see the world, he becomes wise to its ways. Upon his return, seventeen years later, he set out to change the archaic beliefs that hinder the commune of Rumi from entering into the twentieth century. Although he meets with a great deal of rejection from the strongly traditional elders, the new order and truth he represents are, in the end, recognized by the *comuneros*. Benito is eventually elected mayor and the community knows prosperity under his direction. However prosperity does not last in a world ruled by the greed of landowners. The Indians of Rumi – as is the case with the community depicted in Icaza's *Huasipungo* – are massacred down to the last man when the troops are sent in.

The endings of both novels are comparable and yet, thematically speaking, they are very different. Icaza's Indian lives sordidly and dies fruitlessly. He finds neither hope nor help for pain in an alien world that exploits him without respite. In contrast, *El mundo es ancho y ajeno* provided the blueprint for salvation in its *aprista* slate: to preserve the communal values of the past while learning the political and economic structure of the present, in order to end, once and for all, the self-damaging isolation under which Indians had taken umbrage since the Conquest.

The moral of Alegría's drama rings clear: God saves those who save themselves. The Indian must step into modern society of his own accord with the help of those who feel the injustice of his situation. And what is an Indian that has learned the ways of the white man's world? A *cholo*, an *indio ladinizado*, the heroes of the *mestizo* sagas that begin to proliferate after the 1930s, written by the third generation of *Indigenistas*. We have here, as Angel Rama points out in his important *Transculturación narrativa en America Latina*, a literature written for and by the lower middle or *mestizo* classes that are rising socially and economically and feel hampered by the well-rooted and all-controlling landowners.

The 1930s, 1940s, 1950s, and 1960s were trying times for Peru, Mexico, and Guatemala, a time when these countries lived through hazardous changes. The highlands of Peru, for instance, of difficult access since the days of the Conquest, became approachable after a massive road-building campaign in the last years of the 1920s. Commercial culture came knocking at the door of the last bastions of Indian life, some living in a state of semi-isolation since the Conquest. With roads came progress, medicines, books, but also the destruction of communal roots and traditional ways which had cemented together the rural communities since the days of the Inca empire. It was in an attempt to preserve these cultures that the generation of *Indigenistas* of which José María Arguedas was a member shifted its focus of interest from the transcendent civilizations of the past to the fast disappearing ones of the present. The dramatic cultural chasm, the gaping wound which kept Westerners and Indians apart racially, economically, politically, and philosophically was being stitched with rough kitchen thread and the needle of "progress." What Angel Rama refers to as the process of *mesticismo* had begun, even if the combination of cultures was to be more counterpoint than harmony.

The need to save the Indian and preserve his culture held pride of place in the review *Amauta*, directed by prominent politician and theorist, José Carlos Mariátegui (1894–1930), whose *Siete ensayos de interpretación de la realidad peruana* [*Seven Interpretive Essays on Peruvian Reality*] is a cornerstone of the *indigenista* movement to this day. Mariátegui saw in the survival of the *ayllu* (the basic structure in the communal system of the

Inca empire) the key to synchronize archaic economic structures with Marxism. He also explained in his "las corrientes de hoy – El indigenismo" how this literary movement could not give us a strictly accurate version of the Indian because it was literature written by *mestizos* and Whites who viewed the culture from the outside.

The most prominent and influential author of the movement, José María Arguedas, takes issue with the second of these statements and spends his life attempting to translate the authentic voice of the race whose blood he lovingly and painfully shared. As a student, when he read the descriptions of Indian life in the work of López Albújar and Ventura García Calderón, Arguedas had been profoundly shocked by the lack of authenticity and vowed that he would portray the men and women from the Andes as they really were. *Indigenismo* and the reading public are both fortunate, because this portrayal is no mere act of political canvassing. In José María Arguedas the movement finds a committed proselyte who is also an artist of genius.

Here was a man who spoke Quechua since childhood, one who had been a schoolteacher in an Indian village and had become an expert on Andean music and song. An enduring interest in his country and the ways of its people drew him first to the field of ethnology; recognition eventually followed in the form of an appointment as Head of the Institute of Ethnological Studies of Peru's National Museum of History.[2] Clearly, Arguedas was in a good position to discuss Indian culture. But this was not all. He was also adamant about portraying society as he experienced it, even when this meant he had to spend his life rectifying the portrait.

As he matured professionally, the world he pictured resembled a series of concentric circles involving relationships that expanded beyond the overly simplified binomial opposition (between Indians and *ladinos*) that characterized the short stories of *Agua*, his first work of fiction. His progressively more elaborate system of characterization finally culminated (in *Todas las sangres* and in *El zorro de arriba y el zorro de abajo*) in a composite portrait that extended beyond national boundaries in order to describe the relationship between foreign imperialism, national capitalism, and the Peruvian ruling and working classes.

On the basis of his handling and elaboration of character types critics have divided Arguedas's fiction into three separate phases. In the first of these, typified by *Agua* and greatly influenced by the constricting parameters set out as guidelines by the generation of *Amauta* (guidelines that

---

[2] Arguedas has had numerous articles on Quechua folklore, Andean music, and popular art published in newspapers and journals that include *La Prensa* (Buenos Aires), *El Comercio* (Lima), and the *Revista del Museo Nacional de Lima*. A handful of his newspaper articles about Peruvian music have been brought together in *Nuestra música popular y sus intérpretes*. Lima, Mosca Azul and Horizonte Editores, 1967.

include an adherence to Realism, an ideological bent, and a portrayal of the feudal structure of society), Arguedas forged an isolated microcosm in which Indians and landholders – the commune of Tinki and Don Braulio (in "Agua"), or Kutu and Don Froylán (in "Warma Kuyay") – lash out at each other in perpetual antagonism.

In the next phase, characterized by *Yawar Fiesta* and *Los ríos profundos* [*Deep Rivers*], the opposition becomes that between the coast and the mountain region, the *costa* and the *sierra*, understood not merely as geographical opposites but as complex socio-economic and cultural settings that are dramatically different from one another. Not surprisingly, Arguedas repudiated the coast, the region where an aggressive capitalistic system (antagonistic in every way to the collective sense typical of Indian communities) ruthlessly developed.

Finally, in the third phase (represented by *Todas las sangres* and *El zorro de arriba y el zorro de abajo*), the ethnologist turned man of letters contemplated the painful and contradictory coming together of two worlds – *sierra* and *costa* – which had been isolated from each other for centuries. At this point, as if this clash were not enough, the sinister hand of imperialism gripped the reins in the disastrous race for power.

No one has done more to further the aims of the *indigenista* novel or to polish its tools than José María Arguedas. This is why, in a conscientious attempt to portray the social, economic, and cultural forces he witnessed around him, the author of *Todas las sangres* conceived five different character types. As early as the second phase of his work, the Indians and traditional landholders who people his fiction are joined by *mestizos*, students, and a new type of property owner, a sort of *nouveau riche* [the new rich] *latifundista* with political ambitions.

Without a doubt, the greatest innovation Arguedas brought about in terms of these character types was the individualization and development of the *mestizo*. As early as 1952, in a communiqué delivered at the First International Congress of Peruvianists, the Head of the Institute of Ethnological Studies stated that men and women of mixed blood represented a social class that had to be contended with in Peru. Self-evident though this may seem today, such a statement jarred both the sensibility and the credibility of many among Arguedas's contemporaries who viewed the *mestizo* as little more than a thorn in the flesh of national culture. Actually, in the minds of Peruvians influenced by Marxist theory since the 1920s, the redemptive role that Marxism traditionally attributed to the proletariat had been handed over – lock, stock, and barrel – to the full-blooded Indian masses.

Arguedas, more lucid than most, set out to demonstrate how the future of Peru was actually in the hands of the *mestizo* or of the *indio ladinizado* who, like Rendon Willka in *Todas las sangres* or Benito Castro in *El mundo es ancho y ajeno*, has come in contact with the ways of Western culture. In ethnological studies as well as in fiction, he was to reiterate how, left to their own devices and isolated from the world, the Indians would soon be stripped of all they owned and swallowed by the voracious maelstrom of capitalism. More than any other, the isolated communities needed to grasp Western thought and use it to their advantage. It was one of their own who could best mediate between both worlds but only after coming in contact with the ruthless society that was both a pall and a saving mantle for the traditions still maintained alive within the *ayllu*.

With this emphasis on the *mestizo*, the literature of *Indigenismo* evolved into a third phase, one commonly referred to as *Neoindigenismo* because it posits the erstwhile disdained outcast as the redeeming element capable of bringing about a process of acculturation. The figure of the Indian, idealized by the *Indianistas* and exalted by the *Indigenistas* is actually transcended by a growing number of authors who recognize the worth of *mestizo* culture and envision the identity of their respective countries as a congress of cultures.

Not surprisingly, *Neoindigenismo* did not gain ground in Peruvian literature exclusively. It proliferated north of Panama in the expert hands of authors such as Rosario Castellanos (1925–1974) and Miguel Angel Asturias. Long before concerning itself with the role of the *mestizo* in a multiracial and multicultural society, however, the literature portraying native Americans in Guatemala and Mexico evolved – as it did in Peru – through the stages of *Indianismo* and *Indigenismo*. The difference in the literature of Guatemala was that both tendencies were exercised by the same authors, sometimes conjointly. For instance, in his novel *La Gringa*, Carlos Wyld Ospina (1891–1956) relied on the Indian and his customs solely as background color, a tendency that he left behind by the time his collection of short stories, *La tierra de Los Nahuyacas* appeared in print. In this later work, the tone of social protest that typified the literature of *Indigenismo* rang clear. Not only did Wyld Ospina give a striking and sympathetic portrayal of the Kecchi Indians, he also decried the deleterious effect of migration on laborers who end up losing their culture and identity after moving to the coast.

A second Guatemalan writer to portray native Americans in the 1930s was less clear about his aims and, even, it seems, about his convictions. Poet and novelist Flavio Herrera (1895–1968) never quite made a choice between aesthetic descriptions and moralizing. What had formerly been the distinguishing features of *Indianismo* (colorful descriptions, Romanticism, and idealization) and *Indigenismo* (social protest) were lumped together in exuberantly baroque epics such as *El tigre*. Herrera was just as undecided about Indian culture; he criticized the exploitation of native Americans but found them riddled with insurmountable defects and cultural insufficiencies. Like Ventura García Calderón in Peru, he was unable to find a satisfactory solution to the problem of integrating the indigenous inhabitants of his country into the mainstream of society, a riddle that became the main theme of one of the most poignant *indigenista* bugle-calls, written in the upsurge of optimism that followed the demise of dictator Jorge Ubico: *Entre la piedra y la cruz* by Mario Monteforte Toledo (b. 1911).

As the two-edged title indicates, Monteforte Toledo wades here into the murky zone of dual cultures which is to say – for the underdog, at least – of the totally unresolved problem of split identities. Having shared part of his life with a full-blooded Indian woman whose language he learned and in whose village he lived, Monteforte had firsthand experience of his subject.

The Indian, as Ciro Alegría and J. M. Arguedas suggested, must subscribe to Western culture to some degree (the "cross" in Monteforte's title) and learn from it. What the author of *Entre la piedra y la cruz* does is show that once the Indian identifies with this culture, he is neither accepted by the dominant society nor fully satisfied with his native community. The bi-cultural hybrid who is smitten by *ladino* civilization turns into a pariah unless, as Miguel Angel Asturias will come to demonstrate, *mestizo* acquisitions and accomplishments can provide a new system of values, a culture that functions as the living reminder of a past actualized in the daily ritual of the present.

Monteforte's novel strikes a chord of naive optimism in its last pages when its hero, Lu Matzar, is rescued from death by the revolutionary forces that overthrow Ubico in 1944 and joins them in the struggle for a better world. His message is one of brotherhood: the *ladino* must feel responsible for educating the natives and giving them faith in a *mestizo* society they have never trusted. However, this is easier said than done. Racial hatred – as the characters of these Indians' sagas often note themselves – is a burning crucible in all *mestizo* cultures. Besides, why should Indians join revolutions? What will they get out of them? Wishing racial hatred and prejudice to resolve itself in a communal struggle for freedom is praiseworthy but futile as long as concrete solutions to integration are not provided.

Even before the publication of *Entre la piedra y la cruz*, solutions were proposed in Guatemala by the democratic governments that were voted into power after the fall of Ubico. Juan José Arévalo's government (1944–1951) set up farming cooperatives, and widespread educational programs geared to integrating the Indian into the mainstream of national life, while Jacobo Arbenz (president between 1951 and 1954) implemented the Agrarian Reform that Arévalo had spent years setting afoot. Yet even these reforms – as history would take care to demonstrate – could not mitigate racial hatred. Quite the contrary, in fact. Integration had to come about as a more profound transformation in ideology and perception. Indian culture had to be first recognized as worthwhile and then federated into the melting pot that would generate *mestizo* society.

In Peru, the task of praising and showing objectively the worth of Indian culture befell José María Arguedas. In Guatemala, this role was fulfilled by Miguel Angel Asturias. Both authors provided an enlarged concept of the Indian by including extensive glimpses of his own worldview. Unlike earlier works of *Indigenismo* in which native Americans are viewed from the outside, there is in Asturias and Arguedas a desire, as Joseph Sommers so convincingly puts it, "to penetrate beneath the surface of Indian consciousness" ("The Indian-oriented Novel in Latin America," 253). This desire brings with it a more esoteric language and, frequently, a type of syntax that aims to portray native speech patterns and non-Western structures of thought.

The determination to move beyond the former stereotype of superficial Realism and translate the Indian psyche typifies the work of Asturias, who was determined, like Arguedas, to give an accurate portrait of his people. He was admirably suited for this task. To begin with, he had an impressive background in ethnography and sociology. He was also a *mestizo* on his mother's side and had been raised in close contact with the Indian and his traditions from the time his parents were compelled to move to the isolated village of Salamá for political reasons. His interest in the native cultures of Guatemala was early and lifelong, as attested by his doctoral dissertation on "El problema social del indio," written when he was just twenty-four (the dissertation has been reprinted by the Centre de Recherches de l'Institut d'Etudes Hispaniques, Paris, in 1971). Upon reaching Europe in the first of many trips, one of Asturias's most sudden impulses was to enroll on a course on Mayan civilization taught at the Sorbonne by Georges Raynaud, translator of the *Popol Vuh*. Nevertheless, it is true, he did not speak any Indian languages and as regards the sources which inspired his fiction, he only shared political commitment with Arguedas.

In this respect, and like his Peruvian counterpart, Asturias used his work as a platform to denounce the abuse and exploitation of an underdeveloped country by, first, a capitalistic elite, and, subsequently, an industrialized nation. However, the medium for canvassing his message was drastically different from Arguedas's. In 1924, Asturias was dazzled by the theoretical and formal pamphleteering of French Surrealism. This early contact with the most avant-garde artistic movement of the time was responsible in turn for his life-long interest in magic, the esoteric, psychoanalysis, automatic writing, and wordplay, interests that would season his own brand of *Neoindigenismo* with a wholly unique flavor. In terms of formal originality, Asturias stood head and shoulders above his fellow *Indigenistas* whose prose, with few exceptions, was straightforward to the point of being terse. In contrast, his own brand of writing luxuriated in onomatopoeias and alliteration, the reason, no doubt, why critics often refer to him as "the poet–narrator" (Castelpoggi, *Miguel Angel Asturias*, 201).

The very close attention Asturias pays to surface work, to the "texture" of fiction, must not be mistaken for dilettantism or superficiality, however. His *neoindigenista* works, beginning with *Leyendas de Guatemala*, combine magic and reality on many levels, making them as dazzling and hermetic as the writing of James Joyce, whom the Guatemalan émigré to Paris greatly admired.

There is, likewise, a wealth of theoretical and referential background from and through which Asturias's fictional material evolves. Because of his interest in Surrealism and his personal contact with some of the key French intellectuals of the 1920s and 1930s, Asturias discovers the work of Georges Bataille, Freud, Jung, and, eventually, of Claude Lévi-Strauss and succeeds in incorporating a number of their pet notions into the warp and weft of his fiction as, for instance, in his memorable masterpiece of 1949: *Hombres de maíz*.

In this work, pivotal elements in the story (such as corn, water, and fire) are linked with colors, animals, and numbers in keeping with their ascribed spheres of action in Mayan cosmogony. Although this association of elements is not readily apparent, it is, in fact, the unifying principle of a novel which develops neither chronologically nor through its protagonists but, rather, through a character substitution principle that is based on clusters of elements interlinked amongst themselves. By means of such an elaborate pyramid of symbols, Asturias's novel harks back to the *Popul Vuh*, clothing the ancient Quiché manuscript in modern garb and bringing together past and present, tradition and the modern world with a deftness that is only beginning to be understood as one of the most daring experiments in the history of the modern Latin American novel.

For his next *Neoindigenista* novel, *Mulata de tal* [*Mulata*], Asturias recasts one of the mainstays of world folklore, namely, the tale of the poor peasant who trades off his wife to the devil in exchange for wealth. Humorous, zany, and often grotesque, this allegory of the painful dilemma posed by dependency in developing nations translates the author's weariness after the fall of Guatemalan President Jacobo Arbenz.

In 1954, Colonel Carlos Castillo Armas's revocation of the Arbenz Agrarian Reform Law becomes, in Asturias's eyes, a catastrophe announcing the demise of the very same men of maize he had likened to the Mayan corn god in *Hombres de maíz*. This is why *Mulata de tal* ends in a holocaust in which the angry voices of the unborn, of history capsized, as it were, cry out in anger "we want to be born" (p. 297).

Asturias, like José María Arguedas, conceives an angry response to the historical situation around him. For this reason, *Mulata de tal*, like *El zorro de arriba y el zorro de abajo*, is a book that teems with disappointment and rage. Yet, the very fact that these despondent works were written confirms the sustained hope of evolution and reform that typifies both authors, the two men who – along with Mexico's Rosario Castellanos – have done the most to interlace their fiction, written in Spanish, with the idioms, thought patterns, songs, and legends of the Indian cultures of America in order to create a literature that is *mestizo* to the same degree as the characters it portrays. Herein lies their uniqueness as well as their greatness. Theirs is a message for the men and women of America to struggle, unite, and give birth, once and for all, to what Mexican Minister of Public Education (1920–1924) José Vasconcelos referred to as "the cosmic race".

These three authors go much beyond the generation of *Indigenistas* whose work precedes – and sometimes coincides with – the publication of their own. Their brand of writing brings together Western techniques with stylistic elements from Indian literature creating the first major disruption in our hemisphere of the mimetic tradition that typifies European literature. This is why *Neoindigenismo* should be viewed as not merely the most recent phase, but also as the most mature and, stylistically speaking, the most consumately conceived moment in the history of this entire literary tendency.

During the years in which Arguedas and Asturias were advocating social change and translating the struggle for integration, authors further to the north were actively responding to the aims and goals set forth by the Mexican Revolution of 1910 regarding the native population and their civil rights. Mexican literature of this century in which the Indian is portrayed follows three types of approaches. First of all, there are tales of artistic ethnology produced by a handful of anthropologically oriented authors such as Ricardo Pozas (b. 1912); second, there are realistic narratives of social protest – *La bruma lo vuelve azul* by Ramón Rubín (b. 1912) is a case in point – that respond to the traditional model of *Indigenismo*; and third, there are those, namely Rosario Castellanos, who mix techniques and transform language in order to echo what they see as the Indian's inner voice.

In Mexico the interest in the Indian has, in the words of Gabriella de Beer, an almost "scientific" quality (p. 560). A number of anthropologists such as Pozas, or writers, teachers, and journalists with training in anthropology (Carlo Antonio Castro, for instance) have conducted highly wrought interviews which they have later used as a source of inspiration or published, with few changes, as a first person narrative or *novela testimonio*. The best-known example of this technique is the erudite monograph of Chamula Indian[3] culture which Pozas publishes under the title of *Juan Pérez Jolote, Biografía de un tzotzil* after the actual name of one of his Indian informants. Pozas's *novela testimonio* is interesting for many reasons, not least of which is the meticulous objectivity (for instance, the author restricts himself to less than 1,300 words in an effort to accurately portray his informants' adequate but limited knowledge of Spanish) which takes it beyond the ideological manipulation typical of *Indigenismo* in its earlier phases.

This same objectivity allows Pozas to avoid the over-folkloric emphasis that mars many an *indigenista* novel and guides his steps in portraying a Tzotzil Indian's social life as he comes into contact with Western civilization. However, such objectivity must not belie the fact that Pozas uses the informants' reports according to a social plan of his own which, as Jean Franco notes, is "the study of how, in revolutionary Mexico, social change is integrated into the life of a community" (p. 261). *Juan Pérez Jolote* is, therefore, a work of "anthropological recreation" (p. 506), to borrow César Rodríguez Chicharro's terms, and not a case study. Be that as it may, and even if some measure of recreation is involved, Pozas's work allows us to witness the Indian world from the inside: the authorial hand and attitude are almost conspicuous in their absence.

The same is true of Carlo Antonio Castro's short narrative, "Che Ndu: ejidatario chinanteco" (in *La Palabra y el Hombre*), with the one difference that this work is much more universal than Pozas's in its concern with matters of world-wide significance such as life, death, and love, even when its focus is the life of a man in an isolated community. A second interesting contrast between Che Ndu, the protagonist, and Pozas's Juan Pérez is that the former is receptive to the benefits of Western civilization. This is the one exception to the Mexican novels of this period in which authors systematically demonstrate the destructive effect of Western culture on the Indians' way of life.

Indian protagonists, such as Ramón Rubín's Kanamayé (in *La bruma lo vuelve azul*), are torn between two cultures in an identity crisis that is translated, in this specific instance, by portraying the hero's origins as an enigma: is he all Indian or part *ladino*? The enigma is never resolved although the question of identity is explicitly answered by a village elder who tells the confused, humiliated, and, by then, criminal Kanamayé, that he is the worst thing one can be: "an Indian turncoat" (p. 157). The

---

[3] "Chamula" is the name given to a group of over 16,000 individuals who speak Tzotzil and live in the mountains around San Cristóbal, near Ciudad Las Casas. Their center is the town of Chamula – a ceremonial city where political and religious authorities reside.

message, as in Rubín's better known *El callado dolor de los tzotziles* is that *ladino* society destroys the Indian. If Kanamayé had stayed in his village he would have obeyed the law, but, having been contaminated by the outside world, he has lost the moral and spiritual support which the mother culture gave him. As Rubín indicates in the ominous epigraph to *El callado dolor*: "Civilization is like the abyss: it is easy to slide down into it... but whoever tries to crawl out once he has reached the bottom is sadly wasting his time."

This attitude is evident even in the typical example of social Realism that follows the Mexican Revolution, *El Indio* [*El indio*] by Gregorio López y Fuentes. This fascinating study contains all the standard themes, and suffers from the typical flaw, that weaken the literary impact of *Indigenismo*: namely, the tendency to proselytize.

As is customary, Indians in this novel are portrayed as the instrument and object of *ladino* vanity and greed. The element of surprise comes in the last chapters where an *indio ladinizado* begins by becoming a social and political activist and obtains improvements for his people. The reader soon discovers, however, that ambition wears the same colored coat in all cultures. To begin with, the revolutionary *ladino* deputies who are ostensibly helping the Indians need contributions to be re-elected and ask the natives for help. In addition, the Indians, now politically involved in the revolutionary effort, have no time, as they did in the old days, to till the lands they have recently received from the government. López y Fuentes ends the novel by suggesting that while the Indian political activist has improved his lot after receiving an appointment to City Council, traditional Indians find themselves in an extremely defensive position: all they have obtained is impending violence from angered *ladinos* who have lost property and are avidly searching for a scapegoat.

Works of literature that are directly aligned with the novel of the Revolution – such as *El Indio*, and *El resplandor* (1937) by Mauricio Magdaleno (b. 1906) – touch upon ideological questions in a suitably provoking manner without, as Joseph Sommers indicates, "portraying convincing Indian individuals in the context of their own culture" ("The Indian-oriented Novel," 262). In Mexico, the focus on the Indian seen within his own cultural context is the domain of the so-called "Ciclo de Chiapas," a masterful string of novels and short stories in which the action takes place in this southernmost region of the country. The authors whose work merges into the "Chiapas Cycle" are: Ricardo Pozas, Ramón Rubín, Carlo Antonio Castro, María Lombardo de Caso, and Rosario Castellanos, the recognized virtuoso of the group.

Castellanos's *Neoindigenista* novels follow one another in an ever-improving progression that culminates with the widely acclaimed masterpiece of the "Ciclo de Chiapas": *Oficio de tinieblas*. Both her first novel,

Balún canán, and *Oficio de tinieblas* draw on the author's experience in the state of Chiapas, where she spent her childhood. The focus of the earlier work is the tense relationship between Indians and *ladinos* during the presidency of Lázaro Cárdenas when the young narrator's family, like all landowners in Chiapas, suffered major financial setbacks and saw its power and position vis-à-vis the Indians seriously threatened for the first time since the Conquest.

The legends and beliefs of the Tzetzal Indians permeate the narration; in fact, Castellanos incorporates sections from ancient Maya manuscripts including passages from the story of the creation of man that hark back to the *Popol Vuh*. It is true that, as Martin Lienhard observes in a very important article, this use of a highly stylized and ancient rhetoric appears artificial in the mouths of modern-day Indians. In other words, it is totally paradoxical that whenever Castellanos wants to suggest the flavor of contemporary Indian discourse, she resorts to the model provided by the translations of ancient Maya texts (Lienhard, "La legitimación indígena en dos novelas centroamericanas," 115).

The Indian language of *Balún canán* may well be inauthentic but, then again, how could it be otherwise when the narrator is a *ladino* girl? She, as Ernesto in *Los ríos profundos*, acts as a filter through which "reality," even if somewhat disfigured by age and a cultural bias, is portrayed. The merit and advantage of including passages from the *Popol Vuh* is also underscored by Lienhard when he explains how the ancient rhetoric imbues with its prestige the modern and – in the eyes of the *ladinos* – the "impoverished" Indian language, investing it with new dignity. This, of course, is also what Miguel Angel Asturias strove to do all his life: create an American idiom that would actualize the ancient traditions of Mesoamerica. It comes as no surprise, therefore, that Castellanos was a great admirer of the Guatemalan author. That her writing develops in a totally different direction from his, however, is made amply evident in *Oficio de tinieblas*.

Using as her point of departure and source of inspiration the messianic revolt of the Tzotzil Indians (1868–1870),[4] Castellanos conceived a vast frieze of culture in Chiapas at the time of Cárdenas and in the years that followed. The action focuses on the intimate lives of Indians and *ladinos*, both men and women, bringing to light the most thorough and complex study of Indian character in the literature of *Indigenismo*: the *ilol*, or interpreter of the Tzotzil mystic and supernatural beliefs, Catalina Díaz Puiljá.

Catalina's sterility and the frustration that ensues from not conceiving

---

[4] According to Lienhard, Castellanos's source was V. Vicente Pineda: *Historia de las sublevaciones indígenas habidas en el estado de Chiapas. Gramática de las lengua tzel-tal*. Chiapas, Imprenta del Gobierno, 1888.

(a terrible blemish among the Tzotzil) are shown to be at the root of the Indian revolt which she engineers by promising immortality to her people after the immolation of their own Christ figure: the child she had raised and given up to be crucified on Good Friday. The novel depicts passion, ambition, and pride through a dual focus on town (San Cristóbal) and village (San Juan Chamula), on *ladinos* and Indians, demonstrating, much more explicitly than any work of *Indigenismo* before it, that all men are equal even when they refuse to treat each other as such.

Equally dual is the chronological conception of the novel. Western time – specifically, the period of Lázaro Cárdenas's government and the ensuing years in which the aims of the Revolution come of age and efforts are made to implement the Agrarian Reform Law – is historical. Indian time, on the other hand, is cyclical, based on myths which are celebrated as a perpetual re-enactment that guarantees continuity. Besides a dual setting and two conceptions of time, the novel has a deeply religious and mythical backdrop. This religious element transpires already in the title, an overt allusion to the Passion of Christ which is re-enacted by the Indians with a human sacrifice in the church of San Juan Chamula and is not without the suggestion of the eventual likelihood of resurrection (of Indian culture, perhaps?) as Sommers astutely observes ("El Ciclo de Chiapas," 259).

The time for renewal is not the present, however. Induced by Catalina, the Indians revolt and are miserably defeated. Even Cárdenas's official representative – a man who encouraged them and fought on their side – is torn to pieces by the angry mob of Ciudad Real in order to stop the law from sending him to Mexico City where there is no death penalty. Interestingly, the Indian defeat is never described as part of the action; it is merely alluded to after the fact. By abstracting it from the novel, Castellanos qualifies the Indians' revolt as a non-entity, a failed, annulled event.

The Tzotzil that survive take to the high mountains; they have been beaten, the women raped, their brothers massacred. They have lost their sense of unity, their pride, their tribal structure. Only the will to survive remains. Their clothing is torn, they have gone back to wearing barely tanned animal hides. Historical time and "progress" have been relinquished. Only mythic time endures: the tale of their revolt and the events leading up to it become a legend repeated by the Indian *nana* as something which took place long before her charge, Idolina, had been born. Castellanos substantiates how the objectives of the Revolution amount to naught as far as the Indians are concerned. She openly defies official government policy by pointing out that the goals of Cárdenas's government are far from being attained, that many so-called "reforms" have gone awry and that perhaps even the way in which the Indian is being approached is totally insensitive to his culture.

Such defiance of government policy is one of the traits that typify the authors comprising the "Ciclo de Chiapas." Their novels, one and all, amply demonstrate that the Indian stands alone and isolated in spite of all the reforms enacted in order to integrate him into society. As Sommers points out, Juan Pérez Jolote is marginalized by society even though he has risked his life for the sake of the Revolution ("El Ciclo de Chiapas," 260). What becomes rapidly evident is that such critical distance vis-à-vis Revolutionary goals puts a new face on the literature of *Indigenismo.*

After the period of optimism in the decade of the 1940s (one thinks immediately of *El mundo es ancho y ajeno* and *Hombres de maíz,* novels that announce the possibility of a *mestizo* society), we have with the "Ciclo de Chiapas" a more lucid depiction of a situation that is, to this day, highly unresolved.

Nineteenth- and early twentieth-century authors pointed out the need to improve the Indian's lot; the *indigenista* novels from the 1910s to the 1920s showed that in order to improve it, a revolution would be required. Three decades later, the *Neoindigenistas* stepped in to show that the path to salvation must come through the *indio ladinizado.* Closer to our time, the writers of the "Ciclo de Chiapas" suggest that the Indians who have come in contact with Western society either lose their identity and are alienated from both worlds, or settle into white towns to improve their own lives, thinking about their fellow Indians back in the village only when an opportunity arises to get something out of them.

The truth of the matter is that the phase of optimism announced by Alegría in *El mundo es ancho y ajeno* has been superseded by a phase of disappointment grounded in historical fact. The question left unanswered, of course, is: where, at this point, should the Indian turn? How are his goals and needs to be represented in the new literature of *Indigenismo?*

Critics, a vast majority of them, have been announcing the demise of *indigenista* literature for almost three decades. They affirm that this literary tendency has fulfilled its goals when, in fact, as can be readily adduced, the problem it portrays is wholly unresolved. It is in an attempt to come to grips with this problem that a remarkable poet and man of action steps forward.

Before he died in a tragic plane accident in 1983, Manuel Scorza completed one of the towering achievements of *neoindigenista* literature: a five-volume chronicle of peasant revolt in the Peruvian Andes entitled "La Guerra Silenciosa." As Cornejo Polar points out, Scorza's creation responds to the parameters of *Neoindegenismo* through the following features: first, the ubiquitous use of Magical Realism to reveal the mythic dimension of the indigenous world; second, a heightened lyricism; and, third, an amplification and supplementation (when compared with earlier examples of *indigenista* literature) of technical devices and experimentation ("Sobre el 'Neoindigenismo'," *Literatura y sociedad en el Perú* 549).

The manner in which these ingredients are combined is totally new, moreover. To begin with, Scorza, like the authors who engendered the "Ciclo de Chiapas," supersedes, with one exception, the level of propaganda. In addition, he makes no attempt to internalize the style and rhetoric of ancient Indian manuscripts.[5] As a result, the language of "La Guerra Silenciosa" is less ponderous, more light-handedly lyrical, and very often hilarious. The fact that he was a first-hand witness of, and, to some degree, an actor in the Central Andean uprisings described in the saga is in no small measure responsible for the immediacy of the action.[6] So, too, Scorza's interest in the authors of the *Boom* colors his prose; his writing is closer in flavor to that of Gabriel García Márquez (b. 1928), than to that of other *indigenista* authors. This homology is most readily perceived in the handling and portrayal of myth, a constitutive element in the first four novels of "La Guerra Silenciosa."

In *Redoble por Rancas*, for instance, one character speaks to horses and is understood by them; another one, the protagonist of *Historia de Garabombo el invisible*, cannot be seen because, since *ladinos* refuse to see Indians, why shouldn't the hero take advantage of a figure of speech in the action of the novel? Instead of presenting these mythic beliefs through a referent or with a critical distance, Scorza incorporates them into the fiction without in any way passing judgment on either the uproariously outlandish events or the poignantly tragic reality. In other words, the worldview described in these novels is the Indians'; what the *ladino* world qualifies as legend is, in this instance, portrayed as reality. However, this is a statement that must be qualified.

By the time we reach the fifth novel, *La tumba del relámpago*, belief in myths is shown to be insufficient in the face of the all-powerful Cerro de Pasco Corporation that is swallowing up Peru and all its wealth. It is at this point that Scorza's work becomes didactic as well as polemical suggesting "the need to elaborate a revolutionary tactic and strategy that will end the limitations of mythic thought, in this realm" (Cornejo Polar, "Sobre el 'Neoindigenismo'," 556). Mythic discourse shrivels and eventually fades, indicating the need to question and recast revolutionary

---

[5] Specific references are made to the myth of Inkarri but in every other instance, the myths portrayed in the fiction are the author's creations and an attempt to improvise the mental structures that typify Indian thought.

[6] In the prologue to *Redoble por Rancas*, Scorza states: "more than a novelist, the author is a witness." True to his word, in the last installment of "La Guerra Silenciosa" he figures as a character under his own name.

thought in order to make it a working tool for Indians and peasants. This, Scorza advances, must become the goal of the next revolution because, as one character in *La tumba del relámpago* wryly observes, "the scandal of our struggle is that it doesn't coincide with our ideology; rage and courage belong here, on this side, while ideas are theirs and not ours" (p. 225).

The Indian is caught in a culture-shattering quandary: the myth that compensates for a bitter reality is to him both bridle and spur; it keeps him bound and strapped to the traditions of the past while, at the same time, happily invigorated with the culture of his ancestors. Why tear Indians away from the beliefs that nurture them? Yet, it must be done. The question is how?

The ex-*aprista* and Political Secretary of the Communal Movement of Peru echoes J. M. Arguedas's criticism vis-à-vis Communists and *Apristas* who harp on tried-and-false ideologies instead of forging new ones; especially since the problem at hand has not changed significantly since the nineteenth century: how can archaic Indian societies be integrated into the modern world to their own economic advantage but not to the detriment of Indian culture? "La Guerra Silenciosa" remains open-ended regarding this burning question. Like *Todas las sangres*, it posits a need and provides a burning incentive to both society and the writing establishment. What the answer will be remains for America and the *indigenista* novel of the future to resolve.

[5]

Afro-Hispanic American literature

Vera M. Kutzinski

That the 1970s should have been the decade to inaugurate the field of Afro-Hispanic (American) studies is scarcely surprising: the Civil Rights and Black Power movements in the United States had prepared the ground for the founding of numerous Afro-American studies programs while the *Boom* of the Latin American novel – sponsored largely by the United States' aggressive investment in Latin American culture aimed at defusing the political threat of a post-revolutionary Cuba – continued to draw international attention to Latin America's literary production. This, in turn, provided publishing outlets and markets for many poets and novelists of African descent, whose work received special attention and support from newly founded organizations, such as the Afro-Ecuadorian Studies Center in Quito (1979), the Center for the Study of Black Culture in Bogotá (1977), and the Afro-Hispanic Institute at Howard University in Washington, D.C. (1981). Like their predecessors, the Institute for Afro-American Studies in Mexico (1945) and the Society for Afro-Cuban Studies Against Racism in Cuba (1936), these and other institutes also launched new journals: *Cuadernos Afro-Americanos* (Caracas, 1975), *Negritud* (Bogotá, 1977), *Studies in Afro-Hispanic Literature* (Purchase, New York, 1977), and the *Afro-Hispanic Review* (Washington, D.C., 1982, now located in Columbia, Missouri). Conferences were organized, most notably the Colloque Négritude et Amérique Latine (University of Dakar, Senegal, 1974), the Primer Congreso del Negro Panameño (1981), and several Congresos de la Cultura Negra de las Américas (Colombia, 1977; Panama, 1980; Brazil, 1982).

A number of publishing houses, among them Casa de las Américas, Ediciones Universal, and Casa de la Cultura Ecuatoriana, started to reprint "classic" twentieth-century Afro-Hispanic texts, such as Adalberto Ortiz's *Juyungo* (1968); Arnoldo Palacios's *Las estrellas son negras* (1971); Juan Pablo Sojo's *Nochebuena negra* (1972); *Sofía* (1972) and *La familia Unzúazu* (1975) by Martín Morúa Delgado (1856–1910); *Autobio-*

164

grafía de un esclavo (1975) by Juan Francisco Manzano; Nicolás Guillén's *Motivos de son* (1980); Marcelino Arozarena's *Canción negra sin color* (1983); Regino Pedrozo's *Poesías* (1984); and the complete works of Alejo Carpentier, the first volume of which includes all of his "Afro-Cuban" texts. In the United States, an assortment of university and small presses published translations of Ramón Díaz Sánchez's *Cumboto*, Ortiz's *Juyungo*, Nelson Estupiñán Bass's *When the Guayacans Were in Bloom*, short fiction by Carlos Guillermo Wilson (Cubena), two volumes of poetry by Nancy Morejón, and no less than four by Guillén. Unfortunately, the most interesting English translation of Guillén's early poems, *Cuba Libre*, has not yet been reissued.

Similarly, the early 1970s witnessed the publication of several important anthologies of "black" poetry and prose fiction, starting with Rosa E. Valdés Cruz's *La poesía negroide en América* (1970), which was followed by three other collections in 1972: Hortensia Ruiz del Vizo's *Black Poetry of the Americas* and her *Poesía negra del caribe y otras areas*; Enrique Noble's *Literatura afro-hispanoamericana: poesía y prosa de ficción.* Stanley Cyrus's *El cuento negrista sudamericano* followed a year later. Between 1976 and 1982, six major poetry anthologies were added to this list: Jorge Luis Morales's *Poesía afroantillana y negrista: Puerto Rico, República Domínicana, Cuba*, a revised and enlarged edition of which appeared in 1981; Armando González Pérez's *Antología clave de la poesía afroamericana* (1976); José Luis González and Mónica Mansour's *Poesía negra de América*; Aurora de Albornoz and Julio Rodríguez-Luis's *Sensemayá. La poesía negra en el mundo hispanohablante* (1980), and Nicomedes Santa Cruz's *La décima en el Peru*. The writer who continues to draw most attention from critics is of course Cuba's late Poet Laureate Nicolás Guillén (there are at least a dozen book-length studies on him to date, the majority of them written since the mid-1960s). Yet there are many other poets and novelists of African descent whose work has become the focus of countless critical studies attempting to lend shape and definition to the field of Afro-Hispanic literature.

Somewhat ironically perhaps, but consistent with the US-sponsored development of Latin American studies since 1959, most of the comprehensive critical studies of Afro-Hispanic literature since the pioneering work of G. R. Coulthard and Jahnheinz Jahn in the late 1950s and early 1960s have come out of North America and, with rare exceptions, are so far available only in English: Richard Jackson's *The Black Image in Latin American Literature, Black Writers in Latin America*, and *Black Literature and Humanism in Latin America*; Marvin A. Lewis's *Afro-Hispanic Poetry, 1940–1980*; Ian I. Smart's *Central American Writers of West Indian Origin: A New Hispanic Literature*; as well as two essay collections, Miriam deCosta's *Blacks in Hispanic Literature*, and William Luis's

Voices From Under: Black Narrative in Latin America and the Caribbean.
Most notable among the Hispanic American publications in the same
category are Mónica Mansour's *La poesía negrista* and Salvador Bueno's
El negro en la novela hispanoamericana, as well as works of a more
historical and/or interdisciplinary nature, such as José Luciano Franco's
La diáspora africana en el nuevo mundo (his *Afroamérica* had already
appeared in 1961), and the collections *Négritude et Amérique Latine*
(1974) and *Africa en América Latina*, the latter edited by the eminent
Cuban historian Manuel Moreno Fraginals.

This proliferation of literary, critical, and historical works by and
about black Hispanic Americans has serious implications for the writing
of Latin American literary history today. The growing attention these
"minority" writers are receiving not only serves to remind more traditional Latin Americanists, not to mention non-specialist and even non-
academic readers of Latin American literature, that twentieth-century
Colombian literature, for instance, must include the writings of Jorge
Artel, Juan and Manuel Zapata Olivella, and Arnoldo Palacios alongside
the masterful work of Nobel Prize laureate García Márquez. Nor is it
possible any longer, given the poetry of Nicomedes Santa Cruz and
Gregorio Martínez's nationally acclaimed novel *Canto de sirena*, to
dismiss the significance of Blacks in Peruvian literature as easily as José
Carlos Mariátegui could in his 1928 *Siete ensayos de interpretación de la
realidad peruana*. Moreover, the "recovery" of eighteenth- and nineteenth-century writers, such as José Vasconcelos, "El Negrito Poeta
Mexicano" (1722?–1760?), Gabriel de la Concepción Valdés (Plácido)
(Cuba, 1804–1844), Juan Francisco Manzano (Cuba), José Manuel
Valdés (Peru, 1767–1843), Candelario Obeso (Colombia, 1849–1884), and
Martín Morúa Delgado (Cuba), all of whose writings had previously been
dismissed as imitative and generally devoid of identifiable Afro-American
traits, poses the question of there being an actual Afro-Hispanic literary
tradition and, in turn, of the possible existence of a "black discourse" or
"black aesthetic" in Latin America. Yet even if it is exceedingly difficult,
and arguably not even desirable, to construct a unified tradition of Afro-
Hispanic writing that might become the basis for a separate canon, Afro-
Americanist critics, no less increasingly than their Latin Americanist
colleagues, will nevertheless have to take notice of a substantial body of
Afro-Hispanic texts before making general theoretical and/or historical
claims about their New World literatures. These are certainly timely
reminders that neither "majority" nor "minority" canons are as stable as
they are often made to appear.

While no official consensus on the specific parameters of Afro-Hispanic
literature has as yet been established, critical emphases on cultural
authenticity suggest a privileging of racial identification that was much

less of a concern among earlier intellectuals who conflated racial with nationalistic issues even as they distinguished between "inside" and "outside" perspectives. For the most part, then, the authenticating rhetoric adopted today by Afro-Hispanist criticism largely reflects the legacy of the Black Power and Black Arts movements of the immediate North American past, as well as the ideology of the Francophone Négritude groups. The tendency to separate specific works by black writers from the rest of Hispanic American literature and place them within a diasporic, pan-African context resoundingly echoes the cultural nationalism of the 1960s and the equation of the fight against (neo)colonialism in Africa (as well as in Latin America) with the civil rights struggles of North American Blacks. Harold Cruse's influential essay "An Afro-American's Cultural view," published in *Présence Africaine* in 1958, the year after the proclamation of a free Ghana, the Montgomery Bus Boycott, and the desegregation battles in Little Rock, Arkansas, announced a new direction for the artistic projects of Afro-Americans, rejecting the established conception of Negro culture as part and parcel of the American experience. The ensuing controversy over assimilation versus separate identities marked the beginning of a radical redefinition of Afro-American literature in terms of an emerging pan-African vision, a reorientation that initially led writers like LeRoi Jones (soon to rename himself Imamu Amiri Baraka) to denounce the work of previous generations of black American writers as inauthentic, as "Uncle Tom"-ish, identifying instead with the content and spirit of the world revolution. Interestingly, the essay in which Jones traces his incipient radicalization to a visit to Cuba in July 1960, is entitled "Cuba Libre" (1960; in *Home*, 1966).

At the core of this reinvention of Afro-American literature in the United States, as manifest especially in "the new black poetry" of the mid to late 1960s and in the impatience to translate ideological positions into aesthetic principles, is the conceptual need for projecting a unified cultural identity, a kinship based on a shared "black experience" or an "identity of passions." In principle, this is quite similar to the desire for cultural unity that characterizes the mainstream of modern Latin American literature. Clearly, the concept of culture that informs modern Latin American literature implicitly endorses beliefs in cultural bonds established by shared languages. Yet, taken at face value, rather than as a literary mystification, that concept of culture obscures, rather than reveals, the sociopolitical realities of the various Latin American countries, from their intricate and quite rigid caste systems masked by myths of racial democracy to the controversies over Cuban cultural politics that, in the early 1970s, shattered the ideological consensus of the *Boom* years. If such literary projections of a unified Latin American culture must be regarded as acts of self-deception, albeit necessary ones, then any concept of a unified culture governing Afro-Hispanic literature has to be viewed in much the same way. Born at a time of political crisis and dissent among Latin American intellectuals, the very idea of Afro-Hispanic (as opposed to *negrista*) literature testifies precisely to, if anything, the absence of any solid link between language, literature, and culture in Latin America, to the fact that what appear to be languages in common are not reliable indicators of shared cultural values and practices. Such necessary insistence on cultural heterogeneity, combined with the fact that many of the writers in what is, for all intents and purposes, the domain of Afro-Hispanic literature are neither Blacks nor mulattoes, can only compromise the formation of an Afro-Hispanic literary canon, at least one based on race as a guarantor of cultural authenticity. However, by doing so, it brings into focus conflicts between ideological necessities and literary practice that can (and must) be examined from a historical perspective. The remainder of this essay, then, is devoted not to establishing a new literary canon but to charting specific historical developments, with particular emphasis on *negrista* poetry and fiction during and since the 1920s and 1930s, as well as on the more recent rise of the Afro-Hispanic novel.

While the recent interest in Afro-Hispanic literature is a direct result of the political and literary vanguards of the 1960s, it is also part of a much broader historical context. After all, Blacks appeared in the chronicles of the Discovery and Conquest of the New World almost from the very start. The first literary representations of Africans in Hispanic America can be traced back to two epic poems: Alonso de Ercilla y Zúñiga's *La araucana* (1569–1594?) and Silvestre de Balboa's *Espejo de paciencia* (1608), to the latter of which Carpentier alludes in *Concierto barroco* (1974) by making the character Filomeno a descendant of Balboa's heroic slave Salvador Golomón. The literary and critical ventures of the 1970s and 1980s owe as much to earlier periods as to the more immediate past: the debts to the so-called Afro-Antillean or *negrista* movement during the 1920s and early 1930s, and to the nineteenth-century anti-slavery novel in Cuba, are amply acknowledged in many contemporary Afro-Hispanic texts, as well as in the form of substantial numbers of reprinted works from these periods. That Cuban publishing houses such as Casa de las Américas have – as William Luis stresses in his introduction to *Voices From Under* – been instrumental in the promotion of Afro-Hispanic cultures seems consistent with the role Cuban writers and intellectuals have played, since the early nineteenth century, but especially during the 1920s and 1930s, in denouncing racial prejudice and emphasizing the African contributions to American cultures, in the context of their resistance first to Spanish colonialism and later to US military, economic, and cultural imperialism.

If, in 1893, José Martí had issued a hopeful call for racial integration ("Mi raza"), by the turn of the century racial discrimination in Cuba was again on the rise. Racism was fostered in part by the US occupation of the island from 1898 to 1902, when military units were segregated for the first time in Cuban history. Moreover, job discrimination in both the sugar and, especially, the tobacco industries, whose prosperity attracted large numbers of white Hispanic immigrants as well as black workers from Haiti and Jamaica, did much to increase racial tensions. In 1902, the same year that the Platt Amendment made Cuba a virtual protectorate of the United States and a general strike was organized to protest against such discriminatory hiring practices, a group of university-educated black professionals successfully petitioned the government of Tomás Estrada Palma to ban *comparsas* and other forms of Afro-American public performance. The Partido Independiente de Color (PIC) was founded in response to the 1908 elections when, despite both parties' promises to end racial inequality, not a single black politician was elected to office. Ironically, the PIC was outlawed in 1910 mainly due to the efforts of Martín Morúa Delgado, the only person of color ever to become president of the Cuban senate. However, by far the worst confrontation occurred two years later: the government of José Miguel Gómez brutally crushed race riots in Oriente and Havana when faced with the threat of US military intervention. It also banned the secret society of the *ñáñigos* (black mutual protection societies).

During these early years of the Cuban republic, the criminologist/ethnographer Fernando Ortiz (1881–1969) began to explore Havana's "black underworld" and its history. Ortiz's plentiful work was in fact instrumental in promoting Afro-Cuban folklore among Cuban intellectuals. By the mid-1920s, when *ñañiguísmo* had been revived, the Cuban Communist Party and the National Workers' Union (CNOC) had been founded, and Machado had ascended to power, Ortiz, whose initial motives had been to gather scientific support for racist beliefs, had published dozens of articles and three important studies, *Hampa afrocubana: los negros brujos, Los esclavos negros,* and *Glosario de afronegrismos.* He had also founded the Society for the Study of Cuban Folklore, with *Archivos del Folklore Cubano* (1924) as its official organ. All this, combined with the launching of journals such as *Revista de Avance* and *Atuei* by the "grupo minorista," as well as the notes of social protest that began to sound in the poetry of Agustín Acosta, Felípe Pichardo Moya, Lino Novás Calvo, Regino Pedrozo, Félix Pita Rodríguez, and others, between 1926 and 1928, prepared the ground for "Afro-Cubanism" at a time when the mulatto middle class distanced itself from the "uncultured" masses of black laborers whom they perceived as an insult to Cuban civilization.

Although the political situation in Puerto Rico had changed little since Congress's ratification of the Foraker Law in 1900, there was much less opposition to US imperialist ventures. In fact, between 1920 and 1930, all of Puerto Rico's political parties (including the Socialists!) were in favor of Americanization. At the same time, however, "Los seis," a small group of Puerto Rican *modernista* [modernist] writers whose pro-independence sentiments were quite similar to those of Cuba's "minoristas," began to turn to social and racial issues as part of their war on romantic poetry. Even though Luis Llorens Torres (1876–1944) had included a handful of poems about Blacks in his *Sonetos sinfónicos*, the first writer to popularize *poesía negra* in Puerto Rico was Luis Palés Matos (1898–1959), an active member of "Los seis." His early *negrista* poems, "Pueblo negro" and "Danza negra" (possibly inspired by Vachel Lindsay's "The Congo" and by the famous Cuban reciter Eusebia Cosme, who visited Puerto Rico in 1925), appeared in *La Democracia* in 1926 – incidentally, the same year in which Langston Hughes published his influential manifesto "The Negro Artist and the Racial Mountain" in *The Nation*. *La Democracia* also published Pedro J. Brull's "Canto a la negra" in 1927 and Palés's "Canción festiva para ser llorada" in 1928. Palés's "Danza caníbal" appeared in *Poliedro* in 1927. However, the journals that devoted most attention to racial matters were the newly founded *Hostos*, followed by *Indice* which printed "Falsa canción de Baquiné" (1929), "Bombo" (1930), "Elegía del duque de la mermelada" (1930), and "Ñam-ñam" (1931).

In 1928, the conservative *Diario de la Marina*, organ of all anti-nationalist causes and foreign interests in Cuba, and at that time the daily with the largest circulation in the island, printed a public announcement of the founding of the Ku Klux Klan in Camagüey. Only a few months later, Gustavo E. Urrutia's "Ideales de una raza" made its first appearance in the Sunday literary supplement that the paper had carried since 1926. While it is difficult to define an exact starting point for what is now called the Afro-Antillean movement, given that Alfonso Camín's "Elogio de la negra" had appeared in 1925 and several of Palés's poems in 1926, it is safe to say that this modest one-page, presumably unpolitical forum for black culture – which would be discontinued at the beginning of 1931 because, ironically, it was too political – was the first major exponent of *negrismo* and its manifestations in literature, music, and painting. In addition to the column "Armonías," in which Urrutia, despite his initial disclaimer, commented openly on social, economic, and political issues pertaining to Cuban Blacks, "Ideales" published articles on Afro-American history and culture in Cuba, the United States, Colombia, and elsewhere, along with translations from the work of W. E. B. du Bois and Aténor Firmin, and also provided weekly bibliographies devoted to black authors. It spotlighted the work of black Cuban painters and sculptors such as Jaime Valls, Hernando Cárdenas, Teodoro Ramos, Crispín Herrera Jiménez, Pastor Argudín y Pidrozo, and Andrés Alvarez Naranjo, many of whom lived in Paris at the time; reported on the international successes of composers Amadeo Roldán and Alejandro García Caturla, as well as the visits to Havana by Langston Hughes and Federico García Lorca; and it printed *negrista* short fiction by Tomás Savignón (for example, "El bongó,") and Gonzalo Mazas Carballo. However, perhaps most importantly, it, like the literary supplement edited by José Antonio Fernández de Castro, regularly featured *poesía negra*: Ildefonso Pereda Valdés's "Canción de cuna para dormir un negrito" and "La guitarra de los negros" (from *Raza negra*, reviewed in *Revista Bimestre Cubana* that same year); Palés's "Danza negra," which was reprinted twice, in 1927 and 1930; Hughes's "I, Too" and several other poems translated by Fernández de Castro; Ramón Guirao's "Bailadora de rumba," and many other poems by José Manuel Poveda, Regino Boti, Regino Pedrozo, the Panamanian Rogelio Sinán, and, above all, Nicolás Guillén.

Although Guillén (1902–1989) had published at least six poems in *El Diario de la Marina* by 1930, including his "Pequeña oda a Kid Chocolate" (later entitled "Pequeña oda a un negro boxeador cubano"), and, like Alejo Carpentier, regularly contributed articles to "Ideales," nothing equaled the scandalous success of his eight *Motivos de son* (April 1930; three further "Motivos" appeared in July of the same year). Not even Tallet's "La rumba," published in *Atuei* in 1928 and the immediate object of controversy because of its overtly sexual language, had elicited this kind of a response. Guillén was showered with praise by Juan Marinello, Fernando Ortiz, and others who admired the poems' compelling rhythms, and Urrutia exultantly called *Motivos* the only authentic Negro poems ever written in Cuba. Others, including Ramón Vasconcelos and, especially, the mulatto bourgeoisie of Havana's Club Atenas which made up most of the readership of "Ideales," were skeptical, even offended, voicing strong reservations about the propriety of Guillén's poetic use of the vernacular of Havana's poor Blacks in conjunction with the dance form of the *son*. Although the *son*, descended from the famous "Son de la Ma Teodora" (presumably dating back to 1580) and popularized in the 1920s and 1930s by Eliseo Grenet ("Papa Montero") and particularly Miguel Matamoros ("Son de la loma," "La mujer de Antonio"), had by then achieved respectability, its transformation into a literary form was quite a different matter with disturbing implications. While Guillén had already developed something of a reputation as an opponent of the

Machado regime due to his journalistic work with Urrutia, his budding political radicalism had never before entered his poetry in such an explicit fashion.

Guillén's *poemas-son* [*son*-poems] were daring literary experiments in more ways than one. Not only did they emphasize the African contributions to Cuban culture (the *son* is a formal synthesis of Spanish, African, and *taíno* [Arawak] elements), thus indirectly and uncomfortably posing the question of Cuba's national identity. They also, in the voice of black characters descended from those portrayed in anti-slavery novels such as Cirilo Villaverde's *Cecilia Valdés* (1882), addressed unsettling issues: racial shame is targeted in "Negro bembón" ["Thick-Lipped Negro"], "Mulata," and "Ayé me dijeron negro" ["Yesterday Someone Called Me a Negro"], for which Guillén substituted "Hay que tené boluntá" ["One Must Have Willpower"] in later editions of *Motivos*. Poverty, prostitution, and economic injustice are criticized in "Si tú supiera" ["If You Knew"], "Búcate plata" ["Get Some Money"], and "Curujey," and United States imperialism in "Tú no sabe inglé" ["You Don' Know No English"]. Such volatile topics made these *sones* very different from García Lorca's enthusiastic "Son de los negros en Cuba," which was published in *Musicalia* that same April. To many, Guillén's poems amounted to washing Cuba's dirty laundry in public, a charge to which Guillén himself alludes in his tongue-in-cheek "Epístola" [Epistle] to fellow poet Eliseo Diego in *El diario que a diario* [*The Daily Daily*].

However, such criticisms only furthered Guillén's fame. *Motivos* appeared as a booklet soon after its initial publication and was set to music in its entirety by Amadeo Roldán (1900–1939). Alejandro García Caturla, a student of Pedro Sanjuán and Nadia Boulanger who had made a name for himself in Europe with "Danza lucumí," "Danza del tambor," and Carpentier's "Liturgia," completed the music for only two Motivos. The first to compose symphonies with Afro-Cuban themes and rhythms (many inspired by *ñáñigo* ceremonies), and to incorporate on a regular basis typical Cuban percussion instruments in their performance, Roldán had previously collaborated with Carpentier on two ballets/suites, *La rebambaramba* (1928) and *El milagro de Anaquillé* (1929). Both earned him an international reputation: *La rebambaramba*, for example, was performed in Mexico, Paris, Berlin, and California in the early 1930s. Roldán had also written the music for Palés's "Danza negra" (1928). It is quite possible that Roldán's early pieces, especially *Tres pequeños poemas*, partly inspired the poetic use of Afro-Cuban rhythms. The *Motivos* were completed in 1933 and first performed in New York in 1934. Two pieces were performed in Havana in 1937, but the whole set not until 1959.

In 1931 a lottery prize enabled Guillén to print another collection of fifteen "mulatto poems" whose title was derived from the final lines of "Si tú supiera": *Sóngoro cosongo. Poemas mulatos*. In this collection, whose lack of tightness and unity may well be taken as an expression of Cuba's social, political, and cultural fragmentation, Guillén continues his critical examination of social, especially racial, topics, for instance, in "Llegada" ["Arrival"] (clearly an antecedent of his 1954 family elegy "El apellido" ["My Last Name"]), "Canción del Bongó" ["Song of the Bongo Drum"], "Canto negro" ["Black Chant"], "Rumba," "Velorio de Papa Montero" ["Wake for Papa Montero"], "Secuestro de la mujer de Antonio" ["Abduction of Antonio's Woman"], "Pregón" ["Street Cry"], and "Organillo" ["Barrel Organ"]. Guillén offers his poetics of *mestizaje* in resistance to "yanqui" imperialism in the Caribbean, which he explicitly targets in the epigrammatic "Caña" ["Cane"]. This anti-imperialism becomes the main project of *West Indies, Ltd*. and, in fact, most of Guillén's subsequent poems.

The desire for more than nominal national independence was a major catalyst for Afro-Antilleanism, particularly because the ever-present threat of US military intervention had been successfully invoked by a number of Cuban presidents to manipulate the island's internal politics, especially with regard to race issues. However, if the *negrista* work of Ballagas, Guirao, Tallet, Carpentier, Palés, and others cannot be separated from the fight against US imperialism any more than the politically more aggressive poems by Guillén, Arozarena, Boti, and Pedrozo can, the impact on these writers of the "vogue nègre" that swept post-war Europe is equally undeniable. France and Germany's "re-discovery" of non-Western cultures, especially those of Africa, began during the final quarter of the nineteenth century with the wholesale "transferral" of African art objects, primarily sculptures, to museums in London, Paris, Berlin, Leipzig, Dresden, and Brussels. It coincided with a crisis in the visual arts that made painters such as Picasso, Matisse, and Juan Gris (and, to a lesser extent, Kandinski, Modigliani, and Marc) more receptive to African aesthetics. Escalated by the First World War, this modernist crisis, fueled by the work of ethnographers Leo Frobenius and Maurice Delafosse and conceptualized by Oswald Spengler's *The Decline of the West* (1918 and 1919–1922), spread to other areas of artistic representation, especially music (Dvořak, Bartok, Stravinsky) and poetry (Blaise Cendrars, Guillaume Apollinaire, Philippe Soupault, Paul Morand, André Gide). In Latin America, Spenglerian ideas were disseminated mainly through José Ortega y Gasset's *Revista de Occidente*, which also published a translation of Leo Frobenius's *The Black Decameron* (1910) in 1925. Spengler's work was reviewed in the *Revista Bimestre Cubana* the following year.

Yet even before the convergence of ethnographic, aesthetic, and political concerns gave rise to *negrismo* in the Hispanic Caribbean, Afro-

American intellectuals such as Aténor Firmin (*De l'égalité des races humaines*, 1855) and Hannibal Price (*De la réhabilitation de la race noire par le peuple d'Haiti*, 1900) in the French Antilles, as well as W. E. B. du Bois in the United States (*The Souls of Black Folk*, 1903), had initiated "image renovations" that, combined with the advent of Garveyism (1915), culminated in the Harlem Renaissance and Négritude movements. It is also worth noting that René Maran's novel *Batouala* (1921), an important precursor of French West Indian Négritude, appeared in Spanish during the same year it was first published. Afro-Antilleanism's immediate literary antecedents in Hispanic America were poems such as Diego Vicente Tejera's "Dos niños" (1876), Rubén Darío's "La negra Dominga" (1892), Llorens Torres's "El negro" (1914), and Felipe Pichardo Moya's "La comparsa" (1916). Although these and other poems attempted to portray blacks sympathetically, they nevertheless perpetuated the representational conventions of a discursive tradition that ranges from the slavetraders' travelogues and the Enlightenment's exotic "noble savages" to the romantic paternalism of the nineteenth-century anti-slavery novels and pseudo-scientific theories of race. As an avant-garde "movement" that, on the one hand, belonged squarely in the context of Cubism, Fauvism, Futurism, Dadaism, Surrealism, and, especially, Hispanic American *Modernismo* [Modernism] while, on the other, it was deeply entrenched in contemporaneous national struggles for decolonization, Afro-Antilleanism was a conceptual and political battleground. This literary movement was not unified by an aesthetic program, but was made up of many different historical legacies and conflicting political goals.

Little is gained, then, by pursuing the controversy over whether Afro-Antilleanism was indeed an indigenous movement committed to "humanizing" racist stereotypes or whether it was an imported literary fad. Criticizing white *negrista* poets for their "circumstantial tourism," as Guillén himself has done on several occasions (see his *Prosa de prisa*), while privileging writers of African descent for their presumably more "authentic" portrait of Blacks may help consolidate present ideological positions, but it also dehistoricizes and depoliticizes both the issue and the literature. Such a perspective also disregards the fact that the poetry of Afro-Antilleanism, no matter how conservative and "inauthentic" it may seem today, did set an important precedent for writers from other Hispanic American countries. In that regard, it is quite significant that, with the exception of Guillén's first two books of poems, all the major volumes of *poesía negra*, as well as its only novel, Carpentier's *¡Ecué-Yamba-O!* (1933), were published when Afro-Antilleanism was already on the decline: Pedrozo's *Nosotros* appeared in 1933, Ballagas's *Cuaderno de poesía negra*, Guirao's *Bongó*, Gómez Kemp's *Acento negro*, and

Guillén's *West Indies, Ltd.* (in many ways a transitional text that includes few *negrista* poems) in 1934. Palés's *Tuntún de pasa y grifería*, although completed by September 1933, was not published until 1937, the same year that saw the first issue of *Estudios Afrocubanos*, the official organ of the Sociedad de Estudios Afrocubanos Contra los Racismos, founded by Ortiz and others in 1936; and two major anthologies, Ballagas's *Antología de la poesía negra hispanoamericana* and Guirao's *Orbita de la poesía afrocubana 1928–1937*, were not published until 1935 and 1938, respectively. José Sanz y Díaz's *Lira negra* and Ballagas's *Mapa de la poesía negra americana* appeared even later, in 1945 and 1946.

What these dates show is not so much a continuation of *negrismo* in Cuba and Puerto Rico, but the broader dissemination of texts written during the late 1920s and early 1930s, whose initial impact had been mostly in the Caribbean region (and in Europe), and not so much in other Hispanic American countries. This would explain why *poesía negra* written outside the Caribbean did not really begin to flourish until the late 1930s. Most notable among the continental Afro-Hispanic poets who began to publish in the wake of Afro-Antilleanism are the Peruvians Enrique López Albújar (1872–1966) and Nicomedes Santa Cruz Gamarra (b. 1925), the Colombians Jorge Artel (b. 1909), Hugo Salazar Valdés (b. 1926), and Juan Zapata Olivella (b. 1922), the Uruguayans Virginia Brindis de Salas and Pilar Barrios (b. 1889), and the Ecuadorians Adalberto Ortiz (b. 1914) and Nelson Estupiñán Bass (b. 1912).

De la tierra brava. Poemas afroyungas (1938) by López Albújar who is best known for his 1928 novel *Matalaché*, largely continues the *indigenista* Regionalism of his *Cuentos andinos* (1920). Yet it also includes several poems, such as "La abuela gloriosa" and "El culén," that thematize racial mixing in Peru, a country in which only an estimated 1 percent of the population is identifiable as black (*afroyunga* or *chinachola* refers to *mestizos* of black and Indian ancestry). Whereas López Albújar's formal experiments rarely extend beyond the occasional use of vernacular speech (in "¿Jura, china?"), his fellow-countryman Nicomedes Santa Cruz is a veritable virtuoso, Peru's foremost literary *decimero* and the only Peruvian writer who has consistently cultivated black expressive forms. The *décima* is a form of oral poetry that consists of four octosyllabic ten-line stanzas with the rhyme scheme "abbaaccddc," usually preceded by a quartet upon which the rest of the poem elaborates and improvises (*décima glosada* or *décima de pie forzado*). It is traditionally accompanied by guitar music (*socabón*). Practiced in Peru and elsewhere since the early sixteenth century (see the "Verdadera relación de la conquista del Peru," from 1534, included in Santa Cruz's *La décima en el Peru*), the *décima* was relegated in the nineteenth century to the central and northern coastal areas, and, from the second half of the nineteenth century to the early decades of the twentieth, *décimas* were cultivated mainly by the black population. By the 1940s, urban migration and the deaths of Mariano González and Hijinio Matías Quintana, two of the region's greatest *decimeros*, brought this popular poetry to the verge of extinction.

Although Santa Cruz started writing *décimas* as early as 1949, his first books of poems were not published until the late 1950s and early 1960s: *Décimas* (1959, a small private edition, then again in 1960), *Cumanana*, and *Canto a mi Peru*. A 1968 recording of his poetry, *Canto negro* (Lima, FTA) made Santa Cruz known to audiences outside Peru, which resulted in the publication of two anthologies, *Ritmos negros del Peru* and *Décimas y poemas*. The themes of Santa Cruz's *décimas* vary greatly: they range from traditional religious topics ("Lo divino") to social and historical matters ("Lo humano"). The latter category includes satirical and humorous commentaries on everything from love to politics: "Talara, no digas 'yes'," for instance, takes up the cause of the campaign for the nationalization of oil, while "Nochemala" condemns the events of Christmas 1964, when fifty-nine Peruvian miners were killed due to the negligence of a US engineer. Yet other *décimas* deal with the 1879 Pacific War between Peru and Chile. However, Santa Cruz's most frequent reference point is Peru's black population, their history ("Ritmos negros del Peru"), their language ("En la era colonial," "Juan Bemba"), their daily activities. A number of poems ridicule mulattoes who try to hide their black ancestry ("La Pelona," "Hay negra y negra retinta," "De inga y mandinga"). Racial shame as a topic in Afro-Hispanic literature dates back to Plácido's satirical poem "Que se lo cuente a su abuela" (1842). It is also the subject of a number of plays, notably *Sangre azul* (1948) and *Dientes blancos* by the Ecuadorian Demetrio Aguilera Malta, *El color de nuestra piel* (1952) by Celestino Gorostiza, and, more recently, Francisco Arriví's trilogy *Máscara puertorriqueña* (1971).

While the vast majority of Santa Cruz's poems use the traditional *décima* form, he has also written a significant number of pieces on more international topics that employ a wide range of different poetic styles: "Congo libre," "Johannesburgo," "Sudáfrica" (all from 1960), and "Madre Angloa: el retorno," one of his 1976 poems about Angola. "Panalivio," dedicated to Guillén, as was "Johannesburgo," approximates the *son* form to denounce racism and economic exploitation. These targets recur in "Muerte en el ring," a poem about the boxer Benny "Kid" Paret and reminiscent of Guillén's "Pegueña oda a un negro boxeador cubano," and in "De igual a igual," dedicated to George Wallace, "king of racism and governor of Alabama." The poem that invariably closes most of the above collections is "América Latina," which appropriately sums up Santa Cruz's literary and political vision in the neologisms

"Indoblanquinegros / Blanquinegrindios / y negrindoblancos," parallel in their construction to the titles of two poems by Marcelino Arozarena, "Negramaticantillana" (1953) and "Cubandalucia" (1957), both included in *Canción negra sin color*. Santa Cruz has done for the Peruvian *décima* what Guillén did for the Cuban *son*, but his leftist politics have marginalized him in inverse proportion to Guillén's popularity.

Artel, of the same generation as Guillén and often grouped with Afro-Antillean poets, takes an equally strong interest in the poetic possibilities of dance, music, and folklore. *Tambores en la noche: 1931–1934* begins with a section of fifteen poems devoted entirely to Afro-Colombian culture: in addition to invoking the percussive rhythm of the *cumbia*, a dance that combines Indian and African elements ("La cumbia"), Artel focuses on the "flancos inquietantes" ["disquieting thighs"] and "belleza demente" ["demented beauty"] of the mulatta (in "¡Danza mulata!" and "Romance mulata") and celebrates the sensuality of black women (in "Barrio abajo," "Bullerengue," and "Sensualidad negra"). Other poems, such as "Tambores en la noche," "La voz de los ancestros," "Mr. Davi," and "Velorio del boga ausente" – clearly a reference to Candelario Obeso's famous "Cancion del boga ausente" from *Cantos populares de mi tierra* – express a nostalgic longing for a mythic Africa that in the end gives way to a reconciliation of ethnic and personal identities in "Mi canción" and "Canción imposible." The latter two poems may be read as preludes to the social poetry of *Poemas con botas y banderas* – published in 1972, the same year as Guillén's *La rueda dentada* and *El diario que a diario* – and to his *Antología poética*. In addition to previously published poems such as "Este duro salitre que se extiende en mi pecho," which invokes Chile's Salvador Allende as a symbol of political resistance, the anthology also contains seventeen new poems. Many of these, including "Mapa de Africa," "Noche de Choco," "Isla de Baru," and "Palenque," return to African and Afro-American myth and history but are much more vehement in their denunciation of slavery and colonialism than previous ones.

Like *Tambores en la noche*, Juan Zapata Olivella's *Panacea: poesía liberada*, one of the five volumes of poetry he published in the 1970s, devotes a whole section to Afro-Colombian history and culture. *Bullanguero: poesía popular* is an interesting compilation of earlier pieces that includes a handful of *negrista* poems, notably "Eugenesia," whose opening,

> ¿Qué quires, negro bembón?
> ¿que a tí te dá yo mi amó?
>
> [What you want, liver-lipped negro?
> That I give you my lovin'?]

echoes Guillén's "Negro bembón" as much as the revolutionary "híbrido tropical / coctel de razas" ["tropical hybrid / Cocktail of races"] in "Aristocracia criolla" evokes some of the Cuban's later poems. In *Panacea*, "La negra Catalina," "La negrita Claridá," and especially "Negra modelo" carefully avoid sexual stereotypes of black women. Their portraits combine with more folkloric motifs ("Tambores caribeños") and references to Zapata Olivella's unsuccessful bid for the Colombian presidency in the mid-1970s ("El negro sale a votá," "Los negros tienen candidato") as the author attempts to forge a racial and cultural equilibrium. The project of *La hamaca soñadora: poemarios infantiles* could be described in Ralph Ellison's words as "teach it to the younguns," and has as its counterpart Guillén's "Poema con niños" (from *El son entero*).

Salazar Valdés, of the same generation as Zapata Olivella, has published no less than ten volumes of poetry since the late 1940s. While his first *negrista* poems date back to the early 1950s (see the collection *Toda la voz*), his recent *Rostro iluminado del Chocó* actually contains the largest number of poems on black themes. Others can be found in *Pleamar*. Similar to *Dimensiones de la tierra* in its regionalist focus on Salazar Valdés's native Chocó, *Rostro* presents exotic mulattas ("Mulata") and women "dark as Chinese ink" who dance to the rhythms of the *cumbia* and the "tin tan, tin tan, tin tan" of kettle drums ("La negra María Teresa," "Baile negro"). Sexuality, it would seem from these poems, is always African. Meditations on cultural ambivalence, for instance in "El mulato," a poem somewhat reminiscent of "Canción introspectiva" from *Carbones en el alba* (1951), are accompanied by picturesque accounts of Afro-Colombian fiestas and religious ceremonies ("Las fiestas," "El velorio," "San Pancho"). Given that Colombia is one of the few Hispanic American countries with a politically organized black population (since 1975), Salazar Valdés's sexual and racial stereotypes seem curiously anachronistic. This may well account for the fact that, despite the impressive number of his publications, he is much less renowned than either Artel or Juan Zapata Olivella.

Poesía negra in Uruguay, after the publication of Pereda Valdés's *La guitarra de los negros* and *Raza negra*, flourished mainly in a few black-sponsored journals, the most important of which are *Nuestra Raza* (1917; 1933–1948), *Rumbos* (1938–1945; 1948–1950), and *Revista Bahia Hulán Jack* (launched in 1958). For some black poets such as Julio Guadalupe, Carlos Cardozo Ferreira, and Juan Julio Arrascaeta, these journals were the only outlet for their work. Others, notably Virginia Brindis de Salas and Pilar Barrios, were more fortunate in gaining support. The first major book of poems by an Afro-Uruguayan writer, Brindis de Salas's *Pregón de marimorena*, later to be followed by *Cien cárceles de amor*, is in many ways indebted to Guillén's *poesía negra*, both in its thematic focus on the street vendor Black Mary and other working-class figures and in its formal adaptations of *pregones* (street cries), *tangos*, and *madrigales*. Similarly, the call for multi-ethnic continental solidarity under "una bandera / de un sólo color" ["a banner of a single color"], issued in "A la ribera americana," closely parallels the pan-Caribbean vision of *West Indies, Ltd*. While Barrios's early poems are not as explicitly concerned with racial and social issues, the poems of *Piel negra. Poesías (1917–1947)* do not merely pay homage to "tireless fighters" like Guillén and Langston Hughes ("Nicolás Guillén," "Voces"). They also draw attention to the participation of Blacks in Uruguay's wars for independence from Brazil which began in 1825 (in "La leyenda maldita"), the persistence of racism since the abolition of slavery in 1853 (in "¡Negra!" and "Raza negra"), and the tenuousness of racial divisions (in "La lección del abuelo"). Barrios, it ought to be added, was not only editor of *Nuestra Raza* but also one of the founders of the Partido Autóctono Negro in 1937 which, though not legally banned like its earlier Cuban counterpart, suffered a humiliating defeat in the 1938 elections and finally disbanded in 1944.

Novelist-poets Ortiz and Estupiñán Bass, both natives of Esmeraldas, the predominantly black coastal province in northern Ecuador, are among the most prolific of Hispanic American writers of African descent. Unlike the largely neglected work of their Peruvian and Uruguayan colleagues, their writing has been amply supported and promoted by the Casa de Cultura Ecuatoriana, and they are widely recognized as integral parts of Ecuador's national literary tradition. In addition, both have held influential government posts. Ortiz, who is also a naive painter of some repute, published his first poems in Guayaquíl's *El Telégrafo* in 1940. He rose to prominence with his prize-winning novel *Juyungo. Historia de un negro, una isla y otros negros* and has since published several collections of short stories, two more novels, and four books of poetry, including the anthology *El animal herido*. Of the first two volumes of poems, *Camino y puerto de la angustia* and *Tierra, son y tambor*, both initially published in Mexico in 1945, only the latter, reprinted in Ecuador three times (in 1953, 1959, and 1973), is devoted to what Ortiz himself calls *poesía negrista*. Divided into "Cantares negros" and "Cantares mulatos," the poems' themes range from Africa and the slave trade ("Breve historia nuestra," "Contribución," "Romance de la llamada"), and the more contemporary exploitation of Ecuadorian Blacks on the rubber and banana plantations ("Son del trópico"), to Esmeraldan folklore and legend as well as addressing questions of cultural identity posed by a history of miscegenation. Many of the poems in the latter two categories are formally indebted to Guillén, Palés Matos, and Ballagas, whom Ortiz has named as major influences on his poetry. Ortiz's many vernacular poems – notably

"Canción del pescador del río" with its refrain "yo cro que sí" ["I think so"] and the mother's voice in "Antojo," alternating with the daughter's pathetic lament, "¡Ay, mama, yo quiero un blanco! / Un blanco yo quiero, mama" ["Oh, mama, I love a white man, / a white man I love, mama"] – pay homage to Guillén's *Motivos*, as does the "tragic" mulatta in "¿Que tendrá la Soledad?" "Contra'e culebra" specifically recalls Guillén's "Sensemayá. Canto para matar una culebra" (from *West Indies, Ltd.*), "La tunda, tunda que entunda," and "La tunda para el negrito," which also anticipate the stories of *La entundada y cuentos variados* and Guillén's "Balada del güije" from the same volume. "Sobre tu encuentro" evokes "La balada de los dos abuelos," while the set "Mosongo y la niña blanca," "Mosongo y la niña negra," "Mosongo y la iña china" refers back to Ballagas's "Para dormira un negrito" and similar poems. On the other hand, the percussive *jitanjáforas* "¡Talambó, talambó!" (from "Faena y paisaje") and "taca-taca tómb. . . tucu, tucu, túnn" echo Palés's "Danza negra," and the sexually charged "Sinfonía bárbara" is reminiscent of Ballagas's "Comparsa habanera." While the more recent poems of *Fórmulas*, like the metafiction of Ortiz's last two novels, constitute a break with the *negrista* genre, reprinted in this last volume is also an enlarged version of *Tierra* with several new *negrista* poems from the early 1970s: "Invocación," "Consuelo," "Arrullo," and "Negritud con bembosidades." Similarly, the chaotic presence of the "Anima sola," whom Ortiz identifies as the West African trickster god Legba, among the narrative voices in *La envoltura del sueño* attests to Ortiz's continued, though more subtle, mixing of African and European cultural references and forms.

In addition to seven novels and some short fiction, Estupiñán Bass has to his credit several volumes of poetry, the first of which is *Canto negro por la luz. Poemas para negros y blancos*. Now editor of the journal *Meridiano Negro*, he wrote the first Peruvian *negrista* poem, "Canto a la negra quinceañera," published in the socialist paper *la Tierra* in 1934. His preoccupation with lyric portraits of black women continues in the love poems that make up the first section of *Canto negro*. The women we vicariously encounter in "La gualanga," "Negra bullanguera," "Lola Matamba," and even "Tú sabías" are all-too-familiar sexual stereotypes, hip-swaying enchantresses whose elastic bodies smell of cypress nuts, sway in the afternoon breeze, and are juicy like rubber trees. They are not very different from their Caribbean predecessors María Belén Chacón and Rita Barranco. In the second section, however, these images give way to several poems about racial and class consciousness: "Carta al soldado," evocative of Guillén's *Cantos para soldados*; "Rabia"; "Canción del niño negro y del incendio," whose assertive "Negro he sido, negro soy, / Negro vengo, negro voy" revoices the opening of Guillén's "Son número 6" (in *El son entero*); "Mensaje negro para el indio cayapa"; and the title poem, "Canto negro por la luz," whose appeal for ethnic harmony strikes many familiar notes. Formally more interesting perhaps is the popular poetry of *Timarán y Cuabú* and its more recent companion volume, *El desempate*, which place Estupiñán Bass's criticisms of Ecuadorian society in the context of his country's popular oral poetry. If the responsorial structure of these two long poems is in some ways reminiscent of the second part of the Argentinian gaucho epic *Martín Fierro*, portions of which frequently appear in anthologies of *negrista* poetry, it is in many ways even more akin to the "contrapunto" of Nicomedes Santa Cruz's *Cumanana*.

According to the bibliography included in Estupiñán Bass's *Las 2 caras de la palabra* (1981), Esmeraldan writers published twenty-eight literary works between 1960 and 1981, the majority of them poetry. Among these are also *Jolgorio, Más acá de los muertos* (1969), and *Tal como somos*, a poetic trilogy by Antonio Preciado Bedoya, whom Estupiñán Bass calls "un auténtico brujo moderno." Selections from all three volumes are included in *De sol a sol*, an anthology of Preciado's work that also contains a number of new poems. The political and artistic influence of Guillén and Aimé Césaire is acknowledged from the very start in *Jolgorio*, not only in "Un poema a Guillén," "Canto a Cuba amanecida," and "Amanecer," but also in formally more typical *negrista* poems such as "Chimbo," "Rumbera," "Bom," as well as "Matabara del hombre bueno" (from *Más acá*) and "Les toca su tambor" (from *Tal como somos*). The new poems of *De sol a sol*, among them "Carta torrencial a Nelson Estupiñán Bass," return to a more specific focus on Colombia's "Green Province." Above all, however, they testify to Preciado's contention that it is inconceivable to think of Afro-Ecuadorian literature as the exclusive province of Blacks.

Preciado (b. 1941) belongs to a new generation of Afro-Hispanic poets which, in addition to his fellow-countryman José Sosa Castillo, author of *Canciones marginadas* (1976), *Canciones comprometidas* (1977), and *Canción testimonial* (1986), also includes Cuba's Nancy Morejón, Costa Rica's Eulalia Bernard (*Ritmohéroe*), Colombia's Yvonne América Truque (*Proyección de los silencios*, 1986), and Nicaragua's David MacField (*En la calle del enmedio*, 1968; *Poemas para el año del elefante*, 1970). Like MacField, Norberto James Rawlings and Blas R. Jiménez from the Dominican Republic have both published several volumes of poetry. Rawlings's books include *Sobre la marcha* (1969), *La provincia sublevada* (1972), *Vivir* (1982), and *Hago constar* (1983), and he is best known for his prize-winning poem "Los inmigrantes" (1972). The "negritud" poet Jiménez has to his credit *Aquí. . .otro español* (1980), *Caribe africano en despertar*, and *Exigencias de un cimarrón (en sueño)* (1987), a volume that combines poetry with photography. Within the context of their native land, Rawlings and Jiménez are part of a tradition that can be traced back, through Manuel de Cabral's *12 poemas negros* (1932) and *Trópico negro* (1941), Tomás Hernández Franco's "Yélida" (1942), and six books of poetry by Juan Sánchez Lamouth from the 1950s, all the way to Juan Antonio Alix's "El negro tras de la oreja" (1883) and the popular poetry of Manuel ("Meso") Mónica. Due to their Jamaican ancestry, the Panamanians Carlos Guillermo Wilson (Cubena), Gerardo Maloney, and Carlos Russell, all of whom currently live in the United States, have strong ties to the Caribbean which they cultivate in their poetry. Both Maloney and Russell, who, like the little-known Costa Rican Alderman Johnson Roden (1893–1977), writes in English, became known in 1976, when some of their poems were printed in Panama's *Revista Nacional de Cultura* in a special issue about West Indians. Each has published one book of poems, *Juega vivo* (1984) and *Miss Anna's Son Remembers* (1976), respectively.

Although he has to date produced only one book of poetry, *Pensamientos del negro Cubena*, Cubena (b. 1941) has received far more critical attention than most of the above poets, in part because of his short stories, *Cuentos del negro Cubena* [*Short Stories by Cubena*], and his novel, *Chombo*. Cubena's poetry (as much as his fiction) is characterized by an acute sense of history and pan-Caribbean cultural identity (in "Las Américas," "Triangulispono americano"), combined with a penchant for political satire that he shares with many other contemporary Afro-Hispanic writers, specifically Guillén whom he echoes in "In exilium" and, to a lesser extent, Pedrozo whose "Hermano negro" he cites in "Invitación." What makes Cubena's often epigrammatic poems particularly distinctive, however, are the abundant references to West African cultural history as well as the modernist play with language and typography that heightens the ironic and at times sarcastic tone of many of his poems. Particularly striking in their vehement brevity are the lines "No queremos / KOCA / KOLA / KRINGA" from "Gatún," which emphatically resonate with the "Social Club of Masked Men of Kalifornia, Kalabama, and Killinois" from the short story "El bombero" ["The Fireman"]. The violent rage that permeates all of Cubena's writings and links him with the revolutionary poetry of Amiri Baraka, is only briefly alleviated by the tenderness of love poems such as "Negra preciosa," "Mulata linda," and "India encantadora."

While Cubena's reputation is steadily growing, the most prolific and widely known of the new generation of Afro-Hispanic poets remains Nancy Morejón (b. 1944), whose first volumes of poetry began to appear only a few years after the Cuban Revolution. Among these early books, *Ricardo trajo su flauta* (Havana, 1967) is of interest because of its musical references, while *Amor, ciudad atribuida* is notable both for its eroticism, which has been compared to that of Alfonsina Storni and Delmira

Agustini, and for its optimistic recastings of Aimé Césaire's surrealist vision of a Caribbean city at dawn in *Cahier d'un retour au pays natal* (1939). Although Morejón's interest in Cuba's African heritage is undeniable, her more recent poems, such as *Elogio de la danza* (1982), *Octubre imprecindible* (1983), *Piedra pulida* (1986), and especially *Cuaderno de Granada* (1984), tend to follow the path of her mentor Guillén's later social and political poetry much more than that of his *poesía negra*. Interestingly enough, and consistent with the historical legacy of Afro-Antilleanism, many of the post-revolutionary Cuban writers who have most actively cultivated a new "Afro-Cuban" poetry, characterized by a conscious avoidance of *jitanjáfora* and cursory folkloric references, are not of African descent. Among the most interesting texts in that category are Miguel Barnet's *La piedra fina y el pavo real* (1963) and his *La sagrada familia* (1967), Rolando Campíns's *Sonsonero mulato* (1969), José Sánchez-Boudy's *Alegrías de coco* (1970), and Pura del Prado's *Cola de orisha* (1972), which was inspired by Lydia Cabrera's *El monte*. With the exception of Barnet, all these writers live in exile. What is clear, however, from these and many other similar volumes of poetry, is that *poesía negra* or *negrista*, though it has necessarily changed, has not gone out of fashion in Hispanic America. To paraphrase Oscar Fernández de la Vega (*Iniciación a la poesía afro-americana*), those who would have us believe otherwise have little understanding of the poetry or the fashion.

Due partly to the international reputation of Nicolás Guillén, Afro-Hispanic poetry, especially from the Caribbean, has, until very recently, received much more attention and publicity than Afro-Hispanic narrative. On the other hand, it is also true that the early *negrista* writers produced little prose fiction. The most notable exception is Carpentier, who, in 1933, published the novella "Histoire de lunes" (in *Cahiers du Sud*, Paris) and *¡Ecue-Yamba-O!*, the "Afro-Cuban" novel he had begun in prison in 1927 shortly before he left Cuba for France. Also worth mentioning here is Lino Novás Calvo's *El negrero: vida novelada de Pedro Fernández de Trava* (1933), if only because it is one of the rare texts that present the perspective of the nineteenth-century slave trader. Lydia Cabrera's short stories, *Cuentos negros de Cuba*, did not appear until 1940, and Carpentier's "Oficio de tinieblas" (1944), "Vieja a la semilla" (1944) ["Journey Back to the Source"], "Los fugitivos" (1946), and *El reino de este mundo* (1949) [*The Kingdom of This World*] until after Ortiz's *Juyungo* had become established as the Afro-Hispanic novel *par excellence*.

While the *Peregrinación de Bartolomé Lorenzo* by Jesuit historian José de Acosta (1540–1600) would have to be cited as the most remote antecedent of the Hispanic American *negrista* narrative, the most memorable black character to appear in an early *relación* is the Celestinesque *bruja* Juana García, a free black woman whose subversive plots play an important part in Juan Rodríguez Freyle's *El carnero* (1636). Reputed to be the first American novel, *El Periquillo Sarniento* (1816) by the Mexican José Joaquín Fernández de Lizardi (1776–1827), is noteworthy here because of its explicit anti-racist stance, which promptly led to its being banned in Mexico. To elude the strict censorship practiced by colonial governments increasingly fearful of slave insurrections in the wake of the Haitian Revolution (1791–1804), many of the early nineteenth-century protests against slavery were articulated in poetic form, for instance, José María de Heredia's "Himno del desterrado" (1825), Domingo Del Monte's "La patria," (1833), José Jacinto Milanés's "El negro alzado" (1836), Juan Francísco Manzano's "Mis treinta años" (1839), and many of the seemingly innocuous poems by Plácido, who was executed in 1844 for his alleged participation in the Matanzas slave conspiracy of "La Escalera." However, what most characterizes this period is the rise of the Cuban anti-slavery novel, even if it was nearly impossible for abolitionist works to be published in Cuba at the time when they were actually written: Anselmo Suárez y Romero's *Francisco* and Pedro José Morillas's "El ranchador" were both written in 1838 but not published until 1880 and 1856, respectively. Cirilo Villaverde's monumental *Cecilia Valdés* did not appear until 1882 (only the short story version was printed in 1837), and Felix Tanco y Bosmoniel's *Petrona y Rosalía* – also known as *El niño Fernando* and the only surviving portion of the projected *Escenas de la vida privada en la isla de Cuba* – was not published until 1925. Although Manzano's slave narrative (1835) was made available in an ideologically conditioned English translation by Richard R. Madden in 1840 (London), the Spanish original was not printed until much later (*Autobiografía, cartas y versos de Juan Fco. Manzano*, 1937). In fact, the only anti-slavery novel to be published almost immediately after completion was Gertrudis Gómez de Avellaneda's *Sab* (1841), but it was printed in Spain, and she tellingly excised it from her collected works in 1869–1871.

Another precursor of the twentieth-century *negrista* narrative is the 1867 novel *María* by the Colombian Jorge Isaacs (1837–1895), which not only includes an "African episode," whose tepid paternalism is very much in line with Cuban romantic abolitionism, but, more significantly, a *bunde* written in dialect which anticipates Obeso's *Cantos populares de mi tierra* by a decade. However, it was not Colombia but Venezuela that would witness a veritable explosion of *negrista* fiction, from Manuel Vicente Romero García's *Peonía* (1890) to Juan Pablo Sojo's *Nochebuena negra* (1943) and Ramón Díaz Sánchez's *Cumboto* (1950). If both *Nochebuena negra*, an *indigenista* novel that documents the religious traditions of the black population from rural Barlovento, Sojo's native region, and *Cumboto*, which depicts life on a coconut plantation during the second half of the nineteenth century from the ambivalent perspective of the mulatto Natividad, have received the most critical attention from Afro-Hispanist critics, it is because the former is the only Venezuelan novel of that period written by a black author, and the latter, which received the Faulkner Ibero-American Novel Award and was translated into English in 1969, is one of very few narratives in which a white writer effaces himself behind a first-person narrator of African ancestry, a situation suggestive of Miguel Barnet's testimonial novel *Biografía de un cimarrón* (1966). It ought to be added that Sojo (1908–1948) is generally recognized as the father of Afro-Venezuelan studies. He was intimately familiar with the work of Fernando Ortiz and published a series of articles on Afro-Venezuelan culture in the 1940s.

Yet despite their exceptionality in these respects, *Nochebuena negra* and *Cumboto* still have to be viewed within the context of a host of other novels where preoccupation with "venezolanidad" almost inevitably led to an assessment of race relations, both from sociohistorical and metaphysical perspectives. Notable in the latter category are four novels by Rómulo Gallegos, *La trepadora* (1925), *Cantaclaro* (1934), *Canaíma* (1935), and particularly *Pobre Negro* (1937), in which Blacks, preferably mulattoes – who, due to their lower-class, peasant backgrounds were romantically portrayed as representative of the moral and physical vigor of the people – are charged with revitalizing the country's decadent creole aristocracy by reconciling "Civilization" with "Barbarism." Similar upwardly mobile "machista" figures, not all of them as heroic as Gallegos's Hilario Guanipa, Juan Parao, Juan Coromoto, and Pedro Miguel, appear in a series of other novels: Arturo Uslar Pietri's *Las lanzas coloradas* (1931) juxtaposes the mulatto Presentación Campos with the pusillanimous landowner Fernando Fonta. Guillermo Meneses's *Canción de negros* (1934), the first Venezuelan novel with an all-black cast of characters, features the happy-go-lucky, oversexed Julián Ponce. The mulattoes Paulo Guarimba and Miguel Franco from Luis Manuel Urbaneja Achelpohl's *¡En este país!* (1916) and Enrique Bernardo Núñez's *Después de Ayacucho* (1920) belong in the same category. The only novel that effectively explodes the myth of the newfound black social and economic mobility as a vehicle for integration, in this case by focusing on the ruthlessly exploitative side of professional sports (particularly baseball and boxing), is Meneses's *Campeones* (1939). Though its insistent eroticism makes it different from earlier urban novels, such as Manuel Díaz Rodríguez's *Idolos rotos* (1901), Rufino Blanco Fombona's *El hombre de hierro* (1907), José Rafael Pocaterra's *Tierra de sol amada* (1913), Emiliano Hernández's *Vida de Caracas* (1919), and Teresa de la Parra's *Ifigenia* (1924), in all of which Blacks play mostly secondary roles,

Campeones, much like Miguel Toro Ramírez's *Fango* (1936), signifi-cantly continues their overwhelmingly negative attitude toward mulat-toes' social ambitions, portraying them as a "pardocracia" imitating the old creole families ruined by the civil war.

While the increasing prominence of black characters in the Venezuelan novel since 1931 is, on the one hand, inseparable from the influence of Surrealism and its early manifestations in the work of Mariano Picón Salas, Uslar Pietri, and Bernardo Núñez, it must also be remembered that many of these *negrista* novels were written at a time when Venezuela, under the tyrannous reign of President Juan Vicente Gómez (1908–1935), was undergoing radical economic transformations. Massive foreign (especially US) investments in oil led to large urban migrations as well as a constant influx of black workers from Colombia and the Antilles. Though not the first novel to deal with these economic changes and their social ramifications, Díaz Sánchez's *Mené* is notable here for focusing on Caribbean oil workers in the Maracaibo area and the racial discrimi-nation they suffered. It appears that in countries like Venezuela and Cuba, there exist clear links between US economic imperialism and the rise of *negrista* poetry and/or fiction in response to the need to mine national cultural resources to counteract the deterioration of traditional moral and social values. It is not at all surprising, then, that most of these works are pervaded by a romantic idealism that encourages the depoliticization of racial conflict and the creation of nostalgic images of Blacks as a potentially messianic, but nevertheless exotic and "barbaric," race. Sojo's novel, unlike Guillén's poetry, is no exception here. If the characters in *Nochebuena negra*, whose title refers, of course, not to Christmas Eve but to the annual San Juan el Bautista celebrations on June 24, rebel against injustice at all, they invariably do so in the same quiet and solitary manner in which Juan Soledá, protagonist of Díaz Sánchez's nationally acclaimed story *La virgen no tiene cara* refuses to give his picture of the Holy Virgin a white face. Similar scenarios can be found in the work of two Peruvians, the neorealist urban stories and novellas by José Diez-Canseco, collected in 1930 and 1938 under the title *Estampas mulatas* (1967), and the controversial novel *Matalaché* (1928) by Enrique López Albújar, whose "tragic" mulatto protagonist José Manuel is ultimately vindicated at the expense of the black characters.

Much more politically astute, for the most part, than the works by the Venezuelan *negrista* writers and their Peruvian contemporaries are the numerous novels and short stories that, since the early 1950s, have sprung from the pens of Adalberto Ortiz and Nelson Estupiñán Bass from Ecuador, Manuel Zapata Olivella (b. 1920), Juan Zapata Olivella, Jorge Artel, Arnoldo Palacios (b. 1924), and Carlos Arturo Truque (1927–1970) from Colombia, as well as Quince Duncan (b. 1940) from Costa Rica and

Cubena from Panama. While all these novelists, most of whom are also poets, share a commitment to exploring the cultural and social dimensions of their African ancestries, that commitment is also frequently qualified by other concerns.

Ortiz's classic "negrigenista" novel *Juyungo*, for instance, dramatizes the often strained historic relations between Esmeraldan Blacks and the indigenous Cayapa Indians. "Juyungo," meaning "devil," is what the Cayapas call Blacks. However, Ortiz's main concern here is to link racial discrimination and economic exploitation in the evolving social consciousness of the black protagonist Ascención Lastre. We follow Lastre from his childhood in Esmeraldas to his heroic death in Ecuador's 1941 border war with Peru. Yet the novel's real hero, in many ways, is the mulatto Nelson Díaz, a university student and committed Socialist, whose reappearance at the end of the novel signals interracial solidarity as it prophesies the socialist uprisings of 1944. Though *Juyungo* chronicles Ecuadorian history, it does not present that history in the form of a unified narrative. The plot, such as it is, is frequently interrupted by extensive accounts of Afro-Ecuadorian folk traditions, which connects *Juyungo* with *Nochebuena negra*. Sojo's novel, however, lacks the intense lyricism especially of "The Eyes and Ears of the Jungle" sections that open each chapter, and it displays an indebtedness to *negrista* poetry that few other Afro-Hispanic novels have. This poetic super-realism carries over into the language and structure of Ortiz's later novels, *El espejo y la ventana* and *La envoltura del sueño*, subtitled *Novela coral y colérica*. The even greater narrative fragmentation of these two novels, and their often disturbingly macabre humor, place them in close proximity to the "mainstream" of postmodern Hispanic American fiction. Both have formal and, to some extent, thematic affinities with, in particular, Guillermo Cabrera Infante's *Tres tristes tigres* [*Three Trapped Tigers*], Severo Sarduy's *De donde son los cantantes* (1967) [*From Cuba With a Song*], Luis Rafael Sánchez's *La guaracha del macho Camacho* (1976) [*Macho Camacho's Beat*], and Reinaldo Arenas's *La loma del angel* (1987) [*Graveyard of the Angels*], a nightmarish recasting of *Cecilia Valdés*. Like *Tres tristes tigres* for instance, *La envoltura* even has a blank page, in this case for readers' notes.

A similar proclivity for discontinuous narrative forms characterizes many of Estupiñán Bass's later novels, especially *Senderos brillantes*, *Toque de queda*, and *Bajo el cielo nublado*, an "environmental" novel in whose prologue and epilogue personified aspects of the physical environment (the sea, the sky, the river, the old school building, etc.) raise their voices to lament and criticize human actions. The most memorable human voice in this novel is that of the displaced Esmeraldan Rock King/ Roque Quintero ("No me gonoce yu, ya no rimember mí"). Set in the imaginary republic of Girasol on the island Calamares, *Senderos brillantes* is a thinly veiled denunciation of US ("Estados Asociados") imperialist ventures in Latin America. It opens, in Pirandello-like fashion, with a series of letters from the novel's characters, who either congratulate the author or demand public retraction of his vicious "lies." The individual chapters then regress from number 56 to 1, while the subsections move forward in alphabetical order. Appropriately, the novel ends, at 1/z, with yet another letter, this time from the author's "alter ego." *Toque de queda*, Estupiñán Bass's "dictator" novel whose elusive General Espinoza recalls Dr. Melanio Chicande Rentería, better known as Rasputín, from *El paraíso*, is broken up into one-hour intervals representative of the times of the curfew. It is the only one of Estupiñán Bass's novels that dispenses altogether with conventional punctuation. In *El último río* [*Pastrana's Last River*], his best-known novel, Estupiñán Bass employs a more conventional frame-and-tale construction to chronicle the rise and fall of José Antonio Pastrana, governor of Esmeraldas, who gradually progresses from a vehement denial of his blackness ("he was white on the inside") to a violent hatred of Whites and eventually meets with a mysterious death. Shortly before her own death, Pastrana's widow, Ana Mercedes, who had been indicted and jailed for allegedly poisoning her husband, charges Juan, a writer and childhood friend, with reconstructing the true story from the Pastranas' personal papers. Juan's response to her at the end of the prologue, "No, I am not afraid of the truth but of the lies in which we live, that imprison us," could be taken as the motto of all of Estupiñán Bass's novels, from *Cuando los guayacanes florecían* [*When the Guayacans Were in Bloom*] to *El crepúsculo* and, most recently, *Los canarios pintaron el aire de amarillo*. Interestingly, *Cuando los guayacanes* returns to many of the concerns of *Juyungo* but in the context of historical events to which Ortiz only alludes: the Conchist rebellion in Esmeraldas (1913–1916).

The unrelenting criticisms of contemporary social conditions, of the myopia of politicians and bureaucrats, and the frequent attacks on the Catholic church that permeate Estupiñán Bass's novels as much as his poetry, as well as his experiments with narrative perspective, constitute both thematic and formal links between his work and that of several of his Colombian contemporaries: Jorge Artel, whose first and only novel to date, *No es la muerte, es el morir*, is a critical and ultimately quite pessimistic assessment of recent guerrilla movements in Colombia, and, by implication, the rest of Latin America; Juan Zapata Olivella, author of two novels, *Historia de un joven negro* and *Pisando el camino de ébano*, both of which center on black protagonists whose internal or external journeys of self-discovery bring into critical focus racism and prejudice in Colombia; and, last but not least, Manuel Zapata Olivella, psychiatrist, anthropologist, and Colombia's most prolific black novelist and play-wright. With the exception of *Detás del rostro*, Zapata Olivella's first four novels are almost neorealist documentations of Colombia's socio-econ-omic problems, from the exploitation of the rice farmers in the Río Simi region in *Tierra mojada*, and the plight of the urban proletariat in *La calle 10*, to an examination of religious fanaticism in *En Chimá nace un santo [A Saint is Born in Chimá]*. The film version of this last novel is significantly called *Santo en rebelión*. However, it is not until *Corral de negros*, later entitled *Chambacú: corral de negros [Chambacú: Black Slum]*, that Zapata Olivella focuses specifically on the exploitation and suffering of lower-class Blacks, a topic to which he returns in *El fusilamiento del diablo*, to dramatize the events surrounding the arrest and trial of the mulatto Saturio Valencia, nicknamed "The Devil."

The acclaimed *Detrás del rostro*, based on Zapata Olivella's exper-iences as a psychiatrist in a Bogotá hospital, seems like an anomaly, both thematically and structurally. Yet even if it differs from his other novels in that it does not communicate a revolutionary sense of solidarity among the downtrodden (in fact, quite the contrary), its narrative structure foregrounds one of Zapata Olivella's overriding concerns: the social construction of identity. In addition, the use of multiple narrators in *Detrás del rostro* anticipates *Changó, el gran putas*. In preparation for close to twenty years, *Changó* is a novel of epic proportions that uses the legend of Changó's curse as a catalyst for its mythic history of Afro-Americans from the sixteenth century (Part I: "Los orígenes") to the assassination of Malcolm X in 1965 (Part V: "Los ancestros comba-tientes"). Among the countless narrators are not only the *orichas* introduced in the opening poems (one of them, Ngafuá, Changó's messenger appears throughout the novel), but also a host of historical figures, such as Simón Bolívar, José Prudencio Padilla, the Mexican José María Morelos, and the Brazilian sculptor El Aleijandinho, in Part IV ("Las sangres encontradas"), as well as W. E. B. du Bois, Martin Luther King, Jr. (whose famous "I Have a Dream" speech curiously goes unmentioned), Booker T. Washington, Langston Hughes, and Malcolm X in the final and longest part. Part V is set in the United States during the 1960s and centers around Agne Brown, a black anthropologist and the last in a long procession of characters charged by Changó with keeping alive the memory of the African ancestors and the collective fight against racism. So dense is the textual fabric of Part V, so saturated with references, quotations, and allusions, ranging from Estebanico, Nat Love, Frederick Douglass, Harriet Tubman, and John Brown, to Jean Toomer, Bessie Smith, Duke Ellington, Alain Locke, Carl Van Vechten, and Richard Wright, and rhythmically punctuated by the ominous refrain "Malcolm, today you will be killed," that it always teeters on the brink of narrative chaos. What this *tour de force* does communicate, however, is an acute sense of urgency, reinforced by the fact that all of the novel's heroes die betrayed: they are either assassinated or commit suicide. That urgency resounds in the novel's final warning: that, for the living, time is not infinite, indeed a powerful contrast to the apocalyptic ending of García Marquez's *Cien años de soledad* [*One Hundred Years of Solitude*].

If the narrative techniques of *Changó* harken back to *Detrás del rostro*, Zapata Olivella's use of West African mythologies, which continues in *El fusilamiento*, can be traced to *Chambacú*. By the same token, *Changó's* final part returns the reader to the autobiographical essays and stories of *He visto la noche* (1946) and *La pasión vagabunda*, based on Zapata Olivella's extensive travels in Central America and the United States (1943–1947). Other useful reference points are the short story inspired by Frantz Fanon's theories, "Un extraño bajo mi piel," set in Atlanta, Georgia, from the later collection *¿Quién dió el fusil a Oswald?*, as well as the early play *Hotel de vagabundos*, whose background is New York City. More than with the work of other Afro-Colombian writers, *Changó's* invocations of African mythology have more in common with the fictions of Central American writers like Quince Duncan and Cubena, as well as with Manuel Cofiño López's *Cuando la sangre se parece al fuego*, a Cuban novel about the conflict between *ñañiguísmo* and revolutionary ideology. On the other hand, most of Zapata Olivella's earlier writings, including the predominantly rural stories of *Cuentos de muerte y libertad*, show greater affinity to the regionalist Social Realism of Carlos Arturo Truque and even the Naturalism of Arnoldo Palacios. Both Truque, author of two volumes of short stories, *La Granizada y otros cuentos* and the posthumous *El día que terminó el verano y otros relatos*, which rarely focus on the predicament of Afro-Colombians, and Palacios, who has published two novels about his native region of Chocó, *Las estrellas son negras*, whose language and narrative structure has been compared to Richard Wright's *Native Son* (1945), and *La selva y la lluvia*, are relatively little-known outside Colombia.

With the exception of Díaz Sánchez's *Mené*, few novels written outside the Caribbean even made reference to the black workers and their families who, during the late nineteenth and early twentieth centuries, emigrated from the anglophone and francophone parts of the West Indies to various Hispanic American countries, notably Venezuela, Costa Rica, and Panama. It is precisely the history of such immigrant communities that assumes unprecedented prominence in the recent novels and stories by Quince Duncan and Cubena. With the exception of his award-winning *Final de calle*, a novel about ex-revolutionaries corrupted by power that self-consciously refrains from bringing to the fore black issues and themes, Duncan's fiction, from the stories of *Una canción en la madru-*

gada and his first novel, *Hombres curtidos*, concentrates on his native Costa Rican province of Limón. Even today, the population of Limón consists predominantly of working-class Blacks, descended from the large numbers of West Indians who, after the collapse of Jamaica's sugar economy, arrived in Costa Rica between 1872 and the turn of the century to work in railroad construction and, later, on the banana plantations of the United Fruit Company. The historical background of *La paz del pueblo*, for instance, is the strike against United Fruit in 1934, as a result of which the company moved its operations to the Pacific coast and banned black workers from employment in banana production, leaving many of them to look for work in the neighboring Panama. There are two previous Costa Rican novels about the clash between United Fruit and its black workers: Carlos Luis Fallas's autobiographical *Mamita Yunai* (1941) and Joaquín Gutiérrez's *Puerto Limón* (1950). However, Duncan's characters and emphases are quite distinct from those of his predecessors. Reminiscent of the revolutionary José Gordon from "La leyenda de José Gordon" and Jean Paul from "La rebelión pocomía" (both stories are included in *La rebelión pocomía y otros relatos*), Pedro Dull, the protagonist of *La paz del pueblo*, is a vociferous advocate of Garveyism, a movement with enormous popular support in Limón during the 1920s and the specter that disrupts the complacent peace of the people/village. Yet Dull is also, significantly, a member of the African-Jamaican *pocomania* or *pocomía* [Pukumina] cult, into which he is initiated by the priestess Mama Bull, another character from the title story of *La rebelión pocomía*.

The clash between Western science and Afro-Caribbean folk religions plays an important part in almost all of Duncan's fictions. *Los cuatro espejos*, Duncan's second and most ambitious novel, is only one example. Lorena, herself daughter of an obeah-man and the first wife of the anglophone mulatto Charles McForbes, whose racial ambivalence lies at the center of this novel, is attacked by a *dupí* [duppy] in broad daylight and sustains a mysterious illness incurable by contemporary medicine. For many of Duncan's characters, religious rituals also provide important contexts for cultural identification, even though economic and class differences in some cases, such as in *La paz del pueblo*, make racial solidarity seem quite remote. However, Duncan is by no means an advocate of separation but of solidarity across racial lines and of a unified Costa Rica. Since he is descended from a community of West Indian Blacks that has held on to English as a defense against assimilation, Duncan's choice to write in Spanish is certainly telling in this regard.

Duncan's use of Afro-American myth and religion is particularly striking in "Los mitos ancestrales," the final short story in *La rebelión pocomía*, whose narrator is a resident of the *samamfo*, the realm of the dead ancestors. If this links Duncan and Zapata Olivella to some extent, the work to which Duncan's is most closely connected is unquestionably that of his Panamanian contemporary, Carlos Guillermo Wilson (Cubena). Unlike Duncan, however, Cubena has elected to live and work in the United States. In addition to his poetry, he has published a volume of short stories, *Cuentos del negro Cubena*, and a novel, *Chombo*, the first volume in a projected trilogy. The second, entitled *Afroexilados*, has been completed and is forthcoming. *Chombo*, written in a style that Adalberto Ortiz has called "tremendísmo negrista," rages against the "quixotic illusion" of racial democracy in Panama, a country that in 1926 prohibited all further immigration of Antillean Blacks and in 1941 denationalized all Panamanians of West Indian descent. Related targets are the effects of the US presence in Panama since the building of the Canal (1904–1914), among them the wage discrimination of the Gold and Silver Roll system.

Like many of Cubena's short stories, *Chombo* is set in the Canal Zone, though it is by no means the first novel about that area and its West Indian community. However, it differs considerably from previous novels, such as Joaquín Beleño's trilogy *Curúndu*, (1963), *Luna verde* (1951), and *Gamboa Road Gang* (1959), and especially, from Anguilera Malta's *Canal Zone* (1935), all of which, though sympathetic to West Indian Blacks, still represent them in highly ambiguous terms. *Chombo*, on the other hand, meticulously traces the history of black Panamanians of West Indian origin (derogatorily called *chombos*). Its brevity notwithstanding, the novel aspires to be a Panamanian version of *Roots*, which Lito, the young protagonist, is reading in one of the early chapters. Set against the background of the Torrijos–Carter negotiations about the sovereignty of the Panama Canal, *Chombo* takes us back to the nineteenth-century "middle passage" from Jamaica to Panama as Lito meditates on "the matter of the three gold bracelets," symbolic of the history of his family and its African (as well as pre-Columbian New World) origins. The story of Nenén and Papa James Duglin, which eventually returns to the Jamaican maroon stronghold Xaymaca-Nokoro, a mythic homeland of sorts, begins in the third chapter and is told by "the oldest African ancestor." In the final chapter, Cubena even draws figures from traditional African animal fables (tortoise, spider, and serpent) to relate the history of the African family Onítefo and their Inca, Aztec, and Toltec connections, which completes the story of the bracelets.

Even if the novel's black/white symbolism seems often strained, *Chombo* is remarkable not only for its interweaving of minute historical detail and abundant information about West-Indian Panamanian popular culture (including music and cuisine), with Ashanti mythology, but also for its linguistic inventiveness. Its language is a fascinating blend of Twi, Jamaican, and Haitian creoles, and Spanish, as in "pour cuá tú no cocinar like petit sister Aidíta" or "ché ne parle avec tuá," and is frequently laced with emphatic profanity. This hybrid language, no less than the novel's historico-cultural references and the epigraphs drawn from Garvey, Juan Latino, Estupiñán Bass, Guillén, Brindis de Salas, Adalberto Ortiz, and Nicomedes Santa Cruz, self-consciously situates *Chombo* within an Afro-Hispanic context. Yet Cubena's violent rage, and the obsessive proliferation of scatological images in both the novel and his short stories, find by far their closest equivalents in the fiction of Jones/Baraka in the early-to-mid 1960s, especially in the novel *The System of Dante's Hell* (1965). So, for that matter, does Cubena's homophobia. Yet in the midst of images of violence, racial and sexual pathology, and abject poverty with which Cubena inundates his readers to the point of clearly intended nausea, there is also hope for a better future. "Ebeyiye" (a Twi word), "the future will be better," is after all the motto on the Cubena coat-of-arms that adorns each of his books. Perhaps paradoxically, however, neither *Cuentos* nor *Chombo* project visions of social revolution. Instead, they affirm Cubena's profoundly humanistic belief in social improvement through education. In this sense, the epigraph from Ralph Waldo Emerson in *Cuentos* –

> The man is only half himself,
> the other half is his expression

– is more apt, and in a way even more troubling, than the lines from Edward Kamau Brathwaite with which it has been replaced in Ian Smart's English version, *Short Stories by Cubena*:

> And so without my cloth
> shoulders uncovered
> to this new doubt
>
> and desert I return
> expecting nothing;
> my name burnt out,
>
> a cinder on my shoulder.

A detailed history of Afro-Hispanic literature during the nineteenth and twentieth centuries can obviously not be written in so few pages. Not only would it be necessary to include Afro-Brazilian texts, Puerto Rico's *boricua* literature, more extensive discussions of oral poetry and music, not to mention the many plays that have been written and performed since Lope de Rueda's *Eufemia* (1576), areas that have been omitted from this essay for no other reason than lack of space; it is equally imperative, in order to determine what Afro-Hispanic literature actually is (other than simply literature about black themes), to explore more fully the exact position individual texts occupy vis-à-vis what is presumed to be the Latin American literary mainstream, as well as the nature of the historical and conceptual links Afro-Hispanic works claim both with each other and with other literary traditions in the New World, especially from the Caribbean and the United States. Given the extent to which Afro-Hispanic texts are actually intertwined with other mainstream and "marginal" traditions, it may ultimately be neither advisable nor possible to write a separate history of Afro-Hispanic literature, certainly not in any conventional sense. The real challenge is neither to establish a separate canon nor, for that matter, to bring select Afro-Hispanic texts into the fold of already existing canons of Latin American or Afro-American literatures. Both are easily enough accomplished without disturbing the *status quo* in any productive way. What is at issue, then, is our ability (and willingness) to read Afro-Hispanic texts as evidence of the inconsistencies, irregularities, and upheavals that characterize Latin American literary, social, and political history, much more so than any unified critical narrative could even suggest.

[6]

The *criollista* novel
Carlos J. Alonso

The historical depth of the preoccupation with indigenous cultural values in Spanish America makes it difficult to undertake the determination of the precise origins of *criollista* [creole] literary production. During the nation-building stage in the nineteenth century, the leading groups of what would eventually constitute the individual countries of Latin America were busily establishing the discourses and institutions that would preserve an avowed national identity that was, in fact, being created in the process. Hence, one can readily find throughout the century several manifestations of the desire to engender a native literature, from Andrés Bello (1781–1865) through Domingo F. Sarmiento (1811–1888) to José Marti (1853–1895). Indeed the period presents many instances that attest to the conviction that linguistic and literary specificity were regarded as correlatives of the political and cultural distinctiveness that Spanish America had recently achieved through its struggle for independence. One can cite in this regard the many published collections of *cubanismos, argentinismos* or *venezolanismos*, the periodic reformist projects to adjust Spanish orthography to Spanish American phonetics – Bello and Sarmiento are well known exponents of this endeavor – and the founding of *Academias Nacionales de la Lengua* throughout the continent.

Furthermore, although there are essential differences that distinguish the *cuadro de costumbres* [folkloric sketch] from *criollista* literary production, it is no less true that in Spanish America the *cuadro* exhibits a desire for cultural affirmation that differentiates it from its European counterpart and which determines its unusual longevity in the former colonies. It could be argued as well that one of the persistent preoccupations of the practitioners of the late nineteenth-century movement called *Modernismo* [Modernism], notwithstanding the critical notion that affirms its cosmopolitan thrust, ultimately turned out to be a concern for an indigenous literary expression. One would therefore have to agree with the Dominican critic Pedro Henríquez Ureña when he says that "the literary history of our last hundred years could be described as the history of the ebb and flow of aspirations and theories in search of an expression that is most perfectly ours" (*Seis ensayos en busca de nuestra expresión*, 39). In sum, the "origins" of the *criollista* novel, or *novela de la tierra*, as it is commonly called, have a diachronic dimension that cannot be reduced to a concrete point in time.

Nonetheless, the explosive intensity and continent-wide character of the cultural preoccupation with autochthony that marks the first thirty years of this century in Latin America is a phenomenon whose historical coordinates cannot be overlooked. Even while acknowledging that the enterprise of which it is an instance has very extended historical roots, the distinctive response to the question of the autochthonous articulated by the *novela de la tierra* must be examined with a view to establishing its specific nature and the cultural milieu from which it arose.

Traditionally, the *criollista* movement has been regarded as one of several manifestations of that more comprehensive cultural phenomenon that the critic Martin Stabb has called "the rediscovery of America" (*In Quest of Identity*, 58). According to this view, the spirited meditation on cultural essence that characterized the first thirty years of this century in Latin America was a reflection of the Neo-Kantianism or Neo-Spiritualism that in Europe had come to be associated with the Vitalism of Henri Bergson, the contingency of Emile Boutroux, the Nietzschean emphasis on the Will, and the aesthetic influence of Benedetto Croce. However, the uneven diffusion of these ideas throughout Latin America cannot explain the breadth and depth of the nativist explosion throughout the entire continent. The other conventional explanation for the surfacing of a literature of autochthony in this period is that it represents a nostalgia for an agrarian past, in an era of increased immigration and economic expansion that threatened the hegemony of the landed aristocracy throughout the continent. This interpretation is undermined by the dissimilar economic development of the various countries in Latin America, by the widely differing class extractions attributable to the authors involved, and by the conspicuous overtures to modernization present in some of these works (Gallegos's *Doña Bárbara* [*Doña Barbara*] immediately comes to mind in this respect.) Although these two interpretations certainly address significant issues, it could be argued that the context from which the *novela de la tierra* arose entails a more complex conjunction of political, intellectual, and cultural circumstances than they allow. The most salient are addressed in the section that follows.

The broadest of these is the emergence of European Modernism in all its diverse and even contradictory manifestations. European Modernism can be described in very sweeping terms as a composite of two fundamental tendencies – two means through which Modernist aesthetics sought to transcend the impasse, brought about by the critique of nineteenth-century assumptions about representation in art, that sprang up during the *fin de siècle* and the first twenty years of the twentieth century. Both of these arose from the desire to move away from a conception of art as mimesis, and from the attempt to breathe new life into aesthetic canons that were now regarded as contaminated by bourgeois complacence and mediocrity. The first tendency encompassed the desire to put art in contact with what was thought to be a primeval, and therefore more authentic, vital force or essence. This was the origin of the several versions of Primitivism that were engendered by Modernism, and of which Béla Bartòk's explorations of folk music and the Pablo Picasso of *Les Demoiselles d'Avignon* are clear exponents. The other trend represents the enterprise of experimenting within the formal bounds of a given artistic medium in order to arrive at some determination of first principles of composition or expression for that medium. One can think in this regard about Arnold Schoënberg's experiments first with atonal and later with dodecaphonic (twelve-tone) music, or Le Corbusier's attempts to arrive at foundational geometric and functional principles in architecture. These two trends are, to be sure, not entirely unrelated; they are presented here as disconnected in order to make more visible their specific relevance to contemporaneous cultural production in Latin America.

Of these tendencies, the first – the primitivist – was the predominant one in Latin America at the time, and can be readily detected in the three most important cultural developments in the continent during the 1920s and 1930s: Afro-Antillean literature, the *Indigenismo* movement (Indigenism), and *criollista* literary production. All of these cultural projects aspired to put art in general and literature in particular in touch with an avowedly primeval essence whose power derived precisely from its primordial status, and which was construed along various ethnic lines – the Black, the Indian, and whatever figure was deemed to be representative of national identity: the Argentinian gaucho, the Venezuelan *llanero*, the Puerto Rican *jíbaro*, etc. Although the Primitivist intention behind each movement was identical, there were significant differences in the specific rhetoric that the three deployed. The Afro-Antillean and the *indigenista* movements borrowed from anthropology a ready-made discourse about the Other, in order to speak about the Others represented by the Black and the Indian. In contrast – and since it was supposedly addressing what was most intrinsic – the *criollista* narrative invoked the formula for defining cultural identity that formed the core of philology, the discipline that studied cultural monuments in order to unveil the collective spirit that they supposedly embodied. This connection will be the subject of a lengthier discussion below.

Yet another factor that accounts for the emergence of the *criollista* movement was the Latin American reaction against the doctrine of Pan-Americanism, an initiative sponsored by the United States that had as its goal the definition of a bond common to the Americas. Pan-Americanism, the belief in a geographic, economic, and historical order that would encompass both North and South America, became the historico-political myth through which the United States conceived of its relations with Latin America at the close of the nineteenth century and beyond. It represented the resolute advancing by the imperial nation of a powerful myth, a vision regarding the future trajectory of the hemisphere as a totality that was resoundingly heralded throughout the Americas by the United States. The genesis of this formula can be traced to the year 1889, when then Secretary of State James G. Blaine coined the term "Pan-American Conference," and convoked the first of a series of such meetings of representatives of American nations, a conclave that was held in Washington, D.C., late in that year.

To some extent, Pan-Americanism attempted a revival of the anti-European rhetoric of the Monroe Doctrine that understood the New World strictly as the scenario for the development of the nations in it. However, in Pan-Americanism, the emphasis was rather on the formulation of a project for the achievement of a hemispheric order that would only encompass the Americas. A review of the future agenda that was presented to the participants of the first conference in 1889 makes it possible to determine the comprehensive intent of the proposal: adoption of a common currency, provisions for cultural exchange, a uniform system of weights and measures, a continent-wide set of customs regulations, the creation of a Pan-American Bank, the construction of an intercontinental railway, and a number of other similar undertakings. This summary should also leave no doubt that the emergence of the Pan-American ideal must be understood as a decidedly ideological stratagem on the part of the United States meant to facilitate its hegemony over the continent. Nevertheless, what must be underscored is the sense of crisis that the doctrine elicited in Latin American intellectual circles and the cultural strategy through which they attempted to transcend the perceived threat.

The clearest symptom of the crisis represented by the United States' initiative was the ensuing continent-wide controversy surrounding the legitimacy of the very concept of Pan-Americanism as an instrument for envisioning the future of Latin American nations. The enthusiastic espousal and fostering of the Pan-American proposal by the United States did not find a strong echo among countries which perceived the Spanish American War as an abusive conflict deliberately provoked by the United States, and which had witnessed with increasing alarm a series of successive interventions by the northern power in Latin America. Nevertheless, the threatening historical myth of Pan-Ameri canism had to be neutralized with a parallel creation, another cultural narrative that would articulate a particular mytho-poetic reality exclusively for Latin America. This necessity was the wellspring for the affirmation of a continental cultural order that would encompass all Latin American nations, a belief that subsequently circulated under the various labels of *pan-latinismo, pan-iberismo, pan-hispanismo* or *hispanoamericanismo*.

The aspirations represented by *pan-latinismo* were not entirely new in Latin American circles: there had been some feeble and largely unsuccessful attempts to form some sort of union between Latin American nations during the nineteenth century. However, the force and unanimity with which the ideal dominated Latin American intellectual concerns during the first thirty years of the twentieth century attest to its nature as a continent-wide cultural myth, as a collective response to a threat and a challenge issuing from an outside source. This desire to postulate the existence of a cultural order and a historical project specific to Latin America resulted in an enterprise that produced books of major importance such as *Ariel* (1900) [*Ariel*] by José E. Rodó; Manuel Ugarte's *Las nuevas tendencias literarias* (1908), *El porvenir de la América Latina* (1910), and *El destino de un continente* (1923); *La evolución política y social de Hispanoamérica* (1911) by Rufino Blanco Fombona; and Francisco García Calderón's *Les démocracies latines de l'Amérique* (1912) and *La creación de un continente* (1912).

The formulation of a pan-Latin cultural order soon had the opportunity to appropriate for its purposes a historical circumstance that provided an ideal context for its deployment, and which further helps to understand the rise of *criollista* literature: the one-hundredth anniversary of the beginning of the Independence movement in Latin America, in 1910. There is little doubt that the commemoration of the *Centenario*, as it was called, became the most significant cultural event in the decade between 1910 and 1920 in Latin America. The elaborate celebrations of the event that took place in all countries and at various times during the period throughout Latin America attest to that fact. In the context of the desire to affirm a spiritual essence shared by all Latin American nations in order to oppose Pan-Americanism, it was inevitable that the *Centenario* would be interpreted in terms of the possibilities it afforded for that affirmation. In a masterful stroke of historical imagination, Latin American authors and intellectuals claimed to see in 1910 a repetition of the circumstances and possibilities that in their view had characterized the corresponding moment one hundred years previously, in 1810. In other words, the idea of a unity of continental proportions that had surfaced in the first decade of the twentieth century seemed to them to harken back to that historical moment that could be characterized as the very origin of Latin America; that initial moment of avowed continental and cultural unity that preceded the fall into a history of fragmentation and fratricidal dissension known only too well; a moment that had returned – so to speak – in the apotheosis of its centennial celebration. The commemoration of this historical moment – a moment that was reconstructed and refashioned as much as it was celebrated in 1910 – posited also the return of the possibilities that the event had supposedly afforded when seen as the beginning of cultural time. This explains the millennial rhetoric that is typical of the period, and which found expression in formulas such as *mundonovismo*: a concept proposed by the Chilean critic Francisco Contreras to describe the felicitous turn toward indigenous values in the Latin American literature of the times. This rhetoric is also present in the many utopian texts of the period, such as *La raza cósmica* and *Indología* by the Mexican writer José Vasconcelos. Furthermore, it was decidedly not lost on Latin American intellectuals that, at the precise time when Latin America was celebrating this feast of new beginnings, Europe appeared to be signaling its historical exhaustion in the First World War, the apocalyptic "War to end all Wars."

Finally, one would have to mention, as another factor contributing to the appearance of *criollista* concerns, the continental impact of the Mexican Revolution (1910–1920). The cultural enterprise engaged in by the post-revolutionary Mexican intelligentsia (mural art, pedagogical reform, foundational theories about *mestizaje*, etc.) provided a model for the institutionalization of nativist ideology for the rest of the continent. The Mexican Revolution, in conjunction with the events of October 1917 in Russia, was also responsible for inaugurating the rhetoric of social denunciation and reform that henceforth became commonplace in Latin American literary circles, and which is distinctly visible in many of the *novelas de la tierra* as well.

Culling all of the above, and sacrificing nuance for the convenience of dates, the chronological limits of the *novela de la tierra* could be designated as the years of 1910 and 1945. The earlier year reflects the emergence (or reawakening) of a desire to affirm the existence of a national or continent-wide identity through the vehicle of a literary creation; the outer limit reflects the ascendance of existentialist philosophy in Latin America, a development that changed the terms in which both identity and literature were conceived in such a way as to render inoperative the presuppositions on which the *criollista* movement was predicated. From that moment on, the organic relationship between Man and Land posited by the indigenous formula was displaced by a conception of Man based on an inescapable state of rootlessness, and on the belief in his permanent alienation from the world and from himself.

The need to affirm the specificity of a particular Latin American identity created by the historical events and cultural trends discussed above imposed certain demands on literature: to provide a founding myth for the collectivity, and to produce a transcendent text in which the national or continental soul could see reflected both itself and a prophetic vision of its future. Herein lies the stimulus for the project of composing indigenous texts that characterized literary production in Latin America during the first forty years of the twentieth century.

Nevertheless, the problematic nature of that project in Latin America soon made itself evident. This difficulty resided in Latin America's myth of cultural foundation, that is, in its consummate identification with modernity since the beginning of its historical emergence. The resulting affirmation of an absolute break with tradition and the past had the effect of abolishing the history from which the endeavor to produce an indigenous text should supposedly derive its legitimacy and vigor. That creation, that cultural Master Text, could not be compiled and assembled from a presumably ageless reservoir of traditional myths or compositions: if this autochthonous Text were to be at all, it would have to be constructed, produced, *made* (remembering the etymology of the word "poetry" in the Greek *poiein*), rather than be recovered or reconstituted from cultural fragments looming out of an immemorial past.

Hence, if this Text was going to have any claims to authenticity it would have to incorporate within it a discourse that vouched for that legitimacy; in other words, the composition of that literary Text had to take place within the confines of another discourse that could authenticate the Text's claim to being an *indigenous* literary work; a discourse whose precepts would be integrated into the text to certify the latter's pretensions to being truly an indigenous literary creation. This was the role that came to be played by the discipline of philology in *criollista* literary discourse.

The concept of culture that has nurtured Latin America's preoccupation with an autochthonous cultural expression is a synthesis of a number of beliefs that had their first formulation during the last years of the eighteenth century and the first decades of the nineteenth. They include principally the idea of a culture as a closed and *sui generis* entity, whose existence was the deployment in history of an intrinsic and organic plan. Spoken language was the chief vehicle through which this collective spirit was expressed, but by no means the only one; traditions, legends, myths, popular art forms, and common law were other realms where this will manifested itself. Herder, for instance, characterized folk poems as "archives of a nationality," "imprints of the soul of a nation," and as "the living voice of the nationalities." All cultural and political practices and institutions were assumed to be generated organically from a spiritual kernel that manifested itself in history following the dictates of an internal necessity. This development marked all the creations of the community in question, imparting to them a specificity that made it impossible and even undesirable to make cross-cultural comparisons. Expressions such as "national soul," "spirit of the people," and "popular genius" were used to refer to this spiritual monad that unveiled itself throughout the history of a group in an almost impersonal fashion – not unlike a plant – perhaps without ever rising to the consciousness of the individuals that formed the collectivity. Consequently, the creative act, the deed responsible for cultural creations, was conceptualized as anonymous, unreflecting, and collective.

The many botanical and biological metaphors that were used to characterize cultural life and its evolution attest to the organicity that physical and spiritual processes were assumed to have in common; but they are also expressive of the relationship that was presumed to exist between a culture and the physical environment in which it obtained. The spirit of a people manifested itself also in the ways it manipulated and transformed its surroundings – yet the conditions of possibility for that manifestation were determined to an important degree by the physical environment the people inhabited. As a result, the spiritual dimension of a culture reflected and was shaped by the daily contact of the collectivity with the various elements that constituted its environment. Culture and history, then, were to some extent influenced by geography, since the latter invariably left its characteristic imprint on the spiritual make-up of a people that lived within its boundaries. This organic relationship opened the way for a correlative spiritualization of the environment, that is, a conception of the physical milieu as a telluric Agent secretly informing all the creations of the collective being. Geography thus became a Force, a powerful and mysterious spiritual presence that modified the deployment in time of a people's "national soul." The metaphor that described a culture's development as basically similar to that of a plant reflected this "nourishment" that a human collective spirit was deemed to derive from its sustained contact with the national territory.

This conception of cultural identity brought implicit with it the necessity of a comprehensive hermeneutical enterprise: by its very nature, the spirit that was intrinsic to each culture could not be apprehended directly, but rather had to be decoded, reconstructed through the study of that culture's diverse tangible manifestations, particularly those of the culture's remote past, since they were considered to be more spontaneous and less contaminated by contact with other communities. This reconstruction became the project that defined the discourse of philology. From its beginnings in the very late eighteenth century philology underwent a series of internal transformations: from an "intuitive" stage in the Romantic period to Renan's confident definition of it as a (*"science exacte des choses de l'esprit"*) ["exact science of spiritual phenomena"], to the stylistic method that is associated with the more recent names of Karl Vossler and Leo Spitzer. Yet throughout this development the essential objective of philology remained unaltered: to arrive at a determination of the organic spiritual dimension that manifested itself in a culture's creations.

Understanding the foundations of philological discourse is a prerequisite to discerning in turn the various manifestations of the project to write an indigenous literary text that dominated Latin American literature during the early part of this century. One begins to realize then that textualizing a collective spiritual essence is a project that acquires its full intelligibility within the conceptual horizon delimited by the discipline of philology. It could be suggested, in fact, that the Latin American "autochthonous" *oeuvre* would like to fashion itself after the ideal text envisioned by philological interpretive practice: a work that evinces a transparent, unmediated relationship between cultural being (in this instance, Latin American) and writing. Some of the features of the literature produced in Latin America during the period of *criollista* production express this connection quite directly. To begin with, there was an obvious predilection for employing those literary forms that philology had designated as inherently "popular," that is, compositions that had been spontaneously and anonymously produced by the collectivity: the *romance*, the ballad, the epic poem, the legend, etc. A number of the major poets of the period showed their understanding of the possibilities offered by this poetic conception, sometimes effecting as a result radical transformations in their poetic practice and personae. This relationship can also be identified in works such as *El payador*, by Leopoldo Lugones (1874–1938), where there is an attempt to superimpose on Latin American literary history European schemes regarding the formation of a national literary tradition that are derived from philological formulations. Such is in fact the driving force behind the following passage from Lugones's introduction to his treatise, where he expounds in this connection in no uncertain terms:

> I have chosen as the title of this work the name of those wandering minstrels that used to traverse our countryside reciting *romances* and *endechas*, because they were the most important characters in the founding of our race. Just as it happened in all other Greco-Roman

groups, here also that moment coincided with the creation of a work of art. Poetry laid the differential foundation of the Motherland by creating a new language for the expression of the new spiritual entity constituted by the soul of a race as it came into being.   (p. 14)

Similarly, the indigenous Latin American landscape became a privileged literary category, since it was through its constant contact with it that the spiritual essence of the continent's people had been shaped. Here lies the justification for the myriad works produced during this period that aspired to capture the specific geography of a region or country in a cycle of poems, or in a novel or essay. Perhaps the most succinct rendition of this concept is the justly famous essay "Visión de Anáhuac" (1915) by Alfonso Reyes (1889–1959), the source for the following passage:

> Regardless of the historical doctrine one may profess . . . we are in unison with the race of yesteryear not only through our blood, but more importantly through the common effort to dominate the coarse and unyielding nature that surrounds us; such an effort is the foundation of history. We also share with them the profound emotional unanimity that arises from the daily encounter with a similar natural object. The confrontation between human sensibility and a common world carves and engenders a common soul.   (2: 34)

It would be impossible to summarize the total extent and the multifarious forms that this literary endeavor assumed throughout Latin America. What is of particular concern to this essay is the reflection in the novelistic genre of this desire to create an indigenous literary text, a dynamic that produced that large collection of works that have come to be known as the *novela de la tierra*.

The discourse of the autochthonous in these novels represents a rhetorical condensation of the paradigm of cultural interpretation just discussed; that is to say, the discourse of philology provides the essential concepts and relationships that legitimize the writing of these works. This explains why, at the most superficial level, the *novela de la tierra* appears to be an indiscriminate and uncomplicated collection of philological commonplaces: speech as a privileged instance of language; geography as a sempiternal telluric presence; the detailed depiction of a human activity that has arisen in perfect consonance with the environment. Nevertheless, although the basic postulates of philological discourse seem to account for the fundamental characteristics of these texts, that relationship is not as uncomplicated as it would seem at first glance; for the seemingly subordinate relationship between the *novela de la tierra* and philology conceals, nonetheless, a precise inversion of philological operations of interpretation. The philologist's overriding purpose was the revelation of the ultimate spiritual structure that was assumed to be the underlying bedrock or foundation for the text under scrutiny. As a result of this interpretive stance, the work was considered nothing but a more or less transparent screen or veil, with the text's final truth to be arrived at by the critic only beyond it.

However, while philology endeavored to collate and interpret texts in order to arrive at a the collective ontological spirit underlying them, the writers of the *novela de la tierra* take as their point of departure this supposed essence and *then* proceed to write the text that will ostensibly embody it. Therefore, in the *novela de la tierra* there is a reversal of the interpretive trajectory that philology proposed – that is, these novels envision the process of their coming into being as a displacement from spiritual essence to text.

On account of this reversal of hermeneutic paths, one can detect in the *novelas de la tierra* a heightened awareness of their own textuality, of the process that resulted in their writing, that defies all traditional readings of them. This knowledge shows itself in the text as a critical commentary that seeks to guarantee the propriety of the relationship between text and essence that philology simply posited as a given. Hence, the *novela de la tierra* purports to be a literary text that incorporates the autochthonous essence, but it also has alongside it a parallel critical discourse that comments on the legitimacy and validity of the formulation of autochthony that it advances. In this fashion, the autochthonous work is engaged in the ceaseless validation of that which it also assumes to be a given. This situation implies that the autochthonous writer is both author and commentator of his or her own work, a circumstance that belies the customary claims of simplicity and transparency advanced with great consistency by the authors of these works and their critics. The *novela de la tierra* is an attempt to create a genuinely autochthonous work that simultaneously undermines the concept of a spontaneous indigenous text by exposing its discursive nature, its knowledge of itself as a textual effect.

This critical intention surfaces in these works, for instance, as specific moments when the novel lapses into a commentary that tries to elucidate explicitly the relationships that undergird the world it is depicting. One can clearly detect this intention in the following fragment from Gallegos's *Doña Bárbara*:

> The return from work brought the patio in front of the cabins to life. As darkness came on, the cowboys came back in noisy groups, began to banter, and ended by singing their thoughts in ballad form, since for everything that must be said the man of the Plain already has a ballad which says it, and says it better than speech. For life in the Plain is simple and devoid of novelty, and the spirit of the people is prone to the use of picturesque and imaginative forms.
>
> . . .
>
> And between mouthfuls a discussion of the events of the day's work, barbs and boasts, a friendly joke and the quick sharp retort, a story

arising from the picturesque life of the cowboy and guide, the man of hard toil always with a ballad on the tip of his tongue.

And while the watchers by the corrals took turns going around . . . in the cabins, another more boisterous watch was taking place: the guitar and the *maracas*, the *corrido* and the *décima*. The birth of poetry.

(pp. 675–6)

In passages such as this one, the text can be seen to engage in what could be referred to as an explication of its own discursive assumptions. In them, the novels articulate explicitly, and comment on, those relationships that also allow them to conceive the world they recreate as an organic whole in the first place. The critical, explanatory purpose of this particular fragment can be distinguished, for instance, in the causal structure of the first paragraph; but it is also evinced by the manifest exegetical intention of the entire passage. Through it, the text explicates the spontaneous birth of popular poetry (speech) from the interaction between Man's activity and his geographic milieu. This is, of course, a relationship that is presumed by the indigenous text to be an immanent aspect of the universe it portrays. Yet the organic nature of the link that the fragment affirms is compromised by the fragment's very presence in the text, since in order to comment critically on its own procedures the text must have abandoned that organicity in the first place. Hence, the passage points to the problematic rhetorical nature of "autochthonous" discourse, that is, to the way in which its rhetoric undermines the legitimacy of that which it affirms.

Sometimes this commentary assumes a less conspicuous form that nonetheless cannot conceal entirely its interpretive objective. At certain moments the narrative acquires an essentially definitory tone: there is a sudden break in the narrative that allows for the insertion of a detailed commentary on a specific element of the indigenous universe. Another expression of it is the voyage or excursion throughout the privileged landscape that customarily precedes the writing of these novels: an expedition where the author's roaming throughout the land acquires all the trappings of the philologist's field research on language and milieu. Other textual features, such as the glossaries that are appended to the majority of these works and the singling out of particular words or expressions in the text through the use of quotation marks or italics, constitute further signs of the existence of this critical dimension within the text of the *novela de la tierra*.

Therefore, far from simply having a referential or ontological reality, the term "autochthonous" could be used to describe a rhetorical figure encompassing three elements: spoken language, geographical location, and a given human activity. The power of the figure that organizes these categories derives from the fact that any one of the three elements can be subsumed under the remaining two. The three categories are thoroughly intertwined in a complex synecdochical fashion: the land is the scene where the human activity takes place, but it is also the milieu from which the peculiarities of spoken language are supposed to have emerged. Language, in turn, is not only tied to the geography, but is also the lexicon, the argot that is itself an integral component of the human activity depicted. In the *novela de la tierra* then, "the autochthonous" is a discursive mode generated by a complex rhetorical figure that organizes a synecdochical interaction between the three semantic fields described above. The relationships that the figure establishes between the three categories are meant to project discursively the organicity that presumably binds together and relates to the environment every one of a culture's manifestations. The relative importance of each element in the figure can vary from text to text, but a given configuration of it underwrites and sustains the discourse of the autochthonous in each work.

Moreover, the three categories are capable of encompassing a large number of distinct manifestations, a fact that endows the rhetorical figure that contains them with a seemingly inexhaustible generative capacity. Oral language, for instance, can be incorporated in a number of different ways, such as the retelling of legends and tales or the performance of popular poetry and song; it also explains certain textual features, such as the phonetic writing that is so prevalent in the texts, the glossaries that are almost a fixture as addenda to these texts, and the typographical highlighting of certain words by using boldface, italicizing, or enclosing them inside quotation marks. Similarly, the land can subsume the myriad manifestations of non-urban geography, while also sustaining both the detailed descriptions of topographic features and the marked emphasis on spatial organization in the novels. By the same token, the intricate accounts of a given métier and the use of a specialized vocabulary to accomplish this description are some of the textual attributes that arise from the third category, one that can include the many facets and operations of the human activity portrayed. This understanding of the indigenous as a rhetorical figure opens the way for rethinking the nativist literary text as a productivity, that is, as an activity that produces a highly specific discursive performance. The outcome of this performance is "the autochthonous," a discursive construct that is sustained by the figure described above, and not by the worldly, referential status of the essence to which it purportedly alludes.

The rhetorical figure described thus far is the form with which these novels convey textually the wholeness and consonance that are assumed to obtain in the indigenous universe. The overarching assumption at work here is that a balance exists between environment and Man in their mutual interaction and influence.

Nonetheless, once that consonance is assumed, a number of narrative permutations become possible. First, the organic circumstance can be portrayed as a present state of affairs; second, it can be depicted as under threat by some external force or event; or lastly, it can be represented as having been categorically lost. It is probably not a coincidence that the three novels that have been traditionally considered paradigms of the *novela de la tierra* each represents one of these narrative possibilities. These are: *Don Segundo Sombra* [*Don Segundo Sombra: Shadows in the Pampas*], *Doña Bárbara* [*Doña Bárbara*], and *La vorágine* [*The Vortex*].

Don Segundo Sombra by the Argentinian writer Ricardo Güiraldes is a consummate example of the first of these variants. The novel is generally constructed as a *Bildungsroman*, a novel of apprenticeship, in which the young protagonist is tutored in the ways of the gaucho by the larger-than-life man named in the novel's title. The boy, presented in the beginning as a wayward orphan precariously leaning towards an inconsequential adolescence of petty misconduct and boredom, is lifted from this aimless context by his fortuitous encounter with Don Segundo. He joins the latter in his wanderings throughout the pampas in a seemingly carefree search for yet another horse to tame or a new herd of cattle to drive. Patiently he gains from his mentor the knowledge of the métier and the *ethos* of the gaucho way of life. One day, near the close of the novel, the boy discovers that he is not truly an orphan, but rather the illegitimate offspring of a landowning grandee who has recognized him as sole heir in his will. His apprenticeship is finished at this point, and with great sadness and apprehension he abandons his life as a gaucho to assume his new status as landowner and master. As part of his new identity he acquires a more traditional education that allows him to write the autobiographical account that comprises the text of the novel.

Hence, *Don Segundo Sombra* is a work written from a perspective that infuses the narration with a melancholy sensation of nostalgia and a foreboding sense of loss. Yet this narrative situation is, nonetheless, the perfect vantage point from which to depict the organic, interconnected world that the universe of the gaucho is claimed to be. In this fashion, the gaucho's world is considered from the outside, but as a rounded totality – the way one holds at some distance a translucent sphere for examination. There is a continuum of transcendence that envelops the protagonist in his experiencing of that world, from the activities of taming a horse or butchering a cow, to the language that he speaks while in the pampas. Here lies, however, the principal difficulty inherent in this modality of the *criollista* novel: the conflict between the metaphysical stasis of the world portrayed by the text and the change and movement demanded by narrative plot. Indeed, very little actually *happens* in *Don Segundo Sombra*, since the novel is a celebration of the immutable and seamless spirit of the gaucho. This explains why the boy's discovery of his real identity is not portrayed as a loss of that transcendence, but rather as a raising of it to a different, perhaps even higher plane. For the novel strongly suggests that the ex-orphan/ex-gaucho will become an enlightened landowner, one who will administer his property with, and from within, the knowledge that he has painstakingly accumulated as a gaucho.

One can envision readily the ideological implications of this argument, particularly when the novel is considered in the Argentinian context from which it arose. The introduction of an ethical dimension to landowning can be regarded as a call to action by one of its members to an absentee elite which had neglected its patrimony and squandered its resources, and which was rapidly being overtaken by a commercial and industrial urban bourgeoisie. One can also take into consideration the massive influx of immigrants into the country that had peaked towards the turn of the century, and that could be regarded as a threat to the concept of Argentinian identity that had held sway until that time: a concept that, because it had been formulated by that propertied class, predictably revolved around it. These are the particular Argentinian circumstances that may have inflected on the more comprehensive affirmation of autochthonous values that swept the Latin American continent during the period under consideration.

Rómulo Gallegos's *Doña Bárbara* is an instance of the second narrative possibility delineated earlier. Here the balance and symmetry of the autochthonous world is assumed to exist just as clearly as in the first modality, but there is a circumstance or event that threatens with the loss of that equilibrium. Hence, the quintessential situation described by this case is that of crisis. The predominant tone is one of urgency, since the narrative wishes to call attention to an element understood to be deleterious to the presumed ontological permanence of the indigenous world. The understanding of the present moment as a critical juncture determines the particularities of this narrative modality, especially the Manichaean vision advanced by the story. In fact, given both its desire to denounce the *status quo* and the attendant prescriptive intention, it is easy for this kind of work to acquire the fundamental attributes of allegorical narration. The accusation of being simple (and simpleminded) allegories is the charge that is most commonly leveled against novels such as *Doña Bárbara*, an assessment that is difficult to disallow – at least on the most superficial plane of analysis.

The setting for *Doña Bárbara* is the plains or *llanos* of the Apure river in Venezuela. The novel begins with Santos Luzardo, the last heir of a landowning family whose origins go back to the Spanish Conquest, travelling from the city to the plain to sell his property, a vast expanse of land called Altamira. There he discovers that his patrimony is being slowly taken over by a mysterious and ruthless woman by the name of

Doña Bárbara, who has had an illegitimate daughter (Marisela) by Santos's uncle (Lorenzo), and has reduced him to a drunken shadow of his former self. Santos is captivated again by the indomitable power and potentiality of the land, and decides not to sell his property and to struggle against Doña Bárbara instead. In the remainder of the novel Luzardo is shown weakening Doña Bárbara's domination over the *llano* in a number of encounters with her henchmen or with other symbols of her power. Finally, it is intimated that Doña Bárbara commits suicide (in any event she is never heard from again), and Luzardo manages to reconstitute the original family property of Altamira through marriage to Doña Bárbara's sole heiress, Marisela. The work ends hopefully, on a note of resolute affirmation of the country's future triumph over its present ills.

Although the novel's thesis is fairly transparent – modernization will redress the present circumstance of barbarism – the particular attributes of Doña Bárbara make her a contradictory character with regard to the novel's ideological intention of addressing a presumably critical situation. One would expect that the organicity of the autochthonous universe would be endangered by an alien, external force, one whose disruptive presence would serve to provoke the crisis that the novel wishes to underscore. Nonetheless, in Gallegos's work, Doña Bárbara is ambiguously identified *both* as an agent of chaos and as having arisen from the land itself. This ambiguity can also be seen at work in the articulation of Luzardo's reformist project for the plains: he is depicted both as a relentless supporter of progress and change, yet also as thoroughly susceptible to the enchantment of the primordial and violent power of the land. This is why, for all its explicit optimism, the novel's conclusion is paradoxical: it proposes simultaneously an openness to a future of progress *and* the re-enactment of a preterit state of affairs in the reconstitution of Luzardo's ancestral patrimony. One could interpret in this problematic ending the ambivalent juxtaposition of a desire for modernity, on the one hand, and the wish to protect traditional values from the encroachment of the modern, on the other. Such a discordance would appear to stem from an ambivalence toward modernity that is characteristic of societies that regard themselves as eccentric to the metropolitan foci of modern experience. In them modernity is wished for, since it holds the promise of full participation in the world, yet it is also seen with apprehension for the potential it has to render worthless the marginal experience of those societies.

The third narrative modality enacted by the *criollista* novel is represented paradigmatically by José Eustasio Rivera's work *La vorágine*. Here the transcendence of the indigenous universe has been definitively lost on account of some circumstance or event. In this rendering the immanent design of that world acquires now a contrary sign; in other words, there is as much correspondence and continuity between environment and man as before, but this time the outcome is what could be described as a negative transcendence, a state of permanent damnation. The loss of meaning and the breakdown of order is so complete in this case that the world portrayed possesses a paradoxical dystopian wholeness all its own. This is why Rivera's novel has been traditionally accused of ambiguous intentionality, of lack of structure, and of general purposelessness: the loss of significance that the novel assumes in the universe it depicts extends to the text's inner workings as a purveyor of meaning as well.

Arturo Cova, a hypersensitive and melodramatic poet, is the protagonist and narrator of *La vorágine*. Having seduced his mistress (Alicia), he flees with her from an unnamed city to the Colombian plains in order to avoid facing the consequences of his actions. Subsequently Alicia is either kidnapped or willingly charmed by a ruthless rubber entrepreneur (Barrera), whose area of operations is the latex-producing jungle region of the Putumayo. With hurt pride and in a heightened emotional state, Cova travels deep into the thicket, ostensibly to recover his lost mistress and to punish the affront to his honor. But every step into the jungle brings only despair, illness, disaster, and death. The terrible exploitation associated with the Amazonian rubber industry is denounced in a number of scenes or events in which the enormous human toll of the trade is deplored. Yet Nature itself is also an agent of destruction in *La vorágine*: hordes of carnivorous ants, disease, treacherous rapids, etc., conspire against the advance of Cova and the group of men that has accompanied him. The feeling of helplessness and lack of sense is conveyed by the ease with which the party loses its way in the uncharted and unmarked expanses of the jungle. Finally, Cova manages to find his rival; a struggle ensues and Barrera is killed, his body eaten by piranha fish. There is a postscript to the novel by a supposed friend of the poet, who informs the reader that he has received a communiqué from the Colombian consulate in Manaus (Brazil) regarding the fate of the party: not a trace of them is to be found. The justly famous last words of the novel leave no doubt concerning the pessimism and darkness of the work's thrust: "The jungle devoured them!"

Perhaps the greatest difficulty in interpreting *La vorágine* lies in the impossibility of isolating any one argument or purpose as paramount in the text's rhetorical or ideological organization. This quality may stem, as implied earlier, from the novel's attempt to project a negative totality; but the troublesome recalcitrance to exegesis still remains. At times the work appears to be a manifesto against the Amazonian rubber trade, and Rivera often argued for such an intention after the novel's publication. Yet the depiction of Nature as an intrinsically harmful force argues against, or in any event weakens, the corruptive characterization of the rubber industry that the novel would advance: does man invade and pervert Nature, or is Nature itself bent on destruction in the first place? The same can be said, for instance, regarding the novel's ambiguous characterization of the poet Arturo Cova. He is capable of going from intense experiences of lucidity and self-demystification to equally extreme episodes of blindness, melodrama, and self-deceit. This aspect has larger consequences, though, given the first-person narrative perspective employed universally in the novel: the expression "unreliable narrator" cannot begin to do justice to the destabilizing effect that Cova's performance as narrator has on most readers of Rivera's text.

From a more comprehensive perspective, though, the contradictory qualities evinced by *La vorágine* may be illustrative of the quandary that "the autochthonous," as conceived by the *novela de la tierra*, ultimately entailed for Latin American writers and intellectuals of the period under consideration. For these writers the assumption was that national or even continental identity was to be founded on a cultural belief in the correspondence between geography and man. This belief necessarily had to overlook or suppress the fact that, prior to that moment, the distinctiveness of Latin America had been predicated on asserting the existence of an untamed, savage Nature that lent its power and specificity to all New World creations. Already in Sarmiento's *Facundo* (1945) one finds a signal example of this maneuver:

> If any form of national literature shall appear in these new American societies, it must result from the description of the mighty scenes of nature, and still more from the illustration of the struggle between European civilization and native barbarism, between mind and matter – a struggle of imposing magnitudes in South America, and which suggests scenes so peculiar, so characteristic, and so far outside the circle of ideas in which the European mind has been educated, that their dramatic relations would be unrecognized machinations except in the countries in which they are found. (p. 24)

Hence, transforming the Latin American cultural myth of Nature as a violent and wild presence to one in which the latter was perceived as benign and organic could not be an uncomplicated, effortless affair. In point of fact, this internal contradiction is one that the nativist literary discourse never managed to resolve satisfactorily. This is why one finds within the genre a spectrum of works that goes from the transcendent bonding with Nature represented by *Don Segundo Sombra* to the man-eating vortex of Rivera's work. Both conceptions of Nature can be used as foundations for claims of distinctiveness and identity; and indeed, both were – regardless of the resulting and irremediable contradictions – mobilized simultaneously by the *novela de la tierra*.

[7]

The novel of the Mexican Revolution
John Rutherford

The Mexican Revolution was one of the last old-fashioned, pre-industrial wars, in which modern techniques and machinery had only an occasional role to play. It was a war of epic battles and mythical warrior-heroes, two of whom – Pancho Villa and Emiliano Zapata – have achieved fame throughout the world. And since it was a war in which people were more important than machines, it provided a generation of Mexican novelists with an abundant source of inspiration and material.

It began in November 1910. The president, Porfirio Díaz (1830–1915), had ruled, in person or by proxy, since 1876, retaining power for so long by imposing a right-wing dictatorship on a country which, despite some industrialization, retained social and economic structures based on the quasi-feudal system of the hacienda. For some years before 1910 a brave and idealistic northern liberal, Franciso I. Madero (1873–1913), had been campaigning for a revision of the political system and the establishment of a democracy based on the principles of universal suffrage and no presidential re-election. Seeing that his peaceful campaign was achieving nothing, for in fraudulent presidential elections in July 1910 Díaz was re-elected yet again, Madero called for an uprising against the dictator on November 20.

It seemed a hopeless cause. However, Díaz was a tired old man, and his government and his generals had grown old with him. The federal army was incapable of quashing this minor revolt, which gathered support as the months went by. In May 1911 the rebels won their first serious battle, capturing the northern frontier town of Ciudad Juárez. Díaz went into exile and Madero, now a popular hero and "the Apostle of Democracy," entered Mexico City in triumph. He was elected president in October 1911.

Madero believed that his political reform was all Mexico needed, but the events of his brief presidency were to prove him wrong. Disillusion and unrest grew as his supporters realized that the old order was not going to be dismantled, something which would have been difficult because Madero's all too rapid military victory had left the *Porfirista* power structure intact. Yet *Porfiristas* could not forgive Madero for having defeated their leader, and in February 1913 it was a right-wing *coup d'état* which deposed and murdered him and his principal colleagues.

The new president was the federal army general, Victoriano Huerta (1845–1916), a curious mixture of the villain and the buffoon. He attempted to take Mexico back to the days of Don Porfirio and to impose a similar dictatorship backed by army, church, and aristocracy. He was acclaimed by those of like mind as "the iron hand needed to govern Mexico," but the iron hand was too often clutching a bottle of whisky to be capable of governing itself, let alone a country. A revolution – for the first time a national revolution – was soon raging against him. President Woodrow Wilson also wished to rid Mexico of Huerta, but the clumsy method he chose – the occupation of the Gulf Coast port of Veracruz – only aroused a widespread patriotic fury which the dictator did his best to turn to his own advantage. Nevertheless, the federal army was overwhelmed in the battle of Zacatecas in June 1914, and the wretched Huerta fled into exile.

Yet this was not the end. The national revolution had been in reality a coalition of different movements, each with its own interests and aims. The most important were those of Pancho Villa (1878–1923) and of Venustiano Carranza (1859–1920) in the north, and of Emiliano Zapata (1879–1919) in the south. Opposition to Huerta had been the only uniting force, and the revolutionary forces split into their component parts soon after victory. A convention of generals held in Aguascalientes in October 1914 failed to achieve unity. What now developed was a bitter struggle between Carranza and Villa, the latter of whom formed an insecure alliance with Zapata. The struggle reached its bloody climax in the series of battles at Celaya, León, and Aguascalientes in April–July 1915, ending with the decisive victory of the *Carrancistas* over the *Villistas*. Localized fighting was to continue for several years, but by 1916 Carranza was established as the final victor. The old order was defeated and the way cleared for the modernization of Mexico. A nationalistic and reformist but not socialist constitution was drawn up in 1917, and in the same year Carranza was elected president.

Two definitions of the novel of the Mexican Revolution are in use. One is narrow: "novels written by Mexicans about the destructive, military phase of the Revolution, from 1910 until about 1920." Although novels must be set in the military phase to be included, they do not have to narrate military events.

The broad definition is based on the Mexican government's assertion that the Revolution did not end in 1920 but continues pacifically yet dynamically in its constructive phase, as the ruling party's name suggests: Partido Revolucionario Institucional. Any social or political novel set in post-1910 Mexico is, then, a novel of the Revolution. This definition is imprecise and open-ended, and puts disparate novels into the same category.

The definition used in this chapter is, therefore, the former. The only reason why the other one has found any favour seems to be ideological rather than literary: accepting it is held to imply a progressive outlook, a solidarity with the determination of the Mexican people and their government never to tire in their struggle toward a better future; whereas accepting the narrow definition is considered to imply a negative, anti-revolutionary, and reactionary attitude. The choice of definition in this chapter should not be regarded as having any such ideological implications. It is purely practical and literary.

In this context, the word "novel" must be allowed a broader scope than usual. Works which are established as significant novels of the Revolution, such as Martín Luis Guzmán's *El águila y la serpiente* (1928), José Rubén Romero's *Apuntes de un lugareño* (1932) and José Vasconcelos's *Ulises criollo*, would be classed as autobiographies in any other context. However, the division between autobiography and novel is notoriously hazy: Romero inserts at least one fictional character into his book. It would also be perverse to exclude works which it is general practice to include. On the grounds that a word means what its community of users understand it to mean, "novel" includes for present purposes all those autobiographies, memoirs, and biographies which have any aesthetic pretences or qualities. Thus defined, there are some 140 novels of the Mexican Revolution, written by nearly 100 novelists.

The production of the novels of the Mexican Revolution followed a pattern which has been observed by D. G. Thomas in other twentieth-century war fiction, notably in the novels of the First World War and in those of the Spanish Civil War. In each of these three cases there are two distinct periods of productivity.

War novels first appear while the war is being fought. These early novels are written in haste, in difficult circumstances, as vehicles for political propaganda. The novelists are too involved in the catastrophic events and the extreme emotions they describe to be able to turn them into works of art. Furthermore, these often inexpert writers, lacking literary culture, remain close to the traditions of the popular novel, and their works reflect its artlessness in, for example, ponderous melodrama, moral Manicheism, clumsy authorial intervention to deliver simplistic messages, heavy-handed manipulation of plot, crude characterization, forced and inappropriate inclusion of sentimental love intrigues, and language which fluctuates between banality and laboured attempts to reproduce what such novelists regard as elevated literary style.

The first wave of war novels ends as the war ends, or a little later. Such works are an immediate, ephemeral response to a crisis, and their impact, if they have any, is soon forgotten: in the years after the war, people try to forget the recent horrors as they remake their lives. Escapist fiction flourishes during this post-war period.

As life returns to normal and memories of suffering become less acute, novelists and their readers develop a willingness and a need to look back at the war and reassess it. At this point, about ten years after the end of hostilities, the second wave of war novels begins. It lasts for another fifteen years or so, by which time the subject has been worked through and most novelists move on to other matters. These second-wave novels are written in tranquility, with all the advantages of distance and hindsight, often by experienced novelists concerned not to make propaganda but to examine, explore, and reflect. Most of the war novels which survive as works of literature belong to the second wave: those of Erich Maria Remarque, Max Aub, Francisco Ayala, and Ramón Sender.

The novels of the Mexican Revolution follow the pattern of development in two waves in all but one important regard. The exception is Mariano Azuela (1873–1952). He is thus comparable with Henri Barbusse, the First-World-War novelist whose influential work *Le feu* was first published in 1916; but Azuela's writing has lasted better. According to the normal pattern, Azuela should have written his war novels not in the period 1911–1918, as he did, but in 1928–1945, for they possess most of the virtues of second-wave war novels and few of the weaknesses of first-wave ones. Also, as we shall see, Azuela and his novel *Los de abajo* (1916, i.e. written in 1915) [*The Underdogs*] were ignored until 1925, when they set the Mexican second wave in motion. They then so dominated the later writers that most of them took Azuela as a model to be imitated rather than a point of departure.

Azuela was not only a first-wave novelist but in all probability the author of the first novel of the Mexican Revolution, *Andrés Pérez, maderista* (1911). The only rival for this distinction is *La majestad caída* (1911) by Juan A. Mateos (1831–1913), who had gained a certain reputation in the Porfirian period as a prolific writer of plays, poetry, and sentimental historical novels. His treatment of the fall of the dictator, an unintentional parody of the popular romantic historical novel, is a sad reflection of the decline of this writer's limited abilities. Nevertheless, it was *La majestad caída* rather than the intelligent, perceptive, and ironical *Andrés Pérez, maderista* that set the style for the novels of the Revolution – some thirty of them – that were to be written during the next dozen years or so. There were a few exceptions, most notably the other novels by Azuela: *Los de abajo, Los caciques* (1917) [*The Bosses*], *Las moscas* (1918) [*The Flies*], *Domitilo quiere ser diputado* (1918), and *Las tribulaciones de una familia decente* (1918) [*The Trials of a Respectable Family*]. The only other worthwhile novel of the Revolution written during this early period is *En el sendero de las mandrágoras* (2 volumes, 1920) by the journalist Antonio Ancona Albertos (1883–1954). This is an intelligent and thoughtful account of the life during the Revolution of a dissolute but idealistic young newspaperman, yet, like all the other first-wave novels, it fell into obscurity where, like all but those of Azuela, it remains.

It was not until the mid-1920s that a conviction started to develop in Mexican intellectual and literary circles that it was time to abandon the sentimental, escapist fiction which was still fashionable, just as it had been during the Porfirian period, and to write novels that would confront the recent upheavals and address themselves to the realities of contemporary life. Government spokesmen for the arts did much to create this new atmosphere, which provoked a polemic in the Mexican press in December 1924 and January 1925 on the subject "Does a Modern Mexican Literature Exist?" In the course of this polemic the prestigious critic Francisco Monterde based his defense of contemporary Mexican fiction on the literary values of *Los de abajo*. Azuela and his novel became famous almost overnight. Most of the national newspapers published interviews with him, and one of them serialized *Los de abajo*. Important Spanish critics now noticed and praised his novel and a Madrid edition followed in 1927. Azuela, having abandoned the Revolution as a fictional subject nine years earlier, found his reputation established throughout the Spanish-speaking world as the novelist of the Mexican Revolution.

These events set the second wave in motion. The government helped to sustain it, by providing young novelists with undemanding employment yet not attempting to control or censor their novels, despite the fact that most of them, following Azuela's example in this as in many other matters, pointed to the conclusion that the Revolution had done nothing to remove injustice or to make governments less corrupt; which were well-founded accusations. The events of 1910–1920 became the subject-matter of many novels written during the 1930s by new novelists who dominated the Mexican literary scene during this decade, the most noteworthy of which we will examine in as much detail as space allows. First, however, we must consider the undisputed master, Mariano Azuela.

Azuela was a doctor who, by the time he wrote *Andrés Pérez, maderista*, was nearly forty and already had three novels to his name. Each is a naturalistic treatment of contemporary Mexican life and expresses concerns which reappear in Azuela's novels of the Revolution: the inexorable defeat of the idealistic reformer in *Los fracasados* (1908), the suffering of the defenseless poor at the hands of rich landowners and corrupt authorities in *Mala yerba* (1909) [*Marcela: A Mexican Love Story*], and the fatuous aristocratic aspirations of the middle classes in *Sin amor* (1912; but written in 1910 or earlier).

This training can explain the assurance with which *Andrés Pérez, maderista* is written. Andrés tells his own story. He is a lethargic, self-centred journalist from Mexico City on holiday in the provinces who, as a result of events outside his control, and having done nothing to deserve it (having, indeed, done the opposite), finds himself acclaimed as a hero of the *Maderista* rebellion in the state of Zacatecas. Irony accumulates as he realizes that the other local leaders of triumphant *Maderismo* are also yesterday's *Porfiristas*: the only genuine Revolutionary has died in battle. *Andrés Pérez, maderista* is a skillful evocation of the atmosphere of the sedate, self-satisfied Porfirian society which coped with Madero's rebellion by absorbing it.

Los caciques was the next novel Azuela wrote, in 1914. It describes the effects of the Revolution, between its outbreak and early 1914, on the business community of a provincial town, and the ruination of an honest and excessively naive small trader caught in the grips of the unscrupulous men who control the politics and economy of the region. The pessimism of this depiction of the Revolution's failure to deal with injustice is attenuated in the final scene: as the anti-Huerta Revolutionaries occupy the town, the trader's orphaned children take their revenge by setting fire to the bosses' magnificent new warehouse.

Next Azuela wrote the book which was to exert such an influence on the Spanish American novel. In late October 1914 he joined the guerrilla band of the *Villista*, Julián Medina, and he wrote most of *Los de abajo*, a fictional reworking of these revolutionary experiences, while serving under Medina as head of medical services. Azuela claimed to have written one battle scene as he witnessed the events on which he based it. He completed the first version of the novel on going into exile in El Paso, Texas, in October 1915; it was immediately published there in serial form, coming out as a book in December, although the title-page is dated 1916. Azuela later made substantial revisions to his novel, the definitive version of which was first published in Mexico City in 1920.

The story is simple. It concerns the formation, rise, and fall of the guerrilla band of Demetrio Macías, in 1914 and 1915. From its beginning as a handful of discontented friends, the band grows fast, joining the mainstream of the anti-Huerta movement at the battle of Zacatecas, in which Demetrio plays a heroic part. However, then the decline sets in, until Demetrio and the few friends who stay with him are ambushed and killed in the canyon where they had enjoyed their first military success by ambushing and killing a small group of federal soldiers:

The rifle smoke lingers. Cicadas intone their imperturbable and mysterious chant; doves in crevices coo; cows graze peacefully.

The sierra is dressed for a celebration; upon its inaccessible peaks a pure white mist descends, like snowy crepe on the head of a bride.

And at the foot of a gaping cleft, as sumptuous as the porch of an ancient cathedral, Demetrio Macías, his eyes fixed for ever, continues to take aim with the barrel of his rifle.

Azuela's choice of title was an inspired one. *Los de abajo* is a powerful and suggestive title, all the more so for being brief and seemingly simple. It tells the potential reader that this is not just a novel of the Revolution but also, with its collective, lower-class, and therefore largely Indian protagonist, a revolutionary novel (there was, however, a precedent for such a title: *Les Misérables*). The title also identifies a central contradiction of the Revolution, on which this novel focuses: fought by the indigenous peasantry and, in theory, for them, it benefited not them but the bourgeoisie, which it put in the place of the traditional aristocratic ruling classes. Those underneath remained underneath after all their sacrifices and all the promises made to them.

Los de abajo is a realist novel, but in several important ways it distances itself from nineteenth-century fictional practice. There has been much comment on its fragmentary style and structure. In most earlier novels a continuous, flowing narrative provides, often in great detail, all the information which the readers are considered by the narrators to need in order to recreate the fictional world in their imagination. Yet in *Los de abajo* the narrator leaves many gaps which readers must fill for themselves. There are gaps in the description of setting, which is suggested with light and impressionistic touches, often powerful, original, and lyrical, as in the last sentences of the novel. *Los de abajo* avoids the heavy, clichéd rhetoric which clogs much nineteenth-century fiction, preferring a language the strength of which is its evocative brevity. There are gaps, too, in characterization, which emerges, often with fine subtlety demanding close attention from the reader, in the course of dialogue and action rather than being given as descriptive labels, as Clive Griffin demonstrates in his *A Critical Guide to "Los de abajo."* There are also gaps in the telling of the story, which jumps from one episode to another: what lies between – not only the events but also the causal connections – is something the reader has to reconstruct. None of the major events in the Revolution during the period of the novel's action – the battles of Zacatecas and of Celaya, the Convention of Aguascalientes, and the American occupation of Veracruz – is narrated directly, the occupation is not even mentioned.

In its fragmentary discourse, *Los de abajo* foreshadows the Latin American novel of the 1960s and later. However, Azuela never takes fragmentation to the extremes of the later novelists. In his novel events are narrated in chronological order: he does not subvert but merely interrupts the traditional narrative sequence. Attentive readers can easily fill the gaps and make sense of the narration, because the narrator is always considerate enough to provide sufficient information. In this sense, *Los de abajo*, despite its innovatory features, remains within the boundaries of Realism: it tells a coherent story about characters and events which the reader is encouraged to regard as having a real existence. It is also a traditional novel in that it has a clear unity: behind the fragmentation of the surface, there is a precise and symmetrical patterning, in the beginnings at Juchipila, the rise to the climax of success at Zacatecas, and the decline to the end at Juchipila. What is more, the reader is invited to view the novel's action as a microcosm representing the whole Revolution when, just before the final scene in the canyon, Juchipila is identified as "the cradle of the Revolution of 1910" (Part III, Chapter 4). The reader might also notice that the rise to a climax at Zacatecas, after which Demetrio's band declines into purposeless barbarity, reflects what many people, including Azuela, have seen as the Revolution's development as a whole. If the fragmentary narration suggests something about Azuela's view of the haphazard, disorganized nature of the Mexican Revolution, the underlying symmetry reflects his fatalistic belief in the futility of such attempts to improve the lot of the underdog.

Another innovative feature of *Los de abajo* is its use of Mexican, rather than standard peninsular Spanish as approved by the Royal Academy, not only in dialogue – the characters speak a range of lively and convincing varieties of colloquial Mexican Spanish – but also in the narrator's own voice. Azuela was attacked by purists for the ignorant use of barbarisms, but of course this linguistic departure was a necessary feature of the general move away from the dependence on European models in search of a narrative which would be a more adequate expression of the Mexican consciousness and of Mexican realities.

A further innovation is the portrayal of the relationship between Nature and its human inhabitants. In the nineteenth-century fictional tradition the setting is a reflection or projection of themes, moods, and personalities. However, in *Los de abajo* the relationship is more often one of stark opposition, as in the novel's last sentences quoted above, between the beauty and peacefulness of Nature and the brutality of men and women, for whom animal imagery is insistently used.

This extraordinary novel has its weaknesses. Some of the passages that Azuela interpolated during his revision for the 1920 edition are not very happily integrated with the rest of the text. More fundamentally, Azuela's efforts, as a liberal from a bourgeois background, to transcend the race and class barriers that separate him from "los de abajo" are admirable but, perhaps inevitably, not altogether successful: it is noteworthy that this is Azuela's only novel about the revolutionary rank and file. There is middle-class condescension in such statements as "those words kept battering on their sluggish brains like hammers on an anvil" (Part III, Chapter 1). The presentation of the revolutionary peasants' orgies of destruction invites the reader to condemn them from the viewpoint of a bourgeois morality, without any indication that this is a comprehensible expression of class hatred (we do find such indication in the description of the destructive act at the end of *Los caciques* – but this one expresses middle-class hatred of oppressors); or that the typewriters, books, and works of art they destroy cannot have any value for an illiterate peasantry; or that their failure to appreciate a culture from which they are excluded is not their fault. Furthermore, Azuela – who in other ways did so much to free the Latin American novel from nineteenth-century European traditions – was a man steeped in Positivism and Naturalism, and the sympathy he expresses for the suffering poor is opposed by the fatalistic pessimism fostered by these philosophical and literary movements. His preaching of this fatalism, which often takes the form of positivistic racialism, through characters inserted as authorial mouthpieces, is one of the less subtle features of *Los de abajo* and many of his other novels.

Nevertheless, there can be no doubt that *Los de abajo* is a remarkable piece of work, of great importance in the history of Latin American literature.

This concentration on the merits and importance of one novel should not be taken to imply that it is the only one of Azuela's novels worth reading. All his novels of the Revolution – he wrote three more – are fascinating. *Las moscas* portrays the job-hungry bureaucracy that followed Villa's forces. In at least one aspect, its lack of any plot, it is an even more experimental novel than *Los de abajo*. *Domitilo quiere ser diputado* is an accomplished satire of the civilian and military *Carrancista* leaders, whom Azuela ridicules with grotesque dehumanizing caricature. Finally, *Las tribulaciones de una familia decente* portrays, not without sympathy, the reactions of an *hacendado* family to the loss of its wealth.

Of the many novelists of the second wave, none has achieved anything like the enduring success of Azuela.

The first novel of the second wave was by Martín Luis Guzmán (1887–1976) – *El águila y la serpiente* (1928, but serialized in a Mexico City newspaper two years earlier, translated as *The Eagle and the Serpent*, 1930). Guzmán recounts memoirs of his life among revolutionary leaders in 1913 and 1914, making no attempt to fictionalize his narration, which stands well apart both from Azuela's novels and from those of the later novelists. This is the work of an urbane, cultured man, written in careful, studied, elegant Spanish. Descriptions are lengthy and minute, reflecting the attitudes of the detached aesthete caught up in the Revolution, who insists on finding picturesqueness and even beauty there, and on moving away from concrete reality into metaphysical speculations:

> In the military hospital of Culiacán I discovered that . . . there are, without doubt, serious bullets, conscientious bullets, those which kill with an accurate blow and wound with straightforward cruelty; but there are also imaginative, fanciful bullets, those which are no sooner on their way than they succumb to the universal longing to play, and make merry as they carry out their task . . . Each separate casualty was a revelation of the existence of another category of bullet, of a personality alive in each missile at the very moment of delivering its blow.
>
> (Part I, Book 5, Chapter 7)

The theme is elaborated at length. The reader might suspect that the Revolution was, for Guzmán, some kind of theatrical performance, and his indifference in the face of suffering can repel; or maybe such aesthetic distancing was the only way for him to cope with the horrors of war. There is little ethical content in *El águila y la serpiente*, except the occasional lament – frequent in Azuela and nearly all the novelists – that a revolution which started with such high idealism in 1910 ended by merely replacing one corrupt system with another.

The fascination which the personality of Pancho Villa exerted over Guzmán, revealed in many passages of *El águila y la serpiente*, led him to the over-ambitious project of a narration of Villa's life as he imagined Villa would have narrated it: *Memorias de Pancho Villa* (5 volumes, 1938, 1939, 1939, 1940, and 1964).

There was only one significant woman novelist of the Revolution, and she was also one of the most original and imaginative writers of this movement. Her works deserve more recognition than they have received. *Cartucho* (1931) by Nellie Campobello (b. 1909) is a series of brief scenes of the Revolution in the north, in *Villista* territory during the period of Villa's decline, as the narrator remembers having witnessed them as a child. Like Azuela, Campobello achieves expressiveness and freshness with techniques of economic brevity, gap-leaving, fragmentation, suggestion and evocation rather than detailed description, and the use of colloquial Mexican language in both narration and dialogue. However, she goes further than Azuela: the chronological sequence is not just interrupted but subverted, events being recorded in the order in which they are remembered, as a part of an exploration of the relationships between past witnessing and present narrating. Moreover, the gaps are much larger and harder to fill: the child witness can only register the weird things adults keep doing to each other, she cannot begin to account for them. The juxtaposition of innocence and horror is the strength of *Cartucho*:

We saw some soldiers coming, holding up a tray; they walked by, talking and laughing. "Hey, what's that pretty stuff you've got there?" From where we were, above the street, we could see that in the basin there was something pink and quite pretty. They smiled, lowered the tray, and showed us what they were carrying. "Guts," said the youngest one, looking at us to see if we were frightened; when we heard they were guts we got closer and looked at them; they were all rolled up as if they had no end. "Guts, how pretty!" (2, "Las tripas del general Sobarzo")

The entrails are from the embalmed body of an important general, on their way to the cemetery.

Cartucho is an uneven work (Campobello was twenty-one when she wrote it) but at its best, with its fresh, cliché-free, direct language, it has considerable power. *Las manos de mamá* (1937) pushes the experimentation of *Cartucho* still further, but as the title indicates the focus shifts from the Revolution to the narrator's mother.

In *Campamento* (1931), Gregorio López y Fuentes (1897–1967) takes the idea of the collective protagonist to the extreme of not naming any of the characters: "There's no need at all for names, in the Revolution at least. It would be the same as trying to put names to the waves in a river" (Part 1, Section 2). López y Fuentes also adopts the techniques of plotlessness and fragmentation in this montage of scenes during one night in a revolutionary camp – presented as a microcosm of the Revolution – and attempts to emulate Azuela's laconic style, but he does not possess Azuela's gift for choosing the telling detail: all too often he states the obvious and then repeats it. Like *Los de abajo*, *Campamento* contains much dialogue; but López y Fuentes, unlike Azuela, is no master of this art. His use, for the sake of documentary realism, of a rigorously objective, external viewpoint (a narrative present tense is employed throughout) also creates problems which he fails to solve: characters' thoughts and feelings are conveyed with the clumsy device of narrative speculation ("he must be thinking that. . ."), and moral messages are delivered through characters created solely for that purpose.

Tierra (1932), by the same author, is one of the few fictional accounts of Zapata's Revolution. It depicts each of the years 1910–1920, using most of the techniques of *Campamento*, and sharing all its defects.

The year 1931 also saw the publication of *¡Vámonos con Pancho Villa!* (1931), by Rafael F. Muñoz (1899–1972), another novelist who follows Azuela's lead in such matters as episodic construction, economic style, lyrical Nature-description, and minimal characterization. Lacking Azuela's imaginative flair, however, he too often attempts to create interest by dwelling gratuitously on the gory and the macabre, something that Azuela never does. There is more interest in the same writer's *Se llevaron el cañón* *para Bachimba* (1941), a depiction of Orozco's revolt against Madero in 1912, as seen through the eyes of a boy caught up in it. Here sensationalism is abandoned and the possibilities of the first-person narration are thoughtfully exploited.

One of Mexico's best-known novelists of the earlier twentieth century, José Rubén Romero (1890–1952), wrote four novels of the Revolution: the memoirs *Apuntes de un lugareño* and *Desbandada* (1934), and the more fictional *Mi caballo, mi perro y mi rifle* (1936) and *Rosenda* (1946). His reputation does not rest on any of them, however. Romero's real interest is the affectionate and witty description of peaceful provincial life: the Revolution is portrayed as a remote force which ultimately bursts in with disastrous consequences.

The first two volumes of the autobiography of the philosopher and politician José Vasconcelos (1882–1959) concern his activities in the Revolution: *Ulises criollo*, and *La tormenta* (1936). Although they have been praised as important novels of the Revolution, it may be that such praise has more to do with the powerful personality of their eminent author than the quality of his prose, which is fluent but careless and undistinguished.

By the late 1930s so many novels of the Revolution had been written that the movement was showing symptoms of decline from exhaustion and repetition. Various writers made unsuccessful attempts to revive it by approaching the Revolution from new angles. Four of them can be mentioned.

Mauricio Magdaleno (b. 1906) introduced *Indigenismo* [Indigenism] into the novel of the Revolution in *El resplandor* (1937) [*Sunburst*] (1944) and *La Tierra Grande* (1949). However, he overlooked Azuela's lesson about the virtues of subtle suggestive understatement: these protest novels lack power and conviction because they make their points in predictable, repetitive, clumsy ways.

José Mancisidor (1894–1956) has been praised for writing the first and almost only socialist novels of the Revolution: as we have seen, the political stance of most of the significant novelists was that of Azuela, idealistic *Maderista* liberalism lamenting the moral decline of the Revolution and failing to notice what it did achieve. *En la rosa de los vientos* (1941) presents the Revolution in the north through the eyes of a reformed wastrel from Veracruz; *Frontera junto al mar* (1953) is a nationalistic narration of the United States' invasion of Veracruz. These novels, full of noble souls preaching worthy messages to each other, are not socialist works but clumsy, confused attempts to mislead readers into believing that the Revolution was socialist.

General Francisco L. Urquizo (1891–1969) was the only serious novelist of the Revolution to present the federal soldier's viewpoint, in *Tropa vieja*

(1943). This novel is a careful attempt to give a sympathetic and fair account of what it was like to fight against the Revolution. However, Urquizo was another unskilled and unimaginative novelist, and his work is an anthology of all the clichés of the movement. The curse of *costumbrismo* – the description in minute detail of all that which is typical or picturesque, without a thought for its artistic relevance – fell heavily upon Urquizo, as upon many of the less gifted novelists of the Revolution.

The innovation of Francisco Rojas González (1901–1951) in *La negra Angustias* (1944) was to make his protagonist a woman, to give her a powerful, idiosyncratic personality, and to attempt to explore this personality in depth. This psychological novel of the Revolution fails because the writing is laboured and the psychology melodramatic and unconvincing: as a result of childhood experiences Angustias, the fearsome leader of a band of *Zapatista* guerrillas, is both a hater and an imitator of men, but love for the most worthless of men turns her into a sweet, submissive, exploited but uncomplaining wife.

The efforts of these late novelists of the Revolution confirm that the topic was exhausted as far as prose fiction was concerned. Indeed, the whole of the second wave was a disappointing continuation, after Azuela's splendid start.

The importance of the novel of the Mexican Revolution cannot, however, be denied. It was a vital part of the discovery by Mexicans of their corporate identity, of the concept of *Mexicanidad*. Indeed, throughout Latin America the novels of the Mexican Revolution, particularly those of Azuela, showed writers how they could transform the European tradition, and develop ways of writing that were more adequate for the portrayal of American experience.

The Spanish American novel from 1950 to 1975
Randolph D. Pope

A radical shift in the way in which history and literature were conceived, interpreted, and written produced a change in the self-perception of Spanish American novelists between 1950 and 1975. The development of the cities, the coming of age of a large middle class, the Cuban Revolution, the Alliance for Progress, an increase in communication between the countries of Latin America, the greater importance of the mass media, and a greater attention to Latin America from Europe and the United States, contributed to this change. The most important political events of the period were the Cuban Revolution in 1959 and the Chilean *coup d'état* in 1973, but there were also others that affected writing, as they generated explanations, testimonies, or served as a troubling background: the fall of General Perón in Argentina, the protracted violent struggle of the urban guerrillas, brutally repressed in Argentina and Uruguay, and the unending violence in Colombia. These events are more than simply a framework in which to place the literary production of this period. Most of the novelists studied in this chapter believe there is a political and social discourse that only shows its weakness when exposed in the literary text. Their novels are engaged in an intense dialogue not only with other works of literature, but also with oral tradition, speech-writers, police reports, priests, and all defenders of blind orthodoxy. A history of this period must start by stating that history itself became problematic since the new generations questioned the traditional version of history and sought to replace it with their own, a more hesitant, shaded, and distrustful one than the clear-cut oppositions that prevailed before.

Critics continued to publish important and useful studies in which writers were ranked by their date of birth, but novelists themselves were participating in a continental upheaval that affected equally younger and older writers, a crisis centered on the Cuban Revolution and that became known as the *Boom*. While only a few novelists became identified with the *Boom*, as we shall see in detail later, there are many other writers who merit attention, occupied in the mapping of the rapidly changing national reality or in surrealist, existentialist, feminist, or other projects. In general – and considering there are many countries and hundreds of important authors – at the start of the period Realism prevails, with novels tinged by an existentialist pessimism, with well-rounded characters lamenting their destinies, and a straightforward narrative line. In the 1960s, language loosens up, gets hip, pop, streetwise, characters are much more complex, and the chronology becomes intricate, making of the reader an active participant in the deciphering of the text. Late in the period the political adventure goes sour, while the linguistic sophistication reaches a new height, and novelists turn more to a reflection on their own writing, a fiction on fiction or metafiction, while characters and story lines show the corrosive power of a Postmodern society, where all is equally available and insignificant.

More and more there is a shared literary culture in Spanish America that does not depend on the simultaneous reading of European or North American literature. It is safe to say that the major writers of this period are international writers, not only because many of them have been in exile or lived abroad, but because they are read with equal interest in all Spanish-speaking countries.

While any classification is open to criticism, it is useful to envision several categories, so that this critical description may serve the reader as a guide for further study. This chapter shows which writers published works that have merited continued critical attention, and explains briefly why they are important. I have preferred to take a few more lines in order to give a general idea about the works and the narrative strategies of the major writers, rather than to attempt vainly to mention all the active novelists of the period. In the first part of this chapter, I study the *Boom* and some novelists clearly identified with this phenomenon. The second part describes the work of the more traditional narrators, running the gamut from throwbacks to an early period to brilliant experimenters who still have an interest in conveying the illusion that they are reporting about the world. In the last section, I study the work of a few representative authors who have produced extraordinary novels where language and its possibilities prevail. These categories simply stress aspects that coexist in all narrative: a concern for society and the referent of a novel on the one hand, and a creative surge that makes of language itself the referent, on the other.

National literatures should not be neglected, even if they cannot be properly handled in a single essay. It should not surprise anyone that most novels mentioned in this chapter were published in Havana, Mexico City, Buenos Aires, or Santiago. Those have been the sites of important publishing houses and strong centers of cultural innovation. Yet in this period many novels are published in Barcelona, reflecting the new interest of Spanish publishing houses in the Spanish American market. Buenos Aires and Montevideo had their own local stars, such as Murena and Mallea, Bioy Casares or Viñas, but some of their works do not travel well; Santiago, in Chile, is presided by the criticism of Alone, while the older generation of Benjamín Subercaseaux, Eduardo Barrios, Marta Brunet, and Manuel Rojas, is quietly superseded by José Donoso. Other writers, such as Enrique Lafourcade, have a large national readership. Cuba is a lively cultural center, first with the group of *Orígenes*, and then with *Lunes de Revolución*, from Carpentier and Lezama to Arenas and Sarduy. In Central America, Asturias does not find a successor, while in Colombia the rural novels of Caballero Calderón are displaced by García Márquez, who is followed by Alvarez Gardeazábal. Mexico continues a tradition of strong regional writers and diverse schools of writing, from Yáñez to Sainz, with novelists such as Luis Spota or Sergio Fernández, the first a popular, the other a refined, writer, both better-known in Mexico than abroad. I will not be able to account here for these intricate developments and in a few cases I have excluded a writer who is essential in the local scene, but less significant in the Spanish American panorama. Yet, the internationally known authors with whom I am mainly concerned in this chapter are buttressed by a plethora of names of national reputation and sustained by readers who easily juxtapose in their libraries books of Sartre, Buzzati, Marx, Faulkner, and Koestler, with those of Fuentes, Arguedas, Cortázar, Bullrich, Albalucía Angel, and García Márquez.

In brief, the history of the Spanish American novel from 1950 to 1975 saw a change in the standing of the native writers, who went from marginal and tolerated – the center having been earlier Paris and New York – to central and celebrated. Simultaneously there was a shift from the novel as history to history as a novel, from the power of facts to the preeminence of the word.

The greater attention paid to Spanish American novelists and their international success in the 1960s, a phenomenon that was called the *Boom*, affected all writers and readers who lived through this important event. A number of gifted novelists, several international editors in search of a new product, and a growing market were important, but what brought writers together and focused the attention of the world on Spanish America was the triumph of the Cuban Revolution in 1959, which promised a new age. The period of euphoria can be considered closed when in 1971 the Cuban government hardened its party line and the poet Heberto Padilla was forced to reject in a public document his so-called decadent and deviant views. The furor over Padilla's case brought to an end the affinity between Spanish American intellectuals and the Cuban inspirational myth.

Who is and who is not to be included in the *Boom* has been widely debated and never settled. Two books, José Donoso's *Historia personal del "boom"* [*The Boom in Spanish American Literature*], and Emir Rodríguez Monegal's *El boom de la novela latinoamericana* are the best guides in this debate. On the other hand, a few writers exerted wide and undisputed influence. While the names of many other writers may be added to the list, the following may not be omitted: Vargas Llosa, Rulfo, Fuentes, Cortázar, and García Márquez. Vargas Llosa's first novel won the Seix Barral prize in Barcelona in 1962, opening the doors of Europe to Spanish American narrators. European success meant continental visibility and enormous prestige in Spanish America. Rulfo, the author of two books, only one of them a novel, was the acknowledged master incorporated *a posteriori*, a writer who balances social concern, verbal experimentation, and a unique style. Fuentes not only wrote some of the most important novels of the period, but was also an indefatigable and brilliant publicist of Spanish America. Cortázar in one novel brought together Paris and Buenos Aires, poking fun at tradition and opening many new paths. García Márquez wrote the best seller and the masterpiece of the period.

These authors enjoyed immediate popular and critical acclaim. They adopted the avant-garde strategy of proclaiming a new beginning and declaring most of the traditional masters obsolete. Carlos Fuentes in his influential study *La nueva novela hispanoamericana*, argued convincingly that the Spanish American novel had been devoured by the jungle, the mountains, the rivers, in short, by a descriptive passion for Spanish American nature. From our vantage point, what was promoted in the 1960s in Spanish America as a distinct move away from tradition can be traced back to the experimentation of the avant-garde movements in the early part of the century. Macedonio Fernández (Argentina, 1874–1952), for example, anticipated many ideas of the *Boom*, as can be seen in his posthumously published *Museo de la novela de la Eterna*.

The story of the *Boom* could start chronologically with Miguel Angel Asturias's *El Señor Presidente* (published in 1946, but started in 1922) [*El Señor Presidente*] and proceed to recent years relying on the ordered succession of publication dates of the novels that have been mentioned in relation to the *Boom*. Other starting points could be Sábato's *El túnel* (1948) or Onetti's *El pozo* (1939). Or one can go even farther back, to the vanguardist movements of the 1920s. However, the writers of the *Boom* declared themselves orphaned and without any autochthonous model, caught between their admiration for Proust, Joyce, Mann, Sartre, and other European writers and their need to have a Spanish American voice, even if they rejected the most respected Spanish American writers, *Indigenistas*, *Criollistas*, and *Mundonovistas*. Donoso explains in his *Historia personal* that the lack of literary fathers enriched his generation and gave it a great deal of freedom. Obviously, this is not altogether true and its complex and healthy blocking of the father's influence becomes transparent when in a footnote Donoso explains that he has titled his book *Historia personal* after the Chilean critic Alone's *Historia personal de la literatura chilena* (1954). Alone, the pseudonym for Joaquín Díaz Arrieta, had been born in 1891, thirty-three years before Donoso. This illusion of freedom allowed, nevertheless, for a new start, a new game.

In the early 1950s, many critics considered as great Spanish American novels Ciro Alegría's *El mundo es ancho y ajeno*, Eduardo Barrios's *Gran Señor y rajadiablos*, and Agustín Yáñez's *Al filo del agua* (all published in the 1940s). Alegría wrote about the exploitation of the Inca Indians in Peru, Barrios was concerned with the Chilean countryside and mysticism, and Yáñez wrote about a time before the Mexican Revolution. These three novels have a language that is elegant, correct, literary. The narrative progresses by going from first to last, there is a clear understanding of good and bad, and the reader is taken for a tour, carefully guided and pampered. These texts are still echoes of the traditional Spanish American novel, descriptive of the struggle against Nature, militantly concerned with social justice, and lovingly regional.

The triumph of the Cuban guerrillas in January of 1959 over Batista's dictatorship was seen as an affirmation of Spanish American independence. The participation of the Argentinian Ernesto Che Guevara in the insurrectionary movements in Cuba and Bolivia became a symbol of internationalism, while the establishment of a cultural center in 1960, the Casa de las Américas, with its yearly awards and aggressive marketing of the Revolution among Spanish American intellectuals, created a shared sense of purpose. This continental cohesion was validated when Vargas Llosa received the Biblioteca Breve prize of Seix Barral in Barcelona in 1962 for *La ciudad y los perros* [*Time of the Hero*]. Although this novel told a story about a military academy in Lima, and although it was reminiscent of Musil's *Young Törless* (so it could have been read as Peruvian or European), it returned from Europe to the readers in Bogotá, Mexico City, and Buenos Aires as a Spanish American novel. Only Spain had enough publishing power combined with adequate distribution of her books to make a novel simultaneously visible in most Spanish-speaking countries. Her own literature was at the end of a dry period of social realism and readers turned avidly to the complex and daredevil technique and the exotic vocabulary of Vargas Llosa's novel. One of the jurors of the Seix Barral prize, the Spanish poet José María Valverde, was asked to write a prologue to prepare readers for the brutal scenes, the criticism of the army, and the off-color language. Had the action of *La ciudad y los perros* taken place in Madrid, Spanish censorship would not have allowed its publication. The detachable yellow pages with Valverde's prologue and a photograph of Lima's Leoncio Prado Military Academy soon became unnecessary when Vargas Llosa was heralded as a masterful innovator which showed, in contrast, the sorry state of the novel in Spain. Valverde wrote that *La ciudad y los perros* was the best novel *in the Spanish language* since the Argentinian Ricardo Güiraldes's *Don Segundo Sombra*, a novel published in 1926. The brushing aside of over thirty years of novels in the Spanish-speaking world is not completely unjustified. While poets such as Vallejo, Neruda, Huidobro, and Paz had reached international fame and were thoroughly modern and creative in their technique, the novel followed the tired models of the past without much genius. Most readers now lived in the large cities, Mexico City, Buenos Aires, Santiago, and were not primarily concerned about nature, Indians, small towns, nor did they find their own language reflected in the superbly polished prose of Barrios, Ciro Alegría, or Eduardo Mallea. *La ciudad y los perros*, on the contrary, is about the city, prominently displayed in its title, and it presented a challenge to the immense and sophisticated intellectual middle class that had developed in the first part of the century.

Spanish America was also mobilized by John F. Kennedy's election as president of the United States in November of 1960 and the subsequent creation of the Alliance for Progress. The continent had suddenly entered contemporary history and one of the first books to notice the plethora of excellent writers was a collection of interviews, published in 1967, by Luis Harss and Barbara Dohmann, appropriately called *Into the Mainstream: Conversations with Latin-American Writers*. Here Carpentier, Asturias (who won the Nobel Prize in 1967), Borges, Guimarães Rosa, Onetti, Cortázar, Rulfo, Fuentes, García Márquez, and Vargas Llosa shared the limelight.

How was the technique of the major novelists of the *Boom* different from that of their predecessors? It relied on a Cubist superposition of different points of view, it made time and lineal progress questionable, and it was technically complex. Linguistically self-assured, it used the vernacular without apologies. Fuentes's *La muerte de Artemio Cruz* [*The Death of Artemio Cruz*] requires that the reader spend some time adjusting to the mechanism of the storytelling. Time in *Artemio Cruz* flows backwards into the origin of everything, making a statement for the intelligent reader who can follow its tightrope prowess: surely not the happy celebration of life of a Classic period, but the exasperation of a refined society that was sold down the river in the first second in Paradise. In Cortázar's *Rayuela*, the instructions for reading, the intellectual discussions, the defiance of a stable structure, the search for an active reader lead to a homeless and rootless scattering. These novelists, their readers, and their critics started to rewrite the literary tradition, and a new genealogical ABC developed: Miguel Angel Asturias (who repeatedly attacked the *Boom* but revalued indigenous Latin American myths with complex vanguardist prose), Jorge Luis Borges (who never wrote a novel yet became the paragon of a new cosmopolitan writing), and Alejo Carpentier (whose texts are baroque in syntax and language, but flawlessly classical in their structure). Rulfo was incorporated *a posteriori* for his *Pedro Páramo*, Lezama Lima much later, when the power of his *Paradiso* began to be perceived and celebrated. Other writers joined the bandwagon: Cabrera Infante with *Tres tristes tigres* [*Three Trapped Tigers*], and José Donoso with *El obsceno pájaro de la noche* [*The Obscene Bird of Night*], and Manuel Puig, and Severo Sarduy.

Originally, the vanguardist movements, strictly defined, used innovative techniques that were tightly bound to a political message: anti-elitist, progressive, anarchic. In the novels of the 1960s this ideological grounding, lost by then in Europe and North America, reappears. The interrelation of all time, the questioning of one moment by another, the belief in history and reality, the conviction that it is possible to write new literature and that this will have a purifying effect on society, the flights of fantasy, the search for a new language are related to a yearning for an apocalyptic razing of the past to get a new and fresh start. The *Boom* was the culmination of several decades, yet the historical time, the rhetoric of the period, and the talent of its protagonists made it a new beginning of sorts.

I will study here five major authors in the order of publication of their most important novels: Rulfo (*Pedro Páramo*, 1955), Fuentes (*La muerte de Artemio Cruz*, 1962), Cortázar (*Rayuela*, 1963 [*Hopscotch*]), Vargas Llosa (*La ciudad y los perros*, 1963), and García Márquez (*Cien años de soledad*, 1967 [*One Hundred Years of Solitude*]). In the case of Cortázar and Vargas Llosa I follow the alphabetical order.

Juan Rulfo (1918–1986) published only one brief novel, yet it is probably the single most important and influential of this period, *Pedro Páramo* [*Pedro Páramo*]. The setting is rural Mexico, and the action is familiar: the fast rise to power by the ruthless *caudillo*, who flaunts the law and manipulates the Revolution, stopping at nothing to take over the land and enjoy all the women he desires. One woman – the one he loves – resists him, withdrawn into madness and death. Yet the narration takes a fresh angle, following Pedro Páramo's son, Juan Preciado, as he descends into the sun-scorched valley in search of his dead father. He meets his own death amid the rumor of the voices of the dead, never tired of rehearsing their complaint for the suffering brought upon them during their life by love, pride, and power, with the bitter memory persisting beyond the grave. Rulfo builds the story as an enigmatic puzzle, with short fragments of the story following each other in a sequence that does not correspond to their chronology. The language is bare-boned, deceptively simple, rejecting completely the ornate descriptions and adjective-laden sentences of the novels of the first part of the century. *Pedro Páramo* can be read as a Greek tragedy, with the voices of the dead as the choir of the people. There are, as well, many references to a deeper level of myth related to a descent to Hell – like Ulysses, Aeneas, Christ, or Dante – and a return to Paradise and prelapsarian innocence. Yet this is not an intellectual novel or a thesis novel: its power stems from the fact that it is more seen and heard than read, as a telling vision and a mesmerizing whisper of ancestral darkness.

Carlos Fuentes (b. 1928) brought new daring to the Mexican novel, stagnated in rural topics and traditional social realism. With *La región más transparente* [*Where the Air is Clear*], a bravado performance with a multitudinous cast of characters and an immensely rich language bursting the seams of an intricate story line, Fuentes offered the new urban readers a disquieting but recognizable mirror of life in the new Spanish American metropolis. Concerned with history as were his predecessors Yáñez or Azuela, Fuentes introduces not only a more disillusioned view of the Mexican Revolution and its aftermath, and a deeper relation with pre-Hispanic Mexico and with European and North American culture, but also a radically new concept of history, made of options and choices that create simultaneous modes of existence. The brilliant fabric of Fuentes's first novel is woven from a myriad of interrelated stories that reflect the variegated forms that life takes in Mexico City. In the Mexican capital many different spaces, times, and cultures coexist, often in a blind and violent search for power that demands the eradication of any single alternative. Simple binary opposition, innocent belief in progress, exclusive values, all are shaken by the topsy-turvy of the crowded city evoked by Fuentes, a nightmarish and more complex version of John Dos Passos's *Manhattan Transfer*. Fuentes revels in the creative originality of spoken language – including expressions of other Spanish American countries – leaving aside the excuses, the italics, the glossaries, the neat delimitation between educated narrator and characters, and in the trepidation of incurring the displeasure of the Spanish Royal Academy of Language which had handicapped previous narrators. He heard Mexico speaking, and the public liked it, unleashing powerful new creative energies.

La región más transparente chronicles the rise of a corrupt and uninspiring middle- and upper-class, devoted to business and progress, as it faces the resistance of an ancestral Mexico, where magic, cyclical time, and human sacrifice still exist. The eighty-five named characters, in a list added to the 1972 edition, are classified into several groups: families, bourgeois, hangers-on, foreigners, and intellectuals, plus the people, the revolutionaries, and the guardians. The Dantesque description of the city and its many circles owes much to essayists such as Alfonso Reyes, Salvador Novo, and Octavio Paz, but is much more than an amalgam of a great store of information. Fuentes shows a curiosity and a searching mind that delight in amassing information, words, languages, names, puns, in a Joycean swell of untiring celebration of existence. His deep critical insight, his knowledgeable and cosmopolitan view, his uncompromising search for a social and private truth comes from a dissatisfaction that prevents completion, that leaves behind long texts as traces of a frustrated wish to translate all reality into writing. The recounting of the three-year period from 1951 to 1954, that, in the novel, separates the first and last appearances of Ixca Cienfuegos, who acts as the Vergil of this labyrinth, shows that Mexico is not a stable or transparent society but, on the contrary, is fragmented, unreconciled with ancestral wounds and plunging blindly ahead into change.

Las buenas conciencias [*The Good Conscience*] is a more traditional narration about an adolescent coming to terms with the limits imposed on him as a condition of inheriting his family's wealth and the blessing of his social class. The slow description of the rise of the family shows the keen eye for the genealogy of economic and social power that is associated with Balzac in France or Pérez Galdós in Spain. The focus of the novel then centers on the temptations – both social and mystical – of solidarity that would swerve the youngster from pragmatic adaptation to idealistic rebellion.

A similar choice – between passivity and action, between loyalty to the principles of the Mexican Revolution and expedient adaptation to profitable circumstances that call for audacity and the shelving of ideals – torments an aged and dying magnate in Fuentes's best-known novel *La muerte de Artemio Cruz*. The extremely complex structure is a model of purposeful virtuosity that does not upstage the evoked characters and historical period nor turns its back on the reader; on the contrary, the different narrators in first, second, and third person, the segments narrated in past, present, and future tense, the numerous flash-backs, offer a kaleidoscopic view of Artemio Cruz's life and circumstances, characterizing him as villain and hero, as victimizer and victim. Again here, as in *La región más transparente*, many pages read as an inspired transcription of a crowded city, as a network of a language whose referents were in continuous and chaotic motion. Among this rich verbal debris, readers can guess at the tragedy of human beings surviving an implacable society. The novel would not have become an instant classic without the vitality it brilliantly celebrates, from Artemio Cruz himself – refusing to die, recording his voice, searching in his memory for the decisions that allowed him to survive, making love with Regina, plunging into battle – to the lyrical and incantatory enumerations of colloquial expressions. Most critics would probably agree that, with Borges's short stories, Cortázar's *Rayuela*, García Márquez's *Cien años de soledad*, and Rulfo's *Pedro Páramo*, Fuentes's *La muerte de Artemio Cruz* transformed Spanish American literature in a radical and permanent way.

Aura [*Aura*] is a novella where the intelligence, erudition, and masterful craft of Fuentes are powerfully distilled to produce a meditation on writing, magic, and history. *Zona sagrada* [*Holy Place*] analyzes the relation between a young man called Mito (the Spanish word for Myth), and his famous actress mother. Fuentes calls to service here Greco-Roman and Aztec mythology, with a generous serving of Freudian terms and a constellation of emblems of the contemporary myths of the marketplace. *Cambio de piel* [*A Change of Skin*] follows two couples on a trip to Cholula, where they are stranded in the sacred city and where they must face the phantoms of their past. That one of the characters was an architect responsible for building some extermination centers of the Holocaust, and another is an American woman, widens the geographical and chronological scope of the novel. The romantic entanglement of the four main characters and the ritual death of one of them in one of Cholula's pyramids are predictable, yet the novel conceals an intriguing "change of skin" or shift in the narration of the later chapters. *Cumpleaños* is an enigmatic text, rich in references to theology and art, that describes the baffling experiences of a recluse in a sprawling and isolated mansion that seems to expand at will in space and time. A similar brooding and introspective tone is found in Fuentes's monumental *Terra nostra* [*Terra Nostra*], a triptych composed of three interrelated novelistic spaces: an apocalyptic Paris on the verge of the year 2000, the Spain of Philip II and El Escorial, and the New World, especially the conquest of Mexico. Fuentes's learning shines in the many layers of this postmodern historical novel, where history itself is seen as mystification and at best an approximation to a convincing fictive reconstruction of the past. The novel depicts painstakingly the somber atmosphere of the Emperor's monastic palace and playfully provides new versions of glorified moments of Spanish history. Fuentes does away altogether with Charles V – probably too sane and vigorous to inhabit *Terra Nostra* – and makes of Celestina, Cervantes, and Don Quixote intriguing new characters.

Julio Cortázar (1914–1984) distinguished himself first with several books of stunning short stories where the limits of conventional reality were unacknowledged and transgressed with playful freedom. His first published novel, *Los premios* [*The Winners*], tells the story of a group of prizewinners sailing out to sea without knowing their destination and irritated by being excluded from an area in the ship. The setting and action are too allegorical and recognizable as Kafkaesque or French Existentialism, even if some lyrical monologues show Cortázar's trademark of refusing to accept authority and his search – in vain – for a pattern that would explain everything in the old metaphysical tradition.

In *Rayuela* [*Hopscotch*], one of the most famous novels of the Spanish American *Boom*, the uneasiness of the main character, Horacio, is reflected at every level of this decentered and mercurial novel. Readers are invited to read the text as a traditional novel, divided into two parts and an appendix, or to follow a complex order suggested by the author, an order that has readers jumping back and forth and leads them into a trap. The first part follows Horacio as he searches in Paris for a meaning in his life, a rambling existence shared with a woman, Maga, who is in contact with her feelings and can be spontaneous, and an international coterie of intellectual friends. In the second part of *Rayuela*, Horacio returns to Buenos Aires, only to find himself there equally distant from a meaningful life, a life that he sees and envies in his friends Traveler and Talita. The anxiety of Existentialism, the paradox of Zen, the apparent freedom of jazz, the iconoclastic fervor of Vanguardism, and plenty of legitimate humor, happy turns of phrase, and genuine insight drive the novel forth at a dizzying speed. The third part of the novel contains fragments, whole chapters, quotations, as though the neat structure that precedes it had burst its seams from an excess of ideas and a richness of language and imagination that refused to be contained. Some sections of the novel, Rocamadour's death, the piano concert of Madame Trépat, Talita suspended on a makeshift bridge high above the street are masterpieces of narrative. *Rayuela*'s celebration of ordinary language, scorn for pedantry, academicism, and literary posturing, and Cortázar's insistence on the active role that readers should play in reading novels were all lessons that had immediate and deep influence in Spanish America.

62 Modelo para armar [*62: A Model Kit*] is a hermetic novel that develops out of Chapter 62 in *Rayuela*, where an author proposed a novel in which psychological coherence in characters would not exist. *62 Modelo para armar* never reveals the secret of dolls that horrify their owners, even if there are intimations that a vampire may be at large, nor does the map on the cover help much in following the displacements of the characters in Europe. The text, therefore, will always hold a tantalizing possibility for interpretation by the active reader, confronted by a literary puzzle with several pieces missing.

Libro de Manuel [*A Manual for Manuel*], addresses a major problem of a period in which armed insurrection was generalized in Spanish America. The intellectual, in this case Andrés, is confronted with the choice of joining the violence – receding into barbarism – or upholding a peaceful resistance that can be seen as complicity with an extremely violent establishment. The scrapbook of documents that Andrés and his friends are putting together for little Manuel – the next generation – tips the balance in favor of hesitant action. *Libro de Manuel* makes a case for simultaneous revolutions, external, maybe armed, and internal, directed against sexual and cultural prejudices. The same lack of determination of Andrés is found in the genre of the novel, that appears occasionally more like an essay or an autobiography than a traditional novel, and ends pinned down to the time of its writing by all the documents inserted in the text, more an important generational testimony than a work of fiction.

Mario Vargas Llosa (Perú, b. 1936) can tell a story and create a world with the apparent ease of a nineteenth-century master. He holds the attention of the reader and fires the imagination as Balzac, Dumas, or Victor Hugo did in their time. In addition, while the story line is riveting and the characters are clearly visualized with convincing depth, Vargas Llosa gives considerable attention to style, his model being Flaubert, and has an unsurpassed grasp of technical virtuosity – learnt from Faulkner, Dos Passos, Hemingway, and other sources, including romances of chivalry – splicing and mixing time, superposing different spaces, and withholding crucial information until the climactic final revelation. His first novel, *La ciudad y los perros* [*Time of the Hero*] opened the door of the Spanish market to the Spanish American *Boom*. The novel describes life in a military school in Lima, depicting the violence, corruption, and the perverse glorification of supposedly manly virtues condoned by the institution. A series of interior monologues, with recurrent but at first unidentified speakers, and fast-paced action tell a double story of crime and love, of school and city. Stolen exam questions lead to a murder that must be hushed to save the honor of the institution. The cadets learn in the process how to tune down their expectations of themselves and the world. Three of them are romantically involved with the same woman, in an improbable but highly effective way of showing class and personality differences.

La casa verde [*The Green House*] confirmed Vargas Llosa's genius by complicating the action further and magnifying the narrative space with ever-increasing virtuosity. A sequence of story lines brings back with a symphonic effect the tales of two cities and several characters: a city in the jungle, Santa María de Nieva in the Amazon, and one in the coastal, dry region, Piura. In the jungle, young Indian girls are rounded up to be educated by nuns, becoming despoiled of their own tradition and fit only to be maids or prostitutes. The Indians are also being exploited as collectors of rubber sap, and their attempt to bypass the white middleman is ruthlessly repressed with the help of the army. Readers learn part of this story by eavesdropping on the dialogue of a mythical organizer of the jungle criminal trade and his assistant as they float down the river in a canoe, the old kingpin now powerless and sick. In the coastal town, a man of unknown origin sets up a brothel, the Green House, overcoming the resistance of the priest. A soldier who serves in the two cities, and his wife – educated by the nuns at Santa María de Nieva and later a prostitute in the Green House – provide the link between these two stories which paint a grim picture of the church and the army, the supposedly civilizing forces. A masterly use of dialogues switches the story effortlessly from one time and space to a different one.

This practice of nesting past dialogues in present conversations is also brilliantly used in *Conversación en La Catedral* [*Conversation in The Cathedral*], where the central action is a four-hour conversation at a seedy bar called "La Catedral," between a frustrated journalist, Santiago Zavala, and Ambrosio, the former chauffeur and lover of Santiago's father Fermín. A proliferation of memories and the help of a third-person narrator reconstruct the life of the three men, plus a fourth, Cayo Bermúdez, the strong man of the Odría dictatorship (1948–1956). Fermín Zavala represents the white upper class that expects to profit from an alliance with the regime, and he does get preferential treatment for his business, but at the price of a degrading complicity. He is further driven into the underworld by his homosexual practices, considered perverse and despicable in the *machista* world where he lives. Cayo Bermúdez presides over a prostituted society that he baits with money, sex, and power. Ambrosio is a good man, exploited, perhaps driven into crime by friendship, and failed as an entrepreneur. Santiago has rebelled against his social class, studying in the proletarian university, flirting with communist thought, rejecting his family, but finds himself leading a mediocre life without any future. The conclusion is bitter, since the four men exemplify the complete bankruptcy of Peruvian society, but the novel, in its vast cast of characters and different scenarios, uncovers a rich and varied country. The interlocking dialogues are more than an entertaining device, since they show that everyone lives in a continued and necessary relation with others and it is only from an understanding of the social environment that the self can be adequately described.

After the long and somber *Conversación*, Vargas Llosa published a shorter, humorous novel, *Pantaleón y las visitadoras* [*Captain Pantoja and the Special Service*], about a captain in charge of supplying a sexual-relief service to soldiers stationed far from major cities. Pantaleón commands a squadron of prostitutes that criss-crosses the country with military efficiency and admirable logistics. Witty dialogue and a scrap-book of different documents reduces to a minimum the presence of a traditional narrator in this story of military zeal pushed to madness. As a parable of the insanity of blindly obeying orders and of the frenzied efficiency of contemporary organizations, *Pantaleón* delivers more than its entertaining story, by itself an unusual and welcome addition to the generally earnest literature of these decades.

The best-known Spanish American novelist of the *Boom* is the Colombian Gabriel García Márquez (b. 1927), who received the Nobel Prize in 1982. His training as a journalist and screenwriter honed his prodigious ability to tell a story with unequalled skill, with an apparent simplicity and transparency that hide the originality and creativity of his language. His first novel, *La hojarasca* (*Leafstorm*), introduces an imaginary town, Macondo, based partly on the reality of Colombian towns divided by decades of a brutal civil war, and partly on regions invented by the literary mind, such as Faulkner's Yoknapatawpha country, Graham Greene's tropic, or Kafka's dispassionately reported anomalous world. *La hojarasca* presents the conflict between one man, bound by his promise to bury a dead doctor, and the town, which has vowed not to bury him as a revenge for the doctor's refusal to take care of the wounded during an episode of the civil war. While there are many intertextual references to Sophocles' *Antigone* – where Antigone defies her uncle Creon's orders not to bury her brother Polynices – the novel is deeply rooted in Colombian history. The leafstorm is a reference to the swirl created by the banana companies who changed the social fabric of small towns, accelerating history, magnifying space, and multiplying houses, production, and people with a speed disconcerting to the original settlers. The story is told through three voices, an old colonel, his daughter Isabel, and his grandson. The monologues are stilted and undifferentiated, more a report explaining the antecedents of the conflict than true flow of conscience. However, there are in this early work unforgettable images: the boy catching a glimpse of himself in a mirror, the doctor requesting grass to eat for supper, the vapid groom, the defiant maid who turns out in her Sunday best for mass, the extravagant priest who preaches from a farmer's almanac. Many enigmas are left unresolved: who did the colonel's wife believe the doctor was when he arrived in 1903? Was the doctor protecting someone else when he declared himself the father of the maid's child? What would happen once the funeral procession got into the open in 1928? What was the relationship between the doctor and the priest? The reader is left with a burning image of muffled intensity, repressed feelings, and deep, defiant isolation.

El coronel no tiene quien le escriba [*No One Writes to the Colonel*] is a novella about a retired colonel who has been awaiting his pension for fifty-six years. For fifteen years he goes every Friday to the post office expecting a letter from a distant governmental bureaucracy, always in vain. At the start of the narration, on a rainy October day, the colonel is reduced to poverty since he and his wife have eaten up all their savings and sold their possessions. Their son has been murdered nine months before, but he left behind his gamecock that comes to symbolize the resistance against a corrupt and violent establishment. While the colonel is tempted by hunger and destitution to sell the gamecock to a rich friend, he ultimately assumes his position as a leader of a new resistance and courageously faces the future. He is given new life by inheriting his son's mission, the nine months since his son's death transmuted into the successful gestation of the hero. The brilliance of this text stands out when it is contrasted with the many novels of social protest written in Spanish America during the same period, which were heavy-handed, with a profuse rhetoric. *El coronel no tiene quien le escriba* is lean and stark, implying all the violence and terror of an unresponsive and destructive society by telling without excessive sentiment and with dry humor an unpretentious story that is transmuted into an all-encompassing myth.

La mala hora [*In Evil Hour*] takes another, wider view of the same town depicted in *El coronel*, probably inspired by Marshall Sucre. The town is under the authority of a lieutenant who wishes to leave behind his past of criminal repression and to inaugurate a new period of peace, convenient for his burgeoning financial empire. The main distraction is a series of scandalous posters that appear anonymously, escaping the control of the civilian authority – the lieutenant – and the religious authority – a priest who painfully realizes he is unaware of the vital secrets of his parishioners. When violence erupts again towards the end of the novel, when clandestine publications unleash the old resistance and repression, writing is silenced, intimating the horror that replaces the brief cease-fire.

Cien años de soledad is the best-seller and the masterpiece of the *Boom*, the rare case of a novel that is enthusiastically received by the general public and by critics, at home and abroad. The story line is complicated by the number of characters, but it is a straightforward family saga, from the founding of a town, Macondo, to its destruction one hundred years later. The leaders of the first settlers are a married couple of cousins, José Arcadio Buendía and Ursula Iguarán. Her fear of having a child with a pig's tail as a punishment for marrying inside the family delays the consummation of the marriage, brings about a murder, and forces them out of their original town. As did Adam and Eve, they must civilize primal nature and, like them, they carry an original guilt, incest, and violence that they will pass on to their descendants. A roving band of gypsies brings news from the outside world to Macondo, astonishing José Arcadio with such inventions as magnets, telescopes, ice, and alchemy. One of the gypsies, Melquíades, becomes a friend of the family and eventually leaves behind prophetic writings in encoded Sanskrit that are only deciphered at the end of the novel by the last survivor of the Buendías. Much has happened that Melquíades foresaw: the growth from settlement to a bustling plantation town and the bust after a strike that makes the owners leave the region; the long civil war between liberals and conservatives; the last birth in town, a boy with a pig's tail, the son of Aureliano Babilonia Buendía and his aunt; and the end of time in a whirlwind. This path from Arcadia to Babylon is cluttered with hundreds of memorable stories and images: a plague of insomnia, a rain of yellow flowers, an intolerably beautiful woman who ascends to Heaven, a trail of blood that runs across town from a murdered man to his mother, a visit by the Wandering Jew, a levitating priest, a deluge, and so on. García Márquez's prodigious capacity for invention – so great that what he tells always seems natural, more a retelling of ancestral myths and traditional stories than labored literary creation – fills every page with a breathless succession of unforgettable anecdotes, so rich and vivid that one of them would suffice for a whole novel by most writers. Yet, even if he never belabors a point or exhausts a character, the rise and fall of the Buendías is fully conveyed. While part of the charm of the book is its unflappable reporting of amazing events – the exaggerated, outlandish, eccentric, monstrous, dreamlike, fabulous, all made quotidian by the impassive narrator of Magical Realism – García Márquez's timing and his uncanny gift of making every sentence count are matchless, as has been discovered by the many frustrated imitators spawned by *Cien años de soledad*. The novel is highly structured, with a similar anticipatory sentence at the beginning, middle, and end of the book. The repeated names and characters establish the pattern of repetition that ultimately brings history to a halt. Mirrors – a form of repetition – are everywhere: in the bedroom, as identical twins, or as a prophetic text. As a reflection of Spanish American history, the descending spiral of the second part of the novel and the failure of Macondo seem negative. Yet the story is delivered without editorializing, with the implied author almost invisible, to avoid interfering with his created world. Critics are bound to continue to discuss and disagree about the ideological implications of this saga, the symbolic values and the narrative strategies of the text, much as they have done with Homer and Cervantes. Ursula Iguarán, the practical woman that keeps the family together, José Arcadio Buendía, the belated discoverer of the roundness of the Earth, and Colonel Aureliano Buendía, who led thirty-two armed uprisings and lost every time, have found a place among the great characters of literature.

From 1968 to 1975, García Márquez wrote *El otoño del patriarca* [*The Autumn of the Patriarch*]. In six chapters, each starting with a description of the ruinous condition of the palace on the day the dictator dies, several narrators – including the patriarch himself – reconstruct his long reign of terror, prodigiously extended to include in the past the arrival of Columbus to the New World. While the six long paragraphs that constitute the novel and the absence of direct dialogue make the full pages as oppressive as the atmosphere García Márquez evokes, each chapter develops a topic that adds a new, frequently surprising, detail to the dictator's necrology, focusing on the dictator and his double, the murder of his enemies, his loves with a young queen of a beauty contest and with a young nun, a portrait of his mother and the dictator's efforts to have her declared a saint, the sale of the sea to the United States, his life as a recluse and his death. The six chapters can be compared to six days not of creation but of destruction by a perverse god condemned to the loneliness of power. While the fidelity of the novel to its possible historical referents should not be assumed, and the creation of a new stereotype of the Latin American dictator should be resisted, *El otoño del patriarca* clearly excels among the novels dedicated to the figure of the dictator.

The uneasiness found already in the early chronicles of the discovery of America is still present in the mid-twentieth century. The imposing Nature is not so much a topic any longer, but the never-resolved conflicts between different cultures and races, the intractable social inequities, the rebellions and the repressions, the variegated language spoken by many nations and in constant change, continue to challenge novelists and attract readers. Many authors of this period were tempted to fill the vacuum of information left by manipulated or cowed news services and weak social sciences. With a blurry image of themselves as a composite of historians, philosophers, priests, politicians, upholders of Western civilization, and curators of local tradition, novelists were often bogged down by their heady mission, stressing more the instructive than the pleasing aspect of literature. It was a noble cause that brought forth many important novels. In what follows I review by region the notable authors, starting with Mexico in the north and ending with Chile in the Southern Cone.

The Mexican Revolution is far from a closed subject, and most novelists of this period refer to it in their works. More than a simple device to connect to a collective memory and stir up a familiar emotion, it is a constant and critical reexamination of the national myths that still sustain the current political powers.

A continuator of a Realism that starts to sound tired in the 1950s, Agustín Yáñez (1904–1980) describes different regions of Mexico with the ambition of a Muralist, but never repeating his success with *Al filo del agua* (1947). *La creación* deals with the artistic world of Mexico City, reporting the meteoric career of a musician who is a wooden and predictable character. *Ojerosa y pintada* strings together the different rides of a taxi driver through an eventful night in Mexico City. *La tierra pródiga* and *Las tierras flacas* [*The Lean Lands*] both deal with rural topics, the exploitation of the land in the coastal, hot region, and in the cold highlands, respectively. Even if they employ proven techniques, such as the use of italics for interior monologues or flashbacks, the dialogue is stilted and the tone majestic, failing to bring to life the saga of land developers and the hardships of peasants.

Rosario Castellanos (1925–1974) was an essayist of considerable intelligence, a dramatist, poet, university professor, diplomat, and novelist, that is, a true intellectual and a wise observer of Mexican life. She graduated in 1950 from the National University in Mexico City with a controversial thesis called *Sobre la cultura femenina* where she explored some topics she would develop later related to the marginalization of women in a male-dominated society. Her first novel, *Balún-Canán* [*The Nine Guardians*], tells several stories that happen in the 1930s, when President Cárdenas promulgated laws favouring Indian communities. The novel is divided into three parts: the first sees the social unrest from the point of view of the seven-year-old daughter of a farmer in Chiapas, in the mountains of southern Mexico. Her nanny is an Indian woman and the girl hears from her the local legends while she perceives painfully how the Indians are despised by the white population. Torn by her love for her nanny and her sense of belonging to a family of landowners, she is further distressed by her growing understanding of being disenfranchised for being female, since her younger brother is preferred to her as the future heir and continuator of the family lineage. The second section of the novel switches to a third-person narrator, taking away any importance the girl could have in the social upheaval that ensues, an Indian rebellion that chases the family away from their farm. The third part explores the guilt of the girl when her brother dies and she believes it is partly her responsibility. Some monologues of the grown-ups are artificial, but most of the novel recreates forcefully zones of conflict, in the family and in society, between sexes, races, social classes, and generations.

Oficio de tinieblas takes another look at the same period, yet here without the benefit of a first-person innocent narrator. The story unfolds slowly, showing the life of an Indian community in the countryside and of landowners in a small town. The outsiders, an ambitious young priest and an officer of the government, become catalysts of a rebellion fueled by the faith of one of the Indians in the new laws. There are many gruesome details about the exploitation of the Indians and the brutal state to which they have been reduced. The final, apocalyptic chapters, show the crucifixion of a child to create an Indian counterpart of Jesus, and a hellish Indian rebellion. The most interesting aspect of *Oficio de tinieblas* is the women characters and their maneuvers to attain prominence and influence events: Catalina, the visionary Indian woman who pretends to resurrect the cult of the old gods; Julia, who wishes to become powerful by being accepted by the local elitist society; Idolina, who chooses total passivity and then writes letters that undermine the town; and all the wronged, repressed, marginalized women who are caught up in a society built by men on the basis of racial hatred and the exploitation of the poor.

A brief novel, *El viudo Román* (in *Los convidados de agosto*), tells a story of revenge and a returned bride, with intriguing similarities to García Márquez's *Crónica de una muerte anunciada* (1981) [*Chronicle of a Death Foretold*], where Bayardo San Román similarly returns his bride. Of interest in Castellanos's novel are the descriptions of the marriageable girls of the town and her considerations on the status of married women. Ultimately, Castellanos has to be valued not by any one novel but for her whole work, where a clear-headed portrait emerges of the conflicts of Mexican society, especially in regard to Indians and women.

A masterful portrayal of the aftermath of the Mexican Revolution as seen through women's experience is *Recuerdos del porvenir* [*Recollections of Things to Come*] by Elena Garro (b. 1920). The novel is divided into two parts. The first one describes a town in southern Mexico, Ixtepec, occupied by the troops of a northern general, Francisco Rosas. The general is tormented by the mysterious past of his lover, Julia Andrade. The town is obsessed by Julia's beauty and aloofness, until an outsider with magic powers escapes with her in an instant in which time is suspended. Julia, like Helen of Troy, is never described, but her beauty kindles the imagination and is the origin of strife. She lives in the Garden Hotel, an allusion to Paradise and Eve. Her abduction and fall make of women a central yet apparently passive agent of change.

The second part of the novel describes an episode of the *cristero* insurrection (1927–1929), an uprising against the Mexican government's measures to limit the influence of the Catholic church. To save the priest and the parson, the town organizes a party to distract Rosas, but the plan fails. The sister of one of the executed rebels goes over to the other side and becomes the lover of Rosas to be finally punished by becoming a statue of stone. Beyond the interest of *Recuerdos del porvenir* as a historical, existentialist, or mythical novel, its greatest importance lies in the ambiguous and powerful description of women, forced into seclusion and dependence, aggressively passive, and expecting redemption from the love of the same men who oppress them.

Juan José Arreola (b. 1918) was well known as a short-story writer before his novel *La feria* [*The Fair*] appeared in Mexico in 1963. The text is a collection of fragments, mostly dialogues, diaries, and documents of an imaginary town south of Jalisco. The time frame is provided by the efforts of a shoe-maker to become a farmer and cultivate maize. The meticulous description of the tilling of the land, the sowing, the nerve-wracking wait for rain and growth, the fear of birds, pests, and weeds, all take a poetic grandeur when juxtaposed with idle chatter in a town obsessed with the preparation of its festivities, the *feria*, for which the Indians contribute their money and three gold crowns are made for the sacred images in the church. Other events, such as the Indian fight for vindication of their rights to the land, a strong earthquake, the removal of the town priest, the misadventures of the local Athenaeum, all come together from the many voices of the text. *La feria* is the perfect example of Bakhtin's dialogic imagination, since it uses a polyphonic language based in a carnivalesque, irreverential concept of the universe. If Arreola does have a limitation in this novel, it lies paradoxically in his sense of humor, in his wit, that slants the possible tragedy of this town into a celebration of gossip and the down-to-earth perspective of the joke. The long confession where a character – the town itself – accuses herself and himself "of everything," is followed by the absolution of all sins, explicitly showing the implicit author's unflattering yet compassionate portrayal of human evil and foolishness.

The evolution of Vicente Leñero (b. 1933) is illustrative of the shift of interest in this period from the study of the existential crisis of an individual to the recording of the conditions of the life of the working class, and then to a focus on writing itself. Leñero's first novel, *La voz adolorida*, later offered in a revised version as *A fuerza de palabras*, is the monologue of a man who may or may not be mad and who claims he was separated from his wife and had his son stolen from him by his two aunts and his best friend. The indeterminacy of the story and the hostile nature of the world is reiterated in Leñero's second novel, *Los albañiles*, where the murder of a night-watchman is never solved, while almost all characters have motives for killing him. The study of a layer of Mexican society is convincing and well couched in the suspense of the police case. With *Estudio Q*, Leñero explores freedom and writing, using as his subtext Pirandello's *Six Characters in Search of an Author*. A famous soap-opera star is filming a story about his own life and finds that he is unable to function independently from the script, frequently modified to co-opt his impulsive actions. This is a remarkable novel, with much of the humor and critical understanding of pop culture that is also found in some novels by Puig or Vargas Llosa. In *El garabato*, there is a narrative frame that presents the novel of a critic who is reading a novel, in a complex and amusing juxtaposition of styles. *Redil de ovejas* studies Catholicism in Mexico through a convoluted story centered on a priest and his sister, first a young flirt and then an old recluse who baptizes animals and gives Holy Communion to her cat.

The ambition of an all-encompassing novel surfaces in *José Trigo*, by Fernando del Paso (b. 1935), a rhapsodic text about the organizers of a railroad strike in 1960, with two chapters dedicated to an episode of the *cristero* insurrection in the 1920s. However, probably the most moving and effective novel of the younger writers is *Morirás lejos* (Mexico, 1967), by the Mexican poet José Emilio Pacheco (b. 1939). This brief text is brilliantly constructed, alternating paragraphs dedicated to elaborate theories about the identity – or even existence – of a man in an apartment, looking through the blinds at another man in a public square who may be stalking him, with other paragraphs that describe the fall of Jerusalem and the Holocaust. The pages bristle with horrible details laconically stated, as though the infinite proliferation of language and hairsplitting casuistry had to stop when confronted by the horror of undisputable facts. Cabalistic symbols and references to the alchemists, a network of intertextual allusions to film, painting, and literature, and the recurrent reminders of the confusion at Babel (a water tower in the public square, a reproduction of Brueghel's painting "The Tower of Babel" in the recluse's apartment), point to the need to continue the fight against absolute power and the search for a better and more compassionate life. Another writer whose novel was well received in Mexico in this period is Juan Vicente Melo (b. 1932). *La obediencia nocturna* is enigmatic, with scribbled drawings, interspersed Latin – suggesting a confession – and a disillusioned look at the author's generation.

Central American literature in this period is concerned with topics already traditional: dictatorship, the Indian cultures, and exploitation by American companies. Overshadowing other novelists in the region is the 1967 Nobel Prize winner, Miguel Angel Asturias (1899–1974). He found his voice with the surrealist movement in Paris, developing then a theory for analyzing economic and social history in the mirror of myth and psychoanalysis. He returned to live in Guatemala in 1933. *El Señor Presidente* had been written between 1922 and 1932, but was privately published in Mexico in 1946, while Asturias was there as Cultural Attaché. It received wide attention only when Editorial Losada in Buenos Aires published an edition in 1948, becoming extremely influential in the 1950s.

Asturias turned next to the central embodiment of foreign exploitation, the banana plantations of the United Fruit Company. His trilogy starts with *Viento fuerte [Strong Wind]*, where he describes the heroic origins of the banana plantations, when the struggle to bridle Nature's productivity brought together foreigners and natives in a common effort. Later, though, exploitation begins, and the administration of the United Fruit Company is seen as only interested in increasing profits. A rich American shareholder travels undercover to Guatemala to see how the company is operating and is won over by the country and the people, setting up a parallel operation and improving conditions for workers. The novel becomes unavoidably programmatic, despite the complexity of the story, the luxurious language, the spells of magic, and explorations of the deep subconscious. A final storm destroys the work of the planters and kills the helping American couple, anticipating future confrontations. Much of the material is taken from C. D. Kepner and J. H. Soothill's study *The Banana Empire: A Case Study in Economic Imperialism* (New York, 1935).

El papa verde [*The Green Pope*] chronicles the rise of a young American from Chicago, Geo Maker Thompson, to the presidency of the fruit company. The conflict is first between exploitation of the land by a company and its possession by the natives, who are deeply attached to their homes and do not wish to sell. Geo Maker, a creator of sorts, is opposed in his plans by his servant, Chipo Chipó, and his fiancée, Mayarí, who commits ritual suicide by drowning, an action that is considered by the Indians as a wedding ceremony. The rest of the novel follows Geo Maker's rise to power, the constantly threatened success of his banana plantations, and his attempts to have the United States take over Guatemala. The second part of the novel continues the story of *Viento fuerte*, with the inheritance of the American couple and its disruptive effect. The novel closes with Geo Maker's ascent to the presidency of the company. Asturias deploys here a complex structure, with suspense and revelations, yet these turns and twists would turn out to be mechanical if it were not for the sustained beauty of Asturias's writing and the intertwining of Mayan myths.

Los ojos de los enterrados [*The Eyes of the Interred*], as popular wisdom claims, are open until the injustices they have seen are atoned. Here a general strike, based on the historical one of June 1944, brings down the dictator and extracts important concessions from the fruit company. *El alhajadito* shows the fantasy-world of a child who does not know who his mother is, only that she is one of two sisters, facing a similar dilemma to that of Spanish America, undecided between the Indian and the European tradition. Nothing new is added with his other novels. *Mulata de tal* [*Mulatta*] is a Guatemalan version of Faust. *Maladrón* looks at sixteenth-century Guatemalan and Spanish soldiers. In 1972, he published *Viernes de dolores*, in which he recalls the history of the student generation of 1922 in Guatemala.

Alejo Carpentier (1904–1980), the son of a French father and a Russian mother, made of his own problematic identity as a bilingual French–Spanish speaker, a Europeanized Cuban, a scholar interested in architecture and music yet best known as a novelist, the starting point for an Odysseus-like search for a Spanish American home. He wrote an important theoretical statement in the prologue to *El reino de este mundo* (1949)

[*The Kingdom of This World*], where he compared the astonishing reality he had seen in Haiti during a trip in 1943 to the European, especially surrealist, labored attempts to generate the marvelous with tired formulas. America was for Carpentier the continent of the *real-maravilloso*, where simply painting or describing reality presents an extraordinary Nature and history that can only be dreamt about by Europeans. Even if Carpentier later modified his ideas, and introduced the Baroque as a defining trait of Spanish American reality and writing, his concept of *lo real-maravilloso* had lasting influence on novelists and critics, creating a marketing brand that would help the sale of Spanish American novels abroad.

Los pasos perdidos [*The Lost Steps*], his best-known novel, was written in Caracas, where Carpentier lived for a fifteen-year period from 1945 to 1959. The unnamed narrator tells his own story of liberation and loss. Leaving behind in a large metropolis an unfulfilling job and a boring marriage, he goes to the Spanish American jungle to search for a primitive instrument that marks the border-line between magic and science, birdcall and song. His trip becomes a journey in time, as he first happens into the romantic period, and then pushes forth up mountains and down rivers into the lands of the horse and the dog, and ultimately reaches a place where history seems to have begun, the zero hour of human development. He is incapable of simply living in that constant present, and his observations are persistently couched in comparisons with European myth and literature. While he does recover some of the immediacy of childhood and an untroubled pleasure of the senses, he cannot control his mind which seduces him away from a primitive participation in life to the sophisticated roles of a naturalist, historian, or botanist, with an urge to classify and explain. He also experiences a flood of creative ideas for a musical piece, but he runs out of paper to make them last in time, to give them a history. His lover, Rosario, who has in her African, Indian, and European blood, refuses to marry him, explaining that she wishes to preserve her freedom, and the narrator feels irked by this missing document. The excess of ideas and images that he has been unable to leave behind make him accept an offer of a return to the city, from where he will never find the way back to his brief Paradise.

This is an allegoric trip, phrased in European terms, useful as descriptions – for example, the young intellectuals who are so interested in Europe are blinded to their American reality as the victims of the Minotaur – while simultaneously this cultural baggage is rejected as stifling and unnatural. The title *Los pasos perdidos*, that refers to the wasted life of the narrator and to the lost paths that led once to an innocent past, echoes Breton's collection of essays *Les pas perdus* published in 1924 – Carpentier lived in Paris from 1928 to 1939 – while the three V-signs that mark the entrance into the most primitive land could refer to a journal edited by Breton, Duchamp, and Max Ernst in New York from 1942 to 1944, while they were exiled there during the Second World War. In *Los pasos perdidos*, the cloud of butterflies that obscures the sun, the mind-boggling coexistence of all races, of pre-history and every historic period in a Spanish American region, are marvels enough that can be read as a counterpoint to the productions of Breton's, Duchamp's, or Ernst's frenzied imagination.

A note at the end of the novel identifies places and characters with real towns, rivers and people, reinforcing the peculiar tension between a deeply felt historical reality and an archetypal, allegorical universality. On the one hand, as Roberto González Echevarría has proven in *Alejo Carpentier: The Pilgrim at Home*, there is in the novel a carefully modified version of the real trips made by Carpentier in 1947 and 1948. Yet the implicit truthfulness of autobiography is refracted and diluted by the many faces the hero dons over his unnamed self: Jason, Ulysses, Don Quixote, Orpheus, Adam, and others. Even if the novel threatens to collapse under the weight of its many layers of reference and intertextuality, and even if there may be an excess in the deliberate descriptions that imitate the polyphonic and simultaneous richness of a musical composition, this highly structured essayistic novel has ultimately proven convincing to most critics for its depth, imaginative power, and rich, elegant, Baroque language.

El acoso ["Manhunt"] is based on a historical event, the murder of a student-activist in the 1930s. Of extreme narrative complexity with its different narrators and parallel story lines, *El acoso* shows the simultaneous existence of politics, sex, violence, and art in a large city, as the fugitive crosses paths with a humble employee at a concert hall where the orchestra is playing Beethoven's Third Symphony. Neither women, politics, nor art offer final salvation in *El acoso*, yet there is a consolation in the splendor of the senses and the richness of life undiminished by suffering and death, as is suggested by the parallels the novel establishes between the death of the fugitive and Christ's redemptive Passion.

El siglo de las luces [*Explosion in a Cathedral*] is on the surface a traditional historical novel that follows the fate of one family – Carlos, his sister Sofía, and their cousin Esteban – while it describes the period from the events leading to the French Revolution to those preceding Spanish American independence. The cycles of liberation, anarchy, terror, and repression that revolution brings forth are given paradigmatic significance by pointing at similarities between the ideology of modernity in the eighteenth and the twentieth centuries. The spiral progression of history does devour the characters, but not before they have had a chance to decide about their actions in a manner that shows Carpentier's indebtedness to Existentialism. While Victor Hugues – a character based on a historical figure – goes from organizer and revolutionary to tyrant and exploiter, his youthful actions and writings have become an inspiration for others. The opposition frequent in Carpentier's writing between Europe and Spanish America is reduced here to a carefully shaded study of the common ideological bases of change in France and the Caribbean. *El siglo de las luces* is brilliant in its creation of a vast and intricate historical panorama where characters strive to find themselves, while Time runs simultaneously with different clocks and History hides its origins and motives.

El recurso del método [*Reasons of State*] begins in Paris, where an extremely refined and decadent Spanish American dictator enjoys a vacation surrounded by splendor and adulation. After a short visit to his home country to quell a rebellion, he finds when he returns to Paris that the newspapers have informed about his brutal methods and he is given the cold shoulder, until the First World War distracts the attention of the public from his actions. A second rebellion forces him again to resort to the use of methodic violence. His country shifts from French influence to North American as the dictator ages. This alternation between a *here* – the unnamed country that is a composite of several Latin American countries – and a *there* – France or the United States – marks the dependence of this fictional nation on the more developed nations that serve as super-egos because they can hide their own brutality and racism under the veneer of rationality, art, and rhetoric. As usual in Carpentier's novels, much of the action in *El recurso del método* invites allegorical reading and borders dangerously on a parade of stereotypes. The mummies found by the dictator in a cave, the meeting between The Dictator and The Student, the general strike that deposes the dictator, the Spanish American dictator in Paris, are some examples of elements in which the learned essay and literary commonplace lurk uncomfortably under the novelistic surface. Carpentier's dictator corrects the lopsided view of Spanish American strongmen as emanations of an untamed nature and as telluric, savage forces. While he does provide a portrait of the refinements of which such despots have been capable, Carpentier pays less attention – much like the dictator himself – to the internal matters of his invented country, so that it does not come fully to life as a real society.

Concierto barroco [*Concierto Barroco*] is an amusing short novel about the trip to Europe made by a Mexican of Spanish descent and his Cuban servant. The Mexican's disappointment with Madrid is mitigated by a joyous sojourn in Venice, where they meet Vivaldi, Handel, and Scarlatti, and participate in a wild musical soirée with nuns at the Ospedale della Pietà. The rhythm and singing of the Cuban drive the European musicians to a frenzy that celebrates the Spanish American –

Black, Indian, and other – contribution to Western music. Appropriately, the text jumps in time, juxtaposing Handel's trumpets and Louis Armstrong's, Vivaldi's opera on a Mexican theme and Stravinsky, underlining the porous fabric of musical tradition and reaching eventually an epiphany where music and literature, America and Europe, past and present are blended together in an island, Venice, that is presented as a European kindred spirit of Cuba, a utopian place where Carpentier could have felt at home.

For younger writers the only topic, overt or not, became the Cuban Revolution. The most readable novel of those that tried to describe its spirit using the resources of social realism is *La última mujer y el próximo combate* by Manuel Cofiño López (1936–1986). It describes the conflicts arising from implementing a program of forestal and agrarian development, exemplified by the doubts and travails of the new director who arrives from Havana to meet love, solidarity, and death in the countryside. The style is accessible, the structure easy to follow, the characters are neatly divided between the good revolutionaries and the bad counter-revolutionaries. *La última mujer* won the Casa de las Américas prize in 1971 and was re-edited in 1972 by Siglo Veintiuno in Mexico and the Centro Editor de América Latina in Buenos Aires, assuring it a wide readership. However, Cofiño's schematic world and austere prose did not correspond to the mainstream of the period.

More interesting is the work of Edmundo Desnoes, since it captures with unusual equanimity the enthusiasm and the anguish that the Cuban Revolution brought, often to the same person. *El cataclismo* is a triptych, with one story line focusing on a man who leaves for Miami when his properties are expropriated, another where his wife, who stays behind and lives with a bureaucrat of the Revolution, tries to adapt to the new circumstances, but fails, and a final thread where a proletarian couple marry and plan the future with optimism. Desnoes's best-known work is *Memorias del subdesarrollo* [*Inconsolable Memories*], that became a highly praised film under the direction of Tomás Gutiérrez Alea. These memoirs of a man trapped by the Revolution trace his growing sense of despondency and marginality as he discovers he is unable to take part in the change wholeheartedly, but also abhors taking the extreme position of his wife and some of his friends who have fled in blind terror to the United States. This parable of the intellectual's crucible transcends the specific Cuban situation where it originates, since the narrator is not the first or last intellectual to recognize the justice of a cause that threatens to undo the very class that has nurtured him. The underdevelopment here is manifold: from the economic imbalance that has prompted the Revolution, to the exquisite refinement of the Cuban bourgeoisie that did not develop a culture rooted in its own reality and open to others – the poor, the working classes – and also to the narrator's revelation that his love life has been stifled, undeveloped.

Reinaldo (also spelt Reynaldo) Arenas (1943, Cuba) is imaginative and cleverly outrageous in his early novels. *Celestino antes del alba* shows the fragmented and obsessed conscience of a child who lives with his mother, his grandparents, and a cousin, Celestino. The text describes his perceptions and dreams as he is battered and abused by his family. The word "hacha" – his grandfather axes down the trees where the child inscribes his poetry – is repeated as an incantatory denunciation of repressive society. Arenas uses many avant-garde techniques, such as inserting quotations that interrupt (or complement) the text, and providing several possible endings. In the final pages, *Celestino* becomes in part a theatre play, reminiscent of Lorca.

In *El mundo alucinante. (Una novela de aventuras.)* [*Hallucinations*], Servando, the protagonist, is an outsider who is thrown into a world of orgies, sadistic pleasure, and dependency. Learning and books set him apart, leading him to heterodox opinions about the indigenous origin of the Virgin of Guadalupe. Banished to prison in Spain, he manages to escape, experiences the corruption of the Spanish church and Madrid, meets in Europe numerous famous people, and even visits the other world, in the tradition of Dante and Quevedo. At long last he lives to see Mexico's independence from Spain, but only to again reject the imitation of the old ceremonies and the repetition of the old cruelty by the new ruling class. There is a connecting element with the Cuban Revolution, the image of a scientist – a thinly veiled allusion to Carpentier – blindly praising the new government. Arenas's novels transcend the childhood memories or the straightforward adventure novel, offering as an antidote to the repression of an unquestioning society, a free-wheeling text that does not allow any distinction between fantasy and reality.

For a detailed and authoritative guide to the Cuban novel of this period, the reader should consult Seymour Menton's *Prose Fiction of the Cuban Revolution*. Other Cuban writers, more concerned with textual experimentation, will be treated in the fourth section of this chapter.

The struggle in Puerto Rico against a destiny of colonialism is illustrated in an outstanding novel that merits to be better known, *Figuraciones en el mes de marzo* [*Schemes in the Month of March*] by Emilio Díaz Valcárcel (b. 1929). The main character is a Puerto Rican in Spain who is subjected to the arrogance of the faded empire and whose only defense is to reflect on the absurd aspects of language, people, and situations. This funny, creative, sometimes whining, other times angry, novel, that juxtaposes lists, clippings, letters, dialogues, receipts, in a sadly hilarious meditation on the inanity of the human condition, should be counted among the best in the period. *El hombre que trabajó lunes* is a short novel about a bureaucrat exasperated with his perfunctory life, an old and proven topic, handled with humor and insight.

In Colombia, the inheritance of the civil war (1899–1902), that took at least 100,000 lives, and the period known as *la violencia* (1948–1957), a savage confrontation between liberals and conservatives, keeps the topic of violence in center stage.

Eduardo Caballero Calderón (b. 1910, Bogotá) is a Colombian essayist, journalist, diplomat, and novelist who in his best-known novel, *El Cristo de espaldas*, offers a glimpse of the bloody conflict between the conservatives and liberals in a small provincial town. The precipitating factor is the arrival of a young priest, intent on a life of humble sainthood and service. When he arrives he discovers there is no neutral or sacred ground in a political geography fraught with danger and inscrutable to his outsider's eyes. The murder of the head of the conservative party in the region is attributed to his estranged son who, readers soon discover, is innocent. The priest tries to protect him and get a fair trial, but the conservative forces of the region are using the case to imprison and weaken their adversaries, therefore rapidly pushing the priest into an uncomfortable alliance with the liberals. At the request of powerful conservatives, the priest is removed and forced to return to the city, leaving behind a godless whirlwind of violence. The somber and sharp descriptions of the townspeople, the sociologist's eye of the author for unraveling secret alliances and influences give a vivid picture of this town which represents the country torn by civil strife.

The violence is forcefully depicted in *El día señalado*, by Manuel Mejía Vallejo (b. 1923). The novel weaves together the story of a saintly priest and his parishioners with private and social cyclic acts of destruction and regeneration. The dialogue is laconic and the description of the town and the cock-fights generates a stark atmosphere of oppressive heat and tension. Mejía Vallejo's other two novels in this period are more lyrical and less compelling: *Al pie de la ciudad*, an extended vignette of the urban poor, and *Aire de tango*, an evocation of Gardel and the dim portrait of a Colombian tough who excels by his mastery at throwing knives.

The repression of the strike on the banana plantations in December 1928, depicted in a crucial segment of García Márquez's *Cien años de soledad*, is the main event in *La casa grande* by Alvaro Cepeda Samudio (1926–1972). Dialogues of soldiers, documents, monologues by different members of a family divided between supporters of the strikers and opponents to their demands, and an alternation between first-, second-, and third-person narrative give this novel a wide perspective, despite its brevity. The variety in technique and the amplitude of vision are, unfortunately, not matched by a sure hand for avoiding stereotypical characters and situations.

Gustavo Alvarez Gardeazábal (b. 1945), university professor, journalist, politician, and a novelist of great popular success, writes about political violence, corruption, and provincial life with a courage that sets him apart from others who have covered the same topics. His language fluctuates between a rich and complex fabric that borders on the Baroque, and a sparse, journalistic shorthand that gains in urgency and immediacy what it loses in refinement. Deserving of note is *Cóndores no entierran todos los días*, about the rise of the conservative repression in Tuluá during *la violencia*, and the 3,000 dead in that region under the hegemony of a quiet leader, León María Lozano, known as "The Condor." The novel does not dwell on the reasons for the violence, but admirably describes its irrational spread.

Alvarez Gardeazábal's *La tara del papa* is a polyphonic narration of town conflicts, centered on the family saga of the Uribes, that converge into the start of *la violencia*, while *Dabeiba*, using as a pretext the need to abandon the town of Dabeiba, creates a tapestry – from which dialogue is expunged – of sex, power, violence, and memory that borders on gossip, yet manages to convey the suffocating lack of intimacy of a small town. *El bazar de los idiotas* includes some elements of Magical Realism in telling the story of two miraculous brothers who, despite their limited intelligence, possess the gift of curing the sick by the power the brothers receive while masturbating. This striking allegory of political power is told with narrative vigor and subdued lyricism.

Among the younger novelists, Albalucía Angel (b. 1939) wrote her first three novels in Europe. *Los girasoles en invierno* describes the thoughts of a woman waiting for a man in a Parisian café. A second story line about an expedition to Venus is intercalated. The second chapter takes place in Rome, transcribing the chatter of intellectuals in the style of Fellini or Antonioni. This novel, with almost no action and very little psychological insight, represents a search for a way out of the traditional Colombian countryside. In *Dos veces Alicia*, Albalucía Angel follows the model of the detective novel. The narrator observes with disgusted fascination the disintegrating family of the owner of the boarding house where she is staying in London. The story is ingenious, with unexpected interruptions, the titles of chapters inserted in the middle of sections, temporal jumps, intertextual play, suspense, and fantasies. There is a long scene at a Christmas party where (in a parody of a detective novel) the mystery of the life of Mrs. Wilson is revealed. The novel is interesting because it communicates the passion and pains of a small group, seen sarcastically by the exasperated narrator.

Estaba la pájara pinta sentada en el verde limón is a disjointed novel, where public events are a counterpoint to the private life of the protagonist, Ana. The frame of the narration is given by a recurrent situation: Ana refuses to get up in the morning, while the maid, Sabina, receives her confidences and tries to encourage her to get out of bed. The first part is an effective counterpoint between the murder of the liberal leader Jorge Eliécer Gaitán on April 9, 1948, and the secluded life of the girls in a Catholic school run by nuns. The efforts of society to keep women away from power are shown by the fact that they are barred from games, information, and are sexually abused. The novel is made up of voices, with many references to movies, fairy tales, and commercial brands. While there are some letters from prison that explain the motivation of Colombian guerrillas, and a detailed presentation of the murder of several students on June 8 and 9, 1954, with the subsequent censorship of the press, the motives for Ana's participation are sentimental, and her highest contribution to the cause seems to be to make love to her best friend's lover. As a document, the novel is extremely valuable, even if it does read in part as a self-indulgent memoir.

The uneasiness of urban intellectual men is documented in *Crónica de tiempo muerto* by Oscar Collazos (b. 1942). The action happens mostly in Bogotá, with incursions into Paris and Madrid. Sharing his disgust for bourgeois intelligentsia with Cortázar and his anger against signs of identity with Juan Goytisolo, Collazos parades a bored, frequently drunk, leftist writer through several parties and affairs while, as a counterpoint, scenes of student unrest and torture show that a real fight is going on elsewhere. The narrator offers an amazingly crude vision of women, reducing them to sex-obsessed victims of repression longing to be forced into pleasure by a manly man. The moralizing essays, the righteous furor, and the blind behavior and pitiful self-aggrandizement of the protagonist of *Crónica de tiempo muerto* are symptomatic of what could go wrong with revolutionary discourse.

In Ecuador, Demetrio Aguilera Malta (1909–1981) continued to write the sort of journalistic novels that had been successful for him in the past, taking his inspiration from the Spanish novelist Pérez Galdós. While there is certainly some literary merit to these novels – they are eminently readable and informative, even if mannered – their main purpose is to bring history to the reader with a wealth of detail that is harmlessly swallowed with the syrup of entertaining narration. In *Una cruz en la Sierra Maestra*, he tackles the recent events of the Cuban Revolution. *La caballeresa del sol* [*Manuela*] tells the story of Bolívar's lover, Manuela Sáenz. *El Quijote de El Dorado* describes the Amazons and the adventures of Francisco de Orellana. *Un nuevo mar para el rey* is devoted to the navigator Balboa, the Indian princess Anayansi, and the Pacific Ocean.

Aguilera Malta's proven craft as a journalist and a chronicler of the complex reality of Spanish America cannot prepare the reader for the extraordinary quality of his next novel, among the best in the period, *Siete lunas y siete serpientes* [*Seven Serpents and Seven Moons*]. A freshness of style, humor, and a fireworks display of verbal ingeniousness, plus an absorbing plot told with daring craft, retell an old story with a new twist and the force of a classic. In a small town in the jungle, modernity – good and evil – fights the past – equally mixed in value. Medicine and witchcraft mingle freely, as do fantasy and fiction. All the staple characters are here, even duplicated: the good and the bad doctor, the saintly and the corrupt priest, the ruthless entrepreneur, the local *caudillo*. Aguilera Malta adds to the brew the scheming witch-doctor, monkeys, and Christ and the Devil, two of the most amusing characters of the novel. Indigenous religion and Catholicism mix without radical conflict, in a harmonious view of the world where, for a change, things turn out all right without the complexity or seriousness of the issues being simplified. Gregory Rabassa's English translation is brilliant, a creative achievement in its own right.

The exceptional nature of *Siete lunas* in Aguilera Malta's output is further underscored by the heavy-handed satire of a dictator in *El secuestro del general*. The grotesque and parodic elements smother the story, adding little to an already long and crowded tradition of novels about dictatorship and violence in Spanish America.

In Venezuela, the story is the new urban violence. Salvador Garmendia (b. 1928) describes city life as seen from the perspective of the lower middle class. His first novel, *Los pequeños seres*, shows the complete breakdown of a minor office employee after the death of his boss and just at the moment when, after decades of stagnation, he appears to have an opportunity for a promotion. The shifts of the narrative point of view and the protagonist's hallucinations contrasted with his family routine are effective. Garmendia's more ambitious novel with a similar topic, *La mala vida*, is a rambling memoir of an uninteresting life. The insistence on a deteriorating vulgar life, made tolerable to the characters if not to the reader by an existentialist wallowing in anguish, continues in *Los habitantes*, *Díaz de ceniza*, and *Los pies de barro*. *Memorias de Altagracia* shifts to the perspective of a child who grows up in a rural town and later remembers the military feuds, the passional dramas, and the episodes of madness that shaped his otherwise unremarkable life. Angel Rama, in a favorable and excellent study of Garmendia's work, called his style "informalist" and compared it with the free association characteristic of a session with an analyst.

Adriano González León (b. 1933) won the Biblioteca Breve prize of the Seix Barral publishing house in Barcelona in 1968 with *País portátil*. Three parallel stories run through the novel: the first reconstructs the violence in the countryside in the early part of the century, with a patriarchal family and an army general. The second story line shows the repressive violence of the police in Caracas in the 1960s, after the hesitant progress to militant action of a university student, Andrés, who is shown in the third story line as he travels through Caracas to complete a clandestine mission. In *País portátil*, violence is an inheritance that cannot be avoided, reasoned away, or overcome with solidarity or love, when revolutionary violence is easily squashed by the government. The language is rich and the portrait of Caracas has vigor, yet the novel does not have the depth of Cortázar's *Libro de Manuel* nor the vastness of Fuentes's *La región más transparente*.

José María Arguedas (1911–1969) received his degree in ethnology in 1962, and worked as a university professor. His novels present the Indian world, with its traditions, language, music, and conflicts. The narrator keeps in mind the ignorance that his readers would have about the represented world; there is a pedagogical streak in Arguedas's writing, even up to his last diary in which he explains his suicide to friends, editor, employer, students, and readers. Arguedas's novels present a conflicting and divided world, yet the language seems to flow from inside both cultures. Arguedas holds the Indians in high esteem and he does not patronize them or transform them into the exotic aesthetic Other. Notable in Arguedas's works is his language, where Quechua and Spanish words surge together as brought out directly from an experience where they coexist and complement each other. Arguedas's lyricism, syntax, and vocabulary show the contribution the native Indian language that he learnt as a child has had on Peruvian culture.

One of the essential novels of this period is Arguedas's *Los ríos profundos* [*Deep Rivers*]. This *Bildungsroman* about Ernesto, a white boy who has been brought up among the Indians, presents the most convincing appeal for respecting the vigor and creativity of Peru's native culture. Separated from his father, an itinerant lawyer, when he is fourteen years old, Ernesto has to find a space of his own, where the old and the new language, Quechua and Spanish, can coexist. Life in the school at Abancay is wonderfully described (a suffocating yet also nurturing place of acculturation and learning, run by priests), as is Cuzco in the first chapter, when Ernesto visits his powerful uncle, owner of four haciendas, and discovers the sadness of Spanish culture superimposed on the living stones of Inca fortifications. The outside world comes in with an insurrection of the *mestizo* women who sell *chicha*, who complain, at first successfully, against the hoarding of salt. Then the troops arrive to restore order and punish the rebels. Outside and inside, private and public prove to be false distinctions here, because things are magically connected by the deep rivers of culture, blood, and language. The director of Ernesto's school will appease the rebels, playing on their emotions and infusing them with guilt, showing the collaboration between church and feudal landlords. The whirling top with which Ernesto plays, his *zumbayllu*, becomes a symbol of the interconnection of all things in the movement, light, and song of Nature. Ultimately, Ernesto remains an outsider, in a third, imagined space where the past and present of two races, two cultures, and a complex system of social classes could meet. This impasse is transcended only by Nature and music, while the plague that scatters the students in the final pages of the novel is a reminder of the shared fragility of human beings.

El sexto draws on Arguedas's own experience as a political prisoner during one year in a prison in Lima. A student, Gabriel, listens to political speeches and to the squabbles between *apristas* and communists. The narrator does not become a true character and the prisoners appear schematic in this sordid world of naturalist coloring.

In *Todas las sangres*, Arguedas describes a town, San Pedro, located in the southern mountain ranges of Peru. The old, harmonious lifestyle is crumbling under the combined influences of centralism, the collapse of the mining industry, and the weight of accumulated injustice. Indians with their communal lands resist the landowners, represented by Bruno, and the owner of the mine, Fermín, Bruno's brother, while these in turn are pushed aside by the nascent international capitalism of Lima. This lengthy novel shows a plurality of worlds in conflict, of inherited and new structures weighed down by economic interests, in a changing society with greater mobility and more options than the feudal society of regional agriculture and mining. The behavior of the two brothers is brutal and arrogant, reminiscent in tone of Valle Inclán's *Comedias bárbaras*.

El zorro de arriba y el zorro de abajo was published posthumously and it exemplifies a dialectic of mountain/coast, Quechua/Spanish, plus a kaleidoscope of political opinions in a debate that is less vivid than in his previous novels. The interpolated pages of his diary run from May 10, 1968, to October 22, 1969, with moving considerations about suicide and stinging commentaries about other Spanish American novelists. The conflict between different leaders in a fishermen's union is shown, but not resolved. What would seem an interruption of the narrative due only to Arguedas's suicide is also a pessimistic break in the progress of a history stagnated in conflict between those above and those oppressed.

The oppression of the Indians and the racism of the powerful – landowners, doctors, lawyers – in small Peruvian towns are vividly chronicled by Manuel Scorza (1928–1983) in *Redoble por Rancas* and *Historia de Garabombo, el invisible*. Scorza's tendency to caricature and anecdote, his penchant for grotesque humor and heavy-handed parody give to his novels a quality of agitprop dignified with techniques learnt from Ricardo Palma, Ciro Alegría, Asturias, and García Márquez.

The other side of the story, the privileged bourgeoisie caught in a white, European and North American, dream, has been told by Vargas Llosa and by Alfredo Bryce Echenique (b. 1939). Bryce's *Un mundo para Julius* is dreamy and Proustian, less concerned about a story than with the people, their secrets and favorite places. Julius will grow up to realize that the world he was promised does not exist, except as a consoling project, but as Bryce exposes the emptiness of this fabricated world, his ornate prose takes delight in reconstructing an era according to the insightful vision of a participant.

In Argentina the main concern of the period is the unstable and conflictive nature of a society divided between the old money and the mass of immigrants, between the powerful and the dispossessed, and novels tend either to be concerned with describing the apocalyptic condition of the country or to escape into a refined seclusion. Peronists and the army or police roam from novel to novel, but there is no agreement about how they should be judged.

Among the well-known writers who long for order and high culture one finds Manuel Gálvez, Eduardo Mallea, José Bianco, Manuel Mujica Lainez, Ernesto Sábato, Héctor A. Murena, Silvina Bullrich, and Beatriz Guido. Manuel Gálvez (1882–1962), published *Las dos vidas del pobre Napoleón*, a light-hearted story about the transformation of a humble employee into a gambler and an embezzler, as he seeks to imitate the literary portrait of him created by a friend. He also published several historical novels, *Tiempo de odio y angustia*, *Han tocado a deguello*, *Bajo la garra anglo-francesa*, and *Y así cayó don Juan Manuel*, in which he defends Rosas's dictatorship. *El uno y la multitud* describes life in Buenos Aires during the Second World War, *Tránsito Guzmán* is an anti-Peronist novel concentrating on the mob attack on June 16, 1955, against properties of the Catholic church. *Perdido en su noche* is about a Jesuit priest and the crisis of his vocation. *Me mataron entre todos* tells the story of a man who can read other people's minds, and *La locura de ser santo*, published posthumously, is another of his Catholic novels. Gálvez is always a good narrator and his novels are well structured, but his Naturalism and his ideological conservatism were increasingly removed from the mainstream.

Eduardo Mallea (b. 1903), the editor from 1931 to 1955 of the literary supplement of Argentina's leading newspaper, *La Nación*, became well-known for his essay *Historia de una pasión argentina* (1937) [*History of an Argentine Passion*], and his early novels, among them *La bahía del silencio* (1940), but he is a prolific writer who published many novels in the period 1950 to 1975. *Los enemigos del alma* tells the story of a brother and his two sisters, trapped in a conflictive relationship with each other. This novel is discursive and mannered, but provides a detailed portrait of Mallea's native city, Bahía Blanca. In 1951 he published *La torre*, the second volume of a trilogy that had begun with *Las águilas* (1943). *La torre* focuses on the decline of the Ricarte family, exemplified by the hesitations and failures of a young lawyer who searches for the truth of his country and for his true self in the countryside. Mallea's stilted style and repetitive characters – the troubled man, the archetypical outsider, the dominant or enslaved woman, the jealous man, the bitter marriage – and the intellectual, detached, cool narrator, weaken his other novels of this period: *Chaves*, *La sala de espera*, and *Simbad*, a long novel about a writer's career. Three short novels or long stories are included in *Posesión*, where "Los zapatos" shows an uncharacteristic and successful black humor. *El resentimiento* is a triptych of three novels (*Los ensimismados*, *El resentimiento*, and *La falacia*), where Mallea's prologue sums up his wish to distance himself from the world and place himself in the unpopular category of a narrator of ideas. *La barca de hielo* is a collection of stories loosely strung together by the same narrator, while *La penúltima puerta* introduces themes from India. *Gabriel Andaral* is a static portrait of the musings of an Argentinian *homme de lettres*. Mallea portrays, often unintentionally, the exhausted ideology of a French-oriented intelligentsia. His vigor lies more in the essay than in the novel, as proven by *La vida blanca*, written in the early 1940s, and published with a moving prologue and epilogue from 1960, where Mallea laments the passing of a proud Argentina and the collapse of the dreams of a leading and cultured – rich and refined – upper class.

The modernist divide between valued aristocratic art – mostly European – and popular expression – mostly local, disruptive, degraded, and superficial – is brilliantly defended in *La pérdida del reino* by José Bianco (1908–1986). Bianco was the editor of *Sur* from 1938 to 1961, filtering for the Spanish American public the latest and most refined European trends. A prolific essayist, his sparse narrative started brilliantly with two short novels, *Sombras suele vestir* (1941), and *Las ratas* (1943). Bianco describes interpersonal relations with unusual lucidity, exploring with restrained fascination situations where the smoothness of civilized society gives way to sickness, perversion, madness, and suicide. *La pérdida del reino* is divided into two sections of unequal length. The first and shorter one is told from the point of view of an editor who meets Rufino Velázquez, an essayist who has spent several years in Europe and has recently returned to Buenos Aires to die surrounded by his faithful aristocratic friends. Velázquez hands over to the editor the manuscripts of an autobiographical novel and a plethora of documents, from which the second part of *La pérdida del reino* reconstructs Velázquez's life. The care with which Bianco distances writing from truth, his distrust of language in the effort to distill the essence of experience, the enigmatic nature of memory and passion, the gingerly treated homoeroticism are all factors that make this novel reminiscent of Gide, Durrell, Mauriac, and Sartre, while at the same time anticipating some of the metafictional preoccupations of a later period. The portrait of the threatened upper crust of the Argentinian intelligentsia is melancholic and unflattering. Velázquez drifts in and out of an idle life without being able to leave behind his family, especially the double inheritance of his father: money and prestige, on the one hand, the shady memory of a murder, on the other. The seamy side of the elite is thus brought sharply into focus, yet Bianco does not denounce this decadent aristocracy, but more laments the passing of a kingdom of elegant grandeur.

Less discursive than Mallea, not as profound as Murena, Manuel Mujica Lainez (1910–1984) belongs also to a group of Argentinian intellectuals marked by the nostalgia of Europe and mesmerized by the fading grandeur of the landed aristocracy. As a journalist for *La Nación* from 1932 until his retirement in 1969, he was well informed and widely read, receiving many honors for his essays, novels, and translations. His novels from 1950 to 1975 are finely crafted and thoroughly researched, and most are entertaining, but they seldom transcend Mujica Lainez's love of the ornamental, the gossipy, and the titillating. *Los ídolos* is a restrained account of the falsity behind the facade of a famous poet and an aristocratic family. *La casa* and *Los viajeros* are flawed by an artificial narrator – the house – and a diffuse story, respectively. *Invitados en "El Paraíso"* chronicles the sexual excesses of the rich and the bohemian. His best-known novel, *Bomarzo* [*Bomarzo*] lovingly recreates the Italian Renaissance. *El unicornio* [*The Wandering Unicorn*] and *El laberinto* are also historical novels, the first one about the Middle Ages, and the second about one of El Greco's models, a friend of Lope de Vega, and their times. *De milagros y de melancolías* is a pseudo-history of the Southern Cone of Latin America, from the Conquest to the year 3000, a parody of the style of historians and popular myths, and an acerbic criticism of Perón. Ultimately, Mujica Lainez is too refined and civilized, too erudite, to allow the novels to take off with true narrative vigor. It is only in a moving portrait of the Emperor Heliogabalus, sneaked into an autobiographical novel, *Cecil*, that Mujica Lainez allows his fascination with excess and exquisite perversion to surface, but in *El viaje de los siete demonios*, a lively and funny novel, he undercuts sin by reducing the devils to travelling salesmen.

The philosophical essay is only thinly disguised with a novelistic argument in the novels of Ernesto Sábato (b. 1911). *Sobre héroes y tumbas*

[*On Heroes and Tombs*] tells a mystifying love story, with a disconcerted angry young man and a frantic and erratic woman who descends from an illustrious family now in economic, physical, and mental decadence. A counterpoint with heroic events of the past century, and the background of the popular unrest of the 1950s provide depth to a world of uncontrollable violence and insidious madness. The novel incorporates a chilling report, prepared by one of the characters who claims to have discovered the blind have a secret and powerful organization. This paranoid parable can easily be translated into a somber meditation on the leaders of our civilization, their limited vision of the future, and their brutal means of defending their privileges. In *Abaddón el exterminador*, brief episodes and long discussions on literature, politics, art, and literary criticism offer an apocalyptic interpretation of the present. One of the characters is a writer named Sábato, and the characters of his previous novels, critics, journalists, and friends surround him with a maddening babble that distracts him from the important tasks of writing and denouncing the repressive violence of the establishment.

Silvina Bullrich (b. 1915) has an accessible prose that gained her popular success if not critical acclaim. Of the many novels she wrote during this period, noteworthy are *Bodas de cristal*, with a one-sided but moving portrait of a marriage, and *Los burgueses*, depicting a family dinner that becomes an exhilarating occasion for gossip.

An illustrative example of the change, in the period 1950–1975, from the preoccupation with society and ideas to narration and language is provided by Héctor A. Murena (1923–1975), whose early career is marked by his participation in *Sur* and *La Nación*, that is, organs associated with an elitist and refined Argentinian oligarchy. His influential essays, notably *El pecado original de América* (1954), supplied concepts such as parricide, widely used by his and the following generation of Argentinian intellectuals to describe their conflict with their precursors. His novels are grouped into two trilogies, the first one with a strong existentialist mood that owes much to Sartre and Beckett. *La fatalidad de los cuerpos* describes the lonely existence of a bed-ridden industrialist who sees with impotence his world collapse around him, *Las leyes de la noche* (*The Laws of the Night*) is the depressing and brutal story of the industrialist's lover, and *Los herederos de la promesa* centers on the bohemian life of the industrialist's daughter and her lover. The vision of Argentina that emerges from these novels shows her with an aimless and weak leadership threatened by moral disintegration and the violence of the immigrants and the poor. The heirs to the promises of Sarmiento and the liberal, progress-oriented nineteenth century are mired in a shattered dream reflected in the void and pessimism of existentialist rhetoric. Murena's second trilogy, *El sueño de la razón*, proves that he kept abreast of the new trends, since his language becomes innovative and is brought to the fore by ingenious narrators, one of them a story-teller. *Epitalámica* follows the grotesque but amusing adventures of a moronic heir to a large fortune made from selling tainted food products, *Polispuercón* brings the arrogant and exploitative society depicted in the previous volume to an end in an outrageous dictatorship, while *Caína muerte* is a parable of the rise of a populist movement, probably of Peronism. Dogs and cats take over and humans obey them, becoming their lovers, while civilization flounders. Murena's pessimism and his contempt for middle-class values make of both trilogies somber statements of rejection, but the second trilogy is tempered by the playfulness of the language and the intelligence of the grotesque satire. Murena's estrangement in his later years from the Argentinian intellectual mainstream prevented his last novels, among them the posthumously published *Folisofía*, from receiving the attention they merit.

Beatriz Guido (1925–1988) won the Emecé Prize in 1954 with *La casa del ángel* [*The House of the Angel*], the memoirs of a young woman who has grown up in the stifling atmosphere of a rich and conservative household. The dramatic incidents – a duel and a rape – make visible the conflicting society into which she must grow, unprepared for the struggles of sex, class, and politics. In *La caída*, an eighteen-year-old, Albertina, arrives in Buenos Aires to study literature at the university. She is slowly drawn into the life of a peculiar family, daring to replace the mother and falling into a suffocated and voiceless stupor. This striking novel gives a good account of the obstacles to independence for a young intellectual woman. *Fin de fiesta* is a conventional novel about a rural chieftain and his family. The case of a woman incarcerated by her family in her own house and not allowed to live her own life is beautifully handled in the short novel *La mano en la trampa*. *El incendio y las vísperas* [*End of a Day*] shows a very rich and decadent family threatened by Peronist mobs. From the breakfast in the kitchen – the servants are on strike – to the loss of the family farm and the fire at the Jockey Club, the security of the family is eroded by the evil and ugly populace. Many readers, even those who condemn the populist dictatorship of Perón, may find it hard to sympathize with the sufferings of these characters who lead such useless lives among so much wealth and flirt with the working classes only to have sex or to protect their properties. *Escándalos y soledades* is not altogether successful in describing the life of an eccentric family, all males, intercalating documents about the death of Trotsky and the life of his murderer.

On the Peronist side and with corrosive humor, Leopoldo Marechal (1900–1970) offers a brilliant example of how profound ideas can be presented in a captivating way in *El banquete de Severo Arcángelo*. With a talent for the unexpected turn of phrase that cuts down the flights of metaphysical thought without trivializing, Marechal presents enigmatically the preparations for a ritual banquet prepared by a rich Buenos Aires industrialist. The main narrator, a journalist, is in turn seduced and repelled by the series of transcendental symbols with which he is confronted. While the novel owes much to mystery and adventure novels (Salgari is quoted with reverence), and the language is reminiscent of Borges, the madcap frenzy of the action and the depth of the ideas presented are vintage Marechal. *Megafón, o la guerra* is an ambitious novel that passes judgment on Argentinian history and finds it lacking of true martial vigor, commenting negatively on the generals who exiled Perón. Part of *Megafón* is a melancholic return to the places described in Marechal's earlier novel *Adán Buenosayres* (1948). The final chapters are similar to *El banquete*, with the purification and dismemberment of the mythical hero, but *Megafón* is episodic, disjointed, and sermonizing, more in the line of Quevedo's dreams than a traditional novel. Marechal's odd mixture of Medieval Catholicism, Greek mythology, and Homeric epic patterns, suffused by irreverent humor and irony, make him an original and unique writer.

To express a concern for social injustice and the repression of the poor, and to denounce the escapist refinement of the writers associated with the journal *Sur*, several young writers founded *Contorno*, published from 1953 to 1959. One of its founding editors, David Viñas (b. 1929), is also the best known novelist of this group. Of his first novels, *Cayó sobre su rostro, Los años despiadados, Un dios cotidiano*, and *Los dueños de la tierra*, this last one is the best balanced, describing the failed attempts of a Buenos Aires bureaucrat to mediate in a conflict in Patagonia that ends in a massacre. Viñas occasionally reads more as a chronicler than a novelist, and his characters are mostly useful props to tell the story of a period. His sympathies are with the underdog, and there are in his work conflictive and compassionate accounts of the repression of workers, homosexuals, Jews, and women. *Dar la cara* contains a satire of *Sur* (called *La revista* in the novel), and of the Argentinian film industry in the 1950s. *Los hombres de a caballo* is Viñas's most ambitious novel, offering a convincing family portrait of the military and their obsession with power, sex, and fraternity. The intricate network of flashbacks and juxtaposed episodes are more cinematographic than baroque, and allow Viñas to create characters with psychological depth by presenting several generations of army men and showing their importance in Argentinian history. *Cosas concretas* is a bizarre interview of a writer, interspersed with monologues and episodes that throw light on his frustrated career. *Jauría*, despite its complex structure, is the old story of gunmen and the powerful Old Man, more entertaining than revealing. For the period studied in this chapter, *Los hombres de a caballo* is a major accomplishment, surely among the best studies of military psychology in Spanish America and an absorbing, profound, and technically accomplished novel.

Among popular writers, Marta Lynch (1930–1985) outlines important political and social problems of Argentina in her novels. In *La alfombra roja*, she follows the unscrupulous surge to power of a presidential candidate. Her descriptions of the process are detailed and knowledgeable, in part because she had occupied – next to David Viñas and Noé Jitrik, among others – an important position in the presidential candidacy of Arturo Frondizi, between 1956 and 1958. *Al vencedor* looks at the problem of a lost generation, focusing on two men recently discharged from the army. *La señora Ordóñez* describes the life of the bored wife of a doctor, and *Un árbol lleno de manzanas* observes the student unrest of 1972 and the generation gap.

Among novels that reported about being a woman in a male-dominated society, *Las ceremonias del verano*, by Marta Traba (1930–1984), is a passionate portrait of an intellectual struggling to assert her own self, first in Argentina and then in Europe. The novel does not have a strong narrative structure, but is more a series of well-drawn vignettes. Luisa Valenzuela (b. 1938) showed her superior craftsmanship and intelligence from her very first novel, *Hay que sonreír*, on the surface a picaresque novel about a prostitute in Buenos Aires, her subsequent marriage and work in a circus, but on a deeper level a serious consideration of the condition of women as a body for sale or as a severed, smiling head, the whore or the virgin. In *El gato eficaz* she looks at the relationship between women, cats, and discourse, moving to the daring and experimental prose that will become her trademark in later works.

Moving progressively from a lyrical description of the humbler neighborhoods of Buenos Aires to an opaque and lyrical prose, Néstor Sánchez (b. 1935) published *Nosotros dos, Siberia Blues, El amhor, los orsinis y la muerte*, and *Cómico de la lengua*. The first two novels, his most successful, modulate memory and mood in variations that can be compared to the improvisations of a jazz player melancholically reminiscing about a broken marriage or a group of friends involved in petty crime.

A unique vision of Argentina is found in the novels of Haroldo Conti (b. 1925), who describes the rough life of outsiders with the celebration of independence found in Hemingway and Kerouac and a morosity reminiscent of Faulkner and Pavese. *Sudeste* concentrates on fishermen and hunters; *Alrededor de la jaula* follows a boy in his lonely life in Buenos Aires and in his attempt to free his favorite animal from the zoo; *En vida* alternates between the weekly routine of Buenos Aires young bureaucrats and the weekend escapes to the seashore; *Mascaró, el cazador americano* focuses on a circus that becomes the arena in which the protagonist must find his true self. These novels are strong in atmosphere and weak in action, as if the influence of Fellini and Antonioni had magnified the image and the noun at the expense of tension and verbs.

The world of the provinces is recreated in *Aire tan dulce*, by Elvira Orphée (b. 1930). Focusing on three characters who alternate their monologues, the novel looks at the resentment of a poor and violent young man, the loves of a young woman, and the frustrated life of her grandmother. The atmosphere is oppressive and the characters live in an isolation paradoxically aggravated by the rumor mill and the reciprocal surveillance of the bored inhabitants of a small city. A rush of brief sentences, a frenzied and at times confusing action, hatred, and a failure to communicate – especially between the sexes – lead to a violent climax. Orphée does not describe with any detail the physical appearance of her characters or the town, but concentrates instead on the voices and feelings of her characters. She also published in this period the novels *Uno* and *En el fondo*.

Marco Denevi (b. 1922) skillfully combined suspense, perspectivism, reflections on fiction and reality, and a brilliant evocation of different patterns of speech in *Rosaura a las diez* [*Rosa at Ten O'clock*]. The novel offers four versions of puzzling events that lead to murder, and a letter by the victim where she explains the mystery. Denevi's delight in language and narration is an antecedent of Manuel Puig's novels and a reminder of the effectiveness of the traditional detective story in conveying effortlessly the portrait of a segment of society.

Manuel Puig (1933–1990) established himself from his first novel, *La traición de Rita Hayworth* [*Betrayed by Rita Hayworth*], as an original and innovative writer. His portrayal of Argentina's provincial middle class is especially effective because of Puig's knack for recreating dialogue and the voices of women and children, incorporating elements of popular culture, such as soap operas, film, and colloquial language. The voices on the telephone, pages of personal journals, letters, school reports, and interior monologues that proliferate in *La traición* show the shallowness of life and the gap between expectations fueled by the silver screen and the routines of daily life. Puig shows his characters with affection and understanding, but not without a marked irony that invites readers to smile at the pretentiousness and shortsightedness of these modest lives, trivial even to themselves, yet touched by the redeeming grace of camp and kitsch. *Boquitas pintadas* [*Heartbreak Tango*] reconstructs, through the juxtaposition of letters, police reports, dialogues, log books, and other scraps of writing, the life of a small-town seducer. The focus is not on him, a vain and irresponsible character who dies of tuberculosis, but on the women who love him and hate each other in an intricate and suffocating network of actions, gossip, and memories. The texts seem to come directly from the heart of the characters, a heart overflowing with affection and sexual longing but mired in clichés and deception. Puig does away with the traditional narrator, elegant and knowing, and seems to step aside to let the reader gauge the depths of the irony with which these texts are passed on, allowing a wide range of possible readings, from condescending to earnest and compassionate. *The Buenos Aires Affair*, subtitled "Novela policial," reports with a quirky prose the story of two frustrated lovers. While the story line may not compete with the novels of Dashiell Hammett or Ross Macdonald, Puig's verbal dexterity is always dazzling, as can be seen, for example, in the mangled and syncopated language of the recording of a conversation between an informer and the police.

In Uruguay, the dream of a progressive, prosperous, civil republic – the Switzerland of Spanish America – is shattered during this period, as economic pressures mount and violence destroys the peaceful social equilibrium established at the beginning of the century.

Juan Carlos Onetti (1909–1994) is a masterful creator of a novelistic world marked by a gloomy mood and outsider characters trapped in enigmatic circumstances where truth and fiction are hard to disentangle. Onetti's impeccable and terse prose is stretched to the limits of lyricism and obscurity, without ever losing a Naturalistic grounding and more than enough suspense to keep the reader's interest. He brings together in a most effective mix the desolate vision of the world of Kafka and Sartre, Faulkner's poetic perspectivism, and the deadpan cynicism of the American hard-boiled detective novels. *La vida breve* [*A Brief Life*] starts from the situation of Brausen, an employee at a publicity agency in Buenos Aires, whose wife has recently lost a breast because of a mastectomy. The loss is symbolic of falling out of love and of a lack of interest in the routine of his life. Brausen fills in the growing and threatening vacuum by dreaming up two alternative lives. One is played out with a prostitute who moves in next door to his apartment, whose life he reconstructs from the voices and noise coming through the wall of his bedroom. Brausen becomes Arce for her, a violent tough who avenges in her submission, beating, and ultimate murder the irritating independence of Brausen's wife. Also, Brausen fills his hand, orphaned of the motherly breast, with a pen, and tries to write the script of a movie that takes place in Santa María, a mythic blending of Montevideo and Buenos Aires where most of Onetti's characters live. Here, an aggressive and distant woman reduces the man, a doctor, to a provider of morphine – pleasure and dreams – and a servant, but does not allow him any access to her intimacy. The smooth transitions from one story line to the other, the downplaying of symbolism and the understated reporting of events, riddled with gaps and unexplained events, are most effective and show Onetti at his best. *Los adioses* has several people guessing at and thereby inventing the life of a laconic and reclusive patient being treated for tuberculosis in a mountain sanitarium and visited there by two women. The scandal of the unnamed patient is more his obstinate secret than his suspected double life. While some versions are proven to be wrong by the end of this short, beautiful, and very complex novel, the mystery of the man's deeper motivations does not subside. *Para una tumba sin nombre* takes readers again to Santa María, where an unusual burial is variously explained by three of the participants. Not even the name of the dead woman can be ascertained, plunging characters into a darkness that is contemplated with tolerance and even some pleasure for the play it allows to the creative imagination. *La cara de la desgracia*, *Tan triste como ella*, and *La muerte y la niña* offer three cases where a woman dies, murdered by men, or driven to suicide by an unconcerned husband. That in these three short narrations death is the price women pay for their rebellion and independence does point out the problematic and unhappy situation of women in Onetti's world, where violence appears sometimes as a manly and seductive shortcut to the mature relationship that the characters are unable to establish normally.

Onetti's masterpiece is *El astillero* [*The Shipyard*], the story of Larsen, a pimp who clings to the dream of becoming the CEO of a bankrupt and ruined shipyard, while trying to marry the dim-witted daughter of the owner. Larson's salaries go unpaid, his only employees are two plunderers of the remaining carcass of the shipyard, and his work consists of reviewing outdated files. *El astillero* can be read as a parable of the frail foundations of the Uruguayan and Argentinian economies, of the aimless and exploited workers, of the infinite capacity for self-deception and dream that sustains human beings in a time of crisis, or even as a prophetic statement about the collapse of the affluent society in Uruguay and Argentina. However, it is first an unforgettable and haunting story splendidly told. The antecedents of Larsen's life are given in *Juntacadáveres*, where Larsen, as an entrepreneur, brings the first brothel to Santa María, unleashing the ire of the priest and the conservative forces in town. The alternation of first- and third-person narration, the conflict between the town and the outsiders, the wasted effort and the suicide of a sexually aggressive woman, show again in *Juntacadáveres* that in Onetti's world there is no success possible within or without the established norms, except in a detached and amused cynicism that does not exclude a love resigned to the insignificance of human beings and the corrosive swiftness of time.

A minor masterpiece is *La tregua* [*The Truce*], by Mario Benedetti (b. 1920), a perceptive portrait of the brief moment of happiness in the life of a Uruguayan accountant planning to retire. Narrated as a first-person diary, this novel courageously risks being sentimental to tell its love story.

With a restrained prose, Benedetti convincingly explores the relationships of work, family, friendship, and love, intimating that the missing political dimension is what dooms the main character to his final solitude. He also published in this period *Quién de nosotros* and *Gracias por el fuego*.

Cristina Peri Rossi (b. 1941) gives a poetic and forceful account in *El libro de mis primos* of the disintegration of a vast family, symbolic of the collapse of her own country that took her into exile in Spain in 1972. Her lively, playful, and original text mixes prose and verse to describe the world of the family elders (hiding from the world, leaving newspapers unread), a young man who has joined the guerrillas, and the children who imitate the conflictive world of the grown-ups. Memorable chapters include the visit to the doctor of a boy who cries too much, and the surgical rape of a doll.

Augusto Roa Bastos (b. 1917) has created in his many short stories and two novels a monumental, complex, interrelated, and vast world. With a rich, experimental language he rewrites the history of his native land, Paraguay. While Roa Bastos's description of the violence, injustice, and repression of the colonial society of Spanish America has many antecedents, his masterful interweaving of European and Guaraní myths, the depth and openness of his analysis, and the diversity and richness of his literary craft have assured him a position among the best narrators of Spanish America. *Hijo de hombre* [*Son of Man*] has nine chapters, five of them narrated by Miguel Vera, a veteran of the war against Bolivia in Chaco, and four chapters narrated by what seems to be the voice of tradition. Vera's sympathies are with the oppressed – the human being crucified by other human beings – yet he is still serving the oppressors and sheltered in his own self. A final report says that Vera was horrified by suffering, but knew not what to do about it. Roa's novel, by etching the parallel between the life and Passion of Christ and the rebel peasants' leader Cristóbal Jara, is a call to compassion and action, a rejection of uncommitted observers, the Miguel Veras who end up being unwitting accomplices to a situation they detest. The symphonic structure of *Hijo de hombre*, with its apparently independent chapters, proves that time past and present, the individual and society, and peace and war are deeply interrelated, inevitably contaminating the space of the so-called detached observer – Vera or the reader.

Roa's second novel, *Yo el Supremo* [*I the Supreme*], has been considered his masterpiece, and it takes its place alongside other already classic descriptions of Latin American dictators, the Spaniard Ramón María del Valle Inclán's *Tirano Banderas*, Miguel Angel Asturias's *El Señor Presidente*, Alejo Carpentier's *El recurso del método*, and Gabriel García Márquez's *El otoño del patriarca*. The main difference with those other novels is that while they are loosely based on historical facts, their dictator being a composite of several well-known historical villains, Roa's novel closely follows in its story the life of Paraguay's Dr. Francia, who led the country from 1814 until his death in 1840. *Yo el Supremo* presents itself as the compilation by a twentieth-century narrator of a large amount of material about Francia and his period. The narrator adopts from time to time the historian's style of footnotes and the sifting of contradictory evidence. A pretense reminiscent of Cervantes's *Don Quixote* complicates the reliability of the narrative: most of the text pretends to be dictated by Francia himself to his secretary Patiño, who in turn is given to changing a sentence to suit his own convenience. The compiler, Francia, and Patiño, plus the voices quoted from historical documents, struggle in vain to impose one version of the events, to resolve all ambiguities and to arrive at a conclusion, a verdict about Francia's government. Francia delights in puns and etymology, shows himself as a sophisticated and resourceful speaker, sends fatherly and clever "perpetual memos," and shows an excellent grasp of Paraguayan history. While Roa has declared that he was not interested in writing a novel that would follow history in every detail, he has stayed close enough to make the text tantalizing. The reader who is encouraged to turn to history to complement Francia's portrait, will find that "the Supreme" has been the subject of both encomiastic and denigrating biographies, and that even the most trivial documents are suspect in a country where history has been written and rewritten incessantly under the guidance and scrutiny of harsh dictatorships. Since the novel insists on the unreliable nature of all writing, on the supreme power of the author, the discrepancies introduced by Roa confirm that readers must practice an active and questioning reading, never lulled by the false promise of veracity from historians or narrators. Despite the concluding summation of the compiler, where he deplores Francia's big words, fraudulent rhetoric, perverse ambition, and pride, Francia has grown through the novel to be a brilliant and enduring character, in the same category as Sarmiento's Facundo Quiroga or Rómulo Gallegos's Doña Bárbara.

In Chile, Eduardo Barrios (1884–1963) published *Los hombres del hombre*, an introspective study of a jealous man who feels divided into seven voices that reflect different aspects of his personality. However, the younger Chilean writers, moving fast into a period of great social transformation and political unrest, are mostly interested in telling the story of their society, and not the sufferings of a single individual.

Marta Brunet (1897–1967), also an established writer from previous decades like Barrios, published *María Nadie*, in the first section of which she creates the image of a burgeoning frontier town, while the second part of the novel focuses on María López, a professional and independent woman who is rejected by the town. While Brunet is to be commended for her open and courageous treatment of the repression of women in Chilean society and for her pathbreaking openness about sex, her traditional narration and pat psychological portraits limit the effectiveness of her novels. In *Amasijo*, she explains the homosexual tendencies of the protagonist and his eventual suicide as the consequences of a dominant mother's influence. While her dialogues ring true and her description of nature and mood is convincing, she does not escape the stereotypes of *criollista* literature, such as the evil and idle rich, the good prostitute, the exotic foreigners, and the caricature of the lower middle class. Brunet's tendency to explain her characters' actions with a clinical neatness conspires to further dilute her characters.

The main writer of this period in Chile is José Donoso (b. 1924), who describes in his novels the fragile and decadent upper crust of Chilean society, threatened by the mimicry of the middle class and the anger and resentment of workers and the poor. The subtle complexity of his characters and a language that is at once richly local and elegantly transparent characterize Donoso's writing. *Coronación* [*Coronation*] follows the spineless and idle Andrés during his visits to his grandmother's house, where a new maid awakens his sexual urge, driving him to tepid passion, failed action, and feigned madness. The interdependence of masters and servants is brought into sharp relief as the shelter of the ancestral home opens to a vast city of need and violence, masterfully evoked with straightforward language. By leaving aside tiresome descriptions, stereotypic confrontations, and pathetic calls to the reader's allegiance, Donoso short-circuited decades of social realism and established himself as one of the most important voices of the Spanish American novel.

Este domingo [*This Sunday*] combines three story lines. The first offers the point of view of the narrator as a child, visiting his grandparents' house on Sundays and vainly trying to understand the grown-ups, while engaged in the labyrinths created by children's imagination. The second outlines the story of the grandfather, who has remained fixed in his love affair with the maid he had as a young man and is now concerned with a suspected cancer. The third, and most developed, is the story of the grandmother who, unsatisfied with her marriage, has found refuge in social work. She visits a prisoner in jail and helps him establish himself after he is set free, yet the relationship is fraught on both sides with the repression of their feelings caused by the difference in their social class. The tragic ending is narrated without any stridency, underscoring the senseless waste of these aimless characters.

In *El lugar sin límites* [*Hell Hath No Limits*], a transvestite and his daughter are the owners of a rural brothel with a dwindling clientele. They are threatened on the one side by the local landowner, who wants to buy the land where the brothel stands, and on the other by a truck-driver who is a violent repressed homosexual and probably the illegitimate son of the landowner. The ominous vigil for the truck-driver's return and the symbol-laden closing scenes are rescued by the portrait of La Manuela, an aging man who is transfigured when he dances in his red dress and brings illusion to a wasted countryside.

Donoso's best-known novel, *El obsceno pájaro de la noche* [*The Obscene Bird of Night*], is extremely complex, shifting points of view and narrators, making it impossible to pin down an objective truth. While a group of nuns, old women, orphans, and their manservant, in a rambling and vast building which is about to be demolished, await their transfer to a new hospice, an avalanche of voices, memories, documents, and a buzz of legends, gossip, games, songs, and dialogues spin the story of the monstrous son of a rich landowner. The man who used to be his secretary and who wished to emulate him, has now been reduced to a deaf-mute servant of the old, retired maids and to a doll for the orphans. According to his memories, when the monstrous son was born, his father created for him an environment where deformity became the norm and the real world was hidden behind the tall walls of their farm's gardens. The novel lends itself to allegorical interpretations – the Chilean landed aristocracy's obstinate refusal to change and to recognize their anomalous standing in recent history – but is most powerful in exploring the role of imagination in power and sex. The secretary's fascination with his rich employer, his desire to substitute him in his wife's bed, and the landowner's envy of the fertility and sexual prowess of his subordinates are only some threads of a tapestry of frustration, where hiding, wrapping up, storing away, cannibalizing truth, or deflecting it into myth are unable to contain the destructive forces of truth, old age, and history.

Jorge Edwards (b. 1931) also describes the upper middle class and follows in *El peso de la noche* the path of an uncle and his nephew, the former in progressive decadence resulting from his alcoholism, the latter still in school discovering sex and heterodoxy. Edwards's description of the Chilean bourgeoisie is scathing, with an insider's knowledge and a good ear for dialogue.

Enrique Lafourcade (b. 1927) writes popular novels with tantalizing glimpses of the life of the very rich and the very poor described with existentialist and religious undertones. His best novel is *La fiesta del rey Ahab* [*King Ahab's Feast*], a script-like and agile narration of the last day of a dictator reminiscent of Trujillo. Other interesting novels by Lafourcade in this period are *Para subir al cielo*, which includes a good description of night life in Valparaíso, spoilt by a melodramatic story line, and *El príncipe y las ovejas*.

The working class finds a voice in a notable novel of the early part of this period, *Hijo de ladrón [Born Guilty]*, by Manuel Rojas (1896–1973). With a straightforward style and a realist outlook, but with a controlled lyricism and several effective flashbacks, he tells in the autobiographical mode the story of an adolescent forced to strike out on his own when his father is thrown into prison. The travels from Buenos Aires to Valparaíso, life in jail, and the solidarity of the poor are described with humor and compassion. Rojas is an effective storyteller who knows from within the language of his characters, the refuse of society, the working poor, the migrant workers. His later novels expand on this same group of characters, concentrating on their sex life in *Mejor que el vino*, the contrast with the oligarchy in *Punta de rieles*, and political struggles in *Sombras contra el muro*. Rojas's majestic last novel, *La oscura vida radiante*, is an epic but poetic and lively portrait of Chilean workers, anarchists, drifters, and many other characters given life by Rojas's delight in the telling anecdote and the memorable detail.

The darker side of society, the poor, lonely, violent, drunk, is explored in the novels of Carlos Droguett (b. 1915). His best known novel is *Eloy*, the story of the last hours of an outlaw, based on a real case that occurred in 1941. Droguett concentrates on thoughts, memories, and emotions, transcribed in long and convoluted sentences, to the detriment of description or action. His sympathy for the downtrodden and his exaltation of criminals as saintly figures fighting the violence of the establishment serve him well in *Eloy* in making a bewildered and very human victim from the rural bandit. Murderers are also the heroes of two other of Droguett's novels, *El hombre que había olvidado*, and *Todas esas muertes*. *Patas de perro*, about a child who was born with dogs' legs, would have made an excellent short story, in the tradition of Kafka's "Metamorphosis," but it becomes repetitive and sentimental.

Fernando Alegría (b. 1918), a literary critic of great perspicacity with an unerring talent for the synthetic and brilliant descriptive phrase, has written several novels and short stories. Among them, *Caballo de copas [My Horse González]* is outstanding for Alegría's celebration of humble workers. His humor, and his background in Realism and the picaresque mode serve him well to tell a story of mythical proportions: the immigrant to California who strikes it rich at the horse races. The snappy voice of the narrator relishes words as much as eating, drinking, and sex, peppering his descriptions with imaginative expressions from Chile, Spain, and the multilingual San Francisco. The transfiguration of normal people into seekers of the truth (the name of the winning horse), their ability to face defeat, the incessant need to return to the ever-renewed search, gives the novel its significance. Gambling with cards, horses, or love, these men – it is a world of men – can only trust in luck. Alegría's other novels go from a social realism touched with lyricism, to more experimental texts, yet his best work remains *Caballo de copas* for the knowledgeable narration of immigrants' dreams. Other novels by Alegría in this period are *Noches del cazador, Mañana, los guerreros, Los días contados*, and *El paso de los gansos* [*The Chilean Spring*], a moving narration of the military putsch against President Allende in Chile in 1973.

Among the younger writers, Antonio Skármeta (b. 1940) has been the most successful. Well-known as a storyteller who excels in capturing the voice of adolescents, the poor, children, and generally the not-yet-literary language of the new, his novel *Soñé que la nieve ardía* [*I Dreamt the Snow Was Burning*] narrates the adventures of a soccer player from the provinces who comes to Santiago to make it big, only to discover that the country is concerned with the bigger change and turmoil of the Allende government (1970–1973). He discovers love and solidarity just as his dreams, private and social, are interrupted by a brutal *coup*. Skármeta has a unique capacity to deal with important social problems in a lighthearted manner, and to provide a touch of humor and lyricism even to the most desperate or destitute. This first novel seems at first a throwback to the realist tradition, since it does have a clearly delineated set of characters and a well-described space, Santiago, with an action that mixes politics, sports, and sex. What is new is the intertextual play, the sparkling grace of the prose, the gently ironic tone, as if Chilean literature had at last become informal, youthful, and had gone out into the street not to report the drabness of existence, but to have a good time come what may.

A few writers of this period attained success with extremely complex novels, where the twists and turns of language on the page are of greater concern to readers than the referred world. Of course, readers can imagine aspects of Cuban society from the works of José Lezama Lima, Cabrera Infante, and Severo Sarduy, or of Mexico in the novels of Julieta Campos, Salvador Elizondo, and Gustavo Sainz. Nevertheless, what sets them apart is the startling quality of their prose, the density of their intertextual play, and the flaunting of the fictional aspect of the text, characteristics that will endear them to readers of the late 1970s schooled in Poststructuralism and Postmodernism.

José Lezama Lima (Cuba, 1912–1976) is a novelist's novelist, his meandering syntax, baroque intricacy, and profuse references to classical mythology allowing only a select and patient few to fully enjoy *Paradiso* [*Paradiso*]. Yet, not many texts can be more rewarding than this masterpiece by a learned and sensuous poet. In essence a family saga, the text moves as a majestic river incorporating morose and superbly vivid descriptions of asthma (the emblematic suffocation of a whole generation), witchcraft, cooking, school and university life, sex in many variations and carried to mystical excess, music, and madness. Long philosophical discussions on homosexuality bog down a few later chapters and the action is sometimes blurry or dissolves into a contemplative stasis, but the epic vigor of the text is sustained until the end, where the story of José Cemí, Foción, Fronesis, and Oppiano Licario comes to a close with references to the Holy Grail. José Cemí's father was in the army, with discipline and goals supplied by the hierarchy and the organization, but José must find in his quest his own meaningful existence in a Cuban society that is racing to the fall. Traditional mythology, with Eros most frequently named in an avalanche of Greek and Roman names, seems hard put to account for the world described, and in this disjunction a carnivalesque celebration of existence takes over, fired by the experience of the body and the beauty of language.

Guillermo Cabrera Infante (Cuba, b. 1929) used his experience as a film critic, short-story writer, and journalist in Havana to create in *Tres tristes tigres* a refined, decadent, enervating image of a city fragmented into nightclubs, chance encounters, fast-moving cars, a bustling metropolis sustained by youth, talent, culture, sex, and conversation. Cabrera offers a dazzling array of virtuosity, from the sophisticated structure of the novel to his seemingly unending flow of puns that threatens to shake out from every word all possible meanings in a Joycean stream of experimentation. While there is a story line, it is not the primary appeal of the text: a photographer and his friends roam exploring the night life of Havana, where an immensely fat singer appears and disappears, her talent unrecognized by the musical establishment. The suspense arises from what the narrator, and not the characters, will do next: the reader is whisked from voice to voice, each one charged with crackling energy and, while unique and capable of strongly suggesting a true human being, offering also a linguistic tour of the peculiar richness of Cuban language. The displacements are not only from one to another level of speech, but also to extremely fine parodies of the best known Cuban writers. After reading Cabrera Infante's spoof of Carpentier's or Nicolás Guillén's writing it is hard to read these revered writers again with the solemnity they once commanded. *Tres tristes tigres* is an irreverent novel where prerevolutionary Cuba – and especially her language – is treated with revolutionary abandon. Noticeable are the frequent extremely insightful running commentaries of the characters to their own dialogue, constituting literary criticism of the first order and a subtle, entertaining example of metafiction. The intercalated story about a lost walking cane bought by an American tourist is masterful, told first by the man in a straightforward manner, then corrected by his wife; told again modulated into a "literary" style, and again punctured by the in turn more literary corrections of the wife, all four sections shown later to be simply the invention of an unmarried Cuban writer. The segment entitled "Some Revelations," consisting only of four blank pages, the page printed in mirror image, the drawings, and the slowing down of time are reminiscent of the creative genius of Sterne, but Cabrera Infante has managed to make his daring accumulation of tricks into a style of his own. If occasionally cleverness may appear excessive and the appeal of a joke may pale at a second reading, the vitality of the complete novel rescues the trivial and establishes *Tres tristes tigres* among the very best Spanish American novels ever written, as a brilliant and probably extreme case of the celebration of language.

If Postmodernism corresponds to the meaningless jumble and agglomeration of post-industrial society, Severo Sarduy (Cuba, 1937–1993) has taken further and with the greatest refinement the irreducible coexistence of different traditions, the shattering of a stable identity, the opacity of meaning, and the simultaneity or indifference of time found in the contemporary global supermarket. His first novel, *Gestos*, participates in the impersonal narration and the atomistic, detailed description of objects characteristic of the *nouveau roman*. *Gestos* tells the story of a woman who washes clothes during the day and sings by night, and is also rehearsing a Greek tragedy. Her lover persuades her to plant a bomb in the city's main electricity generator. Because of the explosion, the play goes on by candlelight and the theatre burns down. Later, she participates in a political campaign motorcade, which she sabotages, and there are intimations of the messianic arrival of Fidel in Havana. However, the story line is only anecdotal, the deeper meaning and enjoyment to be found in a vanguardist and exhilarating shattering of conventions of which the bombing of the electricity plant is emblematic. His second novel, *De donde son los cantantes* [*From Cuba with a Song*], is a prodigious kaleidoscope that, in four loosely interrelated stories, examines the Chinese, African, and European contribution to Cuban culture. Drugs and sex, violence, and the divine furor of a carnivalesque existence are not presented in any conventional way, but shown in every twist and jump of this unusual narrative where mimetic character presentation and development has been discarded in favor of a deeper proliferation of signs. *Cobra* is a novel of extreme complexity. The names of characters here do not refer to a stable personality, since all is in a state of flux (human beings not being immune to the roller-coaster of history), and new skins or layers of meaning are found by Sarduy in every word. Women become puppets or men in a series of ritual metamorphoses and displacements that take the narrative to Copenhagen, Brussels, and Amsterdam (COBRA). The participation in the frenzied activities of Tibetan monks is not gratuitous, since they are for Sarduy kindred spirits, also forced into exile, as many Cubans were, by communist violence in 1959. Sarduy represents a break with the novelists of the *Boom*, since the splintering of characters, story, and space cannot here be ingeniously reconstructed, as it can, for example, in the works of Fuentes or Vargas Llosa.

Julieta Campos was born in 1932 in Havana, Cuba, but after doing postgraduate work in France she has resided in Mexico since 1955. *Muerte por agua* is an insightful and richly textured psychological novel in which, next to the dialogues of a married couple and the woman's mother, readers are given in alternating paragraphs the secret flow of conscience of the three characters. Campos's style owes much to Virginia Woolf – *Muerte por agua* is reminiscent of *The Waves* – and Malcolm Lowry, authors she has studied in her essays, but she has her own voice and a convincing, original vision. The moments of deep and quiet happiness – a game of cards and a cup of chocolate – among the never-changing days of seclusion and meaningless struggle are movingly described. *Tiene los cabellos rojizos y se llama Sabina* delves into the instant in which a woman contemplates the sea in Acapulco on a Sunday afternoon. She is thinking about writing a novel about a woman who contemplates the sea in Acapulco on a Sunday afternoon. This Escher-like text, a superior example of metafiction and rich intertextuality, displaces the traditional male-oriented interest in solving a reported crime to concentrate on the constellation of feelings, thoughts, emotions, and memories that make up conscience.

Time and its infinite density slows down the pace of the novels of Salvador Elizondo (Mexico, b. 1932) to an obsessive series of glimpses into a reality that, despite reiterated attempts at minute description, recedes from the text leaving the words behind as rhetorical golden chaff. *Farabeuf o la crónica de un instante* makes of torture and the surgical dismemberment of a body an ultimate instance of the lovers' pleasure of offering their bodies to each other. The text itself suffers fragmentation into neat segments that prolong the agony of suspense. Indebted to Sade, Baudelaire, Bataille (*Les Larmes d'Eros*), and Robbe-Grillet, Elizondo's prose also has a hallucinatory cinematographic quality. *El hipogeo secreto* artfully combines metafictional reflections about the writing of the novel with preparations for a night of sadistic love with a woman called Bitch. Elizondo's elegant novels and deep thoughts on literature and art may still repel readers by his equation of suffering, domination, and mysticism, especially since the tortured partner is the woman and in his autobiography Elizondo has confessed to his belief that women attract and wish for physical violence.

At the vanguard of a new wave of writers who express the concerns of a younger generation, greatly sophisticated and more interested in language and its play than in a sociological description of society, is the prolific Mexican novelist Gustavo Sainz (b. 1940). His first novel, *Gazapo*, presents lively dialogues, telephone calls, and tape recordings of a group of young adolescents in Mexico City. The language is witty, streetwise and colloquial. The hectic actions and the mystifications of insecure young people are rendered with an appropriate intricate structure where time warps and truth blends with deception. While the novel shows broken families, sexual obsession and experimentation, the moving death of a grandmother and a parade of Mexico City streets, the true protagonist is the renovated language of youth. In *Obsesivos días circulares*, Sainz moves on, invoking the tutelage of Joyce, to the dense language of young urban intellectuals, studded with fetishistic references to culture. The novel ends with the repetition of a single sentence about decadence, its words more and more magnified until only a single meaningless letter is left on the page. From a language of excess in *Obsesivos días circulares*, Sainz switches to the minimalist and impoverished vocabulary of a young woman in *La princesa del Palacio de Hierro* [*The Princess of the Iron Palace*], a brilliant *tour de force*. As the inane and incessant chatter of the protagonist, an employee at a department store, whirls around the same topics and words, slowly a picture emerges of venality, corruption, and violence.

[9]

The Spanish American novel: recent developments, 1975 to 1990

Gustavo Pellón

The term "*Boom*" has been controversial since it was first coined to refer to the series of Spanish American novels that took the world by storm in the 1960s. At least in one sense, however, it is fortunate that the label has stuck, because it captures the confident, heady, atmosphere of the years when it seemed that Spanish America was finally going to take its place among the nations of the earth, not only culturally, but even politically and economically. The writers of the *Boom* have kept on writing, but it is undeniable that, by the mid-1970s, with the rise of right-wing dictatorships in Argentina and Chile and the economic recession brought on by the oil crisis, the *Boom*, in any sense of the word, had come to an end.

It is significant that after 1975 none of the major authors associated with the *Boom* publish "*Boom* novels." Gabriel García Márquez's *El otoño del patriarca* (1975) [*The Autumn of the Patriarch*], a work whose narrative experimentation brought him closer to the style of other *Boom* writers, is followed by *Crónica de una muerte anunciada* (1981) [*Chronicle of a Death Foretold*], a short work which returns to the clarity of *Cien años de soledad* (1967) [*One Hundred Years of Solitude*], and the Realism of even earlier works like *La mala hora* (1966) [*In Evil Hour*]. Mario Vargas Llosa's *Conversación en La Catedral* (1969) [*Conversation in The Cathedral*], which develops the complex style of *La casa verde* (1966) [*The Green House*], is followed by the humorous and readable *Pantaleón y las visitadoras* (1973) [*Captain Pantoja and the Special Service*]. *Terra nostra* (1975) [*Terra Nostra*], Carlos Fuentes's most ambitious and difficult work, is followed by *La cabeza de la hidra* (1978) [*The Hydra Head*], a much more accessible work that makes an incursion into popular culture. José Donoso's *El obsceno pájaro de la noche* (1970) [*The Obscene Bird of Night*], one of the murkiest and most challenging of the novels of the *Boom*, is followed by the light and easy *Tres novelitas burguesas* (1973). Even Julio Cortázar, whose *Rayuela* (1963) [*Hopscotch*] is often taken as emblematic of the militant experimentalism of the *Boom*, can be said to

279

have made his last contribution to that tendency in the Spanish American novel with *Libro de Manuel* (1973) [*A Manual for Manuel*].

Ultimately the *Boom* novel fell prey to the exigencies of its avant-garde aesthetics. The fact that its leading practitioners themselves realized that they had reached a dead end and successfully wrote themselves out of it is perhaps the best indication of their wealth of creativity. Their subsequent works often explored new avenues opened by the novels of younger writers like Manuel Puig and Severo Sarduy. Although the term "Post-Boom" has been coined in an attempt to describe these new tendencies, there is, in fact, no new movement as such. What one finds is both a development of the *Boom* and a sharp reaction to its worldview and aesthetics. On the part of the younger authors, the recognition of the accomplishment of the *Boom* novelists is coupled with a realization that the game of technical virtuosity is played out and that the mythification of Spanish American reality is an inappropriate response to their historical moment which is marked by unprecedented brutality and political repression.

The writers of the 1970s and 1980s moved away from the ambitious architecture of all-encompassing novels like *Rayuela* [*Hopscotch*], *La casa verde*, and *Cien años de soledad* [*One Hundred Years of Solitude*]. The destructive political and economic environment in which they lived (often in political exile, rather than the cultural self-expatriation of *Boom* writers) did not encourage the self-assured, albeit often pessimistic, vision of Spanish American experience so evident in the works of the previous generation. Their novels drew away from myth towards history even to the extreme of the documentary novel.

The novel from 1975 to the present also reveals a major shift in sociohistorical perspective. Although written by politically liberal and leftist authors, the novels of the *Boom* were written from the social perspective of the center. Male authors of the middle and upper class predominate among the writers of the *Boom*. With the 1970s the perspective of more marginal elements of society increasingly comes to the fore. Women, homosexuals, Jews, and others who live culturally, socially, politically, and economically at the fringe of society and history, become the authors of these novels.

In terms of aesthetics, there is also a movement toward the marginal. The writers of the *Boom* were primarily interested in producing works that would command the admiration accorded to masterpieces of high culture. It was primarily this aspect which helped the Spanish American novel move from the cultural periphery to the center, from Spanish American capitals to those of the developed world: Paris, Rome, London, New York. Starting with Puig and Sarduy, the cultural interest of the novelists of the new generation is in mass media and the genres of popular culture. Their works employ, reflect, and engage the culture of the masses rather than solely that of the elite. Although they do not become producers of popular culture, they face the cultural reality of their times and seek to subvert the value system that draws a sharp distinction between popular and high culture.

While clearly benefitting from the *Boom*'s legacy of narrative sophistication, recent novelists have found it necessary to return to a more overt social and political commitment than was manifested in the works of the *Boom*. Their novels capture, not the voices of mythified *caudillos*, or alienated intellectuals, but the voices of those who for social, economic, and historical reasons have been silenced.

In the heat of the often parricidal *Post-Boom* polemics, the novelists of the *Boom* have been chastised for their alleged political irresponsibility. From the standpoint of the traumatic political events of the 1970s and the 1980s in Argentina, Chile, Central America, and Peru (among other countries), the depiction of Spanish American history in García Márquez's *Cien años de soledad* has been seen as too soft-edged, his portrayal of the dictator in *El otoño del patriarca* [*The Autumn of the Patriarch*] as too sympathetic and even whimsical. Even Vargas Llosa's *La casa verde*, whose social criticism has always been recognized, gives too static a panorama from a patently aloof perspective. To illustrate by means of analogy, one could say that what the novelists of the 1970s and the 1980s have tried to do is to retell *Cien años de soledad* but from the viewpoint of Mauricio Babilonia, or Pilar Ternera, or Petra Cotes, rather than from the viewpoint of the oligarchy represented (however charmingly) by the Buendía family. Rather than deftly manipulate from above the fragmented life stories of characters like Bonifacia, Lituma, and Fushía in *La casa verde* into a monumental mural, more recent writers have sought to liberate them from their cog-like role by giving them two things they never have in real life: a position at center stage and their own voices.

Writers of the *Post-Boom* have also reexamined their target audience and how the choice of a specific reading public implicitly determines the perspective assumed by a novelist. In a lecture delivered at the University of Virginia in 1986 the Argentine novelist, short-story writer, and critic Mempo Giardinelli stated that, along with questioning the desirability of writing the "Great Novel of Latin America," recent writers have grown to distrust a stance that makes Latin American authors into either purveyors of exoticism to readers in developed countries or warrantors of long-held stereotypes about Latin America. It would seem that *Post-Boom* writers have taken very much to heart the epigraph Cortázar affixed to *Rayuela*: "Nothing kills a man like having to represent a country."

The three clearest new currents in the Spanish American novel after the *Boom* are the documentary novel (*novela testimonio*), the historical novel, and the detective novel in its hard-boiled variant. Beyond these it becomes difficult to catalogue the new developments in the novelistic production precisely because of the pluralism that predominates in this period. Nevertheless the fourth major current (made up of many tributaries) could be given the heading: "A more diverse image of Latin American experience." This would include series of novels that break with Spanish American literary and historical stereotypes by giving voice to the experience of women, homosexuals, and Jews.

Although the documentary novel has its origins in the 1960s, it becomes a recognized, powerful trend in the 1970s and 1980s. It is a hybrid genre which combines non-fiction documentary material (most often in the form of tape-recorded interviews) with the novelist's fictive recreation of complementary material. In actual practice, documentary novels fall somewhere within a spectrum that goes from pure documentary (a transcript of interviews) to a fictive narrative where the narrator's speech is an artistic recreation based on the informant's actual speech patterns. The genre exists in a constant tension between non-fiction and fiction, and between the intentions of the informant and those of the author. Even in the most "documentary" of documentary novels, two subjectivities coexist and the friction between them curiously contributes to the aesthetic appeal of the form. From an ethical point of view the documentary novel is also interesting because it constantly prods the reader to consider the concept of "version" and the issue of varying versions of a historical event. This ethical no-man's-land, which makes historians, social scientists, and novelists uneasy, is the ground where the documentary novel thrives.

From 1970 to 1990, as the documentary novel has developed in Spanish America, it is possible to see an evolution in the genre. When it first appeared in the 1960s its major preoccupation was testimonial (as its Spanish name *novela testimonio* bears out), and its urgent task was to give a voice to a different and repressed version of history or contemporary events. A more recent trend is to use the genre of the documentary novel as an occasion to reflect upon the process whereby "official stories" (including documentary novels) form.

Since space does not allow the discussion of even the major exponents of the documentary novel, it will be useful to focus on three authors whose works give an idea of the scope of the genre: the Cuban Miguel Barnet, the Mexican Elena Poniatowska, and the Argentine Tomás Eloy Martínez.

When the anthropologist Miguel Barnet (b. 1940) wrote *Biografía de un cimarrón* [*The Autobiography of a Runaway Slave*], the first-person account of 104-year-old ex-slave Esteban Montejo, he had no intention of writing a documentary novel. As he candidly put it in his introduction: "We know that to present an informant speaking is, in some measure, to create literature. But it is not our intention to create a literary document, a novel" (p. 18). He thought that he had written a contribution to Cuban ethnography. However, the description Barnet gives of his method in the introduction – the rearrangement of anecdotes in a chronological order, the elimination of the informant's repetitions, the use of paraphrase so that the informant would be intelligible to readers, and the use of the first-person narration so that the account "would not lose its spontaneity" and to facilitate the "insertion of words and idiomatic expressions typical of Esteban's speech" – reveals just how far Barnet's ethnographic study went toward becoming a novel. Subsequently, due in large measure to the success of *Biografía*, Barnet decided to create a trilogy. Thus *Biografía*, together with *Canción de Rachel* (the story of an early twentieth-century star of the Havana stage) and *Gallego* (the story of one of the many Galicians who emigrated to Cuba in the first decades of the century) would present a mosaic of Cuban life from the turn of the century up to the Revolution, from the viewpoint of vastly different but socially marginal characters. In terms of the attitude toward the hybrid nature of the genre it is interesting to note that *Canción* is labelled "novela-testimonio" in the blurb, whereas by the time *Gallego* appears the genre is sufficiently established to be called a "novela testimonio" without the self-conscious mediation of a hyphen. Although these subsequent novels lack methodological introductions like that of *Biografía*, they are both pre-ceded by notes that give a brief explanation of the research involved and the procedure followed.

Despite the human and historical interest of both *Canción* and *Gallego*, they pale in comparison with their predecessor *Biografía*, and the reason lies in both their subject matter and the method employed. It is impossible to top the saga of a 104-year-old man, who not only relates his living and working conditions as a slave in a sugar mill in the past century, but also tells the story of his successful escape, years of solitary life as a runaway slave, his participation in the War of Independence, and his disenchant-ment with the Republic's treatment of black veterans, and Blacks in general, after the war. Throughout, Esteban's powerful and eccentric personality permeates the book (this despite Barnet's editing and polish-ing) with his prejudices, his racism (against Chinese laborers but also against whites), and his personal view of Cuban society and history. It is not hard to imagine why this ethnographically valuable book which uncannily allows us to hear the powerful voice of a strong-willed man from another century may have inspired other writers throughout Spanish America to explore the possibilities of the documentary novel. Certainly

Barnet's unwitting but fortunate introduction of Esteban Montejo into literature has significantly altered our concept of Cuban history.

For the creation of the second work of the trilogy, *Canción de Rachel*, Barnet seems to have employed a similar method although his explanatory note is not at all specific:

> The confessions of Rachel, her adventurous life during the scintillating years of the Cuban *belle époque*, the conversations in the cafés, in the streets, have made possible this book which reflects the atmosphere of frustration of Republican life. Rachel was a *sui generis* witness. She represents her time. . . Other characters who appear in this book, complementing the central monologue, are generally men of the theatre, writers, librettists . . . *Canción de Rachel* speaks of her, her life, just as she told it to me and as I later told it to her.

In fact, establishing a procedure he will follow in subsequent works, three informants are fused into the fictional Rachel. *Canción* is rich in show-business anecdotes of early twentieth-century Havana, and through Rachel's reminiscences Barnet captures with a wealth of detail the atmosphere of petty rivalries, envy, and dreams of financial security and social acceptance of the stage world. Despite Barnet's suggestion that the life of this star of the popular stage represents the Cuban experience in the days of the Republic, *Canción* lacks the historical, political, and cultural transcendence of *Biografía*. Barnet's major contribution in *Canción* is to give us access to a period of Cuba's history through the voice of a woman.

The third work of the trilogy, *Gallego*, rights another wrong by highlighting the contribution to Cuban society made by the large group of Spanish immigrants who fled impoverished Galicia and Asturias in the first decades of the twentieth century to make a new life for themselves in the former Spanish colony. Here Barnet departs significantly from his method by creating his protagonist–narrator Manuel Ruiz: "Manuel Ruiz is Antonio is Fabián is José. He is the Galician immigrant who abandoned his village in search of a better life and adventure." The fact that Manuel Ruiz is a fictitious character, albeit a composite of many real *gallegos* whose lives Barnet was able to reconstruct through his research in the archives of the Galician collection at the Instituto de Literatura y Lingüística de la Academia de Ciencias de Cuba, strictly makes *Gallego* more a well-documented novel than a documentary novel. Be that as it may, in *Gallego* Barnet manages to create a voice for Manuel Ruiz that is as convincing and spell-binding in its own way as Esteban Montejo's. Through the life story of Manuel and the account of his struggle to earn a living in a strange and often hostile land, Barnet deals a deathblow to the stereotypical *gallego* of jokes and stage comedy. He captures the culture shock and linguistic isolation suffered by Galician villagers who in most cases had neither been in a city until they embarked nor had ever had occasion to learn Spanish. Through Manuel, Barnet also gives us a view of

Cuban history from 1916 to 1980 from the perspective of a working man. Barnet's most recent novel after the trilogy, *La vida real*, applies the documentary method to the experience of Cubans who emigrated to New York in the 1940s and 1950s.

Elena Poniatowska (b. 1932), possibly the Spanish American author most associated with the documentary novel, has written works that span the whole of the non-fiction/fiction spectrum of documentary literature. Poniatowska is the author of *Hasta no verte Jesús mío, La noche de Tlatelolco* [*Massacre in Mexico*], *Querido Diego, te abraza Quiela* [*Dear Diego*], and *Fuerte es el silencio*. Of these *La noche de Tlatelolco* (a testimonial account of the massacre of Mexican students in 1968) and *Fuerte es el silencio* ought to be considered non-fiction, while *Querido Diego, te abraza Quiela* is an epistolary novel based on the love affair between painter Diego Rivera and the Russian émigré painter Angelina Beloff. *Hasta no verte Jesús mío*, the picaresque life story of a woman from Oaxaca who fought in the Mexican Revolution, most resembles Barnet's documentary novels in its autobiographical structure and in the method of composition followed by the author. Indirectly, the work also has its roots in anthropological research. Poniatowska has given an illuminating account of her method and her relationship with her informant Jesusa Palancares in the article "Hasta no verte Jesús mío" published in *Vuelta* nine years after the publication of her book:

> In order to write the book about Jesusa I used a journalistic procedure: the interview. Two years before, I worked for a month and a half with the North American anthropologist Oscar Lewis, author of *The Children of Sánchez* and other books. Lewis asked me to help him "edit" *Pedro Martínez: A Mexican Peasant and his Family*. . . His informants used to come to see him at his apartment in la calle de Gutenberg: he would turn on his tape-recorder, ask questions, and I had to clean up those narratives from his pile of papers; that is, eliminate useless repetitions and digressions. This experience undoubtedly influenced me when I wrote *Hasta no verte Jesús mío*. However, since I'm not an anthropologist, my work can be considered a testimonial novel and not an anthropological and sociological document. I used the anecdotes, ideas, and many expressions of Jesusa Palancares but I can't affirm that the narrative is a direct transcription of her life because she herself would reject it. I killed off the characters who seemed super-fluous, I eliminated as many spiritualist sessions as I could, I elaborated wherever it seemed necessary, I pruned, I sewed, I patched up, I invented. . . Since I could only use the tape-recorder when she authorized it, every Wednesday night I would reconstruct what she had told me.
>
> (p. 10)

What emerged from Poniatowska's novelistic adaptation of Oscar Lewis's anthropological method is a remarkable literary document. *Hasta no verte Jesús mío* is an account of the life of Jesusa, a woman from Oaxaca who is caught up by the most important event of Mexico's history in the twentieth century, the Revolution, where she fights as a *soldadera* alongside her husband and then sinks back into anonymity and the most grinding poverty. Like Barnet's Esteban Montejo, she is a solitary person who learned long ago not to depend on others for any help. Beyond adding to our understanding of the culture of poverty in the tradition of Lewis's work, probably the most important contribution the book has made is to correct and add to the image of the Mexican Revolution by giving a woman's account. In some ways *Hasta no verte Jesús mío* is the obverse of *La muerte de Artemio Cruz* (1962) [*The Death of Artemio Cruz*]. If Fuentes's novel tells the story of how a peasant betrays and uses the Revolution to rise to a position of great wealth and power by adopting the philosophy of the conquerors: "chingar o ser chingado" ["screw or be screwed"], Poniatowska gives voice to a woman, a "chingada," who outwardly seems a casualty of life but who has always remained proudly true to herself. The image of the *soldadera* in Mexican literature from Azuela's *Los de abajo* (1916) [*The Underdogs*] to Fuentes's *La muerte de Artemio Cruz* and *Gringo viejo* [*The Old Gringo*] is forever altered by the addition of Poniatowska's Jesusa.

Another remarkable extra-generic work that seems to straddle two of the recent currents in the Spanish American novel, the documentary novel and the historical novel, is *La novela de Perón* [*The Perón Novel*] by Tomás Eloy Martínez (Argentina, b. 1934). The ambiguity of the title (is it Perón's novel, or the novel about Perón?) is developed further by the author's statement which appears on the back cover:

> This is a novel in which everything is true. For ten years I collected thousands of documents, letters, voices of witnesses, pages from diaries, photographs. Many were unknown. In exile in Caracas, I reconstructed the memoirs that Perón dictated to me between 1966 and 1972 and those read to me by López Rega in 1970, who explained they were the general's even though he had written them. Later, in Maryland, I decided that the truths of this book could only be told in the language of imagination. Thus there slowly appeared a Perón whom no one had wanted to see: not the Perón of history but an intimate Perón.

Using Perón's return to Argentina from exile in Spain on June 20, 1973, as his narrative axis, Martínez moves back and forth in time to reconstruct an intimate portrait of the elusive Juan Domingo Perón and Argentina's Perón adventure, but also to seek the roots of the traumatic events in Argentina in the 1970s and the 1980s. In the process he traces the careers of Isabel Perón, Héctor Cámpora, and López Rega. Adding a dynamic tension to the novel, which would otherwise have been robbed of cohesion by the heterogeneous materials used to reconstruct Perón's life, is the plotline which describes the events surrounding Perón's return. For as Perón's aeroplane "takes off from Madrid at dawn of the longest day of the year, it flies toward the night of the shortest day in Buenos Aires" (p. 13). A long political night is indeed about to fall on Argentina, and Martínez lets us in behind the scenes as the extreme left and the extreme right of the Peronista party, in their attempts to appropriate the returning leader to their cause, prepare to clash at the airport where millions of Argentines have come to welcome Perón. At the heart of the colossal misunderstandings that led to that conflict lies the greatest insight Martínez offers us regarding Perón as a public figure and as a private person: throughout his life Perón perfected the ability to let others see in him what they wanted to see. Two quotes from Perón (printed on the inside of the jacket and as an epigraph to the novel, respectively) bear out Martínez's thesis and Perón's awareness and exploitation of this trait:

> If I have been a protagonist of history again and again, it is because I contradicted myself. The socialist fatherland? I invented it. The conservative fatherland? I keep it alive. I have to blow in every direction like a weathercock.

> We Argentines, as you know, characteristically always think that we have the truth. Many Argentines come to this house wanting to sell me a different truth as if it were the only one. What do you want me to do? I believe all of them!   Juan Perón to the author, March 26, 1970

Unlike Barnet and Poniatowska who seek to understand the history of their countries and the nature of their societies by seeking informants from the masses, Martínez goes right to the top. Different as his strategy is, it is every bit as demythifying as Barnet's and Poniatowska's. By piercing the bubble of Juan Domingo Perón, whose power to hypnotize the Argentine people is far from spent, Martínez also offers an opportunity to revise his country's history. By alternating the viewpoint from Perón and his gray eminence López Rega to that of the masses, through fictitious characters like Arcángelo Gobbi (one of López Rega's thugs who is preparing to instigate the riot against the leftist Peronistas at the airport) and the *Montoneros* (guerrilla) Nun Antezana and Diana Bronstein who want to claim Perón for their cause, Martínez innoculates the palace intrigue perspective with a solid dose of "history from the ground up." Martínez's *La novela de Perón* is a valuable contribution to the revision of history being carried out by many Spanish American novels. The documentary novel has had a great impact in revising our concept of Spanish American history: another genre, the new historical novel, is adding to the current meditation on the historical process and which versions of that process come to be history.

Practiced by canonized novelists of the *Boom* as well as by younger writers, the new historical novel is perhaps the most important trend in the development of the Spanish American novel in the 1980s. It differs from the traditional historical novel chiefly because it shares the revisionistic spirit of the documentary novel and because in some, though not all cases, it implies or overtly suggests a deconstruction of its own historical discourse. Thus often alongside the historical reconstruction there is a parallel commentary on the process whereby history is constructed. Although there does not seem to be a direct connection, many recent Spanish American historical novels curiously seem to follow the strategies associated with the tendency of literary criticism known as New Historicism. Although varied in their approaches, New Historical critics advocate a rejection of pure formalism in favor of a self-conscious sociohistorical contextualization of literary texts. Spanish American literature seems to be making a similar move from the heightened subjectivity and self-reflexivity of the novels of the *Boom* to the diffident and subtle approach to social and historical objectivity in the documentary novels and in the historical novels of the two decades from 1970. The distinction between fiction and non-fiction is increasingly explored and challenged.

The best example of this new type of historical novel is Fernando del Paso's *Noticias del Imperio*. Fernando del Paso (Mexico, b. 1935), whose earlier novels *José Trigo* and *Palinuro de México* met with critical acclaim, far surpasses his previous work with the haunting evocation of the ephemeral Empire of Maximilian and Carlota in *Noticias del Imperio*. Yet contrary to what one might expect, his evocation of this period in Mexico's past is not haunting principally because of the glamour cast by a nostalgic reconstruction. The haunting quality of *Noticias del Imperio* is akin to Tomás Eloy Martínez's tireless groping for the elusive Juan Domingo Perón. Although del Paso deftly deploys a vast array of sophisticated narrative and rhetorical devices, the mainspring of the novel is the author's obsessive, nearly morbid, probing into the actions and motivations of the main protagonists in one of the most traumatic moments in Mexico's convulsive history.

From a stylistic point of view *Noticias del Imperio* is as ambitious and encyclopedic as any of the masterpieces of the *Boom*. A dazzling variety of fictive and non-fictive narrative registers are marshalled by del Paso in his attempt to present a panoramic whole composed of conflictive and contradictory parts. *Noticias del Imperio*, therefore, requires of its readers constant evaluation of the status of the text at hand and a consequent readjustment of readerly expectations. Reading *Noticias del Imperio* is akin to viewing a historical mural to which photographs have been affixed.

In accordance with a technique often employed in historical films, the text of del Paso's novel is preceded by a paragraph that establishes the historical context for the reader:

In 1861, President Benito Juárez suspended payment of the Mexican foreign debt. This suspension was used as a pretext by the Emperor of the French, Napoleon III, to send to Mexico an army of occupation with the intention of creating a monarchy in that country, at whose head would be a European, Catholic prince. The chosen one was the Austrian Archduke Ferdinand Maximilian of Habsburg who, about the middle of 1864, arrived in Mexico in the company of his wife, Princess Carlota of Belgium. This book is based on that historical event and on the tragic destiny of the ephemeral Emperor and Empress of Mexico.

The generic expectations raised by this traditional introductory statement are immediately challenged by the next words the reader sees: "Chateau de Bouchout 1927." Bouchout was the palace near Brussels where the mad Carlota died sixty years after her husband was executed by a firing squad in Mexico. Twelve chapters with the heading "Chateau de Bouchout 1927" (including the beginning and the ending chapters) report Carlota's circular monologue concerning her ill-fated Mexican adventure and its aftermath. This gripping stream of consciousness (which pays homage to Molly Bloom's in Joyce's *Ulysses*) is intercalated by eleven other chapters reporting the historical events through a series of different narrative registers. Among these registers are: traditional historical novel passages, the correspondence between two French brothers (one a soldier serving in the occupation army in Mexico and the other a Socialist in Paris), a macabre parody of Maximilian's execution imagined according to the meticulous pomp of Imperial court ritual, purely historical narrative, as well as historiographical and metahistorical reflections on the part of del Paso.

With its plurality of voices (fictive, real, lucid, or insane), *Noticias del Imperio* recreates a historical period with a greater degree of complexity than a traditional historical novel and with greater vividness than a straight history. Furthermore it challenges readers and writers to question the established myths of the Spanish American historical experience. Paradoxically, without dispersing the poetic allure of the "ephemeral Emperor and Empress of Mexico," del Paso demythifies them. They, as well as other chief protagonists (particularly Benito Juárez), are stripped of imperialistic self-justification and nationalistic vituperation. Finally del Paso calls for an acceptance of Carlota and Maximilian as Mexican protagonists of Mexican history: "if not Mexican by birth, Mexican by death. By death and madness. And perhaps it would be a good idea to do this so that they will not continue to haunt us: the souls of the unburied always protest our forgetfulness" (p. 643). Throughout the novel, del Paso remains true to his self-imposed double goal: recreation of the historical event and meditation on the "tragic destiny" of its protagonists.

The acrimonious debate unleashed (particularly in Colombia and

Venezuela) by the publication of *El general en su laberinto* [*The General in his Labyrinth*] by Gabriel García Márquez (Colombia, b. 1928) is perhaps the best proof that can be adduced to demonstrate the need for the revisionism of the new historical novel in Spanish America. The novel, an account of the last months of Bolívar's life (May 8, 1830, to December 17, 1830), offers an unprecedentedly human portrait of the "Libertador" and, like del Paso's novel, also attempts to drain another festering historical wound. However, if del Paso seeks to write a belated grandiose requiem for Maximilian and Carlota, García Márquez employs the simpler form of the dirge. All the trappings of power are set aside for this last trip both symbolically and historically for we are given a minute description of the few personal effects that accompanied Bolívar when he left Bogotá for the last time. García Márquez's "valet's-eye-view" of Simón Bolívar was bound to shock readers familiar only with the sanctimonious portrait of the "Libertador" given in school textbooks and the equestrian bronze icon of South American plazas.

El general en su laberinto is a story of dissolution: the dissolution of a body politic (Bolívar's dream of a Spanish American federation) and the dissolution of Bolívar's body. García Márquez's fundamental strategy in this novel is to employ the historical facts and details for poetic effect in order to elucidate Bolívar's final destiny. The most obvious poetic device extracted from historical fact is the last trip itself which in the novel gradually acquires the irresistible force of an archetypal structure. The last voyage from Bogotá to Santa Marta, which readers can follow thanks to the inclusion of a map in the appendix, is also a symbolic descent from power in the height of the Andes to an almost anonymous death at the sea level of the Caribbean. It is also Bolívar's voyage home from the politically and climatically inhospitable city of the Andes toward the warmth of his native Caribbean. As is well known, this topographical imagery, here totally justified by historical events, is a recurrent motif in García Márquez's works and reflects what he sees as an important cultural and historical conflict between Andean and Caribbean Colombia.

Similarly, the focus on the last months of Bolívar's life furnishes García Márquez with an excellent opportunity to satisfy his enduring fascination with the solitude of power. Having previously studied the personal effect of power on those who wield it, in the figures of Colonel Aureliano Buendía in *Cien años de soledad* and the dictator of *El otoño del patriarca*, García Márquez clearly saw the challenge in the possibilities and limitations offered by a historical figure as well-known as Simón Bolívar. Despite the historical basis of the previous fictional characters, García Márquez's imagination was totally unfettered. In *El general en su laberinto* he places himself in the position of having to establish a dialogue between his poetic interpretation of history and the facts of history itself.

In the afterword of the novel, the author explains how he set out to write the work and how the project evolved. García Márquez maintains that he was first attracted to the last days of Bolívar's life because of his experiences as a child in the Magdalena river rather than because of the Liberator himself. Furthermore he explains that he was not very concerned about the historical basis for his novel since "the last trip on the river is the least documented period of Bolívar's life" (p. 269). This expectation that he would have a relatively free hand soon vanished and he found himself immersed in endless research: "from the first chapter I had to do some research into the way he lived, and that research led to more and more and more endlessly. For two long years I gradually sank into the quicksand of a torrential, contradictory, and often uncertain documentation" (p. 270). Eventually García Márquez found himself consulting a whole team of expert historians (whom he acknowledges by name) in order to learn anything from Bolívar's shoe size to the tortuous nuances of his political thought, to the fact that Bolívar, as he says, could not have "eaten mangoes with the childish delight I had attributed to him, for the very good reason that mangoes did not come to the Americas until many years later" (p. 271).

Not surprisingly, in keeping with García Márquez's interest in the Caribbean, his portrayal of Simón Bolívar underscores the "Libertador's" Caribbean-ness. Given García Márquez's concept of Caribbean-ness as heightened sensuality, life-affirming earthiness, suspicion of grandiloquence, and a relaxed attitude toward the mixing of races, the portrait of the Caribbean Bolívar that emerges has a thoroughly demythifying effect with respect to the official myth, although in a different sense, of course, García Márquez is creating a new myth. Appropriately, therefore, on the first page of the novel readers encounter not the uniformed Bolívar of Tito Salas's paintings but the naked body of a sick man floating in a bathtub. A few moments later when his servant has covered Bolívar's naked body with a *ruana* (the poncho of Andean Colombia), the readers are given a perfect emblem of a Caribbean man out of his element.

Throughout the novel, together with the account of the major historical events of Bolívar's last months – Santander's betrayal, Venezuela's secession from Colombia, and Sucre's assassination – García Márquez portrays the general's long-standing love affair with Manuela Sáenz as well as numerous passing love affairs with women of different social classes and races.

Race is another important element in the portrayal of the demythified Bolívar. In the novel Bolívar is described as having hair with "coarse Caribbean curls" (p. 12) and "the coarse sideburns and mustache of a mulatto" (p. 82). Most interesting of all, however, is a brief but explicit account of the pictorial mythification of Bolívar that García Márquez intercalates in a passage where he describes different portraits for which Bolívar sat:

The oldest of his portraits was an anonymous miniature painted in Madrid when he was sixteen years old. At the age of thirty-two another was painted in Haiti, and both were faithful to his age and his Caribbean type. He had inherited African blood through a paternal great-great-grandfather who had a son with a slavewoman, and it was so evident in his features that the aristocrats of Lima called him "El Zambo" [someone of mixed Indian and African blood]. But as his glory grew, painters idealized him little by little, cleansing his blood, mythifying him, until they implanted him in official memory with the Roman profile of his statues.   (p. 184)

The Caribbean man was suppressed in the official portraits of Bolívar just as the Caribbean coast has been discounted from the "official portrait" of Colombia. In his previous novels García Márquez (thanks to his worldwide readership) has corrected the univocal image of an Andean Colombian with Castilian pretensions. *El general en su laberinto*, García Márquez's first historical novel, joins other Spanish American novels in their efforts to demythify history, to reverse the "cleansing" project by facing up to the plurality of visions, the complexity of human character in history. For most Spanish Americans Bolívar was a gold-embroidered uniform with a mask-like face; García Márquez has exhumed and recovered his body.

The new historical novels seem to have a penchant for exhuming corpses even if their purpose is to conduct a rigorous post-mortem and make amends by providing a proper burial. The words of Thomas Browne: "But who knows the destiny of his bones, or how many times he will be buried?" which appear as one of the two epigraphs of *Gringo viejo* by Carlos Fuentes (Mexico, b. 1928) therefore seem particularly appropriate. And *Gringo viejo* does quite a bit of exhuming. Figuratively it exhumes the writer Ambrose Bierce from his unjustly dusty niche in the pantheon of American writers, but it exhumes him in order to kill him again by recreating his possible death in Mexico during the Revolution.

Actually Fuentes portrays two "deaths" of Ambrose Bierce since he is first murdered by the Revolutionary Tomás Arroyo and later he is literally exhumed and his corpse is shot by a firing squad on Pancho Villa's orders. Historically all that is known (as Fuentes states in the "Author's Note" at the end of the novel) is that Bierce went to Mexico in 1913 and disappeared. In Fuentes's novel he disappears into another man's grave because the novel's protagonist Harriet Winslow claims Bierce as her father and has him buried in her own father's tomb. Her father's "tomb" was a pretense to save the family's honor since he had not really died in the Spanish American War but stayed in Cuba to live with a black woman.

In a different sense many other things are exhumed in *Gringo viejo*, chief among them the biggest corpse in twentieth-century Mexico: the Revolution. And in doing so, Fuentes also exhumes the tradition of the novel of the Mexican Revolution, even including his own earlier attempt to understand the betrayal of that process in *La muerte de Artemio Cruz*. Thus *Gringo viejo* is composed of historical and literary corpses, of quotations and allusions to Ambrose Bierce's haunting short stories based on his experiences as a soldier in the American Civil War as well as to Mariano Azuela's *Los de abajo* and Martín Luis Guzmán's *El águila y la serpiente* (1928) [*The Eagle and the Serpent*].

Fuentes employs a third-person narration throughout the novel, but the point of view alternates in the novel's twenty-two chapters. Although the focus of attention is primarily on the old gringo and secondarily on Harriet Winslow and General Tomás Arroyo, Fuentes makes sure to include the perspectives of *soldaderas*, other Revolutionary officers, soldiers, and a boy. The three principal points of view of Ambrose Bierce, Harriet Winslow, and Tomás Arroyo are bound thematically by the preoccupation with fatherhood that has become a hallmark of Mexican twentieth-century literature.

From Octavio Paz's *El laberinto de la soledad* (1950) [*The Labyrinth of Solitude*] to Juan Rulfo's *Pedro Páramo* (1955) [*Pedro Páramo*], and Fuentes's own *La muerte de Artemio Cruz*, the racial and existential condition of Mexicans has been defined by the rape of native Mexican women (symbolized by La Malinche, Cortés's Indian mistress) by Spanish conquerors and their latter-day surrogates in the landed oligarchy. Typical of this novel which mixes the destinies of characters from Mexico and the United States is the playing out of this most Mexican of motifs in the relationship between a Mexican Revolutionary, an old American writer, and a young American woman who, having taken employment as the governess of the wealthy Miranda family, finds herself in the midst of the Revolution. Paternal and parricidal feelings fill the hearts of the old gringo and Harriet Winslow while Arroyo seeks to avenge his illegitimate birth and reclaim his birthright. Arroyo comes to grief precisely because he pursues the quest for his personal birthright (as a red-haired, yellow-eyed Miranda) at the expense of the collective birthright of the peasants and thus betrays the Revolution. Repeated allusions to Ambrose Bierce's own short story "A Horseman in the Sky," a Civil War story of parricide and filial obedience, serve to illuminate the motivations of the three main characters.

By juxtaposing the American Civil War to the civil war Mexicans call their Revolution, by fatally bringing an old gringo and a young gringa into the life of a Mexican Revolutionary, and by delving into the art and Mexican fate of a North American writer, Fuentes is lancing old wounds on both sides of the border and effacing difference.

Although space does not allow its discussion, *El mar de las lentejas* [*Sea of Lentils*] by Antonio Benítez Rojo (Cuba, b. 1931) is yet another excellent example of the new type of historical novel that is written with self-critical open-endedness. Other important historical novels have also made their appearance in this period but they largely seem to follow older patterns. This is the case with Vargas Llosa's *La guerra del fin del mundo* [*The War of the End of the World*] which, despite an implicit dialogical relationship with the historical text *Os sertões* (1902) [*Rebellion in the Backlands*] by Euclides da Cunha, seems in other respects to be a successor of the traditional historical novel. Likewise Antonio Skármeta's novel about the Nicaraguan Revolution against Somoza, *La insurrección* [*The Insurrection*], with its totally uncritical vision seems to hark back to the model of Alejo Carpentier (Cuba, 1904) in a novel like *Consagración de la primavera* (1978).

Another trend that illustrates important thematic and aesthetic changes in the novel after the *Boom* is the new hard-boiled novel. By marrying the generic expectations of a popular genre, the detective novel, especially in the American variant known as the hard-boiled novel, with a thematic structure that subverts the major ideological tenets of the genre, the practitioners of the new hard-boiled novel are taking a cue from Manuel Puig (Argentina, 1932–1990). First perceived as a new addition to the *Boom*, Puig has come to be regarded more and more (together with Severo Sarduy) as an important transitional figure who helped the Spanish American novel out of the dead end to which it had been led by its avant-gardist tendencies. Because of his bold attempts to eliminate all forms of narration that would impose a particular authorial (and authoritative) viewpoint, Puig was naturally considered to be an experimentalist. His narrative experimentation however was ideologically motivated by his agenda to combat structures of dominance in politics, gender relations, and genre relations.

Principally Puig did this through an appropriation of mass culture. His attitude toward mass culture, however, did not share the ironic elitism of the practitioners of "camp" but sprang from the compassionate realization that kitsch often provides the only mode of expression for the vast majority. Motivated by his egalitarianism as much as by a deep nostalgia for the cinema of his childhood, Puig therefore sought to elevate the quality of mass culture genres but always strove to remain accessible to a vast readership. In both regards he was to prove an inspiration to many nascent as well as established Latin American novelists.[1]

Mempo Giardinelli (Argentina, b. 1947) and Osvaldo Soriano (Argen-

---

[1] An example of the use of popular culture forms to combat rather than foment escapism is *La Guaracha del macho Camacho* [*Macho Camacho's Beat*] by Luis Rafael Sánchez (Puerto Rico, b. 1936).

tina, b. 1943) are two practitioners of the new hard-boiled novel who have acquired an international reputation. Despite patent differences in outlook and strategy, the works of Giardinelli and Soriano share important traits. First of these is their common fascination with the hard-boiled variant of the detective novel. From their reading of Raymond Chandler, Dashiell Hammett and Ross Macdonald – but also Ernest Hemingway – they adopt the terse and colloquial narrative style as well as the general plot lines and stock situations. Much as in the case of Puig, their motivation for borrowing the mechanics of the genre is double: personal pleasure mixed with nostalgia for their youthful reading adventures, and a mature realization that the genre can be adapted to fit their aesthetic and ideological goals. Not the least attractive of these particularities is the hard-boiled novel's unsentimental (but romantic) depiction of a fundamentally moral individual fighting without much hope of true success (unlike his counterpart in classic detective stories) to keep his integrity in a corrupt and violent world. As members of a generation that came of age in Argentina at the time of the Montoneros's guerrilla movement and the unprecedented repression and persecution following the military coup of 1976, both Giardinelli and Soriano are obsessed with violence. Scenes of graphic violence recur in their novels, and their blow-by-blow descriptions reveal an ambiguous combination of horror and fascination. Since the context in which this violence occurs in the works of both Giardinelli and Soriano is most often either explicitly or implicitly political, its depiction is as much a form of denunciation as it is a form of therapy.

Giardinelli has published five novels: *¿Por qué prohibieron el circo?*, *La revolución en bicicleta*, *El cielo con las manos*, *Luna caliente*, and *Qué solos se quedan los muertos*. Of these only *Luna caliente* and *Qué solos se quedan los muertos* can be said properly to belong to the genre of the hard-boiled novel, although the other three also bear marks of the influence of the detective story genre.

Luna caliente is a detective thriller in which an eminently civilized and well-educated Argentinian lawyer returns from his studies in Paris to his hometown, Resistencia. Although the year is 1977, one year after the military coup, and there are allusions to fear generated by the state of martial law, Giardinelli goes out of his way not to discuss politics in the novel. The protagonist, Ramiro, seems apolitical and interested only in his local prestige and the possibility of obtaining a teaching position in the provincial university. Yet, as the fast-moving series of events typical of the detective thriller genre is unleashed with just the right measure of sex and violence, the reader is simultaneously led (guided by Ramiro's thoughts) to reflect with horror about how easy it is for a normal human being to commit criminal acts coldly and unscrupulously.

The simplicity of *Luna caliente*, which reads at breakneck speed, is deceptive because it has been elaborately crafted. The use of the indirect free style for the narration of the story is a good example of Giardinelli's care. Since this hybrid style of narration combines the third-person objectivity of what is narrated but can exploit the intimacy of a first-person narration permitting the novel's feverish pitch, Giardinelli can have it both ways. Thanks to the exclusive use of Ramiro's point of view, readers experience the protagonist's mental and moral confusion at close range but are denied the easy solution of declaring him deranged by the effect of objectivity created by the use of the grammatical third person.

Despite the deft handling of all the techniques and commonplaces of the hard-boiled novel, *Luna caliente* is actually a loving reconstruction of the genre applied to a different context. Like the 1947 Ford driven by Ramiro, which has been obsessively restored by his friend Gomulka, the novel's borrowings from the detective genre call attention to themselves with parodic intent. Thus the 1947 Ford which Giardinelli borrows from Raymond Chandler (Fords were Philip Marlowe's favorite cars) is meant to be something ordinary in Chandler's novels but becomes a less than adequate get-away car in 1977 Argentina as Ramiro himself realizes (p. 27). Perhaps the most explicit instance of parody is when Ramiro decides not to return to the scene of the crime because he remembers that is how murderers are always caught in detective novels (p. 80).

Luna caliente, therefore, functions doubly, as a crime thriller and as a meditation on the insight gained from recent Argentine history that the most heinous crimes are not the exclusive purview of monsters but are easily accessible to all. Toward the end Giardinelli leaves the bounds of Realism as it becomes clear that the murdered Araceli, the sexually insatiable thirteen-year-old whose irresistible attraction has triggered the whole chain of events, has come back to life. At this point the thriller becomes allegory: Araceli, the source of so much violence, fascination, and desire who, even when left for dead, comes back to follow Ramiro into exile, is Argentina.[2]

Qué solos se quedan los muertos sticks even more faithfully to the pattern of the hard-boiled novel since its protagonist, José Giustozzi, an Argentine exile in Mexico, takes on the role of detective in order to solve the murder of an old girlfriend. The themes of the accessibility of violence to decent people, the rootlessness of exile, and nostalgia for a lost time and place combine with a fast-moving first-person account of the drug trade and double dealing. Again an ordinary person is suddenly caught up in a whirlwind of violent and extraordinary circumstances. In the tradition of the hard-boiled hero, Giustozzi knows he will probably lose if he stands his ground but has reached the point where he can no longer run away.

[2] In a conversation in the spring of 1988 at the University of Virginia, Mempo Giardinelli told me that for him Araceli was Argentina.

Osvaldo Soriano has written five novels: *Triste, solitario y final*, *No habrá más penas ni olvido* [*A Funny Dirty Little War*], *Cuarteles de invierno* [*Winter Quarters: A Novel of Argentina*], *A sus plantas rendido un león*, and *Una sombra ya pronto serás*. The parody of the hard-boiled novel is more explicit in his work than in Giardinelli's, but Soriano's novels add an element of exaggeration and slapstick to the typical violence of the genre. Soriano's hallmark is the careful preparation of chaotic situations that culminate in cathartic apotheoses of the absurd. The influence of the masters of the hard-boiled genre is matched by that of Laurel and Hardy.

Although Soriano has polished his technique with each succeeding novel and his capacity to imagine and make readers accept the most absurd of situations shows no sign of abating, the potent recipe was already fully present in his first novel. *Triste, solitario y final*, whose title comes from Marlowe's self-description toward the end of Chandler's *The Long Goodbye*, has a promising premise. In 1965, shortly before his death, Stan Laurel hires the aging, unemployed Philip Marlowe to investigate why Hollywood producers won't hire him. Laurel dies before Marlowe can find out and the private detective only resumes the investigation in 1972 when he runs into an Argentinian journalist called Soriano at Laurel's grave. In the rest of the novel Marlowe and his Argentinian sidekick, after receiving countless beatings, discover a conspiracy. The novel reaches a climax when Marlowe and Soriano kidnap Charlie Chaplin at the Academy Awards' ceremony and provoke a monumental fist-fight among Hollywood celebrities in the tradition of the bar-room brawls of Westerns and the pie-throwing scenes of comedies.

Besides the introduction of slapstick and the parodic effect produced by the depiction of the older, poorer, bus-riding Marlowe, Soriano makes a more serious fundamental change. By inserting himself as a character who befriends Marlowe and collaborates with him, Soriano departs from the traditionally individualistic portrayal of the protagonist of North American hard-boiled novels. In *Triste, solitario y final*, as in Soriano's subsequent novels, the solitude of the protagonists (who are always loners) is corrected by solidarity.

Soriano's next two novels, *No habrá más penas ni olvido* and *Cuarteles de invierno*, take place in the fictive Argentinian town Colonia Vela, and although the humor and the alert eye for absurd situations are hardly absent in them, the playfulness of the first novel recedes before the bleaker political subject matter of these novels which depict Argentina in the 1970s. *No habrá más penas ni olvido* and *Cuarteles de invierno* portray how the lives of ordinary people are profoundly changed by the military coup and the political events that led up to it. Soriano seeks the microcosmic rather than the macrocosmic view, the anecdote rather than the panorama, the provincial town rather than the capital. In the prologue to the first edition of *No habrá más penas ni olvido*, after explaining the historical and political context of the events portrayed in the novel (they occur between October of 1973 and July of 1974), Soriano states his strategy: "The action takes place in a small town of the province of Buenos Aires where all the characters know each other. The maneuver of Perón and his minister, José López Rega, thus acquires absurd and grotesque dimensions" (p. 12). Indeed the microcosmic view of the process which prepared the way for the military coup, whereby old-time *Peronistas* were deceived and eliminated at Perón's behest, proves devastating in the setting of a small town. The whole action is reduced to the desperate defense of the city hall by Ignacio, the old-time *Peronista* mayor, and a handful of policemen, against a larger, better-armed force. The climax of absurdity comes when the mayor's "air force" (a crop-dusting plane) sprays the enemy with the only "ammunition" available, manure. The novel ends as the mayor and a corporal he has just promoted to sergeant, the only ones left to defend the city hall, prepare to receive the onslaught.

In *Cuarteles de invierno*, Soriano returns to Colonia Vela but the action now takes place after the military coup has succeeded. A popular singer who has had problems with the regime and a has-been boxer are hired by the authorities to entertain the townspeople at a celebration in honor of the new order. Like Soriano and Marlowe in *Triste, solitario y final* and like Ignacio and Sergeant García in *No habrá más penas ni olvido*, Galván the singer and Rocha the boxer end up supporting each other in an impossible situation. Soriano follows the same strategies in *A sus plantas rendido un león* in which the spurious Argentinian consul and the British ambassador to the fictive African kingdom Bongwutsi try to fight their version of the war over the Falkland/Malvinas islands. The extreme loneliness of the protagonists caught in an absurd situation is only redeemed by moments of human solidarity.

Another significant development in the novels of the 1970s and 1980s is the greater representation of different sectors of society. The repertoire of familiar character types: dictators, revolutionaries, disaffected intellectuals, and budding artists is expanded to include slum-dwellers, factory workers, Jewish immigrants, Middle Eastern immigrants, mailmen, maids, and homosexuals persecuted by right-wing and left-wing dictatorships. Some of these characters, of course, have appeared frequently enough in the literature of the past, but seldom, if ever, as the leading protagonists.

In the two decades since 1970 the greater prominence of women novelists such as Isabel Allende (Chile, b. 1942), Elena Poniatowska, and Luisa Valenzuela (Argentina, b. 1938), of Jewish/Spanish American writers such as Isaac Goldemberg (Peru, b. 1945) and Mario Szichman (Argentina, b. 1945), and of a whole generation of university-educated novelists with a lower-middle-class or proletarian background such as Mempo Giardinelli, Antonio Skármeta (Chile, b. 1940), and Osvaldo Soriano, and of homosexual writers such as Reinaldo Arenas (Cuba, 1943–1990), Manuel Puig, and Severo Sarduy (Cuba, 1937–1993), who defy Spanish American machismo by writing openly about homosexuality in their novels, has resulted in a far less homogenous outlook than ever before.

Unlike Alberto Gerchunoff (Argentina, 1889–1950), whose *Los gauchos judíos* (1910) [*The Jewish Gauchos of the Pampas*], written as part of Argentina's centennial celebration, presented an officially sanctioned account of the immigration of Eastern European Jews, more recent writers have sought to demythify the history of Jewish immigration to Spanish America and to recover a more truthful version of that experience (see Lindstrom *Jewish Issues in Argentine Literature*, and Sosnowski, *La orilla inminente*). The novels of Mario Szichman and Isaac Goldemberg have opened new avenues for the critical examination of what it means to be Jewish and Spanish American.

In his four novels: *Crónica falsa, Los judíos del mar dulce, La verdadera crónica falsa*, and *A las 20:25 la señora entró en la inmortalidad* [*At 8:25, Evita Became Immortal*] Mario Szichman renders a devastatingly demythifying view of Jewish immigration and assimilation by following the fortunes of the fictive Pechof family from Russia to Argentina. Although the time frame of this anti-saga is from 1918 to the death of Eva Perón in 1952, the focus is on the Perón era.

If the Perón era and the Pechof family are constants, there is more change than continuity in terms of style in Szichman's novels. Whereas *Crónica falsa* makes use of the documentary material in Rodolfo Walsh's *Operación masacre* concerning the execution of *Peronistas* on June 10, 1956, as the background for the history of a Jewish family during the Perón years, in the subsequent novels the sociohistorical context, although present as a determining factor, is increasingly distorted through a cultivation of the grotesque and the absurd reminiscent of the novels of Samuel Beckett.

The sanitized lyricism of Gerchunoff's novel is challenged not only by a parody of situations but linguistically by the scatological and hybrid language of the Pechofs. Szichman provides small glossaries to help readers with the Pechofs' Yiddish-sprinkled Spanish, but they are left to their own devices when it comes to deciphering each family member's personal linguistic idiosyncrasies and speech impediments.

Scatology and the absurd reach their zenith (or perhaps nadir would be more appropriate) in *A las 20:25 la señora entró en la inmortalidad*, a novel which revolves around two unburied corpses: Eva Perón and Rifque Pechof. And it literally revolves because the novel's main premise is that all clocks stop at 8:25 p.m. and, day after day, everyone in Argentina is forced to relive the day Evita died. All the while Rifque floats in a bathtub full of formaldehyde because no death certificates can be filed until Eva Perón is buried. The family's attempt to adopt the habits and appearance of Christian Argentinian patricians is presented as one of many desperate strategems to get Rifque buried.

Isaac Goldemberg's novels *La vida a plazos de don Jacobo Lerner* [*The Fragmented Life of Don Jacobo Lerner*] and *Tiempo al tiempo* [*Play by Play*] add another twist to the Jewish/Spanish American dilemma of identity and assimilation. The largely autobiographical novels tell a story of racism, religious discrimination, and culture shock. *La vida a plazos de don Jacobo Lerner* is an account of the immigration of a Russian Jew, Jacobo Lerner, to Lima. By combining a realist narrative style (reminiscent of Vargas Llosa) with the inclusion of other documents, principally newspaper clippings (in the manner of Puig), Goldemberg provides an account of Jewish immigration to Peru that is critical enough to have caused a scandal in Lima's Jewish community.

Efraín, Jacobo's illegitimate son, abandoned in Chepén, furnishes the point of departure for *Tiempo al tiempo*, but in this second novel his name is Marcos Karushansky. The eight-year-old boy, who has been raised in his Peruvian mother's house as a Catholic, is summoned by his father to Lima where he is suddenly expected to acquire a Jewish identity. Marcos's identity crisis is underscored by the treatment he receives in the schools he attends. In León Pinelo, the Jewish school he first attends, his classmates call him "el cholo" (the Indian) and later at the Leoncio Prado military school he is known as "the Jew." Despite the novel's serious subject matter, Goldemberg totally avoids pathos and melodrama through several ironical devices. The clever blend of different narrative points of view (former classmates from either school), and the intercalation of these "straight" chapters with others where a sports announcer narrates Marcos's life in terms of a soccer game between Peru and Brazil, constantly change the ground under the reader's feet and give a vicarious taste of Marcos's bewilderment.

Although women novelists like Rosario Ferré, Cristina Peri-Rossi, María Luisa Puga, Reina Roffé, and Luisa Valenzuela, among many others, have achieved national and international recognition, the only one who has matched the sales records and celebrity status of the writers of the *Boom* is Isabel Allende (Chile, b. 1942). Her three novels *La casa de los espíritus* [*The House of the Spirits*], *De amor y de sombra* [*Of Love and Shadows*], and *Eva Luna* [*Eva Luna*] describe a trajectory that in many ways reproduces the evolution of the Spanish American novel since 1975.

La casa de los espíritus looks both back and forward. Despite its undeniable filiation with García Márquez's *Cien años de soledad*, it is a mistake to follow the critics who have dismissed this work, because it fruitfully points the way in two new directions. First, the importance of women in the work of García Márquez notwithstanding, Allende's book makes a major contribution simply by being a woman's mythification of women. Second, the book does not remain grounded in its derivative Magical Realism but, unlike its predecessor, ends in a starkly realistic mode. If women with green hair and powers of clairvoyance people the early pages of the novel, the latter pages tackle issues of guilt, political irresponsibility, and brutal repression.

De amor y de sombra, centered as it is on the discovery by a politically naive female reporter of a mass grave of the victims of Pinochet's repression is the logical continuation of the end of *La casa de los espíritus*. The fact that the book ends in an almost romance mode is explained by Allende's belief (in this she, like many of her contemporaries, sides with Puig) that popular literary genres can serve means other than escapist entertainment.

Eva Luna, the picaresque adventures of a lower-class girl trying to make her way in the world, is in fact a type of soap opera but with a major difference: Allende breaks with clichés and takes her characters seriously. She invests the character of Eva Luna with a dignity that is totally alien to the stock character of Spanish American soap operas, the country girl who becomes a maid in the big city and is soon seduced by her male employers. *Eva Luna* may have enough elements of wishful thinking to garner the label of a "feminist fable" but as the double ending of the novel makes clear (the reader is actually given a choice between a happy and an unhappy ending) it is a consciously fashioned fable, a fable that takes itself seriously, but not all of the time.

In Spanish American letters the *Post-Boom* represents the crisis of modernity commonly called "Postmodernity." Although the suggestion that the *Boom* corresponds to Modernism and the *Post-Boom* to Postmodernism is strictly untenable, if only because the *Boom* occurred historically in the postmodern era, the crisis of the *Boom* does reflect that of modernity. The major writers of the *Boom* and a younger generation of Spanish American writers realized that the aesthetic paradigm of the Avant-Garde had been taken as far as it would go and they discarded it in favor of a variety of approaches whose common links are greater accessibility and a relationship to the past based more on a dialogue with history than with myth. As a result a strange phenomenon has arisen: a postlapsarian attitude among critics and academics accustomed to the modernist paradigm of the novel. The temptation to measure *Post-Boom* writers by the aesthetics and ethics of the *Boom* needs to be resisted. The Spanish American novel from 1975 to the present demonstrates a bewildering variety and richness. The *Post-Boom* is not a Bust.

Spanish American poetry from 1922 to 1975
José Quiroga

Introduction

The space where language becomes poetry is the zone explored by the voices of the twentieth century poetic tradition. Spanish American poetry in the period from 1922 until 1975 allows us to see texts written in the classical mode or in open defiance of it, using a silent, visual language or one that is twisted into beat syncopation. Expression is colloquial, intimate, populist, and baroque. Poets gaze at figurines in museums, or describe the outlines of a room and the shape of a body; they invent bodies and populate imaginary cities, or walk in their cities and transform them into mythical realms. Poems take place in Burma and Rangoon or in the suburbs of Buenos Aires; they illuminate personal chaos and impersonal order, they question the social order or assert the hidden order of things. The debate on the role of the poem, or of the poet, in the modern world, continues, even after the death of poetry is proclaimed in angry manifestos.

General histories of Spanish American poetry have divided this period into three: a period of radical and violent experimentation from 1922 to about 1940, one concerned with the search for American or national cultures that spans the years from 1940 to 1960, followed by a second experimental period that starts from 1960 and lasts until around 1975. The historical markers fall more or less into place if we consider two pivotal events: the Spanish Civil War from 1936 to 1939, and the triumph of the Cuban Revolution in 1959. The years between these two events form the core of a period of temporary retrenchment, when Spanish Americans turned inward after the more violent ruptures of the 1920s. In relation to European history, the years that followed the First World War find Spanish Americans immersed in the polemics of the Avant-Garde; the effects of the Second World War are signaled by various projects of national or Pan-American aesthetics. Yet, more than these, it was the conflict in Spain and the Cuban Revolution that shaped writers and their aesthetics in very concrete ways, some of which will be discussed during the course of this essay. The critical discourse on Spanish American poetry defines these changes in poetry as cyclical modes within the fabric of the tradition, where a continuing search for specifically Spanish American cultural traits is underscored more or less at different times. The historical Avant-Gardes culminated in the search for national or American specificities within the more political setting of the 1940s; a renewed sense of nationality brought about by the Cuban Revolution, joined with the fact that at least two generations of poets coexist in the 1960s (those established by 1940 and others starting to write in the 1960s), frames a new and polemical beginning that takes us to the present time.

These general lines of development need to be supplemented and refined by a third – namely, the gradual abandoning of national traditions in favor of a more trans-national, cosmopolitan, or generally Spanish American continental poetry. "There is no Argentine, Mexican or Venezuelan poetry: there is a Spanish American poetry or, to be more exact, a Spanish American tradition and style" says Octavio Paz in *Poesía en movimiento* (p. 4). Readers of Spanish American poetry may find similar issues in the many modes and registers of Pablo Neruda, in the baroque profusion of a deeply national Cuban poet such as José Lezama Lima, in the more cosmopolitan Octavio Paz, in the guerrilla poems of Roque Dalton, or in the Nicaraguan vistas of Pablo Antonio Cuadra.

This Pan-American poetic communication is the most direct link that twentieth-century poetry has to *Modernismo* [Modernism]. Since *Modernismo*, poets have translated other cultures into Spanish America's and explained Spanish Americans to themselves. Even if they rejected every central stylistic tenet of *Modernismo*, the Avant-Garde [*Vanguardia*] continued the work of their precursors by repeating its expansive and continental desires. This is at the core of the Avant-Garde's ambivalent attitude to *Modernismo*, although it could also be seen as a critical act vis-à-vis their precursors: the *Vanguardia* eliminated the rhetoric but continued the program. The possibility of a unified aesthetics charged the Avant-Garde to follow the *modernista* example by trying to unify different national voices. It is this program which explains the surprising unity of Spanish American poetry, in spite of the different and contradictory manifestos. For the central argument of Spanish American poetry in this period has been, as in *Modernismo*, a debate as to the shape, outline, and contours of modernity.

All aesthetic and political positions from 1920 to 1975 can be seen as competing versions of a central, yet elusive, narrative that is framed within the encounter of Spanish America with the modern age. The responses to modernity imply questions as to whether poetry serves the social or the personal order, whether it uses colloquial or erudite language, or whether it privileges metaphor or communication. Poetry frames all issues relating to the relationship between poetry, language, and history. History itself appears not only where poetry is meant to serve the greater social order, but even in movements that deliberately turn their back on contemporary political situations, like the Cuban *Orígenes*, or the Mexican *Contemporáneos*. It is the place of the poem and the poet within a historical *way* of understanding history that gives Spanish American poetry its more visible structural principle.

Because the presence of history is so central to the tradition, the notion of generational change that Octavio Paz has explored in his classic *Los hijos del limo* [*Children of the Mire*] becomes an apt model that explains the different cycles of Spanish American poetry. According to Paz, modern poetry is a battle of continuity and rupture waged from one generation of writers to the next. The inheritors of *Modernismo* waged revisionist battles against their precursors, first with *Post-modernistas* like Leopoldo Lugones, Enrique González Martínez, and Gabriela Mistral, and then through the first generation of the Avant-Garde (Vicente Huidobro and Oliverio Girondo), followed by a later generation that comprises Nicolás Guillén, Xavier Villaurrutia, Pablo Neruda, and Octavio Paz. However, this model may be more valid for Paz's generation itself than for the ones that follow him. After 1940, and even more so after 1960, the narrative of generational change collapses, the boundaries between generations blurred because of the continuing presence of major poets like José Lezama Lima, Pablo Neruda, Octavio Paz, and Jorge Luis Borges during the 1960s and early 1970s, signaling the consolidation of at least two generations in the period that coincides with the *Boom* of Spanish American narrative.

Spanish American poems from the 1920s to the 1970s change in time, they are in a constant state of metamorphosis. Modernity's emphasis on language and on the poet as critic has shaped poems into precarious signifying structures that are constantly subjected to revisions and rewriting. These may range from a single comma, to a change in the line breaks or the typographical arrangement of verse, to a complete rewriting of the poem itself. Jorge Luis Borges's first published works, *Fervor de Buenos Aires*, *Luna de enfrente*, and *Cuaderno San Martín* are reissued after 1940 with layers of revisions and rewriting. These take place within a tradition where, since Mallarmé's *Un coup de dés jamais n'abolira le hasard* (1895) [*Dice Thrown Never Will Annul Chance*], a poem's meaning entails not only the signifiers themselves, but the arrangement of the signifiers on the page. Avant-garde poetry cannot be understood unless these revisions take into account the different readings opened up by the position of those same signifiers. For example, Vicente Huidobro's poems from *El espejo de agua* (1916) [*The Mirror of Water*] are fundamentally different from his translation of those same poems into French with a new typographical arrangement a year later in *Horizon carré* (1917) [*Square Horizon*]. The first is still a *post-modernista* book; the second is fully an avant-garde text, and the experience of reading one is not the same as that of reading the other.

The first Spanish American avant-garde poems are eminently visual texts, and as such they are subject to a kind of afterlife, to an interplay between an original text and its reproduction. This tradition culminates in Octavio Paz's prefaces to all editions of *Blanco* [*Blanco*]. In these, Paz reminds his readers of the poem's original edition, where the pages would appear in unnumbered progression like a Tibetan script, with the characters written in ink of different colors. While reminding us of the original, Paz's prefatory gesture also underscores that poetry is a continual transformation, always in a "perpetual present" about which Paz himself speaks in *Viento entero* ["Wind from all Compass Points"].

Modernity has liberated poetry but has also condemned poems to a fragmentary and exiled existence. Published in chap-books that are sometimes visually designed by the authors themselves, poems are residents of a book but citizens of none. They belong in collections that are "books of poems," an organizational structure that has been developed either by the poets themselves or other compilers. The definite contours of these books of poems appear in the modern age with Baudelaire's *Fleurs du mal* [*Flowers of Evil*] and Whitman's *Leaves of Grass*. Spanish American poems of this century hold allegiance to the double origin signaled by these literary fathers. There may be thematic and stylistic unity on the one hand, and on the other a conceptual will: Octavio Paz collects most of his prose poems in *¿Aguila o sol?* [*Eagle or Sun?*], whereas José Lezama Lima publishes the heterogeneous *Enemigo rumor*, where both formal and thematic unities are present in different sections. The Chilean Pablo Neruda has been called fundamentally a poet of books, and his collections strive for the unity of form and content under the guise of a narrative, as in his *Canto general* [*Canto General*], or that of a common form with a multiplicity of objects, as in the various collections of his *Odas elementales*, *Nuevas odas elementales*, or *Tercer libro de las odas*. In a similar vein, but more attuned to conceptual rather than formal organization, the Argentinian Roberto Juárroz since 1963 has written over seven books of poems under the title *Poesía vertical* [*Vertical Poetry*]. In his second, third, and fourth "poesía vertical" (1963, 1965, 1969) each collection consists of a series of sequentially numbered poems. When collected in an anthology – *Poesía vertical, 1958–1975* (1976) – the poet starts anew his numerical sequence. Although the titles of the books might be repeated, the numbers by means of which the poems are recognized change from one collection to the other.

The book of poems as a modern creation works in Spanish America under the principles of unity within difference, of a centrifugal force, signaled by its title, that tempers the centripetal impulse of the poetic fragments, as in Lezama Lima's aptly named *Fragmentos a su imán.* Oliverio Girondo's *Veinte poemas para ser leídos en tranvía* (1922) is structured according to the same unity of time and place as Heberto Padilla's *Fuera del juego*, but they are both different from Rubén Darío's *Cantos de vida y esperanza*, both in their structure and in their aims.

Books of poetry allow for poets' perverse games with their critics or historians. The five editions of Octavio Paz's *Libertad bajo palabra* are a labyrinth of textual tampering, of exclusions and inclusions. The papers that César Vallejo left for posterity have been collected under three different titles, "Nómina de huesos," "Poemas humanos," and, more recently, "Poemas de París," that belie a critical desire for order by their editors. No amount of praise can withstand the modern poet as internal critic of his or her work. A particularly salient example is that of the Cuban poet Cintio Vitier, who in 1938 collects fifty poems in his first book, *Luz ya sueño*, with comments by José María Chacón y Calvo and Juan Ramón Jiménez. When Vitier assembles all of his collections under the title *Vísperas* in 1953, we find a very different version of his first book. Attentive readers will pursue the matter one page *before* the table of contents, where they are informed that poems from *Luz ya sueño* preceded by an asterisk have not been published. With the exception of two poems ("Canción" and "Otro"), all of the texts that were supposed to have been published in 1938 are actually new texts. This Borgesian game with texts and history continues in Vitier's *Antología poética.* Here one finds "El convaleciente" and other poems that seem to have been taken from *Luz ya sueño*, yet did not appear in that book, but instead in the one invented as the source in 1953.

A poem is an essentially unstable text, and its fundamental lack of closure is the key to its history. What Spanish American poets point out with this constant shifting within the text is the paradoxical place of the poem within modernity and historical time, and the critical relationship it has to its creator. Because the poem is an overdetermined verbal construction that changes in time, it is also the mask or the revelation of the self, the particular site where an "I" is also historically grounded. As Guillermo Sucre has pointed out, when poems transparently reveal the mask of their creators, it is the poet as an image that is offered to the readers.

The poetic "personae" of Spanish American poetry are inherited from sources as varied as Ralph Waldo Emerson, Charles Baudelaire, Walt Whitman, Friedrich Nietzsche, and Stephane Mallarmé. Their influence can be found all across the spectrum of twentieth-century Spanish American poetry. From Emerson and Whitman, Spanish Americans received a program for American poetry; translations of Nietzsche into Spanish accentuated the idea of poet as Overman; Baudelaire offered them the tools from which to construct a new critical poetry, and Mallarmé a sense of the ritual mystery of language. Obscurity of language and transparency of means; concern with form and design over meaning, or an aesthetics defined by social responsibility; historical participation by means of armed struggle, or historical participation by means of a negation of history – this confused inheritance is at the root of the tensions of this period. The translation of the (French) Symbolist tradition by the *Modernistas* included Emerson's idea that the poet is the maker of words, and that language is the tool of the maker, as elaborated in his seminal essay "The Poet." Emerson appears quoted in the preface of one of Vicente Huidobro's earliest books, *Adán* (1916), and reappears as an ideal in Borges's *El hacedor*. This Emersonian strain is inseparable from its projection onto Whitman, and most of the earliest poetry of the twentieth century follows a real or imagined body that emanates from the author of *Leaves of Grass*. If Marinetti or Breton in Europe identified themselves as emblems of Futurism or Surrealism, every Spanish American poet who initiated or belonged to a movement also wanted to be, in some way, representative of an American aesthetics. This is as true of Huidobro as it is of Gabriela Mistral. Although Mistral may not have defined her poetry under any manifesto, it was nevertheless her figure as poet that came to stand for the voice of Spanish American women. Likewise, Octavio Paz is not associated with a particular movement but is representative of Mexico itself or of the voracious culture of the Spanish American intellectual – a historically created phenomenon.

The interplay between Emerson and Whitman on the one side, and Mallarmé on the other, gives Spanish American poetry a distinctive place within modernity. Even in moments when the poetic language of the Avant-Garde was more hostile to a "communicative" function, it never lost the belief in the poet as the great communicator, as can be seen in the desire to make of the poet a representative example of America itself. The figure that best exemplifies this voice is of course Pablo Neruda. Yet it could be argued that Neruda himself is the product – if not the apex – of a tradition whose twentieth-century origins are found in Darío's critique of Marinetti's Futurism (1912), copied by Vicente Huidobro and included by the latter in a collection of essays titled *Pasando y pasando* (1914). Both Darío and Huidobro objected to Marinetti's dictum that the avant-garde poet had to abolish the "I." For Darío, this loss entailed agony; for

Huidobro, a threat to the poet's personality. From this point on, Spanish Americans never quite abandon the discourse of poetic personality, or the claims to the *vates* tradition. In spite of the subsequent claims of other *Vanguardistas* on the independence of the image and, consequently, of poetic language, Spanish American poets, from Gabriela Mistral to Pablo Antonio Cuadra and Ernesto Cardenal, have refused to abandon Shelley's dictum that poets are the "hidden legislators of the world."

The other version of modernity, the one inherited from Mallarmé, demands close attention to language as incantatory ritual. While Spanish American poets read their Whitman, they never forgot their Mallarmé, and the most important poems of the tradition tell of a process of *askesis* or purgation where subjects inscribe themselves into language and in the process lose their self within the atemporality of inscription. This loss is the theme of Huidobro's *Altazor*, Gorostiza's *Muerte sin fin* [*Death Without End*], Neruda's "Alturas de Macchu Picchu" ["Heights of Macchu Picchu"], and Octavio Paz's *Blanco*. Even at its most Mallarmean, Spanish American poetry can formally reject the voice of Whitman but can never truly abandon it. Whether poetry works by means of a progressive overloading of elements ["hinchazón y absorción de elementos"], as Neruda classified the method of his *Residencia en la tierra* [*Residence on Earth*] and as would be followed by the neo-baroque aesthetics of José Lezama Lima, or by a return to a less oratorical mode as can be seen in the poetry of Ernesto Cardenal or Heberto Padilla, the daimon of Whitman is an indelible presence, the loss of the poetic "I" too high a price to pay, more often than not at the cost of producing an agony that can be seen in César Vallejo or in Rosario Castellanos. José Lezama Lima's final disappearance into the void that he named the *tokonoma* in *Fragmentos a su imán* closes this cycle of our modernity with a final adieu to the agonies of the "I":

> De pronto, recuerdo,
> con las uñas voy abriendo
> el tokonoma en la pared.
> Necesito un pequeño vacío,
> allí me voy reduciendo
> para reaparecer de nuevo,
> palparme y poner la frente en su lugar.
> Un pequeño vacío en la pared.
>
> (*Poesía completa*, 547)

> [All of a sudden, I remember,
> with my nails I am opening
> the *tokonoma* in the wall
> I need a small void,

there I am reducing myself
in order to reappear again,
feel myself and put my forehead in its place.
A small void on the wall.]

Lezama incorporates himself as image into a space that is invisible and everpresent, where he can, as he says, converse in the streets of Alexandria or among imaginary beings while swimming on a beach. Although Lezama here abandons the overloaded style of his baroque poems, it is precisely the simplicity of the act that accounts for its particular density. Lezama's poetic *oeuvre* ends with the integration of the writer into words. This is the same desire manifested by most major poets in the tradition. The *tokonoma* is the threshold of Huidobro's *Altazor*, it is also the end of Girondo's experimentations with language in *En la masmédula*. It reappears in Borges's story "El Aleph" as a space which is everywhere and nowhere at the same time. "El Aleph," as Enrico Mario Santí has pointed out in "The Accidental Tourist", is framed as a debate between Borges and a poet that sounds surprisingly like Neruda or, at least, a bad imitation of Whitman.

Lezama's poem closes this period of Spanish American poetry, and it does so within the historical scene of the Cuban Revolution, at the point in which poetry has become the unmediated expression of utopian possibilities, where the poet disappears into the collective self. The voice that is closest to Lezama's in this poem is that of Nicolás Guillén's *Tengo*, and in both works individual poets merge with a process that is larger than their own individual selves. *Tengo* is the "other side" of Lezama's project, not its contradiction.

The tradition that is initiated by Vicente Huidobro's *El espejo de agua* is closed by *Fragmentos a su imán*. This magnet ("imán") in Lezama's book is the elusive origin and end that can never be achieved, a dense closure to a tradition that has questioned origin and originality in order to search for the keys to its modernity. When Vicente Huidobro presented the second edition of a small chap-book entitled *El espejo de agua* (1916) to the Spanish vanguardist poets in Madrid, they accused him of falsifying his own preeminence in discovering and experimenting with poetry by printing, in 1917, a false second edition of a book that they said did not exist prior to that second edition. It was the copy that made all poets doubt the existence of the original. It is with this copy that the history of Spanish American poetry in the twentieth century begins.

In what follows, I will center the initial aspects of this history within what we may call the master narrative of the Poet as it is inherited from *Modernismo*, and as it shapes the particularities of the Spanish American Avant-Garde. It is impossible to encompass all of the books by the major poets in the tradition. I have focused on particular authors and pivotal groups in order to proceed from these toward a more comprehensive overview. It is generally agreed that the major figures that cannot go unnamed are Vicente Huidobro, Jorge Luis Borges, César Vallejo, Pablo Neruda, and Octavio Paz, named the "foundational" generation by critics like Yurkievich (*Fundadores de la nueva poesía latinoamericana*). With the exception of Vallejo and Huidobro, these have been a constant living presence throughout the century. It is possible to trace the development of Spanish American poetry simply by taking into account the multiple variations within the texts of these authors. However, this would be done at the expense of other, singular voices that feed from and into the poetry of these founders. It is better then, to keep a loose chronological arrangement as the aesthetic debates proceed throughout these decades. What I am attempting to do here is less a solid narrative construction than a focus on a series of recurring problems that shape Spanish American poetic discourse up to the present.

Projects of modernity

The consolidation of the Spanish American Avant-Garde takes place in the 1920s. While Borges published in Argentina his first book of poems, *Fervor de Buenos Aires*, César Vallejo tore apart the syntax and format of the Spanish language in *Trilce*, and Oliverio Girondo mixed poetry and prose in *Veinte poemas para ser leídos en el tranvía* (1922). These more experimental writers share the literary space of others who were still shedding the last remnants of *Post-modernismo* [Postmodernism]: Gabriela Mistral published her romantic lyrics of *Desolación* in 1922, and Pablo Neruda wrote post-symbolist verses in *Crepusculario*. By 1925, Vallejo was already condemning the Avant-Garde and calling on poets to search for a new poetic expression in the continent, while Luis Palés Matos prefigured a second stage of the Avant-Garde in the Afro-Caribbean poem "Pueblo negro" (1925). In the beginning of this period, the innovations of *Simplismo* or *Estridentismo* – homegrown varieties of the European Avant-Gardes – coexisted with a more "tempered" literary expression, but also with a debate as to the particular contribution of Spanish America to the Avant-Garde that continues after Vallejo. This second moment of the Avant-Garde lasts until the end of the Spanish Civil War.

The two most important movements of the Spanish American Avant-Garde are *Creacionismo*, associated with Vicente Huidobro (1893–1948), and *Ultraísmo* [Ultraism], the work of Jorge Luis Borges and Guillermo de Torre. Both of these movements had a utopian vision of language centered on the poetic image and on an overvaluation of metaphor. *Ultraísmo* wanted to go beyond the received notions of language as representation, and *Creacionismo* sought a language that would rearrange empirical reality in order to fashion a poetic object. Of the two, *Creacionismo* is chronologically the first comprehensive articulation of an avant-garde poetics, and it framed the debate on poetry in Spanish America as a literary reflection on the relationship between poet and language, and language and empirical reality.

As a result of the particular kind of Cubism Huidobro encountered in Paris in 1917, his language constantly referred to the localization of objects in the typographical space of the page, and to the depiction of an object and its place in a representational surface. Like the still lifes of Juan Gris (one of Huidobro's first colleagues in Paris), Huidobro's poetry is charged with the sudden flash of inspiration. Huidobro's first *creacionista* poems were meditations on the visual character of the page: short poems of *El espejo de agua*, translated into French as *Horizon carré*, where the page was a space of play for signifiers. The poems signaled a new poetry that abandoned the *Modernistas'* emphasis on rhythm for a more plastic vision of poetic language. This same procedure was inaugurated by Huidobro himself in *Canciones en la noche* (1913), by Apollinaire's *Calligrammes* (1918), and, quite independently of the two, by the Mexican José Juan Tablada in his *Li-Po y otros poemas* (1920). In longer poems like *Ecuatorial* (1918), Huidobro elaborated on this poetics of space in order to reflect the dismemberment of subject and language as a result of the First World War. In his homage to Robert Delaunay's paintings, *Tour Eiffel* (1918), Huidobro tried to bridge the gaps between literary and pictorial Cubism.

Throughout the late teens and early 1920s, Huidobro promoted himself and his poetry both in Europe and in Latin America. A skillful manipulator of the cultural marketplace, the impact of his writings is directly related to his presence in the poetic discourse of the time, since it is to Huidobro's personal polemics and vendettas that we owe much of the elaboration of the theories of *Creacionismo* [Creationism]. Although there is still open debate as to the relevance of these theories for an understanding of Huidobro's poetry, the fact is that since 1924 they were elaborated in part because of his efforts to distinguish himself from competing movements. For example, his *Manifestes* are published in French mainly as a response to Bréton's Surrealism. Huidobro here argues for a kind of poetry that is precisely the opposite of Surrealism, one in which the poet controls all the elements, metaphors, and design that compose the poem, in order to create a new fact of Nature. Huidobro asserts that this vision of the poet as a magician of language, capable of conjuring new realities by virtue of their appearance on the page, is a return to the true foundations of poetry as incantatory, magical language. The "objective facts" of Nature are filtered through the poet into "new facts" of Nature that do not imitate the external character, but rather the operations, of Nature.

Manifestes arrived too late to make a considerable impact in the marketplace for competing literary programs in the mid-1920s. Huidobro's collection has the appearance of a final swan song to the aesthetics of *Creacionismo*, although the poet never renounced his literary vision. By 1926, not only had Spanish America adopted various individual credos of poetic experimentation in a dizzying array of movements, but Surrealism had by then taken center stage in European literary circles. Aesthetic discourse in Spanish America was shifting toward a more politically committed art, one that participated in a wider search for an "authenticity" inherited from Surrealism itself. Huidobro's riposte to the changing face of the Avant-Garde was his most important text, *Altazor, o el viaje en paracaídas* [*Altazor or a Voyage in Parachute*], a long poem in seven cantos where the relationship between poet, language, and poem is examined by gradually dissecting, or deconstructing, the links of this chain.

Altazor is perhaps the most transgressive poetic text of this period in Spanish American literature. Its main character (Altazor) is a composite word: *alto* (high), *azor* (hawk), a fitting emblem for a poem where Huidobro has language itself undergo countless permutations. By framing a central event – the fall of the celestial voyager Altazor – into a series of cantos, Huidobro plays with our notion of logical and progressive continuities. The reader may follow this general plot in the preface and in the first and second cantos, but after Canto III it is obvious that Huidobro retains only the barest outlines of the plot and hides the celestial voyager in a sea of words. Altazor becomes language thinking of itself and purging itself of its rhetorical mechanisms. For Huidobro, language must first destroy in order to create, and these acts of violence reach their compulsive frenzy in Canto V, where the essence of language is projected into Nature, and where a series of over a hundred lines plays with various combinations added to the word "windmill." In Huidobro's system, language inhabits all objects of Nature, and the poet seeks to uncover the hidden code of a genetic and generative linguistics that nature uses in order to create. In *Altazor*, this code is at the same time veiled and revealed, but always beyond naming. The poem can only point out the moment in which this language is born, for it is impossible for language as it is presently understood to *be* and not to name. It can only name itself by pointing in the direction of the tight and hermetic signifiers of the last two cantos, where the reader stands at a threshold that can only be crossed by silence. These typographical markers at the end of the poem foreshadow a new language:

Io ia
i i i o
Ai a i ai a i i i i o ia
(*Obras completas*, I: 437)

It is this conclusion to the poem that has baffled critics, declaring Huidobro's linguistic adventure either the poet's acceptance of his project's failure or, like Octavio Paz in "Decir sin decir," the index of a Pyrrhic victory. The fact that *Altazor* was elaborated over a period of twelve years (from 1919 to 1931), and that Huidobro himself remarked that it was in many ways a compendium of his whole work, has prompted interpretations that seek to uncover in the poem a final statement on *Creacionismo*. However, this approach does not do justice to the scope and importance of Huidobro's poem. *Altazor* is the first sustained meditation on language by a long poem in the tradition, and it questions the tradition from a threshold that none had dared to cross.

At times overwrought and frustrating, *Altazor* closes off the "heroic" period of the Spanish American Avant-Garde. It systematically assaults preconceptions of the use and abuse of language while it declares, at the same time, its unquestioned faith in the power of words. The polemical debates on poetry's social mission that were contemporaneous to, and that followed, *Altazor*'s publication, seem to have no place within it. Some of these debates after 1925 were actually elaborated with Huidobro as a negative example of a poet who copied European art by paying no attention to his American roots. From a different angle, it is impossible not to see Huidobro's creationist aesthetics parodied by Borges's eminent creators of a surreptitious universe in "Tlön Uqbar, Orbis Tertius" (*Ficciones*, 1944). Borges's cabal is actually a vanguardist conspiracy that creates a universe and a language that belongs in *Altazor*'s Canto VI. By creating a planet whose existence is postulated solely by means of words, they seem to have found the key that leads past the final vowels of *Altazor*.

As an example of a poet whose work was a sustained experimentation in the Avant-Garde, the Argentinian Oliverio Girondo (1891–1967) needs to be included in the roster of Spanish America's more aesthetically defiant poets. His first book *Veinte poemas para ser leídos en el tranvía* (1922) can be considered one of the central texts of the Spanish American Avant-Garde. Originally published with vignettes drawn by Girondo himself, the book is a utilitarian enterprise, the sign of a particularly cosmopolitan way of life: these are poems to be read during a ride in the tram to which the reader is invited. *Veinte poemas* is the diary of a traveller but, unlike a diary, it is not composed as a linear journey to different places in a continuous mode. The poems are dated and assembled according to the principles of Cubist montage (Schwartz, *Homenaje a Girondo*), deliberately breaking up a narrative line. The reader is invited to an instantaneous perception of the multiple locales where this poetry takes place: Paris, Brest, Rio de Janeiro, and others. Here, as in his second book, *Calcomanías*, Girondo writes in verse and in paragraph form of the instantaneous perception of objects that appear as if always in an eternal present in the text itself. The poems are actually plans, projects, "esbozos," designs that seem to possess no ulterior motive or finality.

Whereas Huidobro's influence in the more local national scenes during the initial years of the Avant-Garde was limited because of the fact that he chose to remain in Paris, both Girondo and Borges took center stage in the Argentinian avant-garde circles. Girondo avoided the fractious polemics of his Chilean contemporary, and in 1925 contributed with an irreverent manifesto to the Argentinian review *Martín Fierro* (1924–1927), to which he was a kind of intellectual mentor. For the next thirty years, between 1925 and 1956, Girondo continued his experimentations with language, culminating in *En la masmédula*, his most important book.

Girondo's poetic development is unique, separated from the traditional currents of Latin American poetry, which in general lines retracted from a linguistic experimentation which Girondo himself never abandoned. In this way, he serves as a link between the first Avant-Garde and the second period of experimentation inaugurated in the 1960s. From *Veinte poemas* to *Espantapájaros* to *En la masmédula*, Girondo's experiments with language fall into three distinct moments. In the first, a visual and a verbal code complement each other, words and images point to an external referent. In the second stage of his linguistic journey, Girondo incorporates the visual to the verbal, as in the calligram or visual poem that illustrates the title word of his collection *Espantapájaros*. In the third and most important stage, Girondo does without external meaning altogether: his self-referential words prefigure the later Brazilian concrete poets.

Girondo makes of language its own object by shifting, from the interior landscape of the lyrical subject in its relationship to history, to an exploration of the internal mechanisms of words themselves. *En la masmédula* performs an act of violence to language that had only been seen in the last cantos of Huidobro's *Altazor*. Using Huidobro's procedure, Girondo creates "portmanteau" words – combinations of signifiers like "Altazor" or "masmédula" ("more-than-marrow"). Yet where Huidobro in the last cantos of his masterpiece strips language down to its bare elements, Girondo's process of accumulation and juxtaposition of different words seems to prefigure a language of language, formed by adhesive properties found in different linguistic signs. This language ceases to possess a traditional lyrical "emotiveness" and addresses itself to the word as such (Schwartz, *Homenaje a Girondo*). No other major Spanish American movement has followed Girondo in an experimental project that is still an open proposition, a totally radical approach to language.

If Girondo is, throughout his life, involved in modernist experimentation, Borges's work takes place within and without the shadow of the Avant-Garde. In this sense, the full extent of his original contributions can only be understood by appealing to ever wider nets of textual conspiracies. Not only the Avant-Garde, but also his parodies on it, were carried over to his stories, poems, and essays. Borges seems to relish these parodies, in a game that points the reader away from a particular text to exegetical explorations that need other texts. For example, in the prologue to a late collection of poetry, *El otro, el mismo* Borges recounts how he was asked in Lubbock, Texas, if the poem "The Golem" was a variation of his story "Las ruinas circulares" ["The Circular Ruins"]. Borges responds that he had to "cross the whole continent in order to receive that revelation, which was true" (*Obra poética, 1923–1977*, 174). With his customary self-effacement, Borges alerts readers to indulge in an interpretative operation where poems and stories are variations of each other. His work demands at times to be read by means of comparison and contrast. This is particularly clear in poetry – the genre Borges favored at the beginning and at the end of his literary career. Borges's poems could be seen as a rewriting of concerns that are also expressed in his narrative and in his essays – indeed some of them are stories told in a different way, formatted on the page as verse and, in later years, opting more and more for the traditional rigid constructions of the rhymed sonnet, perhaps because of his blindness.

While Borges's stories have spawned legions of imitators, his poetry has not received the careful attention it deserves. This is because the style of these poems has little or nothing to do with that of his contemporaries. With his peculiar classical rhetoric and the absence of the wilder metaphors found in poetry of the 1930s and 1940s, his poems seem oblivious to the stylistic changes that have prevailed in twentieth-century Spanish American verse. In this sense, Borges has always opted for the deliberate anachronism. His models have always been clearly defined: Quevedo, Whitman, Browning. He never copies their style but internalizes and re-reads them in his own manner, and it is this critical re-reading which makes his poetry inimitable.

Borges begins his literary career with a book of poems, *Fervor de Buenos Aires*, the text of a *flaneur* who strolls around the city. There are recognized itineraries, like "La Recoleta," "El Jardín Botánico," or "La plaza San Martín"; poems dedicated to particularly Argentinian topics, like the card game in "El truco," or "La guitarra," and "Carnicería"; and then poems that signal how Borges's idea of space includes not only the real but also the imagined Buenos Aires, as in "Benarés," where the city is made into a work of the imagination. Borges followed this collection with *Luna de enfrente* and *Cuaderno San Martín*, where his meandering follows the same route: Buenos Aires transformed into a mythical construction, with the occasional added element of exoticism like "Apuntamiento de Dakar."

To a reader in 1923, Borges's books, written in a colloquial language, endeavoured to make poetry out of an ordinary universe. They dazzled the reader with metaphor and emotion expressed in high registers, but also shocked those same readers by their use of Argentinian turns of phrase written in imitation of oral language. This particular version of the Avant-Garde that is revealed in Borges's ultraist books underscores a fascination with the local milieu, it searches for cosmopolitanism within the symbolic framework of the traditional. Borges's Buenos Aires is not like the cities that Girondo depicts in *Veinte poemas*, but one where the survival of ancient traditions offers a respite from the frenetic speed of modern life. This adolescent Borges is lyrical and sentimental, his nostalgia is the theme of his books.

Only after a long hiatus between 1929 and 1943 (during which he makes his incursions into the essayistic genre, culminating in the publication of *Ficciones*, perhaps one of the seminal books of twentieth-century prose), does Borges decide to go back to his poetry. However, in *Poemas 1922–1943*, Borges collects a fundamentally revised poetic *oeuvre*. The revisions range from the elimination of most of the prologue of *Fervor*, the suppression of the one from *Luna de enfrente*, the complete recasting of the Argentinean orthography and general punctuation in *Luna de enfrente*, the elimination of complete poems, and the almost total recasting of the ones that have been left. The act of polishing, writing, and rewriting his poetic works is repeated in 1954 with *Poemas 1923–1953*, and then again in 1958, with *Poemas 1923–1958*. A reader after 1958 who seeks to trace Borges's style as a poet will be disappointed by the lack of development from the first books to the last. Borges himself has warned his readers throughout these later decades against "the predictable monotonies, the repetition of words and perhaps of complete lines" (*Obra poética, 1923–1977*, 173). Borges's poetry seems to deny the fractured history of modernity. Paradoxically, it is this disfigurement that most powerfully situates Borges as Spanish America's most modern poet.

Given this almost complete rewriting of Borges's initial works, the first critical problem is one of accessibility to the production itself. In spite of the diligent search by scholars such as Zunilda Gertel, Guillermo de

Torre, Gloria Videla, and Linda S. Maier, we do not have the full output of Borges's literary work. What we have, instead, is the critical revision that the poet has accomplished, one that has suppressed a considerable body of work disseminated, between 1919 and 1926, in Spanish literary journals like *Alfar, Baleares, Cervantes, Cosmópolis, Grecia, Reflector, Revista de Occidente, Tableros,* and *Ultra.* These texts consist, in the words of one critic, of "thirty poems, three literary manifestoes, six annotated compilations of Spanish American and German expressionist poetry and prose, three essays on the metaphor and six miscellaneous articles" (Maier, "Three 'New' Avant-garde Poems of Jorge Luis Borges").

The young Borges writes of war and socialist ideology, and of the modern city with its accompanying technological progress. He creates neologisms and indulges in the irregular use of line breaks, he shows a marked penchant for metaphorical surprise by forcing his readers to perceive strange and unaccustomed relations between objects. Undoubtedly, these come out of Borges's debt to the German Expressionists, whose works he read while in Switzerland during the First World War. It was an aesthetic to which he was particularly drawn, collecting, translating, and introducing their works to Spanish and Spanish American audiences. Borges's original texts seem to underscore, in a way that his revised texts do not, his narrative of a literary career in the prologue to *El otro, el mismo*: "The fate of the writer is curious. Baroque in the beginning, vainly baroque, after a number of years he can achieve, if the stars are favorable, not simplicity, which is nothing, but a modest and secret complexity" (*Obra poética, 1923–1977,* 174). However, the fact that no trace of this development may be found in the collected volume of Borges's *Obra poética* is precisely what alerts the reader to the constructions of Borges's poetics. It is in this realm of uninterrupted similarity that we might find the key with which to examine Borges's modernity.

Although critics have generally read these revisions, suppressions, and additions as the result of Borges's renunciation of Ultraism in the late 1920s, a second reading clarifies the fact that Borges has in mind much more than a revisionary stance, and that he proceeds to organize his work according to a particular notion of the Book, whose model might be seen in Whitman. Borges's *Obra poética* is a central text to which various different texts are added, it is a labyrinth of sameness to which readers have access on many different levels. From 1923 to 1960, there are basically three books of poems in constant metamorphosis. This process of publication and recollection will continue after 1969, when Borges at seventy re-publishes his first three books and re-reads them by adding new prologues and giving them a definitive form, but also as late as 1979, when a new collection of *Obra poética* is published with new prologues, including one which serves as a general prologue for the rest of the work.

The Book, like Whitman's *Leaves of Grass*, is a kind of encyclopedia of the writer, where different sections are independent of each other but have obsessively similar themes and a style that defies the notion of historical evolution. By means of carefully planned additions and deletions, Borges aimed to have his work under the sign of atemporality. More like Whitman than many of his imitators, all of Borges's poems are written in a similar register, with a deliberate monotony that also recalls Whitman's *Leaves of Grass*.

The rhetorical trope that best describes Borges's poetry is the epiphoric: a repetition of sounds that Borges uses above all in his "Arte poética," where the idea of progression is linked to the notion of repetition:

> Ver en la muerte el sueño, en el ocaso
> Un triste oro, tal es la poesía
> Que es inmortal y pobre. La poesía
> Vuelve como la aurora y el ocaso.
> *(Obra poética, 1923–1977,* 161)

> [To see in death the dream, in dusk
> A sad gold, such is poetry
> That is immortal and poor. Poetry
> Returns like dawn and like dusk.]

It is in this poem that we can find an emblem of Borges's construction of a poetics, with its insistence on a language that goes beyond the metaphor, situated in the infinitive "ver." The poem is an illustration of itself. It says, rigorously, nothing. The initial juxtaposition of one kind of poetry to another collapses: the first is metaphoric and "poor," but the second repeats the metaphor. It is by means of this repetition with variation that time is denied.

Throughout Borges's poetry readers can find the same obsession with violence, the cult of heroes, and the individual lost in the labyrinth of time. He creates an epic of reading, as in "Al iniciar el estudio de la gramática anglosajona," from *El hacedor*, or as presented in "Manuscrito hallado en un libro de Joseph Conrad," from a revised *Luna de enfrente*. He prefers the use of the quatrain and Browning's dramatic monologues; he builds on the same concepts by focusing on an instance that functions as a still-life, a synecdoche that stands for a concept, like Browning's decision to be a poet, or Alonso Quijano's dream. In "Una rosa y Milton", for example, the poem concentrates on a particular situation: a vignette in time that Borges has rescued from the oblivion of literature:

> la postrera
> Rosa que Milton acercó a su cara
> Sin verla.
> *(Obra poética, 1923–1977,* 213)

[the last
Rose that Milton brought nearer to his face
Without seeing it]

The poet invokes for the first time this scene, and borrows the rose for his verse. In this statement we can see that the sheer multiplicity of Borges's archive, of the cultures and languages that he invokes, in different places and times, find precarious and temporary closure in the material space of the page. Reflecting on the moon, in his "Manifesto of Ultraism," Borges shows his classical bent in the center of the Avant-Garde: his moon is an object that is able to possess its old signifieds within a new signifier. The invention of Milton's rose is accomplished by pretending a rewriting, a translation. In this way, a new object is born: Borges's rose is also Milton's, and vice versa.

Like Huidobro, what Borges goes back to is the existence of a universe of words on the page, and Borges's emphasis on the various seductions of symbolic power within the poetic word places him within the avant-garde milieu from which the author later reneged. In spite of his attempts to erase visible changes in his work, the various reformulations of the poems point to a fundamental drama which is played beneath the text. Whereas other Spanish American poets bring their stylistic and agonic preoccupations to the space of the page itself, Borges surrenders them to a supposed ur-space, from which he is reading and from which he is copying.

Borges's Ultraism attempted to bridge the distance between Europe and the Americas by being paradoxically "provincial" and cosmopolitan – Ultraists acted on the national milieu while at the same time they translated other literary experiments into that same context. Since the publication of *Fervor de Buenos Aires* the Argentinian Avant-Garde shows a preoccupation with national culture which is all but absent in the more cosmopolitan Huidobro. However, it is perhaps in the work of César Vallejo (1892–1938) where we can find a meeting of aesthetics and politics, nationalism and cosmopolitanism that has been enormously influential throughout the rest of the century, and that has fostered the division of the Spanish American Avant-Garde into two camps: the political and the aesthetic Avant-Garde. Moving to Lima out of the Andean highlands of his native Peru, and then to his untimely death in Paris, Vallejo's search encompassed some of the most daring experimental poems in the language as well as some of its more politically committed works.

Vallejo published only two books of poems during his lifetime: *Los heraldos negros* [*The Black Heralds*] and *Trilce* [*Trilce*] A third, *España, aparta de mí este cáliz* [*Spain, Take this Cup Away from Me*] was still unpublished at his death and left among a collection of papers with poems that possess no certain order and no verifiable title. For most of their publishing history these texts have been known as *Poemas humanos* [*Human Poems*] and divided into two sections entitled "Poemas en prosa" and "Poemas humanos" according to Georgette Vallejo, the poet's widow, or as "Poemas póstumos" and divided into two sections, "Nómina de huesos" and "Sermón de la barbarie" according to the poet's friend Juan Larrea. The complex history of these papers is admirably rendered in Américo Ferrari's recent edition of the *Obra poética* which groups them under the title *Los poemas de París*.

Los heraldos negros and *Trilce* are separated by four difficult years in Vallejo's life: his mother's death in 1918, followed by the death of a lover in 1919, and his incarceration, under suspicious circumstances, from November 7, 1920 to February 26, 1921. However, no amount of biographical information explains the violent breakdown in poetic language that can be seen from one book to the other. Even if we compare *Trilce* to other texts published during 1922 – T. S. Eliot's *The Waste-Land*, James Joyce's *Ulysses*, Manuel Maples Arce's *Andamios interiores*, Oliverio Girondo's *Veinte poemas* – it stands out for the verbal pyrotechnics that start from the invented word of its title (apparently a play on the number "three" and an allusion to the book's printing costs), and the particularity of its poetic language. The book consists of seventy-seven poems identified by Roman numerals that seem to have been arranged with no particular chronological or thematic order. Like Girondo's *Veinte poemas*, Vallejo's procedure is guided by montage: when one theme seems to predominate, Vallejo jumps and composes poems in a totally different register. Critics have generally seen a number of predominant motifs: the sensation of expulsion from the maternal hearth, the expression of a fundamental orphanhood, and the rupture of the consciousness of the human subject. *Trilce* is an inexplicable text, and no amount of criticism has been able to tame its revolutionary power. The poems play with the spatial configuration of signifiers, they lapse into onomatopoeia, and use a language that is at the same time composed of archaisms and neologisms.

Vallejo seems to have shattered the *modernista* ideal of beauty into innumerable fragments. That he accomplished this is all the more remarkable because of the context in which it takes place. Although by 1917 Peru had experienced its first manifestation of the Avant-Garde with the publication of *Panoplia lírica* by Alberto Hidalgo, Vallejo apparently had little contact with the avant-garde milieu. According to Saúl Yurkievich in *Fundadores de la nueva poesía*, Vallejo's reading of the Avant-Garde could only come from *Cervantes*, the journal edited in Spain by Rafael Cansinos Assens and César E. Arroyo. *Cervantes* in 1918 published texts by Apollinaire and Huidobro, manifestos by Picabia and Tzara, and

Cansinos's translation of Mallarmé's *Un coup de dés*. Yet even readers aware of the most recent trends in European literature were baffled by Vallejo's text, and the poet complained that his book was ignored. Part of the lack of immediate critical response surrounding this text may be due to the fact that, unlike other manifestations of the Avant-Garde, *Trilce* does not come accompanied by any manifesto. Unlike Hidalgo's *Simplismo*, conceived that same year, *Trilce* makes no theoretical claims and does not explain itself.

Not only was Vallejo not tempted into writing a manifesto, but he later attacked the Avant-Garde, in articles like "Poesía nueva" (1926) and "Contra el secreto profesional acerca de Pablo Abril de Vivero" (1927), followed by his condemnation of Surrealism in "Autopsia del superrealismo" (1930), all written after his departure for Europe in 1923. Following the same principle as that employed by Huidobro in his 1914 critique of Marinetti, Vallejo debunks the Spanish Americans' supposed modernity, and accuses his contemporaries of plagiarizing European literature. Vallejo argued for a continuous exploration of the American soul, preferring "the cheap Americanism of themes and names" in José Santos Chocano to the "apelike nightmare" of American *Vanguardistas* like Maples Arce, Neruda, or Borges (Schwartz, *Las vanguardias latinoamericanas*, 513).

Vallejo's essays have fostered a reading of the Avant-Garde as a movement lacking in American concerns. Vallejo assessed that innovation in Europe was one thing, but that the same innovation transported into the Americas was just another example of imitation: "In America, precisely because these disciplines are imported and practiced without modifications, they do not allow writers to reveal and realize themselves, since said disciplines do not respond to peculiar necessities nor have they been conceived by the free and vital impulses of those that cultivate them" (Schwartz, *Las vanguardias*, 514). One can see in these words of Vallejo's the meaning he would have for later writers like Alejo Carpentier, who would perform the same condemnation on Surrealists in the famous prologue to *El reino de este mundo* (1949) [*The Kingdom of this World*].

During the period of composition of the *Poemas humanos*, Vallejo debated and reconceptualized the role of the artist in a revolutionary society, and the position of poetry vis-à-vis politics, particularly after he traveled to the Soviet Union in 1928 and 1929, and during the Spanish Civil War. Yet where other critics would verge on the doctrinaire, Vallejo still attempts to nuance his views. When told by the Peruvian politician and critic Victor Haya de la Torre that artists must help by working in the propaganda of the Revolution, the poet replied that he sympathized with the political intentions of the demand, but that as an artist, "I do not accept any label, mine or from others, that even couching itself with the best of intentions, would submit my aesthetic liberty to the service of this or that political propaganda" (Schwartz, *Las vanguardias*, 481). He distinguished between a revolutionary art and an art that is nominally revolutionary.

In Vallejo's *Poemas humanos* the aesthetic and the political are not opposed. He delves in the sonnet form, resurrects the poem in prose in the tradition of Baudelaire and Rimbaud, incorporates some of the typographical experimentation as well as the nominalizing chaos of his earlier *Trilce*, but above all, he creates a new vocabulary for poetry that uses a poetics of discontinuity and fragmentation applied to proletarian revolt. Even though in "Contra el secreto profesional" he had renounced cheap nationalism, in "Telúrica y magnética" Vallejo creates a new hymn to Peru from the ruins of Santos Chocano's Americanism:

> ¡Mecánica sincera y peruanísima
> la del cerro colorado!
> ¡Suelo teórico y práctico!
> ¡Surcos inteligentes; ejemplo: el monolito y su cortejo!
> > (*Obra poética* (1988) 360)

> [Sincere and Peruvian mechanics
> that of the colored hill!
> Theoretical and practical ground!
> Intelligent furrows; example: the monolith and its retinue!]

Here we can see the ultimate threshold for the carefully wrought poetic language that Vallejo had been searching for since *Los heraldos negros*. Revolution and aesthetics meet and clash at the same time. In "Los mineros salieron de la mina" Vallejo exclaims:

> ¡Era de ver sus polvos corrosivos!
> ¡Era de sus óxidos de altura!
> Cuñas de boca, yunques de boca, aparatos de boca
> (¡Es formidable!)
> > (*Obra poética* (1988) 356)

> [It was a sight to be seen their corrosive dust!
> They were to be heard, their oxides from heights!
> Mouth wedges, mouth anvils, mouth apparatus
> (It is terrific!)]

The exclamatory stance is joined to a more Baudelairian irony in some of the prose poems. In others, a more melancholic Vallejo reigns, as in the justifiably famous "Piedra negra sobre una piedra blanca" and the moving "París, octubre 1936." Here Vallejo's violently fragmented subject offers his readers a moment of lyrical sadness.

With Vallejo's work, the reader feels that these poems are precisely composed of scraps of paper, of the detritus of capitalism in the period during the two world wars. Vallejo allows us to see the poem as it is being written, he is a poet whose rough edges are visible all over the page. His poems at times seem to be made up of sundry heteroclite fragments that make no attempt at logical connection. For example, in one of his posthumous poems, "Sombrero, abrigo, guantes," Vallejo weaves synecdoques sewn into the fabric of a dismembered sonnet written in the Parisian Café de la Regence, across from the Comédie Française. Its first quartet oscillates between Alexandrines and the hendecasyllabic; giving the impression that Vallejo is coming up with the form of the poem at the moment in which he is writing it, as an act of impatience. Much of his work consists of this violent encounter between different elements. This invitation to compose the fabric of the work accounts for many of the misreadings of his critics, who insist on imposing different constructions to a work that is the literary equivalent of one of Tatlin's constructivist monuments.

Critics generally talk about a retrenchment from the experimentation of the Avant-Garde, a period of order that follows the disordered chaos of a poetry that was fundamentally elitist and anti-popular. In Spanish America the break from the period of frenzied experimentation has been placed in 1929 by Nelson Osorio, in 1931 by Jorge Schwartz, in 1935 by Hugo Verani, and in 1939 by Federico Schopf. Regardless of the particular year where this retrenchment takes place, the negation of the Avant-Garde has to be seen as part of the dialectics of modernity. By denying the Avant-Garde, poets were precisely reaffirming its continuing validity.

Vallejo's writing can serve as an index for the growing polarization of Spanish American culture at the end of the 1920s, one that had been prefigured since the beginning of the decade by the formation of communist parties in Argentina (1918), Mexico (1919), Cuba (1925), and Peru (1928). A series of workers' strikes throughout Spanish America occur in the midst of a generalized economic crisis motivated by the economic collapse of 1929, and these in turn were followed by a series of military coups in Peru, Argentina, Brazil, and Cuba, whose consequences would be devastating for culture. Spanish Americans felt that a period was coming to an end. José Carlos Mariátegui, the great theoretician of Peruvian society and culture, died in 1930, and his journal *Amauta* ceased publication. *Martín Fierro* in Argentina closed in 1927, as a consequence of political changes and the *Revista de Avance* folded in Cuba in 1930.

The debate of the 1930s and early 1940s centered on what has been called since then the "classical" opposition within the Avant-Garde of the "politically committed art" and that which appropriates the tenets of "art for art's sake." These debates originate not only from the conception of art itself since the nineteenth century but also from the very definition of the "avant-garde," a term borrowed from the vocabulary of militarism and adopted and adapted by Marx, Engels, and later Lenin in order to speak of a distinct class within society that prepares the advent of the revolutionary struggle. This slippage, between a term that is understood within the province of aesthetics, and the same term understood within the realm of social revolution, would be perverted by Stalinism, which paradoxically identified itself with a political avant-garde while at the same time it frowned on all attempts at artistic independence that were not sanctioned by the Party. In the 1930s and 1940s the doctrine of Socialist realism abolished artistic experimentation, which was then considered the expression of a decadent art. However, it may be misleading to define the Avant-Garde by appropriating the definitions used by the more dogmatic left. From Cubism to Surrealism, the *Vanguardia* was an art of the marketplace, aware of how to scandalize and where to scandalize, conscious of what the audience wanted, and willing to feed the audience its necessary dose of shock and novelty. It is only after a thorough domination of the marketplace that the realignment of forces pointed to a more politically committed art, and to a wider search for national expression.

The readings of the Avant-Garde by the left do not help us to understand the work of Gabriela Mistral (1889–1957), but they do provide a context from which to examine and highlight how Mistral's poetry seemed to be completely alien to the polemics of the time. Although the editors of the *Antología de poesía chilena nueva* exclude her from their ranks and classify her work as fundamentally reactionary and full of nineteenth-century motifs, she may be called upon to provide a bridge between the poetry of the Avant-Garde and the poetry that followed it. Her poetry and her poetic *persona* are present throughout the decades of the 1940s and 1950s, and Mistral was the first Spanish American writer to win the Nobel Prize for Literature in 1945. Her work encompasses the multiple registers of a deeply personal and internal search as well as a Pan-Americanist outlook that will be seen in the later poetry of Pablo Neruda.

Mistral is generally classified as a *Post-modernista*, and her contributions to the poetics of the continent in the 1930s and 1940s have been skirted by a subtle act of chronological sexism. As the term is used in Spanish America, *Post-modernismo* names a moment of cultural impasse that is still not well defined, between the glories of *Modernismo* and the violence of the Avant-Garde, and its emblem is Enrique González Martínez's famous reaction against Darío in "Tuércele el cuello al cisne" (1911). In part, this classification of Mistral occurs because she is an older poet in relation to the younger Avant-Garde generation, but also because she did not quite fit with the other poets of her time. Sucre, in *La máscara, la transparencia*, has defined her work as dominated by a Christological passion – her unadorned style, lacking in the rhetorical flourish or even the penchant for scandal of her peers, does not allow critics to easily classify the poet within the artistic currents of her time. Part of the problem is that Mistral separated herself from the Avant-Garde, and the Avant-Garde condemned her work to premature anachronism. What has been considered her best book, *Desolación*, includes the famous "Sonetos de la muerte," which established the presence of an original voice that evokes erotic loss in a language of a measured elegance:

> Del nicho helado en que los hombres te pusiereon,
> te bajaré a la tierra humilde y soleada
> Que he de dormirme en ella los hombres no supieron,
> Y que hemos de soñar sobre la misma almohada.
> (*Antología poética de Gabriela Mistral*, 47)

> [From the frozen niche in which men have placed you
> I will lower you to the humble and sunlit earth.
> That within her I shall sleep men did not know,
> And that we shall sleep over the same pillow.]

The best poems of Mistral possess this same *chiaroscuro*, the poet draws out of the verse an emotion that meditates on itself with a tone of decision and will that is here signaled by the play between the affirmative acts of the poet, the irregular and fragmented past of both burial and knowledge ("pusieron... supieron"), and the elegant and elegiac construction "he de dormirme." Mistral does not write a poem on the violent contrasts between life and death, but on the mediation of sleep and affection as a space that looks beyond visible oppositions. The body covered in its frozen niche will find a more humble abode in a sunlit earth that for Mistral is both an end and a beginning. Because of the particular mode in which desire, loss, and yearning are expressed, "Los sonetos de la muerte" deserve their own particular place among the best poems of the tradition.

Narrative poems like "Historias de loca," from *Tala* helped Mistral gain a reputation for a poetry that clearly expressed an emotive state with the utmost economy of means. It is a disarming poetry, both for its style as well as for its thematics. *Tala* represents a dramatic journey from the world of the individual to that of the collective American consciousness. The eight sections of the book are constructed by underscoring precisely such a journey: they start with "Muerte de mi madre" and "Alucinación," where Mistral writes in a *post-modernista* voice of intimate reflection, but shift to a populist romantic strain in the latter sections of the book. From the third to the eighth section of *Tala*, Mistral moved towards a divinization of "elementary" objects in "Materias." The theme of these poems to bread, salt, water, and air, and the vistas of the hymnic "América" reappear in Pablo Neruda's *Odas elementales*.

This prefiguration of Neruda's grand theme might be considered her best poetry. Yet whereas Neruda is a poet of everpresent oceanic amplitude, who layers metaphor upon metaphor on objects, what Mistral wants to discover is the symbolic aura of things, reflected in a "simple" language. In "Material," for example, she uses one of her most common stylistic resources, quatrains that flow with unsuspecting ease; in "Cosas," from the section entitled "Saudade," remembrance and loss are joined by a Nature that blurs the distinctions between the space of memory or invention. Mistral's objects acquire an aura of their own, like the allegorical landscapes in mystical Spanish poetry – as when the poet speaks of an "agua silenciosa" whose ripple is felt in spite of the absence of wind. The mystery of this Nature is related to childhood: the magnificence of the Andes and the protection of its valleys. Her sense of romantic loss is not expressed in agonic high registers but by the use of an almost crystalline verse with no deceptive undertones.

The latter sections of *Tala* give an account of the poet as public figure. It is as if Mistral in one book had made her particular symbolic journey, one that continues in *Lagar*. It is impossible to eschew Mistral's contribution to the poetical mythography in Spanish American literature, even if her verses seemed outdated to many of her contemporaries. Like Darío, she was a poet who gave Spanish Americans a collective sense of self. In the narrations written by historians of Spanish American poetry, it seems as if the experimentation of the Avant-Garde flows seamlessly according to the steps traced in the poetic journey that can be seen in *Tala*, where the personal and the political are thematically woven with no visible contradictions. However, it was precisely the articulation of a personal voice that was at issue in the move away from the linguistic experimentation of the Avant-Garde in the 1930s.

Pablo Neruda (1904–1973) moved out of an aesthetics that was similar to early Mistral: under the aegis of *Post-modernismo* he had written his *Crepusculario*, and the classic and consecrated *Veinte poemas de amor y una canción desesperada* [*Twenty Love Songs and a Song of Despair*], where he follows erotic themes explored by *Modernistas* like José Asunción Silva (1865–1896) and Leopoldo Lugones (1874–1938). Yet whereas Mistral did not totally proclaim allegiance to poetic innovation in her verse, Neruda assimilated the Avant-Garde in *Tentativa del hombre infinito*, in order to unite, afterwards, one of the major texts of this period.

The poems in Neruda's best book, *Residencia en la tierra (1925/1935)* [*Residence on Earth*] defy readers' logic. It is a cycle that, upon its completion, can be seen as divided into three parts. The first *Residencia* is published in Chile in 1933 and contains poems from 1925 to 1931. The second appears in a Spanish edition by Cruz y Raya in Madrid in 1935, and adds poems from 1931 to 1935. There is a *Tercera residencia*, that is, according to Emir Rodríguez Monegal in *El viajero inmóvil*, a "bibliographic hybrid" composed of two irreconcilable and distinct books. Only the two initial parts of this volume – from 1933 and 1935 – belong to what Rodríguez Monegal has termed the infernal cycle of *Residencia*, ending with a furiously erotic sequence entitled "Las furias y las penas." The rest of the poems belong to a different cycle, that of the Spanish Civil War. They are, according to Rodríguez Monegal, the account of a different kind of inferno, and the work of a fundamentally different poet, more concerned now with social rather than personal issues.

Neruda published *Residencia* in 1933 and 1935 to considerable critical acclaim. The fact that the eminent Spanish literary critic Amado Alonso wrote *Poesía y estilo de Pablo Neruda* in 1940 reveals that the book was received as an important literary event, even if Alonso misread Neruda as a fundamentally hermetic poet, one whose texts possess a hidden allusive system. *Residencia* is, on the contrary, an illustration of the states of mind within the consciousness of the poet. If it is not structured, like other vanguardist texts, according to the principles of superimposition and montage, the book nevertheless rambles from one state of mind to another as a kind of random poetic diary, Neruda's "saison en enfer." It was written while he was in charge of various diplomatic posts in Asia, principally in Ceylon and Rangoon – but except for the poems about his mistress Josie Bliss and the satiric short portraits of British expatriates, the book makes few references to its Asian milieu.

Neruda is not concerned with form but with objects. These are actually the central elements of *Residencia en la tierra*. The poet's agony is not redeemed by a language that struggles to account for multiplicity and chaos. The disarray of the world implies creation but also the agonic dissolution of the poet's "I." That Neruda was "redeemed" by objects can be seen in the poetics of the natural world that he developed during the period when he composed his book. It finds its most succinct articulation in "Para una poesía sin pureza" published in *Caballo verde para la poesía* (October, 1935). Here Neruda manifests a penchant for "objects in a state of rest: wheels that have traversed long and dusty distances, bearing great vegetable or mineral weights" (Schwartz, *Las vanguardias*, 485) and states: "Let the poetry we search for be like that, worn as if by an acid by the duties of the hand, penetrated by sweat and smoke, with a smell of urine and lilies, splattered by the different professions that are exercised within and outside of the law" (p. 485). Neruda concludes his manifesto brandishing the terrors of ice: "He who flees from bad taste falls on ice" (p. 486).

Neruda's aesthetic darts were directed at the Spanish poet Juan Ramón Jiménez (1881–1958) and his vision of a "pure poetry," an aesthetic that searched for the essence of the sublime removed from the contingencies of time and place. Jiménez is such an important figure in Spanish American poetry of this period that it is difficult to do justice to the ramifications of his poetics in the scope of this essay. He served as an inspiration to certain groups (noticeably, that of José Lezama Lima and *Orígenes* in Cuba), and as a negative example to poets like Neruda, obsessed with decay and the products of the modern urban world. We should add that it was not only Jiménez's works that divided Spanish American poets, but also the strong and temperamental positions of a poet who represented for Spaniards and Spanish Americans the epitome of the aesthete. He is an open book invented and disfigured during the 1930s and 1940s.

The difficult relationship between Neruda and Jiménez continued up to the 1940s, and informs Neruda's condemnation of the passivity and formalism of Mexican poetry in a debate that took place when he was sent as Chilean Consul to Mexico City at the beginning of the decade. The general critique of this kind of "formalism" placed Neruda among the forefront of a generation of Spanish poets like Rafael Alberti and León Felipe, who joined him in a search for a different language. Their concern with social politics arose from the Spanish Civil War; the death of Federico García Lorca (September, 1936) mobilized them. That this was a defining moment for this generation can be seen in the fact that the *Congreso de escritores anti-fascistas* (July, 1937) was the last time the intellectual games of Huidobro met with the vorticist impurity of Neruda; the forcefully revolutionary language of Vallejo with the ongoing discovery of modernity of Octavio Paz. Neruda's shift from Surrealist to Americanist is a complex process that arises from the cultural climate of the 1940s and culminates with his visit to Macchu Picchu in October, 1943 – perhaps one of the pivotal moments of Neruda's life. Few events in the history of literature have been charged with the significance of this particular visit.

Alturas de Macchu Picchu [*The Heights of Macchu Picchu*], published in 1946 and then integrated within the vast panorama of the *Canto general*, is the most lucid moment of the Americanist enterprise. It is *Alturas* that widens the scope of a work that Neruda conceived in 1943, when he published as a separate volume parts of *Canto general de Chile*. From 1943 to 1948 Neruda thought out and planned a more extensive *Canto general*, which was then completed during one year, while the poet was in hiding from the state police of President Gabriel González Videla (Santí, *Pablo Neruda. The Poetics of Prophecy*). This is why the book has been generally read according to one of its central themes, that of the fugitive poet. This figure is as central to the poem as Dante's exile is to the *Divine Comedy*; the structure of both books demands that a poetic self hold the text together as a unifying principle. Neruda speaks as a public figure, as a witness, and as a victim, and it is from this individual voice, from its desire to name and give origin and meaning to life, that the book embarks on the creation of an American founding myth, with a visible plot that is cut into major zones.

Canto general is assembled by means of blocks. Sections range from the history of liberators and tyrants, to descriptions of nature or of historical events, to the adventures of the fugitive poet. This manner of assembling the book resembles the stones of Macchu Picchu itself. Neruda constructed his book with the solidity of stones, and these close one of the more important sections (VII) of the twelve that form "Alturas de Macchu Picchu":

> Cuando la mano color de arcilla
> se convirtió en arcilla, y cuando los pequeños párpados se cerraron
> llenos de ásperos muros, poblados de castillos,
> y cuando todo el hombre se enredó en su agujero,
> quedó la exactitud enarbolada:
> el alto sitio de la aurora humana:
> la más alta vasija que contuvo el silencio:
> una vida de piedra después de tantas vidas.
>
> (*Canto general* [1990], 134)

> [When the clay-colored hand
> turned to clay, when the little eyelids closed,
> filled with rough walls, brimming with castles,
> and when the entire man was trapped in his hole,
> exactitude remained hoisted aloft:
> this high site of the human dawn:
> the highest vessel that has contained silence:
> a life of stone after so many lives.]
>
> (Tr. Jack Schmitt, *Canto General*, 35)

This is one of the more dramatic sections of "Alturas de Macchu Picchu," followed by a shift in tone in Section VIII which Neruda begins by commanding "Sube conmigo, amor americano" (p. 134) ["Rise up with me, American love"] (Schmitt, 36). It represents the culmination of Neruda's historical pathos, as he contemplates lives and histories that have been silenced and destroyed forever. In Canto X Neruda demands: "Macchu Picchu, pusiste / piedra en la piedra, y en la base, harapos?" (*Canto general*, 138) ["Macchu Picchu, did you put / stone upon stone and, at the base, tatters?"] (Schmitt, 39). It is silence itself which Neruda turns into a positive creative force. The lost poet of *Residencia*, with whom "Macchu Picchu" begins, has been able to decipher silence, and to understand it as a creative force that blends the vast panorama which unfolds in Neruda's book. Neruda's chiseled verse, with its rhetorical solemnity, allows for this repetition ("arcilla. . . arcilla"; "piedra. . .

piedra" ["clay. . . clay; stone. . . stone"]). It is a style that gathers its own force and momentum verse after verse.

Neruda did not employ the same style in the books that followed, cycles of love poems like *Los versos del capitán*, and three volumes of *Odas elementales* where he prefers a much shorter line form (in the *Odas* these at times consist merely of one or two words). In these feats of metaphor, Neruda does not write only of literary objects, but includes the whole gamut of creation in his poems: fruits, vegetables, dictionaries, books – objects insignificant enough to be forgotten in everyday life but which Neruda metaphorically reconstructs, in an act of defamiliarization that is admirable for its virtuosity and daring. Neruda overturns the traditional ode of the neoclassical age with irreverence and humor, while transforming each object into a solemn creation. These are some of the more celebrated of Neruda's later poems, written when he was already enormously famous as a poet and political figure, a cultural conscience of Spanish America.

In the *Odas*, Neruda was able to sense a new mode of poetry appearing in Spanish America at the time, principally in Nicanor Parra's *Poemas y antipoemas* [*Poems and Antipoems*]. This poetry was much more colloquial and explored issues that were not generally accepted as "poetic." The odes entail the suppression of the subject; they collapse the distinctions between the poetic and the political by erasing the class distinctions that make certain objects more "poetic" than others (Santí, *Pablo Neruda*, 210). However, this suppression is undertaken as a voluntary gesture, and one only has to look at the prologue to the odes, "El hombre invisible," to notice how this elimination of the poetic "I" does not entail the desperation that was noticed in the more infernal cycles of the *Residencia*:

> yo quiero
> que todos vivan en mi vida
> y canten en mi canto
> yo no tengo importancia
> (*Poesía*, 1:459)

> [I want
> for all to live in my life
> and sing in my song
> I am not important]

Neruda advised younger poets to forgo the painful initiation of the *Residencias*, and to concentrate on the more political aspects of his writing. Parra's "antipoemas," at first a deliberate reaction against the more cosmic and rhetorical Neruda, are closer to the poet of the "odas." Yet Neruda's move to this poetry is also an acceptance of the place of self that prefigures the work of Octavio Paz and the quiet resignation and faith of José Lezama Lima's disappearance into the *tokonoma* of *Fragmentos a sui imán*.

This *persona* that can be seen in the *Odas* ushered in one of the more tragic endings of a poetic career in Spanish American poetry. After this moment of glory, with his Nobel Prize in Literature in 1971, Neruda's death on September 23, 1973, days after the collapse of his friend Salvador Allende's government, gives an ominous symbolic aura to the end of the poet's life. Always prescient of the dangers of complacency, in his last books of poems Neruda turned once again to a visionary, prophetic mode. A long period of introspection sustained in the 1950s and 1960s culminates in *Fin del mundo*, *La espada encendida*, and *2000*, books where Neruda comes face to face with a Blakean apocalypse. His return to a visible prophetic mode is intended as a warning to Spanish Americans, but it also confirms the allegorical character of his work. Neruda's visions are one of the metaphors of closure for this period of Spanish American poetry.

Afro-Caribbean poetry appeared in the late 1920s and early 1930s out of an atmosphere in which the Surrealists' penchant for Primitivism and authenticity was translated by Cuban poets in order to centralize the position of African descendants on the island – from being ethnographic representations of a "backward" society (as they appear in the Cuban ethnologist Fernando Ortiz's first books), to being in the forefront and center of Cuban nationality. It was this inheritance of the Avant-Garde, filtered in Cuba through the work of José Ortega y Gasset, his *Revista de Occidente*, and Spengler's *The Decline of the West*, that prefigured a new aesthetics. During the same period of time (between 1928 and 1931), the poets grouped around the journal *Contemporáneos* in Mexico occupied the center stage in the poetical production of the country. As two versions of a common avant-garde inheritance, the *Contemporáneos* and the Afro-Caribbean movement in poetry might be compared, even if the former were accused as Formalists by Neruda and the latter were concerned with social action. Both groups can be seen within the context offered by Jiménez's "poesía pura," Surrealism, and the Spanish Civil War. A careful study of Afro-Caribbean poetry and that of the *Contemporáneos* would allow a critic to precisely deconstruct the various threads by means of which the cultural presence of Europe is affirmed and denied in Spanish America during the 1930s.

The poets grouped around the journal *Contemporáneos* (1928–1931) in Mexico have been compared to the Spanish "Generación del 27." Like their Spanish contemporaries, they moved away from the more experimental Avant-Garde (in Mexico known as *Estridentismo*) while they also rediscovered the classical Spanish tradition, in order to pave the way for a new poetry that can be seen in the late 1930s in journals like *Taller*, where most recent and contemporary poetry in Mexico begins. The *Contemporáneos* are Bernardo Ortiz de Montellano, Carlos Pellicer, José Gorostiza, Jaime Torres Bodet, Jorge Cuesta, Xavier Villaurrutia, Salvador Novo, and Gilberto Owen. They cannot strictly be called a generation, but a state of mind, as Guillermo Sheridan has remarked. These poets devoured the most experimental currents in Europe and Latin America. They not only founded journals (*Ulises*, 1928; *Contemporáneos* 1928–1931; *Examen*, 1932) but also theatrical groups and cinema clubs. Their cultural action may be seen in their work published in newspapers of the time, in their avid translation of European writers, and in their indefatigable efforts to create an open cultural climate out of an atmosphere of instability arising from the Mexican Revolution.

It was precisely the *Contemporáneos'* demanding sense of aesthetics that accounted for their distance from the more prevalent artistic currents of post-revolutionary Mexico. They were not interested in the novel of the Mexican Revolution and argued instead for a revolutionary novel; they isolated themselves from politically committed literature and inserted Gide, Proust, and Cocteau into the Mexican arena. For these actions they were attacked as anti-nationalist and even as producers of "effeminate" literature, unable to insert themselves in the more "virile" Mexican nationalist and populist arena. Their painful contradictions have been examined by Octavio Paz: they rejected the official line but joined the diplomatic corps; they depended on governmental support but did not extol Mexican nationalism. It is to this group that we owe two of the most important books produced in Spanish American modern poetry: José Gorostiza's long poem *Muerte sin fin* [*Death without End*] and Xavier Villaurrutia's collection *Nostalgia de la muerte*.

In the first book published by José Gorostiza (1901–1973), *Canciones para cantar en las barcas*, the poet discovers the classical Spanish tradition in the use of the "romancillos," where a melodious, chiseled line creates an intellectual poetry that masks itself as popular, simple verse. Gorostiza's preoccupations with form in this first book of poems will lead to his *Muerte sin fin*, perhaps one of the more philosophically complex poems in the Spanish language. Divided into ten unnumbered sections, the poem examines the relationship between form and substance within the context of creation and destruction. Gorostiza tries to capture an essence of objects that can only be apprehended by their sudden immobility in space and time, and postulates that precisely what allows us to intellectually grasp an object is also what condemns it to a "death without end." An eminently phenomenological poem, *Muerte sin fin* belongs to the tradition of Valéry and Mallarmé, of a poetry constructed on the negation of poetry.

Gorostiza's language of philosophical meditation is rigorous – abstraction is a function of the economy of means. Compared to *Altazor*, *Muerte sin fin* is an exercise in form: its carefully measured sentences glide through the page, in blank verses whose subject is lost and recaptured. The differences between *Altazor* and Gorostiza's poem are worth recalling, since they illustrate two different moments of Spanish American modernity. If Huidobro questions and asserts the power of signifiers, Gorostiza concentrates on the signified; whereas Huidobro uses the language of romantic passion, Gorostiza offers us a cool phenomenology. His is a language of philosophical reflection that does not proceed by accumulating metaphor upon metaphor, but by the patient deconstruction of a central image, that of a glass and of the water it contains. The models and echoes of *Muerte sin fin* can be seen in Sor Juana Inés de la Cruz's *Primero sueño* and in Octavio Paz's *Piedra de sol* [*Sunstone*].

Xavier Villaurrutia (1903–1950) divides the second and definitive edition of *Nostalgia de la muerte* into three sections, composed of previously published poems: "Nocturnos," "Otros nocturnos," and "Nostalgias." From its opening epigraph by Michael Drayton, "Burned in a sea of ice, and drowned amidst a fire," Villaurrutia declares his preference for paradox. These nostalgias of death are eminently poems of a desire that is as fleeting and evanescent as Gorostiza's apprehension of things. Villaurrutia is above all a poet of an erotic passion that can be seen in the metaphysical paintings of Giorgio de Chirico and read in Cocteau. They are poems where the obsession with beauty underscores the loneliness that is expressed by the poetic voice. As a poet of desire, what is important in Villaurrutia's poetry is the encounter with a beauty that is not abstract, but whose very corporeality reminds the poet of an unfallen self. Villaurrutia will lapse into wordplay in order to glide the signifiers and their permutations on the page. To the visual aesthetics of the earlier Avant-Garde, Villaurrutia adds a poetics of sound. One of the book's best poems, "Nocturno en que nada se oye," reproduces the voice of nothingness – a voice that Villaurrutia perceives as it is falling between two mirrors. Nothing is heard and nothingness itself is heard. Villaurrutia's fires are muted, intellectual burnings of the flesh that fear the immobility of ice, a prison made of water that is also Breton's nightmare. Cold, water, fire, and thirst are the key elements in Villaurrutia's poetics, where one can notice the presence of Rilke and Novalis. For Villaurrutia, death is the before and after of this interlude of life.

In the Caribbean, what was to become Afro-Antillean or Afro-Caribbean poetry originated out of a similar context of late *Modernismo* and soul-searching lyricism that can be seen in the *Contemporáneos*. Luis Palés Matos (1898–1959), who in 1925 published his poem "Pueblo negro," was until then a *Post-modernista* who had come into contact with the Puerto Rican versions of the Avant-Garde. In Cuba, José Zacarías Tallet, who had written his poem "La rumba" in 1928, and Amadeo Roldán, who penned his *Obertura sobre temas cubanos* and *Ballet negro* in that same year, created an atmosphere that was already mediated by the cultural appropriation of "primitive" art by the European Avant-Garde. One should recall that in the US, Langston Hughes wrote his *Weary Blues* in 1927, and in France the Surrealists' search for non-Occidental ways of thinking had found in African art a purity of expression that did not participate in the constraints of Western rationality. A space had been opened for what was at first a playful depiction of ordinary life, one that erupted first by means of the *jitanjáforas*, a term coined by Alfonso Reyes in 1929 from one of Mariano Brull's *Poemas en menguante* (1928). For Brull, who had traveled to France in 1926 and had come into contact with the Spanish Generation of 1927 and Juan Ramón Jiménez's "poesía pura," the *jitanjáforas* enabled the poet to write in a language that was "originary" in the widest possible sense.

Brull's association with *poesía pura*, as well as his writing of poems with Afro-Cuban motifs deserve to be underscored, particularly because both, *poesía pura* and Afro-Cubanism, are transitional poetic inquiries that foreshadow the poetry of the late 1930s and early 1940s. Brull's *Poemas en menguante* and Emilio Ballagas's *Júbilo y fuga* (1931) and *Cuaderno de poesía negra* (1934) belong to the same context as that of the *Revista de Avance*, which finished its publication in 1930. In retrospect, it might be hard to see the links between the practice of Afro-Cuban poetry and the more intimate amorous lyric produced by these poets, except by stating that the modality of "African" verse was seen by Ballagas and Brull as a linguistic exercise, a way of integrating themselves into an Avant-Garde that their other poetry had forsaken. If the "purity of poetry" that was searched for by Valéry and Juan Ramón Jiménez wanted to strip poetry of extraneous elements in order to capture the evanescent fugacity of an ahistorical poetic essence, Brull's first experimentations in Afro-Cuban verse obey a similar impulse, noticed by Alfonso Reyes in the *jitanjáfora*. According to Reyes, *jitanjáforas* wanted to return words to their "purely linguistic value" because this origin had been lost, "as he who loses the fluid sensation of water after stepping too much on blocks of ice" (*La experiencia literaria*, 190). Reyes saw the liberating potential of these words within a poetry consumed by philosophical speculation, and his reference to "ice," which seems to echo Neruda's critique of Jiménez, attests to the fact that "poesía negra" was to free the poet from the aesthetic distances imposed by Jiménez. It is important to state that the modality as it was practiced in particular by Ballagas and Brull, and later collected by Ramón Guirao in his *Orbita de la poesía afrocubana* (1939), has been seen by critics as emphasizing the exotic aspect of African-

American culture without truly understanding its internal mechanisms (Smart, *Nicolás Guillén: Popular Poet of the Caribbean*).

Afro-Caribbean poetry erupts on the literary scene on April 30, 1930, when the *Diario de la Marina* in Havana publishes eight short poems by Nicolás Guillén (1902–1989) entitled *Motivos de son*. Guillén took this creative leap after reading Langston Hughes's poetry and meeting him in Havana in January, 1930. Guillén's eight "Motivos" are short sketches in which characters speak in the first person with a Spanish "deformed" by the particular manner of black Cuban speech. Guillén writes the poems in order to faithfully reproduce the tone and rhythm of daily speech. His eight voices appear without mediation or contextual setting on the page. No scene is described: these are actually performances that use the black rhythmic idioms of the *son* in order to expand the parameters of what was socially accepted conventional representation. There is no formal syllabic construction in the line of verse, nor is there an obvious preoccupation with rhyme. Guillén prefers to construct according to the laws of rhythm based on repetition. The unfettered sensuality of language and tone in *Motivos de son* strike the reader immediately. Nothing happens in these poems except their own happening. The situations presented here are sharp-edged observations of black life.

From the incidental and anecdotal representations of black Cuban life, Guillén moves in *Sóngoro cosongo* to exploring the implications of his revolution in poetic language. He does away with trying to depict the "talk" of black Cubans, but focuses instead on the rhythmic values of the word. These are the *jitanjáforas*, as codified by Alfonso Reyes: words whose only value consists in the rhythmic aura they possess. In *West Indies, Ltd*. Guillén expands his setting and explores the Caribbean as a region defined by a common history that included slavery and economic and commercial exploitation. This is the book that best represents Guillén's pivotal switch to a poetry that explicitly rejects the imperialist actions of the colonial powers in the Caribbean. His later books continued in this line, as in *Cantos para soldados y sones para turistas*, and *La paloma del vuelo popular*. After the triumph of the Cuban Revolution in 1959, Guillén became a national symbol, and his poetry dealt with the concrete historical situations of revolutionary society.

This post-revolutionary period in Guillén's poetry has been superficially read by critics mainly for its political commitment to the Revolution. Guillén's innovative experimentation with form and poetic language had come to an end in the radical shift of the cultural climate of the later 1930s. As in Neruda, poetry for Guillén becomes a project, a working tool of the poet, one that expresses the political circumstance as registered by an individual subject. Guillén's *persona*, however, is not the solemn witness of history that defines Neruda. Guillén is a trickster, a playful man-about-town portrayed in *Tengo*. The distance between him and Neruda may be seen in Guillén's exploration of history in *El diario que a diario* [*The Daily Daily*] (1972), a collection of poems and papers from the history of Cuba, assembled by a writer who engages in bibliographical games with the reader. Guillén does not assume the voice of Whitman, his "voice" lies in the selection of materials of which his book is composed. It may be seen as part of a wider historiographical project that also appears in Roque Dalton's *Historias prohibidas de Pulgarcito* – texts that mix genres and that play with our notions of history. It is important to state and underscore the importance of late projects such as *The Daily Daily*, because Guillén has been classified only within the confines of Afro-Caribbean poetry. It is Afro-Caribbean poetry, on the contrary, that liberates Guillén into the wider sociopolitical context, one that was not necessarily pursued by other members of Guillén's generation who wrote in the same modality.

The more national Afro-Cuban motif is transformed into the longing for a wider sense of identity in the Puerto Rican Luis Palés Matos's *Tun tún de pasa y grifería*, which opens with "Preludio en Boricua," an invitation to a pan-Caribbean dance. The familiar themes are all here: poems that emphasize rhythm while speaking of sugar cane exploitation, tourists searching for the exotic, and in the center of the tableau the suffering and exploited black man of the Antilles. The emphasis on thematics in this poetry may not underscore strongly enough the fact that both Guillén and Palés excel in variations of classical forms. Palés can create a line of perfect hendecasyllables, but these are accented in the last syllable (in effect, making them dodecasyllabic according to the rules of Spanish syllabic versification) and the beat produces a rhythm unseen since Darío's most daring experiments. Palés's rhythmic experimentation is also accompanied by a strong sense of the social and economic poverty of the Puerto Rican milieu. In "Pueblo" and in "Topografía" Palés assumes the poetic voice of quiet desperation. The trickster-poet, inviting the reader to an Antillean carnival, uncovers its underlying sadness. We can read Palés in these poems prefiguring Lezama Lima's notion of "lejanía," or distance, as one of the major artistic themes of literature produced in islands. Palés dreams of a distant and original place from which the Caribbean self is in exile. In his best poems, he forces us to revisit his work as a desire for that plenitude found somewhere else.

It is impossible not to see the change in aesthetics that will occur around the 1940s without taking Surrealism into account, with its emphasis on both personal and social liberation. Although the other avant-garde movements instigated political action within the realm of the social by imposing their aesthetics as a means to combat stagnant social mores,

Surrealism was the movement that proposed a participation in the political order joined to an aesthetics of liberation. In a sense, most of the poets that have been discussed in this section show traces of a contact with Surrealism, if not in style at least in themes. This is not only the case with Pablo Neruda (whose poetry was nevertheless rejected by the Chilean surrealist group *Mandrágora*), but also with the poets of *Contemporáneos*, who prepared the way for the continuing presence of Surrealism in Mexico after 1950, and with poets like Ballagas, Brull, and Guillén, who did the same for the generation grouped around *Orígenes* in the 1940s.

The relationships between Surrealism and Spanish America are multifaceted and complex – a system of echoes that are more nuanced than can be seen at first glance. The situation in Cuba and in Mexico is exemplary. It is in Havana in 1928 that Alejo Carpentier publishes "En la extrema avanzada. Algunas actitudes del Surrealismo" as a critique of the previous Avant-Garde and a statement of adhesion to the idealist values of Surrealism. The French poet Robert Desnos visited Havana in 1928 and there he met Carpentier and the novelist Miguel Angel Asturias. However, not only did Surrealism not produce a unified movement in Cuba; but, as it appears from the poetry of the generation of Ballagas and Brull, it cannot be found either in their style or in their actions on the cultural scene. In Ballagas it was perhaps the stronger influence of the Catholic church and his feeling of condemnation because of his homosexuality that prevented the poet from adopting a truly liberatory stance. A similar situation to that of Cuba might be seen in Mexico. Although Mexico was the preferred point of entry into America for many European Surrealists (André Breton, Antonin Artaud, Benjamin Péret), its influence can be felt at this time mainly in the visual arts, and not in literature – Mexican surrealist poetry starts only with the generation of Octavio Paz, after 1950.

The unlikely start of a surrealist movement in Spanish America was Argentina, where it appears in the work of Aldo Pellegrini and his journal *Qué (Revista de Interrogantes)* (1928–1930). Even here, there was no continued action upon the literary scene – the avant-garde group of the journal *Martin Fierro*, for example, was indifferent to the new credo propagated by Breton. Chile was the only country with what might be called a proper surrealist movement, although this occurred rather late (1941). Its poets were Braulio Arenas, Enrique Gómez Correa, and Jorge Cáceres. In Peru, José Carlos Mariátegui saw the establishment of the surrealist group with hope and promise, while at the same time he attacked Marinetti and Italian Futurists, who at this point had already allied themselves with Italian Fascism. Vallejo, as we have seen, completely rejected Surrealism.

The Peruvian César Moro (1903–1956) was one of the only poets who totally allied himself with Surrealism. Moro's poems anticipate the erotic vein that is explored later in the work of Octavio Paz, although stylistically their texts are different from each other. Moro's poetry is reiterative, and it proceeds by an accumulation of elements chained to each other in line after line of verse. From within the erotic setting, the poem calls attention to its own surface and texture in a voluptuous sequence of images. It is a poetry of nouns, of gestures that appear in a linguistic chiaroscuro. Moro is a voyeur, and the fleeting images that he sees appear blurred to the eyes of the reader, as in the paintings of the Chilean Surrealist Matta. This may be glimpsed by one of his lines from "Oh furor el alba se desprende de tus labios," one of the poems from *La tortuga ecuestre*: "Yo pertenezco a la sombra y envuelto en sombra yazgo sobre un lecho de lumbre" ["I belong to the shadow and wrapped in shadow I lie over a bed of fire"].

The shadows and smoke that seem to permeate Moro's poetry extend also to a deliberate distance that he sought vis-à-vis the Spanish American tradition. Most of his poetry was written in French, and he published during his life only three books of poems, *Le château de grisou*, *Lettre d'amour*, and *Trafalgar Square*. Although his first poems appeared in 1928 in *Amauta*, he lived in Paris from 1925 to 1934 (roughly contemporaneous to Vallejo), returned to Lima in that year, and in 1938 went to live in Mexico. Here he composed in Spanish some of his best poems. These were published posthumously under the title *La tortuga ecuestre y otros poemas 1924–1949*. We might link Moro's choice of language to his homosexuality and to a desire to express himself openly in a different linguistic code. Yet Moro is still a very reticent poet in French, whereas some of his poems in Spanish explore an eroticism far beyond that which can be seen in Villaurrutia or Salvador Novo.

Moro's influence can be felt in another Peruvian poet, Emilio Adolfo Westphalen (b. 1911). In an autobiographical text of 1974 entitled "Poetas en la Lima de los años treinta" and collected in *Otra imagen deleznable...* – a compendium of his poetry – Westphalen cites the reading of Eguren and of Vallejo's *Trilce* as decisive for the aesthetics of his first poetry, collected in *Las ínsulas extrañas*. Through contact with the poets Martín Adán and Xavier Abril, Westphalen reads at that time Joyce's *Work in Progress*, fragments from Tzara's *L'Homme Aproximatif*, and *Hebdomeros* by Giorgio de Chirico. Later, Westphalen met Carlos Oquendo, Juan Larrea, and Gilberto Owen, and published his second book, *Abolición de la muerte*. These two books and *Belleza de una espada clavada en la lengua*, a third compilation of poems written between 1930 and 1972, but only published within *Otra imagen deleznable*, comprise all of Westphalen's poetic output. Using language as an instrument capable of expressing its own silence, Westphalen explains:

El silencio se pinta una extraña figura
Medita en el destino de una línea para arriba.
(Otra imagen deleznable, 19)

[Silence paints for itself a strange figure
It meditates in the destiny of a line moving upwards.]

Westphalen's poems owe much to Chirico's empty city landscapes. His is a poetry of objects placed discretely on the line; his repetitions mainly fragmentary visions that stand on their own – passionate within their own separation.

The influence of Surrealism may also be felt in the Uruguayan poet Sara de Ibáñez (b. 1910), generally included as a member of the pre-Spanish Civil War generation, although her first book of poems, *Canto*, was published with a prologue by Pablo Neruda, who is generally credited with having "discovered" her. Ibáñez's poetry is more in line with that written by the Cuban group *Orígenes*. Hers is an original combination of Spanish Golden Age *Culteranismo* and Surrealism, a hermetic poetry with classical undertones in its penchant for a well-turned line of verse. Ibáñez's sonnets in *Canto* remind us of Lezama's search for an insular, i.e., Cuban, teleology. These are poems whose constant image is that of light: objects illuminated by a controlled nightmarish vision where passion and discipline are joined.

Languages of poetry

The change in poetic language that critics place around the beginning of the 1940s is the result of a new generation of poets born between 1910 and 1923. These are poets like José Lezama Lima (Cuba, 1910–1976), Pablo Antonio Cuadra (Nicaragua, b. 1912), Octavio Paz (Mexico, 1914), Nicanor Parra (Chile, b. 1914), and Cintio Vitier (Cuba, b. 1921). The work of the poets of this younger generation overlaps with that of older poets like Neruda and Guillén, who at this point change their poetic style and aesthetics to modes that they will continue until the 1970s. The aesthetics of this period range from the hermeticism of Lezama Lima to the colloquialisms of Nicanor Parra, from the Nicaraguan scenes of Pablo Antonio Cuadra to the metaphysical and "simple" language of Vitier. The language of these poets is progressively nearer to "colloquial" language. Because at first it seems impossible to characterize this group, criticism underscored its heterogeneity. Lacking the sense of violent rupture of the first Avant-Garde, this generation was marked at different points and in different ways by their search for history, poetic language, and national expression. Some, like Cuadra, delineate the basic themes of their poetry early on. Others, like Octavio Paz and Nicanor Parra, change their poetics over time.

The poets of 1940 reassess the tradition of *Modernismo* and the Avant-Garde, they construct a new literary mythology as to poetic origins. The political atmosphere of the times forced Spanish Americans to return home from the developing European conflicts that led to the Second World War, and to re-examine their tradition. For established poets at this time, their precursors were the *Modernistas*; for the younger poets, their sense of tradition truly starts with the Avant-Garde, a more cosmopolitan and violent reaction that also spoke the language of poets who lived in what were now the burgeoning cities in Spanish America – cities that were undergoing a publishing boom, with the creation of major editorial houses with a market for poetry. The best example of a change in poetic aesthetics can be seen in anthologies published at this time. Because *Laurel* is the most comprehensive and ambitious of these it is the one we should examine.

Anthologies mask a change in poetic sensibility; they give account of a process. *Laurel* was precisely representative of its time: it unites both sides of the Atlantic in a common poetic tradition, that was highlighted by the emigration of prominent Spanish poets and intellectuals to the Americas after the Spanish Civil War. Although *Laurel* was compiled by a Spanish–American team of Xavier Villaurrutia, José Bergamin, Octavio Paz, and Juan Gil Albert, Paz has recently stated in an afterword that the criteria for inclusion and the aesthetic narrative contained within the anthology were chiefly Villaurrutia's. The history of the exclusions and inclusions (including Neruda's and León Felipe's refusal to participate in the anthology) has been ably rendered by Paz, who was not only a witness of the time but also a member of the younger generation that was excluded, at the last minute, from the anthology.

The different sections of *Laurel* illustrate how poets who were already established in 1940 understood their own tradition. The historical roots of these poets had their point of origin in the *Post-modernismo* of Ramón López Velarde, followed by the various currents of the Avant-Garde, and concluding with the later currents of *poesía pura* as inherited by Spanish American poets from Juan Ramón Jiménez. This change in literary inheritance underscores another that is present not so much in the manner of writing as in the themes and projects that seduce these poets. The poets included in *Laurel* are concerned with the expression of their interior selves in relation to the world. The poets after *Laurel* will be preoccupied with particular acts of poetry within a changing sociopolitical context.

If change is signaled with transparent clarity in *Laurel*, it was already evident in Cuba, where Juan Ramón Jiménez had defined and chronologically framed an aesthetics by creating an anthology of the most important Cuban poets of the time. The generation grouped around the *Revista de Avance* had published its most important books of poetry by 1937: Mariano Brull's *Poemas en menguante* (1928), Emilio Ballagas's *Júbilo y fuga* (1931), Eugenio Florit's *Doble acento* (1937), and Nicolás Guillén's *Cantos para soldados y sones para turistas*. According to Cintio Vitier's recounting of the period in his introduction to the *Obras completas* of José Lezama Lima, Cuban poetry at the time fell into three fundamental categories: *poesía pura*, Afro-Cuban poetry, and poetry of social commitment ("pura, negra y social"), with the latter two fundamentally conflated. In *Lo cubano en la poesía*, a series of lectures Vitier offered at the Lyceum in Havana from October 9 to December 13, 1957 and published in book form in 1958, he devotes a whole chapter to that moment of Cuban poetry. The title of this chapter underscores the importance Vitier attaches to this revisionary generation: "Heightening of Creative Ambition. The Poetry of José Lezama Lima and the Attempt at an Insular Teleology." Even from the distance of almost twenty years, it is evident that what was at stake for this generation was a complete rewriting of the Cuban tradition. *Lo cubano en la poesía* is precisely the account of that teleological revision of Cuban poetry, one that goes back in history in order to discover the essential elements of a Cuban sensibility that was truly defined from 1940 on. In the same way that Paz classifies Villaurrutia's historical narrative of poetry in *Laurel* as the product of the search for precursors by a particular generation, Vitier's book is the testimony of a profound rewriting of Cuban letters. From the philological point of view, 1940 is the point of origin of such a narrative. Little justice can be done here to such a fundamentally pivotal book as *Lo cubano en la poesía*, but we can examine what poets at the time saw in their precursors by reading Vitier's testimony.

Vitier portrays the generation that immediately preceded him (Brull, Florit, and Ballagas) as living within strictly personal and closed spheres, stating that their poetry was confining and that it lacked a sense of impulse. For Vitier, it was fundamentally an epigonic poetry that imitated or drew sustenance from that of Lorca, Alberti, Jorge Guillén, Salinas, Cernuda, and Aleixandre in Spain. The only poet who for Vitier was still relevant for the new generations was Juan Ramón Jiménez, and this is why Vitier dates the beginning of a new poetic discourse to Lezama Lima's *Muerte de Narciso* and his *Coloquio con Juan Ramón Jiménez*. In the former work, Lezama writes an authentic *tour de force*: a long, complex poem that is ambitious and monumental in scope. Lezama's poem is like an object in itself, not a mere representation in language of feelings and ideas, a work of art painstakingly elaborated with a dense rhetorical language that constantly surprises and baffles readers. Lezama's metaphors are conveyed in a language that is highly ornamental and elaborate: it is an attempt to go beyond the historical, to a mythical time of origination. In *Coloquio*, Lezama engages in a fictive dialogue with the Spanish master, and argues for the particular sensibility of the insular condition, one that is inherited from Joyce and Frobenius. It is from this point on that Lezama launches a critique of Cuban culture that amounts to a final death knell for the issues of cosmopolitanism versus nationalism.

How important Lezama's aesthetics were for the new generations of poets can be gauged by Vitier's statement that Lezama reacted to the frustrations of the immediate Cuban situation by submerging himself in the arcane world of culture. Lezama's remoteness is evident in the impressive erudition of his first collection, *Enemigo rumor*. Garcilaso, Góngora, Quevedo, San Juan de la Cruz, Lautreamont, Surrealism, Valéry, Claudel, and Rilke are all part of Lezama's range of allusion. According to Vitier, the title illustrates Lezama's definition of poetry: it is a center that devours, that incarnates as an enemy, but that as an enemy, is able to enter into a communicative act with the poet. This metaphysical definition of poetry separates Lezama from the cultural projects of the 1940s. It is a distance felt more acutely if we compare this poetry to the emerging project of Neruda's *Canto general*, where the poet immersed himself in Western cultural references in order to search for the origins of Spanish America by rejecting the European framework. Lezama, in direct opposition to Neruda, mobilized culture in free verse, in Alexandrine sonnets, in quotations from Rilke and St. Teresa, and in historical scenes like "San Juan de Patmos ante la puerta latina" and "Ordenanza del Marqués de Acapulco." These poems are interspersed with Cuban scenes, in an attempt to capture the essence of a sensibility without concern for its external elements. Lezama, in other words, is not a poet of ecfrasis, that is to say, his poetry does not address an object, but rather tries to incorporate it. As Vitier states in his commentary on "Noche insular: jardines invisibles," Lezama wants to incorporate the essence of night, and not the night as topically rendered. In "El arco invisible de Viñales" from *La fijeza*, Lezama not only writes about what he sees but about how to see:

> Sus ojos, como un canario que se introduce,
> atraviesan la pasta de los olores, remeros del sueño
> . . .
> allí donde la luna entreabre el valle y cierra el portal.
>
> (*La fijeza*, 122–3)
>
> [Their eyes, like a canary that breaks in
> cut across the paste of smells, rowers of dreams
> . . .
> there, where the moon half-opens the valley and closes the porch.]

In "Pensamientos en La Habana," also from *La fijeza*, Lezama addresses the issue of culture in the Americas, in a manner that would reappear in the essays of *La expresión americana* (1957). Lezama not only ends the stanzas of his poem with quotes from Eliot or Mallarmé but argues precisely for a global American expression based on the situation of the poet:

Si no miramos la vitrina, charlan
de nuestra insuficiente desnudez que no vale una estatuilla de Nápoles.
Si la atravesamos y no rompemos los cristales,
no subrayan con gracia que nuestro hastío puede quebrar el fuego
y nos hablan del modelo viviente y de la parábola del quebrantahuesos.
Ellos que cargan con sus maniquíes a todos los puertos . . .
Ellos no quieren saber que trepamos por las raíces húmedas del helecho.

(*La fijeza* 37–8)

[If we don't look at the storefront, they speak
of our insufficient nakedness, not worth a Neapolitan statuette.
If we cross it and do not shatter the glass
they do not underline with grace that our weariness may crack the fire
and they talk to us about the living models and the parabolas of the
lammergeier.
They, who carry their dummies to all ports
. . . They do not want to know that we climb the humid roots of the
fern.]

By means of this dense allegorical poetry Lezama continually surprises his readers. He presents the American poet looking into a kind of window of culture, debating whether to look or not. For Lezama, if American poets do not look, others will talk about their "nakedness." Yet, if poets traverse that transparent space symbolized by the glass of the storefront, where time and place are rendered meaningless, none remark how they can break through the threatening fires of living models. The problem is condensed by Lezama with purposely allusive and obtuse metaphors, since the American poet bites into the "other's" style (meaning the poets of Europe) by surreptitiously climbing "the humid roots of a fern." The poem resembles the project of Eliot's "The Love Song of J. Alfred Prufrock," from which Lezama quotes a number of lines. It is the statement of the poet in relation to his context, and proposes a model for the American poet's exchange with European culture.

If the thoughts and works of this naked American poet that Lezama reveals in "Pensamientos en La Habana" do not have the cultural weight of a Neapolitan statuette, Lezama will create out of the insular condition a point of origin for an imaginary time. His universe is populated by cultural objects apprehended by taking into account all of the objects' cultural associations. Lezama's universe is private and unique paradoxically because of the cultural ground on which it exists, and because of the associations that it evokes. The fabric of Lezama's poems is made up of symbols that, through constant naming and repetition by the poet acquire the consistency of referents that belong to a poetic system of the author's devising. Lezama is a poet of hidden codes, hermetic in a more conventional way than Neruda.

Lezama transmitted his appeal to members of his generation in the vastly important *Orígenes* (1944–1956), a journal where abstract poetics, lyricism, and philosophical speculation meet. Among the contributors to the journal were Cintio Vitier, Fina García Marruz, Eliseo Diego, Lorenzo García Vega, Virgilio Piñera, and Alejo Carpentier. Translations of T. S. Eliot, St. John Perse, and Wallace Stevens appeared next to essays that debated or posited the creation of a national Cuban culture from without the realm of the strictly political circumstance. Although in a number of editorials Lezama did refer to a progressive sense of the disintegration of Cuban life, the journal refused to enter into the polemical situation of insular politics. Instead, Lezama articulated an idea of nationality as a metaphysical construction. This is why *Orígenes* did not emphasize the idea of literary generations and claimed to be a space that was liberated from the chronological dependencies of the generational continuum. Two generations of Cuban poets and artists are represented in *Orígenes*.

The project of *Orígenes* seems to have appeared full-grown, with little if any variations over time, like Lezama's poetry itself. In the *Coloquio con Juan Ramón Jiménez*, Lezama has the Spanish poet state the two dangers of poetry at the time as that of the "escritura informe" versus a "renewed Neoclassicism." These being he two antagonistic poles of writing that Lezama and Vitier faced, they opted for a middle ground. Lezama tempered his Surrealism with a classical bent, while at the same time he developed a long poetic line that is precisely un-musical, guided by a particular a-rhythmia by virtue of its accumulation of words and images. At the same time, Lezama never abandoned the traditional meters of the sonnet, or the *romance*. As Juan Ramón Jiménez says, via Lezama, in the *Coloquio*, the important poetic forms of the time are the *romance*, the "canción," and free verse, all these giving an impression of plenitude, but rendered in a precise language (*Obras completas*, II:63). Although in his use of traditional meters Lezama followed the example of Jiménez and, particularly in his last book of poems, *Fragmentos a su imán*, offered the readers delightful baroque *décimas*, his poetry is characterized by its twisted syntax and unexpected turns of phrase; by the primacy of a metaphor that doubles or triples signifiers to an elusive signified. The influence of this poetry in the wider Spanish American literary scene would not be felt until after the 1960s, particularly with the publication of Lezama's *Paradiso* (1966), a major Spanish American novel of which various chapters had appeared in *Orígenes*. It was then that Lezama was recognized throughout the Spanish-speaking world as a major figure who had, over the course of three decades, developed a unique aesthetics in his poetry and devised a poetic system that rewrote the major issues of American cultural expression.

Although *Orígenes* was Lezama's creation, the poets who collaborated in it did not necessarily follow Lezama's style, nor his complex allusive system. Vitier's poetry was still closer to Jiménez's in the 1930s, and it is only in his second book, *Sedienta cita* (1943), and his third, *Extrañeza de estar* (1945), that we can see the presence of Lezama's style and aesthetics, particularly the themes of distance and nostalgia – hence his references in *De mi provincia* to vaguely mythological echoes of sphinx and king inscribed under the wider mythos of insularity. Some of Vitier's and Lezama's experiments in form occur at similar times – for example, Lezama's exploration of the prose poem in *Aventuras sigilosas* and, more consistently, in *La fijeza*, and Vitier's *Capricho y homenaje* (1946).

Although most of the *Orígenes* poets stayed in Cuba after the Revolution, their situation was drastically altered by the politics of the revolutionary government. Vitier in particular revised the social positions of Lezama and the journal, and responded to the repeated critiques on the ivory tower mentality of *Orígenes*. Vitier explains that their lack of commitment revealed a prescient political instinct, since *"none* of the options available at the time was linked to the real needs of the country" (*Obras completas*, I: xxvii – Vitier's emphasis). However, this is another Vitier speaking, trying to bridge the gap between two different visions of the relationship between poetry and society. The fact is that the poets of *Orígenes* assumed the Cuban condition in a different vein. Lezama's assertion of a poetics that began from an atemporal and ahistorical origin clashed with a different version of modernity as this was practiced by a poetry that after 1959, put its emphasis on the present, in all senses of the word. It might seem paradoxical that a group that wanted to defy the notion of generations felt the impact of a generational change after the Revolutionary years. In relation to the social commitment of the new poets who wrote after 1959, Vitier's idea of community in solitude jars with the poetical sensibility of the 1960s. In "Mundo," Vitier explains:

> El heroismo no es otra cosa que saber
> que la indecible soledad es la comunidad inmensa
> (Antología poética, 100)

> [Heroism is nothing else but to know
> that the unmentionable solitude is the immense community.]

Although the poets and writers of *Orígenes* initiated a revolution in

Cuban culture, theirs was not the vision of revolution nor of society that was at issue after 1959.

A different version of the project for a national poetry that arises from the political circumstances of the 1930s and 1940s can be seen in Nicaragua's Pablo Antonio Cuadra (b. 1912). Cuadra was one of the members of the Nicaraguan *Movimiento de Vanguardia* (1928–1934), which appeared later in Nicaragua than in other Spanish American countries, and was able to incorporate the more daring cosmopolitan experimentation of their precursors to a particular national context. That the Nicaraguan Avant-Garde manifested an early preoccupation with the national situation is undoubtedly due to the fact that it was active in a period of social and political unrest, contemporaneous to the United States' intervention and Sandino's revolutionary struggle. Cuadra's second book, *Poemas nicaragüenses 1930–1933*, illustrates this vanguardist moment by means of a poetry close to the earth and to common speech. As a reaction to his compatriot Rubén Darío's exquisite linguistic plays and exotic locales, Cuadra discovered the landscape and the people of his country. The national "spirit" that Cuadra evokes has been read by equating its emancipatory politics as directed toward that same common man to whom Sandino addressed himself. Cuadra's subsequent books, among them *El jaguar y la luna* [*The Jaguar & the Moon*] have always been firmly rooted in Nicaragua. It is a poetry that transcends the concrete political situation by framing the landscape and its inhabitants within a stylized humanistic understanding. Throughout, Cuadra does not only deal with the present: in *El jaguar y la luna* he rescues Amerindian legends, and in *Cantos de Cifar* [*Songs of Cifar and the Sweet Sea*] he writes of an ahistorical, epic present. From his first books to these latter collections, Cuadra moves from the more concrete Nicaraguan situation to a spiritual search for a syncretic myth that joins the Greco-Roman world with the Mesoamerican universe. In *Cifar*, Cuadra recounts the adventures of Cifar who, like a new Odysseus around the lakes of Nicaragua, encounters situations and characters that resonate with mythical allusions. This might be seen as the culmination of Cuadra's poetic journey, one that originates from an attempt to resolve the oppositions between the regional and the cosmopolitan and that ends with the fusion of the national and the universal, expressed by means of varied modes of expression: from the stylization of popular metric forms, to the long verse line with biblical resonances.

Cuadra's Catholic belief in salvation and redemption invites comparison to the work of Lezama and of other poets of *Orígenes*. In spite of their different styles, both poets proceed from deeply rooted religious convictions, which account for the absence of the sense of violent rupture that was more prevalent in the first Avant-Garde. We should also recall that Cuadra, like many of the Cuban poets, lived to see the national projects of the 1940s realized or reinterpreted in concrete movements of political struggle – in Cuba after 1959 and in Nicaragua after 1979. The position of both these poets within these revolutions, allow critics to examine the different re-writings of the national project from one generation to the next. Although Lezama remained silent in terms of the particular political situation – reverenced but at the same time internally ostracized by the system – Cuadra became an outspoken critic of the Sandinistas without ever leaving Nicaragua. As a critic-from-within, Cuadra's vision of Sandino clashed with the social and political methods of the revolutionary party. Allowing for a number of differences in the political context between 1959 and 1979, the critical space that separates them from the revolutions that they lived within is emblematic of the gap between the idea of culture as it was understood in the 1940s, and the Marxist revision of the 1960s. The difference in Lezama's and Cuadra's responses to the Cuban and Nicaraguan revolutions, the latter vocal while the former passive, belies their own difference from the generation that followed them.

Social concerns, nationalism, and American history can be seen in the poetry of Rosario Castellanos (1925–1974), together with a more ample vision that addresses the specific concerns of women in Spanish American society. Castellanos's poetry moves from nation as myth to that of nation as socially constructed space. In this sense, her poetry adds to the register not only of Gabriela Mistral, but also to that of national projects that were later to be rooted in more abstract ideology. Castellanos specifically attacks the social space of women within the sexist constraints of society by means of wry meditations on social habit and mores, as in "Valium 10" and "Kinsey Report." A poet of different modes, Castellanos is above all an observer and decoder. Her keen eye for detail and language illuminates not only social reality but the relationship between aesthetics and the present. In the Tuxtla Archaeological Museum, Castellanos's encounter with a work of art, entitled "El tejoncito maya," equates the pre-Columbian object with childhood, the Indian universe to an unspoiled, free Nature. The object belongs to the realm of innocence, and the poet asks for its return to the world of objects that a child uses:

> Cubriéndote la risa
> con la mano pequeña,
> saltando entre los siglos
> vienes, en gracia y piedra.

> Que caigan las paredes
> oscuras que te encierran,

que te den el regazo
de tu madre, la tierra;

en el aire, en el aire
un cascabel alegre
y una ronda de niños
con quien tu infancia juegue.

(Poesía no eres tú, 62)

[Covering your laugh
with a small hand,
jumping among the centuries
you come in grace and stone.

Let the dark
walls that confine you fall,
let them give you the lap
of your mother, the earth;

in air, in air,
a joyful bell
and a round of children
with whom your childhood can play.]

In this poem, the laughter of the first verse is also to be understood as a kind of impish malice, joined to the puckish "saltando" of the third line. What the poet asks for in terms of the object is not only its return to a world where the idea of object does not exist (here rendered as childhood) but also, and more importantly, the return of the object to the space of the game. Not only the object without the museum, but the object within the earth. Castellanos is not, however, a naive poet, she is aware of the self-defeating nature of her desire. The three stanzas of the poem are like three distinct moments. They begin in sequence with a certain discursive flow but end in strings of thoughts, with the "ronda" a repetition of that discursive flow of the beginning.

Castellanos's almost Rilkean act of recovery and desire is part of a more general poetics that seems to flow out of Neruda's poems in the 1930s. However, Castellanos does not work only in this mode. She is also a poet of social circumstance, and a keen observer of the social and sexual mores of society. If her early poetry has been characterized as more concerned with the lyrical self, after *Al pie de la letra*, she discovers new registers of liberation both from the models of her symbolist and surrealist precursors and from the "intimate" poetry that has been associated with Spanish American women poets. Yet Castellanos defies the male literary strictures and cultivates a distinctly unsentimental and ironic tone. By the time Castellanos writes her more important work in the 1950s, the language of Spanish American poets had undergone a major change. Lezama was the major exception to this trend. The poetry written in the late 1950s is as different from Lezama's as Lezama's was different from Girondo's.

The change toward a more colloquial language can be dated as far back as 1954, with the publication of the Chilean Nicanor Parra's *Poemas y antipoemas*. Parra begins another poetic cycle in Chilean and Spanish American poetry by deflating the poetics of his major precursors like Huidobro, Mistral, and Neruda with a sharp ironic stance, devoid of the romantic ego that his precursors inherited from Whitman. To read the other Chileans after reading Parra is to experience the power of the destructive turn that Parra makes explicit. In *Poemas y antipoemas* this is done by constructing the book as a kind of poetic narrative: its first section composed of romantic, and *post-modernista* verse, the second of what the poet has called expressionist poems, and the third, finally, of the "antipoemas" – deliberately colloquial and even "prosaic" texts that question the underlying categorizations of poetry. Parra's book illustrates a process of development where models invoked are at first imitated, then appear as a negative presence, from which he liberates himself and achieves his personal and original voice.

This move toward a more colloquial expression has been explained by Parra as a reaction against the "poesía canto" of Mistral and Neruda. Parra seeks to debunk metaphor and strip poems of those elements that make them poetic. What may appear as a simple act of poetic rebellion is actually an experience of a state of being, for Parra's poems do depend upon and refer directly to the precursors' tone and voice. Instead of eliminating verse altogether, Parra's uncanny procedure consists of presenting texts that retain their visual arrangement as poetry. The "anti" is essentially a rejection of content and style. By thus inscribing his poetry as a reaction, Parra is able to create a particular state of being: permanent in its opposition, at best it seeks to compile a totally different dictionary for poetic expression. In "Cambios de nombre," *Versos de salón* is inaugurated by a defiant gesture that recalls that of Huidobro, who defines Altazor as an "antipoet":

> Mi posición es ésta:
> El poeta no cumple su palabra
> Si no cambia los nombres de las cosas

> [My position is this:
> The poet does not stand by his word
> If he doesn't change the name of things]

Parra follows Huidobro's rebellion against poetic language, even if he would probably see Huidobro's procedure as an eminently poetic way of going about effecting a change in poetry. Both poets, nevertheless, inscribe themselves into their poetry – Huidobro by uniting his poems to his image and project as a Vanguardist, and Parra by the constant allusion to his image and self as "everyman." Yet whereas Huidobro's changes obey a particular development and even discourse, Parra's work has a truly dismembered form, as it appears in "Rompecabezas." He expresses his poetics by stating: "Yo digo una cosa por otra" ["I say one thing for another"] (*Poemas*, 1981: 83).

Parra's continuing poetic and antipoetic works, collected in *Obra gruesa*, have followed a similar line without much departure, except for the more lyrical *Canciones rusas*. It would be impossible not to state that Parra is also a poet of humor, and he reminds us that the universe as a whole might feel pleasure or pain, but only human beings are able to laugh. The charged nature of this statement accounts for Parra's eminent humanity, for his self-deprecative humor.

Parra's antipoetry of 1953 almost coincides in historical terms with one of Neruda's multiple changes in poetic form, as shown in *Odas elementales*, and his later *Estravagario*. This urge toward a general stripping down of poetry corresponds to a progressive critique in the search for what poetry is. In other words, if Neruda's *Residencia* seemed impure in 1935, it had become rhetorical in the 1950s.

Translations of history

Throughout the twentieth century, Spanish American poets have rejected the language of their precursors precisely because of the fact that it is *poetic* language. Parra's reaction to the rhetoric of Spanish American poetry is emblematic of the reaction that follows in the 1960s, where "literariness" itself is at issue. This antagonism against literariness is tied to the political commitment of poets like Ernesto Cardenal, Roque Dalton, Fayad Jamís, and Heberto Padilla. These poets are all united by their participation in the social arena. Ernesto Cardenal was Minister of Culture in Nicaragua during the Sandinista Government, Roque Dalton died while a clandestine guerrilla fighter, Heberto Padilla's poetry was published by Fidel Castro's revolutionary government, although the poet was eventually censored and ostracized.

This aesthetic change has been identified with the political turmoil of the 1960s, and is part of a general pattern throughout the United States, Europe, and Spanish America. If the political context is more present in Spanish American poets than in others, it is as a result of events close to home and ideologies that spoke to issues important to Spanish American intellectuals. These were the years of the triumph of the Cuban Revolution, and the promise of more social changes to come, in Bolivia, Chile, Argentina, Nicaragua, and El Salvador. Poets participated in the work of defining Spanish American culture by, in some cases, taking poetry to the streets, or speaking clearly and directly about the social problems at hand. In aesthetic terms, this politicization has to be seen within the context of the Spanish American poetic tradition since *Modernismo*, as exemplified in Rubén Darío's *Cantos de vida y esperanza*, where an explicitly critical vision of the United States is joined to the promises of a united continental ideal. Poets in the 1960s preferred this later version of Darío to the earlier poet of twilight and delirious fancy, even if they also emphasized their distance from Darío's more anachronistic appeals to the Hispanic "race."

While Spanish American poets revised *Modernismo*, the Cuban Revolution reawakened the interest in José Martí as the Revolutionary model of the poet within a political struggle. Martí's *Modernismo* was always Cuban and also Pan-Americanist, and of a much less fantastic nature than Darío's. These two models underscore the shift in Spanish Americans' visions of poetic tradition. The critical revision of *Modernismo* entailed the rejection of the "cosmopolitan" Avant-Garde and its linguistic games; the latter Vallejo was emphasized as the one who overcame the brief temptation of the language poetry of *Trilce*; the latter Neruda erased the more melancholic poet of *Residencia en la tierra*. In an attempt to make their poetry a more immediate object with revolutionary potential, the poets of the 1960s actually continue, in a different mode, the debate as to where poetry fits within the modern world. Since the Avant-Garde, poetry has tried to find a way in which to exist and reflect modernity: Huidobro and José Juan Tablanda made poems that resembled paintings, Girondo wrote poems that could blend with a ride in a city tram, and Borges mapped out the city of Buenos Aires for its citizens.

It would be a mistake to imply that the common aesthetics that unites poets like Cardenal, Dalton, and Heraud was only the desire to fight a revolutionary war or give voice to the dispossessed. Ernesto Cardenal, for example, intends a much more profound meditation on the position of the individual within historical change that borrows from models as disparate as Ezra Pound and Pablo Neruda. Cardenal reads classical poetry as it is filtered by Pound's urge to "make it new." He resurrects the epigram, writes in imitation of biblical psalms, rescues Central American myths, and writes a documentary historical epic, *El estrecho dudoso*. He may start a poem by imitating a classic stanza in rhythm and form, its words imitating sounds from each other, only to undo such classical imitation by naming a random collection of objects from everyday life with an abrupt act of closure that seems to belie the poem's desire for resurrection:

> Detrás del monasterio, junto al camino,
> existe un cementerio de cosas gastadas,
> en donde yacen el hierro sarroso, pedazos
> de loza, tubos quebrados, alambres retorcidos,
> cajetillas de cigarrillo vacías, aserrín

y zinc, plástico envejecido, llantas rotas,
esperando como nosotros la resurrección.

(Cobo Borda, *Antología de la poesía
hispanoamericana*, 324)

[Behind the monastery, next to the road,
there is a cemetery of worn out things,
where there lie corroded iron, pieces
of tile, broken tubes, twisted wires,
empty cigarette packs, sawdust
and zinc, aged plastic, broken tyres,
waiting as we are for the resurrection.]

What is interesting here is Cardenal's rendering of objects that are
emblems for contemporary industrial civilizations as a collection of the
detritus that is produced in the present. These are objects with a utilitarian
function – iron, tubes, wires – or at least that have served their function
(sawdust, broken tyres, aged plastic) but that live in a curious afterlife.
One feels that Cardenal wants these objects to become relics in a museum,
pieces of a destroyed civilization. It is in that sense that he speaks of a
resurrection – the object itself at this point inserted in the inexorable
march of time. We can compare this to Neruda's desire for an impure
poetry, but Cardenal names the objects without metaphorizing them.

The resurrection Cardenal longs for is the resurrection that is already
prefigured in his poem: the resurrection of the object as an image. This is
also prefigured by *Hora o*, where Cardenal speaks of the nights of
Managua by means of a series of linked ideogrammatic scenes of a
mysterious and alluring power. It is also present in a poignant statement in
"Managua 6:30 P.M.," where the poet contemplates the neon signs that
light up the streets of Managua's night. Neon lights, Venus, and the moon
are joined together in this short piece where even the red lights of the
automobiles are "mystical." Cardenal prepares us for the sudden out-
pouring of upper-case signs that imitate the neon signs that he sees. Off-
centered to the right of the page, readers can see in them a static
hieroglyphic of contemporaneity that can only be read by having access to
the codes of transnational capitalism. By the mystical atmosphere created
in the poem, signs become images, and these particular images are
syndecdoques of time, a violent present that is the very definition of
modernity. The particular distance of the observer surmounts the present.
Cardenal exclaims:

Y si he de dar un testimonio sobre mi época
es éste: Fue bárbara y primitiva
pero poética.

(*Nueva antología poética*, 68)

[And if I am to give witness of my age
it is this: It was barbaric and primitive
but poetic.]

What Cardenal implies or means here by poetic is similar to Walter Benjamin's visions of the creations of capitalism: an effect of deliberate and almost willful anachronism and even nostalgia that is reflected in the poem.

The fundamentally religious atmosphere that surrounds Cardenal's poetry would be hard to find in poets of the following generation, who came of age with the Cuban Revolution of 1959. Cardenal himself saw the Revolution with mystical fervor, and after the death of Che Guevara and a visit to Cuba, became totally involved in the defense of revolutionary governments from within a religious stance that links poets to the theology of political and social liberation. In contrast, the best poets of the revolutionary poetry of the 1960s, like Heberto Padilla and Roque Dalton, are less mystical and more ironic.

Heberto Padilla (b. 1932) was one of the first affected by the cultural politics of the Cuban Revolution. His book, *Fuera del juego*, was mired in controversy from the moment of its publication. *Fuera del juego* was awarded a prize in a poetry contest sponsored by the Cuban Artists and Writers Union (UNEAC) in 1968. The organization expressed total disapproval of the judges' decision and published the book with a prefatory note that declared the work "ideologically contrary to the Revolution." Padilla was later forced into an act of self-recrimination and a confession of ideological sins, which created a definitive schism within the Revolution itself and with intellectuals it had courted previously, who wrote public letters on Padilla's behalf. Castro's reply came in a speech on April 30, 1971, to the First National Congress of Education and Culture in Havana, with a more nationalistic line and a rejection of the intellectuals' appeal.

What the judges had found noteworthy in *Fuera del juego* was precisely the fact that it was not apologetic but critical, and that it accurately expressed the dilemmas of poets and poetry within a revolutionary context of rapid social change. Padilla does not write about history as a system of signs or cultural objects. His distance from Lezama can be felt in the fact that Padilla assumes history as power, and his book deals precisely with poetry speaking to, and of, this power, with a language as perversely direct as a weapon. The game referred to in its title is one whose rules are never controlled by poets themselves. This is why Padilla sets the rules for his own in a direct, concise appeal, emanating from a generation that established itself from within the Revolution. Here one can find corrosive acts of self-violence perpetuated by power. In "Homenaje a Huidobro," included in *Fuera del juego*, Padilla debunks Huidobro's utopian project. For Padilla, poets do not need to have the rose flowering in the verse, as Huidobro desired, but just leave it in the garden. It is the sarcastic humor in which this is conveyed that eloquently upholds the scope of Huidobro's utopian project precisely as illusion. Padilla not only criticizes the delusion of poets; his violence is born out of what he feels is the impossibility of his having that delusion himself.

Roque Dalton (1935–1975) was committed to the desire for a socially and politically just order, both in Latin America and in his native El Salvador, and his life coincides with a moment of cultural optimism and struggle. The critical assessment of his poetry has been marked by his life. As a result of his being assassinated by a fringe faction of the left during his involvement as a clandestine guerrilla fighter, Dalton's poetry is only framed according to a political situation. However, what is interesting in Dalton is not only this life in action, but its reflection on paper. Even while he insisted on our reading his poems in the light of his revolutionary commitment, and did not argue for an illusory separation of poetry from the poet – or even of the poet from social circumstance – this monological reading has closed other, more suggestive angles on his poetry. In *La taberna y otros lugares*, Dalton experiments with the typographical rearrangement of verse that he takes from the Brazilian concrete poets in order to give an account of the situation in Prague before the invasion of Soviet troops in 1968. The poem's message is against the atmosphere of pessimistic nihilism that the poet has found in Czech youth, but it is conveyed in a manner that incorporates the form used by Cardenal in *Hora o* and that Dalton also traces to the influence of Ezra Pound.

Some of Dalton's more suggestive voices are found in poetry written during his years as a clandestine poet, collected in *Poemas clandestinos*. For Dalton uses here a procedure not unlike that of Fernando Pessoa's heteronyms, inventing "other" poets that write his poetry. Vilma Flores, Timoteo Lúe, Jorge Cruz, Juan Zapata, and Luis Luna are more than pseudonyms for Dalton. Their poetry is distinguished by tone and theme, and appears with a biography of the authors supplied by Dalton himself. Their mode of writing is a reflection of their social position, with the predominant and best mode of Dalton's the satiric. Luis Luna, for example, had studied architecture and psychology, and had just completed an essay on the narrative of the Latin American *Boom* before writing the poems of his collection, "Poemas para vivir pensándolo bien." Dalton's poems are the most radical example of a total compromise between literature and politics. Because of their status as eminently political poems they stand at the more interesting threshold of the political poetry produced during the 1960s. It is a poetry ferociously incapable of being tamed by any political ideology. Precisely because of

Dalton's total commitment, it is impossible not to read him in his own terms, without at the same time engaging in the hagiographic exercises of his apologists. His poetry is a document of his time; its particular circumstance is what will always speak of a present.

Octavio Paz (b. 1914) is the major presence in Mexican and contemporary Latin American poetry of the 1960s and 1970s. The group of poets that come of age after 1959 in Mexico owe much of their inspiration to him and to the changes that take place in his poetry after the 1960s, surely Paz's most central and prolific decade. Paz started writing poetry in 1933 with a small book of poems entitled *Luna silvestre*, and by 1950 had published his classic essay on Mexico, *El laberinto de la soledad* [*The Labyrinth of Solitude*]. Yet although his poetry is written uninterruptedly after the 1930s, his work consistently places itself as voluntarily epigonic, as the last in line of a particular discourse in Spanish American letters. It is not only because of this strategic rearrangement of causality that Octavio Paz should be placed at the end of this tradition (even if his major work is produced in the 1960s), but because his work and his on-going literature create the sense of an ending for a particular mode of modernity in Spanish American poetry. There is Spanish American poetry after Octavio Paz: generations of poets who reject his legacy, and others that continue his line of experimentation. Nevertheless, the imprint that Paz has given to the tradition as a whole will be with us for years to come.

In awarding Octavio Paz the Nobel Prize for Literature in 1991 for his work's "sensuous intelligence and humanistic integrity," the Swedish Academy recognized the Mexican poet as one of the most influential voices in late twentieth-century letters. It was a recognition long overdue. For the past forty years, Paz has been Spanish America's most public and prolific essayist, cultural historian, poet, philosopher, and translator. In a sense, Paz has shaped and defined the role of the intellectual in contemporary Spanish America; he has been an active participant in the political and poetical battles of his time – a controversial man of letters who has struck a sensitive balance between public discourse and individual poetic expression. Paz's multi-layered texts engage the reader in a sophisticated dialogue between history, literature, and philosophy. As an essayist, Paz is heir to a distinguished tradition in Hispanic letters, one that includes the Spanish philosopher José Ortega y Gasset and the Mexican *homme de lettres* Alfonso Reyes, kindred spirits in the sheer multiplicity of their interests and in the inquisitive tradition of knowledge that their words presuppose. Paz's essays on poetry and poetics, in particular *El arco y la lira* [*The Bow and the Lyre*] (1956) and *Los hijos del limo* (1974) [*Children of the Mire*], define modernity as a fragmented, multi-layered tradition of rupture in Western poetry, a suggestive paradox that for Paz is an emblem of our present condition. To read Paz's writings on literature is to have a feel for connections that are well beyond time and place. He joins in one sweeping phrase Rubén Darío and Matsuo Basho, Apollinaire's calligrams and the surviving codices of early Mexican literature. Paz defines tradition (a much maligned word in the Modernists' canon) not as a set of rules but as an open space for the dissemination and articulation of ideas.

The same intellectual awareness that we find in Paz's essays can be perceived in his poetry, in particular in his major collections to date, *Libertad bajo palabra* and *Ladera este* ["East Slope"]. Poetry grounds the multiplicity of Paz's work: it is a form of expression that Paz has transformed into the point of encounter between philosophy and aesthetics, thought and sensation, especially in his most ambitious poems, *Piedra de sol* ["*Sunstone*"] and *Blanco*. The connections between the poetry and the rest of the work can be seen in particular in Paz's reading of Mexico, a country re-created as a point of encounter between different civilizations. In *El laberinto de la soledad*, Paz has written the definitive work on modern Mexico, a country that is for him as enigmatic as a poem can be.

The traditional chronological arrangement does not offer, by itself, an adequate representation of the variety and consistency of Paz's work at any given point in time. No chronological approach would do justice to the process of elaboration of, in particular, *Libertad bajo palabra*, in its various editions (1949, 1960, 1968, 1975, 1988). Paz's major book of poems grows and branches out like a tree, and the various stages of its ordered composition, of the additions and exclusions, can be related to the different periods in his poetics.

Paz's poetry can be divided into three stages. The first culminates in *Piedra de sol*, where a temporal axis and figural play shape a poem that is grounded on a circular art object: the famous Mexican stone calendar, now housed at the Museo de Antropología in the Mexico Federal District. The second can be seen in Paz's increasingly complex cultural critique of the 1960s, in particular in *Ladera este* and *Blanco*, perhaps Paz's most ambitious poem, in which sense yields to sensation, and in which the category of translation is centralized as a literal metaphor for the act of writing – a poem that shapes Paz's vision of the interplay between East and West, Body and World, Author and Language. The third takes place after his return to Mexico, and can be centered on the most important poem yet of the late period, "Nocturno de San Ildefonso."

Perhaps the most constant feature of Paz's work is poetry of a self-referential mode on language and poet. Many of Paz's poems are meditations on the act of writing and on the power of words themselves, with Paz constantly underscoring to his readers the fact that we are reading a translation of a non-existent original. Paz is a poet who attempts to understand the particular materiality of the word. This can be seen with peculiar clarity in his shorter poems. For example, hieroglyphs or, as Paz also says, "garabatos," are overdetermined signs precisely because their indecipherability gives them a kind of materiality, of body. This is the essence of Paz's poem "Garabato" ["Scrawl"] from *Salamandra*:

> Con un trozo de carbón
> con mi gis roto y mi lápiz rojo
> dibujar tu nombre
> el nombre de tu boca
> el signo de tus piernas
> en la pared de nadie
> En la puerta prohibida
> grabar el nombre de tu cuerpo
> hasta que la hoja de mi navaja
> sangre
>   y la piedra grite
> y el muro respire como un pecho.

> [With a piece of charcoal
> with my broken crayon and my red pencil
> scrawling your name
> the name of your mouth
> the sign of your legs
> on nobody's wall
> On the forbidden door
> engraving the name of your body
> till the blade of my knife
> bleeds
>   and the stone screams
> and the wall breathes like a chest.]
> (Tr. Eliot Weinberger, *The Collected
> Poems of Octavio Paz*, 110–13)

The poet's desire is underscored by the verbal infinitive "dibujar." The act is not what is being described here, but the possibility of the act. The infinitive is not only the mark of a particular elasticity of the present, it is also what separates the desire from the act. The poet is not painting the name of the mouth nor inscribing the name of the body. The infinitive speaks of a possibility, of an act that is being performed in a theatrical space of violence, stolen away the moment violence is committed. Between these syllables and in the interstices of this writing, the act takes place, and the poem is its translation, its oblique desire, and its realization, even if ultimately Paz appeals to another place, beyond language but also within language. The letters of this scrawl are being translated while they are written.

As an inheritor of the linguistic experimentation of the Avant-Garde, Paz constructs verbal objects in which the position of signifiers is as important as what the signs mean. What Paz forgoes are the more obvious traits of the Avant-Garde: instead of experimenting with metaphor, Paz chooses instead to concentrate on form. In *Piedra de sol* and in *Blanco* Paz adjusts the poems to an idea of order and form that, in the former, equates the number of lines to the lunar calendar of the Aztecs, and in the latter structures the poem according to a perversely hermetic interplay between numerology and chance. These experimentations by Paz follow a kind of gnostic belief in the power of the word that he has examined in his *Sor Juana Inés de la Cruz o las trampas de la fé* (Barcelona, 1982) [*Sor Juana Inés de la Cruz or the Traps of Faith*] by projecting these preoccupations onto the work of his Mexican precursor.

Piedra de sol is also a translation, but this time of an Aztec object. It has been, without a doubt, one of the more closely read of Paz's works. It is a long poem on love, memory, war, death, and resurrection, told in 584 hendecasyllabic verses, a number that equals the number of days in the synodic revolution of the planet Venus. Paz's inscription of poetry within Nature is part of his vision of the poem as a kind of poetic talisman, and it is this aspect which frames Paz's preoccupation with form. The closest poem to *Piedra de sol* in the Spanish American tradition is Gorostiza's *Muerte sin fin*, and Paz's vision of cyclical time, of death and resurrection, where history and poetry move like a spiral, may be seen as a version of Gorostiza's apprehension of objects as evanescent impossibilities. Both Gorostiza and Paz inscribe themselves within the context of Heideggerian phenomenology, and Paz's beginnings as a poet are shaped by the generation of *Contemporáneos*.

Piedra de sol underscores a new cycle in Paz's poetry. This new beginning will culminate in *Ladera este* and in *Blanco*. The latter is perhaps one of the more ambitious poems of twentieth-century Spanish American poetry, while the former, *Ladera este*, invites comparisons to Neruda's *Residencia en la tierra*. Both of Paz's books and Neruda's were written in the Orient, although Neruda was much younger when he served in Chile's foreign service while Paz was already a well-known poet, whose resignation from his country's diplomatic service after the government massacred student protesters in Tlatelolco in 1968 was a well-publicized event. Yet Paz's book is not the chronicle of a season in Hell that *Residence on Earth* was for Neruda's stay in Asia. More responsive to their context than Neruda's book, *Ladera este* and *Blanco* testify to a growing fascination with "otherness" in a multicultural perspective.

Paz does not explore his lyrical self in the Orient but the relationship between culture and individuals, between East and West, and between writing and Nature. *Ladera este* is a conscious deciphering of the East, and

CAMBRIDGE HISTORY OF LATIN AMERICAN LITERATURE

the reader needs the textual apparatus provided by Paz's notes on the poems in order to decipher his more particular allusions. During these years in the Orient, Paz works on the Symbolists' notion of correspondence, as it was seen by Baudelaire: the universe is a system of communicating signs and the poet is the one who deciphers the hidden music of things by exploring and revealing their hidden relationships. However, Paz takes this notion a step further: he sees the same system of correspondence, a vast network of rotating signs, not only in Nature but in culture, in books, and in works of art. These ideas, which Paz has elaborated in a number of essays, also appear as themes in his poetry, particularly after *Ladera este* and, in particular, *Blanco*, where the poem at the same time shows direct links to T. S. Eliot, to Tantric art and rituals, to abstract European art, and to Mallarmé.

Paz surrenders himself to what he sees. In Paz's conversational style at this time, the poem is written under a sort of luminous transparency, self-conscious of the fact that it is being written. It is a poetry that purposely introduces itself as self-evident, a revelation in the more exact sense of the word. This is why some poems, like *Piedra de sol* and *Blanco*, obey very rigid constraints. No word can be out of place in these texts, they all seem measured, the elimination of one word would topple the whole edifice.

Blanco's procedure is based on the combination and recombination of different poems, in a scroll that is at the same time folded and unfolded, creating the illusion of multiplicity within an underlying unity to be found once the poem is unscrolled into a single page. Paz's remarks on how to read the poem do not clarify how it was written, but the sequences of poems obey a hidden principle of repetition given in multiples of four. Every four pages Paz writes two columns of poems in red and black ink, and every time these appear they are followed by poems with eleven lines each. Some internal cohesion of the author's own devising can be found in these and other interplays of chance operations that may remind us of the music of John Cage, to whom Paz dedicates one of the best poems of *Ladera este*. *Blanco* is above all an invented poem, as clarified by its compositor:

> El espíritu
> es una invención del cuerpo
> El cuerpo
> es una invención del mundo
> El mundo
> es una invención del espíritu
>
> [The spirit
> is an invention of the body
> The body
> is an invention of the world

The world
is an invention of the spirit]
(Tr. Weinberger, 329)

This chain of continual invention of spirit, body, and world is reminiscent of the perpetually recommencing cycle of *Piedra de sol*. The link of invention has no end but continues its gyrations within its own circularity. It is perhaps a rebellion against closure that gives Spanish American poetry the sense of a new beginning.

That the fractured language of self that inaugurates Spanish American modernity arrives at a teleological moment in Paz's acceptance of the dissolution of the ego and at a similar point in Lezama's *Fragmentos a su imán*, gives the issues of the self and language that have framed Spanish American poetry during this period a temporary sense of closure, at the point in which there is a consciousness of a tradition assumed as a critical problem. It is this aspect which I would like to explore as a way of closing this period and talking about poetry after Paz.

The moment of awareness of a tradition is fundamentally a critical moment. What Paz's poetry underscores is precisely that poetry is a critical act of language. In the work of José Emilio Pacheco (b. 1939), poetry becomes a lucid experiment, a critical questioning, a meditation on the power of later poets in the tradition. His poetry seems to have been created after the resolution of a problem. We do not find here the underlying problems of language and poet that have been a constant in Spanish American poetry, or if we do find them, they appear under a different articulation. Both Paz and Pacheco already work within a tradition that has been assumed as such. Their collective reading of this tradition can be seen in the anthology *Poesía en movimiento, México 1915–1966*, where Paz and Pacheco, along with Alí Chumacero and Homero Aridjis, read their precursors with a critical eye. Octavio Paz, who writes the introduction and appears as the member of a second cluster that chronologically precedes the more recent generation composed by Pacheco and Aridjis, is aware that the originality of contemporary Mexican poetry consists in a critical reading of the tradition itself.

Pacheco posits the role of the poet as a practical problem, his poetry is impersonal and ironic, but always eminently critical. In *No me preguntes cómo pasa el tiempo* [*Don't Ask Me How the Time goes By*] time appears as the concrete experience of history: the poet is an observer of historical time. Pacheco is involved not as a witness but as an observer of historical change. Pacheco refuses to engage in the more obvious rhetorical flourishes of Paz. It is, as critics have termed it, a purposely flattened-out style, a neutral register.

An awareness of this critical impasse where history and aesthetics collide is what characterizes the poetry of Roberto Juárroz (Argentina, b. 1925), the author of seven volumes of poetry, published between 1958 and 1982, all entitled *Poesía vertical* [*Vertical Poetry*]. There are no proper names in this poetry: both the volumes and the poems in them are numbered consecutively. As Sucre has remarked (in *La máscara, la transparencia*), it is a poetry that seems to have no evolution, no change. Julio Cortázar defined it as a poetry that proceeds by the inversion of signs, positing its own negation. Juárroz's poetry is abstract: an experiment in form that avoids cultural reference and oblique or even outwardly "experimental" language. Verticality is assumed both in the geometric shape of poetry as well as in the progressive internalization of the language. Like Girondo's "masmédula," "vertical" for Juárroz is equivalent to an interior of the verse – a kind of falling inside.

In the work of Juárroz we see what is best in the projects of Huidobro, Gorostiza, Borges, and Vallejo – the fact that we have the outlines of an inquiry that is always left unfinished. Whether it is the utopia of a language that erases the distinctions between political and aesthetic commitment, as in Vallejo, or of language chiseling itself out of its own fleeting circumstances into a monument of form, as in Gorostiza and Girondo, or that of a continued and unending verticality, as in Juárroz, these projects of Spanish American poetry belie its manner not only of understanding and translating modernity, but also of coming to terms with a pivotal change that takes place in poetry itself and of which poetry gives an account.

To assume the problem of poetry in a critical manner is to question the very status of the genre and the possibilities of language. The desire of the poets to reformulate the category of poetry itself by defying that which makes language poetic may be seen as another critical operation within language, as part of an inquiry into what makes the poem into a poem. Spanish American poetry since the Avant-Garde defines poetry as something more than a particular rhetoric, but this something more is to be found by stripping that superficial rhetoric and discovering that the poet is not the center of the universe, but another link in a system of relationships that is shown by the permutations of the poetic text.

These written words, on the page, acquire not only a concreteness as words, but a kind of factualness as objects. Poems have become talismans because this is what they had been, before they were poems. The work of Octavio Paz illustrates the "talismanic" aspect of contemporary poetry. However, where this aspect can be seen with particular force is in the work of Alejandra Pizarnik (Argentina, 1936–1972), a poet who truly represents the end of a mode of writing in Spanish America, and the beginning of another, still undefined, way of defining poetry. Pizarnik's suicide in 1972, at the age of thirty-three, is actually the beginning of a work that is still fundamentally unread, or at least read in reverse. Pizarnik's suicide is a figure in the carpet, it shapes and influences any reading that is done of her poetry. It forces critics to read her poetry starting from her death. Yet it was not so much death that Pizarnik always reached for and pursued, but necessity, which entails a different notion of the poetic text.

Pizarnik assumed poetry as an act, and words as fully concrete elements that exist. In "Fragmentos," from *El infierno musical* [*The Musical Hell*], completed months before her death, Pizarnik says:

> No tengas miedo del lobo gris. Yo lo nombré para comprobar que existe y porque hay una voluptuosidad inadjetivable en el hecho de comprobar.   (*El deseo de la palabra*, 26)

> [Do not be afraid of the gray wolf. I named him in order to assert that he exists and because there is an unadjectivable voluptuosity in the fact of asserting.]

Pizarnik's poems assert that all Nature in them is completely language. Even where language is not, the reader is made to think that these spaces need to be, or will be at some point, filled with words. Beyond the particular personal circumstance, Pizarnik forces us to fill her death with the necessary language that explains her silence and that, in a sense, forecloses the possibility of silence itself.

Pizarnik's language resonates in poems that forgo the traditional arrangement of verse forms. A disciple of Rimbaud and Lautréamont, the tone of her poems manages to produce an uncanny resemblance to a colloquial speech that nevertheless points to its own literariness. Pizarnik arrives at a purposely neutral style, where her prose fragments on the page underscore the desire for action more than the desire for expression. In *Extracción de la piedra de la locura* [*Extraction of the Stone of Folly*], her sentences break logical connections from one to the other. In *Los trabajos y las noches* [*Works and Nights*], her short texts, some without punctuation, are instances of time that are configured on the page. One could say that a new Spanish American poetry starts with these words from "La palabra del deseo," a poem out of *El infierno musical*:

> ¿Qué estoy diciendo? Está oscuro y quiero entrar. No sé qué más decir (Yo no quiero decir, yo quiero entrar). El dolor de los huesos, el lenguaje roto a palabras, poco a poco reconstruir el diagrama de la irrealidad.   (*El deseo de la palabra*, 18)

> [What am I saying? It is dark and I want to go in. I don't know what else to say (I don't want to say, I want to go in). The pain in the bones, language broken to words, step by step to reconstruct the diagram of unreality.]

Pizarnik's questions always come with dark and elliptical answers that provoke more questions of their own. There is no place for this poet except the space of the page, where a series of voices speak directly to the readers of this poetic act. They are short and sudden illuminations, sometimes in an ironic mode, where there is always some process of reconstruction taking place. Pizarnik refuses to accept the futility of language. Her poetry is underscored by an act of faith in writing as able to decipher and give an account of a powerful sense of unreality. The writing of culture and of poetry is apprehended as an object, a verbal construction of what will be written, of what there is a necessity to write. This necessity is where Spanish American poetry of the following period begins.

[11]

The modern essay in Spanish America
José Miguel Oviedo

The contemporary Spanish American essay is born simultaneously with the twentieth century in 1900, the year in which José Enrique Rodó (1871–1917) publishes *Ariel* [*Ariel*] in Montevideo. Nearly a century later, it is a book that continues to be read with interest and even debated with passion. While much of what was once at stake in *Ariel* is largely outdated, Rodó's essay has not lost a certain brand of intellectual *mundonovista* charm which still touches something deep within the Spanish American spirit. Before establishing what is today at issue in *Ariel*, it is necessary to situate it within its historical context.

When *Ariel* appeared in 1900, the *modernista* wave that swept America and even extended to Spain was at its apogee. After publishing *Prosas profanas* (1896), a founding text of the *modernista* aesthetic, Rubén Darío travelled to Spain in 1899 and to Paris the following year. It was a moment of apotheosis for the great poet whose revolutionary writing was already a phenomenon internationally known and revered. *Ariel* was at once a reflection and an exaltation of this spiritual climate, as evidenced by its florid, *précieux* language and its gallicized Hellenism, not at all different from that cultivated by Darío. Yet what is striking is that Rodó was among the first harsh critics of *Modernismo* and specifically of Darío, in whom he recognized a superior artistic sensibility but whom he nonetheless eschewed for remaining aloof to the profound intellectual questions of the day. Rodó's 1899 criticism of Darío is perhaps best characterized by its famous accusatory declaration: "He [Darío] is not the poet of America" (Rodó, *Obras completas*, 169). The fact that Darío himself published this critical text as an unsigned prologue to his second, expanded edition of *Prosas profanas* (1901), thereby obliquely validating Rodó's talent while mitigating the force of his critique, is in itself revealing: the poet realized that the Uruguayan essayist was one of the "new spirits" awakened by the *modernista* call.

365

In point of fact, the crux of this opposition is rooted in the aesthetic line that separates two distinct facets of *Modernismo*: on the one hand, a decadent *Modernismo* that tended to shy away from Americanist themes, and on the other, an affirmative Americanism or *Mundonovismo* founded on the new continental conscience. It is tempting to say that Rodó discovered this second phase before Darío – thereby contributing to the dramatic changes evident in Darío's next book of poetry, *Cantos de vida y esperanza* (1905) – and that this early discovery is perhaps one of his most significant merits as well as the primary reason for the sweeping and immediate impact of *Ariel* in the continent. Moreover, there were propitious historical reasons for the book's influence: the Spanish American war over Cuba, Puerto Rico, and the Philippines (1898) represented a moment of crisis for Latin America and for Spain (the well-known "Spanish decadence" which would be laid bare by the Generation of '98), and marked the beginning of US expansionism in Spanish America as foreseen by José Martí. The consequences of this war and the threats it represented for Spanish America embittered Darío himself, thereby prompting his return to Hispanic culture, a culture which he had previously renounced as dry and academic. However, it was Rodó who detected with greater precision – and even poignancy – the change in the environment; he examined this change with a holistic intention and alerted the Spanish American consciousness to it with a tone of alarm and sincere concern. In so doing, he prolonged and renewed the great Americanist polemic, that had been so widely debated by the major essayists of the nineteenth century: Andrés Bello, Domingo Faustino Sarmiento, Martí, and Eugenio María de Hostos.

Ariel is a book that should have been read – and indeed was – first, as a manifesto, and later, in the two decades that followed its publication, as a gospel for action. The text overcomes its generic bounds; it stands out as an expression of a state of mind perfectly synchronized between its author and its projected reader, both of whom had been sensitized by the questions and ideas propagated by *Modernismo*. The moment was ripe for *Ariel*; hence its enormous influence and appeal. Rodó's text is not a treatise or essay with the breadth or complexity of those by Sarmiento or Hostos. It is, rather, a surprisingly brief tract of less than 100 pages, didactic in form, straightforward, and quietly polemical. To better understand it, we should remember its origins: in 1897 Rodó had begun to compile his brief essays and critical texts in a series headed by the title *La vida nueva*. The first series included a short piece "El que vendrá," which can be read as a prefiguration of *Ariel*; the essay speaks of the urgent need for a teacher/master figure – the *maestro* – a spiritual guide to preside over the youth of the day and direct them away from the false lures of decadent *Modernismo*. The series reveals the didactic bent of Rodó's purpose and his perception that there was a very real void to be filled. The second series (1899) included the critical essay against Darío, while the third series of 1900 contained *Ariel*.

The text is inscribed within a broader pedagogical effort; it is, in essence a professorial lesson about Americanism, about the origins, reality, and destiny of Spanish American culture faced by its European heritage and by North American hemispheric hegemony. Because *Ariel*'s target audience was the youth of Spanish America, Rodó resorts to an allegoric strategy commonly used in classical oratory. An old and respected teacher, Prospero, bids farewell to his students who have gathered for their last meeting in his comfortable book-lined study, beneath the protective shade of the bronze statue of Ariel. Ariel is the winged spirit who symbolizes freedom and all that is morally elevated and aesthetically pure; his dark counterpart is Caliban, the embodiment of all selfish and materialist human impulses. Rodó's symbolic figures – Prospero, Ariel, and Caliban – are clear borrowings from Shakespeare's *The Tempest*, but the Shakespearean allusions, although meant to be prestigious, are rather remote ones. Instead, *Ariel* seems to be a response to (or a variant of) the drama by Ernest Renan (1823–1892) entitled *Caliban, suite de La Tempête* (1878) [*Caliban: A Philosophical Drama continuing "The Tempest" of William Shakespeare*], the very title of which already underscores its intertextual connections. Renan had proposed a victory by Caliban; Rodó corrects Renan's conclusions, heralding instead Ariel's triumph. (The intellectual backdrop of this textual dialogue is further complicated by another French thinker – and another of Rodó's intellectual heroes – Alfred Fouillé [1832–1912], who had already criticized Renan in *L'idée moderne du droit*, also published in 1878. What all this proves is that Ariel was already a central figure in the ideological debate of the day into which Rodó inscribes himself.)

The main body of Rodó's essay is subdivided into six chapters (eight according to some editions which include the brief introduction and epilogue as parts of the text). Within the space of the first four chapters, Rodó commends to the continent's youth the defense of the free spirit (1), condemns the modern tendency toward specialization which destroys the integrity and harmony of the spirit (2), underscores the moral function of beauty (3), and criticizes the utilitarian conception of life (4). However, it is the fifth chapter that is the core of its polemic thought and the source of the greatest misunderstanding of Rodó's words: therein appears the characterization of the United States as a great democratic society, filled with energy and devoted to a strong work ethic, but devoured by the narrowness of a utilitarian spirit and by an exercise of freedom that tends toward homogeneity and denies in its wake the best values associated with individuality. Rodó contrasts this social model to that forged by a Latin and Christian America, heir to Hellenic grace and to an uncompromising practice of art; that selfsame society which, under the deceptive spell of the North American mirage, is in danger of forgetting "a sacred link which unites us to the immortal pages of history, trusting to our honor its continuation in the future" (Rodó, *Ariel*, 72). The ambivalence of Rodó's feelings towards the United States ("aunque no les amo, les admiro," p. 76) confused most of his early readers (as well as many of his later ones), leading them to a facile inference not explicitly made by Rodó: namely, that if the symbol of Spanish America is Ariel, then that of the United States must be Caliban. Such a reading dismisses (or simply ignores) Rodó's hopeful outlook for the inevitable role of the United States as a (perhaps unknowing) contributor to the cause of Ariel: "La obra del positivismo norteamericano servirá a la causa de Ariel, en último término" (p. 89). It may be said that *Ariel*'s readers and the historical circumstances at the start of the century assigned the text a semantic and ideological "message" that went far beyond that intended by its author, thereby justifying somehow the legendary aura that still surrounds the essay.

The seductive, though simplistic, image that was most broadly extracted from *Ariel* was this dualism of human societies whose spiritual heritage links them to either Cain or Abel. The consequences that ensued from this image were no less appealing to a vast majority of readers. The antagonistic Ariel–Caliban couple is, to a degree, a refiguration of the civilization–barbarism dichotomy already inscribed in Sarmiento's *Facundo* (1845). For Rodó, the ideals of beauty and freedom which America should represent were inextricably associated with Hellenic culture and, as a result, with Europe; what distinguishes his Caliban from Sarmiento's Facundo is that Ariel's dark counterpart seems to have been extrapolated from his neighbor to the north and not from the gaucho of the south. (It is important to note that "Caliban" is an anagram of "caníbal," Spanish for "cannibal"; the name may also be derived from the word "caribe," meaning native to Caribbean cultures, wherein the most terrible form of barbarity – cannibalism – was practiced to the shock of the European colonizer.) *Ariel* offers an answer to the horror produced by this savage image of America, implicit in Shakespeare and Renan. Other responses would follow thirty years after *Ariel*, in the form of parodies by the Brazilian avant-garde *Antropofagia* movement.

Despite the foregoing, it is evident that the image Rodó had of Spanish America was decidedly European; his text envisions a pure and pristine Spanish America, purged of all its internal contradictions: not a reality, but a moral and aesthetic figuration of a collective entity. The idealism of *Ariel* is incontrovertible: the text offers an intense intellectual perception but also a faith – the faith of an optimist who believed in a future ruled by the guiding principles of good, art, harmony, and justice. Rodó's idealism was not without motivation; it was a symptom of the failure of nineteenth-century Positivism and its blind adherence to science and pragmatism. The positivist model – the dominating philosophical, scientific, and political force of the nineteenth century in Spanish America – is precisely what the *modernista* credo meant to dismantle. The Spanish American bourgeoisie had undoubtedly grown and progressed under its auspices, but this had not made the young republics more just: a liberal economic scheme had paradoxically given rise to a conservative and retrograde military *caudillismo*. While keeping pace with the industrial revolution, societies had achieved material modernization, but were still eluded by the brand of refined modernity that Darío and his followers longed for. *Ariel* expressed this crisis and, moreover, offered a possible solution. There was a certain urgency in it, because the repositioning of political forces at the end of the century put a new threat before Spanish America: the United States.

From the historical vantage point of the present, it may be said today that in his criticism of North America and in his vision of the dilemma that it represented for the rest of the continent, Rodó at once surpasses and falls short of his own agenda. The two Americas are, in effect, two distinct realities (and *Ariel* did well in pointing this out), but not exactly for the reasons proposed by Rodó. It is not the case, for example, that the "principle of disinterest" that is mentioned so frequently in the text is less present in the North than in the South: the ambition for power is a common trait of mankind and there is no modern culture that can declare itself free from it. Furthermore, Rodó's "heroic" concept of history is an overly mechanical construction that oversimplifies the North American formative process as much as it does the Spanish American one. This principle blinds Rodó to what was perhaps the essential problem of the United States: a lack of its own historical sense – an absence of critical consequences in the global political arena. In reality, it may be said that the major problem of the book is its digressive and abstracting tendency, omitting almost all reference to sociological, economic, or political concrete realities. There is no mention whatsoever of some of the most pressing internal questions of the time for Spanish America, such as the status of the native Indian which had already attracted the attention of Manuel González Prada (1844–1918), among others. Wrapped in the wings of Ariel, Rodó glides over a vast panorama which he observes from a distance, seemingly not weighed down by the onus of detail. What Rodó provides is not so much a representation of the true being of America as it is a moral idea of it: a kind of Kantian imperative setting forth what America's collective spirit *should* be, not what it was. The essay is an exquisite manifestation of the philosophical individualism that was adopted at the end of the nineteenth century as a result of the positivist crisis and the advent of *Modernismo*.

Although of different scope and intention, Rodó's publications following *Ariel* generally prolonged the visionary attitude inscribed in the earlier text. *Motivos de Proteo* (1909) reaffirms Rodó's profound Hellenic spiritualism and his somewhat naive certainty that social transformation is the direct result of the human will. Perhaps better than *Ariel*, this book demonstrates Rodó's philosophical capacity: his goal was to develop a psychologic–ethical doctrine that, while clearly based on Bergsonian idealism, would nonetheless reflect a personal vision. The doctrine approaches modern thought inasmuch as Rodó conceived it as a sum of fragments, deliberately denying the work a closed form so the text could freely unfold itself in a constant state of "becoming" (*Ariel-Motivos de proteo*, 59). Even Rodó's prose style has managed to free itself from the heavy-handed oratorical tone of the earlier book; his prose here is tighter, less overwrought. There is an alternation of lyric and reflexive passages, of a purely philosophical discourse with the usual illustrative parables. Despite this, the book remained relatively unknown at that time, perhaps because it was not fully understood by those who had previously read and been moved by *Ariel*; the concerns of the illustrated social sectors seemed to be moving in another direction. Rodó's *El mirador de Próspero* (1913) is a vast collection of articles and previously dispersed pieces which, from its very title, underscores Rodó's insistence on the figure of the teacher as the guiding thread to organize his thoughts.

This didactic intention also affects Rodó's style, which is undoubtedly more outdated for the modern reader than the contents of his work. Pompous, rhetorical, and digressive, *Ariel*'s language suffers from an archaic affectation, more suitable for oratory than for written prose. His is a language that does not want to be read but rather heard: the essay is fundamentally a speech, a civic oration. It is almost surprising to realize Rodó's age when he writes *Ariel*; only twenty-nine years old, he adopted the tone and demeanor of a wise, old professor to convey his message to the youth of his own generation. Rodó loved to make use of the allegorical devices of classical philosophy, further evidenced by his use of fables (such as the one about the Oriental king introduced at the end of Part II of *Ariel*.) By virtue of his cultural background and his spiritualist vocation, Rodó embodies the dominating attitude of the Uruguayan generation which in 1903 would make possible the rise to power of José Batlle y Ordóñez (1856–1929).

Rodó's liberalism seemed to materialize itself in Batlle's, who built an authentically benevolent and provident state in Uruguay, transforming his country into the so-called "Switzerland of America." The message of *Ariel* and its unifying vision of culture are not far removed from the image after which Uruguay and, more broadly, the entire Río de la Plata region molded itself: a largely white, Europeanized, and illustrated collectivity that did not share the same problems that plagued other areas of Spanish America. Rodó remained alien to these problems because they did not figure within his realm of experience. It is *Ariel*'s affirmative strength and its faith in the goodness of the Americanist cause which perhaps best explains the book's enormous reach beyond its historical moment.

In fact, *Ariel*'s influence was so profound that it gave rise to a whole movement of Americanist ideas, propagated under the catch-all name of *Arielismo* [Arielism]. This movement marked the end of the positivist hegemony in Spanish America and although the group is now all but forgotten, it exerted considerable influence in its time. *Arielismo* is far from being a school or even a precise form of Americanist thought; its chronological boundaries are as vague as its ideological ones. In varying degrees, Arielist thinkers shared with their mentor a Gallic sensibility, a formal orientation toward the *précieux*, and cautionary criticism of Anglo-Saxon America. Manifest in *Arielismo* but not in *Ariel* were a pronounced interest in evolutionary theory (which served as a means to address the question of racial diversity) and a markedly conservative and sometimes even reactionary tone. The movement's eventual fascination with local dictatorships and nascent European Fascism would undoubtedly have horrified Rodó.

The greatest aesthete of the Arielist group was the Venezuelan essayist Manuel Díaz Rodríguez (1868–1927) who introduced the decadent tone to Venezuelan literature. Díaz Rodríguez is the author of, among other books, *Camino de perfección* (1908), an elegant collection of essays among which figures an interesting critical portrait of *Modernismo*. A peculiar case is that of the Peruvian Francisco García Calderón (1883–1953). His prolonged residence in France made of him a bilingual writer as well as an avowed Francophile. Influenced by the organicist thought of Gustave Le Bon and Bergsonian idealism, García Calderón devoted various books to the issue of Spanish America confronted by Europe and the United States. His two most important works on the subject are *Les démocraties latines de l'Amerique* (written in French, published in Paris in 1912, and finally translated to Spanish in 1979) and *La creación de un continente* (1913).

Another Peruvian essayist, José de la Riva-Agüero (1885–1944) deserves mention as the founder of modern literary and historiographic studies in Peru. He is the author of *Carácter de la literatura del Perú independiente* (1905) and *La historia en el Perú* (1910) – important books in their respective fields, the first has the added merit of having been a university thesis, written by Riva-Agüero at the age of nineteen. Both are works of profound erudition and personal reflection as well as examples of a polished and precisely worked prose style. *Paisajes peruanos* (1955) is a later text which captures in brilliant images the author's memories of a trip thoughout the interior of Peru. The proud Hispanicism and unyielding defense of Catholicism that characterized Riva-Agüero from early on led him to an acceptance of reactionary positions and, eventually, to the exaltation of Italian Fascism. It is ironic that in his own country Riva-Agüero was considered the visible leader of local Arielism, given that he reproached Rodó for applying Hellenism to a continent which he viewed as irrevocably contaminated by the negative influence of Indians, *mestizos*, and Blacks.

The sad truth is that during this period various important figures of Spanish American thought succumbed to the same pitfalls and to even greater errors. The Argentinian Carlos Octavio Bunge (1875–1918) published in 1903, when the echoes of *Ariel* still resounded loudly, a disconcerting book, *Nuestra América* (1903). The title's echoing to Martí's is completely misleading; Bunge was another follower of Le Bon's theories concerning the influence of racial characteristics in the social physiognomy of a people. His vision of America could not have been any more negative. In sharp contrast to Rodó, Bunge adhered to the principles of scientific determinism and supported a mechanical application of the Darwinian theory of evolution to sociological studies. His rhetoric included, therefore, such terms as superior races, subraces, laws of supremacy, and the like. While Blacks and Indians are presented as socially retrograde beings, incapable of significant intellectual or artistic activity, the *mestizo* is portrayed as the product of a racial mixture which aggravates and degenerates the original typological traits. In Bunge's racist theories, there is even something of phrenology: he goes so far as to judge an individual's spiritual baseness according to his physical constitution. Only the white race, armed with European and authentically Christian values, has any possibility of social progress, which he defines by proposing the United States, and Mexico under the dictatorship of Porfirio Díaz (1830–1915), as models.

Although somewhat more moderate in his approach, the Argentinian essayist José Ingenieros (1877–1925) defended similar ideas in *Sociología argentina* (1910). Ingenieros was a disciple of evolutionary philosopher Herbert Spencer (1820–1903), and although he was also a believer in Socialism, he goes so far as to justify slavery as the juridical manifestation of a biological fact. Among his many books devoted to philosophical, psychological, and social questions (*Hacia una moral sin dogma* [1917], *Ensayos filosóficos* [1917], *Las fuerzas morales* [1922]), *El hombre mediocre* (1913) was the most popular as well as the most influential. It was also the most Arielist of Ingenieros's books, as the Spencerian evolutionism that habitually informs his works is tempered by a brand of social idealism. The essay condemns the conformity and docility of the so-called mediocre individual while it praises the innovative spirit of the superior man who strives for social change.

Another essayist whose thought has connections with the aforementioned is the Bolivian Alcides Arguedas (1879–1946), also known as the author of various indigenist novels. His most widely read essay is *Pueblo enfermo* (1909), closely tied to his narrative work. Arguedas's thought is radical: an unfortunate combination of biological laws, historical factors, and environmental circumstances have made of the Indian race an atrophied and diseased one. Even worse is the problem presented by the *mestizo*, or *cholo*, in whose psyche the genetic faults of his various racial components are multiplied, rendering him incapable of using his own faculties to free himself from the conditioning that enslaves him. There is only one palliative in this disturbing panorama of races condemned to an infrahuman fate: education which, although unable to transform these individuals into truly civilized human beings, is at least capable of converting them into useful ones – good farmers, laborers, or soldiers.

Just as García Calderón represents a perverse extension of the *Arielista* fascination with Europe, the ideas of Bunge, Ingenieros, and Arguedas can be read as a perversion of pre-World War I Scientism; in order to explain the nature of a miscegenated America, all three fell, via different routes, into a deviated sociological determinism founded upon the racial issue.

A healthy rejection of this narrow and retrograde Scientism is that represented by the Mexican thinker Justo Sierra (1848–1912), part of whose work corresponds, more properly, to the nineteenth century. Although marked by contradictions and ambivalence, Sierra is a capital figure of the modern spirit in his country: a liberal thinker born of an intellectual climate dominated by a conservative Positivism, Sierra served as cabinet member first under Porfirio Díaz and later under the regime of Francisco Madero (1873–1913), at the beginning of the Mexican Revolution. As a writer and artist, Sierra was a romantic, admirer of both D'Annunzio and Nietzsche, whose influences are visible in his work. His thought is closer to the humanism of Martí than to the scientists with whom he was associated and although the historical circumstances under which he wrote were completely different from Rodó's, he is a more authentic *Arielista* and has greater affinity with the master than those who formally assumed that name. Essayist, orator, short-story writer and poet, Sierra was also a politician, historiographer, and, above all, an educator. In *Mexico: su evolución social* (1900–1902), Sierra offers the first analysis of the historical and political processes that operate in his country; *Juárez, su obra y su tiempo* (1905) is a brilliant study of the great Mexican reformer. Sierra's modernity resides in his arduous defense of antidogmatism and tolerance in the movement of ideas.

Perhaps it makes sense to close a period that opened with Rodó writing from the very height of *Modernismo* with two writers who embody other important phases of this aesthetic. The first occupies a place of honor in Argentinian literature as a poet, short-story writer, and philosophical and political thinker: Leopoldo Lugones (1874–1938). A contradictory figure, whose politics evolved from an early Socialism to the defense of an ultranationalist militarism, his essayistic work reveals an encyclopedic voracity (that included Hellenism, theosophy, science, and history) as well as the growing intellectual disorder and spiritual anguish that eventually led him to suicide. Lugones's historical essay *El imperio jesuítico* (1904), the fruit of a 1902 trip throughout Misiones accompanied by the great Uruguayan short-story writer Horacio Quiroga, together with *El payador* (1916), part of a vast, unfinished study of *Martín Fierro*, are his two greatest contributions to the genre. They are intensely personal books, somewhat arbitrary and even of unequal quality; they are nonetheless among the finest examples of Lugones's prose – impassioned, baroque, and tightly structured.

The other *modernista* writer to be discussed here is the Venezuelan Rufino Blanco Fombona (1874–1944) whose personality probably contributed at least as much to his fame as his writings. His reputation for indiscretions, sarcasm, and even slander transformed him into the *enfant terrible* of his time. Politics was one of Blanco Fombona's great passions; it was also the primary cause for his long pilgrimage as an exile throughout Europe. He was a fierce polemicist whose formal elegance heightened the artfulness of attacks which were often directed against respected individuals and institutions. Blanco Fombona was a controversial essayist who expressed himself in literary chronicles, and journalistic articles but, almost always, in diatribes against one burning issue or another. The relation between Spain and Spanish America, the fervor for Bolívar, a fascination with the Nietzschean Superman, anarchy, Greek idealism, and the theme of Anglo-Saxon imperialism are among the dominating questions in such books as *La evolución social y política de Hispanoamérica* (1911), *La lámpara de Aladino* (1915), and *El conquistador español del siglo XVI* (1921?). Blanco Fombona also wrote *El modernismo y los poetas modernistas* (1929) and a diary provocatively entitled *Camino de imperfección* (1933).

By the start of the second decade of the twentieth century, the panorama of Spanish American thought was progressing along three separate lines of development: first, the effort to explain and analyze the continent's sociopolitical crisis in light of Marxist theory; second, the renovation of Americanist cultural issues compounded by the Indian question, and finally, the appearance of the first mature attempt at pure philosophical reflection, focused upon the examination of the central problems of humanity. Diagnosis, Americanism, and speculation are the forms which best define the essay of this period, a genre marked by the presence of a number of great figures whose influence is still felt in today's intellectual debate. It can be said that these new contributions closed the idealist cycle of *Arielismo*, presenting a more complex and more problematic view of mankind's situation, both in a social and in a universal context.

Great historical events precipitated the radical change in the direction of Spanish American thought after the century's first decade. It was a particularly dramatic period, marked by the rise of important revolutionary movements (the Mexican Revolution of 1910, the Soviet Revolution of 1917), the First World War, worker and student agitation in both Europe and America (for example, the movement for university reform in Córdoba, Argentina, which had repercussions throughout the entire continent), the intensification of North American intervention, the formation of farmers' unions and the growth of labor organizations in various countries, the exacerbation of the old phenomenon of military dictatorships, etc. Adding to this was the powerful impact of artistic avant-garde movements (which in many instances joined forces with politically radical groups) and the general climate of renovation and contradiction that they propagated throughout the world. This new reality marked the opening of what we can refer to as contemporary thought. It is precisely at this chronological juncture that the great ideological debate which still unsettles us today formally began to take shape.

The essays which characterize the beginning of this period are all recognizable by a tone that is somewhere between optimistic and exasperated, by an explicit degree of militant commitment to concrete causes, and by the rebelliousness and indignation of their discourse. Writers move away from digressions and a purely elegant rhetoric toward a confrontation with the concrete problems of the day filtered through personal experience: essayists perform "diagnoses," "X-rays," "exams." It is evident that the old brand of individualism is outdated: the essay turns instead toward the exterior, in search of the "other," the unknown or the forgotten. The language of the period often sidesteps the private, inner realm of the individual in favor of theoretical considerations regarding social classes or economic structures. Submitted to a wide range of pressures, conditioning, and interests, man is perceived as the embodiment of the values of the "mass", the collectivity within which he lives. The question of the apprehension of reality became a philosophical, aesthetic, and moral problem of enormous proportions in a continent that, to a certain extent, remained unknown to itself.

An important figure in the development of twentieth century Spanish American thought is José Carlos Mariátegui (1894–1930) whose personality, words, and actions can be considered as being particularly representative of his time. Before Mariátegui, and indeed after him, few serious attempts were made in the application of Marxism to the American reality, with two notable exceptions: Juan B. Justo (1865–1928), translator of *Capital* (1867–1885) and director of the socialist newspaper *La Vanguardia*, and Manuel Ugarte (1875–1951), author of *El destino de un continente* (1923), who spread European socialist ideas and anti-imperialist doctrine. Although America's political situation in the beginning of the twentieth century would seem to have been propitious to the development of Marxist thought, its appearance in the continent is rather belated. Despite the efforts of Spanish American Marxists to deny it, neither Marx nor Engels had any significant interest in assimilating the Spanish American case to the body of their historical doctrine; Engels went so far as to rejoice over the territorial plundering that Mexico suffered at the hands of the United States in 1848 – the same year as the Communist Manifesto. In spite of its cultural antiquity, the American continent appeared, even to its most radical figures, as an ahistoric reality – more undeveloped and barbaric even than czarist Russia. Nonetheless, the similarities between the two realities are obvious: Spanish America, like old Russia, was basically an agrarian society, populated by illiterate farmers who were subjected to a regime of feudal exploitation – a subculture at the service of an authoritarian elite. It is precisely the abuse of this subculture that Mariátegui would denounce.

Afflicted by poverty and poor health since childhood, Mariátegui entered the literary arena in the shadows of a decadent *Post-modernismo*, fulfilling the duties of a somewhat frivolous chronicler. Soon thereafter, as early as 1916, his intellectual evolution already began to manifest signs of a deep social unrest, as evidenced by his founding of the newspaper *La Razón*, which was shut down by the Peruvian authorities. In 1920, President Augusto B. Leguía tried to rid himself of the young intellectual by sending him off to Europe. Mariátegui spent the next three years there (from 1920 to 1923), primarily in Italy; this was a fundamental period in his work and in his formulation of an American brand of Marxism. Upon returning to Peru, Mariátegui was a changed man: a doctrinaire Marxist, militant and with a cause to defend.

In the intense years that remained until his early death, and in spite of being confined to a wheelchair, Mariátegui founded and directed *Amauta*, (1926–1930) as well as *Labor* (1928–1929) – literary and ideological journals that were extraordinary in their time; he organized the Peruvian Socialist Party which would serve as the foundation of the Peruvian Communist Party; and he published *La escena contemporánea* (1925) and *7 ensayos de interpretación de la realidad peruana* (1928) [*Seven Interpretative Essays on Peruvian Reality*]. This final collection of essays is

Mariátegui's masterpiece as well as a true milestone for Marxist thought in the American continent.

Mariátegui's brand of Marxism was directly shaped by his European experience and by his Italian readings. Italy was the ideal look-out point for Mariátegui to observe the panorama of global politics, the conflicts of opposing ideologies, their implementation; and above all, to understand the problems of his own country while remaining outside provincial debates. It was the first time since González Prada's indigenist preaching at the end of the previous century, that the problems of Spanish Americans were framed within the context of the struggles of the international proletariat; that is to say, as a specific case but responding to the historical laws common to all oppressed peoples and classes. The national problem was seen, at last, as a chapter in the process of global capitalism. At the beginning of 7 *ensayos*, Mariátegui writes: "My thoughts and my life are one, one single process. And if there is one merit with which I expect and claim to be credited, it is – in accordance with a Nietzschian principle – that of putting all my blood in my ideas" (Mariátegui, 7 *ensayos*, 11) Mariátegui's revolutionary voluntarism and his flexible, humanist conception of Marxism carry the traces of his Italian and French mentors, particularly of Benedetto Croce (in his Marxist stage), George Sorel, and Antonio Gramsci. For these thinkers, Marxism represented a new myth of humanity, capable of radically transforming Europe. Mariátegui conceived as the goal of his new program nothing short of the transformation of America, by means of the liberating forces of Andean peasants in the Peruvian countryside and of worker-organized movements in the cities. Inasmuch as Mariátegui was a true Indigenist, he nonetheless believed that "Indo-American salvation could not be effected without European science and thought" (*ibid.* 12).

Mariátegui's cultural vision formed part of this liberating project. He stands out among both his Spanish American and European fellow Marxists for his comprehensive perception of the role of art in the revolutionary process. Far from being a fanatic cultural commissary, suspicious of the so-called "bourgeois forms" of aesthetic creation, Mariátegui was a sympathetic and enthusiastic promoter of the European and Spanish American Avant-Garde, of Surrealism, and of the discoveries that psychology and science contributed to the art of his times. *Amauta* served as an introductory vehicle to a broad variety of art forms, despite its doctrinaire statement of principles asserting the importance of ideologically committed artistic expression:

> It is not necessary to declare explicitly that *Amauta* is not a tribune open to every fleeting idea. We, the founders of this journal, do not adhere to an agnostic concept of culture and art. We consider ourselves to be a fighting, polemic force... I am a man with an affiliation and a faith. I can

say the same of this journal, that it rejects all that which is contrary to its own ideology as well as that which reveals no ideology at all.

(*Amauta*, no. 1, 1926, 1)

In spite of its militant tone, the magazine was in fact a forum open to the most diverse writers, manifestations, and topics: José María Eguren's symbolist poetry, the baroque "anti-sonnets" of Martín Adán, the works of André Breton and F. T. Marinetti, Mexican Muralism, the psychoanalytic theories of Sigmund Freud, Indigenism [*Indigenismo*], the ideas of José Ortega y Gasset, Louis Aragon, Henri Barbusse. There was a reason for this apparent contradiction: Mariátegui believed that the Avant-Garde corresponded to a phase of Western cosmopolitanism, which would gradually open the way to a superior stage of national affirmation expressed in a realist aesthetic. In this way, literary history too was ordered according to progressive ends. Mariátegui's interest in art and literature is enough to warrant his placement among the most valuable critics and theorists of his time. It is not coincidental that his examination of national literature appears as the final chapter of *7 ensayos*, as a fitting culmination to the social and political issues discussed throughout the previous six essays: the Peruvian economy, the Indian problem, the land situation, education, religion, and the debate of regionalism versus centralism.

No one before Mariátegui had ever submitted Spanish American reality to the kind of multiple examination of *7 ensayos*, much less with the dedication and hopeful vision that inform his effort; the interpretation of reality was conceived as the first step toward action. Possibly the most broadly discussed of the seven essays was the one addressing the land problem; the text proposed an end to the *latifundio* system and to the feudal regime of agrarian exploitation. In his studies of the indigenous communities, Mariátegui discovered in the Quechuan *ayllu* the essential seeds of an "Incan communism"; the political utopia of Peru consisted, therefore, in a return to the past, modelled on the ancient Tahuantinsuyo, and made current by the contributions of modern Socialism and Marxist praxis. This utopian scenario envisioned by Mariátegui was interpreted as heresy by the most recalcitrant factions of Spanish American Marxism and gave rise to a fervent international polemic. Yet another polemic, concerning literary Indigenism, brought Mariátegui face to face with Luis Alberto Sánchez.

Its polemical richness is precisely one of the greatest virtues of Mariátegui's book: it served as a vigorous stimulus for political, economic, and cultural discussion, not strictly in nationalist terms, but also in light of the transformations that were redefining the rest of the world. Mariátegui inscribes contemporary Peruvian history into the impassioned drama that was being acted out on a global stage. His style contributes to the sense of historic urgency and inevitability of his program. Moreover, enough cannot be said of Mariátegui's exceptional talents as a journalist, or of his ability to process what he saw and read, constantly enriching his perspective by assimilating new ideas. He was not so much an organic thinker as a great interpreter, who came across as both sensible and refined. His prose, like that of the best journalism, is functional, clear, convincing, precise, and agile. It is impossible to read Mariátegui with indifference.

Mariátegui's ability to convince and effectively win over his readers has contributed equally to his legendary status and to what may be considered a problem in the reception of his texts, namely the transformation of his thoughts into a massive and monolithic doctrine known by the name of *Mariateguismo*. It is ironic that the work of a great master of intellectual debate has been transformed by some ideologists into an undebatable oracle. Sixty years after its publication, 7 *ensayos* reveals, like all historical texts, its strengths as well as its shortcomings. Mariátegui incorporated Peru and Spanish America into the great current of critical thought that would give rise to contemporary political science. His interpretive scheme – Marxist methodology – allowed him to see clearly what others could not, but in some cases also led to sophisms and simplifications.

For example, Mariátegui's defense of "Incan communism" (developed in an extensive footnote to his essay on the Peruvian land situation and written as a response to *El pueblo del sol* [1925] by Augusto Aguirre Morales [1891–1945]) includes a long digression addressing the problems of the lack of individual freedom and the authoritarianism of the Incan empire. His rejection of Aguirre Morales's thesis as purely idealist and his contention that "the man of Tahuantinsuyo felt absolutely no need for individual freedom" is simply untenable. Mariátegui's faith in Marxism as a messianic formula that would change the world for the better was almost religious in nature: it is worthwhile to remember that as a youth he manifested certain mystical tendencies that were undoubtedly sublimated in adulthood. Mariátegui did not tend toward a rigid conception of Marxism as a science, but he did possess the ardor – and sometimes the blindness – of the providential leader.

It is difficult to situate adequately the work of the Colombian Baldomero Sanín Cano (1861–1957); it is no less difficult to find his peer, except perhaps in Alfonso Reyes (below) whom he calls to mind in his insatiable curiosity and encyclopedic knowledge. First of all, it is necessary to establish that chronologically Sanín Cano is much older than any of the other essayists analyzed in this section; he is in fact only eight years younger than José Martí and is six years older than Rubén Darío. His work begins in the last decade of the nineteenth century and untiringly continues until the middle of the twentieth. Although he shares the general concerns that preoccupied the essayists of the first third of the twentieth century, the most significant aspects of his work clearly diverge in another direction. What is more: Sanín Cano has met the curious destiny of becoming a prestigious and venerable "American classic," yet is hardly read today outside his own country. Sanín Cano stands out as a great thinker to be rediscovered, although he suffers the consequences of a dispersed body of writing, at times inseparable from his journalistic work. There is no centering nucleus to Sanín Cano's work; it was animated, as if by a centrifugal force, by casual and always free encounters with various themes and authors. Sanín Cano was full of ideas, but he lacked theories to defend (which did not preclude a genuine and mutual feeling of admiration between Mariátegui and him). During the almost 100 years of his life, Sanín Cano worked in politics (as a liberal) writing several books on the subject, held important official, diplomatic, and cultural positions, and was both a university professor and correspondent in Madrid and Buenos Aires. However, it is his thirteen-year residence in London (1909–1922) that most strongly marked his destiny as a writer, putting him in contact with a cultural world that would have otherwise remained unknown to him and exposing him to the best of British essayistic and journalistic writing.

The first important collection of Sanín Cano's essays is *La civilización manual y otros ensayos* (1925). The title piece is an exquisite meditation on the importance of the hand in art and culture throughout history. Other texts concerning Nietzsche, Shakespeare, and the English–Argentinian writer William Henry Hudson attest to the breadth of his interests. A review of his other collections of essays – *Indagaciones e imágenes* (1926), *Crítica y arte* (1932), *El humanismo y el progreso del hombre* (1955) – confirm his fine-tuned critical perception for discerning the most valuable work of world literature in order to present it to the Spanish American reading public: Marinetti, George Bernard Shaw, Aldous Huxley, Eugene O'Neill, Giosuè Garducci, John Ruskin, Cyril Connolly, Christopher Isherwood, Evelyn Waugh, and so many others. His attention to foreign literatures did not imply a disavowal of the literature of his own country, as exemplified by *Letras colombianas* (1944), or, much less, of Spanish American literature. It is evident by his tastes, his tone, and his intellectual discretion, that Sanín Cano more closely approaches contemporary sensibilities than many essayists of his time. An admirable note in his writing is the total lack of pretension with which he practiced literary criticism; he believed that "There is no such thing as absolute truth for the critic, whose role is to comprehend and, only in a case of arrogance, to explain" (*Ensayos*, 103). Sanín Cano was a master of the short essay as well as a master of prose, which he managed with elegance, precision, and plasticity. There is a direct line, not well observed, connecting Sanín Cano to Reyes, to Jorge Luis Borges (p. 393) to the youngest essayists of today. In a society like that of Colombia, which was culturally turned upon itself, Sanín Cano's role was vital: he opened windows that allowed a view of world culture and, moreover, he made this culture circulate for the education and enjoyment of others.

There is an entire group of important Mexican thinkers whose ideological cradle was the famous Ateneo de la Juventud (1909–1914), which contributed decisively to Mexico's twentieth-century intellectual history. In the five-year period from the outbreak of the Revolution to the start of the First World War, the Ateneo shaped the intellectual development of José Vasconcelos (1882–1959), Antonio Caso (1883–1946), Alfonso Reyes (1889–1959), and the Dominican Pedro Hénriquez Ureña (1884–1946), whose collective work is fertile in the fields of philosophy, Americanist thought, and literary and aesthetic criticism. The group represents, in general, another manifestation of the humanist reaction against Positivism [*Positivismo*] that elsewhere marked the beginning of the century.

The most complex and polemic of the group is Vasconcelos. He served the revolutionary cause from early on, but later, disgusted by the violence inherent in the Revolution and defeated as a presidential candidate in a fraudulent election (1929), he went on to defend reactionary positions. Throughout various exiles, Vasconcelos came to know Europe and the United States, an experience which gave him a peculiar perspective of Mexican history. He was a sensualist visionary who attempted a fusion of Western thought with Hindu mysticism. Vasconcelos had a utopian, optimistic, and aesthetic conception of American reality, which he imagined as a culture on the march toward a state of greater happiness and of heroic dimensions. His readings of Bergson, Schopenhauer, and Nietzsche reflect his vision of a cosmic race, a miscegenation in a continental melting pot, which would embody the best of all humanity. In Vasconcelos's philosophic vocabulary, words such as "mística limpia" ["clean mysticism"], "vaga impulsión de tránsito" ["vague impulsion of transit"], "consumación en lo absoluto" ["consummation in the absolute"], appear with relative frequency as key moments of a universal epiphany that gives sense to human existence.

Vasconcelos's ideas on race and American reality are perhaps most thoroughly developed in *La raza cósmica* (1925) and *Indología* (1926), a mixture of essays and chronicles that renews the topic of Indigenism and gives it a continental projection. This continental projection is nonetheless diffused by a tendency to fantasize with grandiose or chimeric images, such as those alluding to Atlantis. Vasconcelos's extensive autobiography, beginning with *Ulises criollo* (1935) and continuing with *La tormenta* (1936), *El desastre* (1938), and *El proconsulado* (1939), is filled with valuable pages of historic and philosophic reflection. Furthermore, Vasconcelos's personal work was complemented by his position as Secreatry of Education (1921–1924), an appointment of decisive importance for the cultural and artistic life of his country. Curiously, the optimistic philosopher gave way, especially toward the end of his life, to a writer dominated by rancor and bitterness. His prose, on the whole digressive and rhapsodic, is highlighted, at times, by lyric raptures and pathetic confessions.

Antonio Caso was an accomplished philosopher whose work raises probing questions that are at once permanent and current. His relation with Vasconcelos is particularly interesting; although Caso was deeply influenced by him, especially at the beginning of his philosophic career, he contradicts and even surpasses his forebear in many respects. Like Vasconcelos, Caso utilizes Bergson's ideas on intuition as a foundation, but he submits these to a more organic form of analysis, particularly in *La filosofía de la intuición* (1914). Caso opposes Vasconcelos's brand of vague idealism with a theory that synthesizes the religious with the speculative. In point of fact, what Caso posits is a philosophy to restore the authentically human character of life. Caso's most important work is *La existencia como economía, como desinterés y como caridad* (1919); the title requires an explanation. "Economy" refers to an elemental grade of human life, dominated by immediate interest, efficacy, and the use of the least amount of effort to achieve the greatest benefit. "Disinterest" is a conception of life as a freely assumed sacrifice, whose limitations may be surpassed through the medium of art and the superior expressions of the spirit. "Charity" is an elevated moral concept of existence, inasmuch as it is governed by principles of love and goodness, and divorced from any kind of biological determinism. In much the same way that Caso discusses Schopenhauer's and Nietzsche's ideas concerning the will and transforms them into an original brand of thought, he likewise spans a bridge that will serve as a point of encounter between Bergsonian Vitalism and the phenomenology of Edmund Husserl, whose work he is among the first in America to discover. Caso's 1922 *Discursos a la nación mexicana* proves, together with several other books published in those years, how intuitive philosophy was being applied to a common preoccupation of Caso and thinkers of his generation, namely, the recuperation of the roots of "Mexicanism" at a critical moment in Mexican history marked by a reactivation of the past and a simultaneous conjuring of strengths with the promise of national rebirth.

The most important essayist of the group – and indeed one of the greatest essayists ever to be born in America – is, without a doubt, Alfonso

Reyes. With Reyes, the genre is transformed into an elevated aesthetic manifestation, a marriage of the highest form of art and the most rigorous knowledge. His entire work – consisting of more than twenty massive volumes – could be summarized in the double sense of the word "grace": on the one hand, an exceptional gift and on the other, an elegant, cordial style that extends to even the most profound subjects. In fact, one of his works is entitled *Simpatías y diferencias* (1921–1926), which would seem to point to two essential functions of the critic: to draw differences from among similarities and to do so without pedantry or contrivance. Reyes was a polyglot, a true man of genius, a humanist comparable to the greatest of the Renaissance; someone who was interested in everything and who was able to talk about it with an inimitable personal touch. Miguel de Unamuno observed: "Alfonso Reyes' intelligence is a function of his goodness" (cited by P. Earle and R. Mead, *Historia del ensayo hispanoamericano* 103). Like the Renaissance humanists, he was an admirer of Classical antiquity, which he conceived of not as something distant or exotic, but rather as an immediate example for Spanish Americans to follow if they wanted to remain true to themselves. To define its essence, Spanish America should not renounce its universal heritage, but rather appropriate it and claim it for its own, as has in fact occurred at the greatest moments of human history. The title of one of his poetry books says it all: *Homero en Cuernavaca* (1949); it asserts the bond whereby a Mexican could talk with Homer as if he were just another national poet.

In order to fully appreciate the significance of Reyes's work, it is necessary to recall that during the time in which he lived, Mexico was undergoing a stage of feverish nationalist affirmation that tended toward an exaltation of the telluric and of autochthonous cultural roots. Reyes embodied a secret dilemma between a hedonist personality, devoted to the pure delight of the spirit, and another more austere persona, reclaimed by the exigencies of history and the commitment to those moral questions that were urgent for a Mexican of the first third of the century. Reyes resolved the conflict with characteristic equilibrium: both the seduction of pleasure and the immersion in collective movements, discrete seclusion and active participation were, for him, attitudes that enriched and enlightened human nature. Moreover, the way of achieving harmony between these two realms was through the practice of art, of thought, and of study, each of which constitutes a generous form of giving oneself to the private and the public simultaneously.

While this aesthetic conception corresponded to profound currents in Reyes's own way of being and of writing, one must not forget the decisive influence that certain authors and philosophers exerted upon him (as well as upon other members of the "Ateneo" group), among them Ortega y

Gasset, Unamuno, Waldo Frank, and Max Scheler. The influence of Ortega y Gasset is of particular importance, not only in the case of Reyes, but for the majority of the essayists of his generation, from Mariátegui (above) to Jorge Mañach (1898–1961). Ortega initiated a twentieth-century tradition of influences and reciprocal intellectual borrowings between Spain and Spanish America, the most notable antecedent of which was Hostos's assimilation of Spanish Krausism as a powerful intellectual stimulus in the battle for Puerto Rican independence in the late nineteenth century.

Reyes was personally acquainted with Ortega and they developed a bond of mutual respect and appreciation that is documented in their respective works. Reyes's friendship with Ortega and with so many other peninsular writers can be said to constitute an entire chapter of his intense and fertile relation with Spanish culture. After studying in Madrid, Reyes founded the Mexican "Casa de España" in 1939, which provided shelter to Spanish emigrants after the Civil War (1936–1939) and which eventually developed into the "Colegio de México," a center for advanced studies and research.

One of the central ideas of Ortega's philosophy – that of the interrelation between the individual and his environment that is so well expressed in the formula often cited from the 1941 *Meditaciones del Quijote*, "Yo soy yo y mi circunstancia" ["I am myself and my circumstance"] – had special resonance for Spanish American thinkers and, in particular, for Reyes who sought to define the value of autochthonous cultural creation within the context of the great creations of the human spirit. Perhaps due to the vastness of Reyes's work, readers tend to lose sight of the fact that he, also, formulated his own version of the Americanist ideal. In "Discurso por Virgilio" (1933), for example, he subtly intertwines national issues of the day with the topics of the *Georgics*. The essay presents a viable thesis on the relations between the local and the universal (maintaining that if American art is authentic, it is irrevocably universal as well), and goes so far as to readdress some of the questions that in the nineteenth century were of concern to Bello (the city versus the countryside) and to Sarmiento (civilization versus barbarism), in order to affirm the need for a return to Nature. Among the most beautiful pages attesting to Reyes's devotion to Mexico are those of *Visión de Anáhuac* (1917) in which he writes of the feelings of spirituality that are awakened by natural objects; there is, in this, a marked affinity with Ortegan thought as well as a discrete refutation of the determinism that informs Sarmiento's *Facundo*.

Reyes did not believe that being a rigorous philologist (*Cuestiones gongorinas*, 1927; *Capítulos de literatura española*, 1939), an erudite Hellenist (*La crítica en la edad ateniense*, 1941) or a consummate literary theorist (*El deslinde*, 1944) barred him from also being a graceful conversationalist or a savoury teller of anecdotes and humoristic stories. In *La experiencia literaria* (1942), for example, he manages to define difficult aesthetic concepts at the same time that he entertains his readers with fineries and witticisms such as those found in the essays "La jitanjáfora" or "Aduanas lingüísticas." One of his favorite images for the writer was that of a hunter who ventured far and wide to bring a rich and varied feast to his reader's table. Reyes was able to imbue academic treatises with the engaging style of journalistic writing, critical studies with the tone of intimate biographical sketches, philosophy with personal memory and historic reflection. Although he also wrote poetry, narrative, and theatre, Reyes's most lyric and imaginative passages are to be found in his essayistic work. The art of thinking in images – an art that was mastered by Martí in his time – provides Reyes with instantaneous illuminations that the discourse of the conventional essayist could seldom, if ever, achieve. His prose is punctuated with genteel asides and poetic syntheses which enliven the exposition of ideas and make them clearly visible.

Reyes's capacity to illuminate and make transparent the obscure and complex, to submerge himself in the deepest of waters only to resurface with a rare and memorable treasure in hand, formed part of his humanistic conception of knowledge, wherein everything – great or small, ancient or modern – occupied a precise place. In the vastness of his genius, Reyes is comparable only to such figures as Erasmus, Thomas More, Montaigne, Sor Juana Inés de la Cruz, Diderot, and, perhaps more than anyone else, to Goethe, to whom he dedicated two books (*Idea política de Goethe*, 1954; *Trayectoria de Goethe*, 1954) and with whom he shared more than one intellectual affinity. Like him, Reyes subscribed to an ideal of absolute correspondence between life and knowledge, or better yet, to the knowledge of life, without which learning becomes a dry and insignificant activity. Goethe's characterization of all theory as gray and the tree of life as green could well describe Reyes's attitude toward the interrelation that must operate between the theoretical and the vital. It is perhaps for this reason that Reyes never succumbed to the vanities and miseries that sometimes infiltrate literary circles but always stood out for his generosity and affection. His friends and disciples are innumerable; among them are included literary figures of the importance of Borges and Gabriela Mistral, to name just two. Reading Reyes leaves us with the impression that we are in the presence of a brilliant and yet reasonable man, who is calmly speaking to us about that subject he knows best, in order to make it more clear and amenable. For him, that is precisely the high purpose of the genre he cultivated.

The essayistic work of Pedro Henríquez Ureña (1884–1916) shares certain stylistic elements, themes, and concerns with the work of the Argentinian Ricardo Rojas (1882–1957, below) as well as with the Mexican "Ateneo" group in general and Reyes in particular, although he does not achieve the same degree of breadth and variety. Notwithstanding, Henríquez Ureña's contribution to cultural history and to Spanish American literature is fundamental. At the core of his meditations lies his profound Americanist passion, which gave rise to pages and attitudes that would stimulate entire generations throughout the continent. Henríquez Ureña was, above all, a great teacher, a man of lofty ideals who used the professorate to propagate his intense faith in what he called "the utopia of America." He addressed such essential questions as the existence of a Spanish American culture, its characteristic and distinguishing marks, and its loans to and from other cultures. His two most important books are *Seis ensayos en busca de nuestra expresión* (1928) and *Las corrientes literarias en la América Hispánica* (1949 translation of a book that was first published in English as *Literary Currents in Spanish America*, Cambridge, Mass., 1945), which is the fruit of eight lectures he gave at Harvard University in 1940. The title of the first of these could serve as a rubric to head all of Henríquez Ureña's critical work. It is here that the essay "El descontento y la promesa" is included, a piece which lucidly examines the issues of tradition and rebellion, the problem of language, and the tendency toward Europeanization. His invitation to descend, with rigor and authenticity, to the very depths of one's own personal and cultural experience remains valid even today, as do the basic tenets of Henríquez Ureña's comprehensive vision of the Spanish American literary process, a vision that has served as guide to a great number of modern historians.

Two other cultural historians who contributed to the Americanist cause from a perspective of national values are the Argentinian Ricardo Rojas and the Bolivian Franz Tamayo (1879–1956). Rojas is the author of the ambitious *Historia de la literatura argentina* (1921) as well as of *Eurindia* (1924), wherein he proposes a synthesis of the indigenous and the European as a way to achieve the true essence of what is Argentinian. Tamayo, on the other hand, defends the indigenist cause with an exalted tone and ideas that could be termed Nietzschean, particularly in *La creación de la pedagogía nacional* (1910), a "book of battle and of reflection" (*Obra escogida*, 4) that reacts against the racist thesis of his compatriot Arguedas.

The Mexican Samuel Ramos (1897–1959), the Peruvian Victor Raúl Haya de la Torre (1895–1979), and the Argentinian Ezequiel Martínez Estrada (1895–1964) are very different from each other, but all three represent radical forms of philosophical–political thought. Ramos is a historical philosopher who provides insights on the subject of "Mexicanism." A disciple and a critic of Caso (above), Ramos is a thinker of importance not only for his own country, where his ongoing interest in studying and defining the "Mexican" helped shape perceptions of a national identity, but, moreover, for the movement and dissemination of ideas throughout America, to which he contributed with his knowledge of key philosophers of the twentieth century: Scheler, Nicolai Hartmann, Alfred Adler, and Ortega y Gasset. To a certain extent, Ramos prolongs and synthesizes the humanist philosophical meditations of Vasconcelos and Henríquez Ureña (above). He represents a critical opening toward European thought as a way to understand Mexican culture and, more broadly, human nature as protagonist of culture. The titles of his two best-known books, *Perfil del hombre y la cultura en México* (1934) and *Hacia un nuevo humanismo: programa de una antropología filosófica* (1940), already point to the two outstanding directions of his philosophical work. *Perfil* is an attempt to characterize the social "personality" of Mexico. Inspired by Adler's psychoanalytic theory on complexes, Ramos examines the origins of Mexican culture; he suggests that its imitative and derivative nature in relation to European culture has generated a collective feeling of inferiority and insecurity among Mexicans. These complexes account for the Mexican's distrust, defensiveness, and rigidity in the face of change, as he struggles to preserve the "image" he has created of himself. It is here that Mexican nationalism and *machismo* have their origin. *Hacia un nuevo humanismo* establishes the bases upon which to found a rational neo-humanism, which would free the individual from the irresoluble contradictions of capitalist and bourgeois materialism. One of Ramos's central ideas (which constitutes a middle road between early Marxist humanism and Scheler's axiology) is the creation of a new morality, self-regulated by man's consciousness of his own profound aspirations and not by external concepts or criteria imposed upon him. Ramos's ideas have been fertile: his observations about the Mexican *pelado* and his psychological masks were adopted and expanded by Octavio Paz (b. 1914) in his early analyses of the history and society of his country.

The political and ideological life of modern Peru is dominated by two great figures: Mariátegui (above) and Haya de la Torre. In point of fact, Haya de la Torre's famous polemic with Mariátegui and the consequent break between them over the issue of the *Frente Único* had significant repercussions for the intellectual and political movement of the continent, which Haya termed *Indoamérica*. Born in Trujillo, the city that was also the cradle of the active, youthful bohemia which was crucial to César Vallejo's beginnings as a poet, Haya's early thought was marked by Indigenism, revolutionary fervor, and the anti-imperialist sentiment of the day, convictions he shared with Mariátegui and *Amauta*. Exiled and persecuted, Haya completed his education abroad, in other American countries and in Europe, where his radicalism was quieted and submitted to forthright revision. Haya was a politician who wrote and philosophized, not a true political writer. It is fair to say that his most significant work is not to be found in books, but rather in the 1924 creation in Mexico of the party APRA (Alianza Popular Revolucionaria Americana), a multiclass front whose dramatic and circuitous history could serve as a paradigm of the route followed by non-communist radical groups in the first half of the century. Nonetheless, it is worthwhile to mention at least three of his most important books: *El antimperialismo y el APRA*, *Espacio-tiempo histórico* (1948), and *Treinta años de aprismo* (1956).

Martínez Estrada's essayistic work, though extensive, constitutes only a small fragment of his vast intellectual and creative efforts which include novels, stories, poetry, and theatre. As is the case with other outstanding essayists, Martínez Estrada's moral and emotional profile is clearly inscribed in his work: his voice is grave, somber, disenchanted, and, at the same time, imbued with a prophetic and even messianic passion. The moral and political crises that marked the times in which he lived are clearly reflected in his writing. His revisionism of national history and culture conferred upon him the role of teacher to younger generations. This was not always a fluid relation since Martínez Estrada's thought evolved through various phases that at times violently contradicted each other. There are, however, a number of basic concerns and features in his thought: his admiration for great heroic figures together with his identification with marginalized individuals; his concern for the failure of freedom and justice in the concrete social world; the dehumanizing threat of a technological society; the urgent subject of an Argentina trapped between the rise and fall of *Peronismo* and the two World Wars. The melancholic and pessimistic tone that colors his reflections is strengthened by his readings of Nietzsche, Schopenhauer, Spengler, and Existentialism.

Radiografía de la pampa (1933), *La cabeza de Goliat* (1940), and *Muerte y transfiguración de Martín Fierro* (1948) are frequently cited as Martínez Estrada's three fundamental collections of essays. These books are, without a doubt, his most influential and best-known; however, equally important in understanding Martínez Estrada's complex interior world, his memories and obsessions, and above all, in penetrating the unresolvable conflict between the thinker and the writer which he embodied, is the 1951 *El mundo maravilloso de Guillermo Enrique Hudson*. There are two stages of Martínez Estrada's production, the first lasting until about 1950, and the second marked by a physical distancing from Buenos Aires (which included the brief Cuban interlude from 1961 to 1963), both signs of his growing weariness with Argentina and of his revolutionary hopes.

His work as a whole is somewhat uneven, reflecting the spiritual fluctuations and intellectual tension with which he struggled. *Radiografía* may be read as a critique of Sarmiento's famous "civilization versus barbarism" dilemma. For Martínez Estrada the paradox is a false one, since true civilization consists of harmony with Nature (a Nature observed with Rousseauian affection.) "Civilization" and "Nature," then, are one and the same, and must be considered from within the framework of a dialectic system. Ignoring this fact, the city has grown disproportionately, effectively transforming itself into the focus of a new barbarism: a modern, inhuman, and materialist civilization. Based upon a series of recognizable archetypes and categories (as found in Bacon, Jung, and Spengler), *Radiografía* is testimony to Martínez Estrada's intensely critical vision of the model of Western society that Argentina represented. It is more impressive for the ardour with which it condemns than for the alternatives it offers. *La cabeza de Goliat* falls into the same line of attack; it is his most violent accusation of Buenos Aires as the capital and symbolic center of the Argentinian societal model. The book's thesis generates the graphic and well-known image of Argentina as an octopus, a monstrous figure constituted by powerless and insubstantial legs (the provinces) and a hypertrophic head (the capital) which devours and exhausts the energies of the entire social body. With this work, Martínez Estrada touched a topic that would continue to reappear in the Spanish American essay, namely, the criticism of the modern city as the breeding ground of national evils, portrayed by the glaring contradictions of development and backwardness. The subtitle of *Muerte y transfiguración* ("Ensayo de interpretación de la vida argentina") points to the work of national interpretation that Martínez Estrada sought to write using José Hernández's famous poem as a pretext. Large portions of this extensive essay consist of historical and cultural considerations of rural Argentina, its people, and its customs, reaffirming Martínez Estrada's telluric bond with the pampa and with cultural forms that were either marginalized or near extinction. Yet the pretext grows to assume major proportions: it is an exhaustive study, almost obsessive in its details, which remains valid today and with which few rivals can compete as a masterpiece of devotion and erudition. Martínez Estrada was a prophetic voice as well as a brilliant, if not methodical, thinker. He lived in constant contradiction, trying to understand his world and himself. In the end, it may be said that these contradictions devoured him and that the synthesis promised by his continuous reexamination was never fully achieved.

Among the philosophers, the work of the Argentine Francisco Romero (1891–1962) must be placed together with that produced (since the late nineteenth century) by other Río de la Plata thinkers interested in pure philosophical speculation and representing varying degrees of idealist reaction against Positivism. Two founding figures of that branch of Spanish American thinkers are the Argentinian Alejandro Korn (1860–1936), author of *La libertad creadora* (1920), and the Uruguayan Carlos Vaz Ferreira (1872–1958), whose extensive work includes *Moral para intelectuales* (1910) and *Lógica viva* (1910). Born in Spain but raised in Buenos Aires, Romero was a disciple of Korn, his successor for a university professorship, and later his exegete in the book *Alejandro Korn, filósofo de la libertad* (1956). Romero shares with the Mexican Samuel Ramos (above) both the influence of Scheler and Ortega y Gasset and the humanist orientation. However, Romero's humanist leanings are more purely speculative. He follows a line of thought that could be termed neo-Kantian Personalism, and which carries traces of Korn's teachings. The idea of "transcendence" is essential to his vision of the realization of the being and to the individual's understanding of the high values for which he is destined. Man is confronted by a series of dualities which either tear him apart or confuse him: the individual versus the person, the face versus the mask, and the spirit versus the psyche. These themes are most fully elaborated in *Filosofía de la persona* (1944) and *Teoría del hombre* (1952). Romero was also a historian of American ideas and culture in such works as *Sobre la filosofía en América, Estudios de historia de las ideas* (1953), and *El hombre y la cultura* (1956). His prose style is polished, hallmarked by clarity and precision. Moderate and elegant, Romero is a preeminent thinker who greatly contributed to the development of philosophy on the continent.

A review of Spanish American philosophical essayists cannot be complete without reference to at least two writers who are chronologically at odds and yet fundamentally associated with those thus far examined; while belonging to an earlier period, their mature work coincides in time with that of their younger colleagues. Very different from each other, they are joined only by their rarity and their historic marginalization.

The first is the Cuban Enrique José Varona (1849–1933) whose early *Conferencias filosóficas* date from 1880. As an essayist, Varona was interested in Humanism, history, art, and the question of Cuban independence. The pages of *Desde mi belvedere* (1907) demonstrate his elegance as a prose writer, his intellectual curiosity, and his deep and often skeptic understanding. However it is the aphorisms collected under the title *Con el eslabón* (1927) that truly attest to the modernity and the originality of his thought. It is perhaps worthwhile to remember that, as a genre, the aphorism has traditionally lent itself to philosophical reflection; in the twentieth century alone, it has been cultivated by a number of Spanish

American thinkers, Ramos, Tamayo, and Vaz Ferreira among them. Varona's aphorisms are truly remarkable, the work of a mature thinker of notable verbal precision.

The other is the Argentinian Macedonio Fernández (1841–1922), a disconcerting and unclassifiable author. His written work, dispersed and fragmentary, is brief, something which is reflective of the character of its author: Macedonio (this is the name by which he is best known) was an "oral" creator. He did not believe in the utility of books, rejecting them for fixing at a given moment the free flow of a thought which should remain uninterrupted. Macedonio dedicated his entire life, exemplary for a number of reasons, to the enterprise of thinking what others had not thought of before and to playing with the limits of the absurd and of metaphysical fantasy. Although the word "humorist" does not define him, an eccentric and illuminating humor is an essential element in his work. He was a sort of dime-store philosopher who contemplated the unfathomable mystery of living and sharing the world with others through a prism of skepticism and at the same time warmth. The author of hypothetical novels which end before they begin (or begin as they end), he wrote mysterious and heterogeneous pages that may be read as unorthodox essays, halfway between fiction and metaphysics: *Papeles de recienvenido* (1929 and 1944) and *Miscelánea* (1966). Macedonios's importance can be measured by the indelible impression he left upon disciples of the caliber of Borges and Julio Cortázar, among others.

Most writers born in the late nineteenth and early twentieth century constitute a group that is markedly different from that which preceded them, inasmuch as they were the first whose intellectual background was integrally determined by modern changes and events. Earlier ventures at nationalist and Americanist interpretation were supplanted by a retreat to more profound areas of inquiry as essayists became intimately concerned with aesthetic and moral issues of looming urgency and complexity. Among those figured questions about the nature and function of the essay itself, which was in the process of examining and redefining its various forms in order to coincide with modern challenges. On the one hand, the consequences of the great social and political upheavals of the times demanded a questioning of man's position in the world, of the role of art and culture confronted by the weight of history, and of the possibility of free thought in the midst of doctrinaire ideological determinism. On the other, there was a certain loss of faith, a process of disillusionment, and a subversion of the schemes that had provided an ideological foundation for essayists who had come before.

The essay of the 1930s and 1940s sought to shed light precisely upon the manifestations of the great crisis that afflicted the Western spirit. Beyond the devastating experience of the Second World War, another historical phenomenon had a profound impact on men and women during these years: the Spanish Civil War. Although the conflict that tore Spain apart lasted only three years (1936–1939), it would have lasting repercussions in the field of politics, in the ideological rifts among parties of the Left, and in the intellectual life of all the Hispanic realm. The Spanish tragedy stirred the conscience of the entire world; it engaged intellectuals of all leanings who saw in the war not merely an internal struggle, but rather a heroic defense of basic human rights, of justice, dignity, and culture against the threats of retrograde and intolerant forces. The international hegemony exerted by Stalinism, Fascism, and Nazism was a concrete manifestation of the vilest among the moral plagues of this century: totalitarianism, complete with its usual humiliations and manipulations of intellectual activity. Paradoxically, the loss of human potential that Spain suffered as a result of the massive emigration following the Civil War represented a gain for Spanish American intellectual life. Transplanted to the American continent, numerous writers, thinkers, journalists, and artists not only became assimilated into their new environment, but decisively stimulated it with the creation of a body of work that is perhaps more properly American than it is Spanish. The Mexican philosophical movement, for example, benefitted from the contributions of various exiled Spanish thinkers and philosophers; among them José Gaos (1900–1969), Juan David García Bacca (b. 1901) – both translators of Heidegger – and Eduardo Nicol (b. 1907), all three of whom promulgated and revitalized phenomenological and existentialist thought in Mexico.

One primary philosophical current seems to embody the questioning spirit that marked these years: Existentialism. It imbued intellectual works of the time with notes of anguish, vitality, disquiet, and self-reflection. The other formative intellectual current of this period derived from Marxist revisionism, and proposed commitment, militancy, and the defense of a realist aesthetic as forms of action appropriate to the realms of art and literature. These aesthetic and philosophical options are fraught with sharp moral edges that awakened and even disturbed many people, creating tempestuous polemics some of which remain open today.

All of these issues revitalized the essay in powerful ways. A particular phenomenon of this period (which has as precursor the work of Alfonso Reyes) is the appearance of the so-called "ensayo creador" ["creative essay"]. The term must be understood in two ways: first, in the genre's approach, more marked than ever before, to purely imaginative genres, especially poetry. No longer consecrated solely as a vehicle of undiluted thought, the essay is raised to a high form of artistic expression, erasing the frontiers that previously separated it from more creative genres of literary invention. Elements of fantasy and imagination invade the essay, calling for readers who are both subtle and well-informed. The text seems to direct a wink of complicity to its addressee, offering rich possibilities for reading between the lines and proposing visions of extreme complexity. Secondly, the term can be associated with the emergence of creators who feel the need to assume a critical function, reaffirming the importance of this practice to their artistic enterprise. The integration of diverse, even antagonistic, forms is a hallmark of contemporary literature; the essay does not escape this subversive tendency. Attempts at theorizing are often fraught with creative tension, providing self-reflexive insight into the artistic conscience at work. The criteria that defined the essay, imprecise to begin with, are submitted in this period to a radical revision, producing generic heterogeneity, mutual borrowings, and ambiguities, both formal and semantic. Paradoxically, then, the essay achieves a sort of primacy for its totalizing capacities and is reinterpreted as a "system" that transmits a profound experience or world vision, not so different from totalizing attempts in poetry and the novel. (Classic forms of the essay did not altogether disappear; important essayistic work continued to be produced in the specific fields of history, philosophy, literary criticism, etc.) The essay becomes the playing field for a game between critics with a creative bent and creators with a propensity for critical work, a game of mutual revelations that is particularly suggestive for the reader. Four prominent figures account for the most innovative changes to take place in the essay: Borges, Cortázar, José Lezama Lima and Octavio Paz. Each one shapes and defines the period to which they all belong.

The genius of Jorge Luis Borges (1899–1986) consisted not only in teaching Spanish Americans to write in a way that was not known before, but, moreover, in making people think of literature from a totally new perspective. Borges showed the potential for convergence and harmony that exists between the acts of reading and writing, remembering and imagining, reasoning and dreaming. This potential constitutes a guiding principle of modern literature: the Borgesian principle, unmistakable and yet subject to perpetual reinterpretation and renovation; it postulates a world of infinite invention open to play as well as to profound thought. Emir Rodríguez Monegal (1921–1985), one of Borges's best critics, did well to entitle a general anthology of his work *Ficcionario* (1985) [*Fictionary*].

Although Borges's belated fame is largely ascribed to his production of short stories (which originated in an unplanned manner and then continued intermittently), he began his literary career writing poems and essays, an activity he fostered with growing intensity until the end of his life. In Borges's work, all of these genres, as well as the intermediate forms he cultivated, are mutually explainable within a system of elaborate correspondences and intertextual quotations and echoes which cannot be isolated one from the other. There is no such thing as a Borges the essayist that is distinguishable from Borges the poet or Borges the short-story writer; all parts of the system remit to the center and to each other. His essayistic work is found not only in his essays *per se*, but is dispersed among his stories and poems; to consider any one of these genres by itself constitutes a sort of mutilation which distorts the whole. Furthermore, it is almost impossible to speak of genres with reference to Borges, a writer who continuously violated any and every kinds of frontiers, crossing bounds between philosophy and fiction, between poetry and essays. How, for example, does one classify an exemplary text such as "Borges y yo" ["Borges and I"], except perhaps as a story that is an essay that is a poem.

What would conventionally be defined as Borges's essayistic work is not particularly extensive. Including prologues (a form which gives full reign to his mastery of allusion and synthesis), the texts of his lectures, and brief essays that form part of books of other kinds, the number of titles reaches fifteen, but the pages are scarce in number and heterogeneous in themes, almost lateral diversions of a casual reader. They include reflections about the literature about the gaucho, alongside meditations on the nature of time, the exhumation of a minor poet like Evaristo Carriego (who would hardly be remembered today if not for Borges), or a note on the artificial language invented by John Wilkins. From this disparate ensemble, three are the key books: *Discusión* (1932), *Historia de la eternidad* (1936), and *Otras inquisiciones* [*Other Inquisitions*]. None is an integral work: each book gathers texts, very often brief ones, of diverse origins and intentions. One quality that immediately strikes the reader is that in spite of the overwhelming literary information presented and the precise form in which it is handled, the tone is almost always cordial and serene; erudition is tempered by a self-depreciating irony and by expository simplicity. This was not always the case; the young essayist of *Inquisiciones* (1925) or *El tamaño de mi esperanza* (1926) is surprisingly baroque, bellicose, and overwrought almost to the point of pedantry. These were avant-garde years for Borges, in which he put his *ultraista* ardor at the service of a militant and iconoclastic *Criollismo*, a posture he soon repented of assuming.

No one, with the possible exception of Sanín Cano, had ever written essays like these in America, because no one (or very few) had read texts the way Borges did, or much less written about them with the disconcerting dominion and familiarity that his writing exhibits. As an essayist, Borges managed to incorprate a literary culture that was previously almost unknown to Spanish American literature and which, thanks to him, would come to form an integral part of it; a culture rife with Oriental books, philosophers and mystics of antiquity, Cabalists and Jewish

Gnostics, forgotten French poets, and, especially, English writers. However, it is not only the singularity of Borges's personal library that is so
impressive, but rather his capacity to say something unexpected about
each of its authors, something entirely different from what had been
repeated by literary criticism in the original language of each of these
marginal or canonical works. It may be said, as Paul de Man suggested,
that his were "imaginary essays" (Bloom, *Borges* 22), if we understand the
expression in a precise way: essays of a very personal imagination but
stimulated by the imagination of others. Something that surprises the
reader who recurs to the sources that inspired him is the discovery that, in
his interpretive act, Borges projects as much of himself onto the original
texts as he does of the original authors onto his own readings, a gesture
which effectively infuses the source texts with new meaning. In other
words, Coleridge or Chesterton, after Borges's reading, are quite different
from Coleridge or Chesterton before Borges. The trace of his reading is
deep and extremely personal; so much so that at times it may seem
arbitrary (one need only recall his repeated readings of *Don Quixote*, for
example, a book with which he always maintained an ambiguous
relationship). This arbitrariness ends up being a positive trait, since it is
the stuff with which he moulds a literature that is unmistakably his. His
reading is a form of appropriation and of mirror-trick invention: that
invention to the second power (of indelible magic and suggestiveness) that
is so characteristically Borgesian. As Harold Bloom asserts, "Borges is a
great theorist of poetic influence; he has taught us to read Browning as a
precursor of Kafka" (*ibid.* 2). What we have is a *translation* of his readings
into his own literary language and his distinctive aesthetic universe.

By these means, Borges is able to integrate all the texts he has read and
remembers into an elaborate order, wherein those ideas which are "his"
and those which are borrowed from others participate in a fertile and
highly original dialogue. His books constitute a library created by an
imagination stimulated by other libraries. This is especially visible in his
reading of religious, metaphysical, and philosophical texts; Borges has
said that the theories of writers such as G. Berkeley, Schopenhauer,
Spinoza, and Swedenborg were of interest to him not for whatever truth
they may contain, but rather "for their aesthetic value and even for the
singular, wondrous elements they embody, for their potential to amaze"
(*Otras inquissiciones*, 223). In other words, Borges read religious and
philosophical theories purely as exercises for the mind (valid for themselves and not for their objective correlatives). They were fictions
conceived to explain the world, and fair game, therefore, as the basis for
essays and stories that speculated on these same matters.

Regardless of their subject matter (eternity or the metaphor, Homer or
cyclical time, our conception of Hell or Zeno's paradox) or of their

modest external form (mere book reviews, footnotes, or refutations), Borges's essays are, above all, heterodox propositions, an invitation for the reader to challenge and rethink what is commonly accepted, a benevolent intellectual dissidence. What is striking is that these proposals do not impose a predetermined formula, to be accepted as conclusive. The reader is free to accept or reject any hypothesis offered as a solution. Indeed here, precisely, lies the text's seduction; no matter how far-fetched or improbable a Borgesian hypothesis may seem at the outset, in the end the temptation to succumb to it is irresistible. Borges's essays (like his stories), are an exercise of the free spirit to think and imagine whatever it may. His model argument often proceeds somewhat paradoxically: first, the statement of a problematic theory or question, whether it be literary, philosophical, or cultural; immediately, a recapitulation of the interpretive variants the issue has elicited; next, the proof of some logical error that invalidates these; and finally, the examination of possible alternatives, including Borges's own, accompanied by the suspicion that these too are pervaded by some still undisclosed fallacy. Borges's agnosticism and philosophical skepticism (a legacy of his readings of the Cabalists and English idealists) is the intellectual backdrop for this literary operation which is colored by a running ironic commentary on the laws of human knowledge and its principal instrument, language.

Language is, precisely, the central preoccupation in Borges's work and one that he addressed from his earliest essays. Throughout these, and primarily in *El idioma de los argentinos*, there are visible traces of Croce's ideas concerning the nature of literary language, particularly with respect to the allegory and verbal expression. Very soon, Borges began to distance himself from Croce, underscoring the discrepancies that separate their ideas. The essays "De las alegorías a las novelas" and "Nathaniel Hawthorne" (*Otras inquisiciones*) mark this transition as well as Borges's growing approximation to Chesterton, a writer with whom he felt a great affinity.

It is not difficult to recognize the founding literary principles of Borges's work: the virtual impossibility of Realism in the face of an inexhaustible reality; the conception of writing as an exercise of reduction, selection, and suppression – i.e., to invent, not to produce an impossible copy of lived experience; the notion that allegory is an ideal vehicle for thinking in images, and not, as commonly believed, for abstract thought. Yet the fundamental question underlying all these propositions is an essential one for any reader or writer, namely, what are the limits of language? How can the world be represented through a succession of sounds and conventional signs (or, to quote Borges, quoting Chesterton, through a series of "grunts and screeches" (*ibid.*)? The very nature of language is a sober warning to the writer seeking to create something new: the most we can hope to achieve is a reiteration, with variants, of what has previously been said. In other words, we can only hope to master the instrument of language by working within tradition and not against it. It is easy to understand why modern linguistic theorists and representatives of the French school of theoreticians – from Maurice Blanchot to Michel Foucault – have found Borges's thought so stimulating and have added his name, to Borges's surprise, to the list of precursors of their most sophisticated ideas.

In addition to these essays, the central texts that elucidate Borges's conception of literature (remembering that for him literature is inextricably bound to metaphysical and theological questions concerning such issues as the nature of time or the personality of God) are: "La supersticiosa ética del lector," "La postulación de la realidad," "El arte narrativo y la magia," and "El escritor argentino y la tradición" ["The Superstitious Ethic of the Reader," "The Postulation of Reality," "Narrative Art and Magic," "The Argentine Writer and Tradition"] from *Discusión*; "Las kenningar" ["The Kenningar"] from *Historia de la eternidad*; and "Nuestro pobre individualismo" ["Our Poor Individualism"] from *Otras inquisiciones*. A careful reading of these texts reveals that in spite of their casual air and their pretensionless tone, they constitute a true literary theory, unsystematic but coherent, and attaining the farthest reaches ever attempted in Spanish American thought and literature. After Borges, Spanish American letters would never again be what they once were. The curious reader who scans his pages will be rewarded in yet another way: through the subtle humor that infuses his writings with a grace and wit previously only found in Reyes, with whom Borges maintained close intellectual ties. Borges's irony is a manifestation of his belief that writing is a natural activity and that to associate it with grandiose personalities or ideas is nothing but vanity. His humor is revealed from the very cover of his books; what is more ironic than titling a book *Historia de la eternidad* or another, of scarcely more than one hundred pages, *Historia universal de la infamia* (1935)? What can be said of texts like "Las alarmas del doctor Américo Castro" ["The Alarms of Doctor Américo Castro"] or "Arte de injuriar" ["The Art of Insult"], that are insuperable diatribes, every line of which is filled with barbs as caustic as they are exultant? Borges's irony is, above all, a self-inflicted one; it reflects his conception of his role as writer, practicing his craft with probity, if without hope, as if battling in name of a lost cause. In this light, it is possible to understand why the texts that comprise *Historia universal de la infamia* first appeared in a pastime magazine or why the literary reviews and brief biographies written by Borges between 1936 and 1940 and recently edited under the title of *Textos cautivos* [*Captive Texts*] were originally published in an Argentinian magazine for housewives. Borges is a writer whose intellectual rigor (like that of a geometer or an architect of labyrinths and pyramids) does not prevent him from being gentle and entertaining the way few other writers have been; that is perhaps the greatest compliment that can be paid him. If literary greatness is measured by the pleasure that reading and re-reading a writer's text produces, then Borges is unquestionably among the greatest.

There is an intertwining web of convergences and divergences entangling Borges, Cortázar, and José Lezama Lima (1910–1976). With Cortázar, Borges shares (particularly at the beginning) a vision of the world as a strange and disconcerting place; Borges and Lezama share a common affinity for Francisco de Quevedo, Chesterton, and Valéry, and, moreover, a conception of literary creation as an ordered entity composed of fragments that all remit to a center – the poetic image. Yet the differences separating the three are also significant: Cortázar's mature work is almost the antithesis of Borgesian metaphysics, inasmuch as it attempts to discover the profound sense of historical reality. Lezama's later work, meanwhile, is arduously and almost deliriously baroque, formally at odds with Borges's brand of textual economy and blinding sharpness. Nonetheless, as essayists, all three elaborated texts that in their complexity, their scope, and their richness reveal the existence of an analogous relation between them: their writings are universes of thought and reflection that spin in distinct but overlapping orbits.

While Lezama's first important books of essays, *Analecta del reloj*, *La expresión americana*, and *Tratados en La Habana* date from 1953, 1957, and 1958, respectively, few readers outside Cuba knew of them before 1966, the year of publication of his major novel, *Paradiso*. Its appearance, during that period known as the *Boom* in the Spanish American novel, provoked the rediscovery of his early essays and poems. The obscurity that surrounds Lezama at the start of his writing career and the literary isolation that marked his earlier works contrast sharply with the popularity and intellectual prestige that he has since enjoyed (outside Cuba more so than on the island, where his relation with revolutionary politics grew increasingly strained). After *Paradiso*, Lezama published a huge collection of essays: *La cantidad hechizada* (1970) that confirmed his mastery of the genre.

A distinctive trait of Lezama's work is its inherent "Cubanness," defined in terms of a literary tradition that establishes close ties with its classical peninsular roots (in Lezama's case, particularly through the figure of Luis de Góngora, as well as with the island's African heritage and *criollo* culture. Nation and world, tradition and innovation, spiritualism and sensuality are, for Lezama, parts of the same whole; a totality that is overwhelming, encyclopedic, and complex to the point of seeming babelish and excessive. Lezama absorbs the world of culture with a universal curiosity that is indifferent to boundaries of time, language, or origins. Nothing is extraneous; instead, everything occupies a revered and precise place within a great overall design, like the threads of an unfinished, multicolored tapestry. His is a baroque aesthetic where nothing is wasted and in which each form is a voluptuous composition of materials, tones, and textures of infinite variety.

Lezama is not, nor ever desired to be, easily understood: "Only what is difficult is stimulating" he wrote in the opening lines of *La expresión americana*. If the supreme Borgesian figure is the labyrinth of maddening symmetry, Lezama's is a twisting spiral, decorated to the point of obsession and even impenetrable confusion. He is a fascinating writer, but also one who lets himself be carried away by the proliferating, circular rhythms of his prose and who sometimes gets lost in a void where he hears only his own voice. Like the mythic Narcissus he used as a poetic image, Lezama contemplates himself in a verbal mirror of his own creation, only to fall in love with the feast that satisfies his senses, excited while listening, complacently, to his own Orphic songs. Order is not one of Lezama's virtues; instead, his text proffers the unexpected suggestion, the chance finding of a forgotten treasure, and, above all, the immersion into incandescent levels of the verbal act and of the process of thinking and imagining. For him that process does not consist of ideas, exactly, but of sparks of ideas: brisk collisions of burning materials, violent encounters of historic or fantastic images. Lezama's art is a digressive one wherein Leitmotives and pretexts are often much more important than final propositions. The form in which he weaves relations and analogies between disparate realities attests not only to his vast erudition but also to his powerful imagination. Any one essay of *La expresión americana* suffices as proof. "Sumas críticas de lo americano," for example, opens with a discussion of Pablo Picasso, Igor Stravinski, and James Joyce as models of the innovative spirit of the twentieth century and closes with reflections about the influence of the landscape in Spanish American creative spirit, after references to Egypt, the Middle Ages, and the heroic death of José Martí. Despite the essay's thematic heterogeneity, the argument is visible: American invention involves an exercise in ecumenical synthesis, of which Lezama's own writing is a paradigm.

It may be said that among the myriad images that fly through Lezama's imagination to be illuminated by a penetrating ray of light, there are two fundamental themes: poetry and the conception of Spanish America as cultural creation. His singularity as an essayist consists in marrying the two and reelaborating them as a single utopian proposition that perceives the American continent as the promise of a new "imaginary era," capable of prolonging the universal creations of other times. The very term "imaginary era" is a seed of that promise, inasmuch as it establishes an unheard-of alliance between history and poetic imagery. The essay "Las imágenes posibles" (*Analecta del reloj*) proposes that the image is, in fact, "the last of all possible histories" (Lezama, *El reino imaginario*, 218). This idea presupposes a complete reimagining of Spanish American cultural history and, consequently, of the Americanist question. In a completely free reinterpretation of the ideas of Spengler, Ernst R. Curtius, and Toynbee, Lezama proposes:

> to establish the diverse eras where the image imposed itself as history. That is to say, the Etruscan, the Carolingian, and the Breton imaginations, wherein historical events acquired their reality and gravitation by being born onto the tapestry of an imaginary era. If a culture does not succeed in creating a kind of imagination. . ., it would become grossly undecipherable once burdened with the quantitative freight of millennia. (*ibid.*, 374)

This proposal can only be understood through an appreciation of Lezama's idea of the poetic image as the center of his thought. By creating a new meaning, the image assumes a "new causality"; it proposes a new way of interpreting life and history and, at the same time, of overcoming their limitations. The image is both reason and wonder. This is why Lezama writes that although poetry is "submerged in a pelagic world, it is never illogical" (*ibid.*, 313). His historical conception is Viconian: a system of cycles governed by certain archetypes, myths, or symbols – repeating variations on themes of the imagination that manifest themselves through the poetic language of each period. Human history is the history of human imagination and, in this sense, everything tends toward an ontological or epiphanic vision of human society.

Although his vision seems extreme, it is not unlike theories developed by certain sectors of modern historiography in attempts to explain how humankind imagines and configures its institutions (for example, Cornelius Castoriades's *L'institution imaginaire de la société* [1975] [*The Imaginary Institution of Society*]). In one sense, Lezama installs himself in the rigorous tradition of hermeticism and Catholic-rooted mysticism. Yet he cannot repress a Dionysian, erotic, and jubilant countercurrent that is perhaps best reflected in his sense of humor – Cuban, through and through – and in the liberties of informal chat that his discourse takes. Readers of *Tratados en la Habana*, particularly its second part, are able to savour this freshness firsthand. Logos and Eros, knowledge and play, are the extremes within which his texts orbit, sometimes with dazzling velocity. Lezama's baroque spirit rejoices in contrasts and excesses to such an extent that these sometimes reach the most arbitrary distortions. Like Góngora, he can be admirable, but also irritating. His verbosity sometimes borders on tautology, as when he writes: "The semblance of an image and the image of a semblance, unite the semblance with the image" (*ibid.* 218). Yet this tendency toward obscurity and word play is not a falsely assumed pose but the fruit of an intoxicating knowledge that overflows onto a prose that is almost incantatory and ritual in its incessant flow. No one has ever thought – or written – the way Lezama did; probably no one ever will. His intellectual and imaginary structures found their match in a fertile, reverberating language that was able to embrace and express them and that is truly inimitable.

In contrast to Borges and Lezama Lima, Julio Cortázar (1914–1979) is not "formally" an essayist. However, his exceptional narrative work – and particularly his short stories – led him to write a small number of essays that, while being extremely personal in nature, were also enormously influential in shaping the literary concepts of his time. It is known that he used his novels and stories as means of aesthetic reflection and criticism; conversely, his essays can be read as byproducts of his creative work, but are not for this reason any less original. Cortázar's essayistic texts are, in the first place, exceptionally valuable in order to take a close look at his private laboratory and at the way he conceived of the literary experiments, games, and excursions his work practices. Furthermore, they define the evolution of an aesthetic that distinguished itself for remaining faithful to its central principles, but that nonetheless leaned in the direction of constant change and redefinition. It is an aesthetic that implies not only an intellectual morale, but also an ideological and political stand.

Cortázar published most of his brief essays in miscellaneous volumes in which he put together poems, anecdotes, and anything that was somehow excluded from other books. Genres, and even the concept of books themselves, were empty conventions that aroused his iconoclastic rebelliousness. His most important essays are found in the miscellanies *La vuelta al día en ochenta mundos* (1967) [*Around the Day in Eighty Worlds*], *Ultimo round* (1969) [*Last Round*], and *Territorios* (1978) [*Territories*]; other fundamental essays, such as "Para una poética" (1954) and "Algunos aspectos del cuento" (1962–1963), have appeared in various literary journals. A defining feature of these texts is the intimacy of their tone and the informal manner – irreverent, most of the time – with which they focus on their topics. In a genre that sometimes tends toward solemnity and in a continent where the literary practice can assume annoying pretensions, Cortázar's essays are a breath of fresh air, vivacity, and cordial intelligence; they exemplify the art of expressing profound thoughts without sacrificing daringness, openness, or textual freedom in the process. This is perhaps the result of the passionate and lucid conviction that supported his ideas, which were never systematically learned theories. Cortázar's texts do not want to become crystallized as essays; they are loaded with self-criticism and a playful self-ridicule. *Territorios*, for example, opens with a sort of prologue ("Explicaciones más bien confusas") in which Polanco and Calac, two archetypical figures of mental routine and obtuseness, well-known to Cortázar's readers, reappear to ridicule the author and his decision to publish the book.

Cortázar's thought presents a number of characteristic emblems that are part of the personal mythology of his narrative and which effectively create new bridges between the arts of story-telling and reflection. The figure of the "cronopio," and the sponge and chameleon metaphors he develops each have a precise meaning in his aesthetic formulations. The first is representative of the individual who creates not only through art but also in life, thus resolving an age-old false dilemma; the sponge image serves as a figure for the process of osmosis involved in artistic experience, whereby through an act of transmutation or alchemy, the subject takes hold of an object that was initially alien to him, absorbs it, and incorporates it into his ontological reality. The chameleon is symbolic of our insatiable desire to be something other than what we are and of the risks we are willing to take in order to live in an unknown, but more authentic, dimension. This conception of art and life has a number of significant repercussions; the most critical is the dissolution of subject and object that occurs at the moment of artistic reception, and their subsequent fusion in a place that is neither here nor there. For Cortázar, the aesthetic phenomenon occurs in an interstitial space halfway between the "I" and the "other." The revelation always takes place in an in-between, in a space that did not exist previously and that is the mutual creation of the contemplating subject and the object of contemplation. To experience art requires the abandonment of the self, a realm dominated by habit and passivity. In the essay entitled "Casilla del camaleón," Cortázar defines the poet as the individual who

> renounces the preservation of his own identity in the act of knowing, precisely because the unmistakable sign, that clover mark below the nipple from the fairy-tales, is given to him, from early on, by the experience of feeling himself, at every step, another; of being able to step out of himself to enter the entities that absorb him and to abandon himself to the object that will become a song, to the physical or moral matter whose lyric combustion will provoke the poem.
>
> (*La vuelta al día en 80 mundos*, II: 190)

Although Cortázar cites copiously from Keats, paying a sort of homage to the great English poet, the essay contains a sharp criticism of the notion of the romantic self, as well as an attack on the conceptual simplicity of certain advocates of *engagé* literature. His defense of creative freedom and of the importance of moral responsibility in the exercise of this freedom, culminates with a clearly sarcastic ideological definition:

> That's why, ma'am, I was telling you that many will not understand this chameleon's walk through the variegated rug, even though my favorite color and my preferred route can be discerned merely by looking closely: anyone knows I inhabit the left, [that I am] in the red. But I will never speak about them explicitly, or maybe I will, I neither promise nor deny anything. (*ibid.* 193)

The fluidity of the play of correspondences between the real and the imaginary, the personal and the historic, and even between forms and the undercurrents that move them, is essential to Cortázar's creative enterprise. This is also true for his essays, captivating, above all, because they exist on the very margins of the genre, as personal attempts to establish new routes and new modulations for it. The approximation of literary creation to the act of play, to love-making, and to jazz improvisation is a significant gesture on Cortázar's part. In "Melancolía de las maletas" he writes passionately about the value a jazz fan ascribes to hearing the successive "takes" that are necessary for a recording. He ends up drawing a parallel between practice and "take" that can be read as a poetics:

> Difference between practice and take. A practice leads gradually towards perfection, does not count as product, is present as function of a future. In a take, creation includes its own criticism and for that reason is repeatedly interrupted in order to begin anew; the insufficiency or failure of a take serves as practice for the next one... The best literature is always a take, a risk implicit in performance, a margin of danger that produces the pleasure of driving, of love... I would like to write nothing but takes. (*ibid.* 172)

It is only fair to say that Cortázar the narrator, Cortázar the poet, and Cortázar the essayist were always faithful to this wish. That faithfulness revitalized and enriched Spanish American literature. For his interest in Orientalism, for his focus on the hermetic, the marginal, or the forgotten forms of culture, for his insatiable aesthetic curiosity (which spanned the gamut from neurotic art to strip-tease, from sports to electronic music), he is the Spanish American essayist who most approximates Barthes, particularly the Barthes of *Mythologies* (1957), although without sharing the latter's theorizing passion.

Few in the twentieth century have reached the poetic intensity or the depth of thought that distinguish Octavio Paz (b. 1914). As in Borges and Lezama, there is a sense of totality that unifies Paz's extensive lyrical and essayistic production; it can be said that they constitute a true system of communicating vessels, to borrow Breton's famous image. The poetic act is the experience that most concerns Paz as an essayist; reciprocally, critical reflection is central to his poetic work. Ideas and images, chains of rhythms and of concepts, all remit to a vortex of passion and lucidity that have had profound emotional and intellectual impact both inside and outside the continent. Since the late 1940s, Paz has been one of the most active and influential contemporary literary figures of Spanish America.

For a writer who published journalistic criticism and his first books of poetry in the 1930s, the beginnings of Paz's mature essayistic work are somewhat belated; his first book of essays, *El laberinto de la soledad*, did not appear until 1950 (its English translation, *The Labyrinth of Solitude*, was published in 1961.) Moreover, it was not until the second expanded edition of 1959 that the book – considered Paz's most influential – acquired its present form, marking the birth of a prose and a thought that would become unmistakably his. The genesis and structure of the book deserve attention. Paz's stimulus for writing it was his brief experience as the recipient of a scholarship to the United States (1944). His travels throughout California and New York confronted him with the double strangeness of an unknown country and a Latin (and especially Mexican) culture extrapolated from its place of origin. The book was a search for the historic roots of Mexican culture, a question about its identity, and a portrait of the individuals who keep that culture alive both within and outside its geographic borders. Although centered on historical and sociopsychological issues that define Mexicanness, *El laberinto de la soledad* is a contribution to the unabated Americanist question, inasmuch as it is an impassioned inquiry into the character of Spanish American culture in the face of North American nationalism and hegemony.

The influence of Samuel Ramos (1897–1959), whose theory about the personality of the Mexican Paz defends against detractors, is apparent in *El laberinto de la soledad*; so too is the influence of Existentialism, particularly in its questioning of authenticity, of the dilemma between the individual and the "other," and of the solitude that generates historic alienation. Likewise, a close reading uncovers a change in tone and focus between the first five chapters, tracing the spiritual profile of the Mexican, and the last three, recounting the historical destiny of the country, from its origins through the present. The epilogue, which did not form part of the first edition, is a deep philosophic meditation about love as a path out of the labyrinth of solitude and about the moral responsibility of the Mexican in the modern world. Paz exalts the virtues of myth, poetry, and utopia, as opposed to pure human reason, which has led us to the very borders of annihilation. Everything must be rethought, the labyrinthine path retraced.

The basic repertory of the ideas and formulations which configure Paz's philosophy are already present in *El laberinto de la soledad*: his unshakable faith in poetry as a means to freedom; the play of masks and true realities that challenges the thrust to know; his theory of love as the acknowledgment of the indispensable essence of the "other"; the promise and the failure of revolution; the dialectic between silence and utterance, between the instant and eternity. While some of the sociological observations of *El laberinto de la soledad* have become outdated with time – the 1970 *Postdata* [*The Other Mexico: Critique de la Pyramid*] is an attempt to update these – there is no doubt that the work is seminal.

The long list of books of essays, articles, and critical commentaries that Paz has accumulated over time makes the selection of the most important difficult, not merely because of their sheer abundance, but moreover, because of the breadth of their themes and their far-reaching proposals. His essays are a compendium of all that can interest a modern man of universal aspirations: hermetic poetry, erotic customs, Hinduism, criticism of the totalitarian state, avant-garde art, magic, drugs, translation, myths, history... In this sense, Paz is like Reyes and even more like Ortega y Gasset, both rigorous thinkers who were also witnesses of their times, seduced by the analysis of all current events. The thousands of prose pages that Paz has written constitute a sort of encyclopedia of what a man knows, and especially of what a man hopes to know. In spite of the enormous heterogeneity that colors his work, several books can be singled out as keys to understanding his thought, without forgetting that there are important texts in other collections as well.

El arco y la lira (1956) [*The Bow and the Lyre*] is one of Paz's most beautiful and most important essays. Its subject is poetry (or better yet, the poem), the specific character of poetic revelation, and the function of poetry in our time. The book is at once a rigorous study of the form and meaning of poetry and a meditation that can be read as the personal poetics of a masterful creator. The idea of tension that already appears in the title – objects that vibrate, charged with a sense of imminence and resonance – alludes to Paz's own poetic vision as well as to his deep belief that poetry, far from being a superfluous practice of the minorities, is of critical importance in our times. In the promise of communion it holds, poetry is capable of transforming civilization, making it into something truly human. Once again it is worthwhile noting that it is the second, expanded edition of *El arco y la lira* (1967) that best expresses Paz's thoughts on these matters.

The years that elapsed between the first and second editions of the book were decisive ones for Paz; they coincide with his second stay in Paris (1960–1962) and a stay in India (1962–1968), two cultural experiences that provoked a reformulation of his aesthetic and philosophical beliefs. The traces of Surrealism and postwar European thought that marked his earlier work did not disappear altogether, but were recast and creatively integrated with new ideas, resulting in a syncretism that is perhaps the most outstanding feature of his mature work. It is precisely this capacity for synthesis that best characterizes Paz's writing, together with the power of the images that express it. Everything – from Japanese art to the Avant-Garde, philosophy to anthropology, Oriental cultures to modern poetics – is absorbed by a powerful imagination wherein it is processed and transformed into something new and original. *El arco y la lira* opens a discussion that will be recurrent in Paz's work: the criticism of Western culture. In contrast to Oriental cultures, Western culture has lost the fertile dialogue that links the spirit to the body, religion to eroticism, reason to passion. Our world is a divided one; poetry is the instrument for its reintegration. There is a certain brand of mysticism in Paz, but it is a godless one, based instead on the individual's desires and urgencies to make this life, and not the other, transcendental.

Two relatively brief essays bear witness to Paz's double meeting with Structuralism and the Orient: *Claude Lévi Strauss* (1967) [*Claude Lévi Strauss: An Introduction*] and *Conjunciones y disyunciones* (1969) [*Conjunctions and Disjunctions*]. The first is a valuable summary of the French anthropologist's structuralist theories and of their philosophical, linguistic, and aesthetic repercussions; moreover, it is an updating of Paz's ideas in those same fields. The book is thus an intellectual portrait and self-portrait, simultaneously. The second essay started out as a prologue to a book, which later grew into meditations and digressions about the differences between Eastern and Western sexual customs, between the concepts of *body* and *non-body*, between Buddhist and Medieval art, and between signs and realities. Paz incorporates his observations into a sweeping design that reinterprets Western culture and establishes unexpected relations between all its constitutive elements: science, aesthetics, religion, politics, ethics. The repressive Western spirit accounts for the rebelliousness that has exploded everywhere throughout the modern world. What has been denied for centuries wants to make its presence known, through the promises held in love and poetry.

Paz's most outstanding contribution to the criticism of modern art (which in the last several years, has more than ever attracted Paz's interest) is the 1972 book, *Apariencia desnuda* (second, expanded edition, 1978) [*Marcel Duchamp or The Castle of Purity*]. The collection includes two essays about Marcel Duchamp that are introductions to his art and detailed studies of two of his most important masterpieces. Paz's interest in and admiration for Duchamp come as no surprise: Duchamp embodies the attitudes of total rebellion and critical irony that place modern art at the very limits of its own denial and renovation. These ideas are expanded and reelaborated in *Los hijos del limo* (1974) [*Children of the Mire*], which traces a brief history of the evolution of modern poetry, from Romanticism through the present, and examines the fundamental questions that have defined it: the tendency toward rupture, irony, analogical thought, and revolutionary fascination. The book refined and popularized the concept of "modernity" which, despite having been introduced in the European critical idiom by Jürgen Habermas and others, was generally ignored by Spanish American critics; the word has since been accepted as common currency in critical debate.

Among Paz's most recent productions, several books merit attention. *El signo y el garabato* (1973) is a collection of essays about culture, technology, art and poetry; the first essay expresses an idea that is common to the rest of the book: "If the [atomic] bomb has not destroyed the world, it has destroyed our idea of the world" (p. 14). *El ogro filantrópico* (1979), is another collection of essays and texts of diverse caliber and intention, but all centered on the criticism of the technocratic and totalitarian modern state and its relations with the artist or intellectual. *Sor Juana Inés de la Cruz o las trampas de la fe* (1982) [*Sor Juana or the Traps of Faith*], is Paz's most important work of literary criticism since *El arco y la lira*; it is also a fascinating examination of colonial Mexican society, of the conflicts between church dogmas and intellectual freedom, as well as of the position of a woman, within this context.

However, the most original, unusual, and even radical essay Paz has ever written is, without doubt, *El mono gramático*, (1974) [*The Monkey Grammarian*] (originally published in French, 1972). It is a text that seems to contain all the questions, visions, and images that have disquieted Paz's spirit. To call it an "essay" is perhaps a misnomer, since it trespasses all the frontiers of the genre: it is a prose poem, an account of a ritual journey, and at the same time, a meditation about poetry, art, and about the very act of writing the text. Perhaps, it would be more precise to call it by an expression coined by Paz himself: a "constellation of signs." Paz's ideas about analogy and convergence as essential operations of poetic language are here put into practice. The text blends two separate scenes made homologous by the imagination – an English garden in Cambridge and the road to Galta in India – and sets forth in search of something beyond those realities: an absolute where differences are resolved in the superior reality of poetic revelation, enhanced by artistic visions and by Oriental mysticism. The book is a living metaphor for the act that engenders it: for the acts of reading and writing as paths that entwine and fuse as the bodies of two lovers in a passionate embrace.

The striking unity of Paz's thought and his faithfulness to certain fundamental notions does not imply, however, that his thought has not evolved and undergone revisions over time. The changes that punctuate his work are perhaps most visible in his political writing and in his cultural criticism. Paz has progressively distanced himself from the various ideological positions he has held at different stages in his career (the road to Galta in India – and sets forth in search of something beyond those defense of Republican Spain, Marxist humanism, ideological art, and support of the Cuban Revolution in its early stages); he has adopted, instead, a more guarded or perhaps more skeptical attitude toward contemporary historical events, both inside and outside Spanish America. His horrified vision of Stalinism has resulted in his fear that revolutionary radicalism will lead to a cataclysmic repetition of history. Notwithstanding ideological shifts, Paz's evolution has in no way clouded the lucidity and dialectic transparency of his thought or the exemplary beauty of his prose style. This beauty is double: interior, inasmuch as it presupposes an exact correspondence with the movement of the ideas discussed; exterior in its embellishment of those ideas with an indelible form that we tend to identify with truth. Paz's prose is elastic, intense, made of raw nerve; it moves unabatedly from one thing to another in a succession of transformations, parallels, contrasts, and homologies that awaken powerful convictions. His elegance is intellectual rather than rhetorical, made of daring synthesis and condensations. The suppression of logical or merely explanatory connectives (manifested as colons replacing entire sentences or commas joining opposing levels of discourse) together with the use of enumerative series, litanies, and incantatory formulas lend his prose a swiftness and levity that make it akin to the act of thinking. Paradoxically, this rhetorical concision produces an abundance of images and brings out richness that was previously unperceived. Rigorous and sensual, impassioned and meditative, Paz's prose is like his poetry; or better yet, inasmuch as it is a critical exercise of language, it represents the other face of poetic form.

Two novelists, Ernesto Sábato (b. 1911) and Alejo Carpentier (1904–1980), have each played significant roles in the development of the Spanish American essay in the twentieth century. Sábato is a thinker of the European humanist tradition. His intellectual evolution and his decision to write literature were largely influenced by a number of extraneous factors: his disenchantment with science (he received a doctorate in physics in 1938 and worked in the Curies' laboratory in Paris), his allegiance to and subsequent repudiation of the Communist Party, and his firsthand experience of Europe on the brink of the Second World War. Although he was in contact with the surrealist group in the Paris of 1939 and his intellect, trained in scientific reasoning, succumbed to the fascination of the irrational, Sábato's work is more directly colored by existentialist ideas. This Existentialism is reflected not only in the matters that concerned him – freedom, evil, rebellion against the dehumanizing abstraction of social norms, the dark side of life, the psychological impact of everyday acts – but also in his embittered, somber, and sarcastic tone. His mentors, furthermore, are easily discernible: Kierkegaard, Dostoyevsky, Sartre, and Camus.

Sábato's essays present him as an intuitive and non-conformist philosopher and not as a theoretician. He is a thinker who meditates through his sensibility, finding his way amidst sharp contradictions. The very form of his essay collections attests to this; *Uno y el universo* (1945) and *Hombres y engranajes* (1951) are, for example, repertories of brief notes that cover a wide variety of issues: science, metaphysics, Marxism, sex, religion, culture, language. . . More organic and substantial, *El escritor y sus fantasmas* (1963) focuses on the practice of writing as an art and as a morale. Meanwhile, Sábato's deep concern for the Argentinian reality and its popular culture is reflected in such books as *La cultura en la encrucijada nacional* (1973) and *Tango. Discusión y clave* (1963). A controversial and polemic thinker, Sábato has stressed the point that the writer must have persistence and the courage to remain faithful to his convictions, even when they require the defense of uncomfortable positions.

If Existentialism is the dominating influence in Sábato, then the Avant-Garde (especially the surrealist spirit) is the decisive influence in Carpentier. Somewhat like Lezama (above), Carpentier felt the double attraction of history (particularly of the eighteenth century), on the one hand, and the aesthetic innovations propagated in Europe, on the other. He was doubly seduced by the call of the primitive and the refinement of high culture, by the mysteries of Gothic landscapes and the *criollo* architecture of Havana.

His first essay is the massive and erudite study *La música en Cuba* (1946), fruit of his passion as a musicologist and of careful investigation of Cuban archives and forgotten documents. The book rescues a valuable artistic and anthropological heritage that would have otherwise been lost. Beyond this, and in spite of its highly specialized subject, it is an important text in Carpentier's literary evolution; writing the book required learning the useful art of historical reconstruction (essential to his narrative work) as well as the Baroque prose that would be Carpentier's foremost contribution to Spanish American novel. In *Tientos y diferencias* (1964), a collection of literary and cultural essays, Carpentier reworks a number of Sartre's ideas about novelistic contexts to conclude that "the legitimate style for the Spanish American novelist is the baroque" (Carpentier, 1967, 38). *La novela hispanoamericana en vísperas de un nuevo siglo y otros ensayos* (1981) is a collection of diverse meditations on the novel, culture, music, and art. Carpentier's abundant work as a cultural chronicler has been anthologized recently in several volumes: *Letra y solfa* (1975), *Bajo el signo de la Cibeles* (1979), and *Este músico que llevo dentro* (1980).

Yet the critical repercussions of all these texts together have not surpassed the overwhelming impact of one singular essay: the prologue to his novel *El reino de este mundo* (1949), later revised under the title "De lo real maravilloso americano" and included in *Tientos y diferencias*.

Reread during the 1960s, in the context of the Spanish American novelistic *Boom*, Carpentier's prologue would become at least as famous as the novel it accompanied; it unleashed endless commentaries, finally becoming a sort of aesthetic manifesto of the distinctively American literary phenomenon of "Magical Realism," thereby marking the definitive rupture with the European models that had dominated the literary arena until that time. Before analyzing this crucial text, several observations should be made.

To begin with, the formula "realismo maravilloso" ["marvellous realism"] has clear antecedents: it is most directly associated with the surrealist concept of the *merveilleux*, but in a critical way. The prologue documents Carpentier's disenchantment with the fantastic imagery of Surrealism, which he attacks for both personal and aesthetic reasons. He instead puts emphasis on the term "real," implying that what is truly marvellous already exists in the American reality, if only we are able to contemplate it from a perspective that remains faithful to its essence and originality. Carpentier also ridicules the type of *engagé* literature put in vogue by Existentialism; it is fairly evident that he wants to propose an American alternative not just to one, but to both of the great European philosophical–literary currents of the moment. Secondly, the term "Magical Realism" with which the prologue has so often been connected, was employed for the first time by the avant-garde critic and photographer, Franz Roh (1890–1965) who in 1925 published his *Nachexpressionismus – Magischer Realismus* [*German Art in the Twentieth Century*] in Leipzig. Carpentier undoubtedly knew this text in its Spanish translation, published in the June 1927 issue of *Revista de Occidente*, the literary journal directed by Ortega y Gasset. In contrast, Carpentier seems to have had no knowledge of Borges's important essay "El arte narrativo y la magia," which uses the expression in a different sense altogether, relating it to fantastic literature. In the third place, what sparked Carpentier's interest in defining a new literary canon for the American continent was the integration of these ideas with those discussed by Oswald Spengler in *The Decline of the West* (1918; English translation, 1926). Once more it is worthwhile to note the intervention of Ortega y Gasset, whose publishing house translated Spengler's book into Spanish as early as 1923; this was undoubtedly the edition that Carpentier knew. Carpentier's affirmation that " the feeling of the marvellous presupposes a faith" (*ibid.*, 7) is clearly based on Spengler, for whom the existence of a faith, perceived primarily as a religious element, is the criterion that distinguishes between a culture and a civilization. For Spengler, European civilization had abdicated its cultural reign as a result of its loss of faith; in its place, the primitive world emerged as the cradle of a new culture for modern man. It is within this context that Carpentier's attacks on Surrealism and on manifestations of "the marvellous predicated on disbelief" (*ibid.*, 8) must be considered. Despite the frequent misunderstandings the prologue has generated through the years as well as some of the debatable assumptions it contains, there is no doubt that the text is a captivating one: it is the meeting point of many ideas about art, culture and history, and it has engaged the best American minds for almost half a century.

Argentina's so-called "*Sur* group" was a brilliant assembly of writers and intellectuals congregated around the literary journal of the same name. Founded in 1931, it was, for more than thirty years, a focus of diffusion of the very best of universal culture, with strong leanings toward what came from Europe. Paradoxically, this Eurocentrism (a traditional feature in Argentinian letters) served as a pretext for the numerous attacks the group received from radical factions. It must be said that *Sur* was much more than a journal; it was, in effect, a selective library (not only because it was also a publishing house) in which several generations of Argentinian and Spanish Americans learned to read Kafka, T. E. Lawrence, Graham Greene, Virginia Woolf, and André Malraux, among others. *Sur* is the single, greatest contribution made by the enlightened Argentinian bourgeoisie in the twentieth century.

From this group, whose central figure is Borges, several other names deserve mention. Victoria Ocampo (1890–1979) not only founded the magazine and served as the group's spiritual leader of sorts, but also wrote a number of books in her own right; among them, her memoirs, published in ten volumes under the title *Testimonios* (1935–1977), constitute an important chapter in Argentinian intellectual life. An admirable narrator, José Bianco (1911–1986) served as the journal's chief editor for twenty-three years, during which time he wrote and published numerous notes and essays. *Ficción y realidad (1946–1976)* (1977), for example, is a splendid collection of texts devoted to European and Spanish American literary topics. Two other authors whose influence today is much less than in their own time are Eduardo Mallea (1903–1982) and Héctor A. Murena (1923–1975).

Other Americanist thinkers of this period are of a more liberal intellectual and political bent than these two. There are a number of influential writers who participated in the development of cultural, historical, and literary movements of the time not only through their books, but also through their activities in the fields of politics, journalism, and public education. The Cuban Jorge Mañach is remembered as one of the founders of *Revista de Avance*, an important periodical published from 1927 to 1930, as a biographer of José Martí (*Martí, el apóstol* [1933]), and as author of *Indagación del choteo* (1928), an original anthropological study about the festive and even scoffing attitude with which Cubans respond to the pressures of daily life. Mañach's ideas can perhaps best be compared to those of Ramos and with Paz's observations about the "pachuco" in *El laberinto de la soledad* (above). The Ecuadorian Benjamín Carrión (1898–1976) wrote numerous essays, but none better than his captivating and memorable biography of his country's dictator, *García Moreno, el santo del patíbulo* (1959).

Since the 1920s, the Peruvian Luis Alberto Sánchez (1900–1994) has been producing an abundant and varied work as a literary critic and historiographer, university professor, journalist, politician, novelist, biographer, and ideologue. His prolonged association with the APRA party complicated his intellectual life with exile and persecution, a factor that explains in part the seeming carelessness and hurriedness of some of his writings. His devotion to literature is without question; what is questionable are his judgment and, quite often, his taste. Nonetheless, Sánchez's *La literatura peruana*, a vast literary history that in its most recent edition of 1966 comprised five volumes, is an indispensable summary; in its sociocritical orientation, the work may be read as a reaction against the ideas of Riva-Agüero (above). At the time of its publication, *América: novela sin novelistas* (1933) caused significant stir, but its central thesis, stated in the title, was rapidly disproved. Sánchez's most solid and rigorous critical works are his various studies about González Prada and, above all, his 1960 intellectual biography of the Peruvian poet José Santos Chocano, entitled *Aladino o vida y obra de José Santos Chocano*.

The Colombian Germán Arciniegas (b. 1900) is comparable to Sánchez in the thematic diversity of his work and in his considerable public activity. Arciniegas is dominated, however, by a passion for the historical interpretation of America. In his books, history tends to be reconstructed in a very personal way, colored by a poetic flair and filtered through a hopeful outlook for the future. Over time, that optimistic faith led him to adopt cultural simplifications and somewhat conformist postures in the face of America's social problems. Of all his work, *Este pueblo de América* (1945) captures the best of his thought and his prose.

Two prestigious Venezuelan essayists and public figures who represent other versions of liberal humanism in twentieth-century Spanish America are Mariano Picón Salas (1901–1965) and Arturo Uslar Pietri (b. 1906). Picón Salas was an ambitious cultural historian (*De la conquista a la independencia. Tres siglos de historia cultural hispanoamericana* [1944]) and an impassioned Americanist (*Europa-América. Preguntas a la esfinge de la cultura* [1947]), whose primary concern was for a harmonious relation between man and Nature. However, his most significant and original contributions to the essayistic genre are to be found in the pages of the various books that comprise his intellectual autobiography, as, for example, *Viaje al amanecer* (1943) and *Regreso de tres mundos* (1959). Uslar is the author of novels, chronicles, and essays, among which *Letras y hombres de Venezuela* (1948) and *En busca del Nuevo Mundo* (1969) stand out; the first for making reference to the term "Magical Realism" before even Carpentier (above), and the second as a lucid summary of Uslar's Americanist vision.

Hernán Díaz Arrieta (1891–1984), better known by his pseudonym "Alone," and Ricardo Latcham (1903–1965) are two Chileans who made considerable contributions to the development of literary studies in Chile and throughout Spanish America. Finally, the Mexican Edmundo O'Gorman (b. 1906) analyzed the past as a historian, but with a philosopher's penetration and an artist's creative imagination. His best-known work is the subtle and well-documented *La invención de América* (1958), but he also authored other important studies concerning the history of the Conquest and colonization.

In the field of philosophy, the Mexican Leopoldo Zea (b. 1912) is, without doubt, the one who has posited the most profound questions and problems of contemporary philosophy and applied them to the realities of the American continent. Influenced by the ideas of Ortega y Gasset and existentialist philosophy, Zea conceives of thinking not merely as a speculative and abstract exercise, but as a reflection that takes into account sociohistorical circumstances and the moral responsibilities these impose on Spanish Americans. The subject of Mexicanism, and more broadly, Americanism, is fundamental in his work. His early texts are, primarily a critique of Positivism in Mexico and in Spanish America: *El positivismo en México* (1943), *Apogeo y decadencia del positivismo en México* (1944), and *Dos etapas del pensamiento en Hispanoamérica: del romanticismo al positivismo* (1949). Zea's effort to understand the philosophy of a specific culture within the frame of its historical context does not constitute a resurgence of regionalist or even nationalist ideas; on the contrary, his philosophical Americanism is part of an ecumenical and providential vision that rescues – and unites – the Western humanist tradition and Eastern transcendentalism. It is precisely this sort of double rescue operation that occurs in *América en la conciencia de Europa* (1952) and *América en la historia* (1957). Zea's ideas about America are interesting to compare with those posited by Carpentier in the prologue to *El reino de este mundo*; in both cases America is conceived as a new promised land that arises from the ashes of European civilization. For Zea, when the Mexican thinks or creates, he does so, like men of any nationality, with a universal vocation, as part of a great project that involves everyone. An individual's respect for his own culture is in strict symmetry with his recognition of the dignity of other cultures; mutual access to that which is one's own birthright and that which is patrimony of the other, redeems mankind from spiritual poverty and existential solitude.

Zea's other works, such as *La cultura y el hombre de nuestros días* (1959) and *Latinoamérica en la formación de nuestro tiempo* (1965), reflect even greater concern for the urgent problems of the moment as well as for defining the tasks of an empiric philosophy. The 1969 *La filosofía americana como la filosofía sin más* responds to a disquieting question posited by other philosophers, like the Argentinian Rizieri Frondizi (1910–1983) and the Peruvian Augusto Salazar Bondy (1926–1974): does a Spanish American philosophy truly exist? Somewhat contentiously, Zea suggests that the question is part of the problem, inasmuch as it presupposes the existence of a philosophy (European) that serves as model for all others.

At a midpoint between philosophy and history is the work of another Mexican thinker, Silvio Zavala (b. 1909). Zavala's countless contributions in the field of political history and his investigations concerning the predominating ideas in colonial America are indispensable reflections of how Spanish America's destiny was articulated alongside the universal historical movements of the 1940s and 1950s.

In more recent years, the essayistic genre has undergone a radical transformation both in its form and in its cultural and social significance. On one hand, the extraordinary growth of social sciences has provoked a true revolution, that has not only opened previously unimagined fields of analysis, but that has also questioned the very activity of thought and the position of the thinker. On the other hand, the influence of semiology, Structuralism, Post-structuralism, feminism, psychoanalytic criticism, and other new methodologies, with the breadth of topics they encompass – from language to the revision of cultural statutes to social psychiatry – has profoundly altered the genre's status. Literary essays and social investigations are no longer what they once were. Nevertheless, the advances that have been achieved in the genre are not exempt from problems.

The theorizing fervor of the last several decades has disseminated everywhere, creating a language – a metalanguage, according to its users – that is nothing but a highly specialized technical jargon, inaccessible to the unwary reader. At the hands of the legions of disciples of Lévi-Strauss, Barthes, Jakobson, A. J. Greimas, Emile Benveniste, Julia Kristeva, Jacques Lacan, and Jacques Derrida, the essay has become more ambitious and better informed, but at the same time more hermetic and intransitive, losing, in the process, one of the cardinal virtues of the genre: the free circulation of ideas. The scientific pretensions of these new essayistic models are not modest; they aspire to formulate a unifying theory of human language, that will serve equally well for the analysis of a poem, a journalistic article, or a political slogan. The search for a "new objectivity" has produced works of unquestionable rigor and originality, but has also fallen into a scientific absolutism that tends to suffocate intellectual debates open to other concepts and principles. Methodological precision is without doubt a worthy aspiration, except when used solely to prove the validity of the method, forgetting, in the process, the specificity of the object of study.

Despite these limitations, it is undeniable that contemporary theories of literary criticism have provoked more probing examinations of the phenomena characteristic of the last half of the twentieth century: the questioning of political ideologies, the vertiginous propagation of means of communication, as well as the forms of production and diffusion of a vast popular culture according to complex sets of rules. These questions plainly affect the place that literature is accorded in modern civilization. This holds particularly true for the essay, inasmuch as it is a genre that cannot remain indifferent to the impact of such issues on the thought, imagination, and aspirations of millions. While most of the cultural messages that we receive today are visual, they are not based on reading. What are the repercussions of this on our image- and idea-generating processes? The answer is still elusive, at best. The essay, in response, has adopted – and adapted – new forms in order to incorporate this highly charged problematic and, moreover, in order to survive in a culture that tends more and more toward homogeneity.

If the essayistic genre has, on the one hand, undergone tremendous formal changes in response to evolving modes of thought and perception, it has, on the other, reverted to its origins in its growing approximation to journalism. The North American so-called "new journalism," which represented the possibility of objective and at the same time personal reporting, found a healthy following among Spanish American essayists, particularly in Mexico and Argentina, where important books of socio-political investigative reporting have been published throughout the last several decades. In effect, the boundaries of the essay have become, if not completely erased, then certainly tenuous, resulting in the tremendous overlaps between essays and testimonials, documentaries, and chronicles. Previous attempts to write what could be considered the all-encompassing essay have given way to a privileging of a certain aspect or level of reality that somehow gives sense to the rest. This tendency toward specialization accounts, at least in part, for the relative paucity of essays focusing on Americanist themes during these years. Nevertheless, the expansion of editorial activity and the consequent increase in the production of books, magazines, and newspapers, has also served to stimulate the essay, particularly those concerning social or political issues.

Curiously enough, Spanish American literary studies (which during the 1960s enjoyed a "boom" parallel to the novel's) have significantly benefitted from the impetus provided by North American academia, although it was traditionally France and Germany that were known as centers of Spanish literary investigation abroad. A marked interest in Hispanic literature started at the beginning of the century in the United States, attributable, in large part, to a group of distinguished Spanish professors, many of whom were disciples of Ramón Menéndez Pidal (1869–1968); as a result, the focus was primarily on peninsular literature. Among the pioneers of Spanish American culture and literature in the United States, the most outstanding figure is, undoubtedly, Pedro Henríquez Ureña (above), who, from 1916 on, was professor at the University of Minnesota. After the Spanish Civil War, the diaspora of Spanish intellectuals who emigrated to the United States and occupied professorships in North American universities – Américo Castro (1885–1972), Pedro Salinas (1891–1951), Luis Cernuda (1902–1963), and Francisco Ayala (b. 1908), to name just a few – further helped to promote the diffusion of Spanish American literature in the States. One expression of this renewed interest was the 1934 founding of *Revista Hispánica Moderna* by Federico de Onís (1885–1966), co-directed after 1954 by Angel del Río (1900–1962) and Eugenio Florit (b. 1903), as an organ of Columbia University's Hispanic Society. Another manifestation of the increased attraction held by Spanish American literature was the foundation in 1938 of the International Institute for Ibero-American Literature (Instituto Internacional de Literatura Iberoamericana) and its publication, *Revista Iberoamericana*, at the University of Pittsburgh.

These, then, are the bases that support the notable expansion in the study of Spanish American literature in the United States, as a result of different historical and cultural circumstances. North American universities have profited from the presence and work of many Spanish Americans, primarily Cubans, Argentinians, Uruguayans, and Chileans, escaping dictatorships during the 1970s and seeking respite from the profound economic crises of the 1980s. An unexpected consequence of all this is that new generations of Spanish American critics and investigators have written some of their best work in English, rekindling the question of what criteria serve to frame a determined literary production: is it the author's nationality, the theme of his work, or the language in which he writes?

Finally, North American schools of theory and criticism have served as a channel for the transmission of the new French – and American – critical language to Spanish American essayists. The brands of post-structuralist theories and Derridean deconstruction best known by Spanish American writers are, for the most part, those interpreted and reformulated by the influential Yale school of criticism, whose most prominent representatives are Paul de Man and Harold Bloom (b. 1930). In the social sciences, Spanish American essayists have also made use of ideas and models proposed by North American researchers – although quite often with revisionist intentions.

The list of professors who are also literary critics is a long one, spanning several generations and meriting, therefore, a backwards recapitulation. Before doing so, however, it is necessary to address the resurgent problem of generic boundaries, reincarnated in this case as the fine line dividing the essay, as such, from literary criticism. When a work of literary criticism goes beyond simple textual interpretation or erudite investigation, it becomes an essay. The difference is not merely one of the personal focus or implicit intention of the text in question, but moreover, of the intellectual and even social repercussions that it presents. The factors that imbue literary criticism with essayistic qualities will be taken into consideration in the following selection of authors. It must be recognized, however, that the dividing line between essay and criticism is quite often tenuous at best.

Although the so-called "founders" of Spanish American literary criticism belong to schools of interpretation that have for some time been outdated, their historic significance in creating the discipline is of great importance. The Chilean Arturo Torres Ríoseco (1897–1971), the Mexican Andrés Iduarte, and the Hispano-Cuban Eugenio Florit, among others, provided the documental and historical bases for the study of Spanish American letters as well as the first critical approximations to this literature as a specific field of study. More modern and currently more valid contributions to the discipline were made by the notable group of Argentinian scholars who arrived in the United States after having been trained in philology and stylistics by Henríquez Ureña and Amado Alonso (1896–1952). Among the most prominent members of this group are: María Rosa Lida de Malkiel (1910–1962), who worked primarily in the fields of classic and nineteenth-century literatures; Raimundo Lida (1908–1979), author of *Letras hispánicas* (1958), a book that ranges thematically from linguistic philosophy to readings of Borges; Enrique Anderson Imbert (b. 1910), whose *Historia de la literatura hispanoamericana* (1961) and *La originalidad de Rubén Darío* (1967) continue to be read as indispensable reference works; and Ana María Barrenechea, author of one of the first books about Borges as well as of *Textos hispanoamericanos* (1978), a collection of brief critical essays dating from 1953.

These scholars, and others close to them in age, can be considered the forebears of those Spanish American literary critics whose work is most widely read today. Although the majority are still active, two of the most important in the group have died recently: Emir Rodríguez Monegal (1921–1987) and Angel Rama (1926–1983), both Uruguayans. Very different and, to a certain extent, parallel figures, (both started careers in literary journalism in Uruguay, suffered the hardships of exile, and ended up as professors at Yale and the University of Maryland, respectively),

Rodríguez Monegal and Rama developed their mature work in a climate of constant debate. The rivalry between them exacerbated their differences in sensibilities, backgrounds, and personal convictions; that rivalry has extended – with even greater bitterness – to their disciples. Rodríguez Monegal was trained in England and was a great reader and admirer of Anglo-Saxon literature; Rama, meanwhile, had an inclination for French literature. From a critical perspective, Rodríguez Monegal subscribed to the *nouvelle critique*, while Rama was attracted to Walter Benjamin (1892–1940) and German social criticism. Rodríguez Monegal represented a peculiar form of literary criticism that respected the specificity of the text, without ignoring biographic and psychoanalytic factors. Rama, on the other hand, envisioned literature as one thread in a broader social and historical tapestry; as a good social critic, he could not conceive of literature in any context that did not also make room for questions of ideology, political pressures, and the problematic, changing context of Spanish America. Finally, the styles of the two were extremely different. Rodríguez Monegal's prose was elegant, ironic, and aesthetically pleasing; Rama's, by comparison, tended toward long, dry sentences and overwrought conceptual density. Given all this, it was only natural, then, that Rodríguez Monegal and Rama rivalled and polemicized as they did, quite often brilliantly. Much of their polemic was focused around the Spanish American novelistic *Boom* and resulted in a revitalization and modernization of the critical instruments at hand for reading and understanding the new Spanish American novel.

Without their human presence, Rodríguez Monegal's and Rama's books would perhaps represent something different from what they do, but there is no doubt that they are important contributions. Among Rodríguez Monegal's works, the following must be mentioned: *Narradores de esta América* (1961; second expanded edition: vol. I, 1969; vol. II, 1974), *El viajero inmóvil. Introducción a Pablo Neruda* (1966), *El desterrado. Vida y obra de Horacio Quiroga* (1968), *El otro Andrés Bello* (1969), *Jorge Luis Borges. A Literary Biography* (1978). Rama's more important books are: *Rubén Darío y el modernismo* (1970), *Los dictadores latinoamericanos* (1976), *La novela latinoamericana. Panoramas 1920–1980* (1982), and *La ciudad letrada* (1984). These lists, however, tell only part of the story: the work of both of these critics is also to be found in their innumerable articles in periodicals, reportings, and polemics, and especially, in the creation of journals (such as the decisive *Mundo Nuevo*, which Rodríguez Monegal directed from Paris between 1966 and 1968) and editorial projects (such as the important Biblioteca Ayacucho founded by Rama in Caracas, as testimony of his passion for Spanish America).

The abundance of names that are active today in the field of academic literary criticism allows the mention here of only a few. Some belong to the generation before that of Rodríguez Monegal and Rama, but the fruit of their many years in North American universities continues through today. Among them: the Chilean Eduardo Neale-Silva (b. 1905), diligent interpreter of the work of César Vallejo (1892–1938); the Cubans José Juan Arrom (b. 1910), who has devoted studies to the literary generations in the continent as well as to his own national culture, and José Olivio Jiménez (b. 1926), specialist in *Modernismo* and Spanish American poetry. Immediately following this group chronologically are: Enrique Pupo-Walker (b. 1933), also Cuban and author of important works on colonial chronicles and letters; and the two Argentinians Jaime Alazraki (b. 1934) and Sylvia Molloy (b. 1938), who have made substantial contributions to the study of Borges's work.

The younger academic critics are no less numerous. Two of the most interesting are Roberto González Echevarría (b. 1943) and Enrico Mario Santí (b. 1949), both Cubans and both authors of extensive critical work in English as well as Spanish. González Echevarría, who has been influenced by the Yale school of theory, is the author of *Alejo Carpentier. The Pilgrim at Home* (1977), *Isla a su vuelo fugitiva* (1983), *The Voice of the Master*, and *La ruta de Severo Sarduy* (1987). Santí has published *Pablo Neruda. The Poetics of Prophecy* (1982) and *Escritura y tradición*, as well as a collection of Octavio Paz's early critical work (*Primeras letras*, 1988) and the critical edition of Paz's *Libertad bajo palabra* (1988). The Peruvian Julio Ortega (b. 1942) has written numerous works on Spanish American poetry and the novel, paying especially close attention to Peruvian writers and culture. Puerto Rican and Antillean literature in general, and in particular, the work of Cintio Vitier (b. 1921; below), owe a great deal to Arcadio Díaz Quiñones, whose valuable essays underscore the critical link connecting history and creation. The Uruguayan Jorge Ruffinelli (b. 1943), exiled first in Mexico and currently in the United States, is a disciple of the brand of social criticism practiced by Rama, a fact clearly reflected in his studies of Uruguayan literature, Mexican literature of the Revolution, and the poetry of Nicolás Guillén. An unambiguous manifestation of Ruffinelli's socio-literary concerns is his *Literatura e ideología: el primer Mariano Azuela, 1896–1918* (1982).

Among the academic literary critics doing work in European universities, there are: the Colombian Rafael Gutiérrez Girardot (b. 1928), trained in the German philosophic and critical school, and author of *Horas de estudio* (1976) and *Modernismo* (1983); the Peruvian Américo Ferrari (b. 1929), who wrote *El universo poético de César Vallejo* (1974) and compiled a critical edition of the poet's work; and the Argentine Saúl Yurkievich (b. 1931), another well-known critic of Vallejo and of Spanish American poetry, in general. Educated in the Mexican philological school, Antonio Alatorre (b. 1922) and José Pascual Buxó (b. 1931) have both made solid contributions to Spanish American literary criticism. Alatorre has worked primarily in the field of classical Hispanism and has most recently written provocative essays concerning the excesses of the new Formalism. Buxó has specialized in colonial writings, and in problems of theory and poetics. Finally, Josefina Ludmer (b. 1939), writing in Argentina and now in the United States, has cultivated a psychoanalytic approach to literature, of which her *Cien años de soledad: una interpretación* (1972) is an excellent example.

Beyond the margins of strictly academic circles, the best Spanish American literary criticism of today is marked by the two virtues that Octavio Paz identified as essential to the discipline: rigor and imagination. In its daringness, this brand of criticism can almost be defined as creative literature, something that is not surprising inasmuch as some of its leading practitioners are themselves important novelists or poets. Carlos Fuentes (b. 1928) has written literary criticism (*La nueva novela hispanoamericana*, 1969; *Cervantes o la crítica de la lectura*), reflections on current events (*Tiempo mexicano*, 1971), and a sort of autobiographic testimonial (*Myself with Others*). All these books are infused with the same qualities that characterize Fuentes's creative work: passionate intensity, a contagious enthusiasm for the ideas and the history of the present, and a sensuous, and even burlesque, language. *García Márquez: historia de un decidio* (1971), a critical essay by Mario Vargas Llosa (b. 1936) about García Márquez, is impeccable as a study of an author's complete works (up to the time of its publication) and yet polemic for the theoretic foundations upon which it is constructed. *La orgía perpetua* [*The Perpetual Orgy*], perhaps Vargas Llosa's best-known critical work and fruit of his long-lived devotion to *Madame Bovary*, makes use of three different and contradictory approaches to the classic novel, in an unprecedented critical *tour de force*. *Contra viento y marea* (vol. I, 1983; vol. II, 1986) compiles Vargas Llosa's vast journalistic and critical production, providing, in the process, a synthesis of his literary and ideological evolution. This collection unmasks the obsessions – the "demons" – that inhabit Vargas Llosa's novelistic world at the same time that it confirms the lucidity of his critical thought and the sharpness of his polemic wit as political commentator. Guillermo Cabrera Infante (b. 1929), on his part, is a master of the pun and of all types of linguistic games, as well as a renowned cinematic critic and essayist. His 1985 *Holy Smoke* is an extensive and unusual essay about the history of tobacco inside and outside Cuba, which can be read as a comic or parodic variant of the classic *Contrapunteo cubano del tabaco y el azúcar* (1940) by Fernando Ortiz (1881–1969). His recent *Mea Cuba* (1992) gathers a variety of notes on Cuban history and culture.

Augusto Monterroso, Guatemalan by birth, but transplanted to Mexico, writes in a prose style characterized by a flawless language, measured concision, and subtle humor. His essayistic works, particularly *La palabra mágica*, a collection of brilliant brief essays, and *La letra e* (1987), a sort of casual and fragmentary diary wherein he meditates on his métier, are as demonstrative of these qualities as are his delightful short stories. Severo Sarduy (1937–1993) has written almost all of his narrative and essayistic works while living in France, under the direct influence of the *Tel Ouel* group and of the most sophisticated structuralist theorists. His meditations on homoeroticism, Oriental philosophy, and occultist doctrines tend to be furiously overwrought. His 1974 *Barroco* is a defense of the baroque aesthetic that is so central in Cuban culture (one need only think of Lezama or Carpentier); that essay, together with several others have been collected in the volume *Ensayos generales sobre el barroco* (1987).

The prolific work of Mario Benedetti (b. 1920) is situated at the opposite extreme: while it embraces all genres, from journalism to poetry, it is marked, particularly in the last several decades coinciding with his exile in Cuba and Spain, by a firm, ideological radicalism and the testimonial urgency of an intellectual directly engaged in the political struggle. The very titles of his essayistic and critical books attest to this: *Letras de emergencia* (1981), *Crítica complice* (1988). The most valuable of his works, such as *El ejercicio del criterio* (1981) containing Benedetti's works of literary criticism from 1950 to 1970, and *Literatura uruguaya. Siglo XX* (1963), are intelligent contributions to the essay genre, written in the straightforward, communicative style that characterizes their author. Two essayists interested in poetic theory and formal analysis are the Mexican Tomás Segovia (b. 1927) who published *Poética y profética* (Mexico, 1985) and the Bolivian Renato Prada Oropeza (b. 1937), author of *La autonomía literaria. Sistema y función* (1976) and *El lenguaje narrativo* (1979).

There is yet another group of essayists who share certain affinities: the practice of literary criticism or of art as the manifestation of a "modern" attitude characterized by an openness to contemporary literatures in numerous languages or to other forms of aesthetic expression (such as film) as well as by a receptiveness to various contemporary critical tendencies without falling into any methodological or ideological commitment. Within this group, three Colombian writers, all associated with the journal *Eco*, are notable. The dean of the threesome is Ernesto Volkening (b. 1908), a German born in Ambères and established in Bogotá since 1934. His vast European culture and his Hispanic American intellectual experience are admirably reflected in his critical work, collected in two volumes entitled *Ensayos* (1975, 1976). Hernando

Valencia Goelkel (b. 1928) was founder of the journal *Mito*, which represents an important epoch in Colombian literary life (1959–1962). He is also the author of *Crónicas de cine* (1974) as well as of a splendid collection of brief essays and articles entitled *El arte nuevo de hacer novelas* (1982), about Russian, English, French, and North American writers. The youngest of the group is Juan Gustavo Cobo Borda (b. 1948), poet and editor of *Eco* from 1973 until its disappearance in 1984. Cobo Borda is a voracious and passionate reader who knows how to transmit both his judgments and his enthusiasm for intellectual life in an agile prose and through precise and irreverent images. The title of one of his books says it all: *La alegría de leer* (1976). In *La tradición de la pobreza* Cobo Borda reviewed Colombian literature with a penetrating eye. In Cuba Cintio Vitier's contributions to national literature and identity are considerable; his vision integrates a mystic vein (he is an intellectual with a Catholic foundation), an intimate understanding of the poetic phenomenon, and historic concern, as can be seen in *Crítica sucesiva* and *Ese sol del mundo moral* (1975).

The Venezuelan Guillermo Sucre (b. 1933) is a notable critic of Borges's poetry and author of *La máscara, la transparencia* (1975), a substantial repertory of twentieth-century Spanish American lyric. Although Francisco Rivera (b. 1933), also Venezuelan, studied and worked in North American universities from 1954 to 1963 and was heavily influenced by the *nouvelle critique*, his literary criticism is not academic in nature, but rather personal, and, what is more, open to diverse approaches and methodologies. His essays have been collected in *Inscripciones* (1981) and *La búsqueda sin fin* (1993). Among the Mexicans, the critical and narrative works of Juan García Ponce (b. 1932) stand out for the erotic suggestions, perverse imaginations, and moral strangeness that they embody, presented in a prose style that is as cold and deliberate as the stroke of a scalpel. His essays concern art subjects (*Nueve pintores mexicanos* (1968)) and writers whose worlds the author himself invades as a double, as, for example, in *La errancia sin fin: Musil, Borges, Klossowski* (1981). Another Mexican, José Emilio Pacheco (b. 1939) is a true *homme de lettres* whose critical mind can be appreciated from almost any facet of his work, particularly his poetry, which constitutes its center. Pacheco's critical works are dispersed among prologues, brief studies, reviews, anthologies, translations, and, above all, his intensive – and high quality – production as a cultural chronicler. The Peruvian Julio Ramón Ribeyro (1929–1994) has written a great many stories, but very few, though all insightful, essays. His only publication in the genre is the collection *La caza sutil* (1976). Another Peruvian, but long-time resident of Geneva, is Luis Loayza (b. 1934), an elegant prose writer whose work is relatively unknown. Loayza's essays about Peruvian and European literatures included in *El sol de Lima* (1974) are the offspring of a voracious and discriminating reader. Finally, the Puerto Rican Rosario Ferré (b. 1942) is the author of a polemic book of essays entitled *Sitio a Eros* (1980) that contains texts dedicated primarily to women's writings and feminist issues. More important, however, than Ferré's theoretic positions with respect to feminism, are the passion she puts into her ideas, the brilliance with which she defends forms of expression that are free from erotic censorship, and the authenticity she champions as the primary force that moves literary creation.

In the field of memoirs and diaries, none has been as widely read or as influential to the continental conscience as *Diario del Che en Bolivia* by Ernesto Guevara (1928–1967), wherein the famous revolutionary documents his desperate adventure in the jungles of Bolivia, an adventure whose failure led to his own death. The romanticism of the gesture (regardless of the absurdity of the enterprise), the improvised nature of its writing, and the poetic fervor of many of his notes, make of this political document a text of literary interest, especially if compared to Martí's *Diario de campaña* (1962). The intertwining of literature and politics can also be found in two books hailing from Chile. One is *Confieso que he vivido [Memoirs]* by Pablo Neruda (1904–1973), the memoirs of a great poet, a man of the world, and an active, militant intellectual. Polemic and juicy, contradictory and revealing, it is an indispensable text for knowing both the intimate Neruda and the mask he invented for himself in order to carry the weight of his own glory. The other is *Persona non grata* (1973) by Jorge Edwards (b. 1931), a document of his double experience – as a diplomat and an intellectual – in Havana, during the critical years leading up to the unfortunate "Padilla affaire," a typical confrontation between the interests of the revolutionary state and the artistic freedom of the writer. The ardent denouncement of North American imperialism and the pathetic current situation of Spanish American countries moved the Uruguayan Eduardo Galeano (b. 1940) to write *Las venas abiertas de América Latina*. The text is a good example of political reportage and combat literature, marked by a moving tone and a style of great precision and conviction.

The attack on the central city as nucleus of the ills of a nation is a literary theme that in Hispanic America goes at least as far back as the writings of Bello, who in his poem "La agricultura de la zona tórrida" wrote of the "ocio pestilente ciudadano" ["pestilent idleness of the city"]. In the nineteenth century, the accusation was repeated by González Prada and in the twentieth by Martínez Estrada among others. It is into this tradition that the Peruvian Sebastián Salazar Bondy (1924–1965) inscribed himself with his brief essay *Lima la horrible*. It contains an inclement attack against Lima and its physical and moral horrors, written in a sarcastic prose that tends toward the Baroque. The violence of the attack reflects the ambiguous love–hate relation Salazar Bondy maintained with his city as well as the intellectual crisis he was experiencing at the time of its writing. In his *Buenos Aires: vida cotidiana y alienación* (1964), Juan José Sebreli (b. 1930) made of that city the object of a sociological analysis with Marxist leanings, more valuable for its intuitions than for its methodological rigor.

A militant Marxist, the Mexican José Revueltas (1914–1976) wrote abundant doctrinary and political works in addition to his novelistic work; the best of these are collected in the posthumous publication *México 68: juventud y revolución* (1978). Roberto Fernández Retamar (b.1930), whose critical work frequently represents the official position of the Cuban Revolution on cultural issues, attempted a revision of the topics examined by Sarmiento and Rodó: civilization versus barbarism, North American utilitarianism versus Hispanic American idealism. The author reverses the terms: the American ideal is closer to the barbarous Calibán than to the bourgeois elitism of Próspero. Fernández Retamar's proposal is interesting, but the uncritical use of Marxist materialism hinders his intent, as does the aggressive tone with which he criticizes Spanish American writers, judging them exclusively in terms of their degree of adherence to Cuba. The Chilean Ariel Dorfman (b. 1942), exiled in the United States, presents an even more acute case of intellectual radicalism, which infuses all his work with a tone of Marxist militancy and ideological indoctrination; his works include criticism of political and cultural colonialism, readings of forms of popular expression in his country, literary sociology, campaigns against dictatorships, etc. Of his various books of essays, among the most recent is the collection of critical works somewhat stridently entitled *Hacia la liberación del lector latino-americano* (1984).

12

Literary criticism in Spanish America
Aníbal González

Literary criticism already has a long and distinguished history in Spanish America, one that encompasses such diverse figures as Andrés Bello (1781–1865), José Enrique Rodó (1871–1917), Pedro Henríquez Ureña (1884–1946), Alfonso Reyes (1889–1959), Emir Rodríguez Monegal (1921–1985), and Angel Rama (1926–1983). Nevertheless, Spanish American literary criticism has sometimes had to contend with feelings of inadequacy, not only in comparison to its subject but also to the literary criticism of Europe and the United States.

The inadequacy has often been real, of course, and Spanish American critics have been the first to point out the deficiencies and vices of criticism in Spanish America, as well as the obstacles it has had to face. Among the former, critics note its mimetic character, journalistic superficiality, lack of patience with serious scholarship, and ideological tendentiousness; among the latter are censorship, exile, and sheer lack of financial and institutional support. The absence of any book-length history of Spanish American criticism is probably symptomatic of the unease Spanish American critics and literary historians share with regard to this subject.

Feelings of inadequacy and belatedness are nevertheless endemic to literary criticism wherever it occurs, however much critics may try to hide them beneath an authoritarian rhetoric. In modern literature, which has absorbed criticism into its make-up to a very high degree but without its institutional or ideological constraints, there is always a propensity to surpass the exegetes. This in turn has forced critics to compete with creative writers in the elaboration of ever more probing theories of what literature is and how it achieves its effects.

Lately, poet–critics such as Octavio Paz (b. 1914) and literary theorists such as Roberto González Echevarría (b. 1943) have remarked on the overall weakness of critical thinking in the Hispanic world and have suggested that profoundly critical thought – in the philosophic as well as in the literary sense – can best be found in the works of Spanish America's great poets and narrators rather than in those of scholars or academics. For these two commentators of the critical scene, Spanish American literary criticism, while it has had its share of achievements, lags far behind poetry and narrative fiction in self-awareness, methodological rigor, and questioning ability.

González Echevarría has furthermore suggested that because, as a political and cultural entity, Spanish America is a creation of the modern age, its literature is thus already modern in themes and outlook – that is to say, it deals with the typically modern topics of originality and historical development (*The Voice of the Masters*, 33–40). Unwilling or unable to recognize its "original modernity," however, Spanish American literature has sought modernity as defined by other national literatures, and – if one accepts the identification of criticism with modernity – this has led to a "critical redoubling," or hypercriticism, in Spanish American literature with which ordinary academic or journalistic criticism, subject to ideological, methodological, and institutional limitations, cannot hope to compete. The history of professional (that is, academic or journalistic) literary criticism in Spanish America is therefore a chronicle of delusions, misreadings, and outright falsification, with a few bright areas in the realms of scholarship and literary history.

Nevertheless, the history of criticism is essentially a history of ideas. Even erroneous ideas, if sufficiently widespread, can have an impact on real-world processes and must therefore be studied. The fictions and fantasies of Spanish American literary criticism differ from those of European and US literary criticism mainly in their greater emphasis on forging a coherent image of culture. Buffeted by violent social and political changes, and plagued by doubts about the viability of Spanish America's political independence, literary criticism in Spanish America has developed a vested interest in the creation and preservation of a solidly founded and broadly accepted notion of national culture. It is this cultural conservatism that undermines the critical impulse, since it defines an area that must remain untouched by critical thought. The tension between Spanish American literature and its critics thus arises not only from an old-fashioned criticism straining to catch up with a highly experimental literature, but also from the conflict that arises from Spanish American literature's insistent questioning of the concept of culture in which criticism has such a considerable stake. At present, as González Echevarría has pointed out (*The Voice of the Masters*), the consensus about Spanish American culture that was so important to critical discourse in the region has finally broken down. However, until recently the history of literary criticism in Spanish America was closely linked with the attempt to lay down the foundations of Spanish American culture, with everything this implies in terms of critical blindness and delusion.

Within this process of cultural instauration that is in part the history of Spanish American literary criticism, a series of broad stages or periods can be discerned: Romanticism [*Romanticismo*] (1810–1880s); Modernism [*Modernismo*] (1880s–1920s); Tellurism (1920s–1960s), and Postmodernity (1960–   ). The first covered much of the nineteenth century, from Independence to the 1880s. Representative critics of this period are Andrés Bello, Domingo Faustino Sarmiento (1811–1888), Domingo Del Monte (1804–1853), and Juan María Gutiérrez (1809–1878; some of these writers were, of course, far more than critics of literature). The period is characterized by the importation of some elements of romantic philology, the beginnings of the search for cultural definition, and the invention of a Spanish American literary history following the European model, one in which the colonial period took the place of Europe's Middle Ages. Social and political concerns were also important at this stage, since criticism was seen at the time as an instrument in nation-building.

The second period covered the turn of the century (from the 1880s to the 1920s), essentially coinciding with the Spanish American modernist movement. This period abounded in important critical works, because it witnessed the systematic incorporation of the aims and methods of philology, of literary criticism (as it was embodied in the work of French philologists and critics such as Charles Augustin Saint-Beuve, Ernest Renan, and Hippolyte Taine), into Spanish American literature; thus, many of the major Modernists, such as José Martí (1853–1895) and Rubén Darío (1867–1916), were also important critics. Furthermore, as many have argued, the modernist period is characterized by the increasing professionalization of the Spanish American writers, and this was also the case for the critics. The first major professional literary critic in Spanish America was without a doubt José Enrique Rodó (1871–1917). Other prominent critics of the time were Rufino Blanco Fombona (1874–1944), Ventura García Calderón (1887–1960), Paul Groussac (1848–1929), Baldomero Sanín Cano (1861–1957), and Enrique José Varona (1849–1933). Salient characteristics of criticism in this period were: a tension between aestheticist and positivist approaches to literature, a concern with the relation between ethics and aesthetics, and a strengthening of academic as well as journalistic literary criticism.

The third stage in the history of Spanish American criticism, which may be called the telluric period, extended from the late 1920s to the 1960s. The term "telluric" refers to the renewed preoccupation with social reform and national identity this criticism shared with that of the Romantics and with the "novelas de la tierra." The most common critical approach of this period was the production of broad accounts of Spanish American culture's origin and evolution. The Telluric period produced numerous important professional critics, such as Pedro Henríquez Ureña, Mariano

Picón Salas (1901–1965), and Alfonso Reyes (who, admittedly, was also a broad-ranging "man of letters"). It also witnessed the arrival in Spanish America of a plethora of major Spanish writers and intellectuals, exiled after Spain's Civil War; among these were scholars and critics such as Federico de Onís, Amado Alonso, and Américo Castro. A greater academization of Spanish American literary criticism was also evidenced during these decades, which saw also the growth of academic Hispanism in the United States. The predominant critical methodology during this period was stylistics, the Hispanic equivalent of Anglo-American New Criticism. The importance of social commitment to this critical period is underscored by the appearance of the first important works of Marxist criticism in Spanish America by critics such as José Carlos Mariátegui (1895–1930), Juan Marinello (1898–1977), and Aníbal Ponce (1898–1938).

A crisis in critical methodology was part of the change from the telluric to the current period. If "modernity," both as a concept and as a historical period, is a byproduct of the Enlightenment and of Romanticism, then the current radical critique of the ideological legacy of these two moments of European civilization would have to be labeled "postmodern." The rise of the Spanish American "new novel" during the 1960s (the so-called "Boom") announced a serious questioning of the ideological underpinnings of Telluric criticism. Political events such as the Cuban Revolution gave new impetus to Marxist and sociological approaches to cultural and literary studies. Simultaneously, new European critical methodologies such as Structuralism, semiotics, and Post-structuralism, began to arrive in Spanish America, and a debate ensued between these various methodologies and Marxist literary criticism. The critical consensus achieved during the telluric period was lost, and the current panorama of Spanish American literary criticism is characterized by its diversity. Furthermore, the economic and social crises in Spanish America during the 1970s and 1980s have caused waves of intellectuals from these countries to move to the United States and Europe, eroding the cultural panorama of their home countries and widening the gap, in quantity and quality, between the Spanish American literary criticism produced in the United States and that produced in the Spanish American countries themselves. While much of the best Spanish American literary criticism (like a good deal of Spanish American literature) has always been produced by exiles or expatriates, in the last decades frequent travel or emigration to wealthier countries with richer, more stable academic environments has become almost a necessity for Spanish American literary scholars.

Frequently throughout the history of Spanish American literature, the major writers of a given period have also been among its most important critics (as is the case with Bello, Martí, and Reyes). However, it may be indicative of the recent crisis in criticism that crossover between creative writers and critics has been especially common since the 1950s: the most influential critical figures during this period form a spectrum that encompasses criticism and creative writing in a fluid continuum, from writer–critics such as Jorge Luis Borges (1900–1986), Octavio Paz, José Lezama Lima (1912–1974), and Severo Sarduy (1937–1993), to academic and journalistic critics such as Angel Rama and Emir Rodríguez Monegal, among others.

Before we begin to examine the periods outlined above in more detail, mention must be made of the incipient literary criticism found in the early gazettes, dailies, and journals of colonial Spanish America. This is a poorly studied subject that still awaits serious scholarly research. The rise of regularly published journals or gazettes in Spanish America dates back to the eighteenth century and publications such as the *Gaceta de México* (1728–1738) and the *Gacetas de Literatura de México* (1788–1795), edited by José Antonio Alzate (1729–1799), the *Mercurio Peruano* (1791–1795), edited by Hipólito Unanue (1755–1833), the *Papel Periódico de La Habana* (1790–1804), edited by Diego de la Barrera, Tomás Romay, and José Agustín Caballero, and the *Diario de México* (1805–1817), edited by Carlos María Bustamante (1744–1848). The term "literature" was used rather loosely in those times, and much of what was published under that heading in, for example, the *Gacetas de Literatura de México*, was actually information pertaining to natural history, agriculture, philosophy, economy, and "antiquities" (such as the Mexican ruins of Xochicalco). The *Diario de México*, Mexico's first true daily, did print poetry, essays on manners, and theatre reviews. The latter commented more on the performance than on the texts, and thus fall outside the scope of literary criticism. Much of the poetry published in the *Diario de México* was produced by members of the "Arcadia de México," one of the various "poetic academies" that arose in Spanish America around the mid-1700s in imitation of similar European institutions. In Spanish America, these academies served not only to establish standards of poetic taste, but also to disseminate Enlightenment ideas and to foment patriotic feelings (such as the case with the "Sociedad Patriótica y Literaria" in Buenos Aires and the "Tertulia Eutrapélica" in Bogotá).

The scant criticism that appears in early Spanish American periodicals is usually in the letters addressed to the editor by some of the readers. In these, comments on the poetry published in previous issues or discussion on matters of literary taste can be found. These comments are generally prescriptive, and attempt to follow the dictates of neoclassical poetics such as those of Nicholas Boileau or Ignacio de Luzán. Propriety, idealization, reasonableness, conformity to rules, and avoidance of latinisms or obscure words – indeed, an overt anti-Gongorism – are the literary values stressed in this criticism. Occasionally, there are expressions of an incipient literary regionalism, as when Manuel del Socorro Rodríguez (1758–1818), in the *Semanario de Nueva Granada*, defends the poetry written in the Viceroyalty of New Granada from charges that it is inferior to that written in Mexico or Peru.

Although much of this late eighteenth-century Spanish American criticism – like the literature to which it responded – appears today excessively pedantic, constrained, and conservative, it was perceived quite differently at the time. Instead, it was seen as part of a broad movement of sociopolitical and cultural renewal launched by the French-inspired reformism of the Spanish monarch Charles III. Many of the stuffy neoclassical versifiers and critics who published in the *Diario de México* or the *Papel Periódico de La Habana* were young men, members of the creole elite, who shared a growing cosmopolitan attitude and a hunger for new ideas. It was from this group, in fact, that the founder of modern Spanish American criticism arose: Andrés Bello, who before leaving for England in 1810 had already acquired a solid classical education at the university in Caracas (where he had been an outstanding latinist), participated in the aristocratic salons of the Ustáriz and Bolívar families, and written for the *Gaceta de Caracas*. Moreover, he had conversed at length with Alexander von Humboldt during the latter's visit to Caracas in 1800, and had learned from him about the new ideas in linguistics, literature, and science generated by the European Romantics.

The romantic period of Spanish American literary criticism indeed begins with Bello. Specialists on Bello have divided his life into three stages: the first comprises his birth and education in Caracas (1781–1810); the second, his years of residence in London (1810–1829); and the last and longest stage, his residence in Chile (1829–1865). Most of these specialists agree that his London period was the most fruitful from the point of view of research and publication; it was there that Bello wrote his studies on Spanish medieval literature, his poems "Alocución a la poesía" (1823) and "Silva a la agricultura de la zona tórrida" (1826), and founded and directed the journals *Biblioteca Americana* (1823) and *Repertorio Americano* (1826–1827).

Bello lived and worked in London as a diplomat representing the revolutionary junta of Caracas. London, the capital of European liberalism and of the world's most powerful empire at the time, was a rich repository of culture which Bello tapped to the fullest. In the British Museum, he researched the origins of Spanish poetry in his studies on the Spanish epic, the *Cantar del Mío Cid*, and *romance* versification. During his years in London, Bello followed the polemics provoked by the publication of Lord Byron's *Childe Harold's Pilgrimage* in 1812. He read and commented on the works of Robert Southey, Sir Walter Scott, and

James Fenimore Cooper; he befriended the philosopher James Mill and worked at collecting and organizing Jeremy Bentham's manuscripts; and he of course associated with the community of exiled Spanish liberals such as José María Blanco-White and José Joaquín de Mora.

On the other hand, Bello's Chilean period is generally seen as less creative and more pedagogical. Unable to pursue many of his original researches, Bello took on the role of teacher, founder of cultural institutions such as the Colegio de Santiago, and journalist, in publications such as *El Araucano*. It was during this stage of his life, specifically in the year 1842, that Bello became involved in the famous polemic concerning Romanticism, which pitted him against Sarmiento. In a series of articles entitled collectively "¿Por qué no hay poetas en Chile?," Sarmiento ridiculed Bello's inclinations toward a neoclassical aesthetic and blamed him for the academizing and pro-Spanish trend in the young Chilean writers. Bello replied directly to Sarmiento's criticisms only once, in a gently ironic article published in *El Mercurio* under the pseudonym "Un Quidam." Bello's Chilean disciples took over the rest of the debate against the Argentinian writer.

Like many Spanish American literary debates before and since, this one produced more heat than light, and was politically motivated. Sarmiento saw Bello as an ally of the Chilean conservatives, and unfairly branded him as neoclassical. In fact, both Bello and Sarmiento were romantic to different degrees; Bello's poetic style, as well as his sense of order and rationality, were still neoclassical, but his ideas about language, literature, and culture had been forged in close contact with the English Romantics, whose ideas were generally more innovative and radical than those of their contemporaries in Europe. Sarmiento's Romanticism, in contrast, was strongly French-influenced, and was regarded by Bello and his supporters (also unfairly) as superficial and simply a cover for Sarmiento's political liberalism and anti-Hispanism.

Above and beyond his multifarious contributions to such fields as pedagogy, philosophy, law, political science, historiography, and the natural sciences, Bello's contribution to the tradition of Spanish American literary criticism is threefold. First, he brought a greater awareness of the historicity of language and, consequently, of literature. Second, he brought into Spanish America the European romantic notion of literature as a product of the fusion of human consciousness with the natural environment, which would henceforth become one of the basic tenets of Spanish American literary criticism. Third, Bello conceived of literary criticism as an instrument in the task of nation-building in which he, like many others of his generation, had embarked.

As Amado Alonso (1896–1952) has pointed out, Bello reacted in his philological and grammatical studies against the "logico-generalist" concept of grammar that was common among the Neoclassicists; for Bello, as for the early German romantic philologists such as Friedrich Schlegel, Jakob Grimm, and Franz Bopp, language was no longer studied only in terms of a set of general, universal rules defined by an elite of speakers, but rather in genetic terms. Bello, like his German contemporaries, sought the origins of language and found them in the regionalistic, often irrational, and archaic speech of the common folk. Bello realized that language has a history that can be traced through the study of anonymous and collective forms of literature such as epic poems and folk ballads (the Spanish *romances*). This is, in large measure, the impulse behind his studies of the *Cantar del Mío Cid*, and is part of the ideology underlying his *Gramática de la lengua castellana destinada al uso de los americanos* (1847).

This latter work also reflects Bello's "Americanism" which, although more moderate than Sarmiento's, also showed a desire to stress the cultural particularities of the new Spanish American nation that was being born. Bello's work is an example of how the modern concept of "culture" itself was produced by the Romantics. Like his European counterparts, Bello's concept of culture was based on a botanical, organic metaphor: like a plant, culture arises out of obscure, telluric origins (symbolized by seed and soil); rooted in history, it grows and develops like a living thing. Furthermore, in plant-like fashion, cultures seem to differ according to the diverse geographic regions in which they arise. It is also important that culture's growth and development is not chaotic and unconstrained (like a cancer's) but bound by laws of symmetry and differentiation like those that govern the production of branches, leaves, flowers, and fruits in plants. The organic metaphor of culture was clearly an attempt by the Romantics to reconcile change with order, diversity with uniformity, historicity with permanence.

Bello's work reflects an early stage in the development of this metaphor of culture, when the arbitrariness of the metaphoric link can still be clearly discerned. In his poem *Alocución a la poesía*, which may be considered literary criticism in verse form, Bello apostrophizes Poetry and urges it to abandon Europe in favor of the New World. In the latter, Nature reigns very nearly in its original state; Poetry can thus return to its pastoral, telluric origins and be renewed. It is important to note the imperative tone of Bello's text: the *Alocución* outlines a program for literary renewal that is very much a product of the will and not a "natural," spontaneous consequence of America's "rusticity." Later, in his letter in verse to José Joaquín Olmedo (*Epístola escrita de Londres a París por un americano a otro*, 1827), Bello urges the Ecuadorian poet to "transplant Pindar's laurels" to the "Occidental climes" where "pineapples and tamarinds grow." Bello is the first Spanish American critic to define the uniqueness of

Spanish American literature in terms of its supposed links with the flora, fauna, and geography of the New World.

Considering his "Americanism," surprisingly little of Bello's criticism is directly concerned with the literature of the New World. The vast majority of his critical articles and notes have to do with European writers (from classical authors such as Virgil to contemporary Spanish and British authors such as the Duque de Rivas and Sir Walter Scott). His few critical essays devoted to American subjects deal with José Joaquín Olmedo's poem *La victoria de Junín: canto a Bolívar* (1826), the poetry of José María de Heredia (1803–1899), the poem *Campaña del ejército republicano al Brasil y triunfo de Ituzaingó* (1827) by Juan Cruz Varela (1794–1839), *La Araucana* (1569–1589) by Alonso de Ercilla (1534–1594), an 1844 translation by Sarmiento of a devotional biography of Jesus, and notes on an edition of the *Historia de la conquista de México* (1798) by Antonio Solís, and on Sarmiento's *Viajes* (1845–1847). Of course, not all of Bello's literary criticism is found in his essays and notes; some of his speeches, particularly his well-known "Discurso pronunciado en la instalación de la Universidad de Chile el día 17 de septiembre de 1843" of which more will be said later), contain important critical pronouncements, and we have already commented on the criticism implicit in *Alocución a la poesía*.

This paucity of criticism by Bello on Spanish American topics is understandable if one considers that he spent much of his adult life involved in political, pedagogical, and administrative duties. Significantly, most of Bello's essays on Spanish American works date from his London period, when he had more time to engage in literary and scholarly pursuits. It would have been interesting to know Bello's opinion of works by his contemporaries which would later become classics of Spanish American literature, such as *El Periquillo Sarniento* (1816) by José Joaquín Fernández de Lizardi (1776–1827), "El matadero" (1837) by Esteban Echeverría (1805–1851), or *Civilización y barbarie: vida de Juan Facundo Quiroga* (1845) by Sarmiento. However, works such as these had limited diffusion in their time, and Bello's literary taste privileged poetry over prose: it is unlikely that he would have recognized them as valid subjects for criticism.

Nevertheless, Bello was a precursor in another area of Spanish American literary studies which the Spanish American Romantics would continue to develop: colonial literature. Most of the early Spanish American Romantics who held liberal and anti-Hispanic ideas (as was the case with Sarmiento and the other Argentinian exiles from Juan Manuel de Rosas's dictatorship) viewed the colonial period with distaste, were not interested in researching it, and saw little of value in the surviving texts from that period. Bello's ideas, however, were more conservative, and he strove for a balanced appreciation of Spain's role in Spanish America's historical development. His essay on *La Araucana* is among the first serious and positive evaluations of Ercilla's Renaissance epic of the conquest of Chile. Bello's romantic historicism, which had already led him to seek the origins of Spanish poetry in the popular *romances* and the *Cantar del Mío Cid*, encouraged him to see in Ercilla's poem a literary testimony of Chile's historical origins. For Bello, *La Araucana* was (in his own words) "Chile's *Aeneid*," a foundational text ("*La Araucana*, por Don Alonso de Ercilla y Zúñiga," 360). It should be noted that Bello places *La Araucana* in its appropriate historico-literary context, as a Renaissance epic in the mold of Ariosto and Tasso. However, Bello finds in Ercilla's self-inclusion in the poem, as well as in his familiar and down-to-earth tone, a prefiguration of the new aesthetic freedom brought by Romanticism, with its emphasis on naturalness and spontaneity.

Romanticism, Americanism, and didacticism, Arturo Uslar Pietri (b. 1906) points out, are three constantly interlinked elements in Bello's work. Bello's didacticism was a normal consequence of his increased involvement, during the latter half of his life, in the task of national organization in Chile. Despite Bello's appreciation of colonial literature, he felt that a radical historical break had occurred between the colonial period and his own time, and that the new Spanish American countries were beginning their existence without a strong, clearly defined national literary tradition. In literature, as in many other areas of national life, everything was still to be done. The urgency of nation-building is reflected in Bello's unfinished *Compendio de la historia de la literatura* (1850), written as a textbook for the significantly-named Instituto Nacional, as well as in the pedagogical slant of many of his critical essays and in the exhortations he directed to the students of the University of Chile in his aforementioned "Discurso pronunciado en la instalación de la Universidad de Chile." In this serenely visionary speech, Bello lays out the role of the University in the future development of Chilean culture. Regarding literature, he urges the young Chilean writers to

> write of matters worthy of your country and of posterity. Leave the soft tones of the lyre of Anacreon and Sappho: the poetry of the nineteenth century has a higher mission. Let the great interests of humanity inspire you. Let your works pulsate with moral feeling... And, how many great themes are not already shown to you by your young republic? Celebrate its days of grandeur; weave garlands to its heroes; consecrate the burial shroud of the martyrs of the Fatherland. (p. 20)

Bello's didacticism, as may be seen from the previous quote, is also reflected in his style. Flowing in diction, measured in its use of adjectives, calm and reasonable in tone, Bello's style still bears the clear imprints of

Neoclassicism and the Enlightenment – which, paradoxically, make it seem less dated than the colloquial, neologistic, and self-centered style of younger Romantics such as Sarmiento. It was this younger generation of writers, many of whom were born during the Wars of Independence, who would continue to spread and intensify Bello's transitional critical legacy, linking it (albeit polemically) to the liberal Romanticism of the Argentinian Asociación de Mayo. Indeed, the major difference between Bello and the younger Romantics may well lie in style and language rather than in basic concepts. The younger Romantics were also more disposed to break openly with Hispanic tradition, although, because of the perceived lack of a Spanish American literary tradition, this led them to seek their literary models in France. The reasons for their choice of France over England or Germany were mainly linguistic and political; French was the only other language that many of these writers knew, and they deeply sympathized with the French tradition of antimonarchism and political liberalism. The influential "Dogma Socialista" (1837–1839), by Esteban Echevarría (1805–1851), for example, shows the impact of the social ideas of Henri de Saint-Simon and the philosophy of Victor Cousin.

Needless to say, literary criticism for the young Spanish American Romantics was, even more than for Bello, an instrument in their task of creating a "national consciousness." It is thus not surprising to find that the literary criticism of these writers – leaving aside the journalistic polemics about Romanticism of the early 1840s – is predominantly historiographic: literary history, biography, and bibliography, are its preferred fields of inquiry. In many respects, Spanish American criticism until the 1880s resembled most closely – despite its French models – the literary criticism of European countries like Italy, which was undergoing a similar process of national unification. Until the modernist movement, there were no theorists of literature in Spanish America comparable to Edgar Allan Poe in the United States, much less to major English romantic poet–critics such as Wordsworth or Coleridge. From its beginnings, and even after the rise of Modernism, Spanish American literary criticism was – to use an economic phrase that seems appropriate in this context of exchange – a "net importer" of critical methodologies and ideologies. What is distinctly Spanish American about this criticism, nevertheless, is the particular rate at which foreign critical methods and ideas were adopted, and their frequent transformation into empty rhetoric masking the fundamental obsession of Spanish American criticism with nation-building.

Within the broadly historiographic nature of Spanish American romantic criticism, a distinction should be made between critical works focused on Spanish American texts and those that focused on European literature with the aim of divulging the new standards of literary taste to Spanish

American readers and writers. In both cases, the aim was the same: to establish a distinctly American literary endeavor, although some critics sought to do this by means of the selective adaptation of European literary fashions and others by researching the earliest literary manifestations of the incipient Spanish American identity.

An instance of the former type of romantic criticism is found in the work of Domingo Delmonte in Cuba during the 1830s. A wealthy, Dominican-descended member of the Creole elite, Delmonte had a decidedly pedagogic inclination, and after his return to Cuba in 1829 from a two-year trip to Europe and the United States, he took it upon himself to educate and influence the Cuban writers' literary taste. Delmonte's criticism was disseminated in Havana journals such as *La Moda, o Recreo Semanal del Bello Sexo*, *Revista Bimestre Cubana* (which he directed), *El Plantel*, and *El Aguinaldo Habanero*, among others. In his articles, Delmonte informed readers about subjects such as the historical novels of Sir Walter Scott and his Spanish imitators, about Goethe's *Werther* and Balzac's *Comédie humaine*, about intellectual life in the United States ("Bosquejo intelectual de los Estados Unidos"), and – in a more general vein – about "La poesía en el siglo XIX," and "Los poetas." Yet Delmonte went even further and, as other Spanish American critics then and now have done, put his critical ideas into motion, through his editorship of the *Revista Bimestre Cubana*, his letters to individual writers, and the organization of a literary salon at his home in Havana (the "tertulia delmontina"). His criticism was thus not merely descriptive or analytical but, above all, prescriptive; like Echeverría in Argentina (although more conservative politically), Delmonte was a cultural promoter and innovator who succeeded in transporting elements of Romanticism to the Hispanic Caribbean: his influence extended to Puerto Rico, where Alejandro Tapia y Rivera (1826–1882) began his *Biblioteca Histórica* at Delmonte's suggestion. Like Bello in Chile, Delmonte enjoined Cuban writers to write about "cosas cubanas," such as the Cuban flora and landscape, as well as social customs and problems, such as slavery. Delmonte was responsible in large part for the production of Spanish America's only anti-slavery narratives, from *Francisco. El Ingenio, o las delicias del campo* (1839) by Anselmo Suárez y Romero (1818–1878), to the remarkable *Autobiografía* (1835) by the slave Juan Francisco Manzano (1797–1854), among others.

On the other hand, the most outstanding representative of the literary-historical tendency of Spanish American romantic criticism is the Argentinian Juan María Gutiérrez. Many other critics, of course, produced works of national literary history, such as *Juicios críticos sobre algunos poetas hispanoamericanos* (1859) by two of Bello's disciples, the Chilean brothers Miguel Luis (1828–1888) and Gregorio Victor Amunátegui (1830–1899), *Ojeada histórico-crítica sobre la poesía ecuatoriana* (1868) by Juan León Mera (1832–1894), *Historia de la literatura en Nueva Granada* (1868) by José María Vergara y Vergara (1831–1872), *Historia de la literatura colonial de Chile* (1878) by Toribio Medina (1852–1931), and *Recuerdos literarios* (1878) by the Chilean José Victorino Lastarria (1817–1888). Nevertheless, it is probably Juan María Gutiérrez who singlehandedly did most to stimulate the romantic return to the colonial period. After publishing his ambitious anthology of contemporary poets, *América poética*, in 1846, Gutiérrez broke with the narrow Americanism of his friend Echeverría (who had categorically stated in his "Dogma socialista" that "the social emancipation of America shall only be obtained by repudiating the colonial heritage that Spain left us"), and, true to the Romantics' historicist impulse, proceeded to re-edit and study the Renaissance epic *El Arauco domado* (1596) by the Creole disciple of Ercilla, Pedro de Oña (1570–1643?). This was followed by a series of groundbreaking studies of such notable colonial writers as Sor Juana Inés de la Cruz (1648–1695), Pedro de Peralta Barnuevo (1663–1743), Juan del Valle y Caviedes (1652?–1697?), and Pablo de Olavide (1725–1804), collected in *Estudios biográficos y críticos sobre algunos poetas sudamericanos anteriores al siglo XIX.*

Gutiérrez's interest in colonial writers clearly reflects his desire to bridge the perceived historical divide between the colonial period and the new Spanish American nations; it is an attempt to provide Spanish American literature with historical roots (to use an organic metaphor of which the Romantics were fond) by searching for worthy literary precursors of Creole lineage in colonial letters. All his studies have to do with Creole writers, and are designed to show how, despite Spanish intellectual repression, the native-born intellectuals were able to produce valuable literary and scholarly works.

In a striking passage of his "Advertencia preliminar" in his *Estudios biográficos y críticos*, Gutiérrez compares his research to that of the paleontologists:

> Our colonial biography is a new paleontology whose elements lie hidden in the depths of an unexplored world. Its beings remain unstudied and unclassified, and are only found in fragments under dense layers of indifference and oblivion, to such a degree that however great the care taken in their restoration there is the danger of bringing to the surface skeletons without life or flesh. I have tried to avoid this inconvenience, whenever possible, by placing the characters I study in relation with their epochs, their contemporaries, and the social development of the [Spanish] Metropolis, because for me the portrait is less

important than the background, in my attempt to clarify the moral and
intellectual aspects of the old regime.

("Estudios histórico-críticos sobre la literatura en Sud-América," 42)

However, despite the seemingly positivistic allusion to that nascent
science whose romantic founders were Georges Cuvier and Louis Agassiz,
Gutiérrez's method owes less to paleontology than to the early "socio-
literary" and historicist approaches of Madame de Staël (in *De la
littérature considerée dans les rapports avec les institutions sociales*, 1800)
and Charles Augustin Sainte-Beuve. His essays therefore abound in
broad, picturesque, almost novelistic recreations of life and customs
during the colonial period, often reminiscent of the *Tradiciones peruanas*
that the Peruvian Ricardo Palma began to publish around 1860.

Like Palma, Gutiérrez also turned the colonial period into an analogue
of Europe's Middle Ages; in his 1871 essay, "Estudios histórico-críticos
sobre la literatura en Sud-América," he referred to "the *Middle Age* of the
colonial regime." The reasons for this interpretation are clearly linked to
Gutiérrez's models in romantic historicism. Liberal romantic historiography, whose narrative providentialism required that historical processes
have definite beginnings and endings, taught that the nations of Europe
had originated from popular, agrarian, and vernacular roots during the
Middle Ages. Concurrently, romantic philology affirmed that the old epic
poems and *chansons de geste*, such as the *Cantar del Mío Cid* and the
Chanson de Roland were the early expressions of a growing "national
consciousness." Like Bello in his analysis of *La Araucana*, Gutiérrez's
"Medievalization" of the colonial period arises from his search for
American historical origins parallel to those of Europe. Gutiérrez's view
of the colonial period therefore shows little sensitivity to the peculiarities
of New World history as well as to the baroque period in European and
American cultural history. Despite his praise of Sor Juana and of Peralta
Barnuevo, Gutiérrez was essentially anti-baroque in attitude. Pompous
pageantry, allied to religious obscurantism and political oppression, were
for Gutiérrez the hallmarks of the colonial period; significantly, he refers
to it as "a sort of Carnival in which the most serious acts in the lives of a
people took on a histrionic and theatrical aspect, that was at once
ridiculous and pedantic." As we shall see, some aspects of this view would
remain unchanged – despite a more sympathetic appreciation of the
Baroque – in the Spanish American literary criticism of the 1930s and
1940s.

Although Bello brought the new romantic philology to Spanish America, where it was adopted by the literary critics mentioned above, as well
as by linguists such as the Colombians Miguel Antonio Caro (1843–1909)
and Rufino José Cuervo (1844–1911), it was not until the latter third of the

nineteenth century that the deeper philosophical implications of romantic philology for the study of language and culture began to be assimilated by Spanish American poets and prose writers. Spanish American writers of the late 1870s and 1880s entered a process of professionalization which led them to seek higher artistic standards and a more rigorous use of language and ideas. This was due in general to the increasing prosperity and political stability of Spanish America towards the end of the nineteenth century, but also, more specifically, to the growing prestige of science and technology in Western culture as a whole, a prestige which found systematic expression in the philosophy of Positivism.

The neoclassical ideal of linguistic transparency, of language as an unobtrusive medium of communication for ideas, as well as its opposite, the early romantic fondness for Americanisms and folk expressions (which had figured in the polemic between Bello and Sarmiento in the 1840s), gave way toward the 1870s to a more sophisticated notion of language as a human artifact, as a thing among others in the world, endowed with its own historical depth and an almost palpable materiality. As José Martí declared in a memorable fragment from his unpublished notebooks of 1880:

> There is in words a layer that enfolds them, which is their use: one must, however, go to their very substance (*ir hasta el cuerpo de ellas*). In this examination, something breaks, and one sees into the depths. Words must be used as they are seen in their depths, in their real, etymological, and primitive signification, which is the only robust one, and which assures permanence to the ideas expressed in them. Words must be bright as gold, light as wings, solid as marble.
>
> (*Obras completas*, XIV: 450)

This vision of language as an object (frequently, a precious object) led logically to a notion of culture as artifice. Unlike the Romantics, the Modernists did not view national culture as a process of spontaneous, natural generation from obscure, folkloric roots. Without forsaking altogether the organic metaphors of romantic philology, the Modernists, like their French symbolist and "decadentist" counterparts, regarded national culture (including literature and the arts) as highly refined end-products of a laborious and deliberate historical process. This idea of culture is best summarized by a quote from a speech by Ernest Renan found in one of Martí's "Escenas europeas" (1884): "Human history is not a chapter in Zoology. Man is a rational and moral being. Free will stands above the base influence of the *Volksgeist*. A nation is a soul, a spiritual principle created out of the past, with its life in the present, and any great assemblage of men of sound minds and generous hearts can create the moral consciousness that constitutes a nation."

439

Renan, as philologist and writer, was dear to the hearts of the Modernists (in a way that other philologists, including the Spaniard Marcelino Menéndez y Pelayo, were not), because of his sensitivity to this vision of culture as an artifact. The Modernists also admired Renan's cultivated prose style, his antipositivism, and his sympathy for turn-of-the-century aestheticism. In their journalistic chronicles, essays, and prologues, as well as in their literary works, the modernist poets defended, to varying degrees, the dignity and autonomy of art vis-à-vis politics and science. This attitude was frequently misunderstood as pure aestheticism, or "art for art's sake," but it in fact simply reflected the Modernists' desire to systematize their knowledge about art and literature and raise the contemporary standard of taste.

Yet, even as the Spanish American poets and narrators were showing a greater concern with form and adopting a more sophisticated notion of language in their works, the critics were moving toward a deterministic and moralizing approach that rarely addressed literary form. Unlike the Modernists' literary works, which evidenced an acceptance of philology but a rejection of Positivism, the literary criticism of that period (including that written by modernist authors) was instead powerfully influenced by the positivist approach to literature of Hippolyte Taine, which focused on the extrinsic aspects of the literary work according to his well-known formula: "race, milieu, moment." Despite his rejection of many key positivist notions, Taine, as René Wellek has argued, "was a positivist in a wide and loose sense. The worship of the natural sciences and their methods points in this direction: seen in the wide perspective of XIXth-century intellectual history, Taine seems to belong to the reaction against early idealism. . . He is certainly imbued with the psychological and biological ideas of his time" (A History of Modern Criticism, IV: 35). However, as Wellek also points out, the basic framework of ideas underlying Taine's approach to literature is Hegelian. Taine's concept of history, like Hegel's, is a cyclical process of dynamic change. Also Hegelian are his contentions that great art is both "representative" of its age and nation and the expression of individual personality, and his tendency to seek "ideal types" in fictional characters.

The source of Taine's attraction for Spanish American critics is not difficult to discern. Unlike Ernest Renan, who rejected Positivism's claim to have achieved a thorough systematization of knowledge and studied mostly the literatures of antiquity and the Orient, Taine studied European literature and provided his readers with a seemingly systematic critical vocabulary with which to approach more familiar and contemporary texts. His implicit Hegelianism was probably another source of interest, given the Spanish American writers' constant preoccupation with their national history and its place in a broader historical scheme.

Most of the literary criticism produced by the modernist poets intended to communicate, in an unsystematic manner, the new aesthetic values and ideas about language and literature endorsed by the Modernists. This criticism was contained in their newspaper chronicles, and therefore tended to be journalistic and superficial. Moreover, despite their formalistic inclinations, the modernist poets (as well as the professional critics of the period) were often hampered by the lack of a rigorous terminology for literary analysis. Aside from the jargon of verse theory in which some wrote treatises on versification, such as *Leyes de la versificación castellana* (1912) by Ricardo Jaimes Freyre (1868–1933), the Modernists' critical vocabulary was surprisingly poor. Furthermore, their frequent use of elaborate poetic images to describe literary phenomena made their criticism impressionistic. Thus, even the major modernist poets, such as José Martí and Rubén Darío, found it difficult to avoid the use of Tainean concepts in their critical writings.

The famous conceptual triad of race, milieu, and moment that Taine introduced in his *Histoire de la littérature anglaise* (1864) appears in many of the modernist poets' statements about the relation between literature and society. "Each stage of society brings its own expression to literature; in such a way, that by the diverse phases of their literature the story of nations might be told with greater truth than through their chronicles and annals," declared José Martí in his 1887 essay, "Walt Whitman." For his part, Rubén Darío, even as he criticized the notion of environmental influences, could not avoid using it in his essay on Edgar Allan Poe in his book *Los raros*: "Poe, like Ariel in human form, seems to have spent his life under the spell of a strange mystery. Born in a country where life is materialistic and practical, the influence of his environment worked a contrary effect on him. Such a stupendous imagination arose in a country of numbers and reason."

Nevertheless, in general, the critical writings of the great modernist poets had propagandistic, manifesto-like qualities; they attempted less to elucidate literary works than to promote the modernist aesthetic. Such is the case with Martí's prologue to *Poema del Niágara* (1882) by Juan Antonio Pérez Bonalde (1846–1892), which in style and ideas outshines the rather pedestrian poem it precedes. Darío's choice of authors studied in his collection of literary essays *Los raros* follows the same intention of outlining the modernist creed rather than producing a work of literary history or theory. It profiles major figures such as Poe, Verlaine, Ibsen, Martí, and – in a truly prescient essay – Lautréamont, as well as secondary writers such as Laurent Tailhade and Jean Richepin, all of whom seem to have in common only their "oddity," their distance from the literary mainstream.

An important departure in the modernist poets' criticism exhibited in

Los raros (as well as in other texts) is their well-known "cosmopolitan" attitude. At least until the Spanish(Cuban)American War of 1898, the Modernists were less concerned than their romantic precursors with using literature as an instrument of "nation-building." They were less interested in "building" countries than "building" Literature (with a capital "L"). The exception that proves the rule is, of course, Martí, but even he understood the hierarchical difference between the political and the literary spheres, as the following, much-quoted passage from his notebooks attests: "There is no writing, which is a form of expression, until there is an essence to be expressed by it. Nor will there be Spanish American literature until there is – Spanish America."

Martí's words also prefigure the Modernists' main contribution, after the crisis of 1898, to the ideological background of Spanish American criticism: the search for a compact, clear-cut concept of Spanish American culture (an "essence," in Martí's terms) from which Spanish American writing springs, and through which Spanish American writing assures its uniqueness and originality. In his essay "Nuestra América" (1891) – which is not a work of literary criticism, strictly speaking – Martí proposed a theory of culture which synthesized the romantic idea of culture as an emanation of Nature, with the concept of culture as artifice posited by Renan. For Martí, Spanish American culture is the product of a clash between the Europeans' willpower and American Nature (within which Martí also includes the American Indians). This clash has produced deformities in Spanish American culture which must be corrected by seeking a harmony and balance with Nature. To seek such harmony is for Martí a supremely poetic, creative act: "To be a ruler, in a new nation, is to be a creator." This culturally deterministic theory of Spanish American literature, which still echoed in the works of the telluric critics of the 1930s, was further developed and disseminated, as will be seen shortly, by José Enrique Rodó.

The professional critics during the modernist period, as said before, were even more visibly influenced by the positivistic critical style of Taine than the poet–critics, although most drifted away from it during the early years of the twentieth century. A good example is the Cuban Enrique José Varona, whose Positivism led him to oppose the modernist aesthetic. Taine's strong influence is evident in Varona's *Estudios literarios y filosóficos* and *Seis conferencias*, but gradually Varona grew disenchanted with Taine's propensity toward generalization and dogmatism. Varona's later critical writings, collected in *Desde mi belvedere* and *Violetas y ortigas*, show a moderately aestheticist attitude toward literature and a skepticism toward all forms of dogma that is more reminiscent of the works of Ernest Renan.

In the literary criticism of Argentina at the turn of the century, a more direct French presence was provided by Paul Groussac. A French immigrant who became a Spanish-speaking intellectual and Director of Argentina's National Library, Groussac set to the task of correcting what he saw as the rhetorical excesses of the Spanish American literary idiom, promoting instead the French ideals of clarity and precision. Although in many ways his reformist attitude toward language was similar to that of the Modernists, Groussac was in other respects a confirmed "Americanist" (as his novel *Fruto vedado* [1884] and his travel essays in *Del Plata al Niágara* [1887] attest), and he frequently derided Darío and the Modernists. This did not prevent Groussac, however, from publishing in his journal *La Biblioteca* (founded in 1896) one of Darío's major poems, "Coloquio de los centauros." Groussac's critical methodology was strongly influenced by Taine, but there are echoes of Renan in his concern with stylistic purity (both in Spanish and French); as Darío noted, "sometimes there sings in him a nightingale that is not heard in the mountains of Taine" (*Obras completas*, II: 169).

Renan and Taine, romantic philology and positivist literary history, were both incorporated and to a certain extent reconciled, in the work of the foremost Spanish American critic of the turn of the century, the Uruguayan José Enrique Rodó. Although in 1895 he co-founded a journal with a positivist-sounding title, the *Revista Nacional de Literatura y Ciencias Sociales*, Rodó was sympathetic to the Modernists' aestheticism. Indeed, his first important essay, "El que vendrá" (1896) is a lyrical and – paradoxically – rather detached meditation on the different attitudes taken by turn-of-the-century writers toward the feeling of "decadence" that was widespread in Western culture. Renan and Taine are mentioned together in that essay because of their common interest in – to use Rodó's terms – the "Cult of Truth." The essay, which ends with a call for a new artistic leadership, for a sort of literary Messiah, is preceded by an epigraph from Renan ("Une immense attente remplit les âmes") and its style is evocative of the French philologist's famous "Prière sur l'Acropole" (1876). A veneration of Renan is evident in Rodó's work up to and including *Ariel*, but, as Emir Rodríguez Monegal points out (Rodó, *Obras completas*, 119), Rodó gradually distanced himself from Renan because of the latter's extreme political skepticism in his later years and Rodó's increasing "Americanism."

On the other hand, throughout Rodó's critical work, the Tainean emphasis on environmental determinism, as well as his concept of "representative" artists, reappear. Two of Rodó's best critical essays, "Juan María Gutiérrez y su época" and "Montalvo" (both from 1913) follow Taine's method of historico-literary reconstruction. Significantly, in his well-known essay on "Rubén Darío. Su personalidad literaria. Su última obra" (1899), Rodó criticizes the Nicaraguan poet's fascination with Decadentism in *Prosas profanas* with the assertion "No es el poeta de América;" in other words, denying Darío's status as an artist representative of his time and place. It should be pointed out, however, that many other critics were among Rodó's models; among them, Juan María Gutiérrez, the Spaniards Marcelino Menéndez y Pelayo, Juan Valera, the Countess Pardo Bazán, and *Clarín*, and the Frenchmen Sainte-Beuve, Marie-Jean Guyau, Ferdinand Brunetière, Anatole France, and Paul de Saint-Victor.

Rodó's work, like that of any other writer, cannot of course be reduced to a mere interplay of influences. Leaving aside his extremely important role as a "cultural critic" (in today's terminology) in works such as *Ariel* and *Motivos de Proteo* [*The Motives of Proteus*], Rodó's originality in the history of Spanish American literary criticism lies in his belief that criticism is a form of artistic creation, and that as such, it is worthy of special respect. For Rodó, criticism was not merely a belletristic pastime or a covert way to discuss politics, but (in his words) "the most vast and complex of literary genres" (*Obras*, 169). The ideal critic, according to Rodó in his posthumous *Ultimos Motivos de Proteo*, is a *homo duplex* who is capable of intuitively identifying with the work of art and of re-creating it by means of commentary and paraphrase, while simultaneously judging the value of the work dispassionately.

Rodó's insistence on criticism's artistic side should not be understood simply as an attempt to purposely blur the distinction between criticism and fiction, but as a statement of criticism's inherent value. Terms such as "art" and "artistic" had connotations at the turn of the century which were somewhat different from those of today, and when Rodó speaks of an "artistic" criticism he is referring not only to an unfathomable "creative" element, but also to the intellectual precision and stylistic polish he felt criticism should have – to what today we would call "professionalism." Rodó did more than any other Modernist to exalt literary criticism to its full dignity as an autonomous discipline. It was his respect for the "purity" of criticism that led him to avoid placing it, as his Romantic predecessors had done, fully in the service of a "national consciousness." When Rodó, like many other Modernists after 1898, felt the need to define once more the nature of Spanish American culture, he did so in works of "cultural criticism" such as *Ariel*, *Motivos de Proteo*, and *Liberalismo y jacobinismo* (1906), rather than in works of strictly literary criticism and scholarship.

The rather strict distinction Rodó wished to maintain between cultural criticism and literary criticism tends to break down, of course, when his work and that of other modernist critics is more closely scrutinized. The gnawing question that underlies most Spanish American criticism since Bello is that of Spanish American literature's uniqueness and originality.

At least since Martí and Rodó, this uniqueness is traced to the peculiarity of Spanish American culture vis-à-vis that of Europe. In Rodó's critical work, for example, one can see, as in the other Modernists, two phases: a "cosmopolitan" and an "Americanist" one. Until the crisis of 1898, Rodó, like Darío, seemed to regard Spanish America mainly as a backward province of European culture; the problem for Spanish American literature seemed to be how to "catch up" with the literature of the "civilized nations." After 1898, however, Rodó and the other Modernists moved to a position similar to that of Martí in the aforementioned quotes from his notebook and in essays such as "Nuestra América": Spanish American literature's uniqueness lay in the harmonious and creative interaction between a Europeanized consciousness and the Nature and indigenous peoples of America. (The fact that such harmony was virtually nonexistent did not prevent the Modernists from making it their ultimate goal.) This is essentially what Rodó preached in *Ariel*, although, being from the more Europeanized River Plate region, he paid virtually no heed to the Indians, emphasizing instead the vision of a "regenerated America" (in his words) based on a fusion – achieved by a young and educated elite – of Hispanic and French culture in the ideal of "Latinity."

Other modernist critics in the early years of the century followed Rodó's lead. The Venezuelan Rufino Blanco Fombona's work, for instance, evidences the almost-missionary zeal and broad "Americanist" perspective implicit in Rodó's "Arielism," as some of his titles attest: *Letras y letrados de hispanoamérica*, *Grandes escritores de América*, and *El modernismo y los poetas modernistas*. The name of the highly successful publishing house Blanco Fombona founded in Madrid in 1914 is equally telling: Editorial América. Two of its main series of publications were the "Biblioteca Andrés Bello," which published Spanish American literary works, and the "Biblioteca Ayacucho," devoted mostly to nineteenth-century Spanish American history.

Less ambitious but no less tenacious in their desire to promote a renewed "Americanism" without losing touch with the European cultural legacy were critics such as the Colombian Baldomero Sanín Cano and the Peruvian Ventura García Calderón. Sanín Cano, like Bello, had lived for a long period in Great Britain (he taught Spanish language and literature at Edinburgh University). Perfectly bilingual in Spanish and English, he collaborated in the *Modern English Review*. On his return to Colombia, he found time after his duties as Minister of Finance to write the brief and elegant essays of cultural and literary criticism collected in *La civilización manual*. Ventura García Calderón, on the other hand, exemplified the "Pan-Latin" link with France. A long-time resident of Paris, he began writing "chronicles" in Spanish in the style of Enrique Gómez Carrillo (1873–1927). Many of his narrative works were written directly in French.

Among his salient works dealing with Spanish American literature are: *Literatura peruana* and *Semblanzas de América*. García Calderón's criticism, like Blanco Fombona's or Sanín Cano's, frequently consisted of "profiles" and review essays of contemporary Spanish American writers, which were meant to promote the synthesis of "Americanism" and European aestheticism that lay at the core of Rodó's call to renew Spanish American culture.

The telluric period in Spanish American criticism springs directly from this turn-of-the-century desire for cultural renewal. A great many historical and cultural events form the turbulent background to this criticism; historical events such as the Mexican Revolution (which began in 1910), the First World War (1914–1918), the Russian Revolution (which began in 1917), and the Spanish Civil War (1936–1939), plus the numerous United States interventions in the Caribbean and Central America until the 1950s, which fanned the flames of nationalism; cultural events such as the myriad avant-garde movements that arose between the first and third decades of this century, from Futurism to Surrealism, as well as the rise of new political, social, and philosophical ideologies, from Leninism to psychoanalysis to Existentialism. Already in the early years of the twentieth century, the Modernists had remarked on an apparent "speeding up" of the historical process; technological, social, and epistemological change seemed to be gaining momentum. Such rapid change produced in the Spanish American intellectuals feelings of uncertainty, rather than exhilaration, and gave greater urgency to the "Americanist" project initiated by Martí and Rodó.

The continuity between the late-modernist approach to the problematic of Spanish American culture and that of the Telluric critics is evident at every level: from the titles of their books and essays to the cultural institutions they founded. Two of the major critics of this period, the Mexican Alfonso Reyes and the Dominican Pedro Henríquez Ureña, were among the founders of the "Arielist" Ateneo de la Juventud on the eve of the Mexican Revolution; there, along with the philosopher Antonio Caso (1884–1946) who gave lectures criticizing Positivism (which had become the official ideology of Porfírio Díaz's dictatorship), Henríquez Ureña lectured on "La obra de José Enrique Rodó." Reyes's early book of essays, *Cuestiones estéticas*, bears the stamp of Rodó, and his famous *Visión de Anáhuac* resembles the vivid and colorful recreation of Mexico's indigenous past in Martí's essay, "Las ruinas indias," from his children's magazine, *La Edad de Oro* (1889). Also, echoing the evocation of Greco-Roman culture in the poetry of Manuel Gutiérrez Nájera (1859–1895) and Darío, the works of the "Ateneístas" show a considerable familiarity with, and admiration of, the Greek and Roman classics, as may be seen in

Reyes's play, *Ifigenia cruel* (1924), and his *Discurso por Virgilio*, and in many passages of Henríquez Ureña's critical essays. The Latinism and Hellenism of these writers, their emphasis on a solid knowledge of classical literature, as well as being a modernist inheritance, was a symptom of the telluric critics' insistence on returning to the origins of western culture.

A somewhat different attitude was shown by the Peruvian José Carlos Mariátegui, the first major Marxist critic in Spanish America. Although, as we shall see, Mariátegui shares many ideas with the other less politically radical telluric critics, he openly repudiated the modernist legacy, to which he nevertheless owed his formation as a writer: "Since 1918," he states in a 1927 letter, "nauseated by Creole politics, I resolutely oriented myself toward Socialism, breaking with my early literary attempts, that had been tainted with the turn-of-the-century Decadentism and Byzantinism which were then at their height." It should be recalled that a streak of "utopian Socialism" runs through the writings of many Spanish American liberal Romantics and Modernists, from Alberdi's Saint-Simonian Asociación de Mayo to Martí. Marxian Socialism, however, along with anarchism, arrived in Spanish America at the end of the nineteenth century, brought by European immigrants; already by the 1890s there were "socialist clubs" in all the major Spanish American capitals, from Mexico City to Buenos Aires.

The Modernists had also prefigured the telluric critics' sympathetic approach to Spain. The renewed appreciation of Spain's cultural heritage had begun with Martí, whose style bears a baroque imprint and who, despite being the leader of an anticolonial struggle against Spain, made frequent allusions to the colonial period and the Siglo de Oro. It was further dramatized by Rubén Darío's triumphant trip to the Spanish peninsula in 1892. In the cases of Reyes and Henríquez Ureña, the vicissitudes of exile and the profession of diplomacy took them to Spain during the early decades of the century and allowed them to establish fruitful ties with Spanish intellectuals of the time, from the *noventaiochistas* Miguel de Unamuno, Antonio Machado, and Azorín, to the younger writers such as José Ortega y Gasset and Juan Ramón Jiménez, and philologists such as Ramón Menéndez Pidal. The "Hispanophilia" of the telluric critics, manifested in books such as Henríquez Ureña's *En la orilla de mi España* (1922) and *Plenitude de España* (1940), Reyes's *Cuestiones gongorinas*, *Las vísperas de España* (1937), and *Tertulia de Madrid* (1949), and the Venezuelan Mariano Picón Salas's *Buscando el camino* (1920) and *Europa-América: preguntas a la esfinge de la cultura*, was not merely a consequence of their personal contacts (although this was important) but also part and parcel of their critical ideology: the return to the Spanish roots was an integral part of the search for America's roots.

1910 was a watershed year for the telluric critics, not only because it witnessed the beginning of the Mexican Revolution, but also because it was the first in a series of anniversaries marking the various stages of the struggle for Spanish America's independence. The various centennials of the Wars of Independence commemorated from 1910 to the 1930s were also important elements in the ideological background of the telluric critics. Spanish America was already 100 years old: what had been achieved, these critics asked. After a century of travails and progress, was there a truly Spanish American identity? And had this identity been clearly reflected by Spanish American literature?

In several key books, the major telluric critics presented remarkably similar views of Spanish American literature and its relation to New World society and culture. Among these books are works by Pedro Henríquez Ureña ranging from *Seis ensayos en busca de nuestra expresión* to the posthumous *Historia de la cultura en la América Hispánica*, José Carlos Mariátegui's *7 ensayos de interpretación de la realidad peruana* [*Seven Interpretive Essays on Peruvian Reality*], Alfonso Reyes's *Ultima Tule*, and Mariano Picón Salas's *De la Conquista a la Independencia: tres siglos de historia cultural hispanoamericana*. [*A Cultural History of Spanish America: from Conquest to Independence*].

In many ways, the telluric critics' notion of Spanish American literature was a distillation of the romantic and late-modernist vision, to which was added a leavening of philosophical Vitalism (from Henri Bergson to Oswald Spengler), as well as a strong emphasis on erudition and scholarship. For these critics, Spanish American literature was a unique product of the culture of Spanish America. This culture, in turn, despite regional differences, was assumed to be a coherent entity which derived its uniqueness, its difference, from a deep-seated harmony with New World Nature. True to its romantic background, this theory was also highly historicist in character: Spanish American culture and literature did not arise fully formed once the first *mestizos* were born from their Spanish and Indian parents. Instead, in a basically Hegelian scheme, the telluric critics saw Spanish American literature as the testimony of a process of gradual self-knowledge which eventually gave rise to an "American expression" (to use a phrase from Henríquez Ureña later taken up by Lezama Lima in *La expresión americana*). In his aforementioned book, Mariátegui summarized the stages in the development of Spanish American literature as: "a colonial period, a cosmopolitan period, and a national period. During the first, a people are in terms of their literature nothing but a colony, a dependency of another. During the second, they assimilate simultaneously elements of diverse foreign literatures. In the third, their own personality and their own feelings achieve a well-modulated expression" (p. 239).

In the literary and cultural history of Spanish America presented by the telluric critics, discontinuities and conflicts are smoothed over by their almost-providentialist vision of an overarching historical causality. Faced by the numerous instances of violence, fragmentation, and conflict that have marked Spanish America since the Conquest, the telluric critics needed to support their contention that Spanish American culture had finally "matured" and could "express" itself artistically in an unmistakable fashion. For this, they needed a solid point of origin, or ground, for Spanish American culture. This ground, they believed, could be found in the indigenous pre-Hispanic cultures. The hieroglyph-covered ruins of pre-Hispanic cultures, like those of Greece and Rome for modern Europe, represented a foundation and origin for Spanish American culture, an origin to which it was possible to return again and again due to the continued survival of some of the indigenous groups. However, the present-day condition of the native Americans did not interest these critics (Mariátegui excepted) as much as their ancient ruins, sculptures, and paintings. In Henríquez Ureña's words: "The Conquest decapitated those native cultures; it made religion, art, science (where there was science), and writing (among the Mayas and Aztecs), disappear. But there survived many local traditions in daily and domestic life. There was a fusion of European and indigenous elements which has lasted until today (*Historia*, 30).

Since concepts such as "fusion" and *mestizaje* played such an important role in their theory of culture, it is not surprising that these critics paid a good deal of attention to colonial literature, in which the first testimony of these phenomena could be discerned. The vision of the colonial period found in works such as Henríquez Ureña's *La cultura y las letras coloniales en Santo Domingo* and Picón Salas's *De la Conquista a la Independencia* was more positive than that of the Romantics. Rather than the gloomy American Middle Ages presented by Juan María Gutiérrez and others, the telluric critics saw this period bathed in the light of the Renaissance and the *Chiaroscuro* of the Baroque.

Unlike the Spanish American Romantics, the telluric critics' understanding of the Baroque was more sophisticated and sympathetic, in consonance with the European Avant-Garde's revalorization of this period (of which the tricentennial of Góngora in 1927 was but one manifestation). Reacting to Menéndez y Pelayo's excessively critical (if not prejudiced) assessments of figures such as Sor Juana Inés de la Cruz and Juan Ruiz de Alarcón (1560–1639) in his *Antología de poetas hispanoamericanos* (1893), and following the ideas of turn-of-the-century philosophical Vitalism, the telluric critics presented the Spanish American Baroque as a period of enormous vitality, richness, and splendor. Where Juan María Gutiérrez had only seen a "ridiculous and pedantic" Carnival, the telluric critics – fresh with enthusiasm for the Mexican Muralists of the 1920s and 1930s – pointed with pride and amazement at the mixture of pre-Hispanic and European motifs in colonial church art. Picón Salas went so far as to posit that the rich amalgamation of styles of the Baroque had produced Spanish America's first autochthonous artistic movement, the so-called "Barroco de Indias." For the telluric critics, the colonial period was the crucible in which the synthesis of Spanish American culture was begun, although its flowering would have to wait until the nineteenth and twentieth centuries.

The frequency with which terms such as "fusion," "synthesis," and *mestizaje* are found in this criticism also indicates its constructive, or more precisely, reconstructive nature. The telluric critics were engaged in intellectual tasks which were consonant with those of the heroes of the "novelas de la tierra," particularly in works such as *Doña Bárbara* (1929) by Rómulo Gallegos (1884–1969). Just as Santos Luzardo brought barbed wire and the rule of law to the Venezuelan plains, the telluric critics – authoritative, elitist, and magisterial (as Roberto González Echevarría points out in *The Voice of the Masters*, 33–40), armed with the textual weapons of their scholarship and their eloquence – set out to impose order and method on the ill-defined panorama of Spanish American criticism in the early twentieth century. It is not by chance that one of Reyes's most ambitious works, an attempt at producing a Spanish American literary theory, is entitled *El deslinde* (1944). Certainly these critics (save for Mariátegui, who died prematurely in 1930) were also great teachers and founders of academic institutions, such as El Colegio de México in 1940 (in Reyes's case) or the Faculty of Philosophy and Letters of the Universidad Central de Venezuela in 1946 (in the case of Picón Salas). Their influence was immense, and it was felt also in the United States, in the development of North American Hispanism.

Although Hispanism in the United States during the early decades of the twentieth century was dominated by expatriate Spanish intellectuals such as Federico de Onís, who promoted above all peninsular literature, the cordial relations between the telluric critics and their Spanish counterparts (as well as Washington's "Good Neighbor" policy during the 1940s) made it easy for the Spanish American critics to be invited to lecture and teach at North American universities. Both Henríquez Ureña and Picón Salas taught at Columbia University, Middlebury College, and Harvard, among other institutions, during the 1940s. Henríquez Ureña's *Las corrientes literarias en la América Hispánica* comprises the Charles Eliot Norton lectures he gave at Harvard in 1940–1941, and Picón Salas's *De la Conquista a la Independencia* resulted from courses taught at Columbia, Smith College, and Middlebury College, from 1942–1943. It seems clear that these critics' near-obsession with cultural history is partly attributable to their need to explain Spanish America to "the Colossus of the North."

The telluric critics – like most great critics – were eclectic in their methodology. Nevertheless, they showed a decided tendency to organize their works around the history of culture. Their interpretation of literary works was usually contextual, designed to show the links between literature, culture, and society. Marxist critics such as Mariátegui, Aníbal Ponce (in *Humanismo burgués y humanismo proletario. De Erasmo a Romain Rolland*), and Juan Marinello (in "Americanismo y cubanismo literarios") stressed, of course, the sociological and ideological influences, while Henríquez Ureña, Reyes, and Picón Salas, without ignoring sociology and politics, took into account the history of ideas, art history, and literary periodizations. In the case of the Marxists, a more thorough and consistent application of Marx's theory of class struggle should have led them to question the concept of a unified Spanish American culture, but the need to preserve a "united front" in the struggle against United States interventionism made this undesirable.

Their insistence on contextualization made the telluric critics wary of the linguistics-derived critical methodologies that had been developing in Germany and Spain during the 1920s and 1930s, which eventually, under the name of "stylistics," became a powerful school of literary analysis during the 1940s and 1950s. In his late *Marginalia. (Primera Serie)* (1952), Reyes observes: "So-called pure criticism – aesthetics and stylistics – only considers the specifically literary value of a work, in its form and its content. But this cannot lead to a complete evaluation and understanding of a work. If we do not take into account the social, historical, biographical, and psychological factors, we will never arrive at a just valorization." Nevertheless, there were many points of contact between stylistics and the critical ideology of the telluric critics, and this made it possible for both critical traditions to coexist and interpenetrate. Leaving aside the textual immanentism of the stylistic critics, both critical tendencies – like the Anglo-American "New Criticism" of those same years – stressed the study of literary works as coherent wholes, every detail of which contributed to the work's total effect; they were both intuitive and sympathetic to the works studied, and both paid close attention to the writers' use of poetic and rhetorical devices. Furthermore, both forms of criticism tended to portray literary history as a canon of "great works" by means of which mostly male, white authors "expressed" coherently their feelings, values, and ideas. Stylistics also was able to provide Spanish American literary criticism with the rigorous analytical terminology it had always lacked and which the telluric critics (Reyes's *El deslinde* notwithstanding) had been unable to produce.

The arrival of stylistics as a critical school serves as a bridge between telluric criticism and the postmodern period. Stylistics was the prelude to a series of European critical modalities (such as Structuralism, semiotics, and Post-structuralism) which began sweeping into Spanish America throughout the 1960s and 1970s. Although influenced by the so-called Munich school of Karl Vossler and Leo Spitzer (both of whom wrote extensively on Spanish literature), the Spanish stylistics of Dámaso Alonso and Amado Alonso (who were not related) was also a home-grown product, a result of the philological studies fomented by Ramón Menéndez Pidal in the Centro de Estudios Históricos in Madrid and the *Revista de Filología Española*. Amado Alonso in particular was responsible for the dissemination of stylistics in Spanish America through the Instituto de Filología de Buenos Aires (which he directed from 1927 until his death), the *Revista de Filología Hispánica* (1939–1946), and the *Nueva Revista de Filología Hispánica* (founded in 1947 and still extant). His studies *Poesía y estilo de Pablo Neruda* and *El modernismo en "La gloria de don Ramiro"* were highly influential. Many eminent Spanish American critics from the 1940s to the 1950s were his alumni, from scholars who wrote mostly on peninsular literature, such as Raimundo Lida (1908–1979) and María Rosa Lida de Malkiel (1910–1962), to Spanish Americanists such as Enrique Anderson Imbert (b. 1910) and Juan Carlos Ghiano (b. 1920).

Although the critique of the concept of culture that was to precipitate the postmodern period of Spanish American criticism can be partly attributed to events such as the Cuban Revolution (begun in 1959), some of its main points had been anticipated by Jorge Luis Borges in his 1932 essay, "El escritor argentino y la tradición." There, adopting his typically marginal stance, Borges stated that the relation of literature to national culture was "a rhetorical theme, suitable for pathetic expositions; more than a real mental difficulty I believe it is simply a mirage, a simulacrum, a pseudo-problem." Much later, in the midst of the Cuban Revolution and reflecting its impact on his thinking, Alejo Carpentier (1904–1980) delivered a searing criticism of himself and his generation for their sentimental and utopian *nuestramericanismo* ("Our American-ism"); it was not, he said, "Martí's concept of 'Our America,'" but a vaguely apocalyptic and imprecise 'Our American-ism,' projected towards a future *sine die* [without a specific day for its fulfillment]." In a further break with the telluric ideology, Octavio Paz, whose own research into Mexico's cultural identity from the perspective of Heideggerian Existentialism in *El laberinto de la soledad* [*The Labyrinth of Solitude* 1950] led him to dissolve that identity into an ontological "solitude" common to all humanity, developed during the 1970s a theory of Spanish American literature that emphasized rupture and discontinuity. He expressed it succinctly and eloquently in a 1977 essay, "Alrededores de la literatura hispanoamericana": "Why struggle to define the character of Spanish American literature? Literatures have no character. Or rather, contradiction, ambiguity, exception, and hesitancy are traits which appear in all literatures. At the heart of every literature there is a continuous dialogue of oppositions, separations, bifurcations. Literature is an interweaving of affirmations and negations, doubts and interrogations."

The novels of the Spanish American literary *Boom* of the 1960s also contributed to this questioning of the concept of culture. Although it is true that such questioning has been implicit in Spanish American literary works from the very beginning, in the *Boom* novels the framework of topics and tropes that sustained the telluric concept of culture became even more visible and its artificiality became more apparent. The playful approach to literature and constant narrative shuttling back and forth between France and Argentina in *Rayuela* (1963) by Julio Cortázar (1916–1984) point to the dialectic of unity and fragmentation that underlies the concept of culture. Analogously, the allegory of Peruvian society in the Leoncio Prado military school created by Mario Vargas Llosa (b. 1936) in *La ciudad y los perros* (1963), or his vision of Peru as a whorehouse in *La casa verde* (1966), erode the harmonizing and ennobling aspects of the telluric view of culture. Furthermore, if one considers the fictional Macondo in *Cien años de soledad* (1967) by Gabriel García Marquez (b. 1928) as an allegory of Spanish American history and culture, the revelation of Macondo's detailed inscription in Melquíades's manuscript and its final erasure from the face of the Earth by a "biblical hurricane" are suggestive of the artificial, fictional nature of the concept of culture.

In such a fluid and changeable situation, it is not surprising to find that the two most eminent Spanish American professional critics of the 1960s and 1970s – Emir Rodríguez Monegal and Angel Rama – both came from backgrounds that were more journalistic than academic. Also, both were from Uruguay, a fact which is partly coincidental, but partly explainable by the continuity of the critical tradition laid down by Rodó, and by the social climate in Uruguay during the 1940s and 1950s, which fomented a lively sociopolitical and cultural debate in newspapers and journals such as *Marcha*, *El País*, *El Día*, *Clinamen*, *Escritura*, *Marginalia*, and *Número*. They were both members of what Rama called "the critical generation," a generation whose approach to literature was decidedly cosmopolitan and interdisciplinary (if somewhat dilettantish): they linked literary criticism to art and film criticism, as well as to politics and sociology, and wrote and commented on such diverse topics as the films of Ingmar Bergman, the writings of Borges and Samuel Beckett, Fidel Castro's struggle against Batista in Cuba, and the jazz music of John Coltrane and Miles Davis.

Lifelong adversaries, Rodríguez Monegal and Rama nevertheless made analogous and at times complementary contributions to Spanish American criticism. In the tradition of Domingo Delmonte and other romantic cultural animators, they founded and directed journals which promoted new views of literature as well as the careers of young writers. Rodríguez Monegal founded *Número* in Montevideo in 1945, and was its editor from 1949–1955 and 1963–1964; but his most important directorship was that of *Mundo Nuevo* in Paris from 1966–1968. *Mundo Nuevo* is widely regarded as the main journal that contributed to the promotion and diffusion of the Spanish American narrative *Boom*. It featured texts and interviews by such writers as García Márquez, Carlos Fuentes (b. 1928), Vargas Llosa, Borges, Pablo Neruda (1904–1973), Juan Carlos Onetti (1909–1994), Manuel Puig (1939–1990), and Sarduy, among others.

For his part, Rama founded in 1962 the Arca publishing house in Montevideo, directed the Biblioteca Ayacucho (a publishing venture sponsored by the Venezuelan government) from 1974 until his death, and founded in Caracas the journal *Escritura* in 1975. Through his directorship of the Biblioteca Ayacucho, Rama presided over a wide-ranging effort to republish and make accessible to scholars and students critical editions of classic works of Spanish American narrative prose, essay, and poetry. Similarly, in the two-volume *Borzoi Anthology of Latin American Literature* (1977), published in English, Rodríguez Monegal presented a broad sampling of fragments from works by major authors from Spanish America and Brazil from the colonial period to the present, accompanied by introductions which related each author to both the Spanish American and the Western literary tradition. Whatever reservations one might have about the results, it is unquestionable that Rama and Rodríguez Monegal contributed powerfully to the formation of the present-day canon of Spanish American literature.

Another similarity between Rodríguez Monegal and Rama lies in their contribution to the study of Spanish American Modernism: Rodríguez Monegal with his edition of Rodó's *Obras completas* (Editorial Aguilar, 1957) and various essays on Uruguayan writers of the Generation of 1900, and Rama with ambitious and groundbreaking sociological interpretations of the modernist movement in books and essays such as *Rubén Darío y el modernismo. Circunstancia socioeconómica de un arte americano*, "La dialéctica de la modernidad en José Martí" (1971), and the posthumously published *Las máscaras democráticas del modernismo*.

Differences between these two great professional critics abound, of course. Rama's approach to Spanish American literature was always passionately political (although not partisan). Sometimes, in his fervent "Spanish Americanism" he seemed to return to the ideas of the telluric critics, although his approach to the culture–literature link in Spanish America was less idealistic than that of the earlier critics. In books such as

Transculturación narrativa en América Latina and *La ciudad letrada*, he made use of ideas culled from anthropology and from heterodox Marxist thinkers such as Theodor W. Adorno and Walter Benjamin. At Rama's untimely death, his eclecticism and rather journalistic penchant for following critical fads (another similarity with Rodríguez Monegal) seemed to be giving way to a more systematic and coherent approach, as may be seen in *La ciudad letrada.*

An uncomfortable aspect of Rama's writing, even to his many admirers, was its stylistic awkwardness; as Tomás Eloy Martínez observes, Rama "almost did not stop to correct what he was writing, being excited by the ease with which his thoughts always hit the mark, without realizing that in his haste his language stumbled over too many modal adverbs, and never finished making its way through the tangle of subordinate sentences, and that it therefore lost – because of its untidyness – part of its enormous persuasive force" ("Angel Rama", 645). Rodríguez Monegal's style, on the other hand, was almost always precise, witty, ironic – and usually dispassionate. It was fully appropriate for a critic whose approach to Spanish American literature was less nationalistic and more "extraterritorial." Rodríguez Monegal's criticism, as Roberto González Echevarría has pointed out, "lacks the strident Spanish Americanism of certain academic criticism, or its correlative opposite, a condescending attitude. Rodríguez Monegal can write about little-known Spanish American writers with the same respect and rigor as a scholar in studying a Renaissance humanist, and he can very matter-of-factly state that a Spanish American writer is more important than a great figure of European letters" ("Nota critica sobre *The Borzoi Anthology of Latin American Literature*," 227). Less overtly political, more skeptical (like the many English writers whose works he knew well and, of course, like Borges), Rodríguez Monegal's critical approach was nonetheless eclectic (though borrowing heavily in his later years from Structuralism and semiotics) and tended to stress the writers' biographical context, as may be seen in his well-known studies on Bello (*El otro Andrés Bello*), Neruda (*El viajero inmóvil*), Horacio Quiroga (1878–1937; *El desterrado*), and Borges (*Jorge Luis Borges: A Literary Biography*).

In many ways, the critical trajectories of Rama (Marxist-influenced, politically committed) and Rodríguez Monegal (with his structuralist inclinations and "extraterritorial" perspective) reflect the development of the variegated and turbulent panorama of criticism in Spanish America from 1960 to 1990. It is a panorama, as said at the beginning of this essay, divided into extremely different and competing critical ideologies, from Marxism to Post-structuralism. The Marxist approach has among its salient representatives critics such as Roberto Fernández Retamar (b. 1930; in *Calibán* and *Para una teoría de la literatura hispanoamericana*) and journals such as the Cuban *Casa de las Américas* and the Peruvian *Revista de Crítica Literaria Latinoamericana*. At the other extreme, Structuralism, semiotics, and Post-structuralism are vividly present in works of writer–critics such as Sarduy (in books such as *Escrito sobre un cuerpo*, *Barroco*, and *La simulación*), of professional critics such as Noé Jitrik (b. 1928; in *Las contradicciones del modernismo*) and Sylvia Molloy (b. 1938; in *Las letras de Borges*), among many others, and in journals such as the Mexican *Texto Crítico*, the Venezuelan *Escritura*, and *Dispositio* (published in the United States). Although powerful writer–critics, such as Borges, Paz, Lezama, and Sarduy have come to the fore during this period, their work has been too unsystematic to influence journalistic or academic criticism very strongly, or to create a critical consensus.

Besides ideology and lack of system, another circumstance that obstructs consensus in Spanish American criticism is the current weakened and uncertain socio-economic condition of most Spanish American countries, which has led to a diaspora of intellectuals from the region to the United States and Europe and has left Spanish American universities and research institutions foundering. Arguably, the consensus achieved by the telluric critics can be traced to the moral and institutional support their ideas were given by the Mexican Revolution; a similar (and equally deluded) consensus might have been reached during the 1960s by means of the Cuban Revolution, if the ideological issues in that revolution had not been so polarized by the Cold War. At present, for better or worse, the main center of critical research on Spanish American letters is in the United States, and the effects of this situation are difficult to predict.

An important and interesting development that has taken place mainly in the United States in recent years has been the reinvigoration of the study of colonial Spanish American literature by contact with structuralist and post-structuralist ideas and methodologies, and fields such as anthropology. Because this "boom" in colonial studies is so recent and has taken place mostly among US Hispanists (many of whom are, of course, Spanish American by birth or nationality), a detailed account of it would fall outside the scope of this essay. From the plethora of new critical editions, special issues in professional journals, and book-length essays on colonial themes one must mention José Juan Arrom's critical edition and study of Friar Ramón Pané's *Relación acerca de las antigüedades de los indios* (1498 [1974]), which drew attention to the anthropological dimension of the clash between Europeans and native Americans that gave birth to writing in the New World. Theoretically sophisticated work in a similar vein has been produced with regard to the seventeenth-century Peruvian colonial chronicler Felipe Guamán Poma de Ayala, by scholars such as Rolena Adorno and Mercedes López-Baralt. However, other, better-studied colonial figures have also benefitted from critically mature approaches; such is the case of Sor Juana Inés de la Cruz, whose *Inundación castálida* (1689) received a new critical edition by Georgina Sabat de Rivers in 1982, and whose biography and works were the subjects of a massive study by Octavio Paz, *Sor Juana Inés de la Cruz, o las trampas de la fe.*

Exile or expatriation have not been infrequent, as we have seen, in the history of Spanish American criticism, but the circumstances of exile and work in a foreign academic environment frequently impose on the Spanish American critics different agendas and priorities than they would have at home, and make it extremely difficult, if not impossible, to engage through journalism in the sort of debate that serves to disseminate views and rally critics to a particular set of ideas. It may be argued that one result of exile is precisely to prolong the tendency to explain Spanish American literature in terms of reified and essentialist concepts of literature and culture, because of the exiles' natural tendency to "freeze" their mother tongue at the moment they parted from it, and their propensity to form an idealized vision of their native countries in the distance. On the other hand, the critical ideologies now prevalent in the United States and Europe (from deconstructionism to reader-response theory) work strongly against such a view, and the Spanish American critics are clearly paying attention. If there is any emerging consensus to be found in Spanish American criticism today, it probably lies in the acceptance by many critics of ideological and methodological plurality, and in their attempts to escape – through an appeal to such disciplines as anthropology, semiotics, or sociology – from essentialist notions of both literature and culture.

13

The autobiographical narrative
Sylvia Molloy

Autobiography in Spanish America is a much neglected form. This is not because, as has so frequently and thoughtlessly been asserted, autobiography is unusual, nor is it because Hispanic writers, for elusive "national" characteristics, are not prone to recording their lives on paper. The perceived scarcity of life stories written in the first person is less a matter of quantity than a matter of attitude, for autobiography is as much a way of reading as it is a way of writing. Thus, one might say that, whereas there are and have been a good many autobiographies written in Spanish America, they have not always been read autobiographically: filtered through the dominant discourse of the day, they have been hailed either as history or as fiction, and rarely considered as occupying a space of their own.

First-person narratives abound in Spanish American colonial literature. Chronicles of discovery and conquest, especially those involving some measure of self-awareness on the part of their authors, might be seen as precursors of the autobiographical mode. In the same way, self-reflexive documents such as Juana Inés de la Cruz's letter to the Bishop of Puebla, *Respuesta a Sor Filotea* (1691; pub. 1700), or confessional depositions before the tribunals of the Inquisition, given the vindication of self they propound, may be considered autobiographies. Nevertheless, the fact that the above mentioned texts were conceived primarily for a privileged, institutional, reader (the King, the church) having power over writer and text, and the fact that the narration of self was more a means to achieve a goal than the goal itself, considerably modify the textual self-confrontation and crisis that we have come to recognize as the mark of autobiographical writing.

One might say that autobiography appears in Spanish America as a genre when it becomes a subject of reflection, that is, when questions arise about the validity of self-writing in general, about the forms the exercise should take in particular, and about the purposes it should accomplish.

One of the most captivating examples of early autobiographical awareness may be found in the opening sentences of the Mexican José Miguel
Guridi y Alcocer's *Apuntes de la vida de D. José Miguel Guridi y Alcocer*
(1802); "For days I have been troubled by the thought of making notes
about my life. However much I think of it and examine myself, I have not
been able to ascertain the cause that moves me" (p. 9). That questions
about autobiography should arise in Spanish America at the beginning of
the nineteenth century, at the moment when a received order (that of the
Spanish colonial regime) is replaced by a produced order (that of the
newly independent countries) is not accidental. That these questions
should arise, furthermore, within the context of the more general debates
over national identities and national cultures – debates in which relations
to Spanish, and more generally European, canonical authority are
renegotiated – is also significant. If in the case of colonial writers, self-
writing was legitimated by an institutional Other for whom one wrote, for
the post-colonial autobiographer, those institutions no longer accomplish
their validating function. Indeed, the very notion of institution, as it had
been understood, comes in for serious questioning. If one no longer writes
oneself down for King or church, for whom, then, does one write? The
predicament of the Spanish American autobiographer, the very tentative
figurations of self in which he or she engages, the constant search for
recognition by the reader, give rise to a pattern of provocative ambiguities
that always allude to (but never openly ask) the same question: for whom
am I "I," or rather, for whom do I write "I?" The vacillation between
public *persona* and private self, between communal representativeness
and individual soul-searching, between honor and vanity, between self
and country, between lyrical evocation or factual annotation of the past
are but a few manifestations of the hesitancy that then marked (and may
mark even now) Spanish American self-writing.

From its very inception, then, autobiography suffers from generic
ambiguity. The nineteenth-century Spanish American autobiographer is
hard put to define himself as a subject who writes within the yet unstable
limits of budding national literatures. Often a direct participant either in
the struggle for independence or in the process of consolidation of the
national state, he usually perceives the autobiographical venture as a
didactic and not wholly disinterested task. Beside the purely political
memorialist intent on righting his image for posterity, there is the writer
statesman, postulating himself as an exemplary figure. A civic hero
doubled by a moralist (suffice it to think of Domingo Faustino Sarmiento
and Juan Bautista Alberdi in Argentina, of José María Samper in
Colombia), he writes his life story as a form of service, useful to his
descendants and future compatriots. In spite of its claims to confidentia-
lity – Alberdi subtitles his autobiography *Mi vida privada* [my private life]

– Spanish American autobiography, at the beginning, is a public story: public in the sense that it tells what can and should be told, and public because, more than satisfying the individual's need to speak of himself, it serves the public interest.

Conceived then as a *Bildungsbiographie*, autobiography in the nineteenth century seems a perfect vehicle for history and, more particularly, for the history of the newly formed countries. Now this generic adjudication (autobiography is biography is history), together with its specific characteristics (not only is autobiography history but new national history), imposes a particular slant on the texts. There is little or no room in them – in Domingo Faustino Sarmiento's *Mi defensa*, in his *Recuerdos de provincia*, or in José María Samper's *Historia de una alma*, to give but three examples – for the *petite histoire*, and much desire, instead, to make the text a chapter of the broader History in the making. Indeed, in many cases, what is announced as the story of an individual soon becomes, by metonymy, the story of an emerging country. Such is the case with Sarmiento, who writes in *Recuerdos de provincia*, "I was born in 1811, the ninth month after May 25th" (p. 160). The reference to the first insurrection against Spanish rule as a way of dating his birth unambiguously establishes a genetic, quasi-biological link between the autobiographer and his newly independent country.

This conflation between individual *bios* and national *ethos*, practiced by other autobiographers besides Sarmiento (although the Argentinian writer possibly gave it its most perfect form), conditions personal memory and directs the retrieval of the past. Autobiographers set out primarily to record, less frequently to reminisce. There is little speculation, in early nineteenth-century autobiography, on the workings of memory: memory is a tool not a subject for conjecture, its performance considered as reliable as the perusal of a document. "This is not a novel, it is not a story," writes Sarmiento in *Mi defensa* (p. 5) to stress the accuracy of his account. Nostalgia is a rare luxury in these lives of active political participation; it is an attitude kept in line and controlled by a calculating adult wary of unbridled self-expression, at least in an autobiography. The evocation of childhood is given short shrift, the elegiac tone usually avoided, the usefulness of the memories stressed. Ramón Subercaseaux, in *Memorias de cincuenta años*, pointedly writes: "If, in the first chapters especially, I deal mainly with events of my childhood and early youth, let it be understood that I do this only to make known what the education and customs corresponding to my social sphere in the second half of the past century were like" (p. vi). A similar view of schoolboy recollections (a genre in itself in Europe, from Kipling's *Stalky and Co.* to Musil's *Young Törless*) may be found in the Argentinian Miguel Cané's *Juvenilia*, a revealing account of the education of the Argentinian elite in the late nineteenth century. It is noteworthy that, of all these nineteenth-century autobiographers and ardent admirers of Rousseau's *Confessions*, only one devoted to childhood an account in the spirit of the master. It is also noteworthy that this account was written from a triply marginal position. It was written in exile, in a language that was not the subject's native tongue, and by a woman: *Mis doce primeros años*, first published in French, was written by the Cuban Mercedes de Santa Cruz y Montalvo, Countess of Merlin, whose pretensions to historical documentation were nil. If the Countess of Merlin's autobiography strays from the exemplary model cultivated to perfection by Sarmiento, so does the autobiography of another Cuban writer, Juan Francisco Manzano, albeit for different reasons. An eloquent slave narrative, Manzano's *Autobiografía* (written in 1835–1836; published in Havana in 1937), while also dwelling on childhood with no pretensions to national representativeness, does not cultivate the elegiac mode. Instead, it uses the details of the *petite histoire* both to tell a personal story and to compose a forceful abolitionist document.

If the fiction of national representativeness subsists in twentieth-century self-writing, it often does so in problematic form. José Vasconcelos, in *Ulises criollo* (1935) and in the three autobiographical volumes that were to follow (*La tormenta* [1936], *El desastre* [1938], *El proconsulado* [1939]), doubtlessly repairs to the nineteenth-century exemplary model, presenting a gigantic self-image against the background of revolutionary Mexico, an image that finally merges with that of revolutionary Mexico in one *corpus gloriosum*. Yet where Sarmiento and his contemporaries shunned personal confession in the name of history, Vasconcelos attempts – rather successfully, in spite of his bombastic national rhetoric – to incorporate his personal life, often in quite intimate detail, into that of his country. Notions of the public and the private have changed, as have notions of the tellable and the untellable. (Remarkably though, Vasconcelos would, years later, expurgate his autobiography: for purely ideological reasons, what was deemed tellable in 1935 became untellable in 1958.)

In the twentieth century, the national model may be imitated, as a cliché, in purely utilitarian or opportunistic autobiographies. An early example of such an exercise is the Peruvian José Santos Chocano's *Memorias: Las mil y una aventuras*. In more artful texts, the national model may be accepted even as it is distorted: thus Pablo Neruda, in *Confieso que he vivido* [*Memoirs*] cleverly fuses the *political* identification of self and country with the *poetic* identification of self and country. The monumental status of the subject has not changed in Neruda's text, just the figuration chosen for his autobiographical *persona*: in his pages, the exemplary national statesman is replaced by the exemplary national bard. In a more muted yet equally self-serving vein, Enrique González

Martínez's *El hombre del búho* and *La apacible locura,* advances an equally heroic figuration, that of the exemplary doctor and civil servant. In other cases, the fiction of national representativeness may be denounced for its vacuous rhetoric and resented as an imposition: "Nothing destroys a man more than having to represent his country," writes Cortázar, quoting Jacques Vaché, in the epigraph to the autobiography he does *not* write, that is, his novel *Rayuela* [*Hopscotch*].

Nevertheless, the conception of a national "I" has left its trace in the anxiety of representativeness present in many modern texts. If the openly autobiographical text usually no longer says, "I am my country," it often says, "I am someone writing in the tradition of those who say 'I am my country'." (Or, alternately, "I am someone who cannot get rid of those who say 'I am my country'.") While "I" is no longer a synecdoche for the country itself, it may be a synecdoche for a group, a community, a gender. The latter seems particularly true of the life-stories of members of minority groups, that is, of those whose presence, as individuals, has been routinely marginalized. While not, strictly speaking, autobiographies – these are usually oral *testimonios,* told to, or prompted by, a transcriber – the Cuban Esteban Montejo's *Biografía de un cimarrón* [*Autobiography of a Runaway Slave*] as told to Miguel Barnet, and the Guatemalan Rigoberta Menchú's *Me llamo Rigoberta Menchú y así me nació la conciencia* [*I. . . Rigoberta Menchu. An Indian woman in Guatemala*] as told to Elizabeth Burgos, show a particularly complex tension between an individual "I" and the collective "we" that "I" strives to represent.

If not always perceiving themselves as historians, autobiographers often continue to see themselves as witnesses, usually privileged witnesses to what is no more. Spanish American self-writing continues to resort to what may be seen as a double memory, an exercise in personal reminiscence complemented by a ritual of commemoration, in which individual relics are secularized and re-presented as shared events. This communal memory is often illusory, rarely corresponding to a shared past. What the autobiographer relies on, of course, is the seductive power of bonding illusions whose tropological foundations are often taken from life itself. Thus, in the same way that Sarmiento sought to forge a link with his audience by playing up his family romance – he was the father of his country, the son of his province, etc. – some modern autobiographers court hypothetical siblings, kinsmen who will read and understand them. Mariano Picón Salas's *Viaje al amanecer* and Victoria Ocampo's *El archipiélago,* the first book of her six-volume *Autobiografía,* attempt to create a community of readers that will in some way echo their own, biological family, a community that will participate in their idealization of the past. Ocampo's nostalgia for a patrician past where Argentinian history was a family affair, Picón Salas's fond recollection of his childhood in provincial Mérida, a stronghold of Venezuelan tradition, shows how ideologically charged and how defensive the evocation of the past, in these more recent autobiographies, can still be. Interestingly, María Rosa Oliver, a member of the same class as Victoria Ocampo whose intellectual itinerary would evolve along very different ideological lines, having also experienced history as family gossip during her childhood, pictures herself, in *Mundo, mi casa*, the first book of her three-volume autobiography, questioning the very assertions Gómez Ocampo defends. Oliver's text, as, earlier in Peru, Enrique López Albújar's *De mi casona* and, later on in Cuba, Renée Méndez Capote's *Memorias de una cubanita que nació con el siglo*, looks to another family of readers, one willing to share a revisionary view of the past with the autobiographer. It is interesting to note that, on both sides, either conservative or revisionary, there is a need to historicize, and ideologize, the very references, private in nature, that Sarmiento and other exemplary nineteenth-century autobiographers had banned from their texts as too personal for the wider history of the nation. Here, instead, the personal serves the historical and the *petite histoire* rejoins History.

In the twentieth century, however, there have been considerable attempts to distance autobiography, as a genre, from its primarily historical affiliation. As other discursive practices have invaded its ill-defined domain, autobiography has diversified its forms: new ways of self-writing have been experimented with, the workings of memory have become the subject of inquiry and conjecture, there has been more reflection on the textual fabric of autobiography, more acceptance of its hybrid status, of its unquestionable ties with fiction. The roots of this awareness were already to be found (timidly, it is true) in some turn-of-the-century autobiographies which very tentatively explored other forms for self-writing besides the exemplary. Texts often considered frivolous – such as the Guatemalan Enrique Gómez Carrillo's *Treinta años de mi vida* (1918–1921), which reads like a cross between a picaresque novel and a travelogue, or the Argentinian Lucio V. Mansilla's *Mis memorias*, loosely conceived as a series of light-hearted chats – ultimately opened self-writing to experimentation, by connecting it to other genres (as in the case of Gómez Carrillo) or by suggesting, in pre-Borgesean fashion (as in the case of Mansilla) the impossibility of conceiving the "I" as an organic whole. Also, the genre has gained in diversity as other types of writers, besides statesmen or notables, have engaged in it. As early as 1937, the Argentinian Norah Lange, in her *Cuadernos de infancia*, had turned autobiography into a critical inquiry, questioning its narrative presuppositions and exploring its fictionalizing thrust. In more recent times, some writers of fiction have practiced the genre more or less straightforwardly, such as Sergio Pitol in *Sergio Pitol* and Salvador Elizondo with *Salvador*

Elizondo; others, such as the Cubans Guillermo Cabrera Infante and Severo Sarduy, the Argentinians Manuel Puig and Ricardo Piglia, the Mexicans Elena Garro and Elena Poniatowska, have resolutely turned to fiction as the preferred vehicle for their autobiographical writing. Nevertheless, while it might be tempting to see Spanish American autobiography as a process in which a subject, enmeshed at the beginning in different tactics of self-validation (what must be told in a way that is acceptable to a nation or at least to a community), progressively comes into its own (the story of the self "alone"), it would be ill-advised to conclude that movement from the constraints of the historical document to the freedom of the individualistic, introspective text, is the only goal for Spanish American self-writing. Given the history of the genre, the components that gradually, secretly, have come to integrate what one might term a Spanish American autobiographical tradition (claims to national representativeness, to group bonding, to testimonial service – claims, in short, opening the self to a community) have been naturalized, have been incorporated into an autobiographical rhetoric, and are part of the subject's perception of self, so that they may well be present even in the most ostensibly private or more clearly fictional texts.

[14]

The twentieth-century short story in Spanish America
Daniel Balderston

Story or history

The existing accounts of the Spanish American short story consist almost completely of conventional literary history: the modern short story is said to have been born with Echeverría or Palma or Darío or Quiroga, to have been descended from earlier sources in the Spanish or indigenous or *mestizo* traditions, to have developed or matured or produced such progeny as Borges and Rulfo and Bombal. Attention is not usually called to the organicist metaphors at work in these accounts, the authors seeming to find them beyond question. The literary historian's task, as defined in the manuals by Leal, Menton, and others, consists of a taxonomy by movements (Naturalism, *mundonovismo*, *criollismo*, the fantastic, Neorealism), by generations (the Generations of 1930, 1938, 1940, 1950, and so on, depending on the history of the country in question, or the "first," "second," and "third" generations of writers of the Mexican Revolution), by country or region, or by the gender or ethnic origin of the writers; sometimes, indeed, an uneasy combination of all of the above forms the "history." There is no agreement between the different accounts of this supposed "history," and indeed no agreement would be possible, given the uncertain foundations on which these accounts are built. It is not even very certain that a "history" of the short story genre in Spanish America could be written: the notion of the short story as genre has been vigorously debated internationally, and in Spanish America the constitution and preservation of such a genre is problematized by the uncertain relations between the "short story" and the "*costumbrista* sketch," the "*tradición*," and the "*crónica*." Similarly, the frontiers between the "short story" and the "prose poem" and "novella" or "short novel" are uncertain, waiting to be adjudicated.

Instead, then, of giving an account of a history of something that perhaps never was and certainly resists being told as history, I have chosen here to tell a very different kind of story, the story of the "diverse intonations of a metaphor" or series of metaphors (to paraphrase Borges from "Pascal's Sphere"). The images examined here have been variously proposed as metaphors for narration itself, and their appearances in diverse Spanish American texts have been collected here out of an interest in the poetics of prose.

Circles

A paradigmatic situation: a fat old man tells a story about a place of death, a place that turns out to be the place of the speaker's own death. Within a series of nested narratives, the fat man tells stories, all ultimately variants of the same story. He uses an image to talk about his own storytelling:

> For me reality is what is left when all of reality has disappeared, when the memory of habit has been burnt up, the forest that prevents us from seeing the tree. We can only allude to it vaguely, or dream of it, or imagine it. An onion. You peel off layer after layer, and what's left? Nothing, but that nothing is everything, or at least a stinging vapor that brings tears to the eyes. (*Moriencia*, 90)

The analogy between the onion and the story is repeated three more times. On the following page the fat man says of himself: "I myself talk and talk. For what? To peel off new layers of the onion (p. 91). Later still, the narrator says of the fat man: "You never knew when he was telling a joke or remembering an anecdote, at what point one story ended and another one emerged from it, 'peeling the onion'" (p. 93). Finally, the narrator says: "He told various stories. Perhaps they were all part of the same one, letting go layer after layer and emitting its stinging and fantastic flavor" (p. 95).

Obviously, in this story the onion is a metaphor of the short story itself, and the story has a sort of onion structure due to the seeming divagations of the old man, whose abundant stories turn into variants of a single story. This essential story is told at the end "all at once, without any more interruptions or digressions" (p. 95). It goes like this:

> A man saw the place where he was going to die in a series of dreams. At first he did not understand too well where it was. But the fat man, not in keeping with his usual practice, indulged at the end in a detailed description. He said that afterwards the man lived in fear of coming up in reality with the predestined fatal place. He told the story to various friends. They all agreed that he should not pay attention to dreams. He went to a psychoanalyst who only succeeded in terrifying him still more. He ended up shutting himself up in his house. One night he suddenly remembered the setting of his dream. It was his own room in his house. (p. 95)

The ending, told by the young narrator, is brief: the fat man grows silent, his voice broken and his face ashen, one hand pointing to the empty space of a doorway. Those listening to him suddenly understand that "what the fat man had described point by point was the room where we were sitting" (p. 96). When the narrator and his friends look at the fat man once more he is dead, his eyes staring at them, with a sarcastic smile (p. 96).

The final story thus ends with the death of the fat man, the one who (within the story of the young journalist narrator) tells us the story of his own death, even if he does so in the third person (these are the dreams of "the man" in his stories). To finish telling a story is to die, which means that telling stories is life itself. All of his prior stories, then, put off the essential story, the story that can be told "all at once" because it leads to the end, to nothingness. The central conflict in the story between language and silence is thus part of a dialogue that involves not only the fat man and his interlocutor, our narrator, but also the author and the reader.

The problem set out by the story is the impossibility of uttering the sentence: "I die now, here." This sentence can be transposed into other grammatical persons or verbal tenses, and may be uttered figuratively, but never directly and literally. Thus the story involves the enclosing of an impossible declarative statement in a series of statements that repeat it with a series of differences, or the displacement of it onto the image of the nothingness at the heart of the onion (or the dropping of a hat in *Tristram Shandy*). On a temporal axis, the telling of the series of frame stories precedes the staging of the central anecdote, which is essentially non-narrative and nonverbal. The fact that the central episode requires the death of the speaker makes it impossible for it to be repeated and impossible for it not to be repeated: it is the ultimate story.

The story I have been talking about is by Augusto Roa Bastos (Paraguay, b. 1917), and is significantly called "Contar un cuento" (in *Moriencia* [1984 edn.]). It could easily be the work of a half-dozen other Spanish American writers of short stories. This paradigmatic story unites any number of the most common elements of a dominant tradition of the short story in Spanish America: the concern with the relation between life and death and the analogous concern with the relations between writing and silence, the use of nested narratives, the attempt to recover speech and memory in writing.

Of course, by privileging this story I am suggesting it as a paradigm of "the Spanish American short story," just as any other initial example would predetermine to some extent the categories of the subsequent discussion. I will later return to the question of whether this is one paradigm among many: suffice it to say for the moment that this Roa Bastos story has a number of elements that can be found in other important modern short stories from Spanish America, as for example

Jorge Luis Borges's "Abenjacán el Bojarí, muerto en su laberinto," Juan Rulfo's "Anacleto Morones," Juan Carlos Onetti's "La cara de la desgracia," and Silvina Ocampo's "La furia," to name just a few. In all of these stories, the narration of a death is enclosed within a series of concentric narratives, though the image for this enclosure (onion, spider web, labyrinth, bicycle wheel, pile of stones, drum) may vary.

"Abenjacán el Bojarí, muerto en su labérinto" (*El Aleph*, expanded edn. of 1952) ["Ibn Hakkan al-Bokhari, Dead in His Labyrinth"] is one of Jorge Luis Borges's classic detective stories, and the most famous of his stories to deal explicitly with the labyrinth image associated so often with his name. For Borges (Argentina, 1899–1986), the detective story derives its force from the human desire to know, and is most perfectly exemplified in tales of armchair detectives who learn the truth without a need to experience the world of crime directly. However, even the armchair detective must re-enact the crime (if only in the mind), and an odd complicity is established between the detective and the criminal (most notably in the story "La muerte y la brújula").

"Abenjacán" is a mystery story in a more conventional sense than are several other Borges stories that are sometimes considered examples of the genre – including "El jardín de senderos que se bifurcan" (1941, in *Ficciones*) ["The Garden of Forking Paths"] and "Emma Zunz" (1948, in *El Aleph*) ["Emma Zunz"]. Specifically, it is an example of the "problem of the closed room" alluded to by Borges in several of his essays on crime fiction. In the story, in fact, passing reference is made to Poe and Zangwill (p. 600), reference more specific than may first appear: Poe's "Murders in the Rue Morgue" and Zangwill's *The Big Bow Mystery* are both concerned with murders committed inside closed rooms, and hinge on the identity of those in the rooms. Furthermore, like the examples mentioned, this Borges story is a classic example of an armchair detective story in that Dunraven and Unwin do not have direct access to the crime except through prior narratives: the hypotheses ventured by Unwin are based not on new evidence but on new interpretation of the evidence. The murder itself was committed twenty-five years earlier, and the only access to it is through Dunraven's retelling of the events. What Unwin does in essence is fragment the story as told by Dunraven and then reassemble the parts in a different order. Significantly, Unwin is a mathematician and Dunraven a poet; the mathematical attention to detail and ordering ultimately provides a more adequate explanation than the poet's totalizing dramatic story.

One of the interesting features of "Abenjacán" is the nested story of the two kings and the two labyrinths, printed after the main story as a somewhat discrete entity, though with a note explaining that it is the text of the sermon spoken by Rector Allaby. The nested story takes up the same themes as the larger tale – simplicity versus complexity, the labyrinth as image of the universe – with a quiet ironic touch in that the Anglican minister refers to God as Allah. Borges had in fact already published this brief tale a decade before the composition of "Abenjacán": in his column in the family magazine *El Hogar* in June 1939, he publishes the story exactly as it will later appear in *El Aleph*, attributing it to "the notes that Burton added to his famous translation of the *Arabian Nights*." The tale is not, it seems, actually included in Burton, so it appears that Borges elaborated the longer story out of elements contained in the shorter original, later subordinating the shorter tale to the longer and more complex story.

The epigraph of "Abenjacán" comes from the *Koran*: "they are comparable to the spider, who builds a house." The Koranic original tells a parable of those who worship gods other than Allah, and the comparison to the spider's web turns on the flimsiness of the spider's house, that is, on the weakness of other forms of faith. The spider web image is repeated in the coiled snakes in Zaid's dream and in the labyrinth on the cliff above the sea in Cornwall, and the common element uniting the three images is death. For this to be true, the same "flimsiness" has to be erased from the Koranic passage, and weakness of faith replaced by the fragility of life itself.

Yet another erasure practiced in the story is the obliteration of the faces of the lion, the black slave, and the supposed Abenjacán. This erasure has a similar function to the mute gesture of death in the Roa Bastos story: death itself cannot be narrated here, except *a posteriori* (in the two young men's versions of the story) and *a priori* (in the narrator's implication that the two young men will soon be food for poppies on the battlefields of Flanders). The defaced bodies form an algebraic series which Unwin is professionally equipped to solve, though perhaps his name implies his ignorance of the fact that he too may perhaps soon be inscribed in that series.

"Continuidad de los parques" (in *Final de juego*) ["Continuity of Parks"] is one of the briefest stories by Julio Cortázar (Argentina, 1914–1986). It tells of a character sitting in a chair looking out on a large garden and reading a book about a character sitting in a chair looking out on a large garden. In the novel an assailant creeps up behind the man reading and kills him, just as an assailant creeps up behind the man in the story and kills him. The essential story is the same as the nested narrative of the old man in the Roa Bastos story discussed earlier. Here too the story is told in the third person (though here is an example where first person narration would be equally effective, especially since it would have to stop a moment before the death of the narrator). The circularity of the story is emphasized by the title, which implies that there is continuity between the garden in the story and the garden in the novel (the story within the story). The Spanish phrase "solución de continuidad," usually used in the negative to discuss the lack of a break between one narrative and another, is appropriate for the "solution" here: the narrative "solution" (death of the character in the novel signifies death of the character in the story) implies the dissolution of the narrative itself, hence its brevity.

"La cara de la desgracia" (in *La cara de la desgracia*) ["The Image of Misfortune"] is one of Juan Carlos Onetti's finest stories, and has been termed a masterpiece of Uruguayan literature. Onetti (Uruguay, 1909–1994) often plays in his stories with the theme of dissolution, nowhere to more striking effect than here. The narrator of the story is mourning the death by suicide of his brother Julián a month earlier when a girl appears on the sands of a beach resort riding a bicycle. The two stories – that of the dead brother (and his final conversations with the narrator) and that of the girl on the bicycle – are intertwined in an uncertain way for most of the story. Near the end, after the narrator makes love to the girl, he confesses to her his fears of failure, of having been responsible for his brother's death, of the difference in age between them that may make their love impossible. It is only after the girl has been brutally murdered and the narrator has been charged with the crime that he learns that the girl he supposed was hearing his confession was deaf.

During the confession the narrator remarks: "the girl had turned into the main theme of my story" (p. 242). The uncertainty about the center of the story makes it unstable and circular. The bicycle wheels, the moon, the girl's face in silhouette against the moon: circular objects recur, marking the circularity of the story itself, its inability to progress. The difficulty of overcoming the death that marks the beginning of the story (symbolized here by the narrator's obsession with the newspaper clipping telling of his brother's death) leads finally to paralysis and silence. The story ends, in fact, with a mute gesture. When the narrator agrees to answer the policeman's question about whether he knew that the girl was deaf, he makes his answer conditional on the policeman's telling him whether he believes in God; the policeman ends the story by silently and rather scornfully making the sign of the cross.

Silvina Ocampo (Argentina, 1906–1993) is a prolific writer of poetry and stories whose prose is marked by an odd coexistence of cruelty and innocence. One of her best stories, "Tales eran sus rostros" (in *Las invitadas*) ["Thus Were Their Faces"], which tells of the transfiguration of a group of deaf children into something like angels, contains a phrase that is very telling of much of her work: "In reality we don't know whether it was horrible and then became beautiful, or whether it was beautiful and became horrible" (p. 9). This volatile mixture of cruelty and innocence is especially characteristic of her stories of childhood.

Thus, the story "La furia" (from *La furia*) ["The Fury"] is somewhere on the uncertain edge between *grand guignol* and sentimental farce. The narrator, a young medical student, opens his account with enigmatic references to a drum, a child, and a house: if the child does not stop beating on the drum, he says, he could slit the child's wrists in the bathtub and hide the body under the bed. As it unfolds, the story is the conflation of two stories: the series of Winifred's stories of childhood and the story of her relationship with the narrator. Her ambiguous nature is perceptible in the horror and innocence of her childhood, above all in the episode in which she and her friend Lavinia are dressed as angels for a religious procession and she sets Lavinia on fire; as she says, "it was the happiest and saddest day of my life" (p. 115).

Winifred's relationship with Lavinia was marked by her desire to correct her defects: since Lavinia was scared of animals, Winifred would put live snakes and spiders, and dead rats and frogs, in her bed; since Lavinia was proud, Winifred would cut off part of her hair and pour perfume all over her. Winifred's relationship with the narrator is marked by the same unpredictable qualities: she warns him that she will be cruel to him, flees from his embraces, and when she finally accepts the idea of going with him to a hotel she leaves him alone in the room with the child he will murder at the end of the story.

The narrator comments early in the story, referring to himself and Winifred, "we repeated the same dialogue, with different emphases, one might almost say with different meanings" (p. 114). Near the end of the story the endless dialogue is reestablished, this time between the narrator and the little boy, Cintito. The narrator's problem, in fact, is a difficulty breaking out of the circular narration. He is ultimately forced to kill the child because he has threatened to do so, because of his verbal threat more than because of the pounding on the drum. He reflects at the end on the curious nature of his quandary: he committed the crime in order not to provoke a scandal. The pounding on the drum is maddening to him because he feels taunted for his passivity.

"Anacleto Morones" (in *El llano en llamas*) ["Anacleto Morones"] is a story of pride and jealousy, with a certain family resemblance to the rest of *El llano en llamas* (translated as *The Burning Plain*), the famous collection of stories by Juan Rulfo (Mexico, 1917–1986). In this story, as in "¡Diles que no me maten!" ["Tell Them Not to Kill Me!"] and Rulfo's lone novel *Pedro Páramo* (1955), the murderer (here the narrator, Lucas Lucatero) does not confess his crime directly, but the repeated references to the pile of stones serves to notify the reader of the place of rest of the body of Lucatero's father-in-law Anacleto Morones. The story begins with the arrival of a group of old women, Anacleto's disciples; after a while, Lucas takes refuge in his corral and begins scattering the stones which to him look too much like a grave. They are large round stones from the riverbed, and their shape ("boludas") relates them to the eggs mentioned later (and to the narrator's testicles, which have been alluded to in the sexual double-talk between the narrator and the old women). Stones – eggs – testicles: the sequence alludes to the other story concealed inside this one, the story of the narrator's wife, Anacleto's daughter, who was pregnant with Anacleto's son (and grandson, because the incest confuses the generations). When the narrator says, "Inside Anacleto Morones's daughter was Anacleto Morones's grandson" (p. 128), the text itself turns uncertain, with some editions replacing "nieto" with "hijo." The nesting of the son/grandson inside the daughter mirrors the nesting of the daughter's story inside her husband's story (concealed in turn by the title, which nests the husband's story inside that of the father-in-law). The pile of stones concealing Anacleto's grave and holding in his ghost is an uneasy anticipation of the situation in *Pedro Páramo*: the novel ends with a reference to a pile of stones and concerns the restless souls in the Comala graveyard.

There are many other possible examples of nested narratives, in which the final story concludes not with the narration but with the enactment of a death. I shall consider but one more: Borges's "El hombre en el umbral" (*El Aleph*, 1952 edn.) ["The Man on the Threshold"]. Borges makes striking use of the theme of culture shock, represented spatially as well as psychologically. The initial note tells of the impossibility of telling the story: the British official errs when he cites a verse from Juvenal, Borges and Bioy Casares cannot know the truth of the official's story, and the telling itself is uncertain:

> Among the stories he told that night, I will venture to reconstruct the following one. My text will be faithful: may Allah free me from the temptation of adding circumstantial details or of accentuating the exotic nature of the tale with interpolations from Kipling. (p. 613)

Dewey, the representative of the British Council, tells of his adventures looking for a missing colonial official he calls David Alexander Glencairn, believed kidnapped by religious extremists. Most of the story consists of a conversation he has with an old man sitting in a threshold, who tells him a story from his childhood of the impromptu trial of a cruel British official and of his condemnation to death by a judge who was quite literally insane; when the old man finishes his story and the crowd inside the house disperses, Dewey sees a naked madman dancing around the corpse of Glencairn. The old man's story, told as something far away and long ago, has been enacted before his unwitting eyes.

As in the Roa Bastos story discussed earlier, the frame tale told in the past and in the third person permits the completion of the present story.

This relation is expressed spatially in the story: the house where Dewey interviews the old man consists of a series of enclosed patios, with the conversation taking place at the threshold to the final patio. As in the rest of the stories we have looked at so far, on beyond the threshold lies death; the story is only possible because the conversation between Dewey and the old man takes place outside the space of death.

The initial paragraph of the story, an account of a conversation that Borges and Bioy Casares have in Buenos Aires with Dewey, now of the British Council, restates the motif of the threshold. Just as Dewey could not see what is happening beyond the threshold, and can only reconstruct it afterwards with the benefit of a story that was told supposedly about another time and place, so his Argentinian friends are also on the outside trying to find their way into his story. However, full entry into the story is blocked by the first narrator's ("Borges's") perception of Dewey as an unreliable narrator, by the changes of name and place, and by the insistent use of nested narratives. Though the first narrator says that he is determined to reconstruct Dewey's story as best he can, even at the risk of error, because he feels it would be a shame to lose its "ancient and simple flavor" (p. 612), the simplicity is only apparent at the end when Dewey comes upon the corpse, and brings on the end (the death) of the story.

Lines

In the stories of Horacio Quiroga (Uruguay, 1878–1937), death is also a matter of enclosure and limits in a seemingly open, boundless world. Significantly, in story after story, deaths – and the end of the narrative – are staged at spots where a path is crossed by a barbed wire fence. In the early story "El alambre de púas" the death is that of a bull; the darker later stories "El hijo" and "El hombre muerto" narrate instead the deaths of fathers and sons. Despite the thematic similarities between Quiroga's most important stories about life in the jungle area of Misiones and the stories discussed above, the different disposition of narrative space is a sign of a different concept of storytelling.

Perhaps the best-known set of prescriptive principles for the short story in Spanish America is Quiroga's version of the ten commandments ("Decálogo del perfecto cuentista," 1927). Quiroga's commandments frequently use the metaphor of a horizontal or vertical journey: "Take your characters by the hand and lead them firmly until the end, not seeing anything but the path you traced for them" (*Cuentos*, 308), "Don't start writing until you know from the very first word exactly where you are going" (p. 307). Two less well-known essays, "La retórica del cuento" (1928) and "Ante el tribunal" (1931) confirm the geometrical image, most clearly in the 1931 article, in which Quiroga writes: "I struggled for the short story . . . to have but a single line, traced by a firm hand from beginning to end" (*Cuentos*, 317). Quiroga's practice, however, does not always adhere strictly to this linear model (a model derived, obviously enough, from Poe's "Philosophy of Composition" and the review essay on Hawthorne).

In "El hijo" (first published as "El padre" in 1928, then in its definitive version in *Más allá*, 1935) ["The Son"], for instance, the straightforward action of the story – the son goes out hunting, falls over his gun and kills himself at ten in the morning – is in tension with the ever more extreme hallucinations suffered by the father. These visions – from the first brief mention of the son's still body to the final joyous return of both father and son to the house in the clearing – disrupt the apparent simplicity of the action, and introduce a subject position that is radically different from the more distanced narrator who informs us of the son's death at the end. Even this narrator, however, at the same moment that he confirms the son's death ("the father goes looking for his son who has just died" *Cuentos*, 296) argues that we should cover our ears out of pity for the father's anguish, thus making explicit the tension between a completely cold and objective and a more partial telling of this story.

Quiroga experiments with narrative focalization in a more obvious way in "El hombre muerto" (1920, later collected in *Los desterrados*, 1926) ["The Dead Man"] and "Las moscas" (supposedly written in 1923, but not published until its inclusion in *Más allá*, 1935), two versions of the death of a man. In the first case the father of a family is crossing a barbed wire fence at the edge of his farm when he wounds himself mortally with his machete; the story focuses on his blurring consciousness as he dies, moments before his children reach him. In the latter story, explicitly termed a variation on "El hombre muerto," a man clearing a forest slips on a tree root and falls against a fallen tree, breaking his back in the process; in this version the focus is on the flies buzzing around him, and at the end of the story (when the man is dead) the narration is taken over by one of them.

The theme of limit-situations is often presented in spatial terms in stories of Hispanic life in the United States as well. José Luis González's important story of Puerto Rican life in New York, "La noche que volvimos a ser gente" (in *Mambrú se fue a la guerra*) ["The Night We Became People Again"], for instance, uses the crossing of a spatial limit as an image of a breaking through from atomized and oppressed individuality to a newly discovered solidarity. (Tomás Rivera uses a similar structure in his 1976 story of Chicano migrant farm workers, "Las salamandras.") González (Puerto Rico, b. 1926) creates a character whose broken Spanish and broken self are made whole by adversity experienced not individually but collectively. The story is constructed spatially in the same pattern of ascent as Neruda's "Alturas de Macchu Picchu": the blackout hits Manhattan while the narrator and his friend are in the subway, and continues as they climb out of the subway to the street, then up the stairs of the apartment building to the room where the narrator's wife has given birth to a son. The final ascent is to the roof of the building where the narrator discovers – at the same time that hundreds of other migrants to New York discover on the adjacent rooftops – that the same sky they know from home has been concealed behind the city lights. The darkness and the starlight serve to reconnect Nature and culture, and to reconnect the shattered community.

Julio Ramón Ribeyro's "La juventud en la otra ribera" (collected in *La juventud en la otra ribera*) is also about the act of crossing into another culture, but expresses much greater pessimism about the possibility of preserving humanity or even life in the process. This crossing is represented spatially in terms of physical borders, as well as narratively through the device of narratives that confuse the communication between native and other. Ribeyro (Peru, 1929–1994) takes as his subject the venerable literary construct called Paris. His protagonist is a Peruvian visitor, Dr. Huamán, who is so flooded with prior images of the city that he cannot see the city as it really is when he finally is able to take his grand tour at age fifty. His very literariness makes him gullible, the perfect victim for a group of skilled confidence men (and women). And, because "Paris" signifies "la vie de Bohème" as well as the "capital of the nineteenth century," the sordid and unsavory nature of the life of Solange and her friends makes perfect sense to Dr. Huamán. The Bohemian life is also constructed of cultural codes, and Dr. Huamán is admirably equipped to read them, though like Borges's detective Lönnrot in "La muerte y la brújula" this intellectual ability only makes him easy prey for literate criminals.

The title – and much of the early part of the story – hinges on Dr. Huamán's initial realization that at age fifty he has left his youth behind, that he has finally reached Paris as a stuffy bureaucrat, not a creative Bohemian. This division is represented spatially in the contrast between the bourgeois right bank of the Seine and the Bohemian left bank; when Dr. Huamán tries to go over to the other, Bohemian, side, thanks to his amiable Parisian guide Solange, he gets in trouble. Being able to read the cultural codes is not the same as being able to write them. Dr. Huamán is crippled by his ability to tell the truth and nothing but the truth, while the others prove skillful manipulators of fictions.

When Solange and her friends (all members of a gang led by Petrus Borel) have finally stolen Dr. Huamán's travelers' checks and obtained his signature, he is lured to his death. The place chosen is the forest of Fontainebleau, the favorite retreat of the impressionist painters (and a literary subject for many writers including Robert Louis Stevenson). There, amid the autumn leaves that seem so exotic to this "hombre sincero de donde crece la palma," Dr. Huamán is shot, pushed across to that opposite bank of the river (of life).

Juan Rodolfo Wilcock (Argentina, 1919–1978), in his macabre and humorous story "El caos" (in *El caos*), parodies the existentialist notion that people will encounter their deepest selves when placed in "limit-situations" like those recounted in the González and Rivera stories (though the probable butt of the parody is Ernesto Sabato, whose existentialist novels were much in vogue when the story was written in the 1950s). The philosopher–prince of the unidentified country creates deliberate chaos in his realm so as to force his subjects out of their routine – and also in an attempt to "find himself" in some sense not determined by his role. Thus, he organizes masked balls – one of the most familiar topoi of the European tradition of the Grotesque – in which there are traps and wires set to trip up the revelers, surprising mixtures of sensual pleasures and religious exercises, and the license to play the part of anyone except one's habitual role. What surprises him is that society proceeds more or less intact, despite the fact that former politicians turn hair-stylists, libertines turn chess masters, garbagemen turn government ministers, and marquesses turn greengrocers. It seems ultimately impossible to create chaos: the new chaos so resembles the old order that the very distinction is called into doubt.

The best moments in the story are those reserved for the narrator's revelations of self. The first occurs when some gypsies seize him during carnival to be the King of Carnival, tie him to a long skewer, and proceed to roast him slowly during a hailstorm. The unfortunate prince, caught between fire and ice, resigns himself to his fate:

> Luckily it hadn't occurred to them to pierce me with the skewer, the way it's done with chickens, and besides the coals of the open fire gave off a pleasant heat, which rendered more tolerable my complete nakedness, so inappropriate in all truth to the season of the year. A man with a great black beard, dressed as a gypsy, turned the crank of the skewer with a slow circular motion that allowed me to observe more easily everything that was happening around me. (p. 14)

The peculiar nature of the account is rendered all the more grotesque by the narrator's gratitude at being granted a panoramic view of his circumstances.

The second moment of epiphany occurs on a cliff above the sea where the narrator has been taken in his wheelchair. He has been practicing mystical exercises that promise an overcoming of the self. All at once the cliff gives way, sending narrator and wheelchair tumbling down toward the ocean: "Who would have imagined that at the very moment I thought I was finally detaching myself from the earth, it was the earth that was detaching itself from me!" (p. 20). The narrator of course does not die, since his account must be made to continue.

A variant on the same pattern is the well-known story "Viaje a la semilla" (*Guerra del tiempo*) ["Journey to the Seed"] by Alejo Carpentier (Cuba, 1904–1986). In this story, narrative time runs backwards, so that instead of coming up against the limit-situations (the death of the protagonist and of various members of his family), the story moves away from them. The limit-situation that haunts the end of the story is the disappearance of the protagonist into a different kind of limbo, that which existed before conception.

Borges's famous detective story "La muerte y la brújula" (in *Ficciones*, 1944) ["Death and the Compass"] also plays on the connections between spatial limits and existential or vital ones. The action of the story is arrayed in a rhombus shape over the map of a city that bears an uncanny relationship to Buenos Aires. However, as the detective and victim Erik Lönnrot correctly perceives at the end, the story is not really diamond-shaped but linear. The three dimensions of extensive space are super-fluous; the essential story, the luring of Lönnrot to Triste-le-Roy, is a two-dimensional one. Indeed, the tension between the two models is reenacted in the contest, between Lönnrot and Treviranus, to give an adequate account of the events as they unfold, and also on another level in the duel of wits between Lönnrot and Scharlach. The struggle over the proper dimensions of the story is present also in a number of smaller details. The statue in the garden of the house at Triste-le-Roy is called a "two-faced Hermes" but also a "two-faced Janus": the image of Janus, looking both forward and backward in time, is being confused with those of Hermes the messenger and the boundary god Terminus, often represented in classical times by markers called herms. The conflation of spatial and temporal limits similarly informs the inscription of the message from "Baruj Spinoza" about the fact that the Jewish day begins at sunset on a map of the city emblazoned with an equilateral triangle. Finally, the restatement of Zeno's paradox at the end of the story restates the matter of limits in space and time from the two dimensions of triangles and rhombuses to the one dimension of "that labyrinth that consists of a single straight line . . . invisible, endless" (*Obras completas*, 507). The story plays, then, with the tensions between a simple story and the complex design of nested narratives studied earlier, and the two kinds of stories are explicitly identified with geometric shapes. Though Treviranus is right in seeing the simple story for what it is, Scharlach is a skillful reader of Lönnrot's more intricate plotting, and is able to draw Lönnrot into his own more direct and elemental design.

Photographs, moving pictures

Another well-known statement about the genre is Julio Cortázar's essay "Algunos aspectos del cuento" ["Some Aspects of the Short Story"]. Originally the text of a speech given in Havana in 1962, the Cortázar piece, like the Quiroga commandments, is prescriptive rather than descriptive. Cortázar seeks to persuade his revolutionary Cuban audience that writing short stories is an art with laws of its own, and that it is not sufficient simply to describe things as they are: he argues, then, against a naive kind of Realism. In fact, he says, ordinary people may be more interested in fantastic than in realistic fiction; he gives the example of some rural people whom he and some other writer friends in Argentina befriended, who proved more interested in a ghost story by W. W. Jacobs than in stories on autochthonous themes. (Oddly, Cortázar's speech anticipates the plot of Borges's later story "El Evangelio según Marcos" ["The Gospel According to Mark"] in El informe de Brodie, 1970.)

Cortázar's essay is perhaps best-known for the comparison made between the short story and the photograph on the one hand, and the novel and the film on the other. Particularly because Cortázar uses photography as a theme in stories like "Las babas del diablo" and "Apocalipsis en Solentiname," and includes references to the cinema in his novel Rayuela [Hopscotch], this comparison has seemed to critics to inform his own writing. In the essay, however, this comparison is only one of many; Cortázar also compares the short story to a magnet, the sun, the atom, and so forth. His more important point is that the short story should be endowed with what he calls "intensity," "the elimination of all intermediate ideas or situations, of all the filling or transitional stages that the novel permits and even demands" ("Algunos aspectos," Casa de las Américas, 10). This is a restatement of Quiroga's idea (derived from Poe, Stevenson, and others) that the writer of a short story should concentrate on building a single effect, though Cortázar's intention here (and his practice in his own stories) displays a much greater interest in narrative ambiguity than that sought after by Poe or Quiroga.

In any case, the photograph is a dominant image in Cortázar's own practice of the short story. "Las babas del diablo" (Las armas secretas) ["Blow-Up"] and "Apocalipsis en Solentiname" (Alguien que anda por ahí) ["Apocalypse at Solentiname"] both use the device of a photograph that shows a sharper truth than the one registered by an eyewitness narrator. "Las babas del diablo," which served as inspiration for the Antonioni film Blow-Up, begins with a discussion about whether the story should be told in the first or the third person, and this discussion prefigures the narrative problem later when it becomes increasingly likely that the narrator, Roberto Michel (a Franco-Chilean translator and photographer), is dead, and that at least part of the narration is being carried forward by his camera. The clouds, mentioned throughout the story but with increasing insistence toward the end, imply that the camera has fallen with its lens pointed up toward the sky, and their passing through the field of vision is presented in a completely impersonal and objective way, alien to the human emotion that pervades the story of the love triangle on the Ile Saint-Louis. The cold "camera eye" narration experimented with several decades earlier by Dos Passos and Isherwood serves here as a distancing mechanism that undercuts the melodrama on the island. The camera "casts a cold eye" on the story.

In contrast, the disembodied gaze of the camera in the later story "Apocalipsis en Solentiname" provides a passionate corrective to the narrator's human experience. The narrator has returned from a clandestine trip to Ernesto Cardenal's utopian community in Solentiname on an island in Lake Nicaragua, and when he shows his slides to his friends in Paris the slides reveal a terrible truth that the narrator had not suspected, that Solentiname has been destroyed by a Somocista attack.

Silvina Ocampo uses photographic images as leitmotivs in two important stories: "Las fotografías" (*La furia*) ["The Photographs"] and "La revelación" (*Las invitadas*) ["Revelation"]. "Las fotografías" is the story of a birthday party for Adriana, a girl of fourteen who has just been released from hospital after an accident that left her paralyzed. The story is organized around the eight photographs taken of Adriana and her family and friends by a photographer with the uncanny name of Spirito ("the letter killeth but Spirito giveth life?"). As the story progresses, two other matters increasingly distract from Adriana herself: the rivalry between the narrator and one of the guests, Humberta, and the discourses of self-sacrifice by the various members of Adriana's family. The narrator's ire against Humberta explodes when Humberta discovers that Adriana, whose head has slumped down like a melon, has died shortly after the taking of the eighth photograph: "How unfair life is! Instead of Adriana, who was an angel, that wretch Humberta could have died!" (p. 93).

Much of the power of the story derives from a series of tragi-comic displacements between the photographs and the characters themselves. For the third photograph, for instance, Adriana holds a knife as if to cut the birthday cake, while the guests banter with the photographer that she should stand for the occasion. Spirito replies to an objection that her feet may not look right in the picture by saying: "Don't worry . . ., if they don't look right I'll cut them off later" (p. 91), a sentence in which the cropping of the photograph and the medical interventions on Adriana's body are confused. Throughout the story the photographs are carefully posed to give the impression of happiness and love; the family and friends, and

Spirito himself, clearly understand that a photograph is a simulacrum of a lived experience, not the experience itself. One of the guests says, tellingly: "If this is the happiest day of her life, how can you fail to take her picture next to her grandfather who loves her so much" (p. 92), a phrase in which the "if" clause ranges from certainty to doubt as to Adriana's happiness, but in which her grandfather's love, though not itself subject to doubt, must be posed or staged.

When Adriana's head falls down and hangs from her neck like a melon, the guests are so caught up in their idea of a good time that no one suspects for a while that something is wrong. It is the narrator's rival Humberta who first notices that Adriana is dead, and that discovery brings an abrupt end to the party – and to the story. The photographs will of course remain a lasting tribute to the party that staged Adriana's death, but one imagines that the sadistic nature of the exercise will be lost on future viewers of the memorial album. Perhaps, as in "La furia" by the same author, they will say that this was the happiest and the saddest day of Adriana's life, but Adriana was not allowed to speak that day, and her speech was forever silenced. The staging of the photographs precludes speech to a large extent, and the later examination of them, though it may be occasion for the telling of stories, cannot recover the silenced speech of the protagonist.

In "La revelación," Ocampo uses the usual confidence that photography depicts reality as it is to provide an uncanny proof of a fantastic event. Valentín Brumana, the protagonist of the story and the narrator's cousin, though handicapped by mental and physical disabilities, is gifted with clairvoyance, which he uses to read the thoughts of his cousins (who are also his tormentors). On his deathbed, he asks his cousin the narrator to take a picture of him with "the lady" he is going to marry, "a star." The cousin dutifully takes a picture of Valentín and of an empty space where he insists the lady is. When the roll of film is developed, a blurry image of Death appears, in the guise of the star of the silent screen, Pola Negri. (Note that though Negri is mentioned in her role as film star, the ghostly image that appears has more of the promotional still photograph than of the cinema *per se*.) The twist given to the story is thus a double one: photography is used to prove that Death has taken a human guise, however that guise is associated not with the older stuff of myths but with the commercial world of the entertainment industry (even though Pola Negri is no longer a familiar name to the moviegoer). Miracles themselves, then, succumb to change in what Walter Benjamin calls the age of mechanical reproduction.

Onetti has a pair of stories that utilize photographs in different ways: "El álbum" and "El infierno tan temido." Onetti is known above all as the creator of the fictional city, Santa María, a place that persists in perpetual decadence through a series of short stories and novels since the late 1940s, above all in the major novels *La vida breve* (1950) [A Brief Life], *El astillero* (1961) [The Shipyard], and *Juntacadáveres* (1964) [*Corpse-Gatherer*]. Onetti's stories partake of the same fractured view of the universe. He proceeds through mordant irony and narrative ambiguity to deny his fiction any sort of transcendental meaning, yet the "certainty in degradation" that T. E. Lawrence discovered in the *Seven Pillars of Wisdom* is present in Onetti. Suffering serves as evidence of life.

His procedures are well exemplified in the story "El álbum" (1953, later collected in *La cara de la desgracia*, 1960) ["The Photograph Album"], in which Jorge Malabia, the son of a prominent Santa María family who dedicates his youth to the discovery of everything that has been repressed or silenced by his family and their milieu, tells of his sexual initiation. As occurs very frequently in Onetti, the story is deferred to the last pages with phrases like "The day before the story really began" or "The prologues to the story were . . . ." Since here, as elsewhere in Onetti, the prologues to the story occupy the greater part of the narrative, it is important to inquire how Onetti is distinguishing "the story" from the rest of the narrative. In this case, for instance, Jorge Malabia's sexual initiation, his partner's stories, the matter of the traveling salesman, Tito's rivalry, all of this remains outside the boundaries of "the story." "The story," here, is the narrative of Jorge Malabia's discovery that what he had taken for the fictions of an extraordinarily imaginative liar were in fact accounts of lived experience. The story, then, hinges on the discovery of the photograph album, the apparent proof of the truth of the woman's stories. Out of the multiplicity of stories (the woman's, Jorge's, others') comes the one story that matters, that she really was there:

> Squatting, matured, trying to handle my pipe with obvious pride, I saw the photographs in which a woman – less young and more gullible as I furiously turned the pages – galloped in Egypt, smiled at golfers on a Scottish meadow, hugged movie actresses at a nightclub in California, had forebodings of death at the Ruan glacier, making real and defaming each of the stories that she had told me, all the afternoons I had loved her and listened to her. (*Cuentos*, 172)

What is more, the truth is infamous, for it takes away the magic of mendacity, of invention. The photographs come at the end of "the story," but in effect turn it back from story to mere incident. The truth constitutes a scandal for the young narrator because it dissociates desire and fantasy.

It is interesting that it is precisely the photograph that is posited as the evidence of certainty, of lived experience beyond the possibility of telling stories about it. As Roland Barthes and Susan Sontag have reflected in their books on photography, the photograph has a paradoxical status as the ultimate proof of "the real" (as in Euclides da Cunha's reference to the photograph taken of Antonio Conselheiro's corpse at the conclusion of the Canudos War in Brazil in 1897), yet it is a medium that is far removed from transparency, far from necessary or simple referentiality. Onetti's use of photography is quite different from Cortázar's. For Cortázar, the photograph is an image of the short story, brief, frozen in time; it is a discrete entity subject to multiple interpretations. For Onetti, the photograph is a narrative (like the stories in which it appears), but a narrative which is somehow final and determinate.

Similarly, in Onetti's "El infierno tan temido" (collected in *El infierno tan temido*, 1962) ["Hell Most Feared"], the breakup in Risso's marriage is confused, protracted, and uncertain, yet the photographs that his estranged wife, Gracia César, sends him, obscene photographs of herself with a series of men, have a fierce unambiguity. Yet, according to the narrator (who for a moment seems to visit the wife's mind), the obscene photographs are intended to allude to love, to Risso's reiterated declaration that their love will survive any test or trial. This is an even darker story of the power of photography than the other discussed so far, since the medium has the power to degrade the viewer even more completely than rumor or hearsay: the visual images of Gracia are bits of staged narrative dependent for their very power on being staged in the flesh for the camera.

"Cine Prado" (*Los cuentos de Lilus Kikus*) ["Park Cinema"] by Elena Poniatowska (Mexico, b. 1933) tells of a similar confusion in the mind of the viewer between reality and a narrative formed from visual images. Here, using the cinema instead of the still photograph, Poniatowska gives us an updated version of the episode in *Don Quixote* of Master Pedro's puppet show. The story consists of a love letter written from prison; it is only at the end of the story, with the introduction of a newspaper clipping into the narrative, that we learn that the letter is addressed to the French actress Françoise Arnoul and that the writer of the letter is in prison for having stabbed her cinematic image on the screen of the movie theatre that gives the story its title. The letter itself is the account of the writer's jealousy at seeing his beloved kiss another man with what looks to him like an unnecessary degree of passion. The perversity of the situation is heightened by the narrator's confession that he always insisted on going to the cinema with his wife; according to him, she shares his outrage at the behavior of the beloved actress, though her own account of her feelings as a spectator to her husband's voyeurism and eventual attempted murder is suppressed. Since the husband's perceptions of female subjectivity are so notoriously mistaken in his evaluation of the actress's behavior (whose acting he takes as indicative of her "real feelings"), the reader may reasonably suspect that the wife's perceptions are anything but what the husband says they are.

Virgilio Piñera (Cuba, 1912–1979) was a prolific writer of plays, poems, short stories, and novels whose narrative fiction bears comparison with that of Kafka and Gombrowicz. In fact, he was the head of the translation committee responsible for the Spanish translation of Gombrowicz's *Ferdydurke* (1947), and his later work contains clear gestures of homage to the Polish master. A number of Piñera's early stories, written in Cuba in 1944 before his emigration to Argentina, have the hallucinatory quality associated with the later works of the literature of the Absurd. Piñera's stories are often told in a neutral monotone; they are disquieting because of the cold objective description of atrocious events. In his preface to *Cuentos fríos* (1956) [*Cold Tales*], Piñera writes: "These stories are cold because they limit themselves to the pure exposition of the facts" (p. 7).

"El álbum" (1944, later collected in *Cuentos fríos*, 1956) ["The Album"], for instance, is a masochistic ritual, experienced by (and through) a male narrator caught in the web of a series of women who are cruel in their very indifference to his existence. In this story, the young narrator rents a room. The first night he is unable to sleep because of the cries of the child next door. The next morning, as he is getting dressed to go to his first day at a new job, that of reader to the blind, he is interrupted by the doorman who announces that the best seat has been reserved for him in the session that afternoon when the landlady is going to show her photo album. The new arrival pays the doorman for the seat, only to be interrupted by Minerva, the woman who lives next door with the crying child. Minerva talks interminably of her life, and when she leaves another visitor, a "woman of stone," arrives to beg for the spot the doorman has reserved for the narrator. When the narrator finally goes down to the living room and takes a seat, the landlady opens the photograph album, and begins a description of a photograph from her wedding that will last for eight months. The spectators will sleep, eat, defecate, even die at their places, prisoners all to the expectation of what the landlady may show them.

The absurdly slow pace of the exhibition of the album is due to the digressive nature of the landlady's stories. She takes eight months to describe a photograph of herself cutting the wedding cake because she describes the baking of the cake, the story of the baker, the stories of the presents on the table, the details of the lace on the wedding dress, the story of the dressmaker. Often these stories are the stories of some terrible violence done to the female protagonists by men, and the landlady's stories (like those of Minerva and the "woman of stone") have elements of revenge. The women tell of past events when they were the victims and spectators: Minerva, for instance, tells of the suicide of her husband, who shot his brains out in her presence, and describes her own mute cry of horror, a cry that can only be described in silence, through gesture. The landlady's own story contrasts dramatically with these stories of violence: utterly trivial, she dwells lovingly on such kitsch details as the stuffed puppy given her as a wedding gift by Mrs. Dalmau, a gift that has outlasted the giver: "Look: this is what is left of Mrs. Dalmau (and she put her finger on the point that was no doubt the image of Mrs. Dalmau)" (*Cuentos*, 80). Thus the photograph album, instead of being a means to remember the past, is itself the point of the exercise: the story returns at last to the image which seemed at first its pretext.

Though it has not been thought of in this regard, the famous Borges story "El Aleph" (*El Aleph*, 1949) ["The Aleph"] is also intimately concerned with photography. The story begins with a reference to the posting of new billboards with cigarette advertisements and with the narrator's remark on the relation between the new ads. and the death of Beatriz Viterbo: "the event caused me pain, because I understood that the unending and vast universe was already moving away from her and that that change was the first in an infinite series" (*Obras completas*, 617). It is thus an image (in all probability a photographic image) that sparks his reflection on time and infinite series. (Remember that when the narrator finally comes to see the Aleph, it is as an infinite series of images.) When he visits Beatriz's house he comes face to face with innumerable pictures of her, and says that he studies again and again the "circumstances" of those pictures: her Carnival mask, her first communion dress, her sometime husband, her companions at a lunch at the Jockey Club, her friends, her pekingese. Beatriz Viterbo comes to signify for him, then, not only herself but her circumstances, to paraphrase Ortega y Gasset's maxim, and the figure that produces her significance is metonymy. It is therefore not surprising that the visions provided by the Aleph later in the story should be a kaleidoscopic jumble of images that show the universe in its multiplicity and in its disorder. The famous "chaotic enumeration" ends:

> in a desk drawer I saw (and the handwriting made me tremble) obscene, unbelievable, precise letters that Beatriz had written to Carlos Argentino, I saw a beloved monument in the Chacarita Cemetery, I saw the atrocious relic of what had once deliciously been Beatriz Viterbo, I saw the circulation of my dark blood, I saw the interlocking of love and the modifications of death, I saw the Aleph from all points, in the Aleph I saw the earth, and in the earth I once again saw the Aleph and in the Aleph the earth, I saw my face and my viscera, I saw your face, and I felt vertigo and cried, because my eyes had seen that secret, hypothetical object, the name of which is usurped by men, but which no man has seen: the inconceivable universe. (p. 626)

Though this enumeration has the feel of a cinematic montage, it is a montage in which each discrete element is still: it is a montage of photographic images. What is surprising about the series is the aggressive fragmentation and mutilation of bodies (described so well by Lacan in his essay "On Aggressivity in Psychoanalysis"): first Beatriz Viterbo, then Borges himself, then the reader, are shattered, and out of the broken parts comes the idea of the universe. These images decompose the viewer, and the decomposition marks the death of the narrative.

Bodies, statues, dolls

In a note written to be read aloud together with the text of one of his stories, Felisberto Hernández (Uruguay, 1902–1964) says: "my stories were made to be read by me, just as one might tell someone something strange that one just discovered, in the simple language of improvisation, even in my own natural language full of the repetitions and imperfections that are characteristic of me" (*Obras completas*, III: 277). He adds: "And my problem has been: to try to prune off the ugliest parts, without taking away what is most essential; and I am always afraid that the ugly parts of my writing are perhaps the richest in self-expression" (III: 277).

"Las Hortensias" (*Las Hortensias*, 1949) is Hernández's most important (and most disturbing) exploration of the problems of representation. The main character, Horacio, orders the creation of a series of life-size female dolls, called "Hortensias" after his wife, María Hortensia. His butler, Alex, stages *tableaux vivants* using the dolls in two glass-enclosed rooms. The *tableaux vivants* contain implied stories, but these stories when most effective are ambiguous – was the poisoned bride murdered or did she commit suicide? The stories Horacio imagines can then be checked against the "legends" that Alex leaves in written form. Horacio likes the scenes the best when the meanings are not explicit. Though he likes to guess right, he is often less pleased by those legends that confirm his hypotheses than by those that allow a freer play of the imagination.

The dramatic effect of the story is heightened when the boundaries are erased between the glass cases holding the *tableaux vivants* and the rest of Horacio and María's house and garden. First, María establishes a special relationship with the most important of the dolls, the first Hortensia. Then, Horacio has Hortensia modified so that the doll can serve his sexual pleasure, a modification that provokes María to violence. Finally, Horacio and his associates, sensing the commercial potential in the dolls, sell a line of Hortensias to solitary male citizens. In each of these stages, moral limits, and the limits between imagination and reality, are transgressed. That these transgressions are produced by the interpolation of life-sized dolls into the real world of men and women implies that visual and narrative art serve to confound the limits set by the conscience and the rational mind in their vain efforts to exert control over the world.

Horacio goes mad at the close of the story (though for some readers he was never quite sane earlier on), and his madness has its correlative throughout the story in the noise of the machines from the factory next door to the house. Noise here is the sound of chaos that exceeds rational and artistic discourse, and Horacio's final movement toward the noise marks the failure of his project of a controlled economy of libido and imagination. Similarly, the artifice of the Hortensias is finally revealed as a futile attempt to replace the body, for the body can be represented in and to the mind only as absence and emptiness. The Hortensias, instead of being a mechanism for controlling and subduing frustration, ultimately increase it.

There have been at least two more recent versions of Felisberto's fable of the female body in Latin America. Rubem Fonseca's brilliant story "A Matéria do Sonho" necessarily falls outside the purview of this study (though its absence serves to remind us that a full discussion of the short-story genre in Latin America would necessarily also include Brazil). Rosario Ferré's "La muñeca menor" (*Papeles de Pandora*) ["The Youngest Doll"], however, may be profitably discussed here, since it is an evident reworking of the topos we have examined in the Felisberto Hernández story. (Ferré has published a brief critical book on Hernández, and the relationship between her project and his is obvious enough.) Ferré (Puerto Rico, b. 1942) rearranges the elements of the earlier story, so that now a maiden aunt makes dolls for her nine nieces, one for each year of their lives until they marry. The story focuses on the final doll made for the wedding of the youngest niece, and how that doll ends up taking the niece's place in the house thanks to the husband's inattention. Thus, instead of being a story in which men control women through the manipulation of dolls, this is a story of female vengeance, wreaked through the simulacra of the dolls. Also, since the niece's husband is the son of the doctor who failed to cure the maiden aunt of the parasite that encrusted itself in her leg, the act of revenge is simultaneously that of aunt and niece.

One of Cortázar's most renowned stories is "Final del juego" (*Final del juego*) ["End of the Game"]. The children playing statues by the train track in a slum neighborhood in Buenos Aires (by the train line that goes to the elite northern suburbs) live for fantasy: dreams, readings of adventure books like those about Rocambole, and the postures and statues they assume for the benefit of the passengers on the train. Their game consists of two possibilities: "attitudes," usually abstractions like envy or apathy or indecision (for which no costumes or ornaments are necessary), and "statues," in which the girl chosen is dressed and decorated by the other two and then has to find an appropriate pose. The two games are opposite in kind: the one emphasizes abstraction, the second, individuality.

The narrator of the story has a great deal of intellectual curiosity and some artistic pretensions. She speaks for instance of the "Venus del Nilo," criticizes commonplaces (the example of the scalded cat) for their inaccuracy, and reveals a knowledge of the composition of granite and other information gleaned from the Argentinian children's encyclopedia, Estanislao Zeballos's *Tesoro de la juventud*. She even criticizes the handwriting of Ariel, the young man on the train.

Spatial positioning reflects social class in the story, and the curve of railroad track is described in a way that recalls an amphitheatre, with the actors (the narrator, Hortensia, and Leticia) on a stage enclosed by the curve of the track. Oddly, though, the audience in this case is mobile and the actors are static. Ariel, the boy on the train, is perhaps the (elite) youth of Latin America to whom José Enrique Rodó dedicated his famous essay in 1900, and the spectacle that is arranged for his benefit is one of savagery dressed up as civilization.

The game is an affirmation of the self and the group: the place where it is played is called "nuestro reino" ["our kingdom"] perhaps in echo of the concern in Rodó and Darío for an inner realm of the (elite) psyche preserved from the clutter and confusion of the social world. Rodó's inner realm here, however, has become the province of lower-class girls, and the speaking statue of the master's voice in the Rodó essay has grown mute, replaced by the fantastic contortions of the girls. Leticia may well be the finest "statue" of the three because of her partially paralyzed spinal column. In any case, her defects are considered privileges by the other two girls, envious of the special treatment she is accorded. Her real authority, however, derives from the mute pain she expresses in her statues.

J. R. Wilcock's story "La engañosa" (*El caos*) shows the female body as an infernal machine. The narrator of the story, a young man who keeps the books in an olive plantation near the Andes, falls in love with a sensuous Spanish farmworker named Conchita. (Her name in Argentinian Spanish signifies the female genitalia.) The narrator's attempts to possess Conchita's body, however, are frustrated by the discovery that her breasts come apart when touched, that her buttocks are riddled with little holes surrounded by sharp teeth, and that her genitalia are protected by electrified rabbit traps. When the narrator decides to cease and desist from his courting, it is with the regretful admission that the adventure was one which, though exciting, would have been dangerous to pursue any further (p. 127).

Wilcock's representation of the male body is no less bizarre. "La fiesta de los enanos" (*El caos*) tells of the disruption of the cozy household in which Doña Güendolina lives with her dwarves Présule and Anfio by the arrival of her nephew, Raúl, with whom she initiates an affair. The dwarves, suddenly excluded from the paradise of her table and her company, plot to avenge themselves by poisoning Raúl, but Güendolina takes the poison instead and they are reduced to attacking Raúl and torturing him to death. The description of this event, which occupies much of the story, is orgiastic, since at the same time that the dwarves mutilate the young man's body they indulge in forbidden foods and drink that excite their carnality. The description pauses over the amputation of Raúl's nose, kneecaps, fingers, Achilles tendons, yet the dismembering of his once handsome body is recounted with sensuous glee, as the narrator is infected with the dwarves' enthusiasm. The culmination of the feast tells of their opening several cans of fish: "Delight exalted them beyond the suffering of the flesh, beyond present and past, to a future that might well prove eternal; the fish resolved the contradictions of reality" (p. 63). The mystical language is tinged by its physical substratum: "las miserias de la carne," for instance, is both the religious "sufferings of the flesh" and the all too material suffering of Raúl's flesh.

A sadistic ritual of a different kind is that practiced by Eréndira's heartless grandmother in García Márquez's well-known "La increíble y triste historia de la cándida Eréndira y de su abuela desalmada" (in the book of the same title) ["The Incredible and Sad Tale of Innocent Eréndira and Her Heartless Grandmother"]. When Eréndira at age fourteen inadvertently burns down the grandmother's house, valued at a million pesos, the grandmother insists that she pay back the debt by selling her sexual favors at fifty pesos per client. Though much of the story focuses on the festive atmosphere that surrounds the tent where Eréndira lies in a small town in the desert, there are sudden revelations of her experience when she complains, for instance, that she feels as if she had glass in her bones (p. 112). Thus, though the story is presented largely from the outside looking in at Eréndira in the tent, her voice is heard intermittently, asserting that she is a person who feels, not a doll to be used. Her humanity is called into question, however, by the ending, when she flees from her lover Ulises after they have killed the grandmother; when she runs off into the desert and disappears, the narrator says that nothing was ever heard again of her misfortune (p. 163): her misfortune has become her identity, and the loss of one means the loss of the other.

Silvina Ocampo's "Icera" (Las invitadas) ["Icera"], finally, is the story of a body that aspires to the condition of a doll. The protagonist, little Icera, is a child whose mother cannot afford to give her a doll, but who so insistently admires the dolls' clothes and furniture in the window of a toy store that the salesman gives her one item after another, culminating in the gift of the box in which a doll was delivered to the store. Icera chooses to sleep in the box, and years later it appears that that decision has stunted her growth: when she returns to the store with her mother, now an old lady, the salesman thinks that the old woman is Icera and the younger one her daughter. It is a scandal to his sense of time that Icera has not grown up.

Mirrors

Mirrors are abominable, says Al Moqanna in Borges's version of the story of the Masked Prophet, because they multiply and reaffirm the world (but also because they reflect his own leprous face). This truth, reaffirmed by the heresiarchs of Uqbar, is the belated rejoinder to the biblical injunction "Be fruitful and multiply" (and indeed the Masked Prophet and the heresiarchs are as fearful of copulation as they are of mirrors): in a world of mechanical reproduction, the work of art (and the self) aspires to an older kind of unity, a decorum of wholeness and purity, a freedom from contamination or prostitution. Yet the other fear is also a modern (post-romantic) one: the fear of publicity. *Divulgar*: the verb means to divulge a secret but also to make something known, to spread information, to publicize. As with the laundresses in the Anna Livia Plurabelle sequence of *Finnegans Wake*, who labor by the river to make HCE's private laundry public, there is a transgression of the (always imaginary) border between the private and the public. The mirror challenges the notion of a limit between outside and inside, and opens the face (and the body) to unspeakable inquiries. Moreover, if the individual mirror reveals some of the limits of individuality, the hall of mirrors, with its infinite regression, annihilates the self (as so often in Borges).

"La busca de Averroes" (1947, later included in *El Aleph*, 1949) ["Averroes' Search"] is one example of a story in which the encounter with a mirror brings on the annihilation of the protagonist and the death of the narrative. Borges's narrative focuses on Averroes's attempt to write a commentary on Aristotle's *Poetics*, frustrated by his lack of experience of theatrical representation and his consequent ignorance of the meaning of the words "tragedy" and "comedy." It is the story of an impossibility, then, and one in which Averroes's impossible search for Aristotle is paralleled by the narrator's impossible search for Averroes. That the two impossibilities are the same is dramatized in the story when Averroes looks at himself in the mirror and his world (and self) dissolves; the narrator explains that the story depends on a sort of vicious circle in which to tell the story he had to be the character and that to be the character he had to tell the story (*Obras completas*, 588). His own belief in his project vanishes along with Averroes's image.

Elena Garro's "La culpa es de los tlaxcaltecas" (*La semana de colores*)

["It's the Fault of the Tlaxcaltecas"] is a story of doubles: Laura, a middle-class housewife in modern Mexico City, discovers a shadowy other Indian self when she encounters a bleeding Aztec warrior, her first husband. The story then wobbles back and forth in time as she suffers through the misunderstandings of her modern husband and the accusations of treachery by her Aztec husband. The links established between the two time periods in which the action of the story takes place are not temporal but spatial. Thus, for instance, when Laura goes to the Café Tacuba the scene shifts abruptly to the Tacuba causeway during the final battles between Aztecs and Spaniards for the possession of Mexico-Tenochtitlan. To picture this double and conflictive world, Garro makes frequent use not only of temporal and spatial doubling but also of mirrors.

When Laura returns home, for example, she notes: "When I returned home, I was assaulted by the furniture, pitchers, and mirrors, and they left me sadder even than I was before" (pp. 16–17). Later she (now the Indian self) looks at the eyes of her first (Indian) husband, and they serve as mirrors: "I remembered that I was in front of my father's house, that the house was burning and that there behind me my parents and little brothers and sisters were all dead. I saw it all pictured in his eyes" (p. 22). The images Laura sees of herself also contain all of those others, yet the unstable context in which she finds herself makes her self-image itself highly fluid.

Garro's later story "La primera vez que me vi" (Andamos huyendo Lola) again plays with the mirror image. The "mirror stage" recalled in the title of the story is of a discovery of identity, all right, but the subject of that discovery is not a human being but a little green frog. The frog, who is the narrator of the story, begins the story with an account of a Good Friday when the women were dressed in black and the men wore black ribbons, of a time that some say was a better time though the narrator knows better: "there are no times that are better or worse, all times are the same time although appearances may try to deceive us with their optical illusions" (p. 33). (The frog is a very literate frog, referring with ease to the beginning of A Tale of Two Cities.) The frog enters the house of the Valle family (during the period of the struggle between the Emperor Maximilian and Benito Juárez for Mexico) and hides in a bedroom; there it discovers a deep and dangerous lake, "a pool made prisoner on a wall" (p. 34). When the frog tries to bathe in the pool it discovers that it cannot enter the water, but simultaneously discovers a beautiful figure: itself. Later, during the Mexican Revolution, the frog enters the National Palace and on seeing itself in the many mirrors there "I turned green, so to speak" (p. 40). The story continues with abrupt changes of time and place: late in the story the frog is even deported from the United States as an illegal alien. The one constant is an uneasy contemplation in mirrors – at the deportation office the frog sees a little girl weeping when she sees herself in the mirror, and moments later in the Waldorf Astoria the frog and the little girl see a woman plucking her eyebrows by a large mirror (p. 51).

Garro's use of mirrors is peculiar in that a number of these events occur not when the characters see themselves in the mirror but when they watch others looking at themselves in the mirror, and this vicarious gaze is linked with the frog's (and the other Mexican characters') problematic sense of self. Like much of Garro's later writing, this story is implicitly parodic of Octavio Paz's *El laberinto de la soledad* (1950), which is also concerned with the discovery of identity through difference.

Cortázar's story "Axolotl" (*Final de juego*) ["Axolotl"] again uses the conjunction of an amphibian and a sheet of glass, though in the Cortázar story the glass is the transparent pane of an aquarium, which serves as a mirror only because the narrator chooses to recognize himself in the axolotl. The axolotl is a Mexican amphibian something like a sala-mander; the aquarium is in the Jardin des Plantes in Paris; the narrator is a Latin American in Paris vexed by the same amphibious nature that troubles Roberto Michel in "Las babas del diablo." The story plays, then, with the "amphibious" nature of Latin American identity, with the uncertain relation between self and other.

The climax of the story is the moment of transformation of the narrator into axolotl:

> From very close up I could see the face of an axolotl holding still next to the glass. Without transition, without surprise, I saw my face against the glass, instead of the axolotl I saw my face against the glass, I saw it outside of the tank, I saw it on the other side of the glass. Then my face drew off and I understood. (p. 166)

The delicate play of possessive pronouns here tells the story. The "I" of the narration is constant, but its links to a body and a consciousness shift. The story tells of an odd new "mirror stage" in which the encounter with the self in the mirror simultaneously also becomes an encounter with the other.

"Sombras suele vestir" (*Sombras suele vestir*, 1942) ["Shadow Play"] by José Bianco (Argentina, 1909–1986) is punctuated by two mirrors. The first, when Jacinta Vélez looks at herself in the mirror on the night of her mother's death, is described in these terms:

> And there she was herself in the mirror, her face composed of shifting, mobile surfaces, her features innocent and fine. Still young. But her eyes, of an uncertain gray, were old before the rest of her person. "I have the eyes of a corpse." (*Ficción y reflexión*, 113)

On a second reading of the story this description can be taken as a description of the moment before Jacinta's suicide: according to María

Reinoso and Doña Carmen she killed herself the day of the mother's death by taking digitalis, mentioned (along with a glass and a pitcher of water) in the passage just before the one quoted. Even if this reading is not accepted, however, the description is disconcerting. This description is preceded by the reference to digitalis and followed by allusions to a Shakespeare sonnet and a Carpaccio painting: Jacinta Vélez is not herself, is anything or anyone but herself. The mirror serves to accentuate the strangeness of the revelation.

The second reference to a mirror is at the very end of the story. Sweitzer, who has been trying to decipher what has happened to his partner Bernardo Stocker and is even more perplexed by the desire to know what has become of Jacinta, catches sight of himself when he gets up from bed to turn out the light:

> When he passed the wardrobe he saw himself reflected in the mirror, shorter than usual because barefoot, his double chin quivering. He rejected this far from seductive image of himself, turned off the light, felt his way back to bed in the dark; then, hugging his shoulders through the nightshirt, he tried to sleep. (p. 149)

Sweitzer's function in the story is that of an astute reader who tries to decipher the story of his partner Bernardo Stocker and of Stocker's magnificent obsession, Jacinta Vélez. His unsatisfactory vision of himself in the mirror, which serves to bring the story to a close, is a recognition of his failure and – since he stands for the reader – of the reader's failure to find a coherent, simple story. Sweitzer's rejected mirror image, like Jacinta's estranged vision of herself as a corpse, undermines the very notion of personal identity. Since "Sombras suele vestir" provides for (at least) two mutually exclusive interpretations, the characters' sense of a lack of identity with themselves is in turn mirrored in the reader's experience of estrangement and uncertainty.

Finally, Felisberto Hernández's "El acomodador" (1946, later included in *Cuentos*, 1968) is the story of an usher in a cinema who discovers that his eyes emit a sharp light like that of a flashlight. The initial realization takes place before a mirror – as in many tales of vampires and other monsters – when the narrator looks at himself in a dark room and sees himself with his own light. He sees his own face "divided into pieces that no one could have put together or understood" (*Obras completas*, II). The revelation makes him faint and he resolves never to look at himself again in the mirror. His little world then turns into a sort of mirror, because the amount of light emitted by his eyes varies according to the amount of curiosity he feels. He is witness, then, to the workings of his own imagination. The materiality of much of what he sees in the latter part of the story, particularly that of his host's daughter, is uncertain; no other character in the story verifies the figments of the narrator's imagination. Near the end of the story the narrator's eyes, "like two worms that moved freely inside my eye sockets" (p. 90), see the daughter as a skeleton, "and her facial bones had a spectral glow like that of a star seen through a telescope" (p. 90). Here an identification takes place between self and other, but it is the realization of the death of the self through the death of the other.

Copies

The final device to be explored here is that of the proliferation of copies of a written text, a theme that plays with the materiality of the printed word as well as with the repeatability of oral narrative, and with the very different relations of the two kinds of narrative to "originals." Once again, several interesting examples have to be excluded here for lack of space, including Adolfo Bioy Casares's "El perjurio de la nieve," Roa Bastos's "El pájaro mosca," and Manuel Ramos Otero's recent "Vivir del cuento" and "Descuento."

Elena Poniatowska has been most active as a journalist, and several of her books are collections of eyewitness accounts of events like the Tlatelolco massacre of 1968 (in *La noche de Tlatelolco,* 1971) or the Mexico City earthquake (*Nada, nadie,* 1988). Rather like Oscar Lewis, with whom she worked briefly in the preparation of the oral interviews for *Pedro Martínez,* she seems to place equal weight on letting her informant speak and on having that speech fit into (or even validate) ideas she is trying to express. This form of mediate discourse, like other forms of the testimonial, is terribly fragile: it works only when the reader feels the writer's presence but not too much. The dangers posed by this sort of writing are inauthenticity if the voice of the writer can be too strongly heard, awkwardness and indirection if the informant's words are transcribed too faithfully. In her short fiction Poniatowska plays with the ambiguities of testimonial writing by casting some of her stories as official reports, most notably in "Cine Prado" (discussed above) and "De noche vienes" (*De noche vienes*) ["The Night Visitor"].

"De noche vienes" is a pastiche of the report of a court stenographer, ending with the ritual formula of the Mexican Revolution, "Sufragio Efectivo – No Re-elección." Throughout the story, the judge reproaches the narrator/court stenographer for not making the requisite ten copies of the reports and for omitting the revolutionary slogan. The ironic subtext is that his obsessive bureaucratic concern for precise copies leads to a fundamental misunderstanding of the issues at hand in the case. The accused, Esmeralda Loyden, is married to five husbands, all living and all present in the courtroom. The judge repeatedly asks questions that imply a belief that the five husbands must be carbon copies of one another for Esmeralda; she repeatedly insists that each one is very different for her, as different indeed as the days of the week when she visits them. This misunderstanding – a masculine bureaucratic assumption of sameness versus a feminine assertion of difference – is soon reflected in the court proceedings themselves, as the female employees (including the narrator) come to feel solidarity with Esmeralda and frustration with the judge's rigidity. Instead of carbon copies the story conveys the sense of the characters as unique originals.

Poniatowska's authorial irony is perceptible in the insistence on the Mexican revolutionary slogan about effective suffrage and no reelection. This slogan, adopted by Francisco Madero in his opposition to Porfirio Díaz in the elections of 1910, was pilfered from Díaz himself, who used it to ride to power in the elections in 1876. The slogan too is a copy, and a degraded one at that: its institutionalization as one of the articles of faith of the Institutional Revolutionary Party (PRI) has in the decades since the Revolution come to sound increasingly parodic, as the PRI has used all sorts of means to prevent effective suffrage and to promote the election of one after another of its own party bureaucrats.

The solidarity of the human individuals against the bureaucratic obsession with copies is expressed in the next to last sentence of the story, in which all the parties in the case wish that the judicial action had never gone forward:

> Nonetheless a new case could not be made because accusers and accused, judge and witnesses had repented of having brought the first action, number 479/32/875746, page 68, and everything remained written in the so-called book of life that is very silly and precedes the one now used to record the facts, which has a very ugly name: computer certification. (pp. 230–1)

Thus even the notion of telling stories and writing documents is dependent on copies of the accounts "written" in the "so-called book of life," an unwritten book which all are condemned to write and rewrite. Copies of a lost original, Poniatowska's stories bear humorous witness to the repetition compulsion at the heart of narrative itself.

Borges's "Pierre Menard, autor del Quijote" (1939, later collected in *Ficciones*) ["Pierre Menard, Author of the *Quixote*"] deals with the theme of the copy in a very different vein. Menard, a minor provincial French writer heavily influenced by Symbolism, decides to rewrite Cervantes's novel, and to rewrite it exactly, word for word. When the narrator of the story begins to explain Menard's project with high seriousness (after the burlesque introduction, which concludes with a rather peculiar bio-bibliography of Menard), the project sounds quite reasonable, even interesting. For most readers, the moment of scandal comes when a twenty-nine-word phrase from Menard is compared with the corresponding twenty-nine-word passage in Cervantes, and the reader discovers that the passages are indeed identical, even down to their punctuation. This of course is precisely what the narrator has been telling us all along, but the encounter with the instance of deliberate plagiarism often evokes not just surprise but moral outrage.

The story plays, in fact, with the theme of the writer's social and ethical commitments; the narrator is only too willing to excuse Menard's lapses or his own, but is unforgiving of those of the rest of his circle. What he terms "deliberate plagiarism" and "erroneous attribution" (*Obras completas*, p. 450) may be celebrated for their ludic qualities, but the substrata of the story, the celebration of arms over letters and the violent appropriation of others' lives and works, shed a sinister light on Menard's intellectual games. The story is dated 1939 and the narrator's Fascist inclinations are never in doubt, though the full political implications of Menard's projects are certainly open to debate.

A groundbreaking story by a younger writer, Ricardo Piglia (Argentina, b. 1941), further explores the ethical issues involved in telling (and retelling) stories. Piglia is best known for his novel *Respiración artificial* (1981), widely considered one of the most significant works written from inside the terror of military dictatorship. Piglia's earlier collection *Nombre falso* concludes with a long story/essay called "Homenaje a Roberto Arlt," followed by a supposed Arlt story about a prostitute, "Luba." The frame story tells of the narrator's acquaintance with a friend of Arlt's, Saúl Kostia (mentioned in Onetti's memoir of Arlt), his acquisition of the supposed Arlt manuscript of "Luba," and then of the publication of the manuscript by Kostia before the narrator can publish it himself. A potential pitfall to many early readers of the story was to read with the assumption that "Luba" is in fact a story by Arlt, whereas it might equally be thought that the story is by Piglia or by someone else. (In fact, the story is by the Russian writer Andreyev, who is mentioned several times in passing.) The error is instructive. In the lack of certainty about the authorship of "Luba" it would be better to venture hypotheses, not offer definitive interpretations (much as Wolfgang Luchting was ill-advised to venture a "definitive" interpretation of Onetti's *Los adioses*, and why Onetti had some fun at his critic's expense). The question of truth in narrative has been carefully bracketed by Piglia: the narrator is obsessed with finding "the truth" but writer and reader may well prefer to be skeptical about the possibility (even the desirability) of doing so. The "death of the author" in "Homenaje a Roberto Arlt" is that of Arlt himself, yet – as Barthes and Foucault describe in their essays on the theme – what is really being narrated is the death of narrative authority as a unifying principle.

Conclusions

The images I have studied – concentric circles, lines, photographs, dolls, mirrors, copies – are all duplications. This is not by chance: since storytelling involves either the mirroring of reality (mimesis) or the invention of a separate reality, narration is invariably involved in repetition. The dogma originally espoused by Al Moqanna, the Masked Prophet in Borges's *Historia universal de la infamia* (1935), that "The earth we live in is a mistake, a clumsy parody. Mirrors and paternity are abominable, because they multiply and reaffirm it" (*Obras completas*, 327), and later echoed by Adolfo Bioy Casares in the opening of Borges's "Tlön, Uqbar, Orbis Tertius" (*Obras completas*, 431), is a futile protest against narrative itself, a futile assertion above all because it implies endless stories to justify it.

If this essay has been marked by a refusal of the history of narrative, a refusal to tell the story of the so-called evolution of a disputed genre, that is due to my skepticism that the short story has a "history" in Spanish America, since history would imply continuity and change. I have fragmented my account and traced a variety of paradigms and images, but if there is a story to be told about them I cannot tell it. The initial paradigm provided by Roa's "Contar un cuento" made telling a story impossible (because it leads to death), but makes it possible to talk around a story. Metanarrative, so characteristic of modern fiction in Spanish America, is thus more possible than narrative itself: paradoxically, representation is perhaps only possible when its difficulties are inscribed in the text by the devices we have studied here.

[15]

Spanish American theatre in the twentieth century
Sandra M. Cypess

Until well into the twentieth century most stages in Spanish America were
characterized by plays in which peninsular theatre exerted a dominating
influence. It was not until the 1920s that theatre groups in a number of
Spanish American countries broke definitively with the aesthetic hold of
the nineteenth century and its emphasis on costumbristic realism and
comedy of manners in order to enter a new phase that incorporated
experimentation with expansion and diversification of themes and techniques. Prior to the emergence of these experimental theatre groups in
Mexico, Argentina, and Puerto Rico, the theatre had been dominated
artistically and economically by companies composed largely of Spaniards. Typically, the stage was filled with actors mouthing platitudes in a
peninsular accent, dressed in old-fashioned costumes surrounded by
dated scenery in outmoded theatrical halls. The audiences before which
these commercial companies performed were generally bourgeois and
upper-class, affiliated with the government, and not overly critical of
official political policy. In order to excise a false, out-dated tradition
whose social realism and fixed sense of "dramatic illusion" no longer
matched the reality beyond the theatre, experimental groups in several
countries were formed to create a new dramatic tradition that would
address psychological and metaphysical concerns in an innovative
dramatic idiom based on technical advances.

Individual differences related to sociocultural conditions make genera-
lizations difficult among the countries in Spanish America, and the
number of countries prohibits even a cursory reference to activities in each
area. A brief review of the experiences in three major theatrical regions
will serve as a representative summary of the nature of the transition from
the illusionistic, costumbristic, commercial theatre of the nineteenth
century to the formation of a mature dramatic expression that gives
testimony to the multiplicity of national identities that comprise each of
the nations of Spanish America. The experiences of Mexico, Puerto Rico,
and Argentina will serve as examples.

In Mexico theatrical renovation and innovation was possible after the Mexican Revolution brought greater freedom of expression within the sociopolitical context. In *Historia del teatro en México*, Yolanda Argudín observes that the upheavals of the revolutionary period, 1910 to 1920, affected dramatic productions in a number of ways. On the commercial stage, the comedies and melodramas directed to the populace took advantage of the more liberal freedom of expression resulting from the Revolution to offer outrageous political satire based on stereotyped reflections of Mexican life (pp. 83–4). Some progress toward renovation was achieved through the 1920s by such professional companies as "Grupo de los Siete," which included Francisco Monterde (1894–1985). From the elite, experimental movement, impetus for structural and thematic changes came from groups like *Ulises*, founded in 1928 under the financial sponsorship of Antonieta Rivas Mercado (1898–1932). The central spirits of the new movement were Xavier Villaurrutia (1903–1950) and Celestino Gorostiza (1904–1967), who were joined by other young poets and philosophers, including Salvador Novo (1904–1974) and Gilberto Owen (1905–1952). They were labeled universalists, exotics, Francophiles, as an indication of the international sources of their influences. Their translations made available the important works of playwrights of the avant-garde movement outside Mexico – Jean Cocteau, Henri-René Lenormand, Jean Giraudoux, Eugene O'Neill. In the same period of the aftermath of the Mexican Revolution, the works of the Muralists Diego Rivera and José Clemente Orozco were another manifestation of the charged environment of social reform; despite a shared goal to experiment and reform their respective artistic expressions, the *Ulises* group did not consider the social function of art as their prime motivation. Their productions never attempted to reach a mass public, for they did not view the drama's function to be either moral reform or social change, still one of the most prevalent trends in Spanish American theatre. On the other hand, neither did their explorations of oneiric states and psychological complexes provide the typical evasionist digestifs to soothe the palates of the bourgeoisie.

Although the *Ulises* experiment lasted a brief time, it led to the formation of Teatro Orientación in 1932. Under the direction of Gorostiza, their repertory included not only translations of plays by Sophocles, Shakespeare, Ibsen, Chekhov, Shaw, and Strindberg but original works by national writers who had been stimulated by the new currents brought into Mexico as a result of the *Ulises*–Orientación experimentation. Their approach of filtering international influences through the themes and problematics of national interest, defined broadly, would become the leading pattern of theatrical activity for years to come, both in Mexico and in other countries.

The dramatic career of Villaurrutia is exemplary of the innovators of the period. According to Villaurrutia, their intent was to break with the idea of theatre as a "servile photographic imitation of external models" in order to create a poetic theatre that would capture the internal as well as the external "reality of man" (Dauster, *Xavier Villaurrutia*, p. 77). Villaurrutia played a major role in experimental theatre as a director, translator, and creator of original plays – five one-acters published in 1943 under the title *Autos profanos*.[1] The highly intellectual and metaphysical themes of such plays as *¿En qué piensas?* and *Parece mentira* recall the Freudian approach to time used by the French Vanguardists [*Vanguardistas*] and the exploration of the ambivalence of personality associated with Luigi Pirandello (1867–1936). The expressionistic *Sea Ud. breve* also shows his humor in a broad form that is not usually apparent in the other plays that favor more subtle ironies.

The first phase of his production was followed by several commercially produced three-act plays. As best shown in his most famous play, *Invitación a la muerte* (1940; produced in 1947), Villaurrutia also incorporated experimental dramatic vocabulary and techniques within the more traditional structures used in his three-acters.

The themes of the three-act plays deal with human relations and make use of mythic subtexts: *La hiedra* (1942), for example, is a reworking of the Phaedra story while *La mujer legítima* (1942) and *El yerro candente* (1944) both offer variations on the Electra myth. Myth is used to provide a universe of archetypes that incorporates Mexican experiences and the theatrical structure into the classic tradition, rejecting the marginal status of Mexico or any Spanish American country. Also, characters are used for their symbolic function and settings are concrete manifestations of psychological moods.

The predilection for visual and tactile metaphors noted in his poetry becomes transformed on his stage into visual imagery and the poetic use of objects. For example, Villaurrutia developed an important aspect of the dramatic use of objects that is linked in European theatre to the experiments of Cocteau and Antonin Artaud, whose works he knew.[2]

---

[1] Although the plays were published in 1943, they were written in the 1930s and presented on stage at varying times. The dating of plays in general poses difficulties, since the date of writing, date of publication, and date of staging are often different or not available. Dates used in this chapter reflect the designations usually attributed to the work, unless a change is deemed necessary.

[2] Cocteau's work was known to Villaurrutia since his *Orphée* (1926) was among the first plays chosen for production by Teatro de Ulises. When Artaud visited Mexico in 1936 he was befriended by Villaurrutia and his circle.

Cocteau had alluded to a special kind of "poetic language" for the stage that would endow certain objects with dramatic existence in the way their actions paralleled actions in the plot.[3] Villaurrutia also developed a dramatic existence for objects on stage. The oversized coffin in *Invitación a la muerte* seems to act independently when its lid closes, a visual and aural signal that the protagonist Alberto has just answered the "invitation to death." In *La hiedra*, the playwright pays conscious attention in his stage directions to the movements of the shawl of Teresa so that the shawl becomes a dramatic entity whose actions reveal the state of relationships in the play (Cypess, "Influence," 13).

By introducing philosophical and psychological themes treated by Pirandello, Lenormand, or O'Neill, by incorporating a poetic use of dramatic objects, Villaurrutia and *Ulises-Orientación* educated Mexican audiences to the new trends in theatre and showed that Mexican dramatists could elaborate upon such influence within a viable national theatrical tradition. Subsequent playwrights who explore the mythic subtexts of everyday situations, the surreal world of dreams, and the dialectic between reality and illusion can be derived from their legacy, from Elena Garro (b. 1920) in her 1958 collection of plays to the dramatists of the 1980s – Pilar Campesino (*Superocho*, 1979), Sabina Berman (*Bill*, 1980), Oscar Liera (*La piña y la manzana*, 1982).

After Villaurrutia died in 1950, his contemporaries Novo and Gorostiza along with Rodolfo Usigli (1905–1979), who was never a member of the organized experimental groups, continued to stimulate developments in the national theatre, although the commercial theatre of costumbristic realism tended to dominate the stage of the 1950s.

Usigli became one of the most active dramatists in all of Spanish America, and the numerous plays he wrote remain as texts to be performed and studied. His work is often associated with that of George Bernard Shaw, with whom he corresponded. Both Shaw and Usigli wrote comedies, historical plays, and used pungent satire to censure sociopolitical and sexual hypocrisy, destroying the false myths of their respective societies. Like Shaw in *Mrs. Warren's Profession* (1893), Usigli brings to the Mexican stage subjects previously considered taboo for serious treatment. Usigli is no mere imitator, however, but an original dramatic mind intent on creating both a national theatre and the type of audience to appreciate his aesthetic didacticism. Usigli understood the potential of the dramatic genre for reaching large masses and formulating the culture of a people. Furthermore, like other people dedicated to the theatre in Spanish America, his commitment encompassed the formation of both the type of

---

[3] When Cocteau reworked the Oedipus myth (a practice also found in Spanish America), he imbued Jocasta's blood-red scarf with a dramatic existence so that the scarf leaves blood-red marks on her throat in anticipation of its role as the scarf by which she later hangs herself.

audience and the type of actor that would correspond to his idea of theatre. As a teacher, he trained the next generation of playwrights, including Emilio Carballido (b. 1925), Luisa Josefina Hernández (b. 1928), and Sergio Magaña (1924–1990), among others.

In more than three dozen plays Usigli brought to the Mexican stage a diversity of subjects and techniques, but he remains famous for his historical plays, the *Corona* trilogy and *El gesticulador* (1937). For Usigli non-fiction is not possible, and he considers the facts of history only the basis upon which an interpretation is made by the writer and then conveyed in his text, whether it be a play, a poem, or a so-called non-fiction piece. His plays illustrate the role-playing and fictionalizing strategies human beings engage in as part of their interactions. Although his plays are self-referential, at the same time Usigli also explored all the major national myths, from the Conquest (*Corona de fuego*, 1960), the apparition of the Virgin of Guadalupe (*Corona de luz*, 1963), the French–Austrian intervention (*Corona de sombra*, 1943; produced in 1947), to the Mexican Revolution (*El gesticulador*).

Usigli reaches his Mexican audience as well as an international public not only because of his national themes, but because his plays exhibit a poetic quality in his creation of verbal as well as visual images. *Corona de sombra*, for example, develops imagery based on light and shadows, but as significant is his use of a divided stage space that allows the audience to see the temporal as well as spatial displacements that in the narrative are accomplished by flashbacks. Although *El gesticulador* is famous both as an exploration of the use of masks in Mexican social life and as a metaplay that questions the frontiers between history and fiction, the other plays also deal with historical inventions that form part of a people's reality by virtue of their insertion into national historical discourse. His examination of mythmaking and metatheatre will lead to fruitful areas of inquiry into revisionist historical drama – from Sergio Magaña (*Los argonautas*, 1967) and Carlos Fuentes (*Todos los gatos son pardos*, 1970) to Guillermo Schmidhuber (*Por las tierras de Colón*, 1987) – and the polar forms of documentary drama and self-referential plays to be explored with irony by such writers as Vicente Leñero (*Pueblo rechazado*, 1968; *Compañero*, 1970; *El juicio*, 1972) and Sabina Berman (*Herejía*, 1973).

Spanish theatre companies dominated the Puerto Rican stage until 1938, when the Ateneo of Puerto Rico initiated a contest to stimulate dramatic activity among native playwrights. Two years later Emilio Belaval (1903–1972) formed the Sociedad Dramática del Teatro Popular Areyto. Belaval, the founding father of Puerto Rican national theatre, used the term "areyto," a word of indigenous origin that describes an Amerindian form of dramatic expression, to symbolize the group's mission to create a national theatre with roots in the island's past. Themes, stage settings, ideas, aesthetics, as well as actors and playwrights would reflect "lo puertorriqueño," a thematic concern shared with other genres. While Areyto as a group dissolved in 1942, its brief appearance provided a motivational force for the formation of other groups and for theatrical activity in general. Belaval can be credited with a variety of efforts to stimulate national productions. The writers associated with Belaval – Manuel Méndez Ballester (b. 1909), Fernando Sierra Berdecía (1903–1962), Luis Rechani Agrait (b. 1902), and the younger members of the group, René Marqués (1919–1979) and Francisco Arriví (b. 1915) – also followed his pattern and developed theatrical companies as well as creating original plays that expressed their ideals.

Puerto Rico's anomalous situation as a country with a Hispanic cultural tradition linked politically with the English-speaking United States motivated the dramatists to explore themes relating to Hispanic identity, social stratification, and racial mix, and to present their sociopolitical messages by means of realistic techniques. The efforts of the early national groups were directed not so much to temporal and psychological experimentation nor to associating Puerto Rican theatre with universal representations, as in Mexico; rather, they were more concerned with the idea of theatre as a means of social reform and for political denunciations. Plays like Méndez Ballester's *Tiempo muerto* (1938) and *El clamor de los surcos* (1940) are naturalistic works intent on showing that rural agricultural problems can be the stuff of Puerto Rican theatre. In contrast to the serious Realism of Méndez Ballester's early work, Rechani Agrait's *Mi señoría* introduces another favorite theme as well as a subgenre, farce, that will also prove conducive to creativity especially for the writers who wish to censure sociopolitical behavior. The satirized politicians of *Mi señoría* may be the precursors of Luis Rafael Sánchez's Senator Vicente Reinosa, found in his novel, *La guaracha del macho Camacho* (1976).

The playwrights of the renovation period of the 1930s and 1940s introduce a thematic vocabulary relating to rural life, emigration, unemployment, acculturation, and politics that will be elaborated upon by subsequent writers who will incorporate national cultural concerns with different techniques learned from European theatre. This more technologically sophisticated development of Puerto Rican theatre begins in 1958, twenty years after the first Ateneo productions, when the Instituto de Cultura Puertorriqueña established the Festival de Teatro Puertorriqueño. The first festival offered a retrospective of four plays by the playwrights considered to be major forces on the national dramatic scene at the time. In Belaval's *La hacienda de los cuatro vientos* (first produced in 1940), the historical battle between Spaniard and Creole is re-enacted in the play. Méndez Ballester's *Encrucijada* (first produced in 1940), brings his Puerto Rican protagonists to Spanish Harlem; using such representational techniques as a realistic plot and psychological characterization, he explores the devastating effects of the city on the unsophisticated family which finds its moral values and ways of life, rooted in island ways, attacked and destroyed by the alienating forces in the city; this theme becomes a major point of exploration in theatre and the narrative. Both Francisco Arriví's *Vejigantes*, which introduces the problem of racial discrimination, and René Marqués's *Los soles truncos*, a play combining psychological and political themes, contribute not only new themes but stylistic and structural innovations relating to lighting and music, that bring Puerto Rican theatre out of its purely mimetic, illusionist mold. Arriví and Marqués have continued to play important roles in developing a more sophisticated and varied national theatre and their influence on dramatic productions and young dramatists would be noted well into the 1980s.

The contributions of René Marqués stand out in all the different genres in which he expressed his lifelong concern for the complexities of Puerto Rico's political and cultural status vis-à-vis the United States. With more than a dozen plays, Marqués was recognized at the time of his death in 1979 as one of Puerto Rico's most prominent writers, not only for his thematic ideas, but also for his technical skills, his symbolic use of lighting and auditory details, and his manipulation of shifting levels of time. His theatre provided a range of models for the dramatists who followed, from the Neorealism of *La carreta* (1953), to his imaginative use of stage space and mime in *Juan Bobo y la dama de Occidente* (1955), to the existentialist and absurdist works of the 1960s. His commitment to political independence and his recreation on stage of the speech and lifestyle of the common people in *La carreta* can be said to generate some of the experiments of the New Dramaturgy of Puerto Rico, and the work of such playwrights as Jaime Carrero (b. 1931) (*Pipo subway no sabe reír*, 1973, and *Flag Inside*, 1966), Zora Moreno (b. 1951) (*Coquí coriundo vira el mundo*, 1981), and Nuevo Teatro Pobre de América directed by Pedro Santaliz.

The renovation of the theatre in Argentina, as in Mexico and Puerto Rico, began in earnest in the 1930s, although Argentina and the larger River Plate region to which it belongs benefited from the important contributions of Florencio Sánchez, analyzed by Frank Dauster in the previous volume. Sánchez may be credited with producing the first plays of international stature in Latin America; the way he handled sociopolitical problems without succumbing to easy costumbrism would be a model for subsequent playwrights. Thus in contrast to other countries, in Argentina before the First World War, there was no absence of commercial theatrical productions of successful works by national authors, nor a lack of knowledge of European theatre, for the plays of Ibsen, Maeterlinck, Zola, D'Annunzio, had been presented on the San Martín stage and in the Odeón. The dominant tradition on the stage through the 1920s, however, became fixed in a realist–naturalist, mimetic mold that did not reflect changing aesthetic sensibilities influenced by the intellectual and psychological explorations, developed by Freud, Jung, and Einstein, that were taking place in Europe.

Some scholars overlook the period between the productions of Florencio Sánchez and the establishment of the independent theatre groups initiated by Teatro del Pueblo in 1930. However, the 1923 production of *Mateo* by Armando Discépolo (1887–1971) is considered by some critics to signal an important moment in Argentinian theatre history because of its presentation of the "grotesco criollo." In *El grotesco criollo. Estilo teatral de una época*, Claudia Kaiser-Lenoir presents the argument that it is too simplistic to say that the "grotesco criollo" is a national version of the European Grotesque mated with Pirandello's explorations of multiple personalities in such plays as *Six Characters in Search of an Author* (1921; final version 1925) and *Henry IV* (1922). Rather, the playwrights of the "grotesco criollo" (Discépolo, Francisco Defillipis Novoa [1891–1930], Juan Carlos Ghiano [b. 1920]) produced a unique theatrical response to a particular sociocultural milieu, influencing subsequent writers like Osvaldo Dragún (b. 1929), Ricardo Talesnik (b. 1935), Griselda Gambaro (b. 1928). Since these plays focus on the problems and characteristics of the common people, they are as anti-bourgeois as the texts of the literary group "Boedo," according to David Viñas ("Prólogo," xvii).

The "grotesco criollo" is a syncretic form that incorporates elements of the "sainete criollo" – a short, comic piece usually with a simple plot, stylized characters typical of the period (the immigrants, the *criollos*, the *guapo*), popular language and setting, whose main purpose is to entertain. Unlike the "sainete criollo," the "grotesco criollo" does not romanticize the life of the lower classes who populate its stage, but shows that world to be one of crisis and conflict in which the traditional myths of the dominant social order do not function to maintain the social equilibrium. Word play not only provokes humor but reveals the essential ambiguity of human relations, the lack of congruency between actions and meaning; exploration is begun of the arbitrary nature of the sign, a focus that will reach greater development in the Theatre of the Absurd of the 1960s. The "grotesco criollo" also incorporated the new Freudian psychological theories, as Discépolo shows in *Stéfano* (1928). Although the plots of the plays are generally sad, dealing with the destroyed dreams of the immigrants and other members of the lower classes struggling within an oppressive economic system, the action, gestures, dress of the characters as well as the dialogue are intended to provoke laughter in the spectator. Agustín Cuzzani (b. 1924) will continue their experiments in his creation of the "farsátiras:" *Una libra de carne* (1954), *El centroforward murió al amanecer* (1955), *Sempronio* (1957), and *Los indios estaban cabreros* (1958). The oxymoronic union of the "sad laughter" that so characterizes the contemporary Argentinian stage of Talesnik, Gambaro, Roberto Cossa (b. 1934) – especially in *La nona* – or Eduardo Pavlovsky, also finds its roots in the "grotesco criollo" of this first phase of theatrical renovation.

While the dramatists who contributed innovations in the mode of the "grotesco criollo" also produced other, more traditional forms, it was Leónidas Barletta and his "Teatro del Pueblo," formed in 1930, that attempted to forge an avant-garde theatrical group as a national theatre producing original scripts by national writers. Barletta aspired to mold a new theatrical consciousness by taking theatrical productions out of the traditional elite context, by creating a broad-based audience, by seeking his public beyond the confines of the theatre buildings and in the residential neighborhoods and the plazas, and by encouraging the production of scripts that would demonstrate theatre as a service to society. His goals inspired the dramatic orientation called Teatro Independiente and stimulated theatrical experiments that resulted in a national theatre that remains, despite long periods of political adversities and economic inflation, one of the most stimulating national dramatic movements in Spanish America.

Another noteworthy contribution of Barletta's "Teatro del pueblo" would later be adopted by other groups, especially those engaged in the "collective creations" of the 1960s. The so-called "polemic sessions" held after a performance allowed the audience to express opinions about the performance and discuss aspects of the production. With this approach Barletta anticipates the active role of the audience that is also developed in Brechtian epic theatre and that distinguishes the "collective creations" of the 1960s. Barletta is also credited with encouraging the novelist Roberto Arlt (1900–1942) to write for the stage. Arlt became one of the important dramatists of this first period of theatrical reforms.

Arlt has often been linked to the work of Luigi Pirandello, since both explore the interplay of illusion and reality, the relativity of madness and sanity, the conflict between author and character. One cannot underestimate the decisive impact of Pirandello on the Argentinian stage, his plays having been produced with great acclaim in Buenos Aires by the time he arrived in person (his only Spanish American visit) for a series of successful conferences in 1927. Many writers have attempted to copy his style and themes. Arlt, however, is no mere imitator of the Italian playwright.

Fantasy and dreams are confused with reality by the servant girl who is the protagonist of Arlt's first play, *Trescientos millones* (1932), but unlike Pirandello's *Six Characters in Search of an Author*, in Arlt there is a conflict, between the "real" world and the realm of dreams, that is based on the conflictive reality inherent in the sociopolitical circumstances of Argentinian society. Pirandello, in contrast, rejects the possibility of finding an organic social structure on which to rely, and his characters discover within themselves the dramatic conditions of alienation. Beginning with the expressionistic fantasy of *Trescientos millones* (1932), then, Arlt distinguishes himself from Pirandello by his strong concern with social injustice. At the same time Arlt's plays contain social criticism, they also include elements of the "grotesco criollo" that reflect his Argentinian theatrical roots.

Both playwrights also move away from mimetic art to create self-conscious theatrical expressions. As in Pirandello's *Henry IV*, Arlt's *Saverio el cruel* (1936) explores the conceit of the external deceitful masks that characters create. Arlt's presentation of marginalized heroes and critique of political despotism that degrades the individual anticipate concerns that worried Argentinian writers during the period of the "Dirty War," the so-called "Proceso de Reorganización Nacional" of the 1970s and 1980s. Moreover, Arlt's metatheatrical techniques serve as a precursor of the non-naturalistic strategies favored by many contemporary Argentinian dramatists, including Dragún, Gambaro, Pavlovsky, and Cossa.

Arlt's expressionistic strategies are an example of the innovative accomplishments of the Teatro Independiente groups of the post-1930s. Although they were concerned with reaching a non-elitist public, they did not repeat the trite attempts of their predecessors at realistic representation, called illusionism in the theatre, but made use of expressionistic elements to explore social confrontations and false national myths that assume the integration of immigrants into Argentinian life and that ignore real class and gender distinctions. Even a commercial play like *Un guapo del 900* (1940) by Samuel Eichelbaum (1894–1967) can be said to transcend the costumbristic realism of the "sainete criollo" form it parodies in its deconstruction of traditional *compadrito* stereotypes. Eichelbaum, it should be noted, is often singled out in early histories of Spanish American drama, as is his contemporary Armando Moock (1894–1942) of Chile, for raising the level of commercial theatre and for serving as an important stimulus to theatrical renovation. The presentation of Eichelbaum's *La mala sed* in 1920 introduced a new thematic code influenced by the works of Dostoyevsky, Ibsen, and Strindberg, and the innovative psychological theories of Freud, Adler, and Jung, especially with regard to the influence of dreams and the unconscious on human behavior. His work exemplified the movement away from the description of social reality to a focus on the interior life.

Carlos Gorostiza (b. 1920) is a playwright who began his long dramatic career during the Teatro Independiente period as part of "La Máscara" theatre group and has continued to participate in the active development of the Argentinian theatre. His first play, *El puente* (1949), is basically a neorealist work, unlike many of the plays of the independent groups, which were non-naturalistic. Gorostiza shows the accomplishments of Teatro Independiente in the area of technical advancements and innovative treatment of space and time on stage; he manipulates the theatrical space by means of a turning stage to show the interior scenes of a house and the exterior setting of a street, a physical split that symbolizes the social and economic divisions of the Argentinian class structure.

As exemplified by *El puente*, the innovative mode of Argentinian dramatic activity stimulated by the independent theatre movements was largely in the area of technical enhancements rather than dramatic theory, but even the former subsided during the Peronist period (1943–1955). Nevertheless, the dramatists associated with the Teatro Independiente companies made important contributions that would have an impact on commercial theatre as well as on the experimental theatre groups that began to flourish after the demise of Perón's government in 1955. During the relatively liberal period between 1955 and 1966 the influence of European dramatic aesthetics and theorists like Brecht and Artaud had an important role. When the military took over in 1966, however, the nature of theatrical expression changed in response to the new sociopolitical conditions.

As exemplified by the history of theatrical advancements in Mexico, Puerto Rico, and Argentina, the first phase in the development of a contemporary dramatic tradition was marked by attempts to dissociate the national theatre from the Spanish tradition and the costumbristic mode of conventional illusionism. The formation of national theatre companies and the insertion of a sociopolitical vision and regional language forms, experimentation in dramatic structures and temporal displacements, exploration of psychological states and their exteriorization on stage are some of the elements that would be carried over to characterize the next phases of theatrical evolution. As the writers developed better control of dramatic techniques, they were able to utilize the exciting transformations taking place on the stages of Europe and the United States without losing their own personal accent. New forms of drama emerged in Spanish America under the stimulus of theories associated with Bertolt Brecht (1898–1956) and epic theatre, Antonin Artaud (1896–1948) and the "Theatre of Cruelty," and of the experimentations of the Existentialists and Absurdists such as Jean-Paul Sartre (1905–1980), Samuel Beckett (1906–1989), the Polish "Laboratory Theatre" under Jerzy Grotowski (1933), Julian Beck and Judith Malina's "Living Theatre" (active from 1947–1970), and Augusto Boal and his "Theatre of the Oppressed," among the most notable.

In the Brechtian development of epic as opposed to Aristotelian theatre, the traditional convention of asides becomes direct address by a narrator and often an actor would step out of his character to comment to the members of the audience. The effect of such techniques, the "Verfremdungseffekt" or "alienation effect," is to distance the audience from the characters so that rather than identifying with their universal and unchanging nature, the spectator of epic theatre is conditioned to evaluate the actions presented and temper emotion with knowledge and observation. In addition to focusing on acting techniques of distanciation, epic theatre also stresses the political content of the work, for the presentation of social problems and the education of the audience toward finding solutions are key goals. Brecht introduced posters, slides, songs, and speeches of the chorus to interrupt the action and assert rather than conceal the theatricalism of his enterprise; he devised play structures to incorporate the *commedia dell'arte* tradition of song and clowning, multimedia forms such as slides, tape recorders, and films, and the fragmentation and interruption of the anecdote.

The dramatic theories associated with Brecht and epic theatre were readily accepted among the Spanish American playwrights who were concerned with the immediate social and political context and hoped to apply their theatre toward a solution, or at least an evaluation, of the pressing socio-political problems of their milieus. Beginning in the 1960s, the long list of plays that benefited from the structural and formal innovations promoted by epic theatre would include works by such well-known dramatists as the Argentinians Dragún and Talesnik, the Mexicans Carballido, Jorge Ibargüengoitia (1928–1983), and Luisa Josefina Hernández, the Colombian Enrique Buenaventura (b. 1925), as well as Manuel Galich (1913–1985) of Guatemala, and the Dominican Máximo Avilés Blonda (b. 1931). Fernando de Toro in *Brecht en el teatro hispanoamericano contemporáneo* provides additional names and extensive commentary.

During this same period, psycho-social developments related to post-Second-World-War anxieties about the human position in an irrational and increasingly violent universe influenced European writers, often exiles from their homeland, to produce a series of startling plays that would turn out to be as stimulating of theatrical activity as the psychological breakthroughs of the turn of the century. The works of Samuel Beckett, Eugene Ionesco (b. 1912), Arthur Adamov (b. 1908) are among those which the critic Martin Esslin first grouped under the rubric of "Theatre of the Absurd," a movement which gained popularity in the 1960s in Europe, the United States, and in Spanish America. Although the philosophical premises of the Absurdists do not differ from Existentialism, their theatrical innovations decisively transformed dramatic structure, techniques of presentation, and the exploration of the arbitrary nature of language and its role in human interactions. Whereas epic theatre supported the Spanish American tradition of interest in socially oriented theatre many dramatic expressions stimulated by the Existentialists and the "Theatre of the Absurd" tended to be universalist works, stressing the general characteristics of life in the mechanistic, pessimistic Nuclear Age.

The presence of writers like Arlt and Gorostiza in Argentina, Marqués and Arriví in Puerto Rico, Villaurrutia and Usigli in Mexico, along with Arturo Uslar Pietri (b. 1906) and César Rengifo (1905–1985) in Venezuela, Mario Benedetti (b. 1920) in Uruguay, Sebastián Salazar Bondy (1924–1965) and Enrique Solari Swayne (b. 1915) in Peru, Virgilio Piñera (1912–1979) and Carlos Felipe (b. 1914) in Cuba, attests to the success of the development in these countries of a theatrical tradition based on the works of national playwrights instead of translations by European authors. By their integration of modern theatrical techniques with national themes, they form the foundation upon which would be constructed a contemporary theatrical expression that would show the multiplicity of national identities within each country. Although not every country participated at the same time and to the same extent in this development, by the 1960s some of the figures who would contribute important work for the theatre were already appearing on the scene.

The audiences of Mexico who saw the production of *Rosalba y los Llaveros* in 1950, Emilio Carballido's first full-length play, witnessed the initiation of a theatrical tradition. Carballido, like his predecessor Usigli, has become a director, teacher, journal editor (of *Tramoya*), anthologist – a multi-faceted nurturer of dramatic talent and the theatrical tradition in Mexico. He is among the most prolific of Spanish American dramatists, and certainly one of the more imaginative and profound. A study of his dramaturgy would serve as a synecdoche for the various trends prevalent in the best of Western drama: from Realism to Surrealism, from Artaudian Theatre of Cruelty to Brechtian epic theatre, Absurdism, historical plays, myth, satire and farce, and feminism. This is not to imply that there is an equivalency of one work to one trend, for his works defy traditional labels. In the 1970s alone he wrote five full-length plays, from his original approach to history in *Las cartas de Mozart* (1974) to *Tiempo de ladrones, la historia de Chucho el Roto* (1979), an ambitious spectacle composed of many genres in one, ranging from farce to melodrama, with many subplots, lively stage actions, accompanied by music and dance, which have often distinguished his plays.

Un pequeño día de ira, winner in 1962 of the prestigious Casa de las Américas Prize of Cuba, might be considered a good example of his political realism because of its illusionist set and situations and its critique of the social injustice of the class system in Mexico. Yet Carballido breaks the naturalistic convention of the fourth wall by including a narrator who addresses the audience to comment on the events as an outsider, in the manner of the Stage Manager from *Our Town* (1938), by the American Thornton Wilder; however, he reverses audience expectations again at the end of the play when the narrator enters the action of the play and participates in the events as an actor, blurring the lines of demarcation between the world of everyday reality and the world of the stage.

Although his plays are often rooted in identifiable sociopolitical contexts, Carballido also explores the surreal world of dreams, as in *La hebra de oro* (1955) and in the trilogy entitled *El lugar y la hora* (1956). Margaret Peden has suggested that *La hebra de oro* is a turning point in Mexican theatre because of the way Carballido successfully joins Realistic techniques with an imaginative exploration of the world beyond sleep (*Emilio Carballido*, 129). Also, both texts offer examples of Total Theatre of the type proposed by Antonin Artaud, which is a theatre of sounds, music, gestures, and physical images on stage (Peden, "Theory and Practice in Artaud and Carballido," 133).

Carballido's one-act *Yo también hablo de la rosa* (1965) has generated much critical attention because of the multiplicity of signification it contains. The play asks philosophical questions about the nature of reality at the same time as offering a critique of social injustice, academic hypocrisy, family relations, etc. It is also a spectacle that entertains an audience with humor at the same time that it conveys a serious message. With its regional language, typical characters, folkloric elements, and the allusions to the use of the rose in the Mexican literary tradition, *Yo también hablo de la rosa* is also a good example of the way Brechtian techniques can be utilized to create a uniquely Spanish American play.

Similar to Carballido in their domination of the dramatic genre in all its diversity of styles, settings, and modalities are Jorge Díaz (b. 1930) of Chile and Dragún of Argentina, both of whom also have fame which reaches across borders and languages. The plays of Jorge Díaz, with those of Egon Wolff (b. 1926), brought international attention to the theatre of a country well-known for its poetry.[4] Although there had always been

---

[4] It is interesting that both Pablo Neruda (1904–1973) and Vicente Huidobro (1893–1948) attempted to write for the theatre. Neruda found limited success with *Fulgor y muerte de Joaquín Murieta* (1967), a poetic history play including music and dance. Of Huidobro's two works, *Gilles de Ray* (1925–1926) and *En la luna* (1934), the latter is an exercise in Surrealism on stage and reflects his poetic exploration of multifaceted linguistic signs.

theatrical activity produced by national authors, from Armando Moock (1894–1942) to Luis Alberto Heiremans (1928–1964), no real sense of a national theatrical tradition developed until the 1950s under the auspices of university groups like ITUCH (Instituto de Teatro de la Universidad de Chile) and TEUC (Teatro de la Universidad Católica). Díaz, however, worked with ICTUS, an amateur theatre group in Santiago that soon became the leading avant-garde drama company in Chile. Díaz first became known for his absurdist style, and *El cepillo de dientes*, first produced in 1961, can be cited as a paradigm of the absurdist mode in Spanish America for its cyclical structure, irrational dialogue, generic characters called "El" and "Ella," thematic concern with alienation and incommunication, as well as for its grotesque humor and gratuitous violence. Díaz's attention to word-games, black humor, and political satire is repeated in *Requiem por un girasol* (1961) and will be a constant in his plays. *Topografía de un desnudo*, produced in 1966 in Havana, shows his originality and mastery of dramatic technique. Although he does not use actual documents in the play, Díaz takes his subject matter from a historical event involving the massacre of Brazilian poor, whose marginalized status would ordinarily prevent their story from forming part of official historical discourse. He structures the work by using dramatic techniques and forms considered Brechtian – the mixed media presentation, non-sequential temporal fragments, the direct address to the public. The play also utilizes the resources of Total Theatre: lighting, sound, movement.

Díaz has continued to experiment with new forms and techniques well into the 1970s and 1980s: from the extreme linguistic exercise of *La orgástula* (1970), which is an attempt at "non-language" that recalls Huidobro's final "Canto" in *Altazor*, to the documentary drama *Desde la sangre y el silencio (Fulgor y muerte de Pablo Neruda)* (1984), his homage to Neruda and to the demise of Allende's government in Chile. Neruda's life is also the subject of *En la ardiente oscuridad* (1982) by the novelist Antonio Skármeta (1940); interestingly, the work was conceived as a novel but was mounted as a stage play and then made into a movie directed by Skármeta himself.

In Chile, Díaz's interest in presenting the problems of marginalized people, seen in *Topografía* (1965) as well as in *El lugar donde mueren los mamíferos* (1963), is echoed by Egon Wolff in such plays as *Los invasores* (1964) and *Flores de papel* (1970), and by Isidora Aguirre (b. 1919) in *Los papeleros* (1963) and *Los que van quedando en el camino* (1969). While their techniques vary, from the surreal imagination of Wolff to Aguirre's more obvious political focus, they present the conflict of the oppressed people victimized by the dominant class, using a language that can reach the basically middle-class audiences who are being cautioned, sometimes cajoled, into action.

The coup of September, 1973 that ended Salvador Allende's term as president (and his life), drastically changed conditions in Chile and, of course, the theatre was also affected, as Grínor Rojo registers in *Muerte y resurrección del teatro chileno, 1973–1983*. Commercial theatre thrived by producing plays from other countries while, in the prisons, some of the incarcerated writers were able to create original texts that were enacted for the prisoners and jailers alike. Such previously active playwrights as Aguirre, Wolff, and Sergio Vodanovic (b. 1926) remained silent for a time, and only after 1976 did the Chilean theatre begin to become active again. Through the auspices of an independent theatre movement, revitalized with collective creations, ICTUS and David Benavente (b. 1941) were able to mount *Pedro, Juan y Diego* (1976); in this play, character, language, and anecdote show the effects of the economic reordering of the dictatorship and the need for the Chilean people to build bonds of democratic solidarity.

A recent development of indigenous Chilean theatre is reflected in the prolific output of Juan Radrigán (b. 1937), in such plays as *Testimonios sobre las muertes de Sabina* (1979), *El loco y la triste* (1979), *Redoble fúnebre para lobos y corderos* (1981), *Hechos consumados* (1981), and *Informe para indiferentes* (1982). He elaborated the themes of his predecessors but, in an important change that relates his work to the narrative of testimony, he recreates the perspective of the marginalized characters using their language and worldview; one might call his work a form of the Picaresque tempered by farce and enhanced by the theoretical advances in the field of behavioral psychology. His plays are popular with the working classes and are presented in their neighborhood locales. Radrigán is only one of a number of playwrights and groups of popular theatre in Chile who explore the multi-cultural experiences of their country and attempt to work within the constraints of the political censorship of the military dictatorship. One may add the names of Marco Antonio de la Parra (b. 1952) (with *Lo crudo, lo cocido y lo podrido*, 1979, *La secreta obscenidad de cada día*, 1984, and *El deseo de toda ciudadana*, 1986) and Ramón Griffero (b. 1954) (*Historias de un galpón abandonado*, 1984, *Cinema Utopia*, 1985, and 99 *La Morgue*, 1986) as the active young playwrights of post-coup Chile. In part, their plays continue the bold imagery and violent language of Jorge Díaz, mixed with the grotesque vision of the *esperpentos* of Spain's Ramón del Valle Inclán (1866–1936).

Within contemporary Argentina, the contributions of Osvaldo Dragún and the characteristics of his dramatic world can be used as an illustration of theatrical trends in Spanish America between 1960 and 1990. In the last years of the Teatro Independiente movement, Dragún became associated with the director Oscar Ferrigno and Teatro Fray Mocho, one of the well-known groups of Teatro Independiente. Fray Mocho produced his first play, the historical allegory *La peste viene de Melos* (1956), and in 1957, his *Historias para ser contadas*, a series of three one-act plays that revitalize elements of the "grotesco criollo" within a framework of epic theatre. According to Dragún, the absence of scenery and costumes and the use of four actors (three males and one female), reflected the limited economic resources of the Fray Mocho group rather than a theoretical decision. They overcame any lack of properties and equipment through the richly allusive verbal code.

The *Historias* mark an important achievement in Spanish American theatre for their stylized setting, imagination, and wit in commenting on a sociopolitical agenda. In the *Historias*, the actors play several parts and all act as narrators, creating a complex textual play between the immediacy of the narrative moment and the retrospective state of the dramatic action, the "then" of the represented event. A description of the anecdotes themselves relates aspects of ordinary situations that soon develop into grotesque, farcical experiences that provoke that "sad laughter" already noted in Arlt's plays. Of all the plays grouped under the title *Historias*, the *Historia del hombre que se convirtió en perro* has been reprinted in many different anthologies, including introductory language texts, and produced successfully around the world. Its simple plot, about a man who cannot find appropriate employment and must take the place of the night-watchman's dog in order to earn a living, makes use of the devices of satire and farce to indict the sociopolitical system. Dragún has continued to write a socially committed theatre that relates intimately to the political situation of Argentina and uses the expressive colloquial language of the lower classes of Buenos Aires.

The dramatic practices of Dragún suggest their relationship with the theories of Brecht, perhaps the most influential theoretician for Spanish America. Yet many of these techniques, structures, and themes were already diffuse in early Argentinian cultural expressions. Although his *Heroica de Buenos Aires* may be called an Argentinian *Mother Courage*, the play is rooted in the popular tradition of the "grotesco criollo" and the Picaresque–epic also present in such Argentinian works as Roberto Payró's *El casamiento de Laucha*. Moreover, in contrast to Brechtian theory, even in those plays that show an affinity with techniques popularly associated with epic theatre, like *Y nos dijeron que éramos inmortales* (1963), or *El amasijo* (1968), or the more recent *Al violador* (1981), Dragún succeeds in establishing sympathetic links between his audience and the characters on stage. Just as he was an important member of Fray Mocho, he participated with other major Argentinian dramatists in the revolutionary work of the Teatro Abierto experiments of 1981–1983.

Isaac Chocrón (b. 1932) of Venezuela also responded to the spirit of Vanguardism in Spanish America with *Tric-Trac* (1967), an experiment in

Artaudian Total Theatre and Absurdism that was unlike his previous plays. Its abstruse title, a nonsense phrase that gains connotative value in the play, indicates the play's absurdist characteristics: no logical development of plot, no psychological analysis or individuation of characters, a minimum of realistic motifs. It is a self-referential text in contrast with his earlier plays, *Animales feroces* (1963) and *Asia y Lejano Oriente* (1966), which caused public demonstrations in response to their "too realistic" portrayal of aspects of Venezuelan life.

The première of *Tric-Trac* in Caracas in 1967 marks the initiation of El Nuevo Grupo, whose formation resulted from the collaborations of Chocrón, Román Chalbaud (b. 1931), and José Ignacio Cabrujas (b. 1937), three of the most active and innovative dramatists of Venezuela. When they began El Nuevo Grupo, only one theatre salon enjoyed continuous activity; as a result of their involvement as actors, directors, essayists, as well as playwrights, the contemporary Venezuelan theatre boasts a dynamic group of playwrights creating work in a variety of styles and forms: Rodolfo Santana, Elisa Lerner, Elisabeth Schön, Paul Williams, Mariela Romero, Xiomara Moreno and Grupo Theja, and Rajatabla, a group performing "people's theatre." The repertory ranges from epic theatre to absurdist experiments, from history to the surreal games of Romero's *El juego* (1976).

The successful translation of existentialist thought on the Spanish American stage can be illustrated by dramas of Carlos Solórzano (b. 1922), who was born in Guatemala but lives and works in Mexico. In *Los fantoches* (1958), human actors represent marionettes or puppets whose behavior on stage symbolizes the existentialist idea that human beings exist in an arbitrary universe without meaning and engage in futile activities that have no transcendent meaning. Solórzano's *fantoches* may have European antecedents in the Italian Grotesque and the plays of the Belgian Michel Ghelderode (1898–1962), but he Americanizes his puppets by detailing in the stage directions that the costumes and make-up should liken the actor puppets to the life-size figures of bamboo and colored paper used in Mexican folk festivals. The presence of Judas recalls the traditional role reserved for the figure of the traitor in Holy Week rituals in Hispanic countries. The characters, representing a microcosm of human behavior patterns, have been enclosed in a room together to await the arrival of El Viejo, the maker of the puppets; he periodically enters their room to choose one among them to exit, a liberation that signifies death. While the allegorical level of the play reflects Solórzano's existential message about man's absurd destiny, the folkloric aspect acknowledges the dramatist's need to link his audience in a specific way to the universal message. *Los fantoches* also reflects the contemporary focus on theatricality in drama for at the end, the conventional barrier between actors and audience is negated when the Niña, El Viejo's daughter, in the role of Death, opens the enclosure of the stage to point to members of the audience as her next victims. The image of the Niña with her outstretched finger forms a powerful ending that should shake the complacency of the spectators and assure them of the drama's application to their own lives. Like other writers experimenting with existentialist thought, Solórzano has also produced a number of plays in several forms, and with his anthologies and books of criticism of the theatre, his contributions have continued in a variety of ways.

Some playwrights attempted to convey existential angst in texts that maintained a non-regionalist tone. Whether the play is *El apartamiento* (1964) by the Puerto Rican René Marqués, Maruxa Vilalta's *El 9* (1965) produced in Mexico, or José de Jesús Martínez's *Segundo asalto* (1969), an example from Panamanian theatre, their generic characters suffer the alienation produced by a modern mechanized world devoid of logic or transcendence. The language spoken is not marked by regional distinctions and while expressive of the absurdity of life, the dialogue does not reflect an irrational world as will the verbal exchanges of the absurdist texts.

The irrationality of experience that underpins existentialist theatre as an idea becomes transformed on stage by the Absurdists of the 1960s who portray the absence of a rational universe by rejecting a naturalistic representation, the logical construction of dialogue, and viable anecdotal development. While the works of Beckett, Ionesco, Jean Genet (1910–1986), and Harold Pinter (b. 1930) are often cited as giving definition to the form, one can find Spanish American precursors to the "Theatre of the Absurd." Some critics see antecedents in the plays of the poet Alfonsina Storni (1892–1938); both Dauster and Grínor Rojo in their histories note that her plays *Cimbelina en 1900 y pico* (1931) and *Polixena y la cocinerita* (1931) display absurdist tendencies. Perhaps the work of the Cuban Virgilio Piñera offers the most salient example of absurdist tendencies before the European experiments. Piñera's *Falsa alarma*, written in 1948, had explored the problems of passivity, alienation, and lack of communication that afflict the twentieth-century human condition before these topics were considered characteristics of the Theatre of the Absurd.

Piñera is one of the playwrights of Cuba who participated in the early experiments in theatrical renovation within the context of political censorship in the pre-Castro period, and then was successful in making the transition to the post-Revolution period. The realistic *Aire frío* (1959) and *Dos viejos pánicos*, for which he was awarded the Casa de las Américas Prize in 1968, are Piñera's most famous plays and show his versatility. The first portrays the socio-economic problems of life in pre-revolutionary Cuba, using a realistic manner. The stagnant political atmosphere of the country is symbolized by the constant references to the over-heated environment in which the Romaguera family lives. The members of the family serve as symbols of the different attitudes which beset pre-revolutionary Cuba. The fan that Luz María yearns for to bring them comfort is a concrete dramatic image that symbolizes the need for dynamic movement to save the country from its decomposition.

In *Dos viejos pánicos* Piñera appears to have broadened his depiction of the confined, stagnant existence of Cuban society by his use of Absurdist techniques. The polysemous nature of the non-realistic mode of *Dos viejos pánicos* allows an audience to interpret the work as a generalized statement on the human condition in the Nuclear Age. At the same time, the public in post-revolutionary Cuba, who may prefer to read the play in the manner of social realism, can understand it as a critique of the game-playing and lack of genuine human concern that bourgeois values generate.

Game-playing in place of genuine human contact as a dramatic motif is repeated in the work of another Cuban, José Triana (b. 1932). Many of his plays can be seen as an indictment of the sociopolitical problems of pre-revolutionary governments despite the often absurdist form and structure of the work.

His first play, *El Mayor General hablará de teogonía*, written during his pre-Castro exile in Spain, is a one-act allegory that can be read on many levels. It depicts the lack of communication and alienation prevalent in society on the one hand – in the vein of Ionesco or Beckett – but also contains references to a political reality that is criticized as the cause of the alienation, rather than being the symptom of an absurdist universe. The patriarchal figure of the Major General could well be a reference to one of the infamous dictators of Cuba, Machado, who ruled from 1925 to 1933, and the house of the General a synecdoche for Cuban society. The use of political allegory coupled with absurdist techniques will be repeated in his subsequent works.

La noche de los asesinos (1964), shows the ritualization of contemporary life, a subject also of fellow Cuban Antón Arrufat (b. 1935) in *Todos los domingos* (1965) and *La repetición* (1963). Triana's play continues to be an international success and the object of much critical discussion. Returning to the confined spatial world and the allegorical approach of *El Mayor General*, Triana also makes use of the absurdist two-act structure. Action takes place in the one room of the home of a typical Cuban family. Whereas in *El Mayor General* the protagonists scheme to kill the patriarch, the three children of *La noche* plan the murder of their parents by organizing a rite that they enact daily, recalling the ritual murder enacted in Genet's *The Maids*. Using the technique of a play within a play, the three children undertake the roles of their parents, neighbors, the police, the judge, in order to bring to the stage their perspective of these various institutions and members of society who affect their life. The children criticize the stagnant world of their parents, a theme emphasized in a number of plays that recreate pre-revolutionary Cuban society (*El robo del cochino* by Abelardo Estorino, *La taza de café* by Rolando Ferrer). In *La noche*, however, the universal tone does not localize the work to a particular historical moment. Cuban readers have identified specific historical references and lexical items but Triana successfully created a play that transcends politics, national concerns, historical realities. It is ironic that in the 1980s *La noche* was interpreted by some Cubans as a critique of the *Fidelista* state, the parents being identified with Fidel instead of with Batista or the colonial mother country, Spain. It is a tribute to the polysemous nature of the play that so many diverse readings are possible. It is a political allegory, an exploration of the generation gap, of psychological states, as well as a metatheatrical exercise about the nature of writing.

Another playwright associated with absurdist techniques who has experienced the constraints of political censorship is Griselda Gambaro (b. 1928) of Argentina. When Gambaro first presented her plays in Buenos Aires in the 1960s, her works were soon recognized as important contributions to Spanish American theatre, and she has continued to produce significant dramatic plays. On the basis of her early plays – *El desatino* (1964), *Los siameses* (1967), *El campo* (1967) – which were for a long time the only examples of her plays published and available, critics were quick to associate her with the theoretical writings of Antonin Artaud's "Theatre of Cruelty" as well as with the Absurdists.

Cruelty for Artaud is more than a reference to the depiction of pain and suffering. Rather, his definition broadens the sign to include the cruelty of existence, an oxymoronic state in which suffering yields "joyous harmonies" (Artaud, *The Theater and Its Double*, 103). Gambaro's plays portray the cruelty of existence and make good use of violent physical images as the potent means to express her own vision of the cruelty of existence. In addition, Gambaro's skillful use of non-rhetorical language dominated by gestures and movements along with her manipulation of the space of the stage illustrate her development of theatrical ideas that coincide with Artaud's concept of Total Theatre.

In the manner of the Absurdists, her early plays are divided into two acts, present a simple anecdote of situations rather than a developmental plot, and her characters are generic, lacking the distinctive individuality and psychological subtleties associated with conventional dramas. The references appear devoid of realistic motifs and the dialogue does not reflect the distinctive Argentinian regionalisms found in Dragún's work of the same period. Nevertheless, even in the plays considered as absurd and

Kafkaesque as *Las paredes* or *El desatino*, an allegorical reading of the plays reveals that they do relate to the real sociopolitical milieu of the playwright, not only to the universal scene of human anguish. In *Las paredes*, for example, the young man who is picked up by the authorities after a day in the country is experiencing a Kafkaesque adventure. Also, his kidnapping and subsequent incarceration and mental torture relate to real political occurrences that take place in Spanish American dictatorial regimes and, specifically, anticipate tragically real enactments by the Argentinian military during the so-called "Guerra sucia" ["Dirty War"], in the phrase of the people. Gambaro's plays cannot be considered typically absurdist; unlike the European versions, her use of the grotesque and her concerned attention to a sociopolitical agenda produce a Spanish American configuration of the Absurd. As with Jorge Díaz and José Triana, Gambaro's work follows no imported formula but is well suited to the needs of its audience and author.

Gambaro's productions of the 1970s and 1980s are now being published and disseminated because of the change in government in Argentina and the resulting lack of censorship. Gambaro's plays during the "Dirty War" illustrate the effects of censorship and political oppression on a writer's work. *Información para extranjeros* was written in the early 1970s but not published until 1987 because of its political content. Yet it also shows off Gambaro's ability to create unconventional "Total Theatre." The stage directions call for a house in which the spectators, led by a guide, wander about to view actors in enclosed rooms portraying violent events: kidnappings, murders, trials of political activists, as well as incongruous childish games. As they enter the rooms in which the "play action" takes place the spectators are forced to become more than passive witnesses to the scenes; the boundary between stage and life becomes blurred even further when the actor–guide asks the spectators to comment on their observations. Gambaro's understanding of theatrical spectacle is joined here by a knowledge of the social ills of Argentinian society as she forces the spectators to recognize their general passivity and requires them to question and respond more fully to the nature of events in their environment.

Gambaro's inability to produce her openly political plays during the military regimes, coupled with the real danger she and other writers face in restrictive political systems, led her to write historical plays that use displacement techniques to veil the criticism. *La malasangre* (1982), set in the 1840s during the period of the Rosas dictatorship, ostensibly develops a naturalistic plot that involves a love story. On the allegorical level it describes the awakening of the Argentinian public from its passive state to a new consciousness about its oppressive government. *Del sol naciente* (1984) is set in far-away Japan, yet its samurai warrior and geisha maiden are involved in a power relationship that relates to the military's treatment of the Argentinian people during the Malvinas crisis. The polysemous nature of Gambaro's work illustrates the ways Spanish American dramatists have been able to subvert the repressive regimes under which they live and circumvent suppressive official government policy.

Gambaro represents one of a number of successful dramatists who are also women. The existence and recognition of women dramatists is no longer as anomalous a situation as it was in the seventeenth century for Sor Juana Inés de la Cruz. As the sociopolitical context has developed to provide for greater participation by women, more women dramatists have entered the field in Spanish America, especially in countries that have enjoyed a sustained national theatrical tradition like Argentina, Mexico, Puerto Rico, and Venezuela (Cypess, 'La dramaturgia femenina y su contexto socio-cultural'').

The nature of women's use of dramatic theory and technology is as sophisticated and as varied as their male counterparts. Nevertheless, economic and other extraliterary problems attendant on a dramatic production have generally been obstacles to discourage women from producing plays. More women have been visible in other genres in which socio-economic factors do not play such a major role as in the theatre. Those who have attempted to develop a drama from a written text to a stage production have often written only one or two plays and not maintained the steady dramatic production of Gambaro in Argentina, or Luisa Josefina Hernández of Mexico, Myrna Casas (b. 1934) of Puerto Rico, and Isidora Aguirre of Chile, all of whom have been able to continue working through several decades.

The situation of Puerto Rico illustrates the transformation of the dramatic milieu for women dramatists. In the early days of Areyto, Marta Lomar's plays were produced but not published. In contrast, in 1960, Myrna Casas's first play *Cristal roto en el tiempo*, using sound and lighting techniques reminiscent of the work of René Marqués, was presented and published as part of the Festival de Teatro of the Instituto de Cultura Puertorriqueña; Casas went on to publish many plays in a variety of forms in addition to working as an actress, director, and producer. From the conventional, "well-made play" structure of *Eugenia Victoria Herrera* (1964), to the original use of absurdist techniques in *Absurdos en soledad* (1963), to the vanguardist farces of *La trampa* (1963) and *El "Impromptu" de San Juan* (1963), to the metatheatrical *No todas lo tienen* (1975), she brings an additional perspective to her work by including an exploration of the role of women in society. She has been followed by a succession of women, including Lydia Milagros González (b. 1947), associated with the experimental popular theatre group El Tajo del Alacrán, and Zora Moreno (b. 1951), associated with Flor de Cahillo Productions, both of whom form an active part of Puerto Rican New Dramaturgy. There are also indications of a more enlightened perspective in the criticism of drama; in the work of critics such as Roberto Ramos-Perea, also a dramatist as well as the historian for the New Dramaturgy, the contributions of women are integrated within the general discussion of theatre.

Just as new themes relating to the common people and the realities of their sociopolitical condition have been increasingly an important part of Spanish American theatre, feminism and the role of women in society have also been introduced into the thematic register and developed with sophistication by both male and female dramatists. One can point to the various plays of Carballido, for example, as generally presenting with sensitivity and criticism the constraints imposed upon women in a patriarchal society, as in *Orinoco* (1979) or *Rosa de dos aromas* (1983), or to the plays of Isaac Chocrón (*El acompañante*, 1978) or David Benavente, of Taller de Investigación Teatral of Chile, with *Tres Marías y una Rosa* (1979). However, the issue of women's problems in patriarchal society was an early and consistent theme in the plays of Elena Garro, whether in the realistic mode (*La mudanza* and *Felipe Angeles*) or those presenting a surrealist approach (*Andarse por las ramas, Los pilares de doña Blanca*). Garro's work of the 1950s has been augmented by women working in Mexico and in other countries. Nevertheless, no major group of feminist playwrights has formed in Spanish America. The situation continues to be one in which individual writers make use of a feminist theme as a particular statement in a determined play.

The inquiry into the factors that condition the representations of women on stage – an inquiry that Rosario Castellanos (1925–1974) dramatizes in *El eterno femenino* (1974) – forms part of the larger scrutiny of historical discourse in general. The sophisticated use of the media by interest groups and the acknowledgment of the manipulation of discourse for political purposes have raised issues about the concept of the reliability of historical information. Ideology is no longer viewed as just an aspect of content, but as an inherent factor in the generation of discourse. "Official discourse" has often presented selected information and interpretations that correspond not to a "reality" but to a political ideology. One of the responses of the theatre to the need for revisionist history has been the development of documentary drama.

As implied by its name, documentary drama or "docudrama" refers to the insertion into the dramatic discourse of actual material originating in the real world – newspaper clippings, trial records, interviews – unchanged in content, although they may be selected or adapted. Both historical plays and docudrama refer to real-world counterparts, yet historical drama need only reflect actual situations and not reproduce the actual data and historical figures, as in Gambaro's *La malasangre* or Luisa Josefina Hernández's *La fiesta del mulato* (1970). Stimulated by the documentary dramas of the German playwrights of the post-Holocaust period who attempted to deconstruct the myths of their society, such as Rolf Hochhuth (b. 1932) in *The Deputy* (1963), docudrama also serves as a method of involving the theatre in the ongoing evaluation of reality and national identity.

Vicente Leñero (b. 1939) of Mexico is one of the early practitioners of documentary drama, beginning with the 1968 production of *Pueblo rechazado*, a dramatization of the case brought against Father Gregorio Lemarcier by the Catholic church. His plays *Compañero* (1970) and *El juicio* (1972), the adaptation of Oscar Lewis's *Los hijos de Sánchez* (1972), are also documentary dramas. In the latter play, although restricted to the sociological study of Oscar Lewis, Leñero experimented with the space of the stage, creating four zones as a way to handle the presentation of many scenes and family settings. Leñero demonstrates that the dramatization of documents does not restrict the playwright's use of a variety of other techniques and structures; often, the incorporation of Brechtian elements serves well for encouraging the evaluative process that is part of docudrama. In his *Martirio de Morelos* (1983), he handles with great irony the confluence of documentary drama with history as a way to deconstruct official versions of Mexico's past, recalling the project begun by Usigli in the *Corona* trilogy.

In addition to Leñero's work, *El atentado* (1964) by the Mexican Jorge Ibargüengoitia (1928–1983) also belongs to this current, but he adds the humorist's bite and satire to the evaluation of traditional historical myths. Ibargüengoitia called the work a "farsa documentaria," since he presents the historical events surrounding the assassination of President Obregón with bitter satire, exaggerated comic rhetoric, and an irreverent treatment of authority. Mexico's Marcela del Río (b. 1932) also uses the docudrama form when she turns her attention to the politics of the United States in *El pulpo* (1972). Ostensibly about the events surrounding President Kennedy's assassination, she also shows how the problems afflicting one country pass its boundaries because of pressures from multinational interests that work against the political rights of the masses. Themes based on multinational influences in Spanish American society have been used in several documentary plays, including $S + S = 41$ (1974) from the Ecuadorian group Teatro Ollantay (about international oil companies), *Mear contra el viento* (1974) by the Chileans Jorge Díaz and Francisco Uriz (about the ITT involvement in their country). Clearly, docudrama involves more than using documents from the world of verifiable reality; ironically, the presentation of the real events also re-emphasizes the theatricality of the dramatic form into which it has been incorporated. At the same time, the dramatic production gives a clear message to the public that ideological "illusions" have been masquerading as official reality.

One of the key figures in the development of docudrama and related theatrical experiments in revisionist politics is the Colombian Enrique Buenaventura (b. 1925). His Teatro Experimental de Cali (TEC) presented *La denuncia* (1974), a documentary drama based on the massacre of banana workers in Santa Marta, Colombia, an episode also treated by García Márquez in *Cien años de soledad*. In dramatizing that subject, Buenaventura fulfills one of the goals of docudrama by bringing into the public's consciousness an event that has been either ignored or deformed by the mass media under government control.

As a writer and director, Buenaventura is also considered one of the important motivational forces of "people's theatre" and a related form, collective creations. Like docudrama, these forms recall the pedagogical purposes of colonial theatre, with the important distinction that they often provide a critique of the established patriarchal ideology instead of supporting it. The term in Spanish, "teatro popular," or "popular theatre," is often conflated with "people's theatre" because both refer to the fact that the subject matter, like the audience to which it is addressed, can be described as "pueblo," as opposed to the elite. Both "people's theatre" and collective creations, called the "New Dramaturgy," or "New Theatre," are not text-centered but involve group efforts in which the director with the group replaces the individual writer as the originator of the "text" to be performed. The theories and dramatic work of Augusto Boal of Brazil and his Teatro de Arena have been influential in developing forms of "people's theatre" and collective creations, as the section on Brazilian drama notes.

Buenaventura first became known in 1960 for *A la diestra de Dios Padre*, his humorous dramatization of a folk story based on Colombian Tomás Carrasquilla's narrative version. Buenaventura's use of elements derived from the *mojiganga*, a form rooted in popular sources, anticipates his commitment to popular theatre and his constant recourse to popular themes and experiences as a way to reach an audience. His radical change in style and procedures came about after he lost government funding on the basis of his political position in *La trampa* (1966), a play about political corruption, situated in the Guatemala of dictator Ubico's regime.

Buenaventura and TEC began to develop collective creations in the 1960s at the same time that the influence of the absurdist mode was gaining popularity. Collective creations represent the polar opposite of the absurdist play, which in its pure form rejects the premise that reality can be explained or that the human dilemma can be ameliorated by a change in political structures. Collective creations, in contrast, attempt to show in a number of ways that a relationship exists between the theatrical representation and society. Working together, the several members of the group begin with a social and political agenda which serves as the justification for their existence and for the play produced. Rather than aesthetic or formalist criteria, it reflects the collective reality from which it emerges. The *process* of creation is as important a result as the script created. From researching the background material, drafting the scripts, organizing the technical aspects of the performance to the actual production on stage, the work is performed in the socialist spirit of group cooperation.

The popular theatre groups also redefined the role of the audience. As another important aspect of theatrical development, these groups realized that attention had to be paid to the improvement of the competency level of the public to whom the work was directed. The spectators needed to be educated to accept works that reflected their situation and preoccupations, but without necessarily being openly "realistic" or imitative of everyday experiences. From consumers of entertainment, who looked upon the playwright as a "manufacturer of spectacles" – as Osvaldo Dragún ironically described such writers – the audience had to be transformed into willing participants in a cultural event, members of a ritual during which a society communes with itself. The cultivation of forms of popular theatre and collective creations was aimed at fostering enlightened audiences from spectra of the social hierarchy usually ignored in commercial theatre and elite forms of experimental theatre.

At the same time that interest in the formation of an active audience is essential to collective creations, attention to the audience as an active participant in the theatrical experience has been one of the major developments of post-Brechtian theories. Moreover, popular theatre's redefinition of the relationship between the spectator and the play is also found in other experimental forms, such as Gambaro's *Información para extranjeros* (1972) and *Hablemos a calzón quitado* (1972) by Guillermo Gentile of Argentina.

The process of collective creation can be found in all countries, from the traditionally writer-centered practices of Argentina to socialist post-revolutionary Cuba and Nicaragua. In Argentina, Germán Rozenmacher (1936–1970), Carlos Somigliana (b. 1932), Cossa, and Talesnik experimented with collective creations in *El avión negro*, (1970), a play about Perón's return to Argentina that proved to be prophetic in its predictions about political realities. *El asesinato de X* (1970) is the result of an international collective creation resulting from a group effort of students from both Chile and Argentina who transformed their concern about the political disturbances into a theatrical performance. Of more sustained importance have been the groups like Buenaventura's TEC, La Candelaria, also of Colombia, Chile's ICTUS, and Teatro Escambray of Cuba.

La Candelaria under the direction of Santiago García enjoys an international reputation and has traveled extensively, presenting its collective creations. *Guadalupe años sin cuenta* (1976), a title which plays on its Spanish homonym, "cincuenta," portrays the history of guerrilla activities in the 1950s; *Los diez días que estremecieron al mundo* is the group's version of John Reed's book on the Russian October Revolution. Echoing Buenaventura's approach, La Candelaria believes that the theatre is an arena for social change. They also continuously revise scripts, so that the presentations vary according to their audience and the social context in which they are working.

Although post-revolutionary Cuba has many theatre groups practicing collective creations, the most famous is the Grupo Theatre Escambray (GTE), founded in 1968 with Sergio Corrieri as its director. Named after the region in which the group has its origin, it can no longer be considered a purely local phenomenon, for it has toured throughout Cuba and abroad, including the United States, where it presented *Ramona*, written by Roberto Orihuela, in celebration of International Women's Day, in 1982.

The members of GTE developed new techniques and theatrical language because they had to learn to communicate with an audience untutored in cultural events like theatre. They incorporated the special Cuban *choteo*, or form of humor, music, and customs of the regions, into the theatrical spectacle in order to facilitate identity between the theatre and the community and to integrate the spectator into the spectacle itself.

Popular theatre, in its various forms, is noteworthy for its ability to represent the multiplicity of experiences that comprise the cultures in a given country, and for its incorporation of the public into the theatrical process. The underlying belief that dramatic art is another tool for social change places it on the opposite pole of the postmodernist approach that emphasizes the self-referentiality of a theatrical work. The play *Quíntuples*, presented in 1984 by Luis Rafael Sánchez (b. 1936), represents this new direction.

Despite the presence of six characters divided between two actors, each scene is the monologue of one of the players. No central action takes place, no interaction is posited; rather, each comes on stage to improvise. Unlike the earlier play of Sánchez and the Puerto Rican theatre tradition from which his work emanates, *Quíntuples* eschews the sociopolitical commentary of the Brechtian mode, the nihilism of the Absurdists, the Neorealism of the nationalists. It is not that Sánchez has abandoned his textual and dramaturgical inheritance, but in the creation of a postmodernist piece, the cultural references have been reduced to banal and repetitive decontextualized bits of information, from the language of advertising to the clichés of everyday conversation. The text provides "meaning" only in its mode of function and reception, as a theatrical enunciation. The rhythmic, vocal, intonational, choreographic schema are its reason for being, not plot, characterization, theme. Its focus on theatricality is unquestionably established in the final moments as each actor steps out of character on stage, each removes the make-up that is one of the signs of the theatrical code. Just as their act deconstructs illusionist theatre, they re-emphasize the spectacle and the creativity of the theatrical performance.

Postmodernist plays do not constitute the main tendency of the contemporary Spanish American theatre. As the twenty-first century approaches, the majority of the works are concerned with the most pressing issues of the twentieth century: institutionalization of violence, humankind's capacity for cruelty, political violence, power's corrupting influence, loss of direction in an absurd universe. Issues of class, gender, and ethnic diversity are addressed on stage just as they are being asserted in the political arena. Techniques involving film, videos, revolving stages are becoming integrated with traditional lighting and sound practices when economic conditions permit. Spanish American dramatists have developed a new vocabulary of forms and manners of expression and a thematic register accompanied often by a transfer of focus from the elite to the masses. Theatre itself is being integrated with other cultural practices, creating polyphonic texts that encompass the multiplicity of cultural voices.

16

Latin American (Hispanic Caribbean) literature written in the United States
William Luis

Hispanic Caribbean literature written in the United States is a relatively new field in literary history and criticism. In recent years, Spanish American literature written in the United States has become a reality because of writers who, for economic or political reasons, left their countries to reside in the United States. Authors such as Reinaldo Arenas (Cuba) and Sylvia Molloy (Argentina) write about their homelands; but, as their stay in the United States becomes more permanent, these and other authors such as Luisa Valenzuela (Argentina) and Carlos Guillermo Wilson (Panama) tend to document their experiences in a new environment. They are contributing to an existing body of Hispanic American literature written by Chicanos such as Rodolfo Anaya and Gary Soto, Puerto Ricans such as Nicholasa Mohr and Tato Laviera, and Cuban Americans such as Oscar Hijuelos and Ricardo Pau-Llosa, who write and live in cities like New York, Los Angeles, Miami, and Newark, which have now acquired a distinctly Hispanic character.

Hispanic Caribbean literature written in the United States has profited from the publicity received by the so-called *Boom* of the Latin American novel, which during the 1960s brought Latin American literature to the attention of a world reader. At the same time, Hispanic Caribbean narrative written in the United States appeals to a wide audience which includes English-speaking readers living on the North American continent. Political events have helped to promote aspects of this literature. During the turbulent decade of the 1960s, the Civil Rights and Black Power movements and Young Lords Party drew attention to the plight of Blacks and Hispanics in the United States. Hispanic Caribbean college students, many of them the sons and daughters of immigrants, were instrumental in creating and developing Latin American or Puerto Rican Studies programs throughout New York and other northeastern states. In search of an identity, they demanded relevant courses about life in Puerto Rico, the Dominican Republic, and Cuba, and other Spanish-speaking countries and, equally important, about their own experiences in the

United States. The newly created courses were different from traditional offerings insofar as they were taught from a sympathetic point of view. The enthusiastic efforts of college students on US campuses were paralleled by community activists and organizers who sponsored events to promote ethnic awareness and artistic expressions emerging from the *barrios* and ghettos.

Hispanic Caribbean literature written in the United States can be divided by country of origin and genre, but more appropriately should be divided into two main categories. The first consists of writers who were formed and educated in their native countries and later emigrated or were forced to flee to the United States. While in the United States, they continued to write in the vernacular mostly about themes pertaining to their island of provenance. Some traveled to the United States for brief periods while others stayed longer. Regardless of the reasons for going to the United States or length of time spent there, the writers' presence in the United States has had a lasting effect on them and their works. The second category includes writers who were either born or raised in the United States, and who for the most part write in English. As a group, they write an ethnic literature which responds to concerns about their isolation within a dominant culture that has denied them an identity and access to North American society. For these writers, their parents' country of origin is a distant memory. These Hispanic American or Latino authors write about Hispanic Caribbeans living on the US mainland and their works are at the vanguard of a new literary movement which is both Hispanic and North American and is helping to bring the two literatures and cultures together.

Hispanic Caribbean literature written in the United States is not new. It began as a literature of exile which can be traced to the early and mid nineteenth century, when Cuban and Puerto Rican intellectuals and writers, seeking political asylum from the Spanish colonial government, traveled to and resided mainly in the northeastern part of the United States. New York became the main center of operations against Spanish dominion over the islands. Newspapers and journals contain the political and literary aspirations of generations of intellectuals fighting for their countries' independence, including figures like Cirilo Villaverde (1812–1894), Enrique Piñeyro (1839–1911), and José Martí (1853–1895), of Cuba; and Ramón Betances (1827–1898), Eugenio María de Hostos (1839–1903), Francisco Gonzalo (Pachín) Marín (1863–1897), and Arturo Alfonso Schomburg (1874–1938), of Puerto Rico. In the nineteenth century New York emerged as an important intellectual and publishing center for Hispanic Caribbean authors.

The number of Hispanics traveling to the United States increased after the Spanish-American War of 1898, and during the first decades of the twentieth century. After the Foraker Law of 1900, which made Puerto

Rico a territory of the United States, and in particular the Jones Act of 1917, which gave Puerto Ricans US citizenship, Puerto Ricans began to leave their native island in large numbers to reside in New York and to work mainly in the tobacco industry. Later, after Operation Bootstrap was put into effect, during the 1940s and 1950s, they migrated in still greater numbers and were employed in New York's garment district. These Puerto Ricans were soon joined by a large wave of Cubans who left their homeland shortly after the triumph of the Cuban Revolution in 1959. This group of professionally trained middle-class exiles sought refuge in San Juan but also in Miami, Newark, and New York City. Cubans arrived in three migratory waves: first, from 1959 to 1962; second, from 1965 to 1972; and third, in 1980, as a result of the Mariel boatlift, when they added to a notable presence of Hispanics in the United States, which is increasing by the day. Dominicans are the newest members of a Caribbean population living in the United States. Their numbers have risen as they began to leave their country concomitantly with the first two waves of Cubans, a period which corresponded with the end of the Trujillo dictatorship in 1961 and the US invasion of the Dominican Republic in 1965. However, it was not until the 1970s and 1980s that the Dominicans became a noticeable presence in Hispanic communities. Like the Puerto Ricans, Dominicans fled their homeland to escape declining economic conditions.

Cuban writers were among the first to migrate to the United States; they were at the forefront of their country's liberation movement. José María Heredia (1803–1839) was the first important Hispanic Caribbean writer forced into exile. A leader in the "Orden de los Caballeros Racionales," a branch of the separatist society "Los Soles y Rayos de Bolívar," Heredia was accused of conspiracy in 1823 and, with the help of friends, fled to Boston and lived in New York and Philadelphia. New York became Heredia's temporary home, allowing him to continue his literary career. Two years later, at the invitation of President Guadalupe Victoria, Heredia left for Mexico, a country similar to his own, with a warm climate and the familiar Spanish language. However, before leaving New York, Heredia wrote and published his *Poesías*, which placed him among the leading lyric and Romantic poets of Cuban and Spanish American literatures. This collection includes his most important poem of the period, "Oda al Niágara," a meditation on the New York waterfalls, the poet's own passion, and the yearned-for palm trees of his native Cuba. En route to Mexico, Heredia wrote "Himno del desterrado," a "hymn" about his country, his family, but also about the detestable colonial situation in Cuba. "Himno del desterrado" became a source of inspiration to other Cubans living in exile.

Other Cuban activists soon followed Heredia. Cirilo Villaverde was forced into exile for his political beliefs and activism. A member of the Del

Monte literary circle, Villaverde had produced a considerable body of literature before leaving Cuba and becoming one of the first notable Latin American narrators to seek political asylum in New York in 1849. In 1882 he completed and published in that city the definitive edition of his anti-slavery novel *Cecilia Valdés*. This novel, one of the most important works of nineteenth-century Spanish American literature, would not have been written had Villaverde stayed in Cuba, where slavery was an integral part of the Spanish colonial system. Like most exile-writers, Villaverde's life and literary production can be divided into two parts: his formative years in Cuba, where he published most of his fiction, including two early versions of his *Cecilia Valdés*, and his exile, where he wrote political essays and completed the definitive version of the novel. His later writings include a posthumous homage to General Narciso López, for whom Villaverde worked and who was captured and executed in Cuba in 1851. The manuscript was published under the title *To the Public (General López, the Cuban Patriot)* in New York, in 1850. He also drafted a response to José Antonio Saco's independence ideas, which he entitled *El señor Saco con respecto a la revolución de Cuba*, published in New York in 1852. In addition, he contributed articles to many magazines and newspapers and became editor of *La Verdad* in 1853, *El Espejo Masónico* and *La Ilustración Americana* from 1865 to 1873, *El Espejo* from 1874 to 1894, and *El Tribunal Cubano* in 1878.

At the outset of the Cuban Ten Years' War of Independence (1868–1878), Villaverde renewed his interest in politics, with a slightly different but significant change. Rather than the annexation of Cuba by the United States, he now favored Saco's position, seeking total independence of the island. In a document addressed to Carlos Manuel de Céspedes, entitled *La revolución de Cuba vista desde Nueva York*, Villaverde warns the Cuban patriot of the US intention not to help the rebel forces. By supporting Céspedes and other rebels, Villaverde explicitly embraced the anti-slavery cause. The Constituent Convention of the Guáimaro Assembly, of April 12, 1869, made a provision for the emancipation of slaves in Cuba. Although Villaverde lived to see the liberation of slaves in 1886, he did not witness the events which would lead to the independence of his country.

Villaverde's separation from Cuba, his political concerns, literary freedom, and events unfolding in the United States, in particular the emancipation of slaves in 1865, encouraged him to rewrite his most important novel. The last version of *Cecilia Valdés* is a denunciation of slavery and the Spanish colonial government. Villaverde situates the main action between 1823 and 1832; that is, within the historical context of the corrupt administration of General Francisco Vives. Yet Villaverde also reminds his readers of the Ladder Conspiracy of 1844 in which hundreds of free Blacks and slaves, including artists and writers, were put to death.

José Martí is certainly Cuba's most important literary and political exile. After his second expulsion from Cuba and except for brief periods, Martí resided in New York from 1880 to 1895. Like other intellectuals in exile, Martí continued to write, publishing the chronicles "Cartas de Nueva York; o, escenas norteamericanas" in *La Opinión Nacional* of Caracas, *La Nación* of Buenos Aires, *El Partido Liberal* of Mexico, and *La América* of New York, from 1881 to 1891. Martí also wrote for other New York papers, such as *The Hour* and *The Sun*. In New York, Martí expressed his political beliefs and made plans for Cuban independence. In 1892, Martí became a delegate to the Partido Revolucionario Cubano. He held other political positions including Consul of Argentina, Paraguay, and representative of Uruguay to the American International Monetary Commission in Washington, DC. In 1894, Martí completed the Plan de Fernandina, which outlined the invasion of Cuba in three expeditions, to be coordinated with internal uprisings.

Martí's "Carta de Nueva York," dated August 12, 1886, is addressed to the "Señor Director de La República." The letter refers to a series of New York publications which commented on the wonderful opportunities available to private capital in Honduras, but also to another publication which discouraged it. According to Martí, the country of Honduras was vindicated by another article written by the President of the Central American Workers Union. As a citizen of America in the broadest sense, Martí assumed his patriotic duties and offered his advice to the emerging republic. Martí begins his letter by referring to the sovereignty and natural richness of American soil and the need to work the land. He suggests that jobs and education are the means to assure liberty. Martí supports legitimate investment in Honduras and, with this in mind, he does a close reading of a pamphlet published by the Compañía de Mejora y Navegación del Río Aguán, a model to be applauded. He refers to the company's detailed and public intention to exploit certain natural resources such as lumber, agriculture, and mining and describes the project, which includes cost, profits, and benefits to the host country. The company even desires to return the River Aguán to its original path.

A prolific writer, Martí's most important literary works were written and published in New York; they include his poetry, *Ismaelillo*, *Versos sencillos*, the essay "Nuestra América" (1891), and the novel *Amistad Funesta*, and, from 1878 to 1882, he wrote many of the poems included in his posthumous *Versos libres*. With *Ismaelillo*, which contains fifteen brief poems dedicated to his son, and his prologue to Juan Antonio Bonalde's *El poema de Niágara*, Martí initiates *Modernismo* [Modernism] in Spanish America, a literary movement later associated with the Nicaraguan poet Rubén Darío. Martí's poetry came into fruition with his

Versos sencillos, a sincere expression of emotions related to his homeland, Nature, and mankind. His *Versos libres*, particularly "Amor de ciudad grande" which refers to New York City, represents a period of transition and confusion where he highlights content over form. These poems convey strength and energy which pour from the poet's pen and describe universal symbols. Unlike *Versos libres*, *Versos sencillos* is filled with simplicity and sincerity, with love and reflection about past and friends. Two other collections, *Versos de amor* and *Flores del destierro*, published posthumously in 1930 and 1933, respectively, correspond to the period of *Versos libres*. Martí's presence in the United States allowed him to carry out his political ideas and to understand his adopted homeland. In his much publicized essay, "Nuestra América," Martí warns the nations south of the border about their powerful neighbor to the north. The political and literary writings of Martí, Heredia, and Villaverde were profoundly influenced by their exile to the United States.

New York was also a haven for Puerto Rican activists. By the time Martí arrived in New York, Eugenio María de Hostos had already left his mark there, having lived in the city in 1870 and 1874. He would return later in 1898, and with Julio J. Henna and Manuel Zeno Gandía would publish *The Case of Porto Rico (sic)* (1899), a document in defense of Puerto Rican independence. Although they did not coincide in New York, Hostos and Martí shared the same revolutionary spirit and belonged to the same Partido Revolucionario Cubano. In New York, Hostos was the unofficial editor of *La revolución* for the Comité Republicano Puertorriqueño and called on Puerto Ricans to work for independence. Noting the division between those who supported independence and those who favored annexation, he wrote a manifesto calling for all Puerto Ricans to join the fight for independence. Later he became a leader among workers in the newly formed Club de Artesanos and promoted his ideas against annexation. Hostos's political ideas are gathered in his *Diario*.

In New York, Martí met many Puerto Rican intellectuals, including Francisco Gonzalo (Pachín) Marín who, like the Cuban poet, attended La Literaria, a Hispanic American literary society. During this period of his exile, Pachín Marín wrote a series of articles about New York, published the newspaper *El Postillón* and, under the influence of Béquer but also Martí, he wrote his *Romances*. Like Martí, Pachín Marín worked for independence; he participated in the Liga de Artesanos, was secretary of the Club Pinos Nuevos, and in Cuba gave his life for Cuban independence.

New York, an important theme in later Puerto Rican migration literature, was already visible in the works of Manuel Zeno Gandía (1855–1930), one of Puerto Rico's best-known authors. North Americans are present throughout his works, but New York City becomes his main concern in an inconclusive work *Nueva York*, the fifth of a series of chronicles entitled *Crónicas de un mundo enfermo*, about the Puerto Rican migration to the United States. Needless to say, this work had a profound impact on future generations of writers who developed the theme of migration in Puerto Rican literature.

In the twentieth century, Cubans continued to flee political persecution. The Machado dictatorship resulted in the exile of two of Cuba's most important narrators, Lino Novás Calvo (1905–1973) and Alejo Carpentier (1904–1980). Unlike their nineteenth-century counterparts, they did not live in the United States, but in Europe: Novás Calvo traveled to Madrid as a correspondent for *Orbe*, whose owners also published *El Diario de la Marina*, and Carpentier, after being detained by Machado's henchmen, fled to Paris where he contributed to the surrealist movement and even participated in its disintegration. During the same period, Nicolás Guillén (1902–1989) lived in Cuba but also traveled abroad. Guillén made two brief but important trips to the United States, which influenced some of his poetry. The first was a train ride across the United States, from Mexico to Canada, in 1937; the second was a two-week excursion to New York on his way to Moscow. Guillén was familiar with the racial situation in the United States, but he gained greater insight from his conversations with North Americans, such as Lindem Henry and Lulu B. White, whom he met when he was a delegate to the Congress of Peace in 1949. It was in his travels to the United States that he was able to confirm what he had already known. In an article "De Nueva York a Moscú, pasando por París," published in *Bohemia* in 1949, Guillén describes impressions that would not fade easily from his memory. He writes about the Harlem of luxurious cabarets but also of the misery in which many Blacks lived. Although "Elegía a Emmett Till" was not written until 1956, it captures a part of the Americana Guillén experienced on his visits to the United States. Similar to Neruda's interrogation of the Wilkamayu or Heredia's questioning of Niagara Falls, Guillén speaks to the mighty Mississippi about the death of the black boy. His experience would also serve him when writing other poems including one about black activist Angela Davis.

Batista's dictatorship, from 1952 to 1958, produced a small number of young exile writers for the United States. Incipient authors such as Roberto Fernández Retamar (b. 1930), Edmundo Desnoes (b. 1930), Pablo Armando Fernández (b. 1930), and Ambrosio Fornet (b. 1932) lived and worked in New York, where they furthered their literary careers. For example, Pablo Armando Fernández's second book of poems, *Nuevos poemas*, with an introduction by Eugenio Florit, was published in New York in 1956; Desnoes was the editor of *Visión*, from 1956 to 1959; and Fernández Retamar was a visiting professor at Yale University in 1957. That same year, Fornet was a student at New York University. Of the post Second World War period, Eugenio Florit (b. 1903) is perhaps the best-known writer to occupy a position at a major university in the United States. He arrived in New York in 1940 to work for the Cuban Consulate and in 1945 he joined the faculty at Barnard College of Columbia University. Florit promoted Spanish American literature with anthologies and works of scholarship, and with his own poetry which he wrote but did not publish in the United States. Unlike the poetry written in Cuba by members of *Orígenes* (1944–1956), his poems are devoid of rhetoric and seek to capture the essence of poetic language. One of his best poems is dedicated to New York, "Los poetas solos de Manhattan." This period includes his *Conversación a mi padre, Asonante final y otros poemas*, and *Siete poemas*.

If the younger voluntary exiles returned to Cuba after Fidel Castro's victory to work in the construction of a new society, the same event also produced another wave of exiles, mainly to San Juan, Miami, and New York City, but also to other cities throughout the United States. Every Cuban writer living during the time of the Castro government would be affected in one way or another by Castro's politics. Lino Novás Calvo became the first and most important writer to leave Castro's Cuba; he sought asylum in the Colombian Embassy in 1960, traveled to New York City, and in 1967 joined the faculty at Syracuse University. He taught there until he suffered a stroke in 1973, from which he never recovered.

Novás Calvo acquired literary prominence during the 1930s and 1940s with the novel *El negrero* (1933) and the collections of stories *La luna nona y otros cuentos* (1942) and *Cayo Canas* (1946). In exile, Novás Calvo continued to write in the United States and, like Villaverde, he used his literary and political freedom to denounce events in Cuba. Of the first six stories he published in *Bohemia Libre*, from 1960 to 1963, five narrate events in contemporary Cuba. For example, "Un buchito de café," "El milagro," and "Fernández al paredón," describe the unjust sufferings of innocent people at the hands of supporters of the Revolution.

In 1970 Novás Calvo published *Maneras de contar*, the only collection of short stories from his exile period. Of the eighteen stories, thirteen of them were written in the United States and narrate events in the Revolution; the other five are taken from his earlier collections and include "La noche de Ramón Yendía" and "Aquella noche salieron los muertos," two stories which date back to the Machado years. Novás Calvo's first exile stories were flawed, but he regained the mastery noted in his earlier tales after coming to terms with his condition as an exile. In this second period, Novás Calvo de-emphasizes the antirevolutionary theme and returns to earlier concerns to write, for example, "Peor que un infierno," "El esposo invisible," "Mi tío Antón Luna," and "El secreto de Naciso Campana." In spite of his renewed efforts to write fiction, Novás Calvo was unable to reach the level of recognition he had enjoyed prior to

1959. As a writer, Novás Calvo's reputation was hindered by historical events. He wrote antirevolutionary stories at a time in which the Cuban government enjoyed wide support among intellectuals in Europe, Latin America, and even in the United States, a support which lasted until the "Padilla Affair" of 1971, one year after the publication of *Maneras de contar*.

Perhaps one of Novás Calvo's important contributions to Cuban exile literature written in the United States is contained in "Un bum" and "La noche que Juan tumbó a Pedro," both written in 1964 and whose plots develop not in Cuba but in New York. They narrate the cruel reality exiles must face in the United States, one which Novás Calvo elaborated from personal experiences. The theme of Cubans as foreigners will be repeated by younger Cuban exiles – in particular, in the works of those who were either born or raised in the United States.

If Novás Calvo made an effort to keep his craft alive, other exile writers of his generation were less fortunate. Distinguished writers such as Lydia Cabrera (1900–1991), who left Cuba in 1962 and is known for her treatment of Afro-Cuban themes, Enrique Labrador Ruiz (1902–1990), who abandoned the island in 1970 and is known for his imaginative *novelas gaseiformes*, and Carlos Montenegro (1900–1981), who sought refuge in 1959 and is remembered for his prison narratives, have faded into literary oblivion. After 1959, few younger writers left the island, the majority staying in Cuba. Of those who published in the early years of the Revolution and wrote for *Lunes de Revolución*, edited by Guillermo Cabrera Infante, the literary supplement of the official newspaper of the July 26th Movement, *Revolución*, Matías Montes Huidobro (b. 1931) has remained active. A professor at the University of Hawaii, he has written literary criticism and continues to write plays such as *Ojos para no ver*, which describes the dictator, Castro, as a violent and enraged person. Other exile-writers such as José Sánchez-Boudy (b. 1927) have been active in promoting an anti-Castro literature.

In 1980, another wave of exiles popularly known as the "Marielitos" left Cuba during the Mariel boatlift. Established writers who had achieved recognition in revolutionary Cuba also sought asylum during this period. They included Heberto Padilla (b. 1933), José Triana (b. 1931), César Leante (b. 1928), Reinaldo Arenas (1943–1990), and Antonio Benítez Rojo (b. 1931). In comparison to their literary production in Cuba, this group of exile-writers has published little in their respective genres. Economic imperatives have forced them to devote themselves to other intellectual work, such as publishing and teaching. Of these writers, Arenas, Padilla, and Benítez Rojo reside in the United States, the latter two employed by New York University and Amherst College, respectively. Benítez Rojo has re-edited works previously published in Cuba and has shifted his interest from fiction to criticism. He published *La isla que se repite*, a poststructuralist approach to Caribbean culture, in which he develops the scientific ideas associated with the theory of Chaos and applies them to literature. Within the complexity of this sociocultural region, order and disorder coexist. In *La isla que se repite*, Benítez Rojo studies the plantation system as central for understanding the Caribbean. The plantation has affected all aspects of life and is repeated in the various islands and other parts of Latin America. *La isla que se repite* is a book that will find a place among such great works as Fernando Ortiz's *Contrapunteo cubano del tabaco y el azúcar* (1940), Ramiro Guerra's *Azúcar y población en las Antillas* (1927), and Manuel Moreno Fraginals's *El ingenio* (1978).

Padilla, a poet, published *En mi jardín pastan los héroes* (1981), a novel written in and smuggled out of Cuba. While in the United States, Padilla wrote *La mala memoria*, a testimonial pertaining to events surrounding the "Padilla Affair" in which he states for the record his version of the unfolding of political events in Cuba. Padilla has given much of his time to editing *Linden Lane Magazine*, based in New Jersey, which publishes the works of exile writers.

Reinaldo Arenas, who having tested positive for the HIV virus committed suicide, was the only writer from this group who remained very active and his works have placed him among the leading narrators of Latin American literature. After his arrival in the United States, Arenas founded the magazine and publishing house *Mariel* and published a novel written in Cuba, *Otra vez el mar* (1982). His work in exile included an epic poem, *El central*, a play, *Persecución: cinco piezas de teatro experimental*, a collection of essays, *Necesidad de libertad: testimonio de un intelectual disidente*, and two novels, *Arturo, la estrella más brillante* and *La loma del Angel*. Like many Cuban exile-writers, Arenas was critical of the Castro government. His political position was most explicit in *Necesidad de libertad*. Before his death, Arenas published two other works of fiction – *El portero*, which takes place in New York and describes the protagonist's life in the city, and *Viaje a La Habana*, which gathers three novelettes, each about a different Cuban exile who returns to the island – and two collections of poems *Voluntad de vivir manifestándose*, in which he collects poems written in the last two decades, and *Leprosorio: (trilogía poética)*. He also left four manuscripts which have been published posthumously, three of which are narratives: *El asalto* [*The Assault*] and *El color del verano* [*The Color of Summer*], a collection of short stories *Adios a mamá*, and the autobiography *Antes que anochezca* [*Before Night Falls*], in which the author refers to his literary talents and sexual concerns.

Arenas's *La loma del Angel* is a rewriting of *Cecilia Valdés*. The life and works of one author recall those of the other. Both Villaverde and Arenas opposed their respective governments when each lived in Cuba. For their political beliefs, both Arenas and Villaverde were imprisoned in Cuban jails and escaped from the island, seeking refuge in the United States. Both authors rewrote and published their versions of *Cecilia Valdés* while in the United States. Arenas completed his novel almost one century after Villaverde published the definitive version of *Cecilia Valdés*. Finally, both Arenas and Villaverde died in New York.

In his novel, Arenas joins Villaverde in denouncing slavery and uses the incestuous relationship between the unsuspecting brother and sister to narrate other cultural and political concerns. Just as Villaverde places his narrative time during the corrupt Vives government (1823–1832), but also breaks with it to call attention to the Ladder Conspiracy of 1844, Arenas likewise abandons the chronology of his novel to recall a contemporary time before and during the Cuban Revolution. By including in his narration Lydia Cabrera, José Lezama Lima, and Father Angel Gaztelu, Arenas refers the reader to the 1940s and 1950s and to the periodical *Orígenes* which Lezama edited. Before and after the triumph of Castro, Lezama and other group members were accused of stressing the aesthetic over the political. In Chapter 11, Arenas identifies Lezama as a slave poet, reminding us of the slave poet Juan Francisco Manzano's status during the first third of the nineteenth century and the censorship of anti slavery works.

By including more than one narrator, Arenas's novel decentralizes the authorial voice, and opens the text to multiple interpretations. In so doing, he opposes all monolithic and unidimensional discourses of fiction and history and challenges the view that functionaries of the Castro government are the authorized interpreters of Cuban history and culture. For Arenas, Cuban culture does not develop and flourish exclusively in nineteenth-century Cuba, but exists outside the island, in the works of Villaverde, Martí, and himself, authors who lived and wrote in exile in New York. In *Necesidad de libertad* Arenas states that the real Cuban literature is written outside Cuba.

Of importance to this project is Arenas's *El portero*, a novel which takes place in New York, specifically in a private apartment building in an upper-class neighborhood in Manhattan. The protagonist, Juan, is a Cuban refugee who arrived in New York as a result of the Mariel boatlift and finds a job as a doorman. Juan is an exceptional doorman and does anything to please his tenants, including having sex with men and women alike, but is also interested in talking to them about a metaphorical door. Through Juan's exile perspective, the reader sees life in New York (or perhaps in the United States), represented by rich and eccentric individuals who pay more attention to their pets than to Juan's (human) kindness. Money is not the only factor which produces rudeness and selfishness since the building's superintendent, who is not of the same economic means as the occupants, is also another conspirator against the doorman.

If Part I of the novel describes the people Juan meets on a daily basis, Part II centers on the pets and other animals who are aware of Juan's plight and talk to him about theirs. At a prearranged meeting each animal describes to Juan its own experience and persecution. Like Juan, they are prisoners of men, in general, and their owners, in particular, and conspire with Juan to gain their independence.

This, Arenas's latest novel is a denunciation of the social and political conditions in Cuba which caused him, the doorman, and others to flee from the island. In Cuba, the doorman "lived seventeen years in hunger and humiliation under the communist system and had fled on a boat" (p. 47). In addition, the novel is also a coming to terms with Arenas's exile condition in a foreign land. Juan and the animals speak of their marginal position in society and their desire to seek unity amongst themselves and independence for all. "All who have spoken wish to distance themselves from man, or at least, live in a manner independent from him, and even, if it were possible, to use him as one uses a slave" (p. 113).

In the end, the animals free Juan from an insane asylum; he had been accused of "magnetic ventriloquism" since no one but him believed that animals could speak. He and the animals flee, first to the Mid-West, then to California, later to the Equator, and finally to the sea looking for the magic mountain, a symbol of independence, a magic door which Juan guards. He becomes a St. Peter guarding the door to Heaven, but perhaps more like a bodhisattva who decides not to enter Nirvana in order to guide others.

El portero, which reflects Arenas's own experiences in New York, is sprinkled with English words and references to real characters, some of whom live in the city. It is narrated by a collective "we" who were once Cuban refugees and know every aspect of Juan's life. As a group, they echo the CDR, the Committee in Defense of the Revolution, a neighborhood spy network to "defend" Castro's government, but they live in the United States. The narrator is aware, and informs the reader, of Juan's activities. In the end, the narrative voice recognizes the importance of the movement for liberation of animals and inanimate objects, and also understands Juan's usefulness: he symbolizes hope and can mediate between them and humans.

Antes que anochezca – the title refers to the author's need to write before the evening arrived – is Arenas's best work. Arenas recounts his life in revolutionary Cuba from the perspective of death; he was very sick when he wrote his autobiography and died shortly after completing it. Death is ever-present, from the opening paragraph to the end.

Arenas's life represents an attack on the Castro government. The government objected to his writing, sexual orientation, and political beliefs and Arenas used the same weapons to denounce the injustices to which he and many other Cubans were subjected. The detailed homosexual experiences are a way of desensitizing the reader but also of defying Cuban policy and culture. Arenas challenges the Cuban authorities by suggesting that all Cubans are homosexuals. From a Cuban cultural point of view, only the passive partner in a homosexual relationship is considered to be gay; the active partner is regarded to be exercising his rights as a man. Arenas looks at this relationship from a North American perspective and reveals that everyone in Cuba has had some form of homosexual encounter, including members of Castro's police and military force who feel they are *machos*, but in reality are no different from him.

In Cuba, Arenas is considered to be a marginal writer. Yet outside the island Arenas's work elevates him to canonical stature.

Cuban literature written in the United States is distinctly different from Puerto Rican writing insofar as Cubans write about events and situations on their island. In this respect, Cuban writing both at home and abroad is similar to insular Puerto Rican literature. However, Puerto Rican literature written in the United States describes the life of Puerto Ricans who migrated to New York. The difference between Cuban and Puerto Rican writings in the United States is historical. Cubans traveled to the United States mainly for political reasons and viewed their exile as transitory. Their presence in the United States afforded them a political and literary freedom denied to them in their own country. Puerto Ricans traveled to the United States mainly for economic reasons. The US government's attempt to make Puerto Rico into the showcase of the Caribbean and to industrialize the island offset the Puerto Rican agricultural economy and forced many to leave the rural areas for better-paying jobs in the city. Operation Bootstrap displaced farm workers from the countryside to San Juan and from the capital to New York City. The Puerto Rican rags-to-riches dream turned into a nightmare as a large portion of New York's Puerto Rican population was either unemployed or assumed the lowest-paying jobs. Puerto Rican writers witnessed and some even experienced the migratory pattern created, first by the Jones Act and second by the congressional decision of 1952, making Puerto Rico a Free Associated State.

The large migratory waves to the United States gave the Puerto Rican community a sense of permanence, necessary for the development of a literature of migration. Therefore, Puerto Rican literature in the United States can be divided into two parts: the first is composed by island writers who visited but did not stay in the United States, and is written in Spanish and published abroad. The second, which is more recent, is written by Puerto Ricans who were either born or raised in the United States. Since most of these writers lived in New York City during the 1960s and 1970s, they identified themselves with the city and called themselves Puerto Rican New Yorkers or Nuyoricans, a term which gave identity and meaning to their artistic and literary expressions. Although this term is still relevant today, it does not speak to the experiences of younger Puerto Rican writers who were born or raised in other parts of the United States. Regardless of whether they live in or outside the city, this second group writes mainly in English and publishes in the United States. Nevertheless, both groups write about the Puerto Rican experience in New York. Puerto Ricans and other Hispanics born and raised in the United States share a common background and are also known as Latinos.

Hispanic Caribbean narrative written in the United States acquires an important dimension with the Puerto Rican writers of the Generación del Cuarenta [The Generation of 1940]; that is, with those who began to publish after Operation Bootstrap. Many of them short-story writers, they testify to the effects of Operation Bootstrap on those who were adversely affected by the "Puerto Rican Miracle," that is, the US effort to industrialize the island. The characters are taken from society's lower socio-economic levels. They are poor, uneducated, and marginal elements of society; those who were supposed to benefit from the economic changes become society's victims. For them, pain, suffering, and personal tragedies are an integral part of their migratory experience.

Many of the stories reveal the reason Puerto Ricans left their farms and villages for the city. The theme of displacement is best captured by *La carreta*, by Rene Marqués (1919–1980), a play about a family who abandoned the countryside for the slums of San Juan and ultimately for the ghettos of New York City. The theme of Marqués's play will be explored by other writers. Although it is difficult to state categorically that these authors wrote in the United States, we do know that they, like Puerto Rican writers before them, traveled frequently to New York.

José Luis González (b. 1926) is one of the first to write about the displacement of Puerto Ricans. In his third collection of short stories *El hombre en la calle*, he outlines the Puerto Rican tragedy and signals a new trend in the short story, moving away from rural to urban themes represented by San Juan but also New York City. González's *En este lado* continues the theme of Puerto Rican migration, this time, from San Juan to New York. As he reveals "this side" (the New York side) of the Puerto Rican experience, González shows a keener awareness of society and race both in and outside Puerto Rico, covering Mexico and the Korean War.

González's first story about New York was published in his *En Nueva York y otras desgracias*. In the title story, written in 1948, his protagonist,

Marcelino Pérez, experiences a series of misfortunes from the moment his boat docks in New York harbor, some due to circumstances but others to his own ignorance. Like many of González's characters, Marcelino is a desperate man; despite his ill health, he abandons his bed to rob an elderly woman who happens to be Puerto Rican. He hesitates when hearing her speak Spanish. Marcelino, himself a victim of circumstances, retains a sense of national dignity and does not add to the suffering of his own people.

Many of González's ideas are gathered in *Paisa*, a narrative version of Marqués's *La carreta* in which he describes the same migratory pattern as the play, and the moral and physical destruction of the protagonist. In New York, the story's protagonist, Andrés, is discriminated against and has no other alternative but to turn to a life of crime. In its narrative structure, *Paisa* is González's most experimental story about New York. The two narrations, one present and the other past, come together with the police shooting of Andrés. The ending departs from *La carreta* but is similar to "En Nueva York" and "El pasaje"; for the protagonist, there is no possible return to Puerto Rico, rather he remains in the United States. Through the character Perucho, González proposes that political action is the only solution to the Puerto Rican dilemma in the United States.

Language is important for authors writing about New York and González captures it with varying success. His "En Nueva York" reveals a lack of familiarity with some linguistic aspects of the Puerto Rican experience abroad. For example, the narrator, who describes events in a flawless Spanish, reports the temperature in Centigrade rather than in Fahrenheit and, as Marcelino gets ready to assault a lady, he moves from "house" to "house" instead of from one "building" to another. And except for a scattering of "Spanglish" words, his uneducated characters speak standard Spanish. However, González is more successful in his reproduction of Nuyorican speech in "La noche que volvimos a ser gente," from *Mambrú se fue a la guerra*, which describes the blackout of New York in 1965.

Of the writers of the Generación del Cuarenta, Pedro Juan Soto (b. 1928) has been most preoccupied by the Puerto Rican presence in New York and, with authenticity, has recorded the speech of the poor or working-class Puerto Rican as well as the linguistic phenomenon of mixing Spanish and English. Soto writes from personal experiences, having lived nine years in the Bronx, from 1946 to 1954, and spending much of his time in Spanish Harlem. *Spiks*, whose title is a pejorative term used to describe Puerto Ricans in the United States, contains Soto's best stories. The stories reflect the same migratory pattern the author was exposed to as a child, often contrasting life on the mainland and on the island. With the exception of "La cautiva," all of his stories take place in

New York City. His "Los inocentes" and "La cautiva" describe the change between old and new values, echoing a conflict experienced by many immigrants. However, unlike other immigrant groups, Puerto Ricans are tragic figures as Soto's work suggests. For sociopolitical reasons, their integration into the US mainstream has been more difficult.

Although Soto resides in Puerto Rico, and on occasion travels to New York (he waited thirteen years before returning to New York, and in 1970–1971 taught at the State University of New York at Buffalo), he writes about Nuyoricans and pays homage to them in his *Ardiente suelo, fría estación*. Soto's novel is realistic insofar as it captures the problems experienced by many Puerto Ricans who returned to their native Puerto Rico during the 1960s and 1970s (in part as a result of the racial awareness brought about by the Civil Rights and Black Power movements and by a heightened sense of Puerto Rican nationalism). Puerto Rico symbolizes the origin, but much to the dismay of Nuyoricans, they were not accepted by Puerto Ricans on the island and were treated as Americans; they were foreigners who did not share a common language and culture with islanders. Similarly, Soto's protagonist, Eduardo Marín, is confronted with Puerto Rican chauvinism; for the islanders he is an outsider. The frustrations Eduardo experiences on the island recall those same feelings in New York; he is an outcast both in New York and in Puerto Rico. In the end, the protagonist decides to return to the mainland, to a more familiar situation where he can assert his own individuality. Eduardo's older brother remains in Puerto Rico, thus alluding to the separation of the Puerto Rican family. The theme of Soto's novel will be repeated by Nuyorican writers but, unlike Soto's characters, they will highlight the Puerto Rican experience in the United States.

Unlike *Spiks*, in *Ardiente suelo, fría estación* Soto's characters are better educated and speak standard Spanish and English, which at times he juxtaposes to give authenticity to them. However, only seldom do they code-switch or recreate language to show the imposition and predominance of one culture over the other. The linguistic differences between *Spiks* and *Ardiente suelo, fría estación* can be attributed not only to the level of education of Soto's characters, but to Soto's distance from the mainland. Perhaps Soto also wanted to appeal to a broader Spanish-speaking audience; Soto's novel was not published in Puerto Rico but in Mexico.

Like *Ardiente suelo, fría estación, Harlem todos los días* by Emilio Díaz Valcárcel (b. 1929), a work which brings the experimentation of the *Boom* novel – prevalent in the same author's *Figuraciones en el mes de marzo* (1972) – to the theme of Puerto Ricans in New York, continues the concern of migration so evident in the works of Díaz Valcárcel's generation. In *Harlem todos los días*, the author underscores the anguish experienced by the poor, but also the life of his counterparts; those with the resources exploit the less fortunate. Regardless of the social or economic differences, all are victims of the New York environment. In this nationalistic novel, Díaz Valcárcel is critical of the colonial status under which Puerto Ricans live. However, like other island writers, Díaz Valcárcel is not able to capture effectively the linguistic complexity of Nuyorican speech. (The theme of the two cultures coming together, this time on the island, is continued in his *Mi mamá me ama*, 1981.)

The reproduction of the Nuyorican dialect is best achieved in the works of Nuyorican authors who are at the vanguard of a Puerto Rican or Hispanic Caribbean ethnic literature in the United States; that is, a Latino literature which questions but also accepts its North American environment. These writers, like Sandra María Esteves (b. 1948), Miguel Algarín (b. 1941), and others, write in English and have published their works in the United States. Unlike island-dwelling Puerto Ricans who visit the United States and write for a broad Spanish American audience, Nuyorican authors explore in detail the lives and condition of Puerto Ricans who live in New York. These younger writers use the language of the *barrio* to describe life in the ghetto. In this regard, Nuyorican narrative is not directly influenced by Spanish American literary currents, such as the literature of the *Boom* or *Post-Boom* periods, but by North American literature, in particular, the literature written by Afro-Americans; for example, some share common characteristics with Claude Brown's *Manchild in a Promised Land* (1965). More accurately, Nuyorican literature has no obvious model; rather, it emerges from the socio-economic conditions of Puerto Ricans in the United States. Unfortunately, Nuyorican literature still goes unrecognized by many scholars and critics of Spanish American literature. Moreover, although Puerto Rican writers in the United States celebrate their counterparts on the island, it is not reciprocal; many of the Nuyorican writers are unknown to the island public. This is so, as Soto has pointed out in his novel, because Nuyoricans are not considered authentic Puerto Ricans.

Among Nuyorican narratives, *Down These Mean Streets* by Piri Thomas (b. 1928) is already a classic. However, Thomas's book was not the first and recalls other autobiographical works by Puerto Ricans in New York, in particular *The Son of Two Nations: The Private Life of a Columbia Student* by Pedro Juan Labarthe (1906–1966), but is closer to *A Puerto Rican in New York and other Sketches* By Jesús Colón (1901–1974). Both works were written and published in the United States, but they did not have the impact Thomas's autobiography has had on a Nuyorican and English-speaking public. Only after the publication of Thomas's book are these earlier works receiving attention from critics and readers alike.

Labarthe's and Colón's books provide a framework for understanding works that were to follow. With their autobiographies two patterns emerged: first, Colón's *A Puerto Rican in New York* conveys the hostility with which Puerto Ricans are treated in New York, thus continuing the themes of the writers of the Generación del Cuarenta; second, Labarthe's *The Son of Two Nations* reflects the lives of immigrants in general, the United States representing an opportunity for the characters to improve their social and economic position. One is critical of the American dream, the other accepts it.

The difference in perspective can be attributed to the years in which the works were published. Labarthe published his novel shortly after the Great Depression, when many migrants, regardless of their place of origin, were struggling to survive in American society. Colón's book profited from a different historical setting, marked by political awareness associated with cigar-workers and other union activists, the detainment of nationalist leaders like Lolita Lebrón and Albizu Campos, the failure of the Tydings bill in 1943 to grant Puerto Rico independence, the implementation of Operation Bootstrap, and the prominence of the Civil Rights movement, particularly during the decade of the 1950s.

Colón's collection of sketches, some of which appeared in the *Daily Worker* and *Mainstream*, describe the assault of American society on Puerto Ricans and on the author, in part, often mistaken for a black American because of his dark skin. However, the book is also a testament of Colón's political beliefs and his support for the betterment of Puerto Ricans on the island through independence and Socialism.

In contrast, Labarthe's book is a reflection of the good will and faith of North Americans and of the character's own intelligence. Labarthe's formative years were influenced by his aristocratic and pro-independence father and his humble and pro-American mother. The father's abandonment of the mother, among other reasons, brings Labarthe closer to his mother's ideology; they travel to the United States not for economic reasons, but in search of a better education. In the United States, Labarthe and his mother work hard and with the help of friends, ambition, and a bit of opportunism, the author is able to transcend his condition and attain the "American dream."

Certainly Thomas's *Down These Mean Streets* is the best-known work which describes the Puerto Rican experience in New York during and after the Depression. Unlike Colón and Labarthe, Thomas was born in New York and had no direct connection with the island. Thomas was raised in El Barrio and his life mirrors that of many Nuyoricans who lacked either economic opportunities or a political ideology and were susceptible to drugs, gangs, and crime. Thomas's life represents the United States at its worse; he is the product of a society which has destroyed him and his self-worth. *Down These Mean Streets* allows the reader to look into a window of poverty and discrimination experienced by many Hispanics who have no other choice but to live in the ghetto. From a different point of view, as an author Thomas is a success story; he has transcended his economic and social conditions and has become a known writer within the North American context.

Thomas's subsequent books develop aspects of his life already seen in *Down These Mean Streets*. *Savior, Savior, Hold My Hand* is a continuation of *Down These Mean Streets* and, therefore, of Thomas's life. Here Thomas looks to the Pentecostal church for salvation, and his conversion is precipitated by his aunt and Nita, his wife-to-be. In the end, Thomas's rebellion against institutions results in his separation from Nita. *Seven Long Times* develops in more detail the chapter on prison from his first book, providing accounts of Thomas's life in Comstock. Prison is a home, a family of sorts, and a way of life for those who have difficulty in adjusting to the outside world.

Thomas's autobiography has opened the door for the writing and publishing of works by other Puerto Ricans living in the United States. Of particular historical value is *Memorias de Bernardo Vega*; though Vega (1886–1965) wrote his autobiography in 1947, César Andreu Iglesias did not edit and publish it until 1977. Vega's autobiography offers a chronology of one century, from the American Civil War to the post-Second World War period. This is accomplished through a series of flashbacks narrated first by a fictitious Tío Antonio, who migrated to New York in 1847, and second by Vega himself, who traveled to the same city in 1916. The useful historical information offered by Vega, which includes some statistics, interviews, and newspaper clippings, is part of a historical development to trace the origins of the Puerto Rican independence movement from the nineteenth century to the present. Antonio recalls the role played by intellectuals and workers living in New York, the center of Cuban and Puerto Rican independence movements. With his own experience, Vega shows that in the twentieth century, the independent spirit was kept alive by the unionist activities of cigarmakers. The workers have been at the forefront of the independence movement, though Vega sees marked differences between the Puerto Rican nationalist and communist parties. Vega is concerned with preserving Puerto Rican nationalism and identity.

There are other works which attempt to imitate *Down These Mean Streets*, such as *Una isla en Harlem* by Manuel Manrique, *Nobody's Hero* by Lefty Barreto (b. 1942), and *Run Baby Run* by Nick Cruz (b. 1938). Like Thomas's work, they are "autobiographical" accounts of Puerto Ricans who turned to a life of crime and violence. However, Richard Ruiz's *The Hungry American* and Humberto Cintrón's *Frankie Cristo* follow more closely the pattern set by Labarthe's *The Son of Two Nations* and describe those who grew up in the ghetto and believed in the American dream. For Ruiz, New York is just a resting place to travel to other parts of the United States. Ruiz's life recalls Labarthe's: both authors were born in Puerto Rico, their families had a difficult time making ends meet on the island, they leave hoping to better their lives, and they succeed in making it out of the New York ghetto. Like Labarthe who earned an MA at Columbia University, Cintrón valued education and completed his MA at the University of California.

If Thomas's experience provided a disturbing view of a country in which violence, drugs, crime, and sex were commonplace, the experience of women was much different. In this regard, Nicholasa Mohr (b. 1935), perhaps the first Puerto Rican woman to write fiction in English, represents still another side of the Nuyorican perspective. A painter turned writer, she has been very active, publishing three novels, *Nilda*, *Felita*, and *Going Home*, and three collections of short stories, *El Bronx Remembered*, *In Nueva York*, and *Ritual of Survival: A Woman's Portfolio*, and has completed her memoirs, *In My Own Words: Growing Up Inside the Sanctuary of my Imagination*. Mohr's narratives appeal to a broader English-speaking reader and have received awards such as the *New York Times* Outstanding Book of the Year, *Library Journal* Best Book of the Year, the American Book Award, and others. Because of the simplicity of her language, images, and metaphors, and for marketing purposes, Mohr's books have been unjustly classified as children's literature. According to Mohr, only *Felita* was written for children.

Written from a child's or adolescent's perspective, her works offer a balanced view of reality, describing both positive and negative experiences. Many of Mohr's stories contain autobiographical references, particularly *Nilda* and *Felita*. For example, in *Nilda*, she describes her brother's involvement in crime and drugs and, in *Felita*, the prejudice her family encounters when they move from a crowded neighborhood to a white one and back again. The child narrator is advantageous to Mohr, allowing her to describe the ghetto with objectivity and innocence, tenderness and compassion unknown in the works of her male counterparts. There are no political or social commentaries of an adult narrator, but a description of everyday life: the broken-down buildings, the roaches, the lack of food, the loss of innocence are part of the narrative background. Mohr's works represent a new direction for Nuyorican narrators, away from the violence and assimilation and toward a more balanced view of Puerto Ricans in the United States.

Of the writers, Mohr, but also Algarín and Miguel Piñero (1946–1988), have been outspoken about reappropriating Puerto Rican identity and in their criticism of the treatment Nuyoricans receive when returning to

Puerto Rico. Mohr demystifies the Puerto Rican paradise and accepts New York and the United States as her permanent home. The return to Puerto Rico is the theme of *Going Home*. As in Soto's *Ardiente suelo, fría estación*, Felita experiences difficulty in accepting the island's culture. Mohr contrasts the values of the mainland with those of the island and shows the difference in the treatment of men and women. Felita misses New York and returns "home" to her native city. Mainstream Puerto Rican writers living on the island are also concerned about the question of identity. This is evident in Luis Rafael Sánchez's "La guagua aérea," which describes the daily air shuttles between San Juan and New York, or *allá* and *acá*, and how that frequent migratory travel underscores the dilemma of Puerto Rican identity.

The narrative has played a prominent role in describing the life of Puerto Ricans in the United States, but Nuyorican poetry, although recent, is popular and has received publicity in centers like The Nuyorican Poets Cafe, El Caney, and The New Rican Village. Poetry written in the United States can be traced to Julia de Burgos (1916–1953), who lived in New York from 1942 to 1953 and wrote about the city which occupied an important place in her life; this is particularly evident in her posthumous *El mar y tú, otros poemas*. But her *Obra poética* contains fourteen poems written in New York, though others have been found. Like island writers who traveled to New York, Burgos wrote about the political situation in her native Puerto Rico, as seen in "Una canción a Albizu Campos," "23 de septiembre," and "De Betances a Albizu," though toward the end of her life she wrote in English about "Welfare Island," and "The Sun in Welfare Island," where she died. It would however be left to another group of poets to displace the attention Burgos gave to Puerto Rico and develop further the ideas contained in the poems she dedicated to life in New York.

Puerto Rican poetry in the United States acquires a bilingual dimension with Jaime Carrero (b. 1931) and his *Jet neorriqueño-Neo-Rican Jetliner*, the first work to introduce the term "Neo-Rican" which later gave coherence and identity to a group of younger writers. Carrero also brings to poetry the theme of migration prevalent in the works of the writers of the Generación del Cuarenta. Carrero's poetry is taken one step further by Nuyorican poets who are mainly concerned with the presence of Puerto Ricans in New York. Of this group, Pedro Pietri (b. 1944) is its best exponent. A writer of plays, narratives, and poetry, Pietri is best known for his *Puerto Rican Obituary*; the title poem, "Puerto Rican Obituary," was first published in *Palante: Young Lords Party*, in 1971, and was known to Hispanics in New York City many years before. A descriptive but also symbolic poem, "Puerto Rican Obituary" is the single most important poem in Nuyorican literature. Juan, Miguel, Milagros, Olga, and Manuel are familiar figures who worked hard and believed in the

American dream which they could not attain. As they mirror the conditions under which they lived, the poetic voice condemns them for abandoning their roots and culture. According to the poem, the cycle can be broken if Puerto Ricans develop a sense of national pride and identity. Written in spoken (street) language, which for Pietri includes mixing some Spanish and English, this and other poems are closer to an oral tradition and are meant to be performed or read aloud. Language expresses pride and unity among Nuyoricans, thus rejecting the pressures to assimilate into a "standard" language or way of life. Pietri continues the theme of his best-known work in poems, such as "The Broken English Dream," where he shows that Puerto Ricans did not gain, but rather lost what little they had, including their identity and pride, when they traveled to the United States.

The standards set by Pietri are equaled by Tato Laviera (b. 1951) who, like Pietri, is a playwright and poet. In poetry, Laviera has published *La Carreta Made a U-Turn*, *Enclave*, *AmeRican*, and *Mainstream Ethics*. Laviera's first book continues the ending of Marqués's play, but rather than returning to Puerto Rico, New York is the final destination; that is, there is no lost paradise to which Puerto Ricans return, but a new-found reality. By not completing the full circle, Laviera speaks about his own migratory process; he was born in Puerto Rico and raised in New York City. Despite the difficult life Puerto Ricans must endure abroad, the poem reveals that Puerto Ricans in the United States have undergone a change; although they still identify symbolically with the motherland, they are no longer her children and in reality can never go back. This observation is due to a noticeable predominance of English over Spanish. Yet, ironically, Laviera ends his book with a series of poems in Spanish, suggesting that the problem need not be linguistic but is one of preference. Cultural elements such as those expressed in Afro-Caribbean culture are revered; they allow for an identity of sorts with others struggling in the ghetto and in particular African-Americans. In effect, Puerto Ricans have set the groundwork for the creation of a Hispanic Caribbean subculture within the North American context.

Laviera has the gift of assuming many voices which include the street junkie, the woman, and even the Statue of Liberty. Yet he is most effective when taking on the voice of a fetus about to be born on Christmas Day. Drawing on religious symbolism, "Jesús Papote" is an epic poem about the Puerto Rican experience in the United States. This other Christ figure is born not of a sacred virgin but of a heroin addict who has numerous lovers. The fetus's struggle for survival begins in the womb; he was forced to be a man before he became a child. "Jesús Papote" is certainly a major poem in contemporary Hispanic and American poetry. Younger poets continue to write in the style of Pietri and Laviera. Of these Martín Espada

(b. 1957) should be noted; his works include *The Immigrant Iceboy's Bolero*, *Trumpets from the Islands of Their Eviction*, and *Rebellion is the Circle of a Lover's Hands*.

The woman's perspective among poets is growing and is best represented by Sandra María Esteves whose publications include *Yerba Buena*, *Tropical Rains: A Bilingual Downpour*, and *Bluestown Mockingbird Mambo*. Esteves and other women poets belong to the tradition initiated by Burgos, but also by the women's movement in the United States. The woman's perspective is different from that of the male counterpart insofar as it challenges the dominant Hispanic male culture. Esteves acknowledges Burgos's importance in "A Julia y a mí" and recognizes the poet's strengths and failures. In her best poem "My Name is Maria Christina" Esteves expresses pride in being a Puerto Rican woman from El Barrio. She accepts her traditional role as provider and child-bearer and her new one as creator of different values; she rejects the denigrating aspects of her culture. As a female Christ (Cristina), she is origin and strength, elements necessary for the survival of Puerto Rican identity. Nevertheless, Luz María Umpierre (b. 1947), a recognized poet with works such as *En el país de las maravillas*, *Una puertorriqueña en Penna, y otras Desgracias And Other Misfortunes*, and *The Margarita Poems*, has been critical of Esteves's view of women, believing that she did not go far enough. Umpierre counters Esteves's "My Name is Maria Christina" with her own "In Response," a poem in which the poetic voice denies being María Cristina and, unlike her, is a totally liberated woman. Though Esteves's and Umpierre's poems pertain to Puerto Rican culture, the poets' awareness comes from the North American environment, in general, and the women's movement, in particular.

Puerto Rican identity is certainly important, but some of the poets are beginning to go beyond the familiar themes and include wider concerns. In the case of Laviera, he finds common ground with other Caribbean groups like Jamaicans, but also Chicanos. The attempt to enter the mainstream is exemplified by Miguel Algarín who has published *Mongo Affair*, *On Call*, *Body Bee Calling From the 21st Century*, and *Time's Now*. Algarín begins to branch out and look for common ground among the different cultures as early as his second book which includes his poems "Buddha" and "Balance," representing aspects of Asian culture and religion. His next book is more concerned with sex and the last one with love.

Among the Puerto Rican writers living and writing in the United States, the work of Judith Ortiz Cofer (b. 1952) is of particular interest. She is a poet and novelist and with Mohr, one of the few women narrators writing in English. She has published three books of poems, *Latin Women Pray*, *Peregrina*, and *Terms of Survival*, one book of memoirs, *Silent Dancing*, and one novel, *The Line of the Sun*. Ortiz Cofer was born in Puerto Rico and raised in the United States; after her father joined the Navy, the family moved often and lived in different cities. Her work touches upon some of the themes of other Nuyorican writers but she expresses them from a less marginal perspective, in a language that is more polished and mainstream. Unlike the other writers, Ortiz Cofer is not concerned about the linguistic phenomenon caused by the coming together of Spanish and English nor about the clashing of the two cultures. Many of her poems are of a personal nature, often describing her innermost thoughts, vivid experiences, and members of her family. Poems such as "Housepainter," "Moonlight Performance," "Woman Watching Sunset," and "The Mule" are written with a keen insight of the subject and are composed with much thought and mastery over her expression, but show no trace of her Puerto Rican or ethnic background. There are other poems such as "Visiting La Abuela," "The Gusano of Puerto Rico," and "Latin Women Pray" which suggest a certain Hispanic thematics but although they contain Hispanic names and references to the island, they are written in standard English. Only in a handful of poems does she venture away from English and incorporate a few words of standard Spanish such as "la leche" in "Pueblo Waking" and the vendor's call "frutas hoy, y viandas" in "The Fruit Vendor." Even though she chooses not to use her Spanish, Ortiz Cofer is certainly aware of her parents' language, which the poetic voice will teach others as she reveals in "Lesson One: I Would Sing:"

> In Spanish, "cantaría" means I would sing,
> Cantaría bajo la luna,
> I would sing under the moon.
> Cantaría cerca de tu tumba,
> By your grave I would sing,
> Cantaría de una vida perdida,
> Of a wasted life I would sing,
> If I may, if I could, I would sing
> In Spanish the conditional tense is the tense of dreamers,
> of philosophers, fools, drunkards,
> of widows, new mothers, small children,
> of old people, cripples, saints, and poets.
> It is the grammar of expectation and
> the formula for hope: cantaría, amaría, viviría.
> Please repeat after me.

Ortiz Cofer's poem is concerned with translation and perhaps bilingualism, but is certainly aware of the power of Spanish verbs and tenses, which are antithetical to their less expressive English equivalents. This poem is about marginal people who speak a language, and therefore live in a culture, of hope.

Ortiz Cofer's *The Line of the Sun* is an autobiographical novel of sorts which narrates the story of three generations of Marisol Santa Luz Vivente's family. Marisol, the granddaughter, is Puerto Rican by birth but is raised in the United States after her parents migrate in the 1950s. The novel is divided into two thematic parts: the first pertains to her Puerto Rican village where her father and uncle grew up, and describes rituals and traditions of the island and her uncle Guzman's mischievous life. The second part takes place in El Building in New Jersey and in New York City where she experiences the harsh reality of living on the mainland. A comparison between the two parts shows that the poverty her family endured on the island prefigures that of the mainland. Marisol suffers from an identity crisis created by living in the village of Salud, Puerto Rico, and in Patterson, New Jersey, but also by her father's desire to become Americanized and her mother's knowledge of Puerto Rico and letters about Guzman. Writing takes on a therapeutic meaning: it is a way of staying in touch with her Puerto Rican heritage while living in the United States.

Like poetry and narrative, the Nuyorican theatre is rapidly gaining in popularity, with the emergence of such performing groups as The Puerto Rican Playwrights and Actors Workshops, Teatro Cuatro, El Teatro Ambulante, and Aquarius Theater. This genre is particularly important to the contemporary Puerto Rican and Hispanic communities because it recreates life in the United States, one all too familiar to the Hispanic audience, thus appealing to first-time theatre-goers and providing an alternative for those who customarily take advantage of this art form.

The Hispanic theatre written in the United States has a long history that dates back to the nineteenth century; but in recent times Puerto Rican theatre can be traced to *Esta noche juega el joker* (1939) by Fernando Sierra Berdecía, (1903–1962), a play about the cultural differences between the island and the mainland and the adjustments Puerto Ricans must undergo in New York. It received standing ovations from the public when performed at the Club Artístico del Casino de Puerto Rico and outside the island. Berdecía's tradition was continued by Manuel Méndez Ballester (b. 1909) with *Encrucijada* (1958) and Jaime Carrero with *Caja de caudales F M* (1978). However, Nuyorican theatre is best represented by Miguel Piñero – also known as a poet – and his play *Short Eyes*. Like Mohr's stories, Piñero's play has met with great success, receiving the New York Drama Critics Circle Award and the Obie (Off-Broadway) for 1973–1974, and being produced by Joseph Papp at the Lincoln Center, and reviewed by magazines and newspapers such as the *New York Times*, the *Daily News*, and *Newsweek*, among others. The play received its strongest endorsement by Hollywood when it was made into a full-length motion picture with the same name. Piñero's play recalls the prison theme prevalent in Thomas's *Down These Mean Streets* and *Seven Long Times*. The play reduces the tensions in society to their basic premise, to the racial and ethnic discrimination which Blacks and Puerto Ricans in and outside prison must endure. In prison language (which recalls that of the *barrios* and ghettos), "short eyes" refers to a child molester, the most serious crime of all. Prison life is a mirror of society with racial problems and its own system of justice. However, it is also an inversion of society: the crime is committed not by a Black or a Hispanic but by a White, the black and Puerto Rican prisoners in their overwhelming numbers are in power, and homosexuality plays an important role in prison life. As in society, prison is ineffective in correcting behavior.

As chroniclers of an ethnic culture which is Puerto Rican and North American, Puerto Rican writers in the United States have provided a framework for other Hispanic Caribbean authors who write about their lives and experiences in the same North American environment. As Cubans come to terms with the permanent nature of their condition as exiles, many authors are writing about Cuban American themes. They describe the problems which affect the Cuban American community, even though this community is not homogenous regarding its political views toward Cuba.

It is still early to identify Cuban American figures who will leave a lasting mark, but there are some literary patterns which are emerging. Cuban American narrators write in Spanish and in English. Those who use Spanish bring aspects of the contemporary Spanish American novel into their works; those who use English adhere more closely to North American literary trends. The adopted language suggests an assimilation of sorts, the vernacular represents an attempt to preserve Cuban or Hispanic identity. Although some authors write in Spanish, an increasing number of them are writing in English, and even capturing the influence one language has over the other. These writers are at the forefront of developing a Latino intercultural literature.

In narrative, the theme of the coming together of the two languages and cultures is highlighted by "Nothing in Our Hands But Age" (1979) by Raquel Puig Zaldívar (b. 1950). In this amusing yet tragic story, Puig Zaldívar unites two generations of Cuban exiles, one represented by a teacher educated in the United States, and the other by an elderly exiled couple who must return to school and learn English to revalidate their degrees. The story is about freedom, pride, and perseverance. Similarly, *La vida es un special* by Roberto Fernández (b. 1951), which pertains to Cuban exiles living in Miami, underscores the lack of communication between the younger generation that wants to assimilate into mainstream society, and the adults, who do not speak English and desire to preserve the original culture. In language, the harsh reality is represented by the coming together of Spanish, English, and Spanglish. Also, Fernández's *La montaña rusa*, influenced by the Latin American novel of the *Boom* period, expands on the themes of *La vida*, depicts the life of Cuban Americans in Miami, and is critical of their sexual and anticommunist obsessions as well as their liberal ideas. Most recently he published *Raining Backwards*, a novel which gathers aspects of Cuban culture within the North American environment. In *Los viajes de Orlando Cachumbambé* by Elías Miguel Muñoz (b. 1954), the author uses contemporary techniques to describe a Cuban exile narrator–protagonist who seesaws between two cultures as his mixture of Spanish and English suggests. Muñoz moves closer to the North American culture in his *Crazy Love*, whose title refers to a song by the American pop figure Paul Anka. The novel is written in English and highlights the coming together of the two cultures. By contrast, in "Etruscans" (1981) by María del Carmen Boza (b. 1952), references to Cuba and Miami are part of the protagonist's past; Cuban culture can hardly be discerned, as the protagonist visits a farm in rural Pennsylvania. The story relates to school, friendship, pride, and honesty.

Cuban American writers, like their established exile counterparts, write about Cuba and exile. For example, Pablo Medina (b. 1948) who wrote *Pork Rind and Cuban Songs* and *Arching into the Afterlife*, also published *Exiled Memories: A Cuban Childhood*, an autobiographical account in which the protagonist recollects the first twelve years of his life, which includes his experiences in pre- and post-revolutionary Cuba, and those after his arrival in New York in 1960. Above all, the book is a collective memory of personal experiences, but also family customs and traditions which allow the protagonist to narrate events in the nineteenth and twentieth centuries. The book is a nostalgic account of the past and is accompanied by illustrations of Medina and his family. In "Litany" by Damián Fernández (b. 1957), the protagonist who lives in Cuba is marginal and does not participate in Cuban revolutionary society. In Roberto Fernández's "La encadenada," the characters find it difficult to overcome their condition of exile.

The exile experience is also a theme among the youngest writers of the Mariel Generation. Virgil Suárez (b. 1962), the author of *Latin Jazz* and *Welcome to the Oasis and Other Stories*, also published *The Cutter*, a story about Julián Campos who is at the Havana Airport waiting to leave the island and join his family in the United States when the Cuban security police detain him. Because of the departure of his family five years earlier and his desire to leave the island, Julián is forced to join the Young Pioneers and do additional voluntary work cutting sugar cane. The time of the narration is 1969, one year before the completion of the failed Ten Million Ton Sugar Harvest. In the end, Julián's situation is desperate and he escapes from the island–prison and arrives in Miami. Two other writers of the Mariel Generation worth noting are Roberto Valero (b. 1955) and Miguel Correa (b. 1956).

The representation of two cultures, two languages, and two countries in Cuban American narrative is also reflected in poetry. In her "Para Ana Velfort," in *Palabras juntan revolución*, Lourdes Casal (1938–1981) is caught between two worlds: she refers to New York as her "patria chica," although recognizing that she was not born there. In *Cimarrón*, Ricardo Alonso (b. 1954) is disappointed with the United States but also knows that he is a stranger to the island. In *Sorting Metaphors*, Ricardo Pau-Llosa (b. 1954) looks at Miami with a distant critical eye.

The two most important Cuban American poets are Octavio Armand (b. 1946) and José Kozer (b. 1940), whose works can be understood as responding to the problems of contemporary Latin American writing. Armand's poetry includes *Horizonte no es siempre lejanía*, *Cómo escribir con erizo*, and *Biografía para feacios (1977–1979)*, and although his works are difficult to classify, he attempts to bridge the gap between poetry and prose, at times bordering on one or the other or even a combination of both. His works reveal a preoccupation with the word; not satisfied with its old referents, he desires to attribute to it more than what their tired meanings offer. Other concerns of his include the physical, psychological, and emotional estrangements in which the body, his and that of the text, plays an important role. In *Biografía para feacios*, Armand searches for and escapes to where he is, because there is no "other side."

Other poets go beyond the Cuban American experience. Kozer's most recent works include *La rueca de los semblantes*, *Jarrón de las abreviaturas*, *Bajo este cien*, *La garza sin sombras*, *El carrillón de los muertos*, and *Carece de causa*. The creativity in language noted in Armand's poetry is also present in Kozer's works except that, in the case of the latter, it becomes an eternal quest for answers to questions which have no solutions. The poem becomes an unending search for identity and meaning. He tries to put together a puzzle in which he is just another piece: that of a Cuban Jew in an adopted New York environment. Some of Kozer's poems include Yiddish words with cultural and political referents, thus adding a multicultural dimension to his tropes. For example, in "Kafka" Koser writes about physical isolation and mental escape and makes references to Prague and Lima. In "Julio" the poetic voice describes with nostalgia the past in which childhood and his grandmother were central elements. In an insightful essay on Kozer's works, "Noción de José Kozer," the critic (and poet) Gustavo Pérez Firmat highlights the use of various languages with their multiple referents and studies the grammatical function of parentheses in the poems.

The Cuban American theatre is beginning to make inroads in the

United States. Of the playwrights, Dolores Prida (b. 1943) and her *Beautiful Señoritas*, which was performed many years before it was published, deserves some attention. The play is influenced by the women's movement in the United States and is an attempt to address the issue of Cuban or Hispanic women within the North American context.

Although some writers like Armand and Koser are gaining in popularity, other Cuban American writers are known only in small circles, mainly within the Cuban and Hispanic communities in the United States. Perhaps the exception is Oscar Hijuelos (b. 1951) and his *The Mambo Kings Play Songs of Love*, which was published by a major publisher, Farrar Strauss & Giroux, and earned him a Pulitzer Prize in 1990. Hijuelos had published *Our House in the Last World*, which pertains to the experiences of his family who traveled to the United States in the 1940s, but it was *The Mambo Kings* which made him the star figure of Cuban American writers. Reviewed by all major newspapers and magazines, the novel, set in 1949, narrates the journey of two Cuban musicians, Cesar and Nestor Castillo, who leave Havana and with hard work become musical celebrities of the mambo in New York. After his affair with María, Nestor devotes his life to her memory and writes twenty-two versions of "Beautiful María of My Soul." Music makes the protagonists famous during a period in which Latin music was leaving its mark in the United States; they even appear on the "I Love Lucy" show and play in Desi Arnaz's Tropicana Club. In the author's words: "This is a wonderful book about American history and culture and its intermixing with Cuban culture." With *The Mambo Kings*, Hijuelos has made the transition from a Cuban American writing to mainstream North American literature.

Dominicans are the most recent group of Hispanic Caribbean authors to write in the United States. The Dominican Republic and its writers have been marked by two important events: the end of the Trujillo dictatorship and the US invasion of the island. In the Dominican Republic, these two events motivated a Dominican literature which is obsessed with narrating life under the dictatorship and during the US occupation. The same events opened the door for a new wave of Caribbean immigrants to the United States, increasing in numbers in the 1970s. Only in the 1980s has a Dominican literature written in the United States emerged.

Dominican authors writing in the United States are mainly poets whose works resemble those of first-generation migrants writing in Spanish and publishing in their country of origin. Their presence in the United States has given them greater freedom to continue the Dominican literary tradition abroad. Some writers are merging their native culture with that of their adopted country to form a synthesis of the two. Magazines and anthologies have been responsible for giving publicity to these authors and creating an interested public. Unfortunately, some of the magazines have had limited circulation; they include *Letras e Imágenes* (1981–1982), *Inquietudes* (1981–1982), *Punto 7 Review* (1985–), and *Alcance* (1983–). Of the anthologies, we should mention Franklin Gutiérrez's *Espiga del siglo* (1984), *Niveles del imán* (1983), and *Voces del exilio* (1986), and the bilingual *Poemas del exilio y de otras inquietudes* edited by Daisy Cocco de Filippis and Emma Jane Robinett.

Like other Hispanic Caribbean authors, Dominican writers are beginning to show the influence of North American culture in their works. Leandro Morales (b. 1957) writes about death in "Coplas para la muerte de mi madre" and about Artaud in "Antonin Artaud," a theme also repeated by Alexis Gómez Rosa (b. 1950) in "Cédula métrica"; but in "Cielo pragmático" and "Una y otra vez me preguntaron," Gómez Rosa describes the cemeteries of Newark and Central Park of New York, respectively. The search for an identity created by living abroad is present in English in *Homecoming* by Julia Alvarez (b. 1951). She and Chiqui Vicioso (b. 1948) also offer a female perspective in Dominican poetry. The loss of identity is a concern of Franklin Guitiérrez (b. 1951) in his *Helen*, about a woman whose transformation is evident in her name change from the Spanish Helena to the English Helen. The reality of living in New York and searching for the American dream is best captured by Guillermo Francisco Gutiérrez (b. 1958) in *Condado con candado* (1986). The despair created by exile is present in the works of Tomás Rivera Martínez (b. 1956) and Héctor Rivera (b. 1957). The African American awareness of race and racism is an important influence on Dominican authors. Norberto James Rolling (b. 1945) looks at the issues of race in the Dominican Republic and brings into focus an Afro-Caribbean tradition. Chiqui Vicioso recognizes and defends the Haitian influence on Dominican culture.

Race is also the concern of Miguel A. Vázquez (b. 1942), one of the first Dominican narrators to write in the United States. Vázquez's *Mejorar la raza* is a coming to terms with the racial prejudice of Hispanic Caribbean culture which promotes the betterment of Blacks by "whitening" their skin color. Although the novel takes place in the Dominican Republic, the United States is mentioned briefly, but is more visible in the treatment of race.

Of the Dominican women writers, Julia Alvarez has already found a place among her better-known Hispanic and Latino counterparts with her novel *How the Garcia Girls Lost Their Accents*, published by Algonquin Books in 1991. Like Mohr and Ortiz Cofer who write about their family and childhood memories, Alvarez also describes the dynamic relationships that exist between her mother, father, and their four daughters. Like other immigrants and exiles, she too tries to understand her arrival in the United States from the Dominican Republic at the age of ten and the pressures to assimilate and yet to maintain her own identity. The duality is also reflected in her writing style, in which she brings to English her knowledge of Spanish.

It will only be a matter of time before other Dominican authors follow the path outlined by Puerto Rican and Cuban American writers who use the adopted language to write about the Hispanic experience in New York and other Spanish-speaking cities. Some writers like Morales, Alvarez, Gutiérrez, Rivera, and Gómez Rosa, are already publishing in the United States.

Hispanic Caribbean literature written in the United States forms an integral part of a Spanish American literature of exile and migration. As the conditions of authors living in the United States become more permanent, their literature will include more images about Hispanic life in North American cities. Similarly, as the younger authors continue to express themselves in English, their works will become a part of a Hispanic American ethnic literature which describes the life of the Hispanic or Latino in the United States. Writers such as Nicholasa Mohr, María del Carmen Boza, Judith Ortiz Cofer, and Oscar Hijuelos are beginning to reflect in their works the coming together of a Hispanic Caribbean tradition in a North American context. Hispanic Caribbean literature written in the United States has an impact on both Spanish American and North American literatures. Therefore, it bridges two continents, two cultures, and two languages.

17

Chicano literature

Luis Leal and Manuel M. Martín-Rodríguez

How can the inclusion of a section on Chicano literature in a history of Latin American literature be justified? In order to answer that question it is necessary to examine briefly two topics, the nature of national literature and the nature of Chicano literature itself. Regarding the first, it can be observed that in the field of literary criticism there are two extreme positions: one that denies the existence of a national, regional, or ethnic literature; and another that accepts that concept. Renée Wellek and Austin Warren, in their book, *Theory of Literature*, dedicate a chapter to a discussion of "General, Comparative, and National Literature," in which they state:

> The term "world literature," a translation of Goethe's Weltliteratur, is perhaps needlessly grandiose, implying that literature should be studied on all five continents, from New Zealand to Iceland. Goethe, actually, had no such thing in mind. "World literature" was used by him to indicate a time when all literatures would become one. It is the ideal of the unification of all literatures in one great synthesis, where each nation would play its part in a universal concert. But Goethe himself saw that this is a very distant ideal, that no single nation is willing to give up its individuality. Today we are possibly even further removed from such a state of amalgamation, and we would argue that we cannot even seriously wish that the diversities of national literatures should be obliterated. (Harcourt, 1956: 37)

The same could be said about regional and ethnic literatures, and even for those written in a language other than the national language of a given country. In reference to the study of Medieval English literature, Wellek and Warren state that "A history of literature during the Middle Ages in England which neglected the vast amount of writings in Latin and Anglo-Norman gives a false picture of England's literary situation and general culture" (p. 40).

In his book, *Puertas al campo* (1966), Octavio Paz gives expression to the opposite theory. He states:

Literature or Hispanic-American literature? If we open a book about the history of Ecuador or the Argentine, we find a chapter dedicated to their national literature. Now then, nationalism is not only a moral aberration, but also a deceiving aesthetic. Nothing distinguishes Argentinean from Uruguayan literature, nor Mexican from Guatemalan. Literature transcends frontiers. (p. 12)

If this theory is accepted, Chicano literature could not be studied independently. Yet Chicanos are not ready or willing to give up their own cultural identity, and insist on being considered as an ethnic group whose literature contributes, on the one hand, to the enrichment of the kaleidoscopic nature of North American literature, and, on the other, to the creation of a bridge between that literature and Latin American letters, especially since Chicano literature is written in both English and Spanish, or in a combination of the two languages. Even in Latin America, many intellectuals reject the Pan-Americanist ideas of Octavio Paz, preferring to stress those traits that differentiate national cultures or, at least, the cultures of certain socio-geographical areas (such as the Andes, etc.). Paz himself seems to fluctuate between the internationalism of *Puertas al campo* and a search for the national essences in his earlier *El laberinto de la soledad* (1950) [*Labyrinth of Solitude*]. In the latter, he described Chicano *pachucos* as a sort of aberration of the Mexican national and, in doing so, implicitly alluded to traits of a national culture shared by all Mexicans, as well as to deviations from it: "Whether we like it or not, these are Mexicans, one of the extremes to which a Mexican can get" (p. 13).

The following problem arises, then: to what national literature do the people of Mexican descent who are (or were) citizens or permanent residents of the United States belong? The question is valid only when considering that literature written by Chicanos since 1848 (1836 in Texas). Works produced before those years rightfully belong to the field of Hispanic/Mexican letters, for what is now the Southwest of the United States (hereafter referred to as the Southwest) was first part of the Spanish Empire in America, and later of the Republic of Mexico. These earlier texts can rightfully be considered the antecedent of Chicano literature, as they were written about the same space, the same people, and the same culture as contemporary literature is. It could also be said that this Hispanic/Mexican literature reflects a new sensibility, which is the result of factors that characterize the culture of Mexico's northern frontier. The influence of the landscape, the geography, the climate, and the nature and culture of the inhabitants gave that literature a tonality different from that found in the literature of central Mexico. What is today the Southwest was a region almost isolated from the seat of government in the Mexican capital, and therefore developed its own frontier culture, molded by daily conflicts with the native peoples. The settlers of what are now the borderlands, from the very beginning, developed different attitudes and a different sense of place from that of the inhabitants of other regions of Mexico. With the passing of time, a distinct literary tradition was formed, which has been preserved uninterrupted to this day.

The culture of the Hispanic period (1542–1821) contributed important elements in determining the nature of contemporary Chicano life. It was during that early period that Spanish/Mexican culture was firmly established in the Southwest, with the introduction of the Spanish language, the Catholic religion with the mission system, the political and military (*presidio*) systems, Spanish laws, agriculture and mining. Of course, poetry and the chronicle were also introduced into the Southwest during the sixteenth century by explorers, friars, and secular writers such as Alvar Núñez Cabeza de Vaca (1490?–1559?), Fray Marcos de Niza (?–1558), Gaspar Pérez de Villagrá (1555–1620), Alonso de León (1590–1661), Juan Bautista de Anza (1734–1788), Fray Junípero Serra (1713–1784), and many others. At the same time, the settlers brought with them their *romances*, *pastorelas*, *villancicos*, and other forms of popular literature which they had learned in their places of origin in Mexico – most of them brought there from Spain, although some were of native origin.

Núñez Cabeza de Vaca's *Naufragios* (1542) [*Castaways*] is a narrative which reads very much like a novel of adventures. This is an important work for being the first in which the landscape and nature of the region, as well as the life and customs of the native inhabitants, are described. It is a narrative told from the perspective of a participant in the march across the continent from Florida to Mexico by four survivors of a tragic shipwreck. Some of Cabeza de Vaca's allusions to large communities in the Southwest were associated with the fabled Seven Cities. In turn, these remarks motivated later expeditions by others, and finally led to the colonization of the Southwest.

In his *Relación* (1539), Fray Marcos de Niza also makes reference to the Seven Cities, in highly hyperbolic terms. His description of one of them, Cíbola, presents it as a city rich in gold, precious stones, and natural resources, and with a population larger than that of Mexico City. Niza's depiction of Cíbola incited the greed of the viceroyal authorities, as well as that of other explorers. Of importance to the contemporary Chicanos is Niza's association of communities in New Mexico with the European myth of the Seven Cities, since Aztecs considered a place having seven caves – called Chicomostoc or Aztlán – as their place of origin. This myth of Aztlán, resurrected more recently by the Chicanos, provided a rallying point for the social movement of the 1960s as well as the consequent rebirth of Chicano literature, as we shall see.

The myth of the Seven Cities became a *topos* of this literature and was also retold by Gaspar Pérez de Villagrá, the author of the epic poem *Historia de la Nueva México* (1610) [*History of New Mexico*]. He believed that Aztlán was located in New Mexico, the region explored and conquered in 1598 by Juan de Oñate, in whose army Villagrá held the rank of *procurador general*. "It is well known in fact," he wrote, "that the ancient Mexican races, who in ages past founded Mexico City, came from these regions. They gave the city their name that their memory might be eternal and imperishable, imitating in this the immortal Romulus who first raised the walls of ancient Rome" (1933: 42). Villagrá's poem, in thirty-four cantos of hendecasyllabic verse and one prose passage, is not the history of the Aztecs, but a detailed account of Oñate's expedition. In spite of the poetic form, Villagrá's work is a simple narrative in verse with occasional lyrical passages, especially at the beginning of each canto. It is important in the literary history of the Southwest because it describes the landscape of New Mexico and gives information about its people, thus creating one of the first literary images of the region. Of importance also is Villagrá's account of the staging, in 1598, of a play by Marcos Farfán de los Godos, the first theatrical presentation in the Southwest. "The governor [Oñate] then ordered a large chapel built under a grove of shady trees. Here the priests celebrated a solemn high Mass, after which the learned commissary preached an excellent sermon. Then some of the soldiers enacted a drama written by Captain Farfán. This drama pictured the advent of the friars to New Mexico" (p. 129). In the last eight cantos of his poem, Villagrá relates the fall of Acoma, a description praised by Mabel Major in her book *Southwest Heritage* (1938), with these words: "It is annoying to find American history and letters continually described as a style tradition with its genesis in the Mayflower and the Bay Psalm Book... Villagrá's account of the heroic capture of Acoma by Zaldívar and seventy men bears comparison with the scaling of the heights outside Quebec by Wolfe if one keeps all of the circumstances in mind" (p. 33). Like the epic poem, *La Araucana* (1569, 1578, 1589) by Alonso de Ercilla (1533–1594), considered by many critics to be the antecedent of later Chilean literature, Villagrá's poem represents the precursor of that of New Mexico.

Villagrá's poem, like all other works written before 1848 by the Spanish-speaking inhabitants of the Southwest, has something that identifies it as belonging to the early literature of the region: he contemplated and described a new world never before seen by European eyes. All authors writing at the time in the area described the landscape and gave an account of the native populations, as well as the cultural changes experienced by the explorers and settlers themselves in their confrontation with this new environment. What the Chicano critic Philip D.

Ortego says about New World literatures in general applies perfectly well to the early literature of the Southwest: "In the New World, Spanish literature underwent a unique metamorphosis, integrating alien elements which were to herald a distinct kind of New World literature" ("Chicano Poetry: Roots and Writers," 3). Indigenous elements are found not only in Villagrá's poem, but also in the *Memorial. . .* (1630) of Fray Alonso de Benavides, in which he describes the culture of the Indians of Texas; in the early ethnographic work of Fray Gerónimo Boscana (1776–1831), *Chinigchinich* (1831), about the Indians in the San Diego mission in California; and in the drama *Los comanches*, written between 1774 and 1778 by an unknown soldier, in which the hero, the Comanche chief Cuerno Verde, is presented as proud, brave, dauntless, and aware of his exalted position:

> Yo soy aquel capitán,
> no capitán, poco he dicho.
> De todos soy gran señor.
> (A. L. Campa, "*Los Comanches*,
>   New Mexico Folk Drama," 28)

> [I'm that captain,
> nay, not captain, but more.
> Of all the people I'm the lord.]

By the time of the Mexican Wars of Independence (1810–1821), and due to the neglect of the northern provinces by the central government, the inhabitants of the borderlands had attained a high degree of self-sufficiency. Therefore, a desire for the establishment of an independent political entity became prevalent. As early as 1813, Bernardo Gutiérrez de Lara declared Texas an independent state. However, he did not succeed in his effort, as he was soon defeated by the Spanish armies. However, the sentiment did not disappear, and by 1836 several Mexicans favored the idea of declaring Texas independent from the Mexican republic. Three prominent Mexicans from Texas, among them the writer Lorenzo de Zavala (1788–1836), author of the books *Ensayos. . .* (1831) and *Viaje a los Estados Unidos de Norteamérica* (1834), attended the convention in Washington where the independence of Texas was made a reality on March 22, 1836. Zavala became the first vice-president of the new republic.

By that time the inhabitants of the Southwest were already calling themselves Texans, Californios, and Nuevomexicanos, recognizing that – as in Latin America – different socio-geographic areas had developed differently from a cultural point of view. Rivalries between Texas and neighboring Mexican territories were frequent. This is reflected in the play *Los tejanos* [The Texans], an anonymous New Mexican folk drama written soon after 1841. In that year a Texan expedition, under the leadership of General Hugh McLeod, tried to expand their territory into New Mexico, but was defeated by General Manuel Armijo. The manuscript of the play was found by Professor Aurelio M. Espinosa, in 1931, in the New Mexican town of Chimayó. Since the front page was missing Espinosa gave it the title of *Los tejanos*, and translated it. Of the four characters in the play, McLeod is the only North American; the others are Navarro (McLeod's lieutenant), the New Mexican Don Jorge, and an Indian from Pecos. According to Espinosa, the Indian is "a dramatic character worthy of the play of a master... [He] is so well defined and the story he tells is on the whole so true, however, that we can not dismiss him summarily from the historical scene" (*"The Texans,"* 301). The Indian is presented as a talented fellow, capable of deceiving Navarro and General McLeod and leading them into a trap, where they are made prisoners by Don Jorge. The rivalry between the Republic of Texas and New Mexico, still a part of Mexico when the play was written, is the central theme of this short play.

Mexico was not able to defend the rest of its northern territories, which were lost as a result of the Mexican American War (1846–1848). According to the Treaty of Guadalupe Hidalgo, Mexicans in the "ceded" territories could remain in their lands and become full American citizens or go south to Mexico. Most of them decided to stay, thus creating an ethnic group whose writings mark the beginning of Chicano literature. Due to their isolation from Mexico, they soon began to lose touch with their traditional culture, and especially with the language of their ancestors, since instruction in the schools was in English. There were, of course, conflicts between the two cultures now present in the area, a fact that is reflected in the verses of the New Mexican Jesús María Alarid, who wrote in 1889:

> Hermoso idioma español
> ¿que te quieren proscribir?
> Yo creo que no hay razón
> que tú dejes de existir
> (A. F. Arellano, *Los pobladores
> nuevo mexicanos y su poesía*, 37)

> [Beautiful Spanish language
> do they want to banish you?
> There is, of course, no reason,
> Why you should not exist]

He ended the poem – while discussing the situation of Mexican teachers – with one of the first documented calls for bilingualism:

> pues es de gran interés
> que el inglés y el castellano

ambos reinen a la vez
en el suelo americano.
(Arellano, 37)

[because it is of great interest
that both English and Spanish
prevail one next to the other
in the American homeland.]

Literature written in English did not appear until the second generation of Mexican Americans. Writers from this generation, in general, had been educated in universities outside the Southwest. The influential Otero family could be an example of this. Miguel Antonio Otero (1829–1882) was a professor of classical languages at Fishkill College on the Hudson from 1847 to 1849. His son, Miguel Antonio Otero (1859–1944), during his late years wrote and published his memoirs, two volumes under the title *My Life on the Frontier* (1935, 1939), and a third entitled *My Nine Years as Governor of the Territory of New Mexico, 1897–1906* (1940). In the first volume of the trilogy the presence of folk heroes predominates. There we find interesting accounts of Buffalo Bill, Wild Bill Hicock, and Billy the Kid. To the latter, Otero dedicated an entire book, *The Real Billy the Kid* (1936). In spite of Otero's claim that he confines himself to actual happenings in all of his books, some of the events he narrates are often embellished by his imagination. In any case, although he was not an intellectual but rather a political leader, Otero was able to write an autobiography which is a worthy contribution to the early Mexican American literature written in English. His trilogy remains one of the most important sources of information about life in the Southwest during a critical period: that of the so-called Wild West, when the territories acquired from Mexico were being transformed into rich agricultural states.

In California, María Amparo Ruiz de Burton (1832–1895) published *The Squatter and the Don: A Novel Descriptive of Contemporary Occurrences in California* (1885) under the pseudonym C. Loyal. It is a most interesting narration of the struggle for survival of a Californio family (the Alamares) after the occupation of their land by squatters. In spite of its being centered on the plot of an almost impossible love between the son of "the Squatter" and the daughter of "the Don" of the title, Burton's novel represents an early example of protest literature. Numerous digressions of the main plot deal with the injustices of the legal system of California at that time, the dangerous stereotyping of "Spano-Americans" (as the narrator chooses to call the Alamares), the brutal economic transformation of the state that ended the prosperity of wealthy Californios, and a number of other issues of interest for the study of interethnic relationships. Highly self-reflective, Burton's novel also includes numerous metaliterary digressions that provide a guide for its readers. It is only by paying careful attention to these passages that the meaning of the novel can be fully grasped.

Among the intellectuals of the period who continued to write in Spanish, we could mention the following, all of them from New Mexico: Eusebio Chacón (1870–1948), the author of an unpublished history of the discovery and conquest of New Mexico, and of the novels *El hijo de la tempestad* and *Tras la tormenta la calma* (both published in 1892); Manuel C. de Baca (1853–1915), author of the novel *Vicente Silva y sus cuarenta bandidos* (1896); the poet and novelist Manuel M. Salazar (1854–1900), author of the novel *La historia de un caminante, o sea Gervacio y Aurora* (1881), as well as of two unpublished collections of poetry; and Felipe Maximiliano Chacón (1873–?), author of the novella *Eustacio y Carlota* (n.d.).

By the end of the century, Mexican culture was receding in the Southwest; and so was the public use of Spanish. However, the events of the first two decades of the twentieth century came to reverse the course of history. The Mexican Revolution of 1910–1920, the agricultural and industrial expansion of the Southwest by those dates, and the war efforts during the First World War resulted in a massive immigration from Mexico. This exodus brought not only the much-needed farm-hands and industrial workers, but also new blood to the Mexican community as well as a revitalization of the culture of the *barrios*. In the field of literature, the influence of Mexican writers such as Ricardo Flores Magón (1873–1922), José Vasconcelos (1882–1959), Martín Luis Guzmán (1877–1976), Mariano Azuela (1873–1952), and other exiled Revolutionaries gave impetus to the rebirth of the Spanish language. Some of these writers founded newspapers and editorial houses. The most influential newspapers were those owned by the Lozano family, who founded *La Prensa* in San Antonio, Texas, in 1913, and *La Opinión* in Los Angeles, California, in 1926. The many literary contributions to these and other newspapers constituted a veritable outburst of literary activity among Mexican Americans. Unfortunately, this period has not been sufficiently documented, primarily due to the lack of accessible materials. There are, nonetheless, a number of recent publications that give us access to some of the most influential newspapers of the time. In 1976, Anselmo Arellano reprinted a collection of poems that had appeared in New Mexico's Spanish-language newspapers from 1889 to 1959 with the title *Los pobladores nuevo mexicanos y su poesía, 1889–1959*; in 1982, Juan Rodríguez edited a collection of satirical sketches by Julio G. Arce ("Jorge Ulica", 1870–?), *Crónicas diabólicas*, first published in periodicals of the San Francisco bay area between 1916 and 1926. Finally, in 1984, Nicolás Kanellos edited the novel *Las aventuras de don Chipote o: cuando los pericos mamen* by Daniel Venegas (?), a satirical piece first published by the newspaper *El Heraldo de México* (Los Angeles, California) in 1928. As noted in the introduction by its editor, this is one of the first works in which the narrator adopts an unmistakable working-class perspective, thus anticipating what will become a popular attitude among contemporary Chicano authors. In spite of these publications, there are still many other authors whose texts have not been made available to a wider readership.

The period that spans from the early 1930s – when thousands of Mexicans were deported following the Great Depression – until 1945 is characterized by the preference that Chicano writers gave, once again, to English. Typical of this trend was the poetry and prose of Fray Angélico Chávez (b. 1910), in which religious themes predominate. His most important collections of poems are *Clothed With the Sun* (1939) and *Eleven Lady Lyrics and Other Poems* (1945). Among his prose narratives, worthy of mention are the short stories *New Mexico Triptych* (1940), and the historical novella *La Conquistadora* (1949), in which the narrator is a sculpture of the Virgin Mary brought to New Mexico by the first Spanish settlers.

Another important author of this period was María Cristina Mena (1892–?). She signed her works as Chambers, the name of her husband (Henry Kellet Chambers), a dramatic author and journalist who was editor of the *Literary Digest* from 1920 to 1935. María Cristina wrote a series of five novels, most of them set in Mexico, as were also her numerous stories published in the *Century Illustrated Monthly Magazine*, the *American Magazine*, and *Cosmopolitan*. Her purpose seems to have been to acquaint the young Anglo-American reader with Mexican culture. Two of her most successful novels were *The Water-Carrier's Secrets* (1942), and *The Bullfighter's Son* (1944).

Also set in Mexico were most of the works by Josephina Niggli (b. 1911) who, like Mena, was born in Mexico. She later came to San Antonio, Texas, where she studied at the College of the Incarnate Word, and soon published her first book of poems, *Mexican Silhouettes* (1931). Desiring to continue her studies, she went to Chapel Hill to study drama at the University of North Carolina. In 1938 she published *Mexican Folk Plays*, in 1945 her first novel, *Mexican Village*, and in 1947 a second one, *Step Down, Big Brother*, all of them having a Mexican background. Drawing on her experience as a playwright and teacher of drama, she gave advice to aspiring dramatists in her book *Pointers on Playwriting* (1945).

Toward the end of the 1940s Mario Suárez (b. 1925) wrote several short stories, published in the *Arizona Quarterly*, in which he portrays the people of the *barrios* in Tucson, Arizona. Having an excellent understanding of the psychology of the Chicano/Mexicano people, he was able to create memorable characters like Señor Garza, for whom one of his best-known stories is named. "Señor Garza" (1947), deals with a barber whose personality is revealed through his conversations with *barrio* people who visit his shop. Although he wrote in English, Suárez followed the tradition of the Mexican writers who published in the Spanish-language newspapers of the largest cities in the Southwest. In particular, his stories are related to their *crónicas dominicales*, humorous narrative sketches in which all social classes were satirized. The main difference between Suárez and the Sunday *cronistas* is to be found in the attitude of the narrator toward the Chicanos. While earlier satirists, like the afore-mentioned Jorge Ulica, present the Chicanos in an unfavorable light, criticizing the way they speak Spanish and other traits that differentiate them from Mexican nationals, Suárez – having been born in Arizona – presents his Chicano characters favorably. Chicanos in Suárez's stories are not ashamed of their origin, many reject Americanization, and they are not uprooted, since they consider the Southwest – and not Mexico – to be the home of their ancestors.

The stories written by Suárez, which have not been collected, represent a transition between the early *cronistas* and such writers of the 1970s as Rolando R. Hinojosa-Smith (b. 1929). In that transition, the names of a few other writers should also be mentioned. In particular, Fabiola Cabeza de Vaca (1898–1990) and Sabine R. Ulibarrí (b. 1919) – both from New Mexico – distinguish themselves in their attempts to portray the fast-disappearing way of life that they came to know as children and adolescents. Fabiola Cabeza de Vaca is the author of *We Fed Them Cactus* (1954), which is an account of life in the New Mexican *llano*, with a high dose of autobiography interspersed. Ulibarrí, on the other hand, is best known for several collections of short stories, most of them set in his native Tierra Amarilla county. Closer to *costumbrismo*, his stories are usually retrospective narratives that depict the customs, ways, and folklore of the people of northern New Mexico. Among his many books, mention could be made of *Tierra Amarilla: cuentos de Nuevo México/Tierra amarilla: Stories of New Mexico* (1964), *Mi abuela fumaba puros/My Grandma Smoked Cigars* (1977), *Primeros encuentros/First Encounters* (1982), and the most recent *El cóndor and Other Stories* (1990). Ulibarrí, furthermore, is the only one in this group that writes in Spanish. Most authors, during the decade of the 1950s and in the early 1960s, continued using English in their writings.

Two major works that stand out during this period, announcing what will shortly become a new consciousness among Chicano writers and scholars, are the seminal study, *With His Pistol in His Hand* (1958), by Américo Paredes (b. 1915), and the novel *Pocho* (1959), by José Antonio Villarreal (b. 1924). In his book, Paredes reconstructs the legends that the people of the border have created about Gregorio Cortez. Cortez became a folk hero of the lower Río Grande Valley in Texas when, in 1901, he singlehandedly defied the Texas Rangers. Paredes then compares those legends with the biography of Cortez and, finally, he makes a thorough study of the several variants of the *corrido* written to celebrate Gregorio's daring adventure. *Corridos*, one of the most important forms of the oral tradition in the Southwest and Mexico, are a particular type of ballad that celebrates local heroes, historical events of importance for the community, and the like. In analyzing this particular *corrido*, Paredes presents a theory regarding the origin of the Border ballads, contending that they are the product of the cultural conflicts that resulted after Texas – then Nuevo Santander – was taken over by the Anglo-American settlers. No less important is the fact that his book is the first from a Mexican American scholar to document the life of a Chicano. It has served as a model for many other writers and students of Chicano culture.

Villarreal's novel, *Pocho*, is often considered the first modern Chicano novel. It is a work made significant by the nature of its hero, Richard, who finds himself torn between two cultures: that of his father – a Mexican revolutionary follower of Francisco Villa, who finds refuge in the United States after the defeat of the *villistas* – and that of his friends in the United States. Of similar importance in the novel is the description of internal conflicts in Richard's family as the new values its members learn in the United States challenge those that they brought from Mexico. The rebellious attitude of Richard's sister toward their subservient role is indicative of this process of cultural change.

The publication of *Pocho* by Doubleday also represents the starting point of the first serious attempt to launch commercially the literature written by Chicanos in the United States. Soon after, in 1963, Grove published the very successful *City of Night*, by John Rechy (b. 1934), followed by *Numbers* (1968), *This Day's Death* (1969), *Rushes* (1972), and *The Vampires* (1972), all by the same author. In spite of Rechy's undeniable artistry, the fact that he did not emphasize his characters' ethnicity but rather their unorthodox – in the context of Chicano culture of the time – sexual preference, provoked a silence among Chicano critics that has still to be fully broken. In addition to those titles mentioned, Rechy has also published *The Fourth Angel, Bodies and Souls, Marilyn's Daughter*, and *The Miraculous Day of Amalia Gómez*. Also in the 1960s, Grove published the first two works by Floyd Salas (b. 1931): *Tattoo the Wicked Cross* (1967), and *What Now, My Love* (1969). In 1970, Doubleday published *Chicano*, the best-known of the three novels by Richard Vásquez (b. 1928); and in 1974, the same press produced Villarreal's second novel: *The Fifth Horseman* (1974). That, and Bantam's issuing of *Macho!* (1973) by Edmundo Villaseñor (b. 1940), culminate this wave of

Chicano books in mainstream presses. With the exception of *Pocho* and *City of Night*, most of these works have not resisted the passage of time, as many have seen them flawed by a quasi-stereotypical portrayal of Chicanos, and as they failed to consolidate an impulse toward self-representation and cultural control, which several newly created presses attempted from the early 1970s.

If the action of *Pocho* ended during the early 1940s, when the melting-pot model for understanding ethnic relations was very much in vogue, twenty years later, as a result of the Civil Rights movement, student protests, efforts on the part of César Chávez to organize the *campesinos*, and for other reasons, Chicanos for the first time in their history were able to unite under the banner of "La causa," a powerful nationalistic movement which was noticeable in all regions of the United States. As a result of this new social consciousness, a new type of literature emerged, animated by a rebellious spirit. Characteristic of this new writing was the search for native roots in the Indian past of Mexico, as well as the use of both English and Spanish in the same work, often in a same sentence, thus creating a literary discourse that would reflect the speech patterns of the Chicano population.

This period, usually referred to as the "Chicano Renaissance" or the "*Florecimiento* [Flowering] Chicano," has a more or less precise starting point in 1965 when Luis Valdez (b. 1940), in his efforts to help Chávez and the farmworkers, organized the Teatro Campesino and staged short plays which he called *actos*. These plays were presented in the open fields, where the *campesinos* worked, often in the midst of a *huelga* [strike]. His topics were first inspired by the problems faced by the farmworkers; later he began to make use of historical subject matter, such as the conquest of Mexico by the Spaniards, in order to show the farmworkers the necessity to organize in order to present a united front. In all cases, the *actos* sought to inspire the audience toward social action by raising consciousness and explaining certain abuses on stage. Their aesthetics, always inspired by Chicano popular culture, also borrowed freely from *commedia dell'arte*, agitprop theatre, *teatro de carpa y variedades*, as well as many other sources. Two of the most successful *actos* were "Los vendidos" (1967) and "Soldado razo" (*sic*) (1971). The first is a satire of the Chicanos who live in the city and sell their brothers for the benefit of their employers; in the second play a young Chicano, urged by his father's extreme form of *machismo*, gives his life in Vietnam for a worthless cause. Inspired by the success of the Teatro Campesino, numerous other theatre groups appeared. The most important of them was the Teatro de la Esperanza, organized by critic and director Jorge Huerta in 1971. One of its most notable plays has been "La víctima," which deals with the devastating effects of the economic depression of the 1930s upon the Chicano/

Mexicano communities. Thousands of people were deported to Mexico, sometimes separating families, as depicted in the play. In that same year of 1971, all Chicano theatrical groups united and organized TENAZ (Teatro National de Aztlán), a national organization that coordinated their activities and organized many successful annual festivals, one of them in Mexico City. Most companies (including the Teatro Campesino and the Teatro de la Esperanza) emphasized collective creation of their plays. In fact, Chicano playwrights have been relatively scarce until recently, although the following could still be mentioned: Nephtalí de León (b. 1945) (*Five Plays*, 1972), Fausto Avendaño (b. 1941) (*El corrido de California*, 1979), Alfonso C. Hernández (b. 1938) (*The False Advent of Mary's Child*, 1979), Carlos Morton (b. 1942) (*The Many Deaths of Danny Rosales*, 1983), Estela Portillo Trambley (b. 1936) (*Sor Juana and Other Plays*, 1983), Cherríe Moraga (b. 1952) (*Giving Up the Ghost*, 1986), and others who have published their plays in several collective anthologies or in journals.

The late 1960s also witnessed the foundation of many journals and periodicals that would devote themselves to promoting and disseminating Chicano literature and thought. Three of the earliest, *El Grito* (1967–1974), *Con Safos* (1968–1972), and *Aztlán* (launched in 1970), provided a much-needed forum for creative writing, as well as for social and political analysis of contemporary realities. Of the three, only *Aztlán* is still being published (after a silence of several years), and has been joined by the *Americas Review* (formerly *Revista Chicano-Riqueña*, 1973), *The Bilingual Review/La Revista Bilingüe* (1974), and countless others, among them the disappeared *De Colores* (1973), *Mango* (1976), *Maize* (1977), and *La Palabra* (1979, which devoted itself to literature in Spanish). Yet, by far, the most influential editorial movement of the time was the establishment of the Quinto Sol literary prizes, awarded by the press of the same name. In a promotional effort, at times reminiscent of the Latin American *Boom*, the prize led to the discovery and consolidation of four important writers: Tomás Rivera (1935–1984), Rudolfo Anaya (b. 1937), Rolando Hinojosa-Smith, and Estela Portillo Trambley. Quinto Sol, which was the publisher of the journal *El Grito*, and of the early anthology *El Espejo/The Mirror* (1969), had a clearly defined agenda that included the desire to eradicate stereotypes, the need to promote bilingual publications, and the necessity of having the publication of Chicano books controlled by Chicanos.

Tomás Rivera's most important work is his novel "*. . .y no se lo tragó la tierra*"/"*. . .and the Earth Did not Part*" (1971), the first recipient of the Quinto Sol Prize (in 1970). In a sequence of twelve episodes – preceded by a short prose, "El año perdido" ["The Lost Year"], and followed by a final chapter, "Debajo de la casa" ["Under the House"] – the novel depicts life among migrant Chicano workers from Texas as seen through the eyes of a young boy. Each one of the twelve episodes is introduced by a short vignette whose purpose is to set the tone of the anecdotes; in the prose at the end of the novel the young narrator, under a house, recapitulates the events that took place during the "lost year" with which the novel opens, thus uniting the twelve episodes that make up the core of the work. *Tierra* has been praised for its innovative narrative technique, for its terse style, and for the true-to-life description of the hardships and tribulations of the migrant workers. Rivera is also the author of a collection of verse, *Always and Other Poems* (1973), as well as of several essays dealing with Chicano literature and culture. Recently, Julián Olivares has edited *Tomás Rivera: The Complete Works* (1992), which reunites all of Rivera's previously published works with some unpublished texts.

The second Quinto Sol Prize was awarded, in 1971, to Rudolfo Anaya for *Bless Me, Ultima*, which, unlike *Tierra* – written in Spanish and published with an English translation by Herminio Ríos C. in collaboration with the author – was a novel written in English which has not been translated into Spanish, in spite of its tremendous success. The work deals with life in a northern New Mexico rural area. As in Rivera's novel, the action in *Ultima* is told as experienced by a young boy, Antonio Márez, who is influenced by Ultima's beliefs about life and the supernatural. As a *curandera* [woman healer], Ultima has the necessary wisdom to help Antonio mature. The novel ends with her death, but by that time Antonio has been able to absorb her wisdom. This central narrative thread is given depth by placing it in the context of the Márez family, as well as of Antonio's relations with the youth of the community and its rural environment. In its tone *Ultima* is not too far removed from the magical realism of such Latin American writers as Gabriel García Márquez (b. 1928) and Isabel Allende (b. 1942), also sharing with several Latin American authors a perception of landscape – Southwestern landscape, in this case – as a key to the primeval American world. Other fiction works by Anaya, all with a New Mexican background, are the novels *Heart of Aztlán* (1976) and *Tortuga* (1979), and the collection of short stories *The Silence of the Llano* (1982). Some of his most recent books, however, do not deal with New Mexico but with legendary Mexican topics, as *The Legend of La Llorona* (1984) and *Lord of the Dawn* (1987). He is also the author of a poetry chapbook *The Adventures of Juan Chicaspatas* (1984) and of a travel account entitled *A Chicano in China* (1986).

The third winner of the Quinto Sol Prize, Rolando Hinojosa-Smith, is the author of *Klail City Death Trip*, a series of twelve volumes depicting the daily life and adventures of people living in the fictitious Belken

County, supposedly located in the lower Río grande Valley area. The first of these novels, *Estampas del Valle y otras obras/Sketches of the Valley and Other Works*, winner of the Quinto Sol Prize in 1972, was published the following year in a bilingual edition. It was later "re-created" in English by the author – in what will become a norm for all of his works originally written in Spanish – and published under the title *The Valley* (1983). This first novel set the tone for the whole series, which is still in progress. The second book, *Klail City y sus alrededores* appeared in Havana, Cuba, in 1976 as the recipient of the Casa de las Américas Prize; it was the first occasion on which that prize was awarded to a citizen of the United States. Then followed a book of narrative poetry, *Korean Love Songs* (1980), and a series of books that experiment with different genres in an attempt to explore diverse perspectives in the portrayal of a Chicano community. This generic experimentation also amounts to an encyclopedic attempt to portray the rich heritage that a Chicano author can claim, since the genres used include those most typical of the Mexican/Hispanic tradition, as well as those associated with United States popular culture (including some inspired by television). The rest of the volumes in the *Klail City Death Trip* series are *Mi querido Rafa* (1981) (recreated as *Dear Rafe* in 1985), *Rites and Witnesses* (1982), *Partners in Crime; A Rafe Buenrostro Mystery* (1985), *Claros Varones de Belken/Fair Gentlemen of Belken* (1986), *Los amigos de Becky* (1991, recreated in English as *Becky's Friend*, which was published in 1990, before the Spanish original appeared). The series has an interesting fragmented structure due to the fact that it is presented as a collection of diverse materials brought together by several characters who undertake the task of writing the chronicle of their people by gathering as much information as they can from all the sources available. The resulting open-ended text is then presented to the reader, who must play a very active role in the final configuration of the work. To date, none of Hinojosa's books has been published by a non-Latino-based press, except for a translation to German of *Klail City y sus alrededores*. In the words of one of his critics, José D. Saldívar, Hinojosa "has remained actively committed to the literary development of an American ethnopoetics during the past fifteen years, thus becoming in the eyes of many the foremost exponent of Chicano literature" (*The Rolando Hinojosa Reader*, 44).

The fourth and last Quinto Sol Prize was awarded to Estela Portillo Trambley for her book *Rain of Scorpions and Other Writings* (1975), a collection of stories considered as the first major contribution by a Chicana to contemporary literature. The author was already well known for her play, *The Day of the Swallows* (1971), in which she created a strong character, Josefa, whose desire to keep secret her relationship with a former prostitute leads to her suicide. In recent years Portillo has written several other plays, among them one about the life of the famous seventeenth-century Mexican nun, Sor Juana Inés de la Cruz (included in her *Sor Juana and Other Plays*, 1983). She has also published a novel, *Trini* (1986), the story of a pregnant Mexican Tarascan woman who crosses the border into the United States in search of a better life for her offspring. In both the novel and the stories, Portillo Trambley tries to combine the depiction of everyday realities with a series of symbols that project her narratives onto a transcendent level of reality.

The disappearance in 1974 of Quinto Sol, split into Tonatiuh and Justa, did not lead Chicano literature into a radical change in course as the end of its pioneering role might have made some fear. The fact that other presses were already publishing at a significant pace, and that others would subsequently follow, served to channel the now solid flow of texts that were being produced. Thus, the newly created Editorial Peregrinos published two texts that could have easily been a part of the Quinto Sol program: *Peregrinos de Aztlán* (1974), by Miguel Méndez M. (b. 1930), and *El diablo en Texas* (1976), by Aristeo Brito (b. 1942). Both novels are written in Spanish and use a fragmentary technique (as did those by Rivera and Hinojosa), both adopt a tone of social protest, and they both reject previous stereotypical representations of Chicanos. They are situated in the border area between the United States and Mexico: Méndez's in California and Arizona, and Brito's in the Texas area. Finally, they also share an almost expressionistic tendency to distort reality by creating degraded worlds. In the case of Brito's novel this is less evident, but it occurs in passages in which the devil is the main character, as well as in others where dead characters get together to talk about their lives, in a situation reminiscent of *Pedro Páramo* (1955) by Juan Rulfo (1918–1986). As for Méndez, his novel is closer to the grotesque tradition of Valle-Inclán (1866–1936) and, particularly, to that of Luis Martín Santos (1924–1964). *Peregrinos de Aztlán* deals with the fate of the Yaqui people, who were driven from their homeland in northern Mexico and forced to lead a pariah-like life in the border cities or else to work as peons in the fields of Arizona and California. This novel stands out for its use of colloquial language in its many dialogues, as well as for a skillful manipulation of mythical elements to structure the plot. As opposed to Brito, who has not published any major works after *El diablo en Texas*, Méndez is the author of several collections of short stories and novels, as well as a book of allegorical poetry (*Los criaderos humanos: épica de los desamparados y Sahuaros*, 1975). Many of his stories are inspired by the oral tradition of the Southwest, but others have written sources as old as *Calila and Dimna* (1251). One of his best-known stories is "Tata Casehua." The story is in line with the neoindigenist trend – which we shall soon discuss in detail. Its protagonist is a Yaqui Indian, whose life and death are monuments to his people's endurance and pride. More recently, Méndez has published a second novel, *El sueño de Santa María de las piedras* (1986), in Spanish as are all of his writings. This novel is centered around the memories of a group of elders who get together in the fictional town of Santa María de las Piedras to remember how things were and who people are. It is greatly influenced by Latin American Magical Realism, although Méndez's own voice – particularly his ability to recreate an oral culture in monologues and dialogues – is not lost.

Also from the mid-1970s are two novels that somehow depart from what contemporary Chicano literature had been up to that point, and that announce an imminent expansion of subjects, styles, and voices. We are talking about *The Road to Tamazunchale* (1975), by Ron Arias (b. 1941), and *Caras viejas y vino nuevo* (1975) [*Old Faces and New Wine*], by Alejandro Morales (b. 1944). Arias's text is a radical departure from the previously predominant epistemological obsession showed by Chicano authors. Thus, his novel does not deal with how to understand reality, nor with how to reconstruct history from a Chicano point of view or how to create order out of chaos. Arias's is an ontological novel, in the sense that Brian McHale describes these in *Postmodernist Fiction* (1987): thus, what counts in *The Road to Tamazunchale* is its main character's ability to create – and not interpret – a world or, rather, many different worlds. For that, Arias baptizes his protagonist as Fausto Tejada, a name that immediately recalls two of his most illustrious predecessors: Faustus and Don Quixote. Fantasy is of utmost importance for this text that has also been affiliated with Magical Realism (although it could as easily be placed in the context of the United States' Postmodernism). The wanderings of Fausto, usually in the company of Mario (a *pachuco*-like character) or Marcelino (a Peruvian sheep-herder who suddenly appears on a Los Angeles freeway with his alpacas), take him from an anachronistic colonial Peru to present-day Mexico and the United States; not to mention a number of impossible places in between (like Tamazunchale), some of which belong to different artistic realms (theatre, cinema, and television).

In Morales's case, *Caras viejas y vino nuevo* is also set in an urban atmosphere. Yet, while the novel by Arias departs from everyday reality through fantasy, Morales presents us *barrio* life as if seen through a refracting glass. It is a novel close to *tremendismo* in its strong themes and somewhat imperturbable narrator(s). The presentation systematically distorts reality, be it through a reverse ordering of the plot, through a pervasive use of animalization and reification, or through a very restrictive focalization that reduces people to just parts of their bodies (legs, breasts, etc). In his following novel, *La verdad sin voz* (1979) [*Death of an Anglo*], Morales makes Dr. Logan – an Anglo idealist – the hero and, at the end, the victim of those who resent his helping impoverished Chicano patients. The novel has also several subplots, one of them dealing with the character Profe Morenito's writing of Dr. Logan's story. Morales's third novel, *Reto en el paraíso* (1983) represents one of the most ambitious undertakings in the rewriting of history by Chicano authors. It chronicles the disenfranchisement of Chicanos in California, and the loss of their land grants which began in 1848. The historical dimension of the novel is enriched by the treatment of related topics, such as the problem of identity – explored mainly in symbolic and psychological terms – or that of the social relations between Anglos and Mexicans. In its development, the novel is quite complex due to its fragmented structure, time displacements, and the alternation of English and Spanish. His latest novel, *The Brick People* (1988), returns to the setting of *Caras viejas y vino nuevo*; but what in the latter was apocalyptic, becomes in the former genesis, since *The Brick People* chronicles the foundation of the brick factory and the utopian town intended for its workers, that later in time would become the alienated *barrio* of his first novel. All four of Morales's works are connected by certain repetitions, be it of characters, of settings, or themes, but they are not as integrated as to conform a series, such as that by Hinojosa.

To close our discussion of narrative prose in the 1970s, we have reserved a group of works that are on the boundaries between autobiography and the novel (particularly of the *Bildungsroman* type). One of them, the autobiography *Barrio Boy* (1971) by Ernesto Galarza (1905–1984), contains sufficient novelistic elements to make any classification of the work problematic. It follows the novelistic pattern wherein the protagonist undertakes a journey from Mexico to the United States, either alone or accompanied by his family (as in this case). The initial cultural shock and the process of assimilation are thoroughly documented. Galarza's depiction of this journey is one of the most vivid, from his recreation of life in a remote Mexican village to the observation of life in a series of cities along the way.

If Galarza's text is a fictionalized autobiography, *The Autobiography of a Brown Buffalo* (1972) and *The Revolt of the Cockroach People* (1973), by Oscar Zeta Acosta (1936–?), could be described as autobiographical novels, since fictionalized elements are pervasively interspersed in them with others from the author's life. Both texts are also associated with the journey motif, particularly *The Autobiography of a Brown Buffalo*, but in this case through the filter of the Beat generation. The first volume is a trip (geographically and otherwise) undertaken by its main character in search of himself, while the second is mainly a very unorthodox account of the early years of the Chicano movement, focusing on its main character's participation in it. The question of the subject and, in particular, of the subject who writes (be it his autobiography or the history of his community) becomes a major *topos* for Acosta's texts, as it did for much of the Chicano fiction that we have reviewed; many authors seem to find a need to account for their own coming to terms with writing. Later autobiographical works include *Mi lucha por la tierra* (1978) by Reies López Tijerina (b. 1926), which chronicles the main events of the author's involvement with the Alianza Federal de Mercedes, and *Hunger of Memory* (1981) by Richard Rodríguez (b. 1944), a better-known text, probably due to its polemical ideological position vis-à-vis most other Chicano texts. Written in an often praised style, Rodríguez's text introduced topics and attitudes opposed to those defended by other writers, such as bilingual education, affirmative action, and the public use of the Spanish language, all of which Rodríguez strongly opposes.

The poetry of the late 1960s and early 1970s was clearly characterized by a tone of urgency. A militant tone, counterbalanced sometimes by a desire to recreate collective feelings of pride and brotherhood, was the most easily detectable feature of most poems. Together with an unsurpassed richness in language (poets used English and Spanish – often in the same poem – incorporating at times *caló* – *pachuco* slang – and terms from pre-Hispanic languages), this poetry stands out for its ability to address and reach a non-traditional audience. Although many were published, poems were often conceived for public declamation in community and academic gatherings. In fact, as noted by Cordelia Candelaria in her *Chicano Poetry* (1986), many poems of this era are based upon conventions of oral poetry; thus, marked rhythms, repetitions, clearly demarcated rhymes, and the like, are used to secure an adequate reception in readings. In fact, some poems, like the well-known "Letanía en caló" (1976) by José Antonio Burciaga (b. 1940), require a responsive audience to serve as a chorus in a rosary-like fashion. In others, such as "Stupid America" by Abelardo Delgado (b. 1931) – one of the most widely anthologized poems of these times – a parallelistic construction serves as a base for the variations on the theme of discrimination and stereotyping.

One of the earliest books of poetry published under the aegis of the Chicano movement was *I Am Joaquín* (1967), by Rodolfo "Corky" Gonzales (b. 1928), an epic poem about the complex identity of the Chicanos, which the author traces back to before the conquest of Mexico. Joaquín, the hero of the poem, asserts himself as the descendant of both the last Aztec emperor ("I Am Cuauhtémoc, / proud and noble, / leader of men" [p. 16]) and the Spanish conquerors ("I am the sword and flame of Cortés the despot" [p. 16]). Joaquín, who also identifies with Mexican popular heroes (Juárez, Villa, Zapata, Murrieta), becomes a sort of Chicano everyman, whose identification with Mexican culture was intentionally used by Gonzales in order to instill pride in the rich heritage of Mexican Americans. As a consequence of this book's notoriety, the Teatro Campesino filmed with great success a version of *I Am Joaquín* in 1969.

Somewhat in the epic vein of Gonzales's poem, *Perros y antiperros* (1972) by Sergio Elizondo (b. 1930) resembles *I Am Joaquín* in its structure, its tone, and its content. However, there is less use of symbolic materials (except for the title metaphor of dogs and antidogs), and less emphasis upon Mexican culture, both pre-Hispanic and revolutionary. Also influenced by the ideology of the Chicano movement is the poetry of José Montoya (b. 1932), collected under the title *El sol y los de abajo* (1972). His most famous poem "El Louie" is the elegy of a *pachuco* and, although Montoya's poem is not exempt from ambivalences in the portrayal of Louie, it has come to emblematize the Chicano positing of *pachucos* as cultural heroes of resistance, a trait that – with certain exceptions – continues to date.

However, where the tracing back of the roots to indigenous cultures became consolidated as a nationalistic trend of utmost importance was in the so-called neoindigenist literature of the late 1960s/early 1970s. The poet Alurista (Alberto Baltazar Urista, [b. 1947]), from the beginning of his poetic career, and the playwright Luis Valdez, when he and the Teatro Campesino turned from *actos* to *mitos*, became the leaders of this trend. The *mitos* are plays in which mythical and legendary elements – taken mostly from Aztec and Maya sources – are essential to the development of the plot. Often, Valdez combined both the *acto* and the *mito* in the same play, but not always successfully. The best example of this combination is *La gran carpa de los Rasquachi* (1973), his first full-length play, in which an *acto* deals with the life of Jesús Pelado Rasquachi, a Mexican national who has brought his family to the United States in search of the promised land, only to find discrimination and misery. With this social theme Valdez intermingled two *mitos*, in which he introduces characters from both Christian and pre-Hispanic religions. The resolution of the play is brought about by a miracle, by which the Virgin Mary saves the hero from the Devil. In 1977, in the version presented on television under the title *Corrido*, the two *mitos* were eliminated. Another *mito* by Valdez, which has been staged successfully, is *Bernabé* (1970), a play in which the village idiot (Bernabé) is in love with Mother Earth, the provider of food and life. The presence of pre-Hispanic gods and allegorical characters (the Sun, the Moon, the Earth) are in this play better adapted to the central theme than in other *mitos*. One of the allegorical figures, the Moon, appears as a *pachuco*, a character later made popular by Valdez in his play and film, *Zoot Suit* (1978). While gaining him national recognition, *Zoot Suit* elicited some controversy about Valdez's move from grassroot circles to Broadway and, later, Hollywood (with his acclaimed film *La Bamba*, about the Chicano rock star Ritchie Valens).

Chicano literature

As for Alurista, he is credited as the first to use consistently a blending of English and Spanish in contemporary poetry. He is also credited with authorship of "El Plan Espiritual de Aztlán" ["The Spiritual Plan of Aztlán"], a manifesto that put forward the notion of Aztlán as the Chicano homeland, a very successful unifying metaphor for Chicanos that – although not completely free from controversy – promoted a sense of ethnic pride in the indigenous ancestors while reinvigorating the idea of the Southwest as "occupied America" (a notion fully explored in the history book of that title by Rodolfo Acuña, 1972). Of course, for this nationalistic stance the new language created out of the fusion of English and Spanish represented a sort of national language that conveyed, better than any other linguistic option, the cultural *mestizaje* that had produced contemporary Chicanos. Poets like José Montoya, Juan Felipe Herrera (b. 1948), Luis Omar Salinas (b. 1937), Angela de Hoyos (b. 1940), Tino Villanueva (b. 1941), Ricardo Sánchez (b. 1941), and Bernice Zamora (b. 1938) have perfected this style, but Alurista's poetry is probably the best example of how the combination of the two languages can result in the creation of original and effective poems. At the same time, his poetry represents, better than any other, the close relationship between literature and the social movement known as "La Causa." Although he began to publish poems while he was still a university student in San Diego, California, it was not until 1971 that he became well known with his collection *Floricanto en Aztlán*, a book that marks a high point in the renaissance of Chicano poetry. In it, he created a Chicano world which combines imagery from pre-Hispanic Mexico, the Mexican Revolution of 1910–1920, and contemporary *barrio* life. This trend was continued in his second book, *Nationchild Plumaroja* (1972), in which the values of indigenous America have a prominent place. Alurista's poetry had a major impact on the social and political changes that took place among Chicanos during the late 1960s and early 1970s. Other works by Alurista include *Return: Poems Collected and New* (1982), where the autobiographical element becomes, for the first time, significantly noticeable; *Spik in Glyph?* (1981), his most daring experiment with language thus far, and *A'nque* (1979), where prose and poetry are combined. He has also published an allegorical play, *Dawn* (1974).

The second half of the 1970s brings many important changes to Chicano poetry that extend themselves into the 1980s; among them, an interiorization of poetics and a preference for individual over collective concerns. Together with an emphasis on personal styles, these poets seem to be prone to stressing in their works the differences in the many Chicano communities rather than the communal essences previously sought by others. Thus, class and gender variations begin to surface in their works, as do different conceptions of poetry. English seems to be preferred, overall, to Spanish, but bilingualism continues to be a common option. It

577

was during this period also that women writers, for the first time in large numbers, began publishing extensively and, most importantly, set out to create their own publishing outlets and literary circuits. For the first time also, literary works began to be produced by Chicano writers from the large urban areas of the Midwest, particularly Chicago.

An earlier figure, Tino Villanueva, could be exemplary of the transition from the committed poetry of the 1960s and early 1970s to that of the mid-1970s. In his first work (*Hay otra voz: Poems 1968–1971*, 1972), he already alternated between a socially oriented poetry, and a more personal impulse toward metaphysics, something occasionally seen also in the poetry of Angela de Hoyos. Villanueva's second book, *Shaking Off the Dark* (1984), resolves this duality by reconfiguring the individual in a collectivity that would not negate his own potentiality to both belong and be different. This collectivity is not just the Chicano community or the family recreated in poems such as those in the section "History I must Wake To" (from *Shaking Off the Dark*), but also the community of writers who populate his poems and whose voices Villanueva recalls – sometimes through imitation, sometimes through intertextual allusions. Jorge Guillén (1893–1984), César Vallejo (1892–1938) (quite influential also for Angela de Hoyos and other Chicano poets), Anne Sexton (1928–1974), Pablo Neruda (1904–1973), William Carlos Williams (1883–1963), and Federico García Lorca (1899–1936) are among the easily detectable presences in Villanueva's intertextual quilt. A similarly strong intertextual framework is found in Villanueva's autobiographical *Crónica de mis años peores* (1987), whose title comes from a poem by J. M. Caballero Bonald (b. 1926). In this, his latest book, Villanueva insistently deals with the poles of language and silence, of past and present, in order to chronicle his own transition from being the inarticulate child of migrant workers to becoming a poet who takes control of his own history and his own word.

However, the poet who epitomizes the changes in poetics during the 1970s is Gary Soto (b. 1952), whose influence and reputation in circles beyond the Chicano have been continuously increasing. He is the author of *The Elements of San Joaquín* (1977), and several other collections like *The Tale of Sunlight* (1978), *Where Sparrows Work Hard* (1981), *Black Hair* (1985), *Who Will Know Us?* (1990), and *Home Course in Religion* (1991). His is an imagistic poetry, centered – in his earlier works – in the recollection and observation of his *barrio* childhood and – lately – in a sort of metaphysical questioning of life triggered by everyday nimious incidents typical of a middle-class suburban existence. He has also started a series of autobiographical recollections in prose that include *Living Up the Street* (1985) and *Small Faces* (1986).

As is the case with Soto's, the poetry of Alberto Ríos (b. 1952) (*Whispering to Fool the Wind*, 1982), Bernice Zamora (*Restless Serpents*,

1976), and Lorna Dee Cervantes (b. 1954) (*Emplumada*, 1981) is centered on the imagistic recreation of reality, the exploration of the poets' own subjectivities, and the attempt to reach a wider and more diversified readership. The last two poets mentioned, besides, are in the forefront of a movement toward the engendering of the poetic subject that will become one of the major changes in the literature of the 1980s. This first group of Chicana poets also includes several who choose to write in Spanish, among them Margarita Cota-Cárdenas (b. 1941) (*Noches Despertando InConciencias*, 1977; *Marchitas de mayo*, 1989), Barbara Brinson-Pineda (1956, later Brinson-Curiel) (*Nocturno*, 1979; *Speak to Me from Dreams*, 1989), Lucha Corpi (b. 1945) (*Palabras de mediodía/Noon Words*, 1980; *Variaciones sobre una tempestad/Variations on a Storm*, 1990), Gina Valdés (*Puentes y fronteras*, 1982; *Comiendo lumbre/Eating Fire*, 1986), and Miriam Bornstein (b. 1950) (*Bajo cubierta*, 1976). As suggested by Marta E. Sánchez in her *Contemporary Chicana Poetry*, it could be said that all of them seem to find the need to negotiate their identities by somehow balancing their roles as Chicanas, women, and writers. Most are highly conscious in their poems of the novelty of this latest role, and consistently explore how their being writers affects the perceptions that others have of them.

In most cases, the poetry written by Chicanas is characterized by a fine irony that subverts traditional attitudes toward women; Margarita Cota-Cárdenas or Miriam Bornstein could be representative of this trait. Some poets are also at the forefront of an expansion of the language of Chicano poetry by venturing into the largely sidestepped vocabulary of eroticism and by a daring reclamation of their bodies and their sexualities; Ana Castillo (b. 1953) (*Otro canto*, 1977; *The Invitation*, 1979; *Women Are Not Roses*, 1984; *My Father Was a Toltec*, 1988), Alma Villanueva (b. 1944) (*Bloodroot*, 1977; *Mother, May I?* 1978; *Life Span*, 1985), and María Herrera-Sobek would probably be the best examples of this uninhibited poetry that shuns taboos and euphemisms. Some of these poets embark on a redefinition of terms and historico-mythological figures that radically re-evaluates traditions and social behavior: Tisbe, Penelope, Ariadna, Persephone now appear in poems by Alma Villanueva, Cota-Cárdenas or Brinson telling their stories from a female perspective; the figure of Malintzin/Malinche, in particular, is subject to a systematic revision after the very influential essay by Adelaida R. del Castillo "Malintzin Tenépal: A Preliminary Look into a New Perspective" (1977). She now appears not as the raped mother of the *mestizos*, as frequently portrayed by Mexican and Chicano male authors; she is no longer "la Chingada" – an object – but rather a speaking subject who takes certain decisions concerning herself and, most importantly, a mediator – "la lengua" ["the translator"] – between cultures, as noted by Norma Alarcón in her "Traddutora,

Traditora: A Paradigmatic Figure of Chicana Feminism" (1989). It will be impossible to even list the many essays, poems, and prose works recently devoted to this figure, but among them the reader may consult poems by Lucha Corpi (in *Palabras de mediodía*), Alma Villanueva (in Santiago Daydí-Tolson's *Five Poets of Aztlán*, 1985), and the essays by Gloria Anzaldúa (in *Borderlands/La Frontera*, 1987).

Poetry in the 1980s has followed almost as many paths as there have been poets. Among the most innovative voices, together with those already mentioned, we should highlight Juan Felipe Herrera and Francisco X. Alarcón (b. 1954). Herrera was a major voice in the indigenist trend of the 1970s but, in the 1980s, he has created a type of experimental poetry that approaches the visual arts in his *Exiles of Desire* (1985), *Facegames* (1987), and *Akrílica* (1989), where cinema, graphic design, and painting become necessary points of reference. Alarcón, in turn, is rapidly becoming one of the most respected poets of the 1980s. He is particularly praised for his short poems from *Tattoos* (1985), that are almost limited to the development of one single metaphor. In that sense, his poems inscribe themselves on paper like a tattoo would in somebody's flesh. His most recent *Cuerpo en llamas/Body in Flames* (1990), combines that type of poem with longer ones in which the erotic impulse encounters the political.

In narrative, the abundance and quality of the prose written by Chicanas has been the most noticeable phenomenon during the 1980s. One of the most successful writers is the Chicagoan Sandra Cisneros (b. 1954), whose *The House on Mango Street* (1984) won her an immediate reputation. In a sense, *The House on Mango Street* could be read as an engendered response to Tomás Rivera's *Tierra*, as suggested by several critics. Yet its importance goes beyond that point as it gives us a poetic rendering of social aspects previously almost unheard of in Chicano letters. Cisneros has found a very personal style by appropriating the voice of a young Chicana and following it to maturity. With her second prose book *Woman Hollering Creek* (1991), Cisneros has also joined a very small group of Chicano authors – Cecile Pineda (b. 1942), Arturo Islas (1938–1991) – that are now, once again, penetrating mainstream publication houses.

Ana Castillo's two novels (*The Mixquiahuala Letters*, 1986, and *Sapogonia*, 1990) have also established her as one of the major voices of the most recent Chicano narrative. *The Mixquiahuala Letters* is an epistolary novel, open (*à la* Cortazar) to a number of possible readings suggested by the author. It chronicles the travels (physical and imaginary) of two friends, a Chicana and an Anglo-American woman, as they embark upon a search for themselves, the perfect relationship, and a cultural experience/encounter with Mexico – the Motherland. *Sapogonia*, on the other hand, is a metaphor for the common homeland of all *mestizos*, a sort of follow-up on the idea of Aztlán with a less nationalistic connotation, possibly due to the fact that Castillo grew up in Chicago, a community where Latinos form a heterogeneous group that, to a certain degree, transcends the barriers of nationality.

Much of *The Ultraviolet Sky* (1988) by Alma Villanueva, one of several Chicana poets who, recently, have begun to write novels, is devoted to exploring the painful process of establishing an independent self, free from the constraints of motherhood and marriage – but also free to choose when and how to give birth to a new creature. Another case in point would be that of Lucha Corpi who reconstructs in her *Delia's Song* (1989) the beginning of the Chicano student protests in the Berkeley area, and the difficult position of Chicanas in that movement, being sometimes relegated to secondary roles. Other prose writers who have won praise from most critics are Denise Chávez – who is also a playwright – and Helena María Viramontes (b. 1954), who distinguish themselves for their respective *The Last of the Menu Girls* (1986), a collection of short stories that read as a novel of the coming-of-age of their protagonist, and *The Moths and Other Stories* (1985), which constructs a rich gallery of female characters in a constant struggle for affirmation against social odds as well as their own mistakes.

However, possibly, one of the most novel phenomena taking place in Chicana literature in the 1980s is the creation of a new type of books that transcend the barriers of genre to construct deliberately hybrid texts; their hybridity, in turn, becomes metaphoric of the continuous "border crossings" (as Gloria Anzaldúa would put it) that contemporary Chicanas effectuate; in particular, Chicana lesbians. At least two examples could be cited: those of Cherríe Moraga's *Loving in the War Years* (1983), and of Anzaldúa's *Borderlands/La frontera*. Both books, although different from each other in many ways, switch more or less freely from narrative, to poetry, to essays, to autobiography, in an attempt to engage in the exploration of self and society from different discursive approaches. In both cases, furthermore, the generic experimentation allows for a revindication of the personal as political, and also, is a metaphor for their explicit lesbian sexual identity. Anzaldúa and Moraga are also the editors of the most successful *This Bridge Called My Back* (1981, translated by Ana Castillo as *Esta puente mi espalda* and published, subsequently, in Latin America), which is in the forefront of efforts toward a women-of-color feminism, a movement that claims that European and Anglo-American feminism has traditionally neglected the concerns of women of color, as well as their cultural differences. It also engages in a critical debate with Latin American feminism, since many in the movement feel an important difference in class identification separating them from feminists in Latin America.

Although the prose fiction of Chicanas has been predominantly an English-language phenomenon (with the exception of short stories published in journals), there are at least two novels in Spanish that should be included in an essay like this. The first is *Puppet* (1984) by Margarita Cota-Cárdenas. It is a polyphony of languages, codes, dialects, media discourses, and all kinds of voices that converge in that of Petra Leyva, the narrator. She is trying to elucidate the circumstances of a violent death which occurred in the community. In the process, she is also reconstructing her own personal and cultural history as a Chicana and as a writer. The second text to be mentioned here is *Paletitas de Guayaba* (1991) by Erlinda Gonzáles-Berry (b. 1942), which also reconstructs critically the political, sexual, and social awakening of its protagonist as she travels south (to Mexico) in a train. It is written in an ironic style that, at times, becomes a parody of institutional discourses. The fact that the author has extensive training in linguistics is clearly noticeable in her ability to manipulate language to reflect social and regional particularities, as well as to expose hidden values associated with certain words and attitudes.

Most novels published by Chicanos have also favored English in the 1980s. In English are written even novels like *Rainbow's End* (1988), by Genaro González (b. 1949), which inserts itself in what had been an almost Spanish-only tradition of satirizing the American dream; a tradition that starts with folkloric compositions such as "La tierra de Jauja" or "El corrido del lavaplatos" and continues in novels like Daniel Venegas's *Las aventuras de don Chipote*. Also written in English were Arturo Islas's two novels: *The Rain God* (1984), and *Migrant Souls* (1990). In the first, Islas chronicles the story of several generations of the Angel family through the reflections of Miguel Chico – who is a writer, and who sets out to uncover all the hidden stories, secrets, and lies that try to conceal the less orthodox aspects of his family's life. Of particular interest are Islas's beautiful descriptions of the desert's landscape, as well as the (pre-Hispanic) mythological support of his novel. *Migrant Souls* essentially continues the saga of the Angels, by further narrating their existence at the geographical and historical juncture of two countries and cultures. Both novels show a knowledge on Islas's part of contemporary Latin American literature, from which he drew inspiration at times.

The attention that Chicano literature in general has received from 1970 to 1990 has been due, in part, to the efforts of a growing number of critics and bibliographers, most of them Chicanos, who have been able to apply the latest literary theories and critical approaches in their analysis. Scholars and critics have at hand now for the first time a series of useful monographs which provide complete and up-to-date information regarding the nature of Chicano literature. In 1979, two collections of essays appeared, that had a major impact on the development of Chicano literary criticism: *Modern Chicano Writers*, edited by Joseph Sommers and Tomás Ybarra-Frausto, and *The Identification and Analysis of Chicano Literature*, edited by Francisco Jiménez. During the 1980s Juan Bruce-Novoa collected fourteen interviews under the title *Chicano Authors: Inquiry by Interview*, followed in 1982 by his *Chicano Poetry: A Response to Chaos*. His study is mostly devoted to male authors, and was supplemented in 1985 by Marta E. Sánchez's *Contemporary Chicana Poetry*. To the same genre is devoted *Chicano Poetry: A Critical Introduction*, by Cordelia Candelaria, a survey of major trends and features. The novel has been studied by Salvador Rodríguez del Pino (*La novela chicana escrita en español*), whose work is limited to five novelists who write in Spanish, and by Marvin Lewis, who in the same year published an *Introduction to the Chicano Novel*. More recent studies on narrative include *Contemporary Chicano Fiction: A Critical Survey*, edited by Vernon E. Lattin, and *Chicano Narrative: The Dialectics of Difference*, by Ramón Saldívar, who utilizes a Marxist approach, also influenced by deconstruction. The critics who have dedicated their attention to the theatre are Jorge Huerta (*Chicano Theatre: Themes and Forms*) and Nicolás Kanellos (*Mexican American Theatre: Legacy and Reality* and *A History of Hispanic Theatre in the United States: Origins to 1940*). There are also several reference volumes, among them *Chicano Literature*, by Charles Tatum, *Chicano Literature: A Reference Guide*, edited by Julio A. Martínez and Francisco A. Lomelí, *Understanding Chicano Literature*, by Carl R. and Paula W. Shirley, and *Chicano Writers: First Series* (1989), which is volume LXXXII of the *Dictionary of Literary Biography*, and was edited by Francisco A. Lomelí and Carl R. Shirley. Important bibliographies are those by Ernestina Eger (*A Bibliography of Criticism of Contemporary Chicano Literature*), Roberto G. Trujillo and Andrés Rodríguez (*Literatura Chicana: Creative and Critical Writings Through 1984*), and the *Chicano Periodical Index*, which now comprises five volumes, under the direction of Richard Chabrán.

If we wanted to go back to our initial questions, now that we have summarized what Chicano literature has been like since its antecedents in colonial times, we could suggest that Chicano literature is, indeed, a distinct literature being constantly transformed by its position at the juncture of Anglo- and Latin America. It will be impossible to claim that it belongs exclusively to any of those two traditions – as hard as it will be, for that matter, to conceive of any of them as absolutely fixed entities, or as national cultures in the narrowest sense. A possible way, thus, to approach this particular position of the literature written by Chicanos would be to emphasize its transnational aspect, its being a borderlands culture in continuous reshaping, with continuous (physical and cultural) crossings from one side to the other. In fact, the perception of Chicano literature as border literature has been widely used by scholars and writers, prompting all sorts of performances, publications, and conferences on border aesthetics.

Limiting ourselves now to the question of the relation of Chicano literature with Latin American literature, we could say that they both share a somewhat similar past, characterized by colonization and *mestizaje*. They also share, to a certain degree, a similar oral tradition, which motivates certain similitudes in folklore and popular poetry; this is particularly true, of course, in the case of Mexico, and one should be careful when extrapolating those affinities to the rest of Latin America, where different pre-Hispanic cultures have left a different heritage to present-day societies. What has not been fully shared by Latin America and the Southwest of the United States is the impulse given to the arts and sciences by the process of independence of Latin American nations. As we saw, what is today the Southwest of the United States and California belonged to the independent republic of Mexico for a mere 27-year period. The formation of a national independent conscience was not a major catalyst of cultural change in the Southwest until later, when it was conditioned – in the case of Mexicans in the United States – by their resistance to the new colonial power. In fact, if one excludes the folklore – where resistance and conflict have been continuous attitudes – nationalism has not been a major factor influencing literary aesthetics until the late 1960s/ early 1970s, as we saw. Although nationalism is still an option for many, in recent literature the trend seems to be to emphasize the plural heritage of Chicanos and, with it, their multiple options for national allegiance.

From a different point of view, contemporary Chicano literature has – as has almost any other literature in the world – received influences from the great United States' authors of the nineteenth and twentieth century, as well as from their Latin American counterparts. Yet these influences have seldom been direct, as often it is probably more a question of major changes in contemporary poetry or narrative that affect writers globally in a non-linear fashion. This is particularly true of the oldest generation of writers, some of whom are largely self-taught (Miguel Méndez, for instance). For the youngest, those who hold degrees in Spanish are, obviously, more likely to possess expert knowledge of Latin American literature, as is the case with Ron Arias.

With this restriction in mind, it is still clear that both in Latin America and among Chicanos similar issues have, at times, become major foci of reflection. We have already pointed to some of them, but it may be worthwhile to recall them now to close this essay. Thus, as happened earlier in Latin America, much of the impulse in Chicano theatre, prose, and poetry was aimed at establishing a literary and cultural identity. Some writers (such as R. Anaya) turned to the landscape and to native beliefs as the most autocthonous elements of the Southwest. Others, as Rodolfo Gonzales or Rolando Hinojosa, turned to history (including oral history) from a Chicano point of view. Many poets, following Alurista, set out to explore *the* Chicano language that, for many, was meant to be a combination of English, Spanish, *caló*, and pre-Hispanic languages (mainly Nahuatl, Maya, and Yaqui); a new language that would account for a new national identity. With Alurista and Luis Valdez as leaders, many sought the essence of *Chicanismo* in the indigenous antecedent, not unlike the Latin American *Indigenistas*. In a sense, the processes of transculturation that Angel Rama has so eloquently written about, have also been a key factor for many Chicano writers who seek to render their traditionally oral culture into writing and print, at times in a language other than that historically used by their culture. Last, but not least, some social and literary events in Latin America have had a direct impact on Chicano letters. We have already mentioned the case of the Mexican Revolution, which brought large segments of the population – among them many intellectuals – to the United States, but that also produced an important novelistic movement that influenced some Chicano writers. We could also mention now the impact of the Cuban Revolution of 1959, or the fact that many of the "neoindigenist" writers of the 1970s have been very active – particularly in the 1980s – in the movements of solidarity with Central America, thus creating a series of contacts that did not exist before. Alejandro Murguía, José Montoya, Lucha Corpi, Juan Felipe Herrera, and Francisco X. Alarcón, are among the group that, in one way or another, engage in this socio-poetical dialogue with other writers and militants from El Salvador, Nicaragua, or Guatemala, whether they live in the United States or in their countries of origin.

Links have always existed to keep alive the communication between Latin American and Chicano literatures. Yet those have not been of the cause–effect type, as some form of cultural dependency. They have rather been connected to specific population movements (the last one being the influx of refugees from Central America and immigrants from all over Latin America experienced between 1970 and 1990), and to a broad dissemination of works by Latin American writers in the United States, especially after the 1970s. In the case of Mexico, the contacts have also been kept alive thanks to the constant border crossings in one direction or the other, personal visits to Mexico by Chicano writers, relatives who still live in that country, and cultural exchanges of international scope.

This constant communication, however, has not succeeded in consolidating the dissemination of Chicano literature in Latin America. Chicano authors have experienced difficulties in publishing in Latin American countries, and, if one excludes Hinojosa's *Klail City y sus alrededores* (published by Casa de las Américas in Cuba), there are no Chicano books published in countries other than Mexico. Mexican press Joaquín Mortiz published the first two novels by Alejandro Morales in the 1970s and, in 1980, Fondo de Cultura Económica published Tino Villanueva's *Chicanos*, an anthology of Chicano literature in Spanish, later joined by Oscar Somoza's *Nueva narrativa chicana* (Diógenes, 1983). In the late 1980s, the paucity of publications seems to have changed somehow, and works by Miguel Méndez M. have been published by Ediciones Era (*Peregrinos de Aztlán*, 1989, a reprint of the original 1974 edition) and by the Universidad de Guadalajara (*El sueño de Santa María de las Piedras*, 1986); Ricardo Aguilar (b. 1947) has published his stories *Madreselvas en flor* (Universidad Veracruzana, 1987) and *Aurelia* (Universidad Autónoma de Ciudad Juárez, Colección Premio José Fuentes Mares, 1990); Sergio Elizondo published *Muerte en una estrella* (Tinta Negra, 1984), a novel where the denouncing of social injustices (the killings of Chicano youngsters) is embedded in a highly lyrical and symbolical narrative with musical undertones, a feature also characteristic of *Suruma* (1990), his latest novel. Other authors have been published in journals (*Fem* devoted two issues to Chicana artists), and one book by Gary Soto has appeared in translation (*Como arbustos de niebla* [Latitudes]). What all this means is that Chicano literature, and in particular that which is still written in Spanish, is consolidating its presence in Mexico; hopefully this will mean that, in the near future, publications will also be available in other countries of Latin America.

Index

Index

Index

poetry 64–6
and politics 10, 104
Chocrón, Isaac 513–14, 520
choteo (Cuban department) 524
chronicles (journalistic) 73–82, 88, 112, 124,
    445
    criticism 441
    Martí's 69, 73, 76–8, 88, 530
    overlap with essays/testimonials/
      documentaries 88, 415
    relation to short story 465
chronicles of discovery and conquest 138,
    458
Chumacero, Ali 361
"científicos" 11
cinema:
    Chicano 576
    Contemporáneos and 333
    criticism of 420, 421, 453
    Hispanic Caribbean in USA 511, 550
    impact, nineteenth century 82
    incorporated in theatrical productions 525
    Memorias del subdesarrollo 251
Cintrón, Humberto 544–5
Cisneros, Sandra 580
cities *see* urban development
Ciudad Juárez, battle of 213
Civil Rights movement, US 164, 526, 541,
    543
Clarín 444
Claudel, Paul 343
Clinamen 453
Cobo Borda, Juan Gustavo 422
Cocco de Filippis, Daisy 555
Cocteau, Jean 333, 498, 499
Cofiño López, Manuel 190, 251
Cojo Ilustrado, El 22
Colegio de México 450
Coleridge, Samuel Taylor 13, 19, 89
Collazos, Oscar 255
Colombia:
    Afro-Hispanic literature 166, 177–8, 181,
      186, 188–90
    avant-garde 126, 132
    criticism 438, 445
    novel 228, 253–5, 289–90
    theatre 508, 522–3, 523–4
    see also individual writers
Colón, Jesús 542, 543
colonial period:
    autobiographical narrative 458

Chicano literature 559–61
criticism of literature of 427, 429–30, 433–
    4, 437–8, 449, 456
literature of early 138
periodicals 429–30
Columbia University, USA 416, 450
comanches, Los (eighteenth-century drama)
    561
Communism 6, 324, 408
    see also Marxism
comparsas 169
Comte, Auguste 10–11
Con Safos (journal) 569
Congreso de escritores anti-fascistas (1937)
    329
Congress of Peace (1949) 532
Conquest 2
    chronicles of 138, 458
Conselheiro, Antonio 482
Contemporáneos (poetic group and journal)
    124–5, 332–4
    and history 305
    journal 118, 124, 129, 130, 333
    Paz and 359
    prose narrative 132, 134
    and Surrealism 338
Conti, Haroldo 265–7
Contorno (journal) 264
Contreras, Francisco 200
Contreras, Rafaela 34, 35
Coppée, François 29
Córdoba, Argentina 375
Coronel Utrecho, José 131
Corpi, Lucha 579, 580, 581, 585
Correa, Miguel 553
correspondence, symbolist notion of 360
corridos (Southwest and Mexican ballad)
    567
Corrieri, Sergio 524
Cortázar, Julio 3, 235–7, 255, 398
    death 5
    essays 401–3, 478
    and Existentialism 235–6
    importance 229, 231
    influences on 88, 112, 391
    on Juárroz 362
    novels 235–7
    organization of miscellanies 401
    persona 402
    post-Boom writing 279–80
    Rayuela 231–2, 235, 236, 281, 453, 462, 478

Index

Index

Index

Index